Watford
Season by Season

by
Trefor Jones

Best wishes.
Trefor Jones

'...all seasons shall be sweet to thee...'
(Samuel Taylor Coleridge - *Frost at Midnight*)

Published by T.G. Jones, 10 Brook House,
143 London Road, Twickenham, Middlesex, TW1 1EQ

ISBN 0-9527458-1-X

Designed and typeset by the author

Printed by Ian Allan Printing, Riverdene,
Molesey Road, Hersham, Surrey, KT12 4RG

CONTENTS

Acknowledgements

The author is greatly indebted to **Mandie Beckley** for her unwavering support and technical advice; to **Ed Coan** for his help on behalf of Watford Football Club; to *The Watford Observer* in the person of its Assistant Editor, **Oliver Phillips;** and to **Alan Cozzi** for kindly providing the main cover photograph and also that accompanying the Foreword.

Chronology

1881   The club is formed, as Watford Rovers.

1882   Home games begin in Vicarage Meadow.

1883   Rose & Crown Meadow becomes the venue for home matches.

1886   The first competitive matches - in the FA Cup and the Herts County Cup.

1889   The club moves to Colney Butts Meadow when Rose & Crown Meadow is lost to urban development.

1890   Rovers become the football section of the newly-formed West Herts Club & Ground at Cassio Road.

1893   After three years of internal conflict over the club name, 'West Herts' is universally accepted.

1896   West Herts join Division 2 of the Southern League.

1897   Professionalism adopted.

1898   Rival club Watford St Mary's is absorbed by West Herts, and the name 'Watford' is adopted.

1900   Promoted to Division 1 of the Southern League.

1903   Relegated to Division 2 of the Southern League. John Goodall appointed as the club's first manager.

1904   Promoted to Division 1 of the Southern League.

1909   The club becomes a limited company, and its committee is replaced by a board of directors.

1915   The Southern League championship is won.

1917   After two seasons of wartime activity as a member of the London Combination, the club suspends operations for two years.

1919   Post-war football begins.

1920   The Southern League's First Division (including Watford) becomes Division 3 of the Football League. It is styled 'Division 3 (South)' a year later, when a corresponding Northern section is added.

1922   Vicarage Road becomes the club's new home ground.

1939   Normal competitions cease when war is declared, and the club embarks on seven seasons of football under wartime conditions.

1945   The FA Cup competition is resumed.

1946   Normal League activity is resumed.

1958   Watford are founder-members of Division 4 as the League's lower sections are reorganized.

1960   Promoted to Division 3.

1969   Champions of Division 3, and promoted to Division 2 for the first time.

1970   The club reaches the FA Cup semi-finals for the first time.

1972   Relegated to Division 3.

1975   Relegated to Division 4.

1978   Division 4 champions, and promoted to Division 3.

1979   Promoted to Division 2.

1982   Promoted to Division 1.

1983   By finishing second in Division 1, Watford qualify for entry to the UEFA Cup.

1984   The club's first FA Cup Final appearance.

1988   Relegated to Division 2.

1992   Division 2 of the Football League becomes Division 1, as the top-flight clubs break away to form the FA Premier League.

1996   Relegated to Division 2 (formerly Division 3).

1998   Division 2 champions, and promoted to Division 1 (formerly Division 2).

Foreword by Graham Taylor

THOSE of us involved in football professionally have to concern ourselves with the present and the future, but it's always good to reflect on past performances and achievements whenever we can. And for those whose commitment to the game is as spectators, reminiscing is, of course, a richly satisfying part of the football experience.

Here, on these pages, is a wealth of statistical detail to remind us of all the matches which together make up the long history of Watford FC. Anyone with Vicarage Road affinities is certain to be drawn time and again to the details of games holding personal memories, and to those of earlier times - successful and otherwise - which helped to create the club's character and heritage.

There's plenty here for all of us to relish, and I'm sure you'll find the book a constant source of enjoyment.

Best wishes.

General Manager, Watford FC

PART ONE

Early Years

THE club was founded in 1881 for the simple enjoyment of kicking a ball about. The earliest report of an organized match is of that played on 21st January 1882, but there is nothing to suggest that it was the first fixture the club had undertaken. No competitive games were played until 1886/87, and friendlies continued to constitute the vast majority of games until the club entered the Southern League in 1896. The following list includes all first-team matches until the end of the 1895/96 season of which details are known. Those in **bold type** were competitive matches, for which line-ups and goalscorers are provided at the end of the list.

(Key to competitions: **FA** - FA Cup, **AM** - FA Amateur Cup, **HC** - Herts County Cup, **HE** - Hennessey Cup)

1881/82
Sat	21	Jan	Nascot (a)	W	2-0
Sat	4	Feb	The Cedars (a)	L	0-2
Sat	18	Feb	London Orphan Asylum (a)	W	2-1

1882/83
Sat	14	Oct	The Cedars (a)	L	0-6
Sat	21	Oct	The Rev D. Patterson's XI (h)	W	2-1
Sat	28	Oct	St Albans (h)	L	1-2
Wed	8	Nov	Bourne Hall (h)	W	5-2
Sat	11	Nov	Berkhamsted Grammar School (a)	L	1-2
Sat	18	Nov	London Orphan Asylum (a)	W	6-0
Wed	22	Nov	Silesia College (a)	L	0-4
Sat	2	Dec	St Albans Grammar School (a)	D	0-0
Sat	23	Dec	Oxhey & New Bushey Recreation Society (a)	W	3-1
Sat	6	Jan	Uxbridge Caxtonians (h)	W	2-0
Sat	3	Feb	The Cedars (h)	D	2-2
Wed	7	Feb	Silesia College (h)	D	2-2
Sat	24	Feb	Uxbridge Caxtonians (a)	L	0-2
Sat	3	Mar	The Rev D. Patterson's XI (a)	W	13-0
Wed	7	Mar	Bourne Hall (h)	W	3-1
Sat	10	Mar	The Cedars (a)	L	0-4
Sat	17	Mar	St Albans (a)	L	0-3

1883/84
Sat	13	Oct	Berkhamsted Grammar School (h)	L	1-4
Sat	20	Oct	Oxhey (h)	W	3-0
Sat	27	Oct	The Rev D. Patterson's XI (a)	W	2-1
Sat	3	Nov	Silesia College (a)	W	3-0
Sat	10	Nov	Uxbridge Crescents (h)	W	3-1
Sat	17	Nov	St Albans (h)	L	2-3
Sat	24	Nov	Woodville (h)	W	3-0
Sat	1	Dec	Nascot (h)	L	1-2
Sat	15	Dec	St Albans Grammar School (h)	W	4-1
Wed	26	Dec	Mr W.A. Sargent's XI (h)	D	3-3
Sat	29	Dec	Hemel Hempstead (a)	L	0-3

Sat	12	Jan	Uxbridge Crescents (a)	L	0-2
Sat	19	Jan	Oxhey (h)	L	0-2
Sat	23	Feb	St Albans Grammar School (a)	W	6-0
Sat	8	Mar	The Rev D. Patterson's XI (h)	W	3-0
Sat	15	Mar	Hemel Hempstead (h)	L	1-3

1884/85
Sat	11	Oct	St Albans (a)	L	1-4
Sat	18	Oct	Christ Church Rangers (a)	W	3-1
Sat	25	Oct	Berkhamsted School (h)	L	0-1
Sat	1	Nov	The Rev D. Patterson's XI (a)	L	0-3
Sat	8	Nov	City Ramblers (h)	W	9-0
Sat	15	Nov	Oxhey (h)	L	1-3
Sat	22	Nov	Hemel Hempstead (a)	D	1-1
Sat	29	Nov	St Albans (h)	W	3-0
Sat	6	Dec	Berkhamsted School (a)	L	2-5
Thu	11	Dec	University College (h)	W	3-0
Sat	13	Dec	Boxmoor United (h)	W	4-0
Sat	20	Dec	North Western Swifts (a)	W	3-1
Fri	26	Dec	Remington (h)	W	3-0
Sat	27	Dec	Mr Wellings's Team (h)	W	3-0
Sat	3	Jan	Woodville (a)	W	3-0
Sat	10	Jan	Mr Wellings's Team (a)	W	2-1
Sat	17	Jan	Boxmoor United (a)	L	1-2
Sat	24	Jan	St Albans (a)	W	2-1
Sat	7	Feb	Woodville (h)	W	2-0
Sat	14	Feb	Oxhey (h)	D	1-1
Sat	21	Feb	Christ Church Rangers (h)	W	7-0
Sat	7	Mar	Hemel Hempstead (h)	W	2-1
Sat	14	Mar	City Ramblers (a)	D	1-1
Sat	21	Mar	South Hackney (h)	W	3-1
Mon	6	Apr	St Albans (a)	W	2-1

1885/86
Sat	3	Oct	West End 2nd XI (a)	W	11-0
Sat	10	Oct	Boxmoor United (h)	W	1-0
"	"	"	South Hackney (a)	W	8-0

Sat	24 Oct	Old St Mark's (h)	W	3-1
Sat	31 Oct	City Ramblers (h)	W	2-0
Sat	14 Nov	Hemel Hempstead (a)	W	3-1
Sat	21 Nov	St Albans (a)	W	3-2
Sat	28 Nov	Oxhey (h)	D	2-2
Sat	5 Dec	Luton Town (h)	W	1-0
Sat	19 Dec	Boxmoor United (a)	D	1-1
Sat	26 Dec	(am) Mr Fairman's Team (h)	W	6-0
"	" "	(pm) Remington (h)	W	3-1
Sat	2 Jan	Harrow Town (h)	W	7-1
Sat	16 Jan	Hotspur 2nd XI (h)	W	5-1
Sat	30 Jan	Oxhey (h)	W	2-1
Sat	6 Feb	Acton (a)	W	8-2
Sat	13 Feb	Harrow Town (a)	W	7-1
Sat	20 Feb	Hemel Hempstead (h)	D	2-2
Sat	27 Feb	Civil Service Wanderers (h)	W	4-0
Wed	17 Mar	Berkhamsted School (h)	W	1-0
Sat	20 Mar	Luton Town (a)	W	3-0
Sat	27 Mar	Old St Mark's (h)	L	0-3

1886/87

Sat	2 Oct	Civil Service Wanderers (h)	W	6-0
Sat	9 Oct	Harrow Town (a)	W	4-3
Sat	16 Oct	Luton Town (h)	L	1-4
Sat	**23 Oct**	**Swindon Town (h) (FA)**	**L**	**0-1**
Sat	30 Oct	Hotspur 2nd XI (h)	W	6-2
Sat	**6 Nov**	**St Albans (h) (HC)**	**W**	**3-0**
Sat	13 Nov	Berkhamsted School (h)	W	4-0
Sat	27 Nov	West End (a)	W	2-1
Wed	1 Dec	Aldenham School (h)	D	1-1
Sat	4 Dec	United London Scottish (a)	L	0-1
Sat	11 Dec	St Albans (h)	W	2-0
Sat	18 Dec	London Caledonians (h)	D	1-1
Wed	12 Jan	Guy's Hospital (h)	L	1-2
Sat	29 Jan	Hemel Hempstead (h)	W	4-3
Mon	31 Jan	Middlesex Hospital (h)	D	0-0
Sat	**5 Feb**	**Hitchin Town (a) (HC)**	**W**	**5-3**
Sat	19 Feb	Berkhamsted School (a)	L	0-3
Sat	5 Mar	Aldenham School (a)	W	2-0
Sat	12 Mar	St Albans (a)	W	7-0
Sat	19 Mar	W.A. Sargent's XI (h)	L	0-3
Sat	**26 Mar**	**Hoddesdon (at Hertford) (HC)**	**L**	**2-5**
Sat	16 Apr	London Caledonians (h)	W	2-1

1887/88

Sat	1 Oct	Clapton (h)	L	1-3
Sat	8 Oct	Amherst (h)	W	10-0
Sat	**15 Oct**	**Chesham (a) (FA)**	**L**	**2-4**
		(replay ordered by FA)		
Sat	**22 Oct**	**Chesham (h) (FA)**	**W**	**3-1**
Sat	**5 Nov**	**Old Carthusians (h) (FA)**	**L**	**1-3**
Sat	**12 Nov**	**Aldenham School (h) (HC)**	**W**	**3-1**
Sat	3 Dec	Aldenham School (h)	D	0-0
Mon	26 Dec	Champion Hill (h)	W	10-0
Sat	14 Jan	Harrow Town (h)	(result unknown)	
Sat	21 Jan	Guy's Hospital (h)	W	2-1
Sat	**28 Jan**	**Berkhamsted (h) (HC)**	**W**	**10-0**
Sat	**10 Mar**	**Croxley (h) (HC)**	**W**	**8-0**
Sat	**17 Mar**	**Hoddesdon (at Hertford) (HC)**	**L**	**3-4**
Wed	21 Mar	A.T.B. Dunn's XI (h)	L	2-4
Sat	7 Apr	West End (h)	L	1-2
Sat	14 Apr	St Albans (h)	W	2-0

1888/89

Sat	22 Sep	London Caledonians (h)	L	2-3
Sat	29 Sep	Clapton (h)	W	2-1
Sat	6 Oct	Hampstead (h)	W	7-0
Sat	13 Oct	St Albans (a)	D	2-2
Sat	20 Oct	Aldenham School (a)	W	5-3
Sat	**27 Oct**	**Old Foresters (h) (FA)**	**W**	**6-0**
Sat	3 Nov	Harrow Town (h)	W	7-0
Sat	10 Nov	Aldenham School (h)	W	3-1
Sat	**17 Nov**	**Great Marlow (h) (FA)**	**L**	**0-2**
Sat	1 Dec	Hendon (a)	L	3-5
Sat	**8 Dec**	**Windsor Phoenix (a) (HE)**	**D**	**1-1**
Wed	26 Dec	Old St Paul's (h)	L	2-3
Sat	12 Jan	Berkhamsted (a)	W	7-0
Sat	19 Jan	St Martin's Athletic (h)	W	2-0
Sat	**26 Jan**	**Windsor Phoenix (at Uxbridge) (HE)**	**W**	**2-0**
Sat	2 Feb	Harrow Town (a)	W	5-4
Sat	9 Feb	Aldenham School (a)	W	4-0
Sat	16 Feb	Kensington Rangers (h)	W	5-1
Sat	**23 Feb**	**Hitchin Town (at St Albans) (HC)**	**W**	**6-0**
Sat	**2 Mar**	**Uxbridge (a) (HE)**	**L**	**1-4**
Sat	16 Mar	Casuals (h)	W	2-0
Sat	**23 Mar**	**Hoddesdon (at St Albans) (HC)**	**W**	**2-0**

1889/90

Sat	21 Sep	London Caledonians (h)	L	1-5
Sat	28 Sep	Vulcans (h)	D	0-0
Sat	**5 Oct**	**Swindon Town (h) (FA)**	**W**	**5-3**
Sat	12 Oct	Mr A.T.B. Dunn's XI (h)	D	4-4
Sat	19 Oct	Hampstead (h)	W	5-0
Sat	**26 Oct**	**Schorne College (a) (FA)**	**W**	**2-1**
Sat	2 Nov	St Albans (h)	W	5-0
Sat	9 Nov	Chesham (a)	L	2-3
Sat	**16 Nov**	**Swifts (h) (FA)**	**L**	**2-5**
Sat	23 Nov	Aldenham School (a)	D	2-2
Sat	30 Nov	St Bartholomew's Hospital (h)	L	0-2
Sat	**14 Dec**	**Berkhamsted (h) (HC)**	**W**	**9-0**
Sat	**28 Dec**	**Uxbridge Caxtonians (h) (HE)**	**W**	**3-2**
Sat	4 Jan	Old Harrovians (h)	L	1-5
Sat	18 Jan	Shaftesbury Westminster (h)	W	4-0
Sat	25 Jan	St Albans (a)	W	12-0
Sat	**1 Feb**	**Windsor Phoenix (a) (HE)**	**L**	**0-1**
Sat	8 Feb	Aldenham School (h)	W	3-1
Sat	15 Feb	Chesham (h)	W	3-1
Sat	**22 Feb**	**St Albans (at Bushey) (HC)**	**---**	**2-2**
		(match abandoned)		
Sat	1 Mar	Old Cranleighans (h)	W	7-0
Wed	12 Mar	Mr A.T.B. Dunn's XI (h)	D	1-1
Sat	15 Mar	Berkhamsted (a)	W	5-0
Sat	5 Apr	Clapham Pilgrims (h)	W	8-0
Mon	7 Apr	Clapton Wanderers (h)	W	3-1
Sat	12 Apr	London Caledonians (h)	D	1-1
Sat	19 Apr	Uxbridge (h)	D	3-3

1890/91

Sat	27 Sep	A.T.B. Dunn's XI (h)	L	1-2
Sat	**4 Oct**	**Chesham (a) (FA)**	**W**	**2-1**
Sat	11 Oct	Chatham (a)	L	1-5
Sat	18 Oct	Vulcans (h)	W	8-2
Sat	**25 Oct**	**93rd Regt (Highlanders) (h) (FA)**	**L**	**2-3**
Sat	**1 Nov**	**Uxbridge (a) (HE)**	**W**	**5-0**
Sat	8 Nov	St Mary's Hospital (h)	D	0-0

Sat	15	Nov	Harrow Town (h)	W	12-1
Sat	22	Nov	Aldenham School (a)	L	1-2
Sat	6	Dec	Old St Mark's (h)	W	3-1
Sat	17	Jan	Watford St Mary's (h)	W	7-4
Sat	**24**	**Jan**	**2nd Scots Guards (a) (HE)**	**L**	**1-3**
Sat	31	Jan	Swifts (h)	W	6-2
Sat	7	Feb	93rd Regt (Highlanders) (h)	L	0-5
Wed	11	Feb	Aldenham School (h)	W	6-0
Sat	21	Feb	Guy's Hospital (h)	L	0-4
Sat	**28**	**Feb**	**Watford St Mary's (h) (HC)**	**W**	**6-0**
Sat	14	Mar	Old Cranleighans (h)	W	3-1
Sat	**28**	**Mar**	**St Albans (at Hatfield) (HC)**	**W**	**6-2**
Mon	30	Mar	Mr W.H. Dixon's XI (h)	W	4-0
Sat	4	Apr	Chatham (h)	L	2-5

1891/92

Sat	26	Sep	Crouch End (h)	W	14-1
Sat	**3**	**Oct**	**Maidenhead (a) (FA)**	**W**	**5-0**
Sat	10	Oct	Casuals (h)	W	6-0
Sat	17	Oct	London Welsh (h)	W	7-0
Sat	**24**	**Oct**	**London Caledonians (a) (FA)**	**L**	**1-2**
Sat	31	Oct	Aldenham School (h)	W	3-2
Sat	14	Nov	Wolverton L&NWR (h)	W	6-3
Wed	25	Nov	St Mary's Hospital (h)	W	1-0
Sat	28	Nov	Luton Town (a)	W	4-3
Sat	5	Dec	Chesham (a)	L	3-5
Sat	12	Dec	Old St Mark's (h)	D	2-2
Wed	16	Dec	Bank of England (h)	W	7-1
Sat	2	Jan	St Albans (a)	D	2-2
Sat	9	Jan	Chesham (h)	D	2-2
Sat	23	Jan	Millwall (h)	L	0-6
Sat	30	Jan	Luton Town (h)	D	2-2
Sat	**6**	**Feb**	**Watford St Mary's (h) (HC)**	**W**	**8-0**
Sat	13	Feb	Bowes Park (h)	W	7-1
Sat	**5**	**Mar**	**St Albans (at Hatfield) (HC)**	**D**	**3-3**
Sat	**12**	**Mar**	**St Albans (at Hatfield) (HC)**	**W**	**5-1**
Sat	19	Mar	St Mary's Hospital (h)	W	3-0
Sat	26	Mar	Old Cranleighans (h)	W	6-2
Sat	**2**	**Apr**	**Hoddesdon (at Ware) (HC)**	**W**	**5-2**
Sat	9	Apr	Chatham (h)	D	1-1
Sat	16	Apr	Stroud Green (h)	W	5-1
Mon	18	Apr	Crewe Alexandra (h)	L	1-9

1892/93

Sat	10	Sep	Chatham (a)	L	2-7
Sat	17	Sep	Casuals (h)	W	4-2
Sat	24	Sep	Condors (h)	W	2-0
Sat	1	Oct	Luton Town (a)	L	1-4
Sat	8	Oct	Berkhamsted School (h)	W	11-0
Sat	**15**	**Oct**	**Crusaders (h) (FA)**	**L**	**2-6**
Sat	22	Oct	Uxbridge (h)	W	5-1
Sat	29	Oct	Aldenham School (h)	W	2-1
Sat	5	Nov	Fulham St Clements (h)	W	4-0
Sat	12	Nov	Millwall (a)	L	4-8
Wed	16	Nov	St Mary's Hospital (h)	W	6-0
Sat	19	Nov	Wolverton L&NWR (a)	L	1-3
Sat	26	Nov	Ilford (h)	W	6-1
Sat	3	Dec	Luton Town (h)	L	0-3
Sat	10	Dec	London Caledonians (h)	D	1-1
Sat	17	Dec	Hoddesdon (a)	W	4-1
Sat	24	Dec	City Ramblers (h)	W	5-1
Sat	14	Jan	Hoddesdon (h)	W	5-0

Sat	21	Jan	Bowes Park (h)	W	2-1
Sat	28	Jan	St Bartholomew's Hospital (h)	L	3-4
Sat	4	Feb	Romford (h)	W	2-1
Sat	11	Feb	3rd Grenadier Guards (h)	W	5-2
Sat	18	Feb	St Bartholomew's Hospital (h)	W	3-0
Sat	25	Feb	2nd Coldstream Guards (h)	W	4-0
Sat	4	Mar	Old Cranleighans (h)	W	4-1
Sat	18	Mar	Guy's Hospital (h)	W	2-1
Sat	25	Mar	London Welsh (h)	L	0-1
Sat	1	Apr	Chesham (h)	W	4-0
Mon	3	Apr	Wolverton L&NWR (h)	W	6-1
Sat	8	Apr	Old St Stephens (h)	D	1-1

1893/94

Sat	16	Sep	3rd Grenadier Guards (h)	W	4-1
Sat	23	Sep	Old St Stephens (h)	W	8-0
Sat	30	Sep	2nd Coldstream Guards (h)	W	4-3
Sat	7	Oct	Bowes Park (h)	W	7-1
Sat	14	Oct	Chesham (h)	W	8-0
Sat	21	Oct	Uxbridge (h)	W	5-0
Sat	28	Oct	Crouch End (a)	L	1-7
Sat	4	Nov	Aldenham School (a)	W	3-1
Sat	**11**	**Nov**	**Norwich Thorpe (a) (AM)**	**W**	**6-2**
Sat	18	Nov	Chesham Generals (h)	W	4-3
Sat	25	Nov	Old St Mark's (h)	W	6-3
Sat	**2**	**Dec**	**Ilford (a) (AM)**	**L**	**0-2**
Sat	16	Dec	RE Training Battalion, Chatham (h)	L	0-4
Sat	23	Dec	Chatham (h)	L	1-4
Tue	26	Dec	3rd Grenadier Guards (h)	W	5-2
Sat	30	Dec	Chesham (a)	L	2-3
Sat	20	Jan	Luton Town (h)	L	2-3
Sat	27	Jan	Uxbridge (a)	L	0-2
Sat	3	Feb	Aldenham School (h)	W	4-2
Sat	10	Feb	Luton Town (a)	L	1-3
Sat	24	Feb	Chatham (a)	L	2-3
Sat	**3**	**Mar**	**St Albans (a) (HC)**	**W**	**3-2**
Sat	10	Mar	Old St Mark's (h)	W	5-1
Sat	**17**	**Mar**	**West Herts FA (at St Albans) (HC)**	**W**	**5-1**
Sat	24	Mar	Chesham Generals (h)	W	2-1
Mon	26	Mar	Wolverton L&NWR (h)	W	4-1
Sat	7	Apr	Crusaders (h)	L	1-4
Sat	21	Apr	London Welsh (h)	W	6-1

1894/95

Sat	22	Sep	RE Training Battalion, Chatham (h)	L	0-5
Sat	29	Sep	St Albans (h)	W	7-0
Sat	6	Oct	Chesham (h)	W	3-1
Sat	**13**	**Oct**	**Tottenham Hotspur (a) (FA)**	**L**	**2-3**
Sat	20	Oct	Vampires (h)	W	4-1
Sat	27	Oct	Uxbridge (a)	W	2-1
Sat	**10**	**Nov**	**Wycombe Wanderers (h) (AM)**	**W**	**5-1**
Sat	17	Nov	Wolverton L&NWR (a)	L	1-4
Sat	24	Nov	1st Grenadier Guards (h)	L	0-2
Sat	**1**	**Dec**	**Maidenhead (h) (AM)**	**D**	**1-1**
			(abandoned in extra time)		
Sat	**8**	**Dec**	**Maidenhead (a) (AM)**	**L**	**2-4**
Sat	15	Dec	2nd Grenadier Guards (h)	D	1-1
Sat	22	Dec	St Albans (a)	W	1-0
Thu	27	Dec	Darwen (h)	L	2-4
Sat	19	Jan	Chesham Generals (h)	L	2-3
Sat	26	Jan	Wellingborough (h)	W	1-0
Sat	23	Feb	City Ramblers (h)	L	1-3

Sat	2	Mar	Watford St Mary's (h) (HC)	D	2-2	
Sat	9	Mar	1st Grenadier Guards (h)	W	5-2	
Sat	16	Mar	3rd Grenadier Guards (h)	L	2-3	
Wed	20	Mar	Uxbridge (h)	W	2-1	
Sat	23	Mar	Watford St Mary's (a) (HC)	D	2-2	
Sat	30	Mar	Luton Town (a)	L	0-8	
Wed	3	Apr	Watford St Mary's (h) (HC)	---	1-2	
			(abandoned in extra time)			
Sat	6	Apr	Watford St Mary's (at St Albans) (HC)	L	1-5	
Sat	13	Apr	Liverpool Casuals (h)	L	2-3	
Mon	15	Apr	Wolverton L&NWR (h)	W	3-2	
Sat	20	Apr	Casuals (h)	W	3-1	

1895/96

Sat	21	Sep	Bradfield Waifs (h)	W	6-0
Sat	28	Sep	Dunstable Town (h)	W	3-0
Sat	5	Oct	Wolverton L&NWR (a)	L	1-5
Sat	12	Oct	Norwich CEYMS (h) (FA)	W	2-1
Sat	19	Oct	Casuals (h)	L	1-2
Sat	26	Oct	Old Harrovians (h)	W	6-0
Sat	2	Nov	Old St Stephens (h) (FA)	L	0-1
Sat	9	Nov	Aldenham School (h)	W	4-2

Sat	16	Nov	St Albans (h)	D	1-1
Sat	23	Nov	Crouch End (a)	W	3-2
Sat	7	Dec	1st Coldstream Guards (h)	W	2-1
Sat	14	Dec	Watford St Mary's (h)	W	4-0
Thu	26	Dec	London Caledonians (h)	L	1-3
Fri	27	Dec	Maidenhead (h)	W	5-2
Sat	28	Dec	Chesham Generals (h)	W	5-1
Sat	4	Jan	2nd Grenadier Guards (h)	D	3-3
Sat	11	Jan	City Ramblers (h)	L	1-2
Sat	25	Jan	St Albans (a)	L	1-2
Sat	1	Feb	Wolverton L&NWR (h) (AM)	W	4-3
Sat	8	Feb	Hammersmith Athletic (h)	W	5-0
Sat	15	Feb	Maidenhead (a) (AM)	L	0-1
Sat	29	Feb	London Welsh (h)	W	2-0
Sat	7	Mar	Crouch End (h)	W	4-0
Sat	14	Mar	Southall (h)	W	4-2
Sat	28	Mar	Watford St Mary's (a)	L	0-1
Sat	4	Apr	Wolverton L&NWR (h)	L	0-4
Mon	6	Apr	Woolwich Arsenal Reserves (h)	L	2-6
Sat	11	Apr	West Croydon (h)	D	2-2
Sat	18	Apr	Bowes Park (h)	W	3-1

THE COMPETITIVE MATCHES IN DETAIL

Figures in brackets after players' names indicate goals scored. Scorers' identities are not entirely reliable for early matches; in some cases there are conflicting accounts, and sometimes a goalscorer is not credited at all.
The Hennessey Cup was a competition organized by Uxbridge FC for clubs within a ten-mile radius of Uxbridge.

23/10/1886 FA Cup, 1st Round v Swindon Town (h) lost 0-1
A.A. Sargent (goal); H.J. Capell & H.W. Grover (backs); H.J. (or W.J.) Pickin, S.J. Poulton & C.H. Peacock (half-backs); E. Halsey, S.J. Valentine, H. Wheeler, W.H. Wellings & G. Waterman (forwards)

6/11/1886 Herts County Cup, 1st Round v St Albans (h) won 3-0
A.A. Sargent (goal); H..J. Capell & H.W. Grover (backs); W.A. Sargent, S.J. Poulton & C.H. Peacock (half-backs); F.A. Sargent **(2)**, E.Halsey **(1)**, W.H. Wellings, S.J. Valentine & G. Waterman (forwards)

5/2/1887 Herts County Cup, 2nd Round v Hitchin Town (a) won 5-3
A.A. Sargent (goal); W.N. Roe & H.J. Capell (backs); S.J. Poulton, W.A. Sargent & C.H. Peacock (half-backs); P.H. Morton **(1)**, W.H. Wellings **(1)**, F.A. Sargent **(2)**, S.J. Valentine & G. Waterman (forwards) (+ 1 goal unattributed)

26/3/1887 Herts County Cup, Final v Hoddesdon (at Hertford) lost 2-5
A.A. Sargent (goal); W.N Roe & H.J. Capell (backs); W.A. Sargent, C.H. Peacock & S.J. Poulton (half-backs); F.A. Sargent, G. Waterman **(1)**, P.H. Morton, E. Halsey & W.H. Wellings **(1)** (forwards)

15/10/1887 FA Cup, 1st Round v Chesham (a) lost 2-4
A.A. Sargent (goal); C.H. Peacock & H.J. Capell (backs); W.F. Horton, H.W. Grover & W.A. Sargent (half-backs); W.E. Gardner, H. Wheeler **(1)**, W.S. Coles **(1)**, S.J. Poulton & G. Waterman (forwards)
(Chesham fielded an unregistered player, and the FA ordered a replay at Watford)

22/10/1887 FA Cup, 1st Round v Chesham (h) won 3-1
A.A. Sargent (goal); W.N. Roe & H.J. Capell (backs); W.A. Sargent, C.H. Peacock & S.J. Poulton (half-backs); P.H. Morton **(1)**, W.H. Wellings, W.S. Coles **(1)**, G. Waterman & E. Halsey **(1)** (forwards)

5/11/1887 FA Cup, 2nd Round v Old Carthusians (h) lost 1-3 attendance 800
A.A. Sargent (goal); W.N. Roe & H.J. Capell (backs); W.A. Sargent, S.J. Poulton & C.H. Peacock (half-backs); E. Halsey, G. Waterman, W.S. Coles **(1)**, P.H. Morton & W.H. Wellings (forwards)

12/11/1887 Herts County Cup, 1st Round v Aldenham School (h) won 3-1
A.A. Sargent (goal); W.A. Sargent & H.J. Capell (backs), H.W. Grover, C.H. Peacock **(1)** & S.J. Poulton (half-backs); G. Waterman, W.S. Coles, F.A. Sargent **(2)**, A.H. Town & S.J. Valentine (forwards)

28/1/1888 Herts County Cup, 2nd Round v Berkhamsted (h) won 10-0
A.A. Sargent (goal); W.N. Roe & H.J. Capell (backs); S.J. Poulton, C.H. Peacock & W.A. Sargent (half-backs); G. Waterman **(1)**, H. Wheeler **(4)**, F.A. Sargent **(3)**, W.S. Coles & P.H. Morton (forwards) (+ 2 own goals)

10/3/1888   Herts County Cup, Semi-Final   v Croxley (h)   won 8-0
A.A. Sargent (goal); W.A. Sargent & H.J. Capell (backs); C.H. Peacock, H.W. Grover & S.J. Poulton (half-backs);
G. Waterman, H. Wheeler (1), F.A. Sargent (4), P.H. Morton (1) & W.S. Coles (2) (forwards)

17/3/1888   Herts County Cup, Final   v Hoddesdon (at Hertford)   lost 3-4
A.A. Sargent (goal); W.N. Roe & H.J. Capell (backs); S.J. Poulton, C.H. Peacock & W.A. Sargent (half-backs);
G. Waterman, H. Wheeler, F.A. Sargent (3), W.S. Coles & P.H. Morton (forwards)

27/10/1888   FA Cup, 2nd Qualifying Round   v Old Foresters (h)   won 6-0
A.A. Sargent (goal); W.N. Roe & J. Woods (backs); E.E. Villiers, C.H. Peacock & W.A. Sargent (half-backs);
W.S. Coles (1), P. Coles, F.A. Sargent (3), S.J. Poulton & J.W. Dickson (2) (forwards)

17/11/1888   FA Cup, 3rd Qualifying Round   v Great Marlow (h)   lost 0-2   attendance nearly 2,000
A.A. Sargent (goal); W.N. Roe & J. Woods (backs); E.E. Villiers, C.H. Peacock & W.A. Sargent (half-backs); J.W. Dickson,
S.F.P. Moore, F.A. Sargent, S.M. Stanley & W.S. Coles (forwards)

8/12/1888   Hennessey Cup, lst Round   v Windsor Phoenix (a)   drew 1-1   attendance 200/300
A.A. Sargent (goal); C.H. Peacock & W.A. Sargent (backs); J.R. Dukes, E.E. Villiers & H.W. Grover (half-backs);
W. Gibson, F. Parkes, W.S. Coles (1), P. Coles & S.J. Poulton (forwards)

26/1/1889   Hennessey Cup, 1st Round replay   v Windsor Phoenix (at Uxbridge)   won 2-0
A.A. Sargent (goal); J. Woods & C.H. Peacock (backs); W.A. Sargent, E.E. Villiers & H.W. Grover (half-backs); P. Coles,
W.S. Coles (1), F.A. Sargent (1), J.A. Stuart & S.J. Poulton (forwards)

23/2/1889   Herts County Cup, Semi-Final   v Hitchin Town (at St Albans)   won 6-0
A.A. Sargent (goal); J. Woods & C.H. Peacock (backs); W.A. Sargent, E.E. Villiers & S.J. Poulton (half-backs); G.R. Bacot,
J.A. Stuart, F.A. Sargent (3), W.S. Coles (1) & P. Coles (2) (forwards)

2/3/1889   Hennessey Cup, Semi-Final   v Uxbridge (a)   lost 1-4
A.A. Sargent (goal); J. Woods & C.H. Peacock (backs); W.A. Sargent, E.E. Villiers & W.H. Grover (half-backs);
W.S. Coles, P. Coles (1), F.A. Sargent, J.A. Stuart & S.J. Poulton (forwards)

23/3/1889   Herts County Cup, Final   v Hoddesdon (at St Albans)   won 2-0   attendance 1,000
A.A. Sargent (goal); Rev J. Kennedy & C.H. Peacock (backs); E.E. Villiers, S.J. Poulton & W.A. Sargent (half-backs);
W.S. Coles (1), G.R. Bacot (1), F.A. Sargent, P. Coles & J.A. Brown (forwards)

5/10/1889   FA Cup, 1st Qualifying Round   v Swindon Town (h)   won 5-3   attendance 300
A.A. Sargent (goal); W.A. Sargent & C.H. Peacock (backs); E.E. Villiers, G.D. Morrison (1) & S.J. Poulton (1) (half-backs);
J.A. Stuart, J.W. Dickson, F.A. Sargent (1), W.S. Coles (1) & P. Coles (1) (forwards)

26/10/1889   FA Cup, 2nd Qualifying Round   v Schorne College (a)   won 2-1
A.A. Sargent (goal); E.H. Mariette & W.A. Sargent (backs); S.J. Poulton, G.D. Morrison & E.E. Villiers (half-backs);
J.W. Dickson, J.A. Stuart, F.A. Sargent (1), P. Coles (1) & W.S. Coles (forwards)

16/11/1889   FA Cup, 3rd Qualifying Round   v Swifts (h)   lost 2-5   attendance 2,000
A.A. Sargent (goal); E.H. Mariette & W.A. Sargent (backs); E.E. Villiers, G.D. Morrison & C.H. Peacock (half-backs);
J.A. Stuart (1), J.W. Dickson (1), F.A. Sargent, P. Coles & W.S. Coles (forwards)

14/12/1889   Herts County Cup, 1st Round   v Berkhamsted (h)   won 9-0
A.A. Sargent (goal); W.A. Sargent & A. Tooms (backs); E.E. Villiers, C.H. Peacock & S.J. Poulton (half-backs);
P. Coles (3), W.S. Coles (2), F.A. Sargent (4), F. Parkes & J.A. Stuart (forwards)

28/12/1889   Hennessey Cup, 2nd Round   v Uxbridge Caxtonians (h)   won 3-2
A.A. Sargent (goal); A.M. Low & W.A. Sargent (backs); C.H. Peacock, G.D. Morrison & H.W. Grover (half-backs);
J.A. Stuart (1), S.J. Poulton, F.A. Sargent (1), W.S. Coles & P. Coles (1) (forwards)
(Watford Rovers had a bye in the 1st Round)

1/2/1890   Hennessey Cup, Semi-Final   v Windsor Phoenix (a)   lost 0-1
A.A. Sargent (goal); C.H. Peacock & W.A. Sargent (backs); E.E. Villiers, G.D. Morrison & S.J. Poulton (half-backs);
F. Parkes, F.A. Sargent, W.S. Coles, J.A. Brown & P. Coles (forwards)

22/2/1890   Herts County Cup, Semi-Final   v St Albans (at Bushey)   match abandoned at 2-2   attendance 1,200
A.A. Sargent (goal); A.M. Low (1) & W.A. Sargent (backs); G.C. Clark, C.H. Peacock & E.E. Villiers (half-backs);
J. Stokes, F.H.S. Iles, F.A. Sargent, W.S. Coles (1) & P. Coles (forwards)
*(Match abandoned following a pitch invasion when a third St Albans goal was disallowed. Watford Rovers subsequently
withdrew from the competition "to prevent further ill-feeling" between the clubs.)*

4/10/1890   FA Cup, 1st Qualifying Round   v Chesham (a)   won 2-1
A.A. Sargent (goal); W. Woodward & W.A. Sargent (backs); E.E. Villiers, C.H. Peacock & H.J. Dewey (half-backs);
J.W. Dickson, A. Horton, F.A. Sargent (2), P. Coles & J.B. Wildman (forwards)

25/10/1890   FA Cup, 2nd Qualifying Round   v 93rd Regt (Highlanders) (h)   lost 2-3   attendance 600/800
G.D. Morrison (goal); W.A. Sargent & J. Woods (backs); E.E. Villiers, C.H. Peacock & H.J. Dewey (half-backs); P. Coles,
W.S. Coles, F.A. Sargent, J.W. Sharpe (1) & J.W. Dickson (1) (forwards)

1/11/1890   Hennessey Cup, 1st Round   v Uxbridge (a)   won 5-0   attendance 400
W.W. Brunt (goal); J. Woods & W.A. Sargent (backs); E.E. Villiers, C.H. Peacock & H.J. Dewey (half-backs);
W. Woodward, A. Horton, F.A. Sargent (3), W.S. Coles (2) & P. Coles (forwards)

24/1/1891   Hennessey Cup, 2nd Round   v 2nd Scots Guards (a)   lost 1-3   attendance 300
W.W. Brunt (goal); W.A. Sargent & G.C. Clark (backs); E.E. Villiers, C.H. Peacock & H.J. Dewey (half-backs); F. Parkes,
A. Horton, F.A. Sargent, W.S. Coles (1) & P. Coles (forwards)

28/2/1891   Herts County Cup, Semi-Final   v Watford St Mary's (h)   won 6-0
W.W. Brunt (goal); G.C. Clark & W.A. Sargent (backs); E.E. Villiers, C.H. Peacock & H.J. Dewey (half-backs);
J.C. Hibbert, F. Parkes, F.A. Sargent (3), F.H.S. Iles (1) & A. Horton (1) (forwards) (+ 1 own goal)

28/3/1891   Herts County Cup, Final   v St Albans (at Hatfield)   won 6-2   attendance 1,000
W.W. Brunt (goal); E.H. Mariette & W.A. Sargent (backs); E.E. Villiers, C.H. Peacock & H.J. Dewey (half-backs);
A. Horton (1), F.A. Sargent (2), A.T.B. Dunn (2), E. Beevor & F. White (1) (forwards)

3/10/1891   FA Cup, 1st Qualifying Round   v Maidenhead (a)   won 5-0
J. Woods (goal); W.A. Sargent & E.H. Mariette (backs); S.J. Poulton, C.H. Peacock & J. Penney (half-backs); J. Munn,
W.S. Coles (3, inc 1 pen), F.A. Sargent, H. Culverhouse (2) & A. Horton (forwards)
   (The law providing for penalty kicks had just been introduced, and Coles's kick in this match was the club's first.)

24/10/1891   FA Cup, 2nd Qualifying Round   v London Caledonians (a)   lost 1-2   attendance 2,000
J. Woods (goal); W.A. Sargent & E.H. Mariette (backs); C.H. Peacock, J. Penney & A.M. Low (half-backs); W.S. Coles (1),
P. Coles, F.A. Sargent, A. Horton & H. Culverhouse (forwards)

6/2/1892   Herts County Cup, 1st Round   v Watford St Mary's (h)   won 8-0
J. Woods (goal); W.A. Sargent & H.G. Wardale (backs); E.E. Villiers, C.H. Peacock & J. Penney (half-backs); P. Coles,
W.S. Coles (6), F.A. Sargent (2), J.C. Hibbert & A. Horton (forwards)

5/3/1892   Herts County Cup, Semi-Final   v St Albans (at Hatfield)   drew 3-3
J. Woods (goal); W.A. Sargent & E.H. Mariette (backs); E.E. Villiers, C.H. Peacock & J. Penney (half-backs); P. Coles,
W.S. Coles (2), F.A. Sargent, E. Beevor & M.J. Cottam (1) (forwards)

12/3/1892   Herts County Cup, Semi-Final replay   v St Albans (at Hatfield)   won 5-1   attendance 2,000
J. Woods (goal); W.A. Sargent & E.H. Mariette (backs); E.E. Villiers, C.H. Peacock & J. Penney (half-backs); P. Coles,
W.S. Coles (1), F.A. Sargent (1), A.T.B. Dunn (1) & E. Beevor (forwards) (+ 1 goal "rushed through by the brothers Coles")

2/4/1892   Herts County Cup, Final   v Hoddesdon (at Ware)   won 5-2
J. Woods (goal); W.A. Sargent & E.H. Mariette (backs); E.E. Villiers, C.H. Peacock & J. Penney (half-backs); P. Coles,
W.S. Coles (3), F.A. Sargent (1), M.J. Cottam (1) & E. Beevor (forwards)

15/10/1892   FA Cup, 1st Qualifying Round   v Crusaders (h)   lost 2-6   attendance 1,000
J. Woods (goal); E.H. Mariette & J.R. Paull (backs); J. Penney, C.H. Peacock & A.J. Houghton (half-backs); C. Wheeler
W.S. Coles (1), S.C. Wilks, C. Pretty (1) & T.B. (or J.) Wilkinson (forwards)

11/11/1893   FA Amateur Cup, 2nd Round   v Norwich Thorpe (a)   won 6-2   attendance 300/400
S. King (goal); W. Spearing & A. Coles (backs); A. Burr, C.H. Peacock & J. Penney (half-backs); P. Coles, W.S. Coles (3),
C. Harrison (2), W. Dodds (1) & C. Wheeler (forwards)
                              (West Herts had a bye in the 1st Round)

2/12/1893   FA Amateur Cup, 3rd Round   v Ilford (a)   lost 0-2   attendance 1,000
J. Woods (goal); W.S. Coles & H.M. Harford (backs); J. Penney, C.H. Peacock & A. Burr (half-backs); P. Coles,
F.A. Sargent, C. Harrison, W. Dodds & C. Wheeler (forwards)

3/3/1894   Herts County Cup, Semi-Final   v St Albans (a)   won 3-2   attendance 2,000/3,000
S. King (goal); J.R. Paull & H.M. Harford (backs); J. Penney, C.H. Peacock & G.E. Green (half-backs); C. Wheeler (1),
R. Slaughter, W.S. Coles, S.S. Taylor (1) & F.A. Sargent (forwards) (+ 1 goal unattributed)

17/3/1894   Herts County Cup, Final   v West Herts FA (at St Albans)   won 5-1   attendance 700
S. King (goal); J.R. Paull & H.M. Harford (backs); G.E. Green, C.H. Peacock & J. Penney (half-backs); C. Wheeler (1),
R. Slaughter, W.S. Coles (1), S.S. Taylor (2) & F.A. Sargent (1) (forwards)

13/10/1894   FA Cup, 1st Qualifying Round   v Tottenham Hotspur (a)   lost 2-3   attendance 2,500
S. King (goal); J.R. Paull & J.S. Lidderdale (backs); G.E. Green, F.C. Robins & J. Penney (half-backs); R.C.M. Strouts,
S.S. Taylor, J.O. Anderson, R.G. Wright (1) & S.G. Hobbs (1) (forwards)

10/11/1894   FA Amateur Cup, 2nd Qualifying Round   v Wycombe Wanderers (h)   won 5-1
S King (goal); J.S. Lidderdale & A.O. Ardley (backs); G.E. Green, F.C. Robins & J. Penney (half-backs); C. Wheeler (1),
A.R.L. Wright, S.G. Hobbs (2), R.G. Wright (2) & F.A. Sargent (forwards)
                         (West Herts had a bye in the 1st Qualifying Round)

1/12/1894   FA Amateur Cup, 3rd Qualifying Round   v Maidenhead (h)   drew 1-1   attendance 700
S. King (goal); J.R. Paull & J.S. Lidderdale (backs); A.O. Ardley, F.C. Robins & J. Penney (half-backs); C. Wheeler,
J.O. Anderson, S.G. Hobbs (1), R.G. Wright & F.A. Sargent (forwards)
                         (Match abandoned in extra time, owing to bad light)

8/12/1894   FA Amateur Cup, 3rd Qualifying Round replay   v Maidenhead (a)   lost 2-4   attendance 400
S. King (goal); J.S. Lidderdale & J. Penney (backs); F. Watson, F.C. Robins & A.O. Ardley (half-backs); A. Harrison,
S.G. Hobbs (1), J.O. Anderson (1), E.H. Mariette & C. Wheeler (forwards)

2/3/1895   Herts County Cup, Semi-Final   v Watford St Mary's (h)   drew 2-2
S. King (goal); J.R. Paull & H.M. Harford (backs); J. Penney, F.C. Robins & H.A. Rauthmell (half-backs); C. Wheeler,
R.C.M. Strouts, R.G. Wright (1), W.S. Coles (1) & F.A. Sargent (forwards)
                         (West Herts were exempt until the semi-finals)

23/3/1895   Herts County Cup, Semi-Final replay   v Watford St Mary's (a)   drew 2-2   attendance 1,000/1,500
S. King (goal); J.R. Paull & H.M. Harford (backs); A.O. Ardley, F.C. Robins & J. Penney (half-backs); C. Wheeler (1),
R.C.M. Strouts, R.G. Wright, F.A. Sargent (1) & G.E. Green (forwards)

3/4/1895   Herts County Cup, Semi-Final, 2nd replay   v Watford St Mary's (h)   1-2 (ab)   attendance 1,200

S. King (goal); J.R. Paull & H.M. Harford (backs); A.O. Ardley, F.C. Robins & J. Penney (half-backs); R.C.M. Strouts, W.S. Coles, P. Coles, R.G. Wright (1) & F.A. Sargent (forwards)

(Match abandoned in extra time, owing to bad light)

6/4/1895   Herts County Cup, Semi-Final, 3rd replay   v Watford St Mary's (at St Albans)   lost 1-5

S. King (goal); H.M. Harford & P. Coles (backs); G.E. Green, F.C. Robins & A.O. Ardley (half-backs); F.A. Sargent, R.G. Wright, W.S. Coles, C. Wheeler (1) & R.C.M. Strouts (forwards)

12/10/1895   FA Cup, 1st Qualifying Round   v Norwich Church of England Young Men's Society (h)   won 2-1   attendance 700

S. King (goal); H.M. Harford & J.R. Paull (backs); G.E. Green, F.C. Robins (1) & A.O. Ardley (half-backs); B.H. Joy, R.G. Wright, S.G. Hobbs, C.F. Maclachlan (1) & R. Blyth (forwards)

2/11/1895   FA Cup, 2nd Qualifying Round   v Old St Stephens (h)   lost 0-1

S. King (goal); H.M. Harford & J.R. Paull (backs); G.E. Green, F.C. Robins & A.O. Ardley (half-backs); J. Brandon, R.G. Wright, S.G. Hobbs, C.F. Maclachlan & W. Lovett (forwards)

1/2/1896   FA Amateur Cup, 1st Round   v Wolverton London & North Western Railway (h)   won 4-3

S. King (goal); J.R. Paull & A.O. Ardley (backs); R. Blyth, F.C. Robins & G.E. Green (half-backs); H.G. Anderson, C.F. Maclachlan (2), S.G. Hobbs (1), R.G. Wright (1) & F.M. May (forwards)

15/2/1896   FA Amateur Cup, 2nd Round   v Maidenhead (a)   lost 0-1   attendance nearly 500

S. King (goal); A.O. Ardley & J.R. Paull (backs); G.E. Green, F.C. Robins & R. Blyth (half-backs); F.M. May, R.G. Wright, S.G. Hobbs, C.F. Maclachlan & H.G. Anderson (forwards)

THE FIRST KNOWN ELEVEN

The earliest known line-up is that which defeated The Rev D. Patterson's XI by two goals to one in Vicarage Meadow on 21st October 1882:

H. Wheeler (goal)
W. Horton, H.J. Capell & H.W. Grover (backs)
S.J. Valentine & W. Hurndall (1) (left forwards)
G. Waterman & H.T. Horton (right forwards)
T. Smith (1), A. Christmas & W. Grace (centres)

PART TWO

A Man for All Seasons

THERE is no single theme to the following gallery of Watford worthies. Some were irrefutably the outstanding figure of the season in question (who else but Cliff Holton could possibly be chosen to represent 1959/60?); some earn inclusion for particularly valuable service to the club over a longer period; whilst others have been selected to mark a notable feat or milestone.

1896/97
Against Old St Stephens,
**Micky Wood** scored the
club's first Southern
League hat-trick

1897/98
Later a director of the
club, Scotsman **Johnny Hill**
first came down to Cassio
Road as a player

1898/99
A son of Bushey,
**Bobbie Slaughter** was the
club's last locally-born
leading scorer

1899/1900
**Jack McNee** took his career
total of Southern League
goals to 32, a club record
until Charlie White beat it

1900/01
**Wally Eames** was the
youngest débutant until
Arthur Grimsdell ten
years later

1901/02
Robust and popular, full-back
**Jack 'Darkie' Cother** was
one of four players who
appeared in every game

1902/03
**Jimmy Tennant** missed only
two Southern League games
in his three seasons at
Cassio Road

1903/04
*The appointment of
John Goodall as the club's
first manager brought instant
and emphatic success*

1904/05
*After emigrating to Canada,
George Badenoch was to
return to Europe and lose his
life in the Great War*

1905/06
***George Fyfe** arrived from
Hibernian of the Scottish
First Division and stayed for
five years*

1906/07
*After this, the last of his four
seasons, **Joe Brooks** moved
to the top flight with
Sheffield United*

1907/08
***Jack Foster** was sold to
Sunderland in December, but
still easily headed the list
of goalscorers*

1908/09
*The Amateur caps won in
May by **Tiny Fayers** were the
club's only England honours
at any level before 1955*

1909/10
***Billy Biggar** made more
Southern League
appearances for the club
(217) than anyone else*

1910/11
***Arthur Grimsdell** set out on
a senior career which would
bring him the captaincy of
England*

1911/12
*Despite protests from the
public, **Arthur Lockett**, once
of England, was released at
the end of the season*

1912/13
***Val Gregory** and his brother
Fred were now both
established as first-team
players*

1913/14
***Thomas Ashbridge** led
the scorers with 14 goals -
and nine of them came in
two games*

1914/15
*This season's championship
win was the high point of
Harry Kent's 16 years as
manager*

1919/20
***George Edmonds** picked
up where he left off before
the war - as the club's
top scorer*

1920/21
*The club's first senior cap
was won this season by
Welshman **Frank Hoddinott***

1921/22

*His brother had moved on,
but **Fred Gregory** continued
a Watford career which
spanned 15 years*

1922/23

***Fred Pagnam** had been
signed to score goals, and
that's what he did*

1923/24

***George Toone** completed a
sequence of 175 appearances
in all competitions - a club
record which still stands*

1924/25

***Charlie White** ended his
career - and very soon his
life - with record totals of
appearances and goals*

1925/26

*The goalkeeping character
Skilly Williams was ever-
present in his final season at
Vicarage Road*

1926/27

*Right-half **Frank Smith**
completed a run of 116
consecutive appearances*

1927/28

***George Prior**, a stalwart of
the defence, took his total
of first-team games into
three figures*

1928/29

*Scotland international
defender **Neil McBain**
arrived at the club he was
destined to manage twice*

1929/30

***Frank McPherson**, record-
scorer in 1928/29, continued
in prolific vein until he left
for Reading*

1930/31

*McPherson had been
exchanged for **George James**,
but the goals still flowed*

1931/32

***Harry Lowe** failed with a
penalty kick in the last game
of the season, just a few
hours after getting married*

1932/33

*Right-back **Bill Brown**,
rarely absent in the early-
1930s, made 249 first-team
appearances without scoring*

1933/34

*He arrived already a veteran,
but **Jim McLaren** was to
be first choice in goal for
five years*

1934/35

*Only Frank McPherson had
hit more goals in a season
before **Billy Lane**'s
35 in 46 games*

1935/36

*Tireless **Arthur Woodward**
played in every game; his
final tally of appearances
was 432*

1936/37

*Against Gillingham
Taffy Davies performed his
best scoring feat in a Watford
career lasting 20 years*

1937/38

*In the seasons leading up to
the war, **Jimmy Armstrong**
was a solid figure at the
heart of the defence*

1938/39

*War ended **Tommy Barnett**'s
career, but not before he had
set record goalscoring and
appearance totals*

1946/47

***Bill Findlay** began still in
charge, but couldn't
reproduce the form of
pre-war seasons*

1947/48

***Tommy Eggleston** was easily
the most successful of five
mid-season signings from
Leicester City*

1948/49

*Hard-tackling defender
Harry Oliver quickly became
a crowd favourite*

1949/50

*No other Watford goalie has
matched **Geoff Morton**'s feat
of eight consecutive clean
sheets in the League*

1950/51

*The elegant **Tony Collins**
began the first of his two
spells at Vicarage Road*

1951/52

***Cyril Thompson** achieved the
highest goals tally in
peacetime since 1934/35*

1952/53

***Frank Mitchell** was an
influential left-half and
captain with experience at
the top level*

1953/54

*This season's leading scorer,
Roy Brown, was equally at
home as the defensive pivot*

1954/55

*The dashing **Maurice Cook**
enjoyed the best goalscoring
season of his career*

1955/56

***Freddie Bunce** made his
début in the Football
League, and also for the
England Youth team*

1956/57
*The genial **Dave Underwood** returned for the second of his three Watford spells*

1957/58
***Bobby Bell** came down from Scotland for a Vicarage Road career which would encompass over 300 games*

1958/59
***George Catleugh** was in the process of compiling a run of 129 consecutive appearances*

1959/60
*No player before or since has dominated the club so completely as **Cliff Holton***

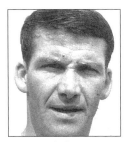

1960/61
***Ken Nicholas** was as near as possible to being an automatic selection at left-back*

1961/62
***Vince McNeice**, a cultured centre-half, had no goals to show for his 231 Football League appearances*

1962/63
*Results fell away badly, but **Dai Ward** scored more League goals than anyone else in Division 3*

1963/64
***Bill McGarry**'s impact was such that the club attained its highest Football League position to date*

1964/65
***Dennis Bond**, aged 17, began a senior career which would bring him 301 Watford appearances*

1965/66
*This was **George Harris**'s fourth and last season of outstanding service on the left wing*

1966/67
*The long-serving **Johnny Williams** became a fixture in the left-back position*

1967/68
***Stewart Scullion** - individualist supreme in an otherwise efficiently organized team*

1968/69
*To **Ken Furphy** fell the distinction of taking the club into Division 2 for the first time*

1969/70
*For the fifth season running, **Duncan Welbourne** played in every League game*

1970/71
This season the wholehearted
Tom Walley *won his only*
senior cap for Wales

1971/72
Keith Eddy *was a tower*
of strength in good times
and - as now - bad

1972/73
Club history was made when
schoolboy ***Keith Mercer***
made his League début at 16
years and 125 days

1973/74
No other Division 3 player
scored as many League goals
this season as ***Billy Jennings***

1974/75
Manager ***Mike Keen*** *had*
continued his long playing
career, but this season was
his last in the dual role

1975/76
Only Skilly Williams has
made more appearances in
the Watford goal than
Andy Rankin

1976/77
Strong and dependable in
defence, ***Alan Garner*** *was on*
course for a run of 134
consecutive appearances

1977/78
Graham Taylor *announced*
himself at Vicarage Road
with a runaway
championship win

1978/79
His League tally made
Ross Jenkins *the 92 clubs'*
leading scorer in this second
successive promotion season

1979/80
Ian Bolton *was a powerful*
influence and a magnificent
striker of the ball

1980/81
At the age of 18,
Nigel Callaghan *was*
beginning to make the No 7
shirt his own

1981/82
John Barnes *began a swift*
rise to fame which extended
far beyond the confines of
south-west Herts

1982/83
In Watford's top-flight début,
Luther Blissett *scored more*
League goals than anyone
else in the four divisions

1983/84
Wilf Rostron *should have*
led the team out Wembley,
but missed the big day
through suspension

1984/85

*Signed to stabilize a shaky defence, **John McClelland** was an instant success*

1985/86

***Tony Coton** was a dominating presence between the posts for nearly six years*

1986/87

***Gary Porter** established himself this season, and went on to accumulate 472 senior appearances*

1987/88

*One of the few consolations of a dismal season was the skill and vision of **Glyn Hodges***

1988/89

*Twin brother Dean had to leave to get his career going, but **David Holdsworth** stayed to give long service*

1989/90

*With the club's appearances record in his sights, injury ended the playing career of 28-year-old **Kenny Jackett***

1990/91

***Paul Wilkinson** became the first player to lead the club's goalscorers in three consecutive seasons*

1991/92

***David James** was transferred to Liverpool after two years in the Watford goal*

1992/93

*After coming late to full-time football, the energetic **Andy Hessenthaler** enjoyed a good career*

1993/94

***Paul Furlong** was by some way the club's leading scorer in both his seasons at Vicarage Road*

1994/95

*The New Year brought nine successive clean sheets, and **Kevin Miller** was in goal for eight of them*

1995/96

*The burgeoning career of sharpshooter **Kevin Phillips** was interrupted by injury*

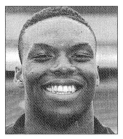

1996/97

*At 16 years and 314 days, **Gifton Noel-Williams** became the youngest scorer in the club's history*

1997/98

*After 15 years as a first-team player, **Nigel Gibbs** was rewarded with a championship medal*

PART THREE

Season by Season

THE following pages provide tabulated details of all competitive matches played whilst the club has been a member of the Southern League (from 1896/97 to 1919/20) and Football League (from 1920/21), except during the two world wars. For all home matches, the opposing club is listed in capital letters.

Notation for team line-ups and goalscorers

Tactical formations are now so varied and flexible, and players' roles have extended so far beyond the simple old 'right-back-to-outside-left' sequence (eg 'wing-back', 'in the hole', 'just in front of the back four', etc) that shirt numbers have become almost irrelevant except as a means of identification during the game. For the team line-ups, therefore, 'X' has been used to denote all outfield players. (A guide to each player's normal function in the team is included in Part Six.) The full notation for line-ups and goalscorers is as follows:

G	goalkeeper
X	outfield player in the starting line-up
R	outfield player replaced by a substitute
S	substitute who took part in the match
SR	substitute replaced by another substitute
GR	goalkeeper replaced by a substitute
SG	substitute goalkeeper
1,2,3 etc	goal(s) scored
p	one penalty goal - included in the goal(s) scored
#	two penalty goals - included in the goals scored

(NB: No substitutes at all were allowed in competitive matches until 1965/66, when a single substitution was permitted in League matches - and then only in the case of injury.)

Names of competitions

For purposes of continuity and ease of reference, temporary commercial sponsors' names have not been used in the titles of the following competitions:

FOOTBALL LEAGUE - also known as the Canon League, Today League, Barclays League, Endsleigh Insurance League and Nationwide League

FOOTBALL LEAGUE CUP - also known as the Milk Cup, Littlewoods Cup, Rumbelows Cup and Coca-Cola Cup

FOOTBALL LEAGUE FULL MEMBERS CUP - also known as the Simod Cup and Zenith Data Systems Cup

FOOTBALL LEAGUE ASSOCIATE MEMBERS CUP - also known as the the Freight Rover Trophy, Sherpa Van Trophy, Leyland Daf Cup, Autoglass Trophy and Auto Windscreens Shield

The South-Eastern League

For some fixtures in this competition (1902/03 to 1907/08) the club fielded its first team and for others its reserve team. Only the former are included here.

Use of shading

For ease of reference, shading is used to highlight matches in competitions other than the Southern League and Football League. The totals of appearances, substitutions and goals above each player's name are separated into Southern League (or Football League) and other competitions. For the latter, shading has again been used.

Players' first and last appearances

A player's name is shaded to indicate the season in which he made his first peacetime appearance for Watford. The season of his <u>final</u> peacetime appearance is denoted by a double slash (//) after his name.

Attendances

Published attendances over the years have often been at variance with audited (and unpublished) Football League gate returns, which exist from 1924/25. In the past there has also been confusion over season tickets - sometimes included in published attendances, and sometimes not. Where discrepancies are apparent, audited Football League figures are given.

Southern League position: 9th out of 13 in Division 2
Manager: None

	Pl	W	D	L	For	Ag	Pts
Dartford	24	16	4	4	83	19	36
RETB (Chatham)	24	11	9	4	49	37	31
Uxbridge	24	11	5	8	62	37	27
* Freemantle	24	12	4	8	58	40	26
Wycombe Wanderers	24	10	6	8	37	54	26
Chesham	24	11	3	10	41	55	25
Southall	24	9	6	9	55	52	24
1st Scots Guards	24	9	6	9	49	50	24
WEST HERTS	24	11	1	12	41	49	23
Warmley	24	10	2	12	44	43	22
Old St Stephens	24	5	7	12	36	52	17
Maidenhead	24	4	8	12	33	64	16
1st Coldstream Guards	24	3	6	15	30	66	12

Home-and-away league doubles
For – 1 (Maidenhead)
Against – 2 (1st Scots Guards, Uxbridge)

Divisional changes at end of season: Royal Artillery (Portsmouth) & St Albans elected in place of 1st Coldstream Guards, 1st Scots Guards & Freemantle; division reduced to 12 clubs

All Matches: Won 14, Drew 1, Lost 14, Goals 52-60

Highest Score: 6 (Match 15)

* Two points were deducted from Freemantle's total for fielding an ineligible player in a Test Match

No	DATE			COMPETITION	OPPONENTS	HOME	AWAY	ATTENDANCE	
1	September	Sat	19	Southern League, Division 2	WYCOMBE WANDERERS	5-0 W		400	
2		Sat	26	Southern League, Division 2	SOUTHALL	2-0 W		400	
3	October	Sat	3	Southern League, Division 2	Chesham		L 2-3		1,000
4		Sat	17	Southern League, Division 2	Old St Stephens		L 1-6		600
5		Sat	31	FA Cup, 2nd Qualifying Round	Maidenhead		L 1-2		
6	November	Sat	7	FA Amateur Cup, 2nd Qualifying Round	BRADFIELD WAIFS	3-1 W		600	
7		Sat	14	Southern League, Division 2	RETB (Chatham)		L 0-1		
8		Sat	21	FA Amateur Cup, 3rd Qualifying Round	Cheshunt		L 2-5		
9		Sat	28	Southern League, Division 2	WARMLEY	1-0 W			
10	December	Sat	5	Southern League, Division 2	Southall		L 1-4		
11		Sat	12	Southern League, Division 2	UXBRIDGE	0-1 L		300	
12		Sat	19	Southern League, Division 2	Dartford		L 1-6		600
13	January	Sat	9	Southern League, Division 2	Wycombe Wanderers		L 1-2		500
14		Sat	16	Southern League, Division 2	1st SCOTS GUARDS	0-3 L		300	
15		Sat	30	Southern League, Division 2	OLD ST STEPHENS	6-2 W		200	
16	February	Sat	6	Southern League, Division 2	RETB (CHATHAM)	2-0 W		500	
17		Sat	13	Herts Senior Cup, Semi-Final	Apsley (at Berkhamsted)		(W 3-2)		500
18		Sat	27	Southern League, Division 2	MAIDENHEAD	4-0 W		1,000	
19	March	Sat	6	Southern League, Division 2	Warmley		L 0-2		1,000
20		Sat	13	Southern League, Division 2	FREEMANTLE	3-1 W			
21		Wed	17	Southern League, Division 2	1st COLDSTREAM GUARDS	4-0 W			
22		Sat	20	Southern League, Division 2	Uxbridge		L 0-5		1,500
23		Sat	27	Herts Senior Cup, Final	Hitchin Town (at Hatfield)		(W 2-1)		600
24	April	Thu	1	Southern League, Division 2	Maidenhead		W 2-1		
25		Sat	3	Southern League, Division 2	CHESHAM	1-0 W		1,000	
26		Wed	7	Southern League, Division 2	DARTFORD	2-1 W		500	
27		Sat	10	Southern League, Division 2	Freemantle		L 0-5		100
28		Wed	14	Southern League, Division 2	1st Scots Guards		L 0-3		
29		Sat	17	Southern League, Division 2	1st Coldstream Guards		D 3-3		
					(the final match was an away fixture, but played at Watford)				

League ever-presents: S. King, W. Saunders
Most appearances in total: S. King & W. Saunders 29 out of 29   **Most goals in total:** W. Saunders 15
Hat-tricks: H. Wood (Match 15)   **Penalty goals:** W. Saunders 2, R.G. Wright 1
Sent off: None
Full international appearance(s) this season: None

	Anderson, H.G.	Ardley, A.O.	Ayling, A.W.	Blyth, A.	Blyth, R.	Bradford, A.D.	Bradford, H.	Busby, E.	Button, J.T.	Clarke, T.W.	Davenport, G.	Dow, H.J.	Green, F.	Green, G.E.	Harrison, H.	Hill, M.	Hobbs, S.G.	Hollingshead, H.	Iles, J.H.	Joy, N.H.	King, F.	King, S.	Maclachlan, C.F.	Paris, H.J.	Paten, R.B.J.	Paull, J.R.	Putterill, F.T.	Robins, F.C.	Saunders, W.	Weedon, J.	Wilson, J.	Wise, R.K.	Wood, H.	Wright, A.R.L.	Wright, R.G.
Apps	8	4	3	3	18	1	1	10	3	8	23	5	1	3	8	1	18	4	1	1	1	24	1	6	1	10	4	6	24	12	13	5	22	1	10
Subs																																			
Goals	2							2		2	1				1		8									1			13				7		4
Apps	3		1		5			2			4				2	1	2	3				5	1			5	1		5	2	2	1	5		4
Subs																																			
Goals			1												1		1									1			2				3		2
1	X1	X			X						X			X								G				X		X	X2				X		X2p
2	X1				X						X			X			X1			X		G							X	X			X		X
3	X		X		X						X			X			X1					G							X	X1			X		X
4	X		X		X						X											G		X					X	X1		X	X		X
5	X				X						X							X				G		X		X			X				X	X	X1
6	X		X1		X						X						X1	X				G							X				X	X	X1
7	X		X		X						X				X		X	X				G							X				X		
8	X				X						X						X	X				G				X	X1		X				X		X1
9	X				X						X		X				X	X				G				X		X	X1				X		
10			X		X						X1	X					X					G		X					X			X	X		
11	X				X	X	X				X						X	X			X	G							X				X		
12	X				X						X				X		X	X				G							X	X		X	X		
13					X					X	X	X			X1							G							X	X	X		X		
14			X		X					X	X	X			X		X					G		X					X				X		
15					X						X	X			X		X1					G		X		X			X1				X3		X1
16					X			X				X			X	X	X					G		X		X			X2	X					
17					X			X							X	X						G				X			X2p	X	X		X1		X
18					X			X1			X						X					G				X			X1p	X	X		X1		X1
19			X		X					X	X						X					G				X			X	X	X		X		X
20					X			X			X						X1					G				X			X1	X	X1		X		X
21								X1			X						X1					G				X	X	X	X	X	X		X2		X
22		X						X		X	X											G				X			X	X	X		X	X	
23					X			X			X				X1							G				X			X	X	X		X1		X
24		X						X		X					X							G							X2	X	X	X	X		
25					X					X	X						X1					G				X			X	X	X		X		X
26					X			X		X	X						X2					G							X	X	X	X	X		
27								X		X	X				X		X					G							X	X	X	X	X		
28		X						X		X	X									X		G		X					X	X		X	X		
29								X	X	X2	X				X							G		X	X1				X	X	X				

1897/98

Southern League position: 3rd out of 12 in Division 2
Manager: None

	Pl	W	D	L	For	Ag	Pts
RA (Portsmouth)	22	19	1	2	75	22	39
Warmley	22	19	0	3	108	15	38
WEST HERTS	22	11	6	5	50	48	28
Uxbridge	22	11	2	9	39	57	24
St Albans	22	9	5	8	47	41	23
Dartford	22	11	0	11	68	55	22
Southall	22	8	2	12	49	61	18
Chesham	22	8	2	12	38	48	18
Old St Stephens	22	7	2	13	47	66	16
Wycombe Wanderers	22	7	2	13	37	55	16
Maidenhead	22	4	4	14	27	81	12
RETB (Chatham)	22	4	2	16	26	62	10

New league opponents: Royal Artillery (Portsmouth), St Albans

Home-and-away league doubles
For – 3 (Chesham, Southall, Wycombe Wanderers)
Against – none

Divisional changes at end of season: Royal Artillery (Portsmouth) to Division 1; Wolverton London & North Western Railway from Division 1; Brentford, Fulham, Shepherds Bush & Thames Ironworks elected in place of Dartford, Old St Stephens, Royal Engineers Training Battalion (Chatham) & Warmley

All Matches: Won 11, Drew 6, Lost 6, Goals 54-55

Highest Score: 6 (Match 21)

(After this season the club changed its name from West Herts to Watford)

No	DATE			COMPETITION	OPPONENTS	HOME	AWAY	ATTENDANCE
1	September	Sat	18	FA Cup, Preliminary Round	3rd GRENADIER GUARDS	4-7 L		
2	October	Sat	2	Southern League, Division 2	Uxbridge		L 0-2	200
3		Sat	16	Southern League, Division 2	Dartford		L 0-8	
4		Sat	23	Southern League, Division 2	RA (PORTSMOUTH)	2-2 D		
5		Sat	30	Southern League, Division 2	RETB (CHATHAM)	3-1 W		1,500
6	November	Sat	6	Southern League, Division 2	Wycombe Wanderers		W 2-1	700
7		Sat	20	Southern League, Division 2	OLD ST STEPHENS	2-2 D		1,200
8		Sat	27	Southern League, Division 2	Chesham		W 2-1	900
9	December	Sat	4	Southern League, Division 2	SOUTHALL	4-2 W		1,000
10		Sat	11	Southern League, Division 2	St Albans		D 2-2	
11		Sat	18	Southern League, Division 2	Warmley		L 0-11	700
12	January	Sat	1	Southern League, Division 2	Southall		W 1-0	200
13		Sat	15	Southern League, Division 2	WARMLEY	4-0 W		3,000
14		Sat	22	Southern League, Division 2	UXBRIDGE	0-0 D		
15		Sat	29	Southern League, Division 2	RETB (Chatham)		L 0-2	100
16	February	Sat	5	Southern League, Division 2	RA (Portsmouth)		L 0-2	2,000
17		Sat	12	Southern League, Division 2	CHESHAM	5-1 W		1,500
18	March	Sat	5	Southern League, Division 2	ST ALBANS	2-2 D		2,500
19		Sat	19	Southern League, Division 2	Maidenhead		D 2-2	250
20	April	Sat	2	Southern League, Division 2	WYCOMBE WANDERERS	4-2 W		1,000
21		Wed	13	Southern League, Division 2	Old St Stephens		W 6-1	
22		Sat	23	Southern League, Division 2	DARTFORD	4-2 W		1,000
23		Mon	25	Southern League, Division 2	MAIDENHEAD	5-2 W		500

	Ardley, A.O.	Auld, D.S.	Baker, A.G.	Beach, T.H.	Burgess, R.	Clarke, T.W.	Davenport, G.	Glew, J.W.	Hall, H.A.	Hendry, W.H.	Hill, J.	King, S.	Lister, F.S.	McNee, J.	Marsh, I.	Myers, J.E.	Nock, W.	Osborn, F.J.	Osborne, E.J.	Paull, J.R.	Ray, W.	Richardson, J.W.	Robins, F.C.	Saunders, W.	Varley, E.A.	Wakefield, J.	Wilson, J.	Wood, H.	Wright, R.G.	Own goals	Unattributed goals
Apps	5	2	14	16		4	21	11	2	5	20		10	19	20	3	3	5	2	2	20	2	20	4	4	1	7	19	1		
Subs																															
Goals				11			7						3	5	5		3				10		2							2	2
Apps	1	1			1	1			1			1										1	1	1			1	1			
Subs																															
Goals						2																1		1							
1	X	X			X	X2			X			G										X1	X	X1			X	X			
2	X	X				X	X		X		X							G	X			X	X	X			X				
3	X						X		X		X		X		X			G	X				X		X		X	X			
4	X					X	X			X	X		X	X	X2			G			X		X					X			
5	X					X	X			X	X		X	X	X			G			X2		X					X			1
6		X				X	X			X1	X		X	X	X1			G			X		X					X			
7	X			X1		X	X				X		X	X		G					X1		X					X			
8				X		X	X				X		X1	X	X	G					X		X					X			1
9				X2		X	X				X		X2	X	X	G					X		X					X			
10			G	X			X				X		X		X1					X1			X		X		X	X			
11			G	X			X				X		X	X	X						X		X					X			
12			G	X	X	X	X				X			X	X						X		X	X	X1						
13			G	X1		X	X				X		X	X1	X						X		X					X			
14			G	X	X		X				X			X	X			X	X		X						X	X	X		
15			G	X	X	X	X				X			X	X						X		X	X				X			
16			G	X			X				X			X	X					X	X		X				X	X			
17			G	X1			X				X			X	X1						X1		X	X1			X	X			1
18			G	X1			X				X			X1	X		X		X	X	X		X					X			
19			G	X2p			X		X		X			X	X						X		X		X			X			
20			G	X1			X		X		X			X1	X		X1				X		X					X		1	
21			G	X			X		X		X2			X1	X						X3		X		X			X			
22			G				X		X		X			X1	X		X2				X1		X		X			X			
23			G	X2			X		X		X			X	X						X1		X		X			X			

1898/99

Southern League position: 3rd out of 12 in Division 2 (London Section)
Manager: None

	Pl	W	D	L	For	Ag	Pts
Thames Ironworks	22	19	1	2	64	16	39
Wolverton L&NWR	22	13	4	5	88	43	30
WATFORD	22	14	2	6	62	35	30
Brentford	22	11	3	8	59	39	25
Wycombe Wanderers	22	10	2	10	55	57	22
Southall	22	11	0	11	44	55	22
Chesham	22	9	2	11	45	62	20
St Albans	22	8	3	11	45	59	19
Shepherds Bush	22	7	3	12	37	53	17
Fulham	22	6	4	12	36	44	16
Uxbridge	22	7	2	13	29	48	16
Maidenhead	22	3	2	17	33	86	8

New league opponents: Brentford, Fulham, Shepherds Bush, Thames Ironworks, Wolverton London & North Western Railway
Home-and-away league doubles
For – 5 (Brentford, Chesham, Shepherds Bush, Southall, Uxbridge)
Against – none
Divisional changes at end of season: Thames Ironworks to Division 1; St Albans & Uxbridge resigned; Dartford & Grays United elected; division reduced to 11 clubs
All Matches: Won 25, Drew 4, Lost 8, Goals 114-50
Highest Score: 15 (Match 1)

Watford finished 1st out of 6 clubs in the Bucks & Contiguous Counties League, Division 1 (Won 8, Drew 1, Lost 1, Goals 43-12, Points 17)

No	DATE			COMPETITION	OPPONENTS	HOME	AWAY	ATTENDANCE	
1	September	Wed	14	Bucks & Contiguous Counties Lge, Division 1	WYCOMBE WANDERERS	15-0 W		300	
2		Sat	24	FA Cup, Preliminary Round	CHESHAM	1-0 W		2,000	
3	October	Sat	1	FA Cup, 1st Qualifying Round	CHESHAM GENERALS	4-0 W		2,000	
4		Sat	8	Southern Lge, Div 2 (London Section)	Brentford		W 4-2		1,000
5		Sat	15	FA Cup, 2nd Qualifying Round	LOWESTOFT	2-0 W		2,000	
6		Sat	22	Southern Lge, Div 2 (London Section)	SHEPHERDS BUSH	7-0 W		1,500	
7		Sat	29	FA Cup, 3rd Qualifying Round	Luton Town		D 2-2		3,000
8	November	Wed	2	FA Cup, 3rd Qualifying Round replay	LUTON TOWN	0-1 L		2,000	
9		Sat	19	Southern Lge, Div 2 (London Section)	Wolverton L&NWR		W 3-1		1,000
10		Sat	26	Southern Lge, Div 2 (London Section)	THAMES IRONWORKS	0-0 D		1,000	
11	December	Mon	5	Bucks & Contiguous Counties Lge, Division 1	Wycombe Wanderers		W 2-1		
12		Sat	10	Southern Lge, Div 2 (London Section)	CHESHAM	7-1 W		1,500	
13		Sat	17	Southern Lge, Div 2 (London Section)	Thames Ironworks		L 1-2		500
14		Sat	24	Southern Lge, Div 2 (London Section)	BRENTFORD	2-1 W		1,500	
15	January	Sat	7	Bucks & Contiguous Counties Lge, Division 1	AYLESBURY UNITED	4-1 W		1,000	
16		Sat	14	Southern Lge, Div 2 (London Section)	Uxbridge		W 4-1		1,000
17		Sat	21	Southern Lge, Div 2 (London Section)	WYCOMBE WANDERERS	1-3 L		1,000	
18		Sat	28	Southern Lge, Div 2 (London Section)	FULHAM	6-3 W		1,000	
19		Mon	30	Bucks & Contiguous Counties Lge, Division 1	Chesham		D 1-1		500
20	February	Sat	4	Southern Lge, Div 2 (London Section)	Shepherds Bush		W 2-1		1,000
21		Sat	11	Southern Lge, Div 2 (London Section)	ST ALBANS	2-1 W		2,000	
22		Sat	18	Southern Lge, Div 2 (London Section)	Chesham (an away match, but played at Watford)		W 3-2		2,000
23		Sat	25	Southern Lge, Div 2 (London Section)	SOUTHALL	5-0 W		1,000	
24		Mon	27	Bucks & Contiguous Counties Lge, Division 1	Chesham Generals		W 3-0		200
25	March	Sat	4	Southern Lge, Div 2 (London Section)	Wycombe Wanderers		D 2-2		
26		Sat	11	Southern Lge, Div 2 (London Section)	WOLVERTON L&NWR	0-2 L		1,500	
27		Thu	16	Southern Lge, Div 2 (London Section)	Maidenhead		W 5-1		
28		Sat	18	Southern Lge, Div 2 (London Section)	St Albans		L 1-3		2,000
29		Thu	23	Southern Lge, Div 2 (London Section)	Fulham		L 0-2		
30		Sat	25	Southern Lge, Div 2 (London Section)	MAIDENHEAD	0-3 L		400	
31		Fri	31	Bucks & Contiguous Counties Lge, Division 1	CHESHAM	4-1 W		2,000	
32	April	Sat	1	Southern Lge, Div 2 (London Section)	UXBRIDGE	4-2 W		1,500	
33		Sat	8	Southern Lge, Div 2 (London Section)	Southall		W 3-2		
34		Wed	12	Bucks & Contiguous Counties Lge, Division 1	WOLVERTON L&NWR	4-2 W		400	
35		Mon	17	Bucks & Contiguous Counties Lge, Division 1	CHESHAM GENERALS	3-2 W			
36		Sat	22	Bucks & Contiguous Counties Lge, Division 1	Wolverton L&NWR		L 0-3		400
37		Thu	27	Bucks & Contiguous Counties Lge, Division 1	Aylesbury United		W 7-1		100

	Ardley, A.O.	Baker, A.G.	Beach, T.H.	Brunt, W.W.	Catlin, W.	Cother, E.	Cother, J.W.	Davenport, G.	Edwards, H.R.	Fellows, W.	Hare, C.B.	Hill, J.	Janes, W.H.	Jordan, H.	Lister, F.S.	McNee, J.	Marsh, I.	Paull, J.R.	Robins, F.C.	Saunders, W.	Sharp, A.	Slaughter, R.	Steel, T.	Turner, A.D.	Varley, E.A.	Wilson, J.	Wood, H.	Wright, R.G.	Unattributed goal
Apps	1	21	19	1		8	19	3	7	1	18	22	2	1	1	22	3	1	19	2	18	17	1	4	8		21	2	
Subs																													
Goals			5			1					10	11	1			11			2	1	1	12		1	3		1	2	
Apps		15	14		1	7	9	2	2	2	14	15	2	2	1	15	6	1	10	1	11	13	2	1	5	1	12	1	
Subs																													
Goals			6			1	1				12	9				8	2		1			9			1		1		1
1		G	X3				X				X4	X4				X1	X1		X		X	X2					X		
2		G	X			X					X	X	X			X	X1				X	X					X		
3		G	X2p				X				X	X1				X	X				X	X1	X				X		
4		G	X1				X				X	X1				X			X		X	X2					X		
5		G					X				X	X			X	X			X		X	X2					X		
6		G					X				X3	X				X1			X		X	X2					X	X1	
7		G	X				X				X2	X				X			X		X	X					X		
8		G	X				X				X	X				X			X		X	X				X			
9		G	X1		X1		X				X	X				X1			X		X	X					X		
10		G	X		X		X				X	X				X			X		X	X					X		
11		G	X	X				X			X1p	X		X		X						X			X1		X		
12		G					X				X2	X2				X1					X	X			X1		X	X1	
13	X	G	X				X				X	X1				X			X		X	X					X		
14		G	X				X				X1	X1				X			X		X	X					X		
15		G	X			X	X				X2	X1				X			X			X					X		
16		G	X			X					X	X				X			X		X	X3			X1		X		
17		G	X			X	X				X	X				X1			X		X	X					X		
18		G	X				X				X	X4				X1		X	X		X1			X1			X		
19		G	X			X	X				X	X1	X			X				X	X						X		
20		G	X1				X	X			X	X				X					X	X1		X1			X		
21		G	X				X				X1	X				X					X	X1		X			X		
22		G					X				X1	X1				X			X		X	X1		X			X		
23		G	X						X	X	X	X2p				X2		X1			X	X					X		
24		G	X						X		X	X1	X	X		X					X	X2					X		
25		G	X				X	X			X2	X				X					X	X					X		
26		G	X				X	X			X	X			X	X						X					X		
27		X2	G		X	X						X	X1			X		X1		X1	X						X		
28		G	X		X	X						X				X1					X	X		X			X		
29		G	X		X	X					X	X				X			X		X	X					X		
30		G	X		X	X					X	X				X			X		X			X			X		
31		G	X				X			X1		X1				X1					X1	X1	X	X			X		
32		G	X				X				X1	X1				X						X1	X1	X1	X1		X		
33		G				X	X				X	X				X1			X			X1			X1		X		
34		G	X				X				X2	X				X1			X			X			X		X		1
35		G	X			X	X1				X	X				X1			X1p			X			X		X		
36		G	X				X			X	X	X				X						X			X	X	X		
37		G	X1			X	X					X				X4			X			X		X1	X			X1	

1899/1900

Southern League position: 1st out of 11 in Division 2 – promoted to Division 1
Manager: None

	Pl	W	D	L	For	Ag	Pts
WATFORD	20	14	2	4	57	25	30
Fulham	20	10	4	6	44	23	24
Chesham Town	20	11	2	7	43	37	24
Wolverton L&NWR	20	9	6	5	46	36	24
Grays United	20	8	6	6	63	29	22
Shepherds Bush	20	9	4	7	45	37	22
Dartford	20	8	3	9	36	44	19
Wycombe Wanderers	20	8	3	9	35	50	19
Brentford	20	5	7	8	31	48	17
Southall	20	6	3	11	21	44	15
Maidenhead	20	1	2	17	16	64	4

New league opponents: Grays United
Home-and-away league doubles
For – 4 (Dartford, Fulham, Maidenhead, Shepherds Bush)
Against – none
Promotion to Division 1: Watford were promoted after beating Sheppey United, who finished bottom of Division 1, in a Test Match
All Matches: Won 25, Drew 2, Lost 6, Goals 112-36
Highest Score: 11 (Match 21)

Watford finished 1st out of 5 clubs in the Bucks & Contiguous Counties League, Division 1 (Won 7, Drew 0, Lost 1, Goals 40-6, Points 14).

No	DATE			COMPETITION	OPPONENTS	HOME AWAY	ATTENDANCE	
1	September	Sat	9	Southern League, Division 2	Chesham Town	D 2-2		500
2		Wed	27	Bucks & Contiguous Counties Lge, Division 1	AYLESBURY UNITED	10-0 W	200	
3		Sat	30	FA Cup, 1st Qualifying Round	HITCHIN TOWN	7-1 W	1,000	
4	October	Sat	7	Southern League, Division 2	BRENTFORD	4-0 W	1,500	
5		Sat	14	FA Cup, 2nd Qualifying Round	WOLVERTON L&NWR	1-0 W	2,000	
6		Wed	25	Southern League, Division 2	Dartford	W 4-2		
7		Sat	28	FA Cup, 3rd Qualifying Round	Crouch End Vampires	W 3-0		500
8	November	Sat	4	Southern League, Division 2	Shepherds Bush	W 3-1		1,000
9		Sat	11	Bucks & Contiguous Counties Lge, Division 1	CHESHAM GENERALS	5-0 W	500	
10		Sat	18	FA Cup, 4th Qualifying Round	Luton Town	L 2-3		4,000
11		Sat	25	Southern League, Division 2	Wycombe Wanderers	L 1-2		700
12	December	Sat	9	Southern League, Division 2	SHEPHERDS BUSH	4-0 W	700	
13		Mon	25	Southern League, Division 2	SOUTHALL	6-1 W	1,000	
14		Sat	30	Bucks & Contiguous Counties Lge, Division 1	Chesham Town	L 0-2		
15	January	Sat	6	Southern League, Division 2	FULHAM	2-1 W	1,500	
16		Sat	13	Southern League, Division 2	Wolverton L&NWR	L 1-4		300
17		Sat	20	Bucks & Contiguous Counties Lge, Division 1	CHESHAM TOWN	5-0 W	1,500	
18		Sat	27	Southern League, Division 2	Brentford	D 2-2		800
19	February	Sat	10	Southern League, Division 2	WOLVERTON L&NWR	1-0 W	700	
20		Sat	17	Southern League, Division 2	DARTFORD	5-1 W		
21		Sat	24	Southern League, Division 2	MAIDENHEAD	11-0 W	800	
22	March	Sat	3	Southern League, Division 2	Fulham	W 1-0		2,000
23		Sat	10	Southern League, Division 2	WYCOMBE WANDERERS	1-0 W	2,000	
24		Thu	15	Bucks & Contiguous Counties Lge, Division 1	Aylesbury United	W 8-3		
25		Sat	17	Bucks & Contiguous Counties Lge, Division 1	Chesham Generals	W 1-0		200
26		Thu	29	Southern League, Division 2	Maidenhead	W 1-0		300
27		Sat	31	Southern League, Division 2	Grays United	L 1-6		
28	April	Tue	3	Southern League, Division 2	GRAYS UNITED	4-0 W		
29		Fri	13	Southern League, Division 2	CHESHAM TOWN	2-1 W	2,500	
30		Sat	14	Bucks & Contiguous Counties Lge, Division 1	WANDSWORTH	6-0 W		
31		Tue	17	Southern League, Division 2	Southall	L 1-2		
32		Sat	21	Bucks & Contiguous Counties Lge, Division 1	Wandsworth (an away match, but played at Watford)	W 5-1		200
33		Mon	30	Southern League Test Match	SHEPPEY UNITED	2-1 W	500	

The following match became void when Wolverton L&NWR subsequently resigned from the Bucks & Contiguous Counties League:

	December	Sat	2	Bucks & Contiguous Counties Lge, Division 1	WOLVERTON L&NWR	2-0 W	1,000	

	Baker, A.G. //	Bayley, J.T. //	Beach, T.H.	Brunt, W.W. //	Cother, J.W.	Cox, A.G. //	Fellows, W.	Good, M.	Gran, J.J. //	Hare, C.B.	Hill, J.	McNee, J. //	Richardson, J.W.	Robins, F.C.	Saunders, W.	Sharp, A.	Slaughter, R. //	Tervit, W.	Varley, E.A.	White, H.W.	Wilson, J. //	Wood, H.	Own goal	Unattributed goal
Apps	16	4	5	5	18	1	16	17		20	21	21	1	1	3	19	16	1	15	7	3	21		
Subs																								
Goals								5		11	6	16			3		6		5	5		1	1	
Apps	10	2	6	1	12		6	9	1	11	12	12	3		4	10	8		11		1	12		
Subs																								
Goals					1			5		21	3	4	1		5		7		3			1		2
1	G		X		X					X1	X	X		X		X	X		X1			X		
2	G		X		X			X2		X4	X1	X2				X	X1		X			X		
3	G		X		X					X3	X	X				X	X4		X			X		
4	G		X		X					X1	X	X				X	X2		X1			X		
5	G		X		X			X1		X	X	X				X	X		X			X		
6	G		X		X			X1		X1	X1	X1				X	X		X			X		
7	G		X		X					X2	X	X				X	X1		X1			X		
8	G		X		X					X	X1	X				X	X1		X			X		1
9	G		X		X			X2		X2	X	X	X				X		X	X	X		1	
10	G		X		X			X		X2	X	X	X			X			X			X		
11			G				X	X		X	X	X1	X						X	X		X		
12	G				X	X		X		X1	X	X2			X1	X	X					X		
13	G				X		X	X1		X	X1	X1				X	X3		X			X		
14			G		X		X	X		X	X	X				X	X		X			X		
15	G				X		X			X	X	X				X	X			X1		X		
16	G				X		X			X	X	X1				X	X		X	X		X		
17	G				X		X	X		X2	X	X			X1	X			X1			X		1
18	G				X		X			X	X	X			X1	X			X1			X		
19	G				X		X			X1	X	X				X		X	X			X		
20	G	X					X	X1		X	X1	X1					X		X	X2		X		
21	G				X		X	X1		X2	X1	X4					X		X1	X1		X1		
22	G				X		X	X		X1	X	X				X	X			X		X		
23	G				X		X	X		X	X	X1				X	X			X		X		
24					X1			X	X	X3	X1	X1			X2	G			X			X		
25	G				X		X	X		X	X	X			X		X		X			X1		
26		X	G		X		X			X	X	X1				X	X		X			X		
27		X	G	X			X			X1p	X	X				X	X			X		X		
28		X	G	X			X			X2	X	X1				X	X		X1			X		
29	G				X		X	X		X	X1	X1				X			X	X		X		
30	G	X			X			X		X3	X1	X1	X1			X	X					X		
31			G		X		X	X		X	X	X			X1	X			X			X		
32	G	X			X			X		X	X	X			X2	X	X2		X1			X		
33	G				X		X			X1	X	X				X			X	X1		X		
	G				X		X	X1		X1	X	X				X	X	X				X		

1900/01

Southern League position: 14th out of 15 in Division 1

Manager: None

	HOME					AWAY					
	Pl	W	D	L	For	Ag	W	D	L	For	Ag	Pts
Southampton	28	13	1	0	44	12	5	4	5	14	14	41
Bristol City	28	12	2	0	40	6	5	3	6	14	21	39
Portsmouth	28	12	2	0	33	7	5	2	7	23	26	38
Millwall	28	11	1	2	36	10	6	1	7	19	22	36
Tottenham Hotspur	28	12	1	1	35	8	4	3	7	20	25	36
West Ham United	28	10	2	2	28	10	4	3	7	12	18	33
Bristol Rovers	28	10	3	1	29	8	4	1	9	17	27	32
Queens Park Rangers	28	9	1	4	29	21	2	3	9	14	29	26
Reading	28	7	2	5	16	10	1	6	7	8	15	24
Luton Town	28	9	1	4	32	20	2	1	11	11	29	24
Kettering	28	7	4	3	21	12	0	5	9	12	34	23
New Brompton	28	5	4	5	20	19	2	1	11	14	32	19
Gravesend United	28	5	5	4	23	27	1	2	11	9	58	19
WATFORD	28	6	3	5	17	16	0	1	13	7	36	16
Swindon Town	28	3	6	5	15	18	0	2	12	4	29	14

New league opponents: Bristol City, Bristol Rovers, New Brompton, Gravesend United, Kettering, Luton Town, Millwall, Portsmouth, Queens Park Rangers, Reading, Southampton, Swindon Town, Tottenham Hotspur

Home-and-away league doubles

For - none

Against – 5 (Bristol City, Millwall, Portsmouth, Queens Park Rangers, West Ham United)

Divisional changes at end of season: Bristol City to Football League; Gravesend United resigned; Brentford from Division 2; Northampton Town & Wellingborough elected; division increased to 16 clubs

All Matches: Won 7, Drew 6, Lost 19, Goals 36-57

Highest Score: 10 (Match 9)

No	DATE			COMPETITION	OPPONENTS	HOME	AWAY	ATTENDANCE
1	September	Sat	8	Southern League, Division 1	Bristol City		L 1-6	7,000
2		Sat	15	Southern League, Division 1	SWINDON TOWN	1-1 D		3,000
3		Sat	22	Southern League, Division 1	Queens Park Rangers		L 0-1	4,500
4		Sat	29	Southern League, Division 1	Luton Town		L 0-2	4,000
5	October	Sat	6	Southern League, Division 1	TOTTENHAM HOTSPUR	2-1 W		5,000
6		Sat	13	Southern League, Division 1	West Ham United		L 0-2	3,000
7		Sat	20	Southern League, Division 1	PORTSMOUTH	2-4 L		4,000
8		Sat	27	Southern League, Division 1	New Brompton		L 1-2	1,000
9	November	Sat	3	FA Cup, 3rd Qualifying Round	LEIGHTON CEE SPRINGS	10-0 W		2,000
10		Sat	10	Southern League, Division 1	Reading		L 0-1	2,000
11		Sat	17	FA Cup, 4th Qualifying Round	QUEENS PARK RANGERS	1-1 D		3,000
12		Wed	21	FA Cup, 4th Qualifying Round replay	Queens Park Rangers		L 1-4	3,000
13		Sat	24	Southern League, Division 1	Gravesend United		L 2-4	1,000
14	December	Sat	1	Southern League, Division 1	MILLWALL	1-2 L		2,000
15		Sat	8	Southern League, Division 1	Southampton		L 0-1	2,000
16		Sat	29	Southern League, Division 1	Swindon Town		D 1-1	3,000
17	January	Sat	5	Southern League, Division 1	QUEENS PARK RANGERS	0-1 L		2,000
18		Sat	12	Southern League, Division 1	LUTON TOWN	2-0 W		3,000
19		Sat	19	Southern League, Division 1	Tottenham Hotspur		L 0-7	3,200
20		Sat	26	Southern League, Division 1	WEST HAM UNITED	0-1 L		2,000
21	February	Sat	9	Southern League, Division 1	Portsmouth		L 0-2	4,000
22		Sat	16	Southern League, Division 1	NEW BROMPTON	2-1 W		1,500
23		Sat	23	Southern League, Division 1	Bristol Rovers		L 1-4	
24	March	Sat	2	Southern League, Division 1	READING	1-0 W		
25		Sat	9	Southern League, Division 1	Kettering		L 1-2	1,500
26		Wed	20	Southern League, Division 1	BRISTOL ROVERS	2-1 W		500
27		Sat	23	Southern League, Division 1	Millwall		L 0-1	1,500
28		Sat	30	Southern League, Division 1	SOUTHAMPTON	1-1 D		3,000
29	April	Sat	6	Southern League, Division 1	GRAVESEND UNITED	2-0 W		1,500
30		Wed	17	Southern League, Division 1	BRISTOL CITY	1-3 L		2,000
31		Sat	27	Southern League, Division 1	KETTERING	0-0 D		1,500
32		Mon	29	Southern League Test Match	GRAYS UNITED	0-0 D		500

				The following matches became void when Chatham resigned from the Southern League in December 1900:				==========
	September	Sat	1	Southern League, Division 1	CHATHAM	2-1 W		2,500
	December	Sat	15	Southern League, Division 1	Chatham		D 1-1	

				The following match was abandoned after 75 minutes, owing to bad light:				
	December	Sat	22	Southern League, Division 1	BRISTOL CITY	0-0		3,000

League ever-presents: R.W. Hammett, H.M. Wilcox
Most appearances in total: R.W. Hammett & H.M. Wilcox 32 out of 32   **Most goals in total:** J.L. Price 9
Hat-tricks: C.B. Hare (Match 9)   **Penalty goals:** T. Farnall 1, J.L. Price 1
Sent off: None
Full international appearance(s) this season: None

	Allan, W.	Colclough, E.	Cother, J.W.	Eames, W.	Farnall, T.	Fellows, W.	Ferne, G.E.	Gale, A.E.	Good, M.	Hamilton, A.	Hammett, R.W.	Hare, C.B.	Hill, J.	Jeffrey, A.	Nidd, G.F.	Parkinson, R.	Price, J.L.	Sharp, A.	Varley, E.A.	White, H.W.	Wilcox, H.M.	Wood, H.
Apps	18	17	22	2	21	2	4	1	25	6	29	5	2	18	27	15	26	21	15	3	29	11
Subs																						
Goals	1	1			1		1		1	1	2	1			5		6		1	1	2	
Apps	1				3				3		3	3	1	3	3		3	3	2	2	3	
Subs																						
Goals					1							3					3	2		1	2	
1		X	X		X1		X		X		G				X		X		X		X	X
2		X	X		X		X1		X		G				X		X		X		X	X
3		X	X		X		X		X		G	X		X	X		X				X	
4		X	X		X		X		X		G				X		X		X		X	
5		X	X		X				X		G				X		X1		X	X	X1	
6	X	X			X	X					G				X		X		X	X	X	
7					X				X		G	X	X1	X	X		X		X1	X	X	
8					X				X		G	X	X	X	X		X1		X	X	X	
9					X1p				X		G	X3	X	X	X		X2	X2	X		X2	
10	X	X			X					X	G	X			X				X		X	X
11	X				X				X		G	X			X		X1p	X		X	X	
12					X				X		G	X			X		X	X	X	X1	X	
13			X						X	X	G	X2			X		X	X	X		X	
14			X		X				X	X1	G				X		X	X	X	X	X	
15	X				X				X	X	G				X		X	X		X	X	
16	X		X						X		G				X	X	X1	X			X	X
17	X		X						X		G				X	X	X	X			X	X
18	X		X						X		G				X	X	X1	X	X1		X	
19	X		X						X		G				X	X	X	X	X		X	
20	X	X	X						X		G				X	X	X	X			X	
21	X				X				X	X	G				X	X	X	X			X	
22	X	X	X		X				X1		G				X	X1	X	X			X	
23	X	X	X		X				X		G				X	X	X1	X			X	
24	X1	X	X		X				X		G				X	X	X	X1			X	
25	X	X	X		X				X		G				X	X	X1	X			X	
26	X	X	X		X				X		G				X	X	X1	X			X1	
27	X	X	X		X				X		G				X	X	X1				X	X
28	X	X	X		X				X		G				X	X	X1				X	X
29		X1	X		X				X		G				X	X1	X	X			X	X
30		X	X		X				X		G				X	X1	X	X			X	X
31	X		X					X	X		G				X		X	X	X		X	X
32	X		X	X		X					G				X		X	X	X		X	
		X	X		X		X		X		G				X		X1		X		X1	X
		X			X				X1	X	G		X	X	X		X	X			X	
		X		X					X	X	G		X	X	X		X	X		X		

- *33* -

1901/02

Southern League position: 13th out of 16 in Division 1
Manager: None

New league opponents: Northampton Town, Wellingborough

Home-and-away league doubles
For – 1 (Swindon Town)
Against – 5 (Millwall, Portsmouth, Southampton, Tottenham Hotspur, Wellingborough)

Divisional changes at end of season: None

All Matches: Won 10, Drew 4, Lost 18, Goals 39-63

Highest Score: 4 (Match 4)

		HOME					AWAY					
	Pl	W	D	L	For	Ag	W	D	L	For	Ag	Pts
Portsmouth	30	11	4	0	35	5	9	3	3	32	19	47
Tottenham Hotspur	30	11	2	2	42	11	7	4	4	19	11	42
Southampton	30	12	2	1	54	10	6	4	5	17	18	42
West Ham United	30	10	2	3	27	13	7	4	4	18	15	40
Reading	30	10	4	1	38	9	6	3	6	19	15	39
Millwall	30	9	3	3	35	13	4	3	8	15	18	32
Luton Town	30	8	5	2	16	10	3	5	7	15	25	32
Kettering	30	9	4	2	31	12	3	1	11	13	27	29
Bristol Rovers	30	11	1	3	37	10	1	4	10	6	29	29
New Brompton	30	10	2	3	27	8	0	5	10	12	30	27
Northampton Town	30	7	3	5	40	30	4	2	9	13	34	27
Queens Park Rangers	30	6	5	4	21	16	2	2	11	12	39	23
WATFORD	30	7	2	6	21	19	2	2	11	15	41	22
Wellingborough	30	8	2	5	23	18	1	2	12	11	54	22
Brentford	30	7	2	6	23	21	0	4	11	11	40	20
Swindon Town	30	2	3	10	13	27	0	0	15	4	66	7

No	DATE			COMPETITION	OPPONENTS	HOME	AWAY	ATTENDANCE
1	September	Sat	7	Southern League, Division 1	Queens Park Rangers		W 1-0	5,000
2		Sat	14	Southern League, Division 1	READING	0-2 L		4,000
3		Sat	21	Southern League, Division 1	Southampton		L 0-5	4,000
4		Sat	28	Southern League, Division 1	BRISTOL ROVERS	4-0 W		3,000
5	October	Sat	5	Southern League, Division 1	New Brompton		L 1-2	3,000
6		Sat	12	Southern League, Division 1	NORTHAMPTON TOWN	2-1 W		2,500
7		Sat	19	Southern League, Division 1	WEST HAM UNITED	0-0 D		4,000
8		Sat	26	Southern League, Division 1	Tottenham Hotspur		L 1-8	7,500
9	November	Sat	2	FA Cup, 3rd Qualifying Round	West Hampstead		W 2-1	2,000
10		Sat	9	Southern League, Division 1	Portsmouth		L 0-2	
11		Sat	16	FA Cup, 4th Qualifying Round	LUTON TOWN	1-2 L		5,000
12		Sat	23	Southern League, Division 1	Millwall		L 1-4	2,000
13		Sat	30	Southern League, Division 1	MILLWALL	1-2 L		2,000
14	December	Sat	7	Southern League, Division 1	Luton Town		L 0-1	2,000
15		Sat	21	Southern League, Division 1	QUEENS PARK RANGERS	1-1 D		2,000
16		Sat	28	Southern League, Division 1	Reading		D 1-1	3,000
17	January	Sat	4	Southern League, Division 1	SOUTHAMPTON	1-2 L		2,000
18		Sat	11	Southern League, Division 1	Bristol Rovers		L 0-3	2,500
19		Sat	18	Southern League, Division 1	NEW BROMPTON	3-0 W		3,000
20		Sat	25	Southern League, Division 1	SWINDON TOWN	3-0 W		2,000
21	February	Sat	1	Southern League, Division 1	West Ham United		L 2-3	1,000
22		Sat	8	Southern League, Division 1	TOTTENHAM HOTSPUR	0-3 L		3,000
23		Sat	15	Southern League, Division 1	Wellingborough		L 0-3	700
24		Sat	22	Southern League, Division 1	LUTON TOWN	2-0 W		3,000
25	March	Sat	1	Southern League, Division 1	Swindon Town		W 3-1	600
26		Sat	8	Southern League, Division 1	BRENTFORD	2-1 W		3,000
27		Sat	15	Southern League, Division 1	Kettering		L 1-3	1,000
28		Fri	28	Southern League, Division 1	PORTSMOUTH	0-5 L		4,000
29		Mon	31	Southern League, Division 1	WELLINGBOROUGH	0-1 L		4,000
30	April	Sat	5	Southern League, Division 1	KETTERING	2-1 W		1,500
31		Sat	12	Southern League, Division 1	Brentford		L 3-4	2,000
32		Sat	19	Southern League, Division 1	Northampton Town		D 1-1	1,200

League ever-presents: J. Chalmers, J.W. Cother, J. Hamilton, H. Lyon
Most appearances in total: J. Chalmers, J.W. Cother, J. Hamilton & H. Lyon 32 out of 32   **Most goals in total:** H. Lyon 14
Hat-tricks: None   **Penalty goals:** H. Lyon 1
Sent off: E.H. Cottrell (Match 23)
Full international appearance(s) this season: None

	Brown, W.	Chalmers, J.	Cother, J.W.	Cottrell, E.H.	Drake, C.F.	Greenslade, R.P.	Hamilton, J.	Hammett, R.W.	Harding, A.	Harvey, H.	Hogan, C.	Horner, F.Y.	Lyon, H.	Morgan, J.S.	Munn, S.	Nidd, G.F.	Pangborn, T.	Waller, G.	Wragg, W.	Own goal
Apps	15	30	30	19	1	20	30	4	7	28	2	15	30	2	20	28	24	7	18	
Subs																				
Goals	1	5		5			3			3			12	1			5		1	
Apps	2	2	2				2		2	2			2			2	2	2	2	
Subs																				
Goals		1											2							
1	X	X	X				X	G		X	X		X1			X	X		X	
2	X	X	X	X			X	G		X	X		X			X			X	
3	X	X	X				X	G	X		X		X			X	X		X	
4	X	X1	X				X	G	X		X		X1			X	X2		X	
5	X	X	X				X		X	X			X1			X	X	G	X	
6	X	X1	X	X			X		X				X			X	X1	G	X	
7	X	X	X				X		X	X			X			X		G	X	
8	X	X	X	X			X		X	X			X1			X		G	X	
9	X	X	X				X		X	X			X2p			X		G	X	
10	X	X	X	X			X						X		X	X	X	G	X	
11	X	X1	X				X		X	X			X			X	X	G	X	
12		X	X	X			X			X1			X			X	X	G	X	
13		X	X	X1		X	X			X			X			X	X	G	X	
14	X	X	X	X		X	X			X			X		X	G			X	
15		X	X	X		X	X			X1			X		X	G	X		X	
16		X	X	X		X	X			X			X1		X	G	X		X	
17		X1	X	X		X	X			X			X		X	G	X		X	
18		X	X	X		X	X			X		G	X		X	X	X			
19		X1	X	X1		X	X1			X		G	X		X	X	X			
20		X	X	X1		X	X			X		G	X2		X	X	X			
21		X	X	X1		X	X			X		G	X1		X	X			X	
22		X	X	X		X	X			X		G	X			X	X		X	
23		X	X	X		X	X			X		G	X			X	X		X	
24		X	X	X		X	X			X		G	X		X	X	X1			1
25		X1	X	X		X	X1			X		G	X1		X	X	X			
26		X	X	X1		X	X			X		G	X1		X	X	X			
27	X	X	X			X	X			X		G	X		X	X	X1			
28		X	X		X	X	X			X		G	X		X	X	X			
29	X	X	X			X	X			X		G	X		X	X	X			
30	X	X	X			X	X			X		G	X2		X	X	X			
31	X1	X	X			X	X			X1		G	X	X1	X	X				
32	X	X	X			X	X1		X	X		G	X	X	X					

1902/03

Southern League position: 15th out of 16 in Division 1 – relegated to Division 2
Manager: None

		HOME					AWAY					
	Pl	W	D	L	For	Ag	W	D	L	For	Ag	Pts
Southampton	30	12	2	1	53	7	8	6	1	30	13	48
Reading	30	12	2	1	47	14	7	5	3	25	16	45
Portsmouth	30	11	2	2	36	13	6	5	4	33	19	41
Tottenham Hotspur	30	10	5	0	34	9	4	2	9	13	22	35
Bristol Rovers	30	9	5	1	33	12	4	3	8	13	22	34
New Brompton	30	9	4	2	24	9	2	7	6	13	26	33
Millwall	30	9	2	4	33	16	5	1	9	19	21	31
Northampton Town	30	7	3	5	23	19	5	3	7	16	29	30
Queens Park Rangers	30	8	3	4	25	16	3	3	9	9	26	28
West Ham United	30	8	5	2	25	14	1	5	9	10	35	28
Luton Town	30	8	3	4	28	14	2	4	9	15	30	27
Swindon Town	30	8	5	2	24	13	2	2	11	14	33	27
Kettering	30	5	8	2	19	12	3	3	9	14	28	27
Wellingborough	30	9	2	4	27	15	2	1	12	9	41	25
WATFORD	30	5	1	9	22	33	1	3	11	13	54	16
Brentford	30	2	1	12	10	36	0	0	15	6	48	5

New league opponents: None
Home-and-away league doubles
For – 1 (Brentford)
Against – 6 (Bristol Rovers, Luton Town, Millwall, Queens Park Rangers, Reading, Southampton)
Relegation to Division 2: In Test Matches against the joint-champions of Division 2, Watford lost and Brentford beat Fulham. Promotion and relegation nevertheless were still decided by vote, and Fulham were promoted at Watford's expense.
All Matches: Won 8, Drew 5, Lost 23, Goals 49-101   **Highest Score:** 6 (Match 32)

Watford finished 7th out of 12 clubs in the South-Eastern League, but fielded the first team in only three of the 22 games.

No	DATE			COMPETITION	OPPONENTS	HOME	AWAY	ATTENDANCE
1	September	Sat	6	Southern League, Division 1	WELLINGBOROUGH	3-1 W		3,000
2		Sat	13	Southern League, Division 1	Bristol Rovers		L 1-5	5,000
3		Wed	17	South-Eastern League	GRAYS UNITED	2-1 W		200
4		Sat	20	Southern League, Division 1	NORTHAMPTON TOWN	1-0 W		3,000
5		Sat	27	Southern League, Division 1	Millwall		L 0-8	5,000
6	October	Sat	4	Southern League, Division 1	Brentford		W 3-2	1,500
7		Sat	11	Southern League, Division 1	TOTTENHAM HOTSPUR	1-2 L		4,000
8		Sat	18	Southern League, Division 1	West Ham United		L 1-3	3,000
9		Sat	25	Southern League, Division 1	PORTSMOUTH	1-4 L		4,000
10	November	Sat	1	FA Cup, 3rd Qualifying Round	FULHAM	1-1 D		2,000
11		Thu	6	FA Cup, 3rd Qualifying Round replay	Fulham		L 0-3	2,000
12		Sat	8	Southern League, Division 1	SWINDON TOWN	5-3 W		1,500
13		Sat	22	Southern League, Division 1	LUTON TOWN	0-1 L		3,000
14		Sat	29	Southern League, Division 1	Reading		L 2-5	2,000
15	December	Sat	6	Southern League, Division 1	QUEENS PARK RANGERS	0-2 L		1,500
16		Sat	13	Southern League, Division 1	Southampton		L 0-11	
17		Sat	20	Southern League, Division 1	Wellingborough		L 1-2	1,000
18		Sat	27	Southern League, Division 1	BRISTOL ROVERS	1-2 L		2,000
19		Mon	29	Southern League, Division 1	Kettering		D 1-1	2,000
20	January	Sat	3	Southern League, Division 1	Northampton Town		L 0-3	1,500
21		Sat	10	Southern League, Division 1	MILLWALL	1-7 L		3,000
22		Sat	17	Southern League, Division 1	BRENTFORD	3-1 W		1,200
23		Sat	24	Southern League, Division 1	Tottenham Hotspur		D 1-1	4,000
24		Sat	31	Southern League, Division 1	WEST HAM UNITED	2-1 W		2,000
25	February	Sat	14	Southern League, Division 1	NEW BROMPTON	2-2 D		2,500
26		Sat	21	Southern League, Division 1	Swindon Town		L 0-3	3,000
27		Sat	28	Southern League, Division 1	KETTERING	0-2 L		2,000
28	March	Sat	7	Southern League, Division 1	Luton Town		L 1-4	2,000
29		Sat	14	Southern League, Division 1	READING	1-2 L		1,500
30		Sat	21	Southern League, Division 1	Queens Park Rangers		L 0-3	5,000
31		Sat	28	Southern League, Division 1	SOUTHAMPTON	1-3 L		2,500
32	April	Sat	4	South-Eastern League	BRIGHTON & HOVE ALBION	6-1 W		400
33		Wed	15	South-Eastern League	Grays United		L 2-3	300
34		Sat	18	Southern League, Division 1	Portsmouth		D 1-1	
35		Sat	25	Southern League, Division 1	New Brompton		L 1-2	
36		Mon	27	Southern League Test Match	Brighton & Hove Albion (at West Ham United)	(L 3-5)		200

League ever-presents: **J. Tennant**
Most appearances in total: J. Tennant 36 out of 36   **Most goals in total:** J. Tennant 10
Hat-tricks: J.S. Morgan (Match 12)   **Penalty goals:** W. Dackers 1, H.M. Matthew 1
Sent off: J. Murray (Match 11)
Full international appearance(s) this season: None

Appearances / Goals summary

	Allan, E.	Beach, T.H.	Brown, W.	Cother, J.W.	Cottrell, E.H.	Dackers, W.	Eames, W.	Farnall, T.	Greenslade, R.P.	Harding, A.	Harvey, H.	Higgins, H.W.	Horner, F.Y.	Lyon, F.	McAvoy, F.	Matthew, H.M.	Morgan, J.S.	Mumn, S.	Murray, J.	Padley, R.	Proudfoot, J.	Smith, G.	Tennant, J.	Turner, R.	Walmesley, ---	Welch, C.F.	Own goal
Apps	20		22	19	19	26	19	9	11	4	11	18	12	14	23	10	11	16	27		12	3	31	2	1	1	
Subs																											
Goals				7		1	3				1				2		6		6		5		6			1	
Apps	4	1	2	5	3	3	2	2	1	2	2	2	3		2	2	2	5	4	1	1	1	5				
Subs																											
Goals				1			2									1		2					4				1

Match appearances

Match	Allan	Beach	Brown	Cother	Cottrell	Dackers	Eames	Farnall	Greenslade	Harding	Harvey	Higgins	Horner	Lyon	McAvoy	Matthew	Morgan	Mumn	Murray	Padley	Proudfoot	Smith	Tennant	Turner	Walmesley	Welch	OG
1	X			X	X			X	X		X		G						X1		X1		X1	X			
2	X			X	X1			X	X		X		G						X		X		X	X			
3	X			X	X			X	X	X	X		G					X				X	X1				1
4	X			X	X1	X		X			X		G						X		X		X				
5	X			X				X	X		X		G						X		X		X				
6	X			X	X	X					X		G						X		X2		X				
7	X			X	X			X			X1		G						X		X		X				
8	X			X				X	X		X		G						X		X		X1				
9	X			X				X	X		X		G						X		X		X			X1	
10	X			X				X			X		G				X	X	X		X		X1				
11		X	X	X	X	X		X					G		X								X				
12			X	X		X	X					G		X	X1		X3	X	X1				X				
13			X	X		X	X					G		X	X		X	X	X				X				
14			X	X		X	X					G		X	X				X		X2		X				
15			X	X		X	X					G		X	X				X		X		X				
16			X			X	X		X	X		G			X				X		X		X				
17	X		X				X	X1	X		X	G			X				X		X		X				
18			X				X	X	X	X		G			X		X1		X			X	X				
19			X			X1	X	X	X	X		G			X				X			X	X				
20			X				X	X	X	X		G			X				X			X	X				
21			X	X		X1	X	X						X	X				X				X		G		
22			X	X		X	X	X1				G		X	X1				X1				X				
23	X		X	X		X	X1	X				G		X	X				X				X				
24	X		X	X1		X						G		X	X			X	X				X1				
25	X		X			X1p	X					G		X	X	X	X		X1				X				
26	X		X	X	X	X	X					G			X	X			X				X				
27	X		X	X	X	X	X					G			X	X			X				X				
28	X		X			X						G		X	X	X	X1		X				X				
29	X		X			X	X					G		X	X	X	X1		X				X				
30	X		X			X	X					G		X	X	X	X		X				X				
31	X		X			X	X					G		X	X	X			X				X1				
32	X		X	X			X2					G			X	X1p		X	X2	X			X1				
33	X		X	X1	X	X	X					G				X	X	X	X				X1				
34	X		X	X								G			X	X	X	X	X				X1				
35	X			X	X1		X					G			X	X	X	X					X				
36			X	X	X1	X	X					G			X	X	X	X	X1				X1				

- 37 -

1903/04

Southern League position: 1st out of 11 in Division 2 – promoted to Division 1
Manager: John Goodall

	Pl	W	D	L	For	Ag	Pts
WATFORD	20	18	2	0	70	14	38
Portsmouth Reserves	20	15	2	3	85	25	32
Millwall Reserves	20	9	4	7	35	39	22
Southampton Reserves	20	9	3	8	59	35	21
Grays United	20	9	3	8	25	55	21
Fulham Reserves	20	8	4	8	40	34	20
Swindon Town Reserves	20	8	3	9	50	44	19
Reading Reserves	20	8	2	10	43	42	18
Wycombe Wanderers	20	5	5	10	29	64	15
Southall	20	4	2	14	25	62	10
Chesham Town	20	1	2	17	19	65	4

New Southern League opponents: The reserve teams of Fulham, Millwall, Portsmouth, Reading, Southampton & Swindon Town
Home-and-away league doubles
For – 8 (Chesham Town, Grays United, Millwall Reserves, Portsmouth Reserves, Reading Reserves, Southall, Swindon Town Reserves, Wycombe Wanderers)
Against – none
Promotion to Division 1: Kettering resigned from the Southern League, and Watford were elected to take their place in Division 1
All Matches: Won 30, Drew 2, Lost 3, Goals 133-34   **Highest Score:** 10 (Match 18)

(Watford finished 4th out of 12 clubs in the South-Eastern League, but fielded the first team in only 13 of the 22 games.)

No	DATE			COMPETITION	OPPONENTS	HOME	AWAY	ATTENDANCE
1	September	Sat	5	Southern League, Division 2	Grays United		W 3-1	
2		Sat	12	Southern League, Division 2	PORTSMOUTH RESERVES	6-1 W		2,500
3		Sat	26	Southern League, Division 2	WYCOMBE WANDERERS	9-0 W		2,000
4	October	Sat	3	South-Eastern League	Tottenham Hotspur Reserves		W 3-2	
5		Sat	10	Southern League, Division 2	Portsmouth Reserves		W 2-1	3,000
6		Sat	17	Southern League, Division 2	READING RESERVES	2-1 W		2,000
7		Mon	19	South-Eastern League	Woolwich Arsenal Reserves		L 1-3	1,500
8		Sat	24	South-Eastern League	HITCHIN TOWN	9-0 W		
9		Sat	31	FA Cup, 3rd Qualifying Round	Redhill		W 6-0	2,000
10	November	Sat	14	FA Cup, 4th Qualifying Round	Luton Town		L 1-4	7,000
11		Sat	21	Southern League, Division 2	FULHAM RESERVES	2-0 W		1,500
12		Sat	28	Southern League, Division 2	Chesham Town		W 1-0	
13	December	Sat	5	Southern League, Division 2	SWINDON TOWN RESERVES	6-1 W		1,000
14		Sat	12	Southern League, Division 2	Fulham Reserves		D 3-3	
15		Sat	19	South-Eastern League	GRAYS UNITED	8-0 W		
16		Fri	25	South-Eastern League	QUEENS PARK RANGERS RESERVES	4-2 W		
17		Sat	26	South-Eastern League	Queens Park Rangers		W 3-0	
18	January	Sat	2	Southern League, Division 2	SOUTHALL	10-0 W		
19		Sat	9	South-Eastern League	CHESHAM GENERALS	6-0 W		
20		Wed	13	South-Eastern League	LUTON TOWN	4-3 W		1,000
21		Sat	16	Southern League, Division 2	Reading Reserves		W 2-1	700
22	February	Sat	6	Southern League, Division 2	MILLWALL RESERVES	3-0 W		
23		Sat	13	Southern League, Division 2	Grays United	1-0 W		2,000
24		Sat	20	South-Eastern League	WOOLWICH ARSENAL RESERVES	3-1 W		2,500
25		Sat	27	South-Eastern League	TOTTENHAM HOTSPUR RESERVES	1-0 W		
26	March	Sat	5	Southern League, Division 2	Wycombe Wanderers		W 5-0	1,000
27		Sat	12	Southern League, Division 2	SOUTHAMPTON RESERVES	3-0 W		2,000
28		Sat	19	Southern League, Division 2	Swindon Town Reserves		W 2-0	1,500
29		Wed	23	Southern League, Division 2	CHESHAM TOWN	3-1 W		
30	April	Tue	5	Southern League, Division 2	Millwall Reserves		W 3-2	1,000
31		Sat	9	South-Eastern League	WAR OFFICE	8-1 W		
32		Sat	16	South-Eastern League	BRIGHTON & HOVE ALBION RESERVES	4-1 W		1,000
33		Mon	18	Southern League, Division 2	Southampton Reserves		D 2-2	
34		Sat	23	Southern League, Division 2	Southall		W 2-0	2,000
35		Sat	30	South-Eastern League	Luton Town		L 2-3	

The following match was abandoned after about an hour, owing to fog:

	January	Sat	23	Southern League, Division 2	CHESHAM TOWN	5-0		

League ever-presents: J. Brooks, W. Brown, J. Goodall, H.W. Higgins, D. McCartney, W. Morgan, J. Tennant
Most appearances in total: J. Brooks, H.W. Higgins & W. Morgan 35 out of 35   **Most goals in total:** H.E. Banks 33
Hat-tricks: H. Barton (Match 1, 6 goals Match 3, Match 14, Match 18 & Match 31), H.E. Banks (Match 2, Match 8, Match 13, Match 15, Match 18 & Match 26), J. Goodall (Match 8), W. Eames (4 goals, Match 19)   **Penalty goals:** W. Morgan 12
Sent off: None   **Full international appearance(s) this season:** None

	Badenoch, G.H.	Banks, H.E. //	Barton, H.	Brooks, J.	Brown, W. //	Cother, J.W.	Davis, J. //	Eames, W.	Goodall, J.	Harding, A. //	Higgins, H.W.	Lindsay, W.	McCartney, D.	Morgan, J.S.	Morgan, W. //	Mumn, S. //	Reading, E.	Tennant, J.	Trainer, P. //	Own goal
Apps	19	19	19	20	20		1	1	20	1	20	18	20	1	20	1		20		
Subs																				
Goals	1	21	19		3				4				3	2	9			7		1
Apps	14	13	14	15	12	1	1	3	13		15	13	14		15	4	3	14	1	
Subs																				
Goals	2	12	12	1	3			4	13				1		5		1	7	2	

Match	Badenoch, G.H.	Banks, H.E. //	Barton, H.	Brooks, J.	Brown, W. //	Cother, J.W.	Davis, J. //	Eames, W.	Goodall, J.	Harding, A. //	Higgins, H.W.	Lindsay, W.	McCartney, D.	Morgan, J.S.	Morgan, W. //	Mumn, S. //	Reading, E.	Tennant, J.	Trainer, P. //	Own goal
1	X	X	X3	X	X				X		G	X	X		X			X		
2		X3	X1	X	X				X1		G	X	X		X	X		X1		
3	X	X1	X6	X	X1				X		G	X	X		X1			X		
4	X	X	X	X	X				X1		G	X	X1		X			X1		
5	X	X1	X	X	X				X		G	X	X		X1p			X		
6	X	X2	X	X	X				X	X	G		X		X			X		
7	X	X	X	X	X				X1		G	X	X		X			X		
8	X	X3	X2	X	X		X		X3		G				X	X		X1		
9	X	X1	X	X	X1				X1		G	X	X		X1p			X2		
10	X	X	X	X	X				X		G	X	X		X			X1		
11	X	X1	X	X	X				X		G	X	X		X1p			X		
12	X	X	X1	X	X				X		G	X	X		X			X		
13	X	X3	X	X	X				X1		G	X	X1		X1p			X		
14	X		X3	X			X	X	X		G	X	X		X			X		
15	X	X3	X2	X	X1				X1		G	X	X		X			X1		
16	X	X1	X1	X	X				X		G	X	X		X2p			X		
17	X	X	X1	X	X				X1		G	X	X		X1p			X		
18	X1	X3	X3	X	X1				X		G	X	X1		X			X1		
19	X		X1	X	X1	X		X4			G	X	X		X			X		
20	X1	X2	X1	X	X				X		G	X	X		X			X		
21	X	X	X	X	X1				X		G	X	X		X			X1		
22	X	X1	X	X	X				X		G	X	X		X2#			X		
23	X	X	X	X	X				X		G	X	X		X			X		
24	X	X	X1	X					X2		G	X	X		X		X	X		
25	X	X	X	X					X		G	X	X		X1p		X	X		
26	X	X3	X	X	X				X		G	X	X		X1p			X1		
27	X	X1	X	X	X				X		G	X	X1		X1p			X		
28	X	X1	X	X					X1		G	X	X		X			X		
29	X	X1		X	X	X			X		G		X	X2	X			X		
30	X	X1	X	X	X				X		G	X	X		X1p			X1		
31	X	X2	X3	X1	X				X1		G	X	X		X			X1		
32	X1			X					X		G	X	X		X	X	X1	X	X2	
33	X	X	X1	X	X				X		G	X	X		X			X1		
34	X	X	X	X	X				X1		G	X	X		X			X	1	
35		X	X	X	X			X	X2		G	X	X		X	X		X		
	X	X2	X2	X	X				X		G1	X	X		X			X		

1904/05

Southern League position: 9th out of 18 in Division 1
Manager: John Goodall

	HOME					AWAY					
	Pl	W	D	L	For	Ag	W	D	L	For	Ag	Pts
Bristol Rovers	34	13	4	0	51	11	7	4	6	23	25	48
Reading	34	13	3	1	36	12	5	4	8	21	26	43
Southampton	34	9	4	4	29	21	9	3	5	25	19	43
Plymouth Argyle	34	14	3	0	38	11	4	2	11	19	28	41
Tottenham Hotspur	34	10	3	4	34	15	5	5	7	19	33	38
Fulham	34	10	5	2	32	9	4	5	8	14	25	38
Queens Park Rangers	34	10	2	5	36	19	4	6	7	15	27	36
Portsmouth	34	12	1	4	39	19	4	3	10	22	37	36
WATFORD	34	12	0	5	30	19	3	3	11	14	26	33
New Brompton	34	8	7	2	25	13	4	4	10	15	28	33
West Ham United	34	9	3	5	30	15	3	5	9	18	27	32
Brighton & Hove Albion	34	9	2	6	25	15	4	4	9	19	30	32
Northampton Town	34	8	4	5	26	17	4	4	9	17	37	32
Brentford	34	5	7	5	17	14	5	2	10	16	24	29
Millwall	34	7	6	4	26	15	4	1	12	12	32	29
Swindon Town	34	11	4	2	30	17	1	3	13	11	42	29
Luton Town	34	11	1	5	35	18	1	2	14	10	36	27
Wellingborough	34	4	3	10	16	37	1	0	16	9	67	13

New Southern League opponents: Brighton & Hove Albion, Plymouth Argyle

Home-and-away league doubles
For – 2 (Northampton Town, Reading)
Against – 4 (Bristol Rovers, Southampton, Tottenham Hotspur, West Ham United)

Divisional changes at end of season: Wellingborough resigned; Norwich City elected

All Matches: Won 26, Drew 5, Lost 19, Goals 93-60

Highest Score: 10 (Match 31)

Watford finished 4th out of 13 clubs in the South-Eastern League, but fielded the first team in only 11 of the 24 games.

No	DATE			COMPETITION	OPPONENTS	HOME	AWAY	ATTENDANCE
1	September	Sat	3	Southern League, Division 1	Millwall		W 2-0	5,000
2		Mon	5	South-Eastern League	Queens Park Rangers		D 1-1	2,000
3		Wed	7	South-Eastern League	LUTON TOWN	1-0 W		2,000
4		Sat	10	Southern League, Division 1	TOTTENHAM HOTSPUR	0-1 L		5,800
5		Sat	17	Southern League, Division 1	Luton Town		L 1-2	6,000
6		Wed	21	South-Eastern League	GRAYS UNITED	3-0 W		
7		Sat	24	Southern League, Division 1	Swindon Town		1-0 W	5,000
8		Wed	28	South-Eastern League	BRIGHTON & HOVE ALBION	1-3 L		
9	October	Sat	1	Southern League, Division 1	New Brompton		L 0-1	5,000
10		Wed	5	South-Eastern League	QUEENS PARK RANGERS	1-0 W		500
11		Sat	8	South-Eastern League	WOOLWICH ARSENAL RESERVES	4-2 W		2,500
12		Wed	12	South-Eastern League	Brighton & Hove Albion		L 0-4	1,500
13		Sat	15	Southern League, Division 1	Southampton		L 1-2	5,000
14		Sat	22	Southern League, Division 1	FULHAM	2-1 W		5,000
15		Sat	29	FA Cup, 3rd Qualifying Round	BIGGLESWADE	7-1 W		1,500
16	November	Sat	5	Southern League, Division 1	Plymouth Argyle		D 0-0	10,000
17		Sat	12	FA Cup, 4th Qualifying Round	Grays United		W 3-1	1,000
18		Sat	19	Southern League, Division 1	Reading		W 3-1	4,000
19		Sat	26	FA Cup, 5th Qualifying Round	HITCHIN TOWN	2-0 W		2,000
20	December	Sat	3	Southern League, Division 1	Northampton Town		W 2-1	3,000
21		Sat	10	FA Cup, 6th Qualifying Round	LINCOLN CITY	1-1 D		5,000
22		Wed	14	FA Cup, 6th Qualifying Round replay	Lincoln City		L 1-2	1,000
23		Sat	17	Southern League, Division 1	Brentford		D 1-1	
24		Sat	24	Southern League, Division 1	QUEENS PARK RANGERS	1-0 W		6,000
25		Mon	26	Southern League, Division 1	Wellingborough		D 1-1	4,000
26		Tue	27	South-Eastern League	Luton Town		W 1-0	1,500
27		Sat	31	Southern League, Division 1	MILLWALL	0-1 L		3,500
28	January	Sat	7	Southern League, Division 1	Tottenham Hotspur		L 0-2	10,000
29		Sat	14	South-Eastern League	HASTINGS & ST LEONARDS UNITED	6-0 W		600
30		Sat	21	Southern League, Division 1	Swindon Town		L 0-2	
31		Wed	25	South-Eastern League	EASTBOURNE OLD TOWN	10-0 W		
32		Sat	28	Southern League, Division 1	NEW BROMPTON	2-0 W		4,000
33	February	Sat	11	Southern League, Division 1	SOUTHAMPTON	0-4 L		5,000
34		Sat	18	Southern League, Division 1	PLYMOUTH ARGYLE	3-1 W		4,000
35		Wed	22	Southern League, Division 1	Fulham		L 1-2	2,000
36		Sat	25	Southern League, Division 1	Brighton & Hove Albion		L 0-1	3,000
37	March	Sat	11	Southern League, Division 1	West Ham United		L 0-2	3,000
38		Wed	15	South-Eastern League	SOUTHERN UNITED	7-0 W		
39		Sat	18	Southern League, Division 1	READING	3-2 W		3,500
40		Wed	22	Southern League, Division 1	PORTSMOUTH	4-1 W		2,000
41		Sat	25	Southern League, Division 1	Bristol Rovers		L 1-3	6,000
42		Wed	29	Southern League, Division 1	BRISTOL ROVERS	1-4 L		2,000
43	April	Sat	1	Southern League, Division 1	NORTHAMPTON TOWN	1-0 W		3,000
44		Sat	8	Southern League, Division 1	Portsmouth		L 0-1	6,000
45		Sat	15	Southern League, Division 1	BRENTFORD	1-0 W		4,000
46		Fri	21	Southern League, Division 1	LUTON TOWN	3-0 W		7,500
47		Sat	22	Southern League, Division 1	Queens Park Rangers		L 1-4	8,000
48		Mon	24	Southern League, Division 1	WELLINGBOROUGH	3-0 W		
49		Tue	25	Southern League, Division 1	WEST HAM UNITED	0-3 L		700
50		Sat	29	Southern League, Division 1	BRIGHTON & HOVE ALBION	5-1 W		2,500

League ever-presents: W. Biggar, J. Brooks, P. Turner
Most appearances in total: W. Biggar & P. Turner 50 out of 50   **Most goals in total:** J. Goodall 17
Hat-tricks: W. Eames (Match 15), P. Turner (Match 29), H. Barton (Match 31), J. Goodall (Match 38)   **Penalty goals:** D. McCartney 4
Sent off: None
Full international appearance(s) this season: None

	Badenoch, G.H.	Barnes, C.	Barton, H. //	Biggar, W.	Bray, C. //	Brooks, J.	Broughton, M.	Cother, J.W. //	Croom, W. //	Eames, W.	Field, S. //	Goodall, J.	Grieve, T. //	Jones, J. //	Lees, W. //	Lindsay, W.	McCartney, D.	Main, A.	Morgan, J.S. //	Ralston, A.T. //	Reading, E.	Richardson, J.W. //	Simons, G.F. //	Smith, G.	Tennant, J. //	Tierney, T.T. //	Tooley, A.E.	Turner, P.	Wigzell, -- //	One player short
Apps	28	5	15	34		34	8	3		11		29	1	7	6	27	31	27	1	2	6	30	1		32		1	34		1
Subs																														
Goals	7	1	7							2		10			2		5	1		1		1			2			5		
Apps	9	3	9	16	1	15	1	1	1	5	1	11		4	8	12	15	12	1		1	12	1		16	2	2	16	1	
Subs																														
Goals	2	1	5				1			7		7			5		5	1							7			8		

Match	Badenoch	Barnes	Barton	Biggar	Bray	Brooks	Broughton	Cother	Croom	Eames	Field	Goodall	Grieve	Jones	Lees	Lindsay	McCartney	Main	Morgan	Ralston	Reading	Richardson	Simons	Smith	Tennant	Tierney	Tooley	Turner	Wigzell	OPS
1	X		X2	G		X									X	X	X	X	X						X			X		
2	X		X	G		X									X	X	X	X	X						X1			X		
3			X1	G		X				X					X	X	X	X							X	X		X		
4	X		X	G		X										X	X	X	X						X			X		
5	X			G		X										X	X	X	X1	X					X			X		
6		X		G		X				X2					X1	X		X				X			X	X	X	X		
7		X		G		X						X1				X	X	X				X			X			X		
8				G		X				X					X	X	X	X	X1						X			X	X	
9	X		X	G		X						X				X	X	X				X			X			X		
10				G		X				X		X				X1	X	X				X			X			X		
11		X		G		X						X1				X2	X					X			X	X1		X		
12		X		G		X						X				X	X	X				X			X	X	X	X		
13		X		G		X						X				X1	X	X				X			X			X		
14				G		X				X1		X	X			X	X	X				X			X			X1		
15		X1		G		X				X3		X				X	X1	X				X			X			X1		
16	X			G		X						X				X	X	X				X			X			X		
17	X			G		X				X2		X1				X	X	X				X			X			X		
18	X		X2	G		X						X1				X	X	X				X			X			X		
19	X1		X	G		X						X				X	X	X				X			X1			X		
20	X		X1	G		X						X1				X	X	X				X			X			X		
21	X		X	G		X						X1			X	X	X					X			X			X		
22	X		X	G		X						X				X	X	X				X			X			X1		
23	X		X	G		X						X				X	X	X				X			X1			X		
24	X		X1	G		X						X				X	X	X				X			X			X		
25	X		X1	G		X						X				X	X	X				X			X			X		X
26	X		X	G		X	X	X				X					X1	X				X			X			X		
27	X		X	G		X						X				X	X	X				X			X			X		
28	X			G		X	X									X	X	X			X	X			X			X		
29	X			G		X	X			X1		X		X	X1			X				X			X1			X3		
30	X			G		X				X		X				X	X	X			X	X			X			X		
31	X1		X3	G		X									X	X1	X	X2	X		X				X2			X1		
32	X			G		X						X1			X	X	X	X				X			X			X1		
33	X			G		X	X					X				X	X	X							X			X		
34	X2			G		X	X					X1				X	X	X							X			X		
35	X1		X	G		X						X				X	X	X				X			X			X		
36			X	G		X				X						X	X	X				X			X			X		
37	X		X	G		X						X				X	X	X				X			X			X		
38	X		X1	G		X						X3				X	X1	X				X			X			X2		
39	X1		X	G		X						X				X	X1p	X1				X			X			X		
40	X1		X	G		X						X1				X	X	X				X			X			X2		
41			X	G		X						X1				X	X	X			X	X			X			X		
42	X		X	G		X						X				X	X1p					X			X			X		
43				G		X	X			X		X1				X	X	X							X			X		
44				G		X				X		X			X1	X	X	X							X			X		
45	X1			G		X				X		X		X		X	X	X				X			X			X		
46	X			G		X	X	X		X		X1					X1p					X			X		X1	X		
47	X			G		X	X	X		X		X					X1P					X			X			X		
48	X		X	G		X	X	X		X1		X2	X								X	X			X			X		
49	X		X	G		X				X		X	X							X	X	X						X		
50	X1		X1	G		X						X	X							X1	X1				X		X	X	X1	

1905/06

Southern League position: 14th out of 18 in Division 1
Manager: John Goodall

	HOME						AWAY					
	Pl	W	D	L	F for	Ag	W	D	L	For	Ag	Pts
Fulham	34	10	7	0	22	6	9	5	3	22	9	50
Southampton	34	13	2	2	32	11	6	5	6	26	28	45
Portsmouth	34	13	3	1	39	11	4	6	7	22	24	43
Luton Town	34	13	2	2	45	13	4	5	8	19	27	41
Tottenham Hotspur	34	13	2	2	36	11	3	5	9	10	18	39
Plymouth Argyle	34	11	3	3	32	13	5	4	8	20	20	39
Norwich City	34	9	8	0	31	11	4	2	11	15	27	36
Bristol Rovers	34	11	1	5	37	23	4	4	9	19	33	35
Brentford	34	11	3	3	28	19	3	4	10	15	33	35
Reading	34	9	7	1	34	15	3	2	12	19	31	33
West Ham United	34	12	2	3	30	9	2	3	12	12	30	33
Millwall	34	9	4	4	26	16	2	7	8	12	25	33
Queens Park Rangers	34	9	3	5	39	14	3	4	10	19	30	31
WATFORD	34	7	6	4	28	20	1	4	12	10	37	26
Swindon Town	34	6	4	7	21	23	2	5	10	10	29	25
Brighton & Hove Albion	34	8	5	4	24	24	1	2	14	6	31	25
New Brompton	34	5	5	7	10	20	2	3	12	10	42	22
Northampton Town	34	5	4	8	17	22	3	1	13	15	57	21

New Southern League opponents: Norwich City
Home-and-away league doubles
For - none
Against – 2 (Brighton & Hove Albion, Queens Park Rangers)
Divisional changes at end of season: Crystal Palace & Leyton from Division 2; division increased to 20 clubs
All Matches: Won 23, Drew 15, Lost 22, Goals 101-89
Highest Score: 10 (Match 42)

Watford finished 1st out of 10 clubs in the United League (Won 13, Drew 4, Lost 1, Goals 49-15, Points 30). In the South-Eastern League, the club finished 11th out of 13 clubs, but fielded the first team only five times in the 24 games.

No	DATE			COMPETITION	OPPONENTS	HOME AWAY	ATTENDANCE	
1	September	Sat	2	United League	LUTON TOWN	2-1 W	6,000	
2		Mon	4	Southern League, Division 1	PORTSMOUTH	2-2 D	3,000	
3		Wed	6	United League	CRYSTAL PALACE	1-0 W		
4		Sat	9	Southern League, Division 1	Tottenham Hotspur	L 0-1		7,000
5		Wed	13	South-Eastern League	BRIGHTON & HOVE ALBION	0-2 L		
6		Sat	16	Southern League, Division 1	BRENTFORD	1-0 W	5,000	
7		Wed	20	United League	LEYTON	2-1 W	500	
8		Sat	23	Southern League, Division 1	Norwich City	D 1-1		6,000
9		Mon	25	United League	New Brompton	L 1-2		300
10		Sat	30	Southern League, Division 1	PLYMOUTH ARGYLE	0-2 L	5,000	
11	October	Thu	5	South-Eastern League	Leyton	L 3-4		
12		Sat	7	Southern League, Division 1	Southampton	L 1-2		4,000
13		Wed	11	United League	NEW BROMPTON	2-0 W	300	
14		Sat	14	Southern League, Division 1	READING	1-0 W	4,500	
15		Wed	18	United League	Swindon Town	W 3-1		500
16		Sat	21	Southern League, Division 1	Northampton Town	L 1-2		5,000
17		Sat	28	United League	Brighton & Hove Albion	W 2-0		
18	November	Sat	4	Southern League, Division 1	WEST HAM UNITED	3-1 W	4,000	
19		Sat	11	Southern League, Division 1	Fulham	D 0-0		9,000
20		Sat	18	Southern League, Division 1	QUEENS PARK RANGERS	3-4 L	4,000	
21		Wed	22	South-Eastern League	WOOLWICH ARSENAL RESERVES	1-4 L		
22		Sat	25	Southern League, Division 1	Bristol Rovers	L 1-6		
23		Thu	30	United League	Southern United	W 4-1		500
24	December	Sat	2	Southern League, Division 1	NEW BROMPTON	2-2 D	3,000	
25		Sat	9	FA Cup, 4th Qualifying Round	SOUTHPORT CENTRAL	3-1 W	3,000	
26		Sat	16	Southern League, Division 1	SWINDON TOWN	1-2 L	3,000	
27		Sat	23	Southern League, Division 1	Millwall	L 0-1		
28		Mon	25	Southern League, Division 1	Luton Town	L 0-2		9,000
29		Tue	26	Southern League, Division 1	Brighton & Hove Albion	L 0-2		
30		Sat	30	United League	Crystal Palace	W 3-2		1,500
31	January	Sat	6	Southern League, Division 1	TOTTENHAM HOTSPUR	0-0 D	5,000	
32		Sat	13	FA Cup, 1st Round	Worcester City	W 6-0		4,000
33		Thu	18	United League	Leyton	D 3-3		
34		Sat	20	Southern League, Division 1	Brentford	L 0-3		5,000
35		Sat	27	Southern League, Division 1	NORWICH CITY	1-0 W	3,500	
36	February	Sat	3	FA Cup, 2nd Round	Woolwich Arsenal	L 0-3		11,000
37		Sat	10	Southern League, Division 1	SOUTHAMPTON	4-1 W	3,000	
38		Wed	14	South-Eastern League	Brighton & Hove Albion	L 1-3		4,000
39		Sat	17	Southern League, Division 1	Reading	L 1-3		2,000
40		Wed	21	United League	Grays United	W 3-0		
41		Sat	24	Southern League, Division 1	NORTHAMPTON TOWN	5-3 W	4,000	
42		Wed	28	United League	GRAYS UNITED	10-1 W		
43	March	Sat	3	United League	BRIGHTON & HOVE ALBION	2-1 W	3,000	
44		Mon	5	United League	Clapton Orient	W 2-1		
45		Sat	10	Southern League, Division 1	West Ham United	D 0-0		7,000
46		Wed	14	United League	CLAPTON ORIENT	1-1 D	500	
47		Sat	17	Southern League, Division 1	FULHAM	0-0 D	7,000	
48		Wed	21	United League	SWINDON TOWN	0-0 D		
49		Sat	24	Southern League, Division 1	Queens Park Rangers	L 0-6		9,000
50		Wed	28	South-Eastern League	LEYTON	0-0 D		
51		Sat	31	Southern League, Division 1	BRISTOL ROVERS	1-1 D	3,000	
52	April	Wed	4	United League	SOUTHERN UNITED	8-0 W	400	
53		Sat	7	Southern League, Division 1	New Brompton	L 0-2		3,000
54		Fri	13	Southern League, Division 1	LUTON TOWN	1-1 D	8,000	
55		Sat	14	Southern League, Division 1	Portsmouth	L 2-4		6,000
56		Mon	16	Southern League, Division 1	BRIGHTON & HOVE ALBION	0-1 L	5,000	
57		Tue	17	United League	Luton Town	D 0-0		3,000
58		Sat	21	Southern League, Division 1	Swindon Town	D 0-0		3,000
59		Wed	25	Southern League, Division 1	Plymouth Argyle	W 3-2		
60		Sat	28	Southern League, Division 1	MILLWALL	3-0 W	3,000	

League ever-presents: None
Most appearances in total: W. Biggar & P. Turner 56 out of 60
Most goals in total: J. Reid 16
Hat-tricks: F. Spiksley (Match 41), J. Foster (4 goals, Match 42)
Penalty goals: D. McCartney 3, W. Biggar 1, F. Kelly 1
Sent off: None
Full international appearance(s) this season: None

	Aston, C.L.	Badenoch, G.H.	Barnes, C.	Biggar, W.	Brooks, J.	Broughton, M.	Brown, G.F.	Eames, W.	Eaton, S.L.L.	Foster, J.	Fyfe, G.	Goodall, J.	Harper, --	Higgins, H.W.	Howard, G.A.	Kelly, F.	Lindsay, W.	McCartney, D.	Main, A.	Pheby, F.	Reid, J.	Richardson, J.W.	Sans, A.E.	Spiksley, F.	Turner, P.	Walter, J.	Own goal
Apps	31	33		33	23	1	3	14	11	13	9	12		1		24	14	31	27		19	32		11	31	1	
Subs																											
Goals		1						4	1	3	1					2		5			7			5	8		1
Apps	20	22	1	23	22		2	11	13	7	15	3	1	3	1	22	11	21	21	1	16	20	1	1	25	3	
Subs																											
Goals		4		1	1			8	3	6	4	2				9		3			9	4			9		
1		X		G	X					X						X	X	X1	X		X1	X			X		
2		X		G	X		X									X1	X	X1p	X		X	X			X		
3		X		G	X							X1				X	X	X	X		X	X			X		
4	X	X		G	X		X									X	X	X	X		X	X			X		
5	X	X		G	X		X									X	X	X	X		X	X			X		
6	X	X		G	X				X	X						X		X1	X		X				X		
7	X	X		G	X				X	X						X		X	X			X1			X1		
8	X	X		G	X				X	X						X		X	X		X				X		1
9	X	X		G	X					X		X1				X		X	X		X				X		
10		X		G	X					X			X			X	X	X	X		X				X		
11	X	X		G	X					X1						X	X	X	X			X			X2		
12	X	X		G	X					X						X		X	X		X1	X			X		
13	X	X		G	X					X	X1	X				X		X			X1	X					
14	X	X		G	X					X	X	X				X		X			X1	X					
15	X	X		G	X					X		X				X1		X			X1	X1			X		
16	X	X		G	X					X	X	X				X		X			X1				X		
17	X	X		G						X1	X1					X	X	X	X		X				X		
18	X	X		G						X1						X	X	X	X		X1	X			X1		
19	X	X		G							X					X	X	X	X		X	X			X		
20	X	X		G						X1						X	X	X1p	X		X	X			X1		
21	X	X			X					X		X		G		X1	X					X			X	X	
22	X	X		G						X						X	X	X	X		X	X			X1		
23	X	X1		G	X					X		X1				X1	X				X1	X			X		
24	X	X		G	X					X		X1				X	X				X1	X			X		
25	X	X		G	X					X1		X				X1			X		X	X1			X		
26	X	X		G	X					X						X		X1p	X		X	X			X		
27	X			G		X			X	X						X	X	X	X		X	X			X		
28	X			G						X						X	X	X	X		X	X			X		
29	X	X		G						X						X	X	X	X		X	X			X		
30	X	X		G				X		X1						X	X	X	X			X			X2		
31	X	X		G						X						X	X	X	X			X			X		
32	X	X		G				X1								X2	X	X	X		X2	X1			X		
33		X1		G	X		X	X1								X1	X	X	X		X2	X			X		
34	X	X		G		X		X		X						X	X	X							X	X	
35	X	X		G				X								X	X	X1			X	X			X		
36	X	X		G				X								X	X	X			X	X			X		
37	X	X		G			X2					X					X	X	X			X		X1	X1		
38	X	X		G	X			X		X						X					X1	X		X	X	X	
39	X	X		G				X		X	X								X					X	X1		
40	X	X		G				X2		X									X			X1			X	X	
41	X	X		G	X			X1		X	X								X			X		X3	X1		
42				G1p	X1				X	X4	X					X1p	X	X1	X		X1				X1		
43	X			G	X			X1	X			X					X	X			X			X	X1		
44	X			G	X			X	X			X				X1	X	X			X			X	X		
45	X	X		G	X			X				X					X	X			X			X	X		
46	X	X		G	X			X1				X					X	X		X	X			X	X		
47	X	X		G	X			X				X					X	X			X			X	X		
48	X	X	X	G	X					X							X	X			X	X			X		
49	X	X		G	X			X				X					X	X			X			X	X		
50		X			X					X	X	X		G	X	X	X				X	X	X		X		
51	X	X		G	X			X				X					X	X			X			X	X1		
52	X	X2		G	X			X2			X1	X1				X		X1	X						X1		
53	X	X		G	X				X	X	X	X						X			X			X	X		
54	X	X		G	X			X			X	X						X				X		X	X1		
55		X		G	X			X1			X	X				X		X				X		X1	X		
56	X	X		G	X			X				X				X		X				X		X	X		
57		X			X			X	X			X			G	X		X	X		X	X			X		
58	X	X		G	X			X								X		X	X		X	X			X		
59	X	X1		G	X					X1						X1		X	X		X	X			X		
60	X	X		X	X					X1				G		X		X	X			X		X2	X		

- 43 -

1906/07

Southern League position: 9th out of 20 in Division 1
Manager: John Goodall

	HOME					AWAY					
	Pl	W	D	L	For	Ag	W	D	L	For	Ag	Pts
Fulham	38	13	5	1	34	12	7	8	4	24	20	53
Portsmouth	38	15	3	1	45	11	7	4	8	19	25	51
Brighton & Hove Albion	38	10	4	5	33	16	8	5	6	20	27	45
Luton Town	38	12	4	3	38	22	6	5	8	14	30	45
West Ham United	38	12	5	2	39	12	3	9	7	21	29	44
Tottenham Hotspur	38	13	4	2	46	12	4	5	10	17	33	43
Millwall	38	14	3	2	53	11	4	3	12	18	39	42
Norwich City	38	9	6	4	34	21	6	6	7	23	27	42
WATFORD	38	9	7	3	31	18	4	9	6	15	25	42
Brentford	38	14	3	2	39	16	3	5	11	18	40	42
Southampton	38	9	6	4	31	18	4	3	12	18	38	35
Reading	38	12	3	4	42	11	2	3	15	16	36	34
Leyton	38	9	6	4	26	23	2	6	11	12	37	34
Bristol Rovers	38	10	4	5	41	20	2	5	12	14	34	33
Plymouth Argyle	38	7	9	3	26	14	3	4	12	17	36	33
New Brompton	38	9	4	6	30	21	3	5	11	17	38	33
Swindon Town	38	11	7	1	28	8	0	4	15	15	46	33
Queens Park Rangers	38	9	5	5	32	16	2	5	12	15	39	32
Crystal Palace	38	7	4	8	29	28	1	5	13	17	38	25
Northampton	38	5	8	6	22	24	0	1	18	7	64	19

New Southern League opponents: Crystal Palace, Leyton
Home-and-away league doubles
For – 3 (Brighton & Hove Albion, Crystal Palace, Reading)
Against – 2 (Brentford, Norwich City)
Divisional changes at end of season: Fulham to Football League; Bradford (Park Avenue) elected
All Matches: Won 17, Drew 17, Lost 21, Goals 64-88
Highest Score: 6 (Match 36)

Watford finished 8th out of 8 clubs in the United League (Won 3, Drew 1, Lost 10, Goals 15-38, Points 7). In the South-Eastern League, the club finished 12th out of 13 clubs, but fielded the first team only once in the 24 games.

No	DATE			COMPETITION	OPPONENTS	HOME	AWAY	ATTENDANCE
1	September	Sat	1	Southern League, Division 1	Brentford		L 0-2	8,000
2		Wed	5	Southern League, Division 1	TOTTENHAM HOTSPUR	1-1 D		4,000
3		Sat	8	Southern League, Division 1	MILLWALL	2-1 W		4,000
4		Mon	10	United League	Luton Town		L 0-2	1,200
5		Sat	15	Southern League, Division 1	Leyton		D 1-1	4,000
6		Wed	19	United League	LUTON TOWN	0-1 L		1,000
7		Sat	22	Southern League, Division 1	PORTSMOUTH	2-0 W		5,000
8		Wed	26	United League	NORWICH CITY	1-1 D		
9		Sat	29	Southern League, Division 1	New Brompton		L 0-2	5,000
10	October	Wed	3	United League	LEYTON	2-1 W		500
11		Sat	6	Southern League, Division 1	PLYMOUTH ARGYLE	2-2 D		5,000
12		Thu	11	United League	Leyton		L 1-4	1,000
13		Sat	13	Southern League, Division 1	Brighton & Hove Albion		W 3-0	6,000
14		Wed	17	United League	CRYSTAL PALACE	1-2 L		500
15		Sat	20	Southern League, Division 1	READING	1-0 W		5,000
16		Thu	25	United League	Norwich City		L 0-3	2,000
17		Sat	27	Southern League, Division 1	BRISTOL ROVERS	0-0 D		5,000
18		Mon	29	United League	New Brompton		L 0-4	
19	November	Sat	3	Southern League, Division 1	Northampton Town		D 1-1	4,000
20		Wed	7	United League	HASTINGS & ST LEONARDS UNITED	4-1 W		
21		Sat	10	Southern League, Division 1	QUEENS PARK RANGERS	1-0 W		5,000
22		Wed	14	United League	Brighton & Hove Albion		L 1-4	1,000
23		Sat	17	Southern League, Division 1	Fulham		D 0-0	10,000
24		Wed	21	United League	Crystal Palace		L 1-6	
25		Sat	24	Southern League, Division 1	SOUTHAMPTON	1-1 D		5,000
26		Wed	28	United League	Hastings & St Leonards United		L 1-5	
27	December	Sat	1	Southern League, Division 1	West Ham United		D 1-1	7,000
28		Sat	8	FA Cup, 5th Qualifying Round	Stockton		W 2-0	8,000
29		Sat	15	Southern League, Division 1	Swindon Town		D 0-0	5,000
30		Sat	22	Southern League, Division 1	NORWICH CITY	0-2 L		4,000
31		Tue	25	Southern League, Division 1	Luton Town		L 0-2	8,000
32		Wed	26	Southern League, Division 1	CRYSTAL PALACE	2-0 W		3,000
33		Sat	29	Southern League, Division 1	BRENTFORD	1-4 L		3,000
34	January	Sat	5	Southern League, Division 1	Millwall		L 1-10	4,000
35		Sat	12	FA Cup, 1st Round	Southampton		L 1-2	3,886
36		Sat	19	Southern League, Division 1	LEYTON	6-2 W		3,000
37		Sat	26	Southern League, Division 1	Portsmouth		L 0-1	5,000
38	February	Sat	2	South-Eastern League	Brighton & Hove Albion		L 0-5	2,000
39		Sat	9	Southern League, Division 1	Plymouth Argyle		W 2-1	6,000
40		Sat	16	Southern League, Division 1	BRIGHTON & HOVE ALBION	1-0 W		4,000
41		Sat	23	Southern League, Division 1	Reading		W 1-0	3,000
42	March	Sat	2	Southern League, Division 1	Bristol Rovers		D 1-1	5,000
43		Sat	9	Southern League, Division 1	NORTHAMPTON TOWN	5-0 W		5,000
44		Sat	16	Southern League, Division 1	Queens Park Rangers		D 0-0	5,000
45		Wed	20	Southern League, Division 1	NEW BROMPTON	2-2 D		2,000
46		Sat	23	Southern League, Division 1	FULHAM	0-1 L		7,000
47		Fri	29	Southern League, Division 1	LUTON TOWN	2-2 D		9,000
48		Sat	30	Southern League, Division 1	Southampton		D 0-0	3,000
49	April	Mon	1	Southern League, Division 1	Crystal Palace		W 3-1	10,000
50		Sat	6	Southern League, Division 1	WEST HAM UNITED	2-0 W		4,000
51		Wed	10	United League	BRIGHTON & HOVE ALBION	1-4 L		
52		Sat	13	Southern League, Division 1	Tottenham Hotspur		D 0-0	10,000
53		Sat	20	Southern League, Division 1	SWINDON TOWN	0-0 D		4,000
54		Wed	24	United League	NEW BROMPTON	2-0 W		200
55		Sat	27	Southern League, Division 1	Norwich City		L 1-2	2,500

League ever-presents: W. Biggar, A. Hitch
Most appearances in total: W. Biggar 53 out of 55   **Most goals in total:** J. Foster 16
Hat-tricks: T.B. Niblo 36   **Penalty goals:** P. Turner 1
Sent off: None
Full international appearance(s) this season: None

Season totals

	Aston, C.L.	Badger, H.O.	Biggar, W.	Brooks, J.	Broughton, M.	Foster, J.	Furr, G.M.	Fyfe, G.	Goodall, J.	Grimes, W.J.	Higgins, H.W.	Hitch, A.	Hosier, L.G.	Law, W.	Main, A.	Niblo, T.B.	Orr, W.	Richardson, J.W.	Soar, T.A.	Tooley, A.E.	Turner, P.	Walter, J.
Apps	35	23	38	29	5	31		29		15		38		31	13	30	5	34	28		34	
Subs																						
Goals	1	2				14		1		3		1		5		8		1	3		7	
Apps	12	12	15	9		14	3	15	3	7	2	10	2	17	7	12	7	11	12	2	11	4
Subs																						
Goals		2				2	3			1		1	2	1		3			1		1	1

Match-by-match

#	Aston, C.L.	Badger, H.O.	Biggar, W.	Brooks, J.	Broughton, M.	Foster, J.	Furr, G.M.	Fyfe, G.	Goodall, J.	Grimes, W.J.	Higgins, H.W.	Hitch, A.	Hosier, L.G.	Law, W.	Main, A.	Niblo, T.B.	Orr, W.	Richardson, J.W.	Soar, T.A.	Tooley, A.E.	Turner, P.	Walter, J.
1	X	X	G	X								X		X	X	X		X	X		X	
2	X	X	G	X								X1		X	X	X		X	X		X	
3	X		G	X		X2						X		X	X	X		X	X		X	
4	X		G	X		X				X		X		X	X			X	X		X	
5	X		G	X		X						X		X	X	X1		X	X		X	
6			G	X		X		X				X		X	X	X	X	X	X		X	
7	X1		G	X		X1		X				X			X	X		X	X		X	
8	X		G			X		X		X			X1	X	X			X	X		X	
9	X		G	X		X						X		X	X			X	X		X	
10	X	X2	G	X		X						X		X		X	X	X	X			
11	X		G	X		X1		X				X			X	X		X1	X		X	
12	X	X	G	X				X		X				X		X1	X		X		X	
13	X		G	X		X1		X		X		X		X	X				X		X2	
14	X	X	G	X		X		X						X			X		X		X	X1
15	X		G	X		X		X		X1		X		X	X				X		X	
16		X	G			X		X				X		X	X				X		X	X
17			G	X		X		X				X		X	X	X			X		X	
18		X	G	X		X		X				X		X		X			X	X	X	X
19	X	X	G	X		X		X				X				X			X		X1p	
20		X		X		X		X	X	G		X1		X1		X1		X			X1	
21		X	G	X		X		X				X				X		X	X	X	X1	
22		X	G			X1		X		X		X		X		X		X	X			X
23		X	G			X		X		X		X		X		X			X		X	
24	X	X	G	X				X	X	X		X	X1	X		X						
25	X	X	G		X	X		X		X		X		X1		X		X				
26	X	X					X1	X	X	X	G			X	X				X	X		
27	X	X	G		X	X1		X		X		X		X					X	X		
28	X		G			X1		X		X1		X		X	X	X	X		X	X		
29	X	X	G			X						X		X	X	X	X		X	X		
30	X	X	G			X						X		X	X	X	X		X	X		
31	X	X	G					X				X		X		X			X	X	X	
32	X	X	G	X				X				X		X		X1		X	X	X1	X	
33	X	X	G	X						X		X		X		X1		X	X	X	X	
34	X	X	G			X1						X		X	X	X		X	X	X	X	
35	X	X	G			X		X				X		X		X		X	X	X1	X	
36	X	X	G			X2		X				X		X		X3		X	X	X1	X	
37	X	X	G			X		X				X		X		X		X	X	X	X	
38	X		G			X		X				X		X	X	X		X	X	X	X	
39	X		G	X				X		X2		X		X		X		X	X	X	X	
40	X		G	X				X		X		X		X		X1		X	X	X	X	
41	X		G	X		X		X				X		X		X		X	X	X1	X	
42	X	X	G	X		X		X				X	X1	X		X			X		X	
43	X		G	X		X2		X				X	X2			X1		X	X		X	
44	X		G	X		X		X				X		X		X		X	X		X	
45	X	X2	G	X		X		X				X		X				X	X		X	
46	X		G	X	X	X		X				X		X				X	X		X	
47	X		G	X	X	X1		X				X		X		X			X		X1	
48	X	X	G	X		X		X				X		X		X			X		X	
49	X	X	G	X		X		X1				X		X			X	X	X		X2	
50	X	X	G	X		X2		X				X		X			X	X	X		X	
51	X	X	G	X		X	X1	X						X		X	X	X	X			
52	X	X	G	X		X		X				X		X			X		X		X	
53	X	X	G	X	X	X		X				X		X					X		X	
54	X	X	G			X	X1	X						X		X1	X	X	X		X	
55	X	X	G			X		X		X		X		X1			X	X	X		X	

1907/08

Southern League position: 14th out of 20 in Division 1
Manager: John Goodall

	HOME						AWAY					
	Pl	W	D	L	For	Ag	W	D	L	For	Ag	Pts
Queens Park Rangers	38	12	4	3	46	26	9	5	5	36	31	51
Plymouth Argyle	38	13	5	1	33	13	6	6	7	17	18	49
Millwall	38	10	5	4	24	10	9	3	7	25	22	46
Crystal Palace	38	10	4	5	35	28	7	6	6	19	23	44
Swindon Town	38	12	6	1	41	12	4	4	11	14	28	42
Bristol Rovers	38	11	5	3	36	19	5	5	9	23	37	42
Tottenham Hotspur	38	11	2	6	33	18	6	5	8	26	30	41
Northampton	38	9	5	5	30	17	6	6	7	20	24	41
Portsmouth	38	14	1	4	43	19	3	5	11	20	33	40
West Ham United	38	9	6	4	27	16	6	4	9	20	32	40
Southampton	38	11	5	3	32	21	5	1	13	19	39	38
Reading	38	12	1	6	38	18	3	5	11	17	32	36
Bradford (Park Avenue)	38	6	7	6	30	27	6	5	8	23	27	36
WATFORD	38	9	4	6	31	23	3	6	10	16	37	34
Brentford	38	8	4	7	31	22	3	6	10	16	37	34
Norwich City	38	13	3	3	38	15	1	2	16	11	37	33
Brighton & Hove Albion	38	9	6	4	29	19	3	2	14	17	40	32
Luton Town	38	9	4	6	21	17	3	2	14	12	39	30
Leyton	38	6	6	7	30	31	2	5	12	21	42	27
New Brompton	38	7	3	9	24	29	2	4	13	20	46	25

New Southern League opponents: Bradford (Park Avenue)
Home-and-away league doubles
For – 2 (Brighton & Hove Albion, Northampton)
Against – 3 (Bradford [Park Avenue], Brentford, West Ham United)
Divisional changes at end of season: Tottenham & Bradford (Park Avenue) to Football League; Southend United from Division 2; Coventry City & Exeter City elected; division increased to 21 clubs
All Matches: Won 12, Drew 10, Lost 19, Goals 51-67
Highest Score: 4 (Matches 9 & 41)

In the South-Eastern League, Watford finished 17th out of 18 clubs, but fielded the first team only twice in the 34 matches.

No	DATE			COMPETITION	OPPONENTS	HOME	AWAY	ATTENDANCE
1	September	Sat	7	Southern League, Division 1	PORTSMOUTH	1-0 W	5,000	
2		Wed	11	Southern League, Division 1	BRADFORD (PARK AVENUE)	1-3 L	3,000	
3		Sat	14	Southern League, Division 1	Bradford (Park Avenue)		L 2-3	13,000
4		Sat	21	Southern League, Division 1	MILLWALL	1-0 W	5,000	
5		Wed	25	South-Eastern League	CLAPTON ORIENT	2-4 L		
6		Sat	28	Southern League, Division 1	Brentford		L 1-4	6,000
7	October	Sat	5	Southern League, Division 1	BRISTOL ROVERS	1-2 L	4,000	
8		Sat	12	Southern League, Division 1	Leyton		W 2-1	5,000
9		Sat	19	Southern League, Division 1	READING	4-0 W	4,000	
10		Sat	26	Southern League, Division 1	New Brompton		L 1-3	6,000
11		Thu	31	South-Eastern League	Clapton Orient		L 2-3	
12	November	Sat	2	Southern League, Division 1	Norwich City		L 0-2	5,000
13		Sat	9	Southern League, Division 1	NORTHAMPTON TOWN	2-1 W	4,000	
14		Sat	16	Southern League, Division 1	Southampton		D 1-1	5,000
15		Sat	23	Southern League, Division 1	PLYMOUTH ARGYLE	3-0 W	5,000	
16		Sat	30	Southern League, Division 1	West Ham United		L 0-2	6,000
17	December	Sat	7	Southern League, Division 1	QUEENS PARK RANGERS	0-3 L	6,000	
18		Sat	14	Southern League, Division 1	Tottenham Hotspur		L 0-5	5,000
19		Sat	21	Southern League, Division 1	SWINDON TOWN	0-0 D	3,000	
20		Wed	25	Southern League, Division 1	Luton Town		D 1-1	
21		Thu	26	Southern League, Division 1	Brighton & Hove Albion		W 1-0	10,000
22		Sat	28	Southern League, Division 1	Crystal Palace		L 1-3	7,000
23	January	Sat	4	Southern League, Division 1	Portsmouth		L 0-2	9,000
24		Sat	11	FA Cup, 1st Round	Gainsborough Trinity		L 0-1	4,000
25		Sat	18	Southern League, Division 1	Millwall		D 0-0	4,000
26		Sat	25	Southern League, Division 1	BRENTFORD	1-2 L	3,000	
27	February	Sat	8	Southern League, Division 1	LEYTON	2-2 D	4,000	
28		Sat	15	Southern League, Division 1	Reading		L 0-3	8,000
29		Sat	22	Southern League, Division 1	NEW BROMPTON	1-1 D	1,500	
30		Sat	29	Southern League, Division 1	NORWICH CITY	1-0 W	3,000	
31	March	Sat	7	Southern League, Division 1	Northampton Town		W 1-0	5,000
32		Sat	14	Southern League, Division 1	SOUTHAMPTON	0-1 L	5,000	
33		Sat	21	Southern League, Division 1	Plymouth Argyle		D 1-1	8,000
34		Sat	28	Southern League, Division 1	WEST HAM UNITED	2-3 L	3,000	
35		Mon	30	Southern League, Division 1	Bristol Rovers		D 1-1	
36	April	Sat	4	Southern League, Division 1	Queens Park Rangers		D 3-3	8,000
37		Sat	11	Southern League, Division 1	TOTTENHAM HOTSPUR	2-2 D	5,000	
38		Fri	17	Southern League, Division 1	LUTON TOWN	2-1 W	9,500	
39		Sat	18	Southern League, Division 1	Swindon Town		L 0-2	4,000
40		Mon	20	Southern League, Division 1	BRIGHTON & HOVE ALBION	3-0 W	4,000	
41		Sat	25	Southern League, Division 1	CRYSTAL PALACE	4-1 W	3,000	

League ever-presents: C.L. Aston, W. Biggar
Most appearances in total: C.L. Aston 41 out of 41   **Most goals in total:** J. Foster 14
Hat-tricks: J. Foster (Match 9), H. Smith (Match 41)   **Penalty goals:** G. Fyfe 2, J. Foster 1, A. Hitch 1
Sent off: None
Full international appearance(s) this season: None

	Aston, C.L.	Badger, H.O.	Betts, A.C.	Biggar, W.	Eames, W.	Ebden, A.W.	Fayers, F.	Foster, J.	Furr, G.M.	Fyfe, G.	Goodall, J.	Higgins, H.W.	Hindmarsh, J.L.	Hitch, A.	Howard, G.A.	Hubbard, A.	Law, W.	Palmer, F.	Pillon, W.	Reynolds, J.	Richardson, J.W.	Sharpe, I.G.	Smith, H.	Soar, T.A.	Walker, T.	Wright, J.	Young, G.
Apps	38	31	25	38	14		7	13	20	27	1		10	31	1	11	32			27	35	7	2	5	15	27	1
Subs																											
Goals		3			2			12	3	3			4	1		4	2			4		1	3		5		
Apps	3	3	3	2	1	2		1	3	1		1		1	2		3	1	1	2	1					2	
Subs																											
Goals					1				2									1									

	Aston, C.L.	Badger, H.O.	Betts, A.C.	Biggar, W.	Eames, W.	Ebden, A.W.	Fayers, F.	Foster, J.	Furr, G.M.	Fyfe, G.	Goodall, J.	Higgins, H.W.	Hindmarsh, J.L.	Hitch, A.	Howard, G.A.	Hubbard, A.	Law, W.	Palmer, F.	Pillon, W.	Reynolds, J.	Richardson, J.W.	Sharpe, I.G.	Smith, H.	Soar, T.A.	Walker, T.	Wright, J.	Young, G.
1	X	X	X	G				X1	X	X				X			X				X					X	
2	X	X	X	G				X1		X				X			X			X	X					X	
3	X	X	X	G	X			X1	X	X1	X			X			X									X	
4	X	X	X	G	X				X	X1				X	X		X									X	
5	X	X	X		X1	X			X			G				X	X	X1	X								
6	X	X	X	G	X			X!	X	X				X			X			X							
7	X	X	X	G	X				X	X			X1p				X				X					X	
8	X	X		G	X			X1	X	X				X			X1				X					X	
9	X	X1		G	X			X3p	X	X				X			X				X					X	
10	X	X		G	X1			X	X	X				X			X				X					X	
11	X	X	X	G		X		X2	X							X	X			X						X	
12	X	X		G	X				X	X				X			X			X						X	
13	X	X		G	X1			X1		X				X			X			X	X					X	
14	X	X		G	X			X1		X				X			X			X	X					X	
15	X	X		G	X			X2		X				X			X1			X	X					X	
16	X	X		G	X			X		X				X			X			X	X					X	
17	X	X		G	X				X	X				X			X			X	X					X	
18	X	X		G	X					X			X	X			X			X	X					X	
19	X	X		G					X	X			X	X			X			X	X					X	
20	X	X1		G					X	X			X	X			X			X	X					X	
21	X	X		G					X	X			X1	X			X			X	X					X	
22	X	X	X	G					X	X1p				X			X			X	X					X	
23	X	X		G					X	X				X			X			X	X					X	
24	X	X	X	G					X	X				X			X			X	X					X	
25	X	X	X	G										X			X			X	X	X		X		X	
26	X	X	X	G										X			X			X1	X	X		X		X	
27	X	X1	X	G										X		X1				X	X	X	X	X		X	
28	X	X	X	G										X			X			X	X		X	X		X	
29	X	X	X	G										X			X			X	X			X	X1		
30	X	X	X	G										X			X			X	X			X1	X		
31	X	X	X	G										X			X			X	X			X1	X		
32	X	X	X	G										X			X			X	X			X	X		
33	X		X	G						X			X	X						X1	X	X			X		
34	X		X	G						X			X	X						X1	X	X1			X	X	
35	X	X	X	G			X		X					X			X			X	X				X		
36	X	X	X	G			X		X				X2							X	X				X		
37	X		X	G			X		X1	X			X1							X	X	X				X	
38	X		X	G			X		X1p					X		X1	X			X	X					X	
39	X		X	G			X		X							X	X			X	X					X	X
40	X		X	G	X				X1	X						X	X			X	X				X		
41	X		X	G	X				X	X						X	X			X	X		X3			X	

1908/09

Southern League position: 14th out of 21 in Division 1
Manager: John Goodall

	HOME					AWAY					
	Pl	W	D	L	For	Ag	W	D	L	For	Ag	Pts
Northampton Town	40	15	3	2	51	14	10	2	8	39	31	55
Swindon Town	40	18	0	2	68	15	4	5	11	28	40	49
Southampton	40	13	4	3	44	26	6	6	8	23	32	48
Portsmouth	40	13	5	2	42	17	5	5	10	26	43	46
Bristol Rovers	40	13	5	2	39	20	4	4	12	21	43	43
Exeter City	40	13	5	2	37	28	5	4	11	19	37	42
New Brompton	40	12	2	6	30	22	5	5	10	18	37	41
Reading	40	7	9	4	33	19	4	9	7	27	38	40
Luton Town	40	16	1	3	45	14	1	5	14	14	46	40
Plymouth Argyle	40	9	6	5	28	16	6	4	10	18	31	40
Millwall	40	14	3	3	37	18	2	3	15	22	43	38
Southend United	40	12	6	2	33	14	2	4	14	19	40	38
Leyton	40	13	3	4	35	12	2	5	13	17	43	38
WATFORD	40	12	7	1	37	16	2	2	16	14	48	37
Queens Park Rangers	40	10	6	4	41	24	2	6	12	11	26	36
Crystal Palace	40	10	4	6	42	23	2	8	10	20	39	36
West Ham United	40	16	1	3	43	13	0	3	17	13	47	36
Brighton & Hove Albion	40	11	4	5	46	20	3	3	14	14	41	35
Norwich City	40	10	4	6	42	21	2	3	15	17	54	35
Coventry City	40	9	4	7	44	37	6	0	14	20	54	34
Brentford	40	10	5	4	40	26	3	2	15	19	48	33

New league opponents: Coventry City, Exeter City, Southend United

Home-and-away league doubles
For – 1 (Leyton)
Against – 1 (Luton Town)

Divisional changes at end of season: Croydon Common from Division 2; division increased to 22 clubs

All Matches: Won 15, Drew 10, Lost 18, Goals 57-69

Highest Score: 5 (Match 43)

No	DATE			COMPETITION	OPPONENTS	HOME	AWAY	ATTENDANCE	
1	September	Wed	2	Southern League, Division 1	SWINDON TOWN	1-0 W		3,000	
2		Sat	5	Southern League, Division 1	Portsmouth		L 0-2		8,000
3		Mon	7	Southern League, Division 1	Queens Park Rangers		L 0-2		5,000
4		Sat	12	Southern League, Division 1	EXETER CITY	3-1 W		4,000	
5		Wed	16	Southern League, Division 1	QUEENS PARK RANGERS	0-0 D		3,000	
6		Sat	19	Southern League, Division 1	Northampton Town		L 0-7		8,000
7		Sat	26	Southern League, Division 1	NEW BROMPTON	2-1 W		3,000	
8		Wed	30	Southern League, Division 1	WEST HAM UNITED	2-1 W		2,500	
9	October	Sat	3	Southern League, Division 1	Millwall		L 1-2		7,000
10		Sat	10	Southern League, Division 1	SOUTHEND UNITED	2-2 D		4,000	
11		Sat	17	Southern League, Division 1	Coventry City		L 2-3		7,000
12		Sat	24	Southern League, Division 1	BRISTOL ROVERS	4-1 W		3,000	
13		Sat	31	Southern League, Division 1	PLYMOUTH ARGYLE	1-1 D		4,000	
14	November	Sat	7	Southern League, Division 1	Norwich City	D 2-2			6,000
15		Sat	14	Southern League, Division 1	READING	0-0 D		3,500	
16		Sat	21	Southern League, Division 1	Southampton		L 0-1		5,000
17		Sat	28	Southern League, Division 1	LEYTON	1-0 W		3,000	
18	December	Sat	5	FA Cup, 5th Qualifying Round	WEST STANLEY	4-1 W		3,000	
19		Sat	12	Southern League, Division 1	BRIGHTON & HOVE ALBION	1-1 D		3,000	
20		Sat	19	Southern League, Division 1	Crystal Palace		L 1-3		7,000
21		Fri	25	Southern League, Division 1	Brentford		L 1-3		6,000
22		Sat	26	Southern League, Division 1	Luton Town		L 0-1		9,000
23		Mon	28	Southern League, Division 1	Swindon Town		L 1-4		4,000
24	January	Sat	2	Southern League, Division 1	PORTSMOUTH	1-1 D		3,000	
25		Sat	9	Southern League, Division 1	Exeter City		L 0-1		6,000
26		Sat	16	FA Cup, 1st Round	LEICESTER FOSSE	1-1 D		5,545	
27		Wed	20	FA Cup, 1st Round replay	Leicester Fosse		L 1-3		8,000
28		Sat	23	Southern League, Division 1	NORTHAMPTON TOWN	4-1 W		4,000	
29		Sat	30	Southern League, Division 1	New Brompton		L 1-5		
30	February	Sat	13	Southern League, Division 1	Southend United		L 0-2		4,000
31		Sat	20	Southern League, Division 1	COVENTRY CITY	3-1 W		2,500	
32		Wed	24	Southern League, Division 1	MILLWALL	1-0 W		1,500	
33		Sat	27	Southern League, Division 1	Bristol Rovers	D 1-1			5,000
34	March	Sat	6	Southern League, Division 1	Plymouth Argyle		L 0-2		4,000
35		Sat	13	Southern League, Division 1	NORWICH CITY	1-1 D		3,000	
36		Sat	20	Southern League, Division 1	Reading		L 0-3		2,500
37		Sat	27	Southern League, Division 1	SOUTHAMPTON	3-0 W		4,000	
38	April	Sat	3	Southern League, Division 1	Leyton		W 1-0		3,000
39		Fri	9	Southern League, Division 1	LUTON TOWN	0-3 L		9,000	
40		Sat	10	Southern League, Division 1	West Ham United		L 1-3		7,000
41		Mon	12	Southern League, Division 1	BRENTFORD	2-0 W		4,000	
42		Sat	17	Southern League, Division 1	Brighton & Hove Albion		W 2-1		4,000
43		Sat	24	Southern League, Division 1	CRYSTAL PALACE	5-1 W		4,000	

	Betts, A.C.	Biggar, W.	Cleaver, F.L.	Farrow, A.E.	Fayers, F.	Furr, G.M.	Fyfe, G.	Hubbard, A.	Kelly, F.	Lockett, A.	McKinley, D.	MacLaine, J.	Moffat, J.	Palmer, F.	Richardson, J.W.	Riddell, F.W.	Saunders, H.J.	Skilton, A.H.	Smith, H.	Squires, A.	Woods, H.A.	Own goals
Apps	36	38	21	9	33	17	30	39	22	37	23	37	18	15	32	6	2	5	14	3	3	
Subs																						
Goals		1	6		2			14	3		5	10					1	4	3		2	
Apps	3	3	2		3	3	3	3	1	3	3	3			3							
Subs																						
Goals			1					2			1	2										
1	X	G			X1	X	X	X	X	X		X			X				X			
2	X	G			X	X	X	X	X	X		X			X				X			
3	X	G	X		X	X	X			X	X		X	X					X			
4	X	G			X	X	X	X1		X		X			X	X			X2			
5	X	G		X	X	X	X	X		X			X			X			X			
6	X	G		X	X		X	X		X			X	X		X			X			
7	X	G			X		X	X	X1	X	X1	X	X			X			X			
8	X	G			X		X	X	X	X	X1	X1	X			X						
9	X	G			X		X	X1	X	X	X	X			X							
10	X	G			X		X	X2	X	X	X	X			X							
11	X	G			X			X	X1	X	X		X	X		X1						
12	X	G			X	X		X	X1	X	X2	X1	X	X		X						
13	X	G			X	X		X1	X	X	X		X									
14	X	G			X1	X	X	X	X		X	X		X					X1			
15	X	G			X	X	X	X	X		X	X		X					X			
16	X	G			X		X	X	X	X		X	X		X							
17	X	G			X		X	X1p	X	X	X		X			X			X			
18	X	G			X	X	X	X2	X	X	X1	X1		X								
19	X	G			X	X	X	X		X	X		X			X1						
20		G	X		X	X	X	X1		X	X	X		X								
21		G	X1		X		X	X	X	X	X		X			X						
22		G	X	X	X	X	X	X			X	X		X	X							
23		G	X	X	X	X	X	X		X1	X		X	X								
24	X	G	X	X		X		X	X1		X	X	X		X							
25	X	G	X	X	X		X	X		X	X	X		X								
26	X	G	X1		X	X	X	X		X	X	X		X								
27	X	G	X		X	X	X	X		X	X	X1		X								
28	X		X2		X	X	X	X1		X	X	X		X		G					1	
29	X		X		X	X		X	X		X	X1		X	X	G						
30	X	G	X			X	X		X	X	X	X	X		X				X			
31	X	G1p			X	X1		X	X1	X	X	X	X		X			X	X			
32	X	G			X	X1		X	X	X	X	X	X		X			X	X			
33	X	G	X		X	X1		X	X	X	X	X	X		X							
34	X	G	X		X		X	X		X	X	X	X		X							
35	X	G	X		X	X	X1		X		X	X	X		X				X			
36	X	G	X		X	X	X	X		X		X	X		X							
37	X	G	X1		X	X	X1	X	X		X1		X	X		X						
38	X	G	X1		X		X	X	X		X	X	X	X		X						
39	X	G	X			X	X	X		X	X	X	X		X							
40	X	G	X			X	X	X		X1	X	X	X		X							
41	X	G	X	X		X	X	X		X2	X			X					X			
42	X	G	X1	X	X		X	X	X		X	X							X1			
43	X	G	X	X	X		X	X	X		X2	X							X2		1	

1909/10

Southern League position: 19th out of 22 in Division 1
Manager: John Goodall

		HOME					AWAY					
	Pl	W	D	L	For	Ag	W	D	L	For	Ag	Pts
Brighton & Hove Albion	42	18	2	1	50	11	5	11	5	19	17	59
Swindon Town	42	15	3	3	63	20	7	7	7	29	26	54
Queens Park Rangers	42	12	5	4	41	28	7	8	6	14	19	51
Northampton Town	42	16	3	2	66	11	6	1	14	24	33	48
Southampton	42	11	7	3	35	23	5	9	7	25	30	48
Portsmouth	42	13	5	3	43	18	7	2	12	27	46	47
Crystal Palace	42	13	3	5	48	19	7	3	11	21	30	46
Coventry City	42	11	6	4	47	24	8	2	11	21	36	46
West Ham United	42	10	7	4	43	23	5	8	8	26	33	45
Leyton	42	11	4	6	43	21	5	7	9	15	24	43
Plymouth Argyle	42	14	5	2	42	8	2	6	13	21	46	43
New Brompton	42	16	2	3	52	21	3	3	15	23	53	43
Bristol Rovers	42	13	5	3	25	8	3	5	13	12	40	42
Brentford	42	13	5	3	33	13	3	4	14	17	45	41
Luton Town	42	10	6	5	45	34	5	5	11	27	58	41
Millwall	42	9	6	6	24	17	6	1	14	21	42	37
Norwich City	42	11	5	5	42	24	2	5	14	17	54	35
Exeter City	42	12	4	5	46	21	2	2	17	15	47	34
WATFORD	42	8	8	5	32	24	5	1	15	19	52	33
Southend United	42	10	4	7	30	19	2	5	14	25	73	33
Croydon Common	42	8	2	11	33	39	5	3	13	23	58	31
Reading	42	7	6	8	27	25	0	4	17	11	48	24

New league opponents: Croydon Common

Home-and-away league doubles
For – 2 (Bristol Rovers, Southend United)
Against – 3 (Brighton & Hove Albion, Coventry City, Millwall)

Divisional changes at end of season: Croydon Common & Reading to Division 2; division reduced to 20 clubs

All Matches: Won 15, Drew 13, Lost 21, Goals 68-83

Highest Score: 8 (Match 18)

No	DATE			COMPETITION	OPPONENTS	HOME	AWAY	ATTENDANCE
1	September	Wed	1	Southern League, Division 1	Queens Park Rangers		L 3-4	5,000
2		Sat	4	Southern League, Division 1	SWINDON TOWN	0-1 L		5,000
3		Wed	8	Southern League, Division 1	QUEENS PARK RANGERS	1-1 D		2,000
4		Sat	11	Southern League, Division 1	Crystal Palace		D 1-1	6,000
5		Wed	15	Southern League, Division 1	Luton Town		L 2-4	3,000
6		Sat	18	Southern League, Division 1	BRIGHTON & HOVE ALBION	1-2 L		4,000
7		Wed	22	Southern League, Division 1	LUTON TOWN	1-1 D		3,000
8		Sat	25	Southern League, Division 1	West Ham United		L 0-2	6,000
9		Wed	29	Southern Charity Cup, 1st Round	LUTON TOWN	2-1 W		1,000
10	October	Sat	2	Southern League, Division 1	PORTSMOUTH	3-3 D		4,000
11		Sat	9	Southern League, Division 1	Bristol Rovers		W 3-1	6,000
12		Sat	16	Southern League, Division 1	NORWICH CITY	1-1 D		4,000
13		Sat	23	Southern League, Division 1	Brentford		L 0-2	5,000
14		Thu	28	Southern Charity Cup, 2nd Round	Northampton Town		W 2-1	2,000
15		Sat	30	Southern League, Division 1	COVENTRY CITY	0-3 L		3,000
16	November	Sat	6	Southern League, Division 1	Exeter City		D 1-1	
17		Sat	13	Southern League, Division 1	Reading		L 0-2	
18		Sat	20	FA Cup, 4th Qualifying Round	BROMLEY	8-1 W		3,000
19		Sat	27	Southern League, Division 1	Leyton		L 0-3	5,000
20	December	Sat	4	FA Cup, 5th Qualifying Round	Wycombe Wanderers		W 4-0	4,000
21		Sat	11	Southern League, Division 1	Southampton		D 2-2	2,000
22		Wed	15	Southern League, Division 1	SOUTHEND UNITED	3-1 W		1,000
23		Sat	18	Southern League, Division 1	CROYDON COMMON	1-0 W		3,000
24		Sat	25	Southern League, Division 1	New Brompton		L 0-2	6,000
25		Mon	27	Southern League, Division 1	Millwall		L 0-3	
26		Tue	28	Southern League, Division 1	Northampton Town		L 0-3	9,000
27	January	Sat	1	Southern League, Division 1	NORTHAMPTON TOWN	2-0 W		3,000
28		Sat	8	Southern League, Division 1	Swindon Town		D 3-3	5,000
29		Sat	15	FA Cup, 1st Round	Woolwich Arsenal		L 0-3	8,700
30		Sat	22	Southern League, Division 1	CRYSTAL PALACE	3-0 W		3,000
31		Sat	29	Southern League, Division 1	Brighton & Hove Albion		L 1-3	4,000
32	February	Sat	12	Southern League, Division 1	Portsmouth		L 0-5	5,000
33		Sat	19	Southern League, Division 1	BRISTOL ROVERS	4-0 W		3,000
34		Sat	26	Southern League, Division 1	Norwich City		D 2-2	4,000
35	March	Wed	2	Southern League, Division 1	WEST HAM UNITED	2-1 W		1,000
36		Sat	5	Southern League, Division 1	BRENTFORD	0-0 D		4,000
37		Wed	9	Southern Charity Cup, Semi-Final	QUEENS PARK RANGERS	1-0 W		
38		Sat	12	Southern League, Division 1	Coventry City		L 0-5	5,000
39		Sat	19	Southern League, Division 1	EXETER CITY	1-3 L		3,000
40		Fri	25	Southern League, Division 1	NEW BROMPTON	2-2 D		4,000
41		Sat	26	Southern League, Division 1	READING	1-0 W		3,000
42		Mon	28	Southern League, Division 1	MILLWALL	0-2 L		5,000
43	April	Sat	2	Southern League, Division 1	Southend United		W 1-0	3,000
44		Mon	4	Southern Charity Cup, Final	Brighton & Hove Albion (at Chelsea – after extra time)	(L 0-1)		3,000
45		Sat	9	Southern League, Division 1	LEYTON	1-1 D		4,000
46		Sat	16	Southern League, Division 1	Plymouth Argyle		L 0-2	1,500
47		Wed	20	Southern League, Division 1	PLYMOUTH ARGYLE	3-0 W		1,000
48		Sat	23	Southern League, Division 1	SOUTHAMPTON	2-2 D		3,000
49		Sat	30	Southern League, Division 1	Croydon Common		L 0-2	2,000

	Barsby, E.	Beaumont, S.	Becton, M.	Betts, A.C.	Biggar, W.	Cleaver, F.L.	Cotterill, F.	Crownshaw, H.	Fayers, F.	Fyfe, G.	Grieve, J.	Higgins, H.W.	Horne, O.A.	Kent, H.	Kyle, P.	Lockett, A.	McArdle, P.	MacLaine, J.	Moore, J.	Palmer, F.	Shinner, J.H.	Skilton, A.H.	Smith, H.	Squires, A.	Wheeler, W.	White, C.W.	White, T.H.	Own goal
Apps	4	12	20	32	36	18	13		24	24	34	6	5	35	12	37	1	42	20	1	18	10	5	22	12	16	3	
Subs																												
Goals		2			2	4			2	1		4		4				11	2			4	3	6		5		1
Apps		2	4	6	7	3	3	1	3	4	5		2	5	1	5		7	3	2	4	2		3	4	1		
Subs																												
Goals		3				2								3				4	2	1				1	1			
1			X	X	G	X			X	X	X					X		X2	X					X1				
2		X	X		X				X	X	X	G				X		X	X					X				
3	X		X		G	X			X	X				X	X	X		X	X					X1				
4			X		X1				X	X	X	G		X		X		X	X					X				
5			X		X				X	X	X	G		X		X		X	X1					X			1	
6			X		G	X			X	X				X		X		X1	X					X		X		
7			X		G	X			X					X		X		X	X			X	X1			X		
8			X		G				X					X		X		X	X			X	X			X		
9		X	X		G			X	X				X					X		X1	X	X		X1				
10		X1	X		G				X	X			X	X		X		X				X2		X				
11			X		G				X	X			X	X				X1			X	X1		X1				
12	X	X1	X		G					X	X		X	X				X			X	X		X				
13			X		G					X	X		X	X				X			X	X		X				
14		X2	X		G	X	X		X	X		X	X					X				X						
15		X	X		G				X	X		X	X					X			X	X						
16		X	X		G	X			X				X			X		X1	X			X				X		
17		X	X		G	X			X				X			X		X	X			X				X		
18			X		G				X	X			X2			X		X3	X2					X		X	X1	
19			X		G				X	X	X		X	X	X	X		X							X	X		
20		X	X		G	X2			X		X		X1			X		X1	X							X		
21			X		G	X			X	X	X		X1	X1		X		X							X			
22			X		G	X2			X	X	X		X	X1		X		X							X			
23			X		G	X1			X	X	X		X	X		X		X							X			
24			X		G	X	X		X	X	X					X		X							X			
25			X		G	X	X		X	X	X					X		X							X			
26			X		G	X	X		X	X	X					X		X	X									
27		X	X		G	X			X	X	X					X		X2	X									
28			X		G	X			X	X1	X1			X1		X		X	X									
29			X		G	X			X	X	X			X	X	X		X	X									
30					G	X1			X		X			X	X1	X		X1	X			X			X			
31					G	X			X		X			X	X1	X		X	X			X			X			
32			X	X	G				X	X	X			X	X	X		X										
33		X	X		G					X1				X		X		X	X			X		X2		X1		
34		X	X		G				X		X			X		X		X	X1			X		X		X1		
35		X	X		G				X		X			X		X		X1	X			X		X		X1		
36	X	X	X		G				X					X		X		X				X		X		X		
37		X1	X		G	X								X		X		X			X	X		X		X		
38		X	X		G	X								X		X		X			X	X		X		X		
39			X		G				X	X	X			X1		X		X				X		X		X		
40		X	X	X	X							G		X		X		X						X2	X	X		
41		X	X	X	X							G		X		X		X						X	X	X1		
42	X	X	X	X					X			G				X		X						X	X	X		
43		X			G				X		X			X		X		X			X	X1		X				
44			X	X	G	X			X		X					X		X			X	X		X				
45			X		G	X					X			X		X	X	X			X	X		X1				
46		X	X		G	X					X			X		X		X	X			X		X				
47			X		G	X1			X		X			X		X		X2						X	X			
48			X		G	X			X		X			X1		X		X				X		X1p	X			
49	X	X	X		G						X			X				X				X	X	X	X			

- 51 -

1910/11

Southern League position: 14th out of 20 in Division 1

Manager: Harry Kent

	HOME					AWAY					
Pl	W	D	L	For	Ag	W	D	L	For	Ag	Pts
Swindon Town	38	16	2	1	54	9	8	3	8	26	22	53
Northampton Town	38	14	3	2	39	7	4	9	6	15	20	48
Brighton & Hove Albion	38	15	2	2	41	12	5	6	8	17	23	48
Crystal Palace	38	11	5	3	35	23	6	8	5	20	25	47
West Ham United	38	12	6	1	44	17	5	5	9	19	29	45
Queens Park Rangers	38	11	6	2	37	16	2	8	9	15	25	40
Leyton	38	13	3	3	37	15	3	5	11	20	37	40
Plymouth Argyle	38	10	6	3	37	14	5	3	11	17	41	39
Luton Town	38	13	4	2	42	18	2	4	13	25	45	38
Norwich City	38	12	5	2	31	13	3	3	13	15	35	38
Coventry City	38	12	4	3	47	21	4	2	13	18	47	38
Brentford	38	12	5	2	32	13	2	4	13	9	29	37
Exeter City	38	8	5	6	32	29	6	4	9	19	24	37
WATFORD	38	10	5	4	32	23	3	4	12	17	42	35
Millwall	38	10	5	4	21	20	3	6	10	21	34	31
Bristol Rovers	38	6	6	7	24	23	4	4	11	18	32	30
Southampton	38	8	3	8	25	28	3	5	11	17	39	30
New Brompton	38	10	5	4	19	15	1	3	15	15	50	30
Southend United	38	7	4	8	28	26	3	5	11	19	38	29
Portsmouth	38	6	10	3	21	15	2	1	16	13	38	27

New league opponents: None

Home-and-away league doubles
For – 2 (Bristol Rovers, Plymouth Argyle)
Against – 3 (Coventry City, Leyton, Swindon Town)

Divisional changes at end of season: Southend United & Portsmouth to Division 2; Reading & Stoke from Division 2

All Matches: Won 17, Drew 9, Lost 18, Goals 64-74

Highest Score: 6 (Match 17)

No	DATE			COMPETITION	OPPONENTS	HOME	AWAY	ATTENDANCE
1	September	Sat	3	Southern League, Division 1	Northampton Town		L 0-2	8,000
2		Sat	10	Southern League, Division 1	BRIGHTON & HOVE ALBION	2-1 W		5,000
3		Wed	14	Southern Charity Cup, 1st Round	BRENTFORD	3-2 W		1,000
4		Sat	17	Southern League, Division 1	Exeter City		L 0-2	6,000
5		Sat	24	Southern League, Division 1	SWINDON TOWN	1-3 L		4,000
6	October	Sat	1	Southern League, Division 1	Bristol Rovers		W 1-0	3,000
7		Sat	8	Southern League, Division 1	CRYSTAL PALACE	1-1 D		4,000
8		Sat	15	Southern League, Division 1	Brentford		L 0-2	7,000
9		Wed	19	Southern Charity Cup, 2nd Round	LUTON TOWN	2-1 W		1,000
10		Sat	22	Southern League, Division 1	LEYTON	1-2 L		3,000
11		Sat	29	Southern League, Division 1	NORWICH CITY	3-0 W		3,000
12	November	Sat	5	Southern League, Division 1	Plymouth Argyle		W 2-0	
13		Sat	12	Southern League, Division 1	SOUTHAMPTON	1-1 D		4,000
14		Sat	19	FA Cup, 4th Qualifying Round	ILFORD	3-2 W		3,000
15		Sat	26	Southern League, Division 1	COVENTRY CITY	0-2 L		3,000
16		Mon	28	Southern Charity Cup, Semi-Final	Brighton & Hove Albion (at Millwall)	(L 1-2)		1,000
17	December	Sat	3	FA Cup, 5th Qualifying Round	CLAPTON	6-0 W		2,000
18		Sat	10	Southern League, Division 1	MILLWALL	3-3 D		3,000
19		Sat	17	Southern League, Division 1	Queens Park Rangers		L 1-4	4,000
20		Sat	24	Southern League, Division 1	WEST HAM UNITED	1-3 L		
21		Mon	26	Southern League, Division 1	LUTON TOWN	1-0 W		6,000
22		Tue	27	Southern League, Division 1	Luton Town		L 1-3	6,000
23		Sat	31	Southern League, Division 1	NORTHAMPTON TOWN	2-2 D		7,000
24	January	Sat	7	Southern League, Division 1	Brighton & Hove Albion		L 0-5	7,000
25		Sat	14	FA Cup, 1st Round	BARNSLEY	0-2 L		5,679
26		Sat	21	Southern League, Division 1	EXETER CITY	2-2 D		3,000
27		Sat	28	Southern League, Division 1	Swindon Town		L 1-5	
28	February	Sat	4	Southern League, Division 1	BRISTOL ROVERS	1-0 W		3,000
29		Sat	11	Southern League, Division 1	Crystal Palace		L 0-1	6,000
30		Sat	18	Southern League, Division 1	BRENTFORD	1-0 W		3,000
31		Sat	25	Southern League, Division 1	Leyton		L 2-3	3,500
32	March	Sat	4	Southern League, Division 1	Norwich City		L 1-5	3,000
33		Sat	11	Southern League, Division 1	PLYMOUTH ARGYLE	2-0 W		3,000
34		Sat	18	Southern League, Division 1	Southampton		D 2-2	4,000
35		Wed	22	Southern League, Division 1	New Brompton		D 1-1	3,000
36		Sat	25	Southern League, Division 1	SOUTHEND UNITED	2-1 W		3,000
37	April	Sat	1	Southern League, Division 1	Coventry City		L 1-4	5,000
38		Sat	8	Southern League, Division 1	NEW BROMPTON	3-0 W		3,000
39		Fri	14	Southern League, Division 1	Portsmouth		D 0-0	10,000
40		Sat	15	Southern League, Division 1	Millwall		W 3-0	10,000
41		Mon	17	Southern League, Division 1	PORTSMOUTH	3-2 W		6,000
42		Tue	18	Southern League, Division 1	Southend United		L 0-2	
43		Sat	22	Southern League, Division 1	QUEENS PARK RANGERS	2-0 W		4,000
44		Sat	29	Southern League, Division 1	West Ham United		D 1-1	8,000

League ever-presents: A. Lockett, A. Stewart
Most appearances in total: A. Lockett & A. Stewart 44 out of 44   **Most goals in total:** C.W. White 12
Hat-tricks: None   **Penalty goals:** A. Stewart 3
Sent off: None
Full international appearance(s) this season: None

	Beaumont, S.	Davies, R.	Flint, W.	Gale, A.E.	Grieve, J.	Grimsdell, A.	Kelly, W.B.	Kent, H.	Lockett, A.	McArdle, P.	MacLaine, J.	Middleton, H.	Prentice, H.	Saunders, J.E.	Smith, C.	Smith, H.	Squires, A.	Stewart, A.	Tattersall, W.S.	Theobald, F.	Webster, J.	Wheeler, W.	White, C.W.	Own goal
Apps	15	15	17	3	28	2	29	27	38	10	20	13	1	4	21	9	21	38	30	3	34	12	28	
Subs																								
Goals	1		4				8	2			6	4					4	2	2	6			9	1
Apps	1	3	6	2	6		5	3	6	3	3			1	2	1	1	6	6		5	2	4	
Subs																								
Goals			6				1				2					1		1				1	3	
1	X		X		X		X	X	X		X			G			X	X	X					
2	X1		X		X		X	X	X		X			G			X1	X	X					
3	X		X1		X		X1		X	X				G	X	X1		X	X					
4	X		X		X		X	X	X		X			G			X	X	X					
5	X		X		X		X1	X	X	X	X			G				X	X					
6			X		X		X	X	X		X					X		X	X		G	X		1
7			X		X		X	X	X		X					X	X	X1			G	X		
8			X		X			X	X		X					X	X	X		X	G	X		
9			X1		X		X		X	X	X					X		X	X		G	X1		
10			X1		X		X		X	X	X					X		X	X		G	X		
11			X		X		X	X	X		X1					X		X	X1		G	X		
12			X1		X		X		X		X1						X	X			G	X	X	
13			X		X		X	X	X		X1						X	X			G	X	X	
14			X1		X		X	X	X		X							X1p	X		G	X	X1	
15		X	X				X	X	X		X		X					X	X		G	X		
16		X	X1				X		X	X	X						X	X	X		G		X	
17		X	X2				X		X	X2	X							X	X		G		X2	
18		X	X		X				X		X2				X			X1p	X		G		X	
19		X	X1	X			X		X		X							X	X		G		X	
20	X	X	X1					X	X		X							X	X		G	X	X	
21	X	X	X					X	X		X							X	X		G	X	X1	
22	X	X	X					X	X		X1						X	X			G		X	
23	X	X						X	X		X2							X		X	G	X	X	
24		X		X			X	X	X		X							X		X	G	X	X	
25	X	X	X				X		X		X						X	X	X		G		X	
26	X		X		X1		X	X	X		X				X		X	X			G		X1	
27	X		X		X1		X	X	X		X				X		X	X			G		X	
28	X		X		X	X	X	X	X		X				X		X	X			G		X1	
29	X		X				X	X	X		X				X	X		X	X		G		X	
30	X		X		X		X		X		X				X	X1	X	X	X		G		X	
31	X	X	X		X			X	X		X1				X	X1		X			G		X	
32	X		X		X			X	X		X				X	X		X1p	X		G		X	
33			X		X1	X	X	X	X		X				X		X	X	X		G		X1	
34			X		X1	X	X	X	X		X				X		X	X	X1		G		X	
35			X		X	X	X	X	X		X1				X		X	X	X		G		X1	
36			X		X	X	X	X	X		X1				X		X	X	X		G		X	
37			X		X	X	X	X	X		X				X		X	X	X1		G		X	
38			X		X	X1	X	X	X		X				X		X	X	X		G		X2	
39			X		X	X	X	X	X		X				X		X	X	X		G		X	
40	X				X	X	X	X	X		X				X		X	X	X1		G		X2	
41	X				X1	X	X	X	X		X1				X		X1	X	X		G		X	
42	X	X			X		X	X	X		X				X			X	X		G		X	
43	X			X	X		X	X			X				X			X	X2		G		X	
44	X			X	X		X		X		X				X	X1	X	X	X		G		X	

- 53 -

1911/12

Southern League position: 9th out of 20 in Division 1
Manager: Harry Kent

New league opponents: Stoke

Home-and-away league doubles
For – 2 (Bristol Rovers, West Ham United)
Against – 2 (New Brompton, Plymouth Argyle)

Divisional changes at end of season: Luton Town to Division 2; Leyton left the Southern League; Merthyr Town & Portsmouth from Division 2

All Matches: Won 15, Drew 12, Lost 17, Goals 65-82

Highest Score: 6 (Match 13)

		HOME					AWAY					
	Pl	W	D	L	For	Ag	W	D	L	For	Ag	Pts
Queens Park Rangers	38	12	5	2	36	14	9	6	4	23	21	53
Plymouth Argyle	38	16	2	1	42	7	7	4	8	21	24	52
Northampton Town	38	16	2	1	57	15	6	5	8	25	26	51
Swindon Town	38	14	3	2	52	19	7	3	9	30	31	48
Brighton & Hove Albion	38	15	2	2	54	12	4	7	8	19	23	47
Coventry City	38	14	3	2	47	13	3	5	11	19	41	42
Crystal Palace	38	11	5	3	43	14	4	5	10	27	32	40
Millwall	38	11	6	2	43	19	4	4	11	17	38	40
WATFORD	38	10	5	4	35	20	3	5	11	21	48	36
Stoke	38	10	3	6	35	26	3	7	9	16	37	36
Reading	38	10	7	2	35	14	1	7	11	8	55	36
Norwich City	38	7	11	1	27	18	3	13	13	12	41	34
West Ham United	38	10	3	6	40	27	3	4	12	24	42	33
Brentford	38	10	5	4	43	18	2	4	13	17	47	33
Exeter City	38	8	6	5	30	22	3	5	11	18	40	33
Southampton	38	9	3	7	29	27	1	8	10	17	36	31
Bristol Rovers	38	7	8	4	24	18	2	5	12	17	44	31
New Brompton	38	7	6	6	23	23	4	3	12	12	49	31
Luton Town	38	7	5	7	32	28	2	5	12	17	33	28
Leyton	38	6	8	5	15	19	1	3	15	12	43	25

No	DATE			COMPETITION	OPPONENTS	HOME	AWAY	ATTENDANCE
1	September	Sat	2	Southern League, Division 1	EXETER CITY	0-0 D		5,000
2		Mon	4	Southern League, Division 1	Leyton		D 1-1	2,000
3		Sat	9	Southern League, Division 1	Brentford		L 2-4	6,000
4		Wed	13	Southern Charity Cup, 1st Round	LUTON TOWN	0-1 L		
5		Sat	16	Southern League, Division 1	QUEENS PARK RANGERS	0-3 L		5,000
6		Sat	23	Southern League, Division 1	Millwall		L 0-6	10,000
7		Sat	30	Southern League, Division 1	WEST HAM UNITED	2-0 W		3,000
8	October	Sat	7	Southern League, Division 1	Bristol Rovers		W 2-0	5,580
9		Sat	14	Southern League, Division 1	SWINDON TOWN	2-0 W		5,000
10		Sat	21	Southern League, Division 1	Northampton Town		D 2-2	6,000
11		Sat	28	Southern League, Division 1	BRIGHTON & HOVE ALBION	3-3 D		5,000
12	November	Sat	4	Southern League, Division 1	Stoke		L 0-1	10,000
13		Sat	11	Southern League, Division 1	COVENTRY CITY	6-2 W		4,000
14		Sat	18	FA Cup, 4th Qualifying Round	Custom House		W 5-0	1,000
15		Sat	25	Southern League, Division 1	NORWICH CITY	3-1 W		5,000
16	December	Sat	2	FA Cup, 5th Qualifying Round	BARROW	2-2 D		5,000
17		Thu	7	FA Cup, 5th Qualifying Round replay	Barrow		W 2-1	4,500
18		Sat	9	Southern League, Division 1	SOUTHAMPTON	0-0 D		4,000
19		Sat	16	Southern League, Division 1	Plymouth Argyle		L 1-5	
20		Sat	23	Southern League, Division 1	READING	1-1 D		
21		Mon	25	Southern League, Division 1	Luton Town		D 1-1	8,000
22		Tue	26	Southern League, Division 1	LUTON TOWN	0-1 L		6,000
23		Sat	30	Southern League, Division 1	Exeter City		W 1-0	5,000
24	January	Sat	6	Southern League, Division 1	BRENTFORD	3-0 W		2,000
25		Sat	13	FA Cup, 1st Round	WOLVERHAMPTON WANDERERS	0-0 D		7,538
26		Sat	20	Southern League, Division 1	Queens Park Rangers		D 1-1	6,000
27		Wed	24	FA Cup, 1st Round replay	Wolverhampton Wanderers		L 0-10	8,751
28		Sat	27	Southern League, Division 1	MILLWALL	1-1 D		3,000
29	February	Sat	10	Southern League, Division 1	BRISTOL ROVERS	2-1 W		3,000
30		Sat	17	Southern League, Division 1	Swindon Town		L 0-4	5,000
31	March	Sat	2	Southern League, Division 1	Brighton & Hove Albion		L 1-7	5,000
32		Sat	9	Southern League, Division 1	STOKE	4-2 W		3,000
33		Mon	11	Southern League, Division 1	West Ham United		W 3-1	4,000
34		Sat	16	Southern League, Division 1	Coventry City		L 1-3	5,000
35		Wed	20	Southern League, Division 1	CRYSTAL PALACE	2-0 W		2,000
36		Sat	23	Southern League, Division 1	LEYTON	3-2 W		2,000
37		Sat	30	Southern League, Division 1	Norwich City		D 1-1	4,000
38	April	Fri	5	Southern League, Division 1	New Brompton		L 0-1	5,000
39		Sat	6	Southern League, Division 1	Crystal Palace		L 0-2	
40		Mon	8	Southern League, Division 1	NEW BROMPTON	0-1 L		5,000
41		Wed	10	Southern League, Division 1	NORTHAMPTON TOWN	3-0 W		2,000
42		Sat	13	Southern League, Division 1	Southampton		L 1-2	6,000
43		Sat	20	Southern League, Division 1	PLYMOUTH ARGYLE	0-2 L		4,200
44		Sat	27	Southern League, Division 1	Reading		L 3-6	

League ever-presents: None
Most appearances in total: T. Dixon, J. Webster & C.W. White 43 out of 44   **Most goals in total:** T. Dixon 13
Hat-tricks: None   **Penalty goals:** A. Squires 3, A. Lockett 1
Sent off: J. Blythe (Match 24)   **Full international appearance(s) this season:** None
(In Match 28, the opponents' goal was conceded after C. Bulling had replaced the injured J. Webster as goalkeeper.)

Summary (League / Cup):

	Blythe, J.	Bulling, C.	Bulling, H.M.	Cousins, A.C.	Dixon, T.	Gregory, F.J.	Gregory, V.F.	Grimsdell, A.	Lockett, A.	Middleton, H.	Ness, J.R.	Norman, G.W.	Orme, J.H.	Pantling, H.H.	Smith, C.	Smith, H.	Squires, A.	Stewart, A.	Tattersall, W.S.	Webster, J.	White, C.W.	Own goals
Apps	29	32	9	2	37	20	16	34	29	10	4	8	1	2	11	2	36	28	34	37	37	
Subs																						
Goals		1			12	4	2	3	1	1	2	4			1		7		5		11	3
Apps	5	6	1	1	6	5		6	4	1	1				1		6	6	5	6	6	
Subs																						
Goals					1	4		1									2				1	

Match	Blythe, J.	Bulling, C.	Bulling, H.M.	Cousins, A.C.	Dixon, T.	Gregory, F.J.	Gregory, V.F.	Grimsdell, A.	Lockett, A.	Middleton, H.	Ness, J.R.	Norman, G.W.	Orme, J.H.	Pantling, H.H.	Smith, C.	Smith, H.	Squires, A.	Stewart, A.	Tattersall, W.S.	Webster, J.	White, C.W.	Own goals
1					X			X	X	X	X				X		X	X	X	G	X	
2					X1			X	X	X					X		X	X	X	G	X	
3		X			X			X			X2				X	X	X	X	X	G	X	
4		X	X	X	X			X		X	X						X	X		G	X	
5		X			X			X	X	X	X				X		X	X	X	G		
6	X	X		X	X			X	X						X		X	X	X	G	X	
7	X	X			X	X		X									X	X	X1	G	X1	
8	X	X			X1	X		X	X								X	X	X1	G	X	
9	X	X			X1	X		X	X1p								X	X	X	G	X	
10	X	X			X1	X		X1	X								X	X	X	G	X	
11	X	X			X1	X		X1	X								X1	X	X	G	X	
12	X	X			X	X		X	X								X	X	X	G	X	
13	X	X			X1	X1		X	X								X	X	X1	G	X1	2
14	X	X			X	X2		X	X								X2p	X	X	G	X1	
15	X	X			X1	X		X	X								X	X	X	G	X1	1
16	X	X			X	X2		X	X								X	X	X	G	X	
17	X	X			X1	X		X1	X								X	X	X	G	X	
18	X	X		X	X			X	X				G					X	X		X	
19	X	X			X1	X		X	X								X	X	X	G	X	
20	X	X			X	X1		X								X	X	X	X	G	X	
21	X				X	X	X	X	X								X	X	X	G	X1	
22	X				X	X	X	X	X								X	X	X	G	X	
23	X	X			X		X1	X	X								X	X	X	G	X	
24	X	X1			X		X	X1	X								X1p	X	X	G	X	
25	X	X			X	X		X	X								X	X	X	G	X	
26	X				X1			X	X	X					X		X	X	X	G	X	
27	X	X			X	X		X							X		X	X	X	G	X	
28	X	X	X		X	X		X	X								X1		X	G	X	
29		X			X	X	X1	X	X	X							X	X		G	X1	
30	X	X			X	X	X	X									X	X	X	G	X	
31	X				X	X	X	X	X			X					X	X	X	G	X1	
32	X	X				X		X				X2				X	X	X	X1	G	X1	
33	X	X			X	X1		X				X1				X	X1p	X		G	X	
34	X	X			X			X				X				X	X1	X	X	G	X	
35		X	X		X	X		X	X								X1		X1	G	X	
36		X	X		X1	X	X	X				X1					X		X	G	X1	
37		X	X		X	X	X	X				X					X		X	G	X1	
38	X	X	X		X		X	X	X								X		X	G	X	
39	X	X			X	X	X	X	X								X		X	G	X	
40	X	X			X	X	X	X									X	X	X	G	X	
41	X	X	X		X1			X	X							X	X1		X	G	X1	
42	X	X	X		X	X		X				X					X		X	G	X1	
43	X	X	X		X	X	X	X				X					X			G	X	
44	X	X			X1	X1		X	X1					X		X	X			G	X	

1912/13

Southern League position: 14th out of 20 in Division 1
Manager: Harry Kent

New league opponents: Merthyr Town

Home-and-away league doubles
For – 2 (Southampton, Swindon Town)
Against – 2 (Queens Park Rangers, West Ham United)

Divisional changes at end of season: Brentford & Stoke to Division 2; Cardiff City & Southend United from Division 2

All Matches: Won 14, Drew 11, Lost 18, Goals 52-56

Highest Score: 5 (Match 18)

		HOME					AWAY					
	Pl	W	D	L	For	Ag	W	D	L	For	Ag	Pts
Plymouth Argyle	38	15	2	2	47	9	7	4	8	30	27	50
Swindon Town	38	13	5	1	44	16	7	3	9	22	25	48
West Ham United	38	11	6	2	39	15	7	6	6	27	31	48
Queens Park Rangers	38	14	4	1	33	10	4	6	9	13	25	46
Crystal Palace	38	13	3	3	38	13	4	8	7	17	23	45
Millwall	38	14	0	5	36	17	5	7	7	26	26	45
Exeter City	38	13	3	3	29	16	5	5	9	19	28	44
Reading	38	12	3	4	34	20	5	9	5	25	35	42
Brighton & Hove Albion	38	12	5	2	39	19	1	7	11	9	28	38
Northampton Town	38	11	4	4	42	17	1	8	10	19	31	36
Portsmouth	38	11	5	3	28	15	3	3	13	13	34	36
Merthyr Town	38	8	9	2	27	18	4	3	12	15	42	36
Coventry City	38	9	4	6	42	27	4	4	11	11	32	34
WATFORD	38	8	5	6	28	24	4	5	10	15	26	34
Gillingham	38	7	7	5	19	21	5	3	11	17	32	34
Bristol Rovers	38	9	6	4	37	23	3	3	13	18	41	33
Southampton	38	7	6	5	28	25	3	4	12	12	47	31
Norwich City	38	8	7	4	27	20	2	2	15	13	33	29
Brentford	38	10	3	6	27	17	1	2	16	15	38	27
Stoke	38	8	3	8	21	17	2	1	16	18	58	24

No	DATE			COMPETITION	OPPONENTS	HOME	AWAY	ATTENDANCE
1	September	Sat	7	Southern League, Division 1	Exeter City		L 0-1	5,000
2		Wed	11	Southern League, Division 1	BRISTOL ROVERS	2-1 W		2,000
3		Sat	14	Southern League, Division 1	WEST HAM UNITED	0-2 L		5,000
4		Wed	18	Southern League, Division 1	NORTHAMPTON TOWN	2-0 W		3,000
5		Sat	21	Southern League, Division 1	Brighton & Hove Albion		L 0-3	7,000
6		Sat	28	Southern League, Division 1	COVENTRY CITY	1-1 D		4,000
7	October	Sat	2	Southern League, Division 1	Bristol Rovers		D 2-2	
8		Sat	5	Southern League, Division 1	STOKE	2-4 L		4,000
9		Wed	9	Southern League, Division 1	BRENTFORD	1-0 W		2,000
10		Sat	19	Southern League, Division 1	CRYSTAL PALACE	1-1 D		4,000
11		Sat	26	Southern League, Division 1	Plymouth Argyle		D 0-0	6,000
12		Mon	28	Southern League, Division 1	Merthyr Town		W 3-0	4,000
13	November	Sat	2	Southern League, Division 1	SOUTHAMPTON	2-0 W		4,000
14		Sat	9	Southern League, Division 1	Reading		L 0-2	5,000
15		Sat	16	Southern League, Division 1	NORWICH CITY	2-0 W		4,000
16		Sat	23	Southern League, Division 1	Gillingham		L 0-2	
17		Sat	30	FA Cup, 4th Qualifying Round	Brentford		D 0-0	8,000
18	December	Wed	4	FA Cup, 4th Qualifying Round replay	BRENTFORD	5-1 W		2,000
19		Sat	7	Southern League, Division 1	Queens Park Rangers		L 0-2	6,000
20		Sat	14	FA Cup, 5th Qualifying Round	Chesterfield Town		L 1-3	8,000
21		Sat	21	Southern League, Division 1	Millwall		L 0-1	7,000
22		Wed	25	Southern League, Division 1	Swindon Town		W 2-1	
23		Thu	26	Southern League, Division 1	SWINDON TOWN	2-1 W		5,000
24		Sat	28	Southern League, Division 1	EXETER CITY	1-0 W		4,000
25	January	Sat	4	Southern League, Division 1	West Ham United		L 0-2	8,000
26		Sat	18	Southern League, Division 1	BRIGHTON & HOVE ALBION	3-1 W		
27		Sat	25	Southern League, Division 1	Coventry City		L 1-2	
28	February	Sat	1	Southern Charity Cup, 2nd Round	Coventry City		W 2-0	2,000
29		Sat	8	Southern League, Division 1	Stoke		W 2-1	7,000
30		Sat	15	Southern League, Division 1	MERTHYR TOWN	1-3 L		3,000
31	March	Sat	1	Southern League, Division 1	PLYMOUTH ARGYLE	0-1 L		3,000
32		Sat	8	Southern League, Division 1	Southampton		W 1-0	6,000
33		Sat	15	Southern League, Division 1	READING	3-3 D		
34		Fri	21	Southern League, Division 1	PORTSMOUTH	1-2 L		5,500
35		Sat	22	Southern League, Division 1	Norwich City		D 1-1	4,000
36		Mon	24	Southern League, Division 1	Portsmouth		D 1-1	12,000
37		Sat	29	Southern League, Division 1	GILLINGHAM	1-1 D		
38	April	Sat	5	Southern League, Division 1	Northampton Town		D 1-1	3,000
39		Sat	12	Southern League, Division 1	QUEENS PARK RANGERS	1-2 L		3,000
40		Thu	17	Southern Charity Cup, Semi-Final	BRIGHTON & HOVE ALBION	1-2 L		
41		Sat	19	Southern League, Division 1	Brentford		L 0-2	5,000
42		Wed	23	Southern League, Division 1	Crystal Palace		L 1-2	4,000
43		Sat	26	Southern League, Division 1	MILLWALL	1-1 D		2,500

League ever-presents: A. Jebb
Most appearances in total: A. Jebb 43 out of 43   **Most goals in total:** T. Dixon 13
Hat-tricks: A. Squires (Match 18)   **Penalty goals:** C. Bulling 1, A. Stewart 1
Sent off: None
Full international appearance(s) this season: None

	Blythe, J.	Bulling, C.	Bulling, H.M.	Carr, J.E.C.	Dixon, T.	Edmonds, G.W.N.	English, J.C.	Evans, J.	Gemmell, G.	Green, A.	Gregory, F.J.	Gregory, V.F.	Jebb, A.	Kilner, E.	Mitchell, T.W.	Orme, J.H.	Pantling, H.H.	Robinson, E.	Smith, H.	Squires, A.	Stewart, A.	Webster, J.	White, C.W.
Apps	15	26	30	3	35	2	33	11	6	7	19	35	38	5	33	12	8	1	3	24	9	26	37
Subs																							
Goals		3			9	1		1	1	1	5	3			9				1	2			7
Apps	1	4	5		4		4	4			1	1	4	5		5	1	1		5	1	4	5
Subs																							
Goals					4															3	1		1
1		X			X		X	X				X	X	X						X	X	G	X
2		X			X1		X	X				X	X	X						X	X	G	X1
3		X	X		X		X	X				X	X	X						X		G	X
4		X	X		X		X			X		X	X		X1	G				X			X1
5	X	X	X		X		X	X					X		X					X		G	X
6		X	X		X		X	X	X1			X	X		X							G	X
7		X	X		X1		X				X1	X	X		X				X			G	X
8	X1p	X			X		X			X		X	X		X				X1			G	X
9	X	X	X		X1		X			X		X	X		X							G	X
10	X	X	X		X		X			X		X	X		X1							G	X
11	X	X	X		X		X				X	X	X		X							G	X
12	X	X	X		X		X				X2	X	X		X							G	X1
13	X	X	X		X1		X				X	X	X		X							G	X1
14	X	X	X		X		X				X	X	X		X							G	X
15	X	X1	X		X		X				X1	X	X		X							G	X
16	X	X	X		X		X				X	X	X		X							G	X
17		X	X		X		X	X				X	X		X					X		G	X
18		X	X		X2		X	X				X	X		X					X3		G	X
19		X	X		X		X	X				X	X		X					X		G	X
20		X	X		X1		X	X				X	X		X					X		G	X
21		X	X		X		X	X				X	X		X					X		G	X
22		X	X		X1		X	X				X1	X		X					X		G	X
23		X	X		X		X				X1	X	X		X2					X		G	X
24		X	X		X		X				X	X	X		X					X		G	X1
25		X	X		X		X				X	X	X		X					X		G	X
26		X			X		X		X		X1	X			X1			X		X1		G	X
27	X	X			X		X	X				X	X		X1					X		G	X
28	X	X			X1		X	X				X	X		X					X		G	X1
29	X	X			X			X1				X1	X		X	X				X		G	X
30		X1	X		X					X		X	X		X	X				X		G	X
31		X	X		X		X					X	X	X						X		G	X
32		X	X		X						X	X	X		X	G				X			X1
33	X		X	X	X2		X			X	X	X	X		X1	G							X
34	X		X		X		X				X	X	X		X1	G				X			X
35	X		X		X		X				X	X	X		X1	G				X			X
36	X				X		X				X	X	X		X	G				X	X		X1
37					X1		X			X		X	X		X	G	X			X	X		X
38					X1		X			X		X	X		X	G	X			X	X		X
39		X			X		X			X		X	X		X	G	X			X1	X		X
40	X	X									X	X	X		X	G	X			X	X1p		X
41		X									X	X	X	X	X	G	X	X	X	X	X		X
42			X		X1						X	X	X	X		G	X			X			X
43			X		X						X1	X	X	X		G	X			X			X

1913/14

Southern League position: 18th out of 20 in Division 1
Manager: Harry Kent

New league opponents: Cardiff City

Home-and-away league doubles
For – 1 (Southampton)
Against – 4 (Gillingham, Portsmouth, Southend United, Swindon Town)

Divisional changes at end of season: Merthyr Town & Coventry City to Division 2; Croydon Common & Luton Town from Division 2

All Matches: Won 11, Drew 9, Lost 21, Goals 60-60

Highest Score: 10 (Match 18)

		HOME					AWAY					
	Pl	W	D	L	For	Ag	W	D	L	For	Ag	Pts
Swindon Town	38	14	3	2	57	11	7	5	7	24	30	50
Crystal Palace	38	12	5	2	41	13	5	11	3	19	19	50
Northampton Town	38	11	8	0	31	9	3	11	5	19	28	47
Reading	38	14	4	1	32	11	3	6	10	11	25	44
Plymouth Argyle	38	11	6	2	25	12	4	7	8	21	30	43
West Ham United	38	9	7	3	39	22	6	5	8	22	38	42
Brighton & Hove Albion	38	12	5	2	31	16	3	7	9	29	29	42
Queens Park Rangers	38	10	6	3	27	14	6	3	10	18	29	41
Portsmouth	38	10	7	2	31	13	4	5	10	26	35	40
Cardiff City	38	10	6	3	27	11	3	6	10	19	31	38
Southampton	38	11	2	6	35	22	4	5	10	20	32	37
Exeter City	38	7	8	4	21	11	3	8	8	18	27	36
Gillingham	38	10	6	3	36	15	3	3	13	12	34	35
Norwich City	38	7	10	2	34	19	2	7	10	15	32	35
Millwall	38	10	6	3	34	20	1	6	12	17	36	34
Southend United	38	7	7	5	29	28	3	5	11	12	38	32
Bristol Rovers	38	10	5	4	32	25	0	6	13	14	42	31
WATFORD	38	9	4	6	37	20	1	5	13	13	36	29
Merthyr Town	38	7	7	5	23	18	2	3	14	15	43	28
Coventry City	38	4	8	7	28	28	2	6	11	15	40	26

No	DATE			COMPETITION	OPPONENTS	HOME	AWAY	ATTENDANCE
1	September	Thu	4	Southern League, Division 1	Norwich City		L 1-3	5,000
2		Sat	6	Southern League, Division 1	SOUTHEND UNITED	1-2 L		4,000
3		Wed	10	Southern League, Division 1	NORWICH CITY	2-0 W		2,000
4		Sat	13	Southern League, Division 1	Brighton & Hove Albion		D 0-0	6,000
5		Wed	17	Southern League, Division 1	READING	0-0 D		3,000
6		Sat	20	Southern League, Division 1	PORTSMOUTH	0-2 L		4,000
7		Wed	24	Southern League, Division 1	COVENTRY CITY	7-0 W		
8		Sat	27	Southern League, Division 1	Millwall		D 2-2	
9	October	Wed	1	Southern Charity Cup, 1st Round	Luton Town		L 0-3	1,500
10		Sat	4	Southern League, Division 1	EXETER CITY	0-1 L		4,000
11		Sat	11	Southern League, Division 1	Cardiff City		L 0-2	14,000
12		Sat	18	Southern League, Division 1	SWINDON TOWN	1-2 L		5,000
13		Sat	25	Southern League, Division 1	Bristol Rovers		L 1-2	
14	November	Sat	1	Southern League, Division 1	MERTHYR TOWN	3-0 W		4,000
15		Sat	8	Southern League, Division 1	West Ham United		D 1-1	15,000
16		Sat	15	Southern League, Division 1	PLYMOUTH ARGYLE	0-1 L		
17		Sat	22	Southern League, Division 1	Southampton		W 3-1	9,000
18		Sat	29	FA Cup, 4th Qualifying Round	BOURNEMOUTH	10-0 W		2,000
19	December	Sat	6	Southern League, Division 1	Crystal Palace		L 0-3	5,000
20		Sat	13	FA Cup, 5th Qualifying Round	Gillingham		L 0-1	6,000
21		Sat	30	Southern League, Division 1	Queens Park Rangers		L 2-3	6,000
22		Thu	25	Southern League, Division 1	GILLINGHAM	0-2 L		
23		Fri	26	Southern League, Division 1	Gillingham		L 0-3	7,000
24		Sat	27	Southern League, Division 1	Southend United		L 0-1	6,000
25	January	Sat	3	Southern League, Division 1	BRIGHTON & HOVE ALBION	3-1 W		2,000
26		Sat	17	Southern League, Division 1	Portsmouth		L 0-1	7,000
27		Sat	24	Southern League, Division 1	MILLWALL	2-1 W		
28		Sat	31	Southern League, Division 1	Reading		L 0-3	5,000
29	February	Sat	7	Southern League, Division 1	Exeter City		D 1-1	4,000
30		Sat	14	Southern League, Division 1	CARDIFF CITY	3-2 W		2,000
31		Sat	21	Southern League, Division 1	Swindon Town		L 0-3	
32		Sat	28	Southern League, Division 1	BRISTOL ROVERS	1-1 D		2,500
33	March	Sat	7	Southern League, Division 1	Merthyr Town		L 0-1	7,000
34		Sat	21	Southern League, Division 1	Plymouth Argyle		D 1-1	6,000
35		Sat	28	Southern League, Division 1	SOUTHAMPTON	2-1 W		3,000
36	April	Sat	1	Southern League, Division 1	WEST HAM UNITED	6-0 W		2,000
37		Fri	10	Southern League, Division 1	NORTHAMPTON TOWN	3-3 D		5,000
38		Sat	11	Southern League, Division 1	CRYSTAL PALACE	1-1 D		3,000
39		Tue	14	Southern League, Division 1	Northampton Town		L 0-2	5,000
40		Sat	18	Southern League, Division 1	Coventry City		L 1-3	4,000
41		Sat	25	Southern League, Division 1	QUEENS PARK RANGERS	2-0 W		5,000

The following match was abandoned after 38 minutes, owing to a waterlogged pitch:

	March	Sat	14	Southern League, Division 1	WEST HAM UNITED	0-1		3,000

League ever-presents: V.F. Gregory
Most appearances in total: V.F. Gregory & A. Stewart 40 out of 41   Most goals in total: T.E. Ashbridge 14
Hat-tricks: G.W.N. Edmonds (4 goals Match 7), T.E. Ashbridge (5 goals Match 18, 4 goals Match 36), V.F. Gregory (Match 18)
Penalty goals: W. Dryden 1, A. Stewart 1   Sent off: None   Full international appearance(s) this season: None
(In Match 23, one of the opponents' goals was conceded after H.H. Pantling had replaced the injured J. Webster as goalkeeper.)

	Ashbridge, T.E.	Bulling, C.	Bulling, H.M.	Carr, J.E.C.	Cramb, J.	Crownshaw, H.	Donald, D.M.	Dryden, W.	Edmonds, G.W.N.	Frankish, J.J.	Green, A.	Gregory, F.J.	Gregory, V.F.	Grimsdell, E.F.	Kennedy, J.J.	Kent, H.	Kingham, W.	McLauchlan, J.I.S.	Mahon, L.	Mitchell, T.W.	Pantling, H.H.	Stewart, A.	Webster, J.	White, C.W.	Williams, R.G.	Own goal
Apps	21	2	25	15		1	22	20	12	2	18	29	38	9	19	1		14	10	27	25	37	34	33	4	
Subs																										
Goals	9		1				3	8	8		4	1	3					5				1		6		1
Apps	2		1	1	1		2	1	2	1	3	3	2			1	1		1			3	3	2	3	
Subs																										
Goals	5								2				3													
1			X				X	X		X			X					X	X	X		X	G	X		1
2	X1		X				X	X		X			X					X	X	X		X	G			
3			X				X	X1				X	X					X	X	X		X1p	G	X		
4			X				X	X				X	X					X	X	X		X	G	X		
5			X				X	X				X	X					X	X	X		X	G	X		
6			X				X	X	X			X	X						X	X		X	G	X		
7	X						X		X4	X1	X		X2									X	G	X1		
8			X	X			X	X1			X	X										X	G	X1		
9			X	X	G		X			X	X	X					X					X	X	X		
10			X	X			X	X			X	X	X									X	G	X		
11							X	X	X	X	X									X				X	G	
12	X1						X	X			X	X	X							X	X	X	G	X		
13	X					X	X	X1			X	X	X							X		X	G	X		
14	X1						X	X1			X1	X	X	X						X		X	G	X		
15	X						X			X1	X	X	X									X	G	X		
16	X						X			X	X	X	X	X								X	X		G	
17	X1						X			X1	X	X	X	X								X	G	X		X1
18	X5						X		X2		X	X	X3							X		X	G	X		X
19	X						X		X		X	X	X									X	G	X		X
20	X						X		X		X	X	X				X					X	G	X		X
21			X						X1	X	X1	X	X	X		X				X		X	G			
22			X						X	X	X	X	X	X	X					X		X	G			
23			X						X		X	X	X		X					X		X	X	X		
24		X	X						X		X	X			X					X		X		X	G	
25	X	X	X						X2		X1	X	X		X					X				X	G	
26		X	X						X		X	X	X		X					X		X	G	X		
27	X	X	X				X2p					X	X		X							X	G	X		
28	X	X	X								X	X	X		X							X	X	X		
29		X	X									X	X		X			X				X	X		G	X1
30		X	X									X	X		X			X2				X	X		G	X1
31		X	X									X	X		X			X				X	X		G	
32		X	X									X	X		X			X1				X	X		G	
33	X	X	X									X			X			X				X	X		G	
34	X	X					X					X1			X			X				X	X	X	G	X
35	X1	X					X					X			X			X1				X	X	X	G	X
36	X4	X					X					X			X			X1				X	X	X	G	X1
37	X		X1				X2					X			X			X				X	X	X	G	X
38	X		X				X1				X	X			X							X	X	X	G	X
39	X	X	X				X				X	X										X	X	X	G	X
40	X	X					X				X1	X	X									X	X	X	G	X
41	X						X		X1		X	X	X									X	X	X	G	X1
	X		X	X								X						X				X	X	X	G	X

1914/15

Southern League position: 1st out of 20 in Division 1
Manager: Harry Kent

New league opponents: None

Home-and-away league doubles
For – 7 (Bristol Rovers, Cardiff City, Croydon Common, Crystal Palace, Gillingham, Millwall, Portsmouth)
Against – 1 (West Ham United)

Divisional changes before 1919/20 season: West Ham United to Football League; Croydon Common wound up; Brentford, Merthyr Town, Newport County & Swansea Town from Division 2 (Division 1 increased to 22 clubs)

All Matches: Won 22, Drew 8, Lost 10, Goals 68-50

Highest Score: 5 (Matches 29 & 31)

	HOME						AWAY					
	Pl	W	D	L	For	Ag	W	D	L	For	Ag	Pts
WATFORD	38	12	4	3	37	15	10	4	5	31	31	52
Reading	38	12	4	3	37	16	9	3	7	31	27	49
Cardiff City	38	16	1	2	51	12	6	3	10	21	26	48
West Ham United	38	14	4	1	42	18	4	5	10	16	29	45
Northampton Town	38	11	5	3	37	23	5	6	8	19	28	43
Southampton	38	14	3	2	56	28	5	2	12	22	46	43
Portsmouth	38	10	5	4	26	14	6	5	8	28	28	42
Millwall	38	9	4	6	28	23	7	6	6	22	28	42
Swindon Town	38	11	5	3	55	21	4	6	9	22	38	41
Brighton & Hove Albion	38	11	5	3	29	16	5	2	12	17	31	39
Exeter City	38	10	3	6	32	16	5	5	9	18	25	38
Queens Park Rangers	38	8	4	7	30	28	5	8	6	25	28	38
Norwich City	38	10	6	3	33	16	1	8	10	20	40	36
Luton Town	38	6	3	10	27	34	7	5	7	34	39	34
Crystal Palace	38	8	4	7	24	25	5	4	10	23	36	34
Bristol Rovers	38	8	4	7	42	28	2	1	16	11	47	33
Plymouth Argyle	38	12	2	5	34	25	0	7	12	17	36	30
Southend United	38	8	5	6	27	20	2	3	14	17	44	28
Croydon Common	38	7	6	6	28	18	2	3	14	19	45	27
Gillingham	38	6	6	7	32	29	0	2	17	11	53	20

No	DATE			COMPETITION	OPPONENTS	HOME	AWAY	ATTENDANCE	
1	September	Wed	2	Southern League, Division 1	CARDIFF CITY	2-1 W		1,500	
2		Sat	5	Southern League, Division 1	Portsmouth		W 3-2		7,000
3		Sat	12	Southern League, Division 1	SWINDON TOWN	3-0 W		3,000	
4		Wed	16	Southern League, Division 1	BRIGHTON & HOVE ALBION	0-0 D		1,500	
5		Sat	19	Southern League, Division 1	Southend United		D 0-0		4,000
6		Sat	26	Southern League, Division 1	QUEENS PARK RANGERS	2-2 D		5,000	
7	October	Sat	3	Southern League, Division 1	Millwall		W 3-0		15,000
8		Sat	10	Southern League, Division 1	BRISTOL ROVERS	2-0 W		3,000	
9		Sat	17	Southern League, Division 1	Croydon Common		W 1-0		6,000
10		Sat	24	Southern League, Division 1	READING	0-1 L		5,000	
11		Sat	31	Southern League, Division 1	Southampton		L 1-3		
12	November	Wed	4	Southern Charity Cup, 1st Round	Luton Town		L 0-2		
13		Sat	7	Southern League, Division 1	NORTHAMPTON TOWN	0-0 D		6,000	
14		Sat	14	Southern League, Division 1	CRYSTAL PALACE	1-0 W			
15		Sat	21	Southern League, Division 1	Plymouth Argyle		D 1-1		
16		Sat	28	Southern League, Division 1	WEST HAM UNITED	0-1 L			
17	December	Sat	5	Southern League, Division 1	Norwich City		L 0-2		3,000
18		Sat	12	Southern League, Division 1	GILLINGHAM	4-0 W		2,500	
19		Sat	19	FA Cup, 6th Qualifying Round	Rochdale		L 0-2		4,000
20		Fri	25	Southern League, Division 1	EXETER CITY	1-1 D		2,000	
21		Sat	26	Southern League, Division 1	Exeter City		L 1-4		6,000
22	January	Fri	1	Southern League, Division 1	Cardiff City		W 3-2		1,900
23		Sat	2	Southern League, Division 1	PORTSMOUTH	2-1 W		3,000	
24		Sat	23	Southern League, Division 1	Reading		D 1-1		
25	February	Wed	3	Southern League, Division 1	SOUTHEND UNITED	2-1 W		1,000	
26		Sat	13	Southern League, Division 1	Bristol Rovers		W 3-2		1,000
27		Sat	20	Southern League, Division 1	CROYDON COMMON	3-0 W		3,000	
28		Sat	27	Southern League, Division 1	MILLWALL	4-0 W		3,000	
29	March	Sat	6	Southern League, Division 1	SOUTHAMPTON	5-2 W			
30		Sat	13	Southern League, Division 1	Northampton Town		D 1-1		10,000
31		Thu	18	Southern League, Division 1	Queens Park Rangers		W 5-2		5,000
32		Sat	20	Southern League, Division 1	Crystal Palace		W 1-0		
33		Sat	27	Southern League, Division 1	PLYMOUTH ARGYLE	2-0 W		3,000	
34	April	Fri	2	Southern League, Division 1	LUTON TOWN	2-4 L		8,000	
35		Sat	3	Southern League, Division 1	West Ham United		L 0-2		10,000
36		Mon	5	Southern League, Division 1	Luton Town		W 2-0		7,000
37		Tue	6	Southern League, Division 1	Swindon Town		L 0-6		1,000
38		Sat	10	Southern League, Division 1	NORWICH CITY	2-1 W			
39		Sat	17	Southern League, Division 1	Gillingham		W 3-2		
40		Sat	24	Southern League, Division 1	Brighton & Hove Albion		W 2-1		3,000

League ever-presents: F.J. Gregory, R.G. Williams
Most appearances in total: F.J. Gregory & R.G. Williams 40 out of 40   **Most goals in total:** G.W.N. Edmonds 17
Hat-tricks: T. Waterall (Match 7)   **Penalty goals:** J.J. Kennedy 2
Sent off: None   **Full international appearance(s) this season:** None
(In Match 22, two of the opponents' goals were conceded after T. Waterall had replaced the injured R.G. Williams as goalkeeper.)

	Barnshaw, R.J.	Bulling, H.M. //	Edmonds, G.W.N.	Green, A. //	Gregory, F.J.	Gregory, V.F.	Grimsdell, E.F.	Hastings, W. //	Hatton, S.T. //	Kennedy, J.J. //	McGuire, R. //	McLauchlan, J.J.S. //	McMorran, F.A. //	Ronald, P.M.	Stewart, A. //	Waterall, T.	White, C.W.	Williams, R.G.	Own goals
Apps	11	35	35	23	38	32	1	34		32	3	6	6	35	37	33	19	38	
Subs																			
Goals			17	8	2	3		6		3			3	9		10	4		3
Apps	2	1		2	1			2	1	2		2	1	1	1	2	2	2	
Subs																			
Goals																			
1		X	X	X	X	X		X		X				X1	X		X1	G	
2		X	X1	X	X	X		X		X				X1	X		X1	G	
3		X	X1	X	X	X		X		X				X	X		X1	G	1
4	X		X	X	X	X		X		X				X	X		X	G	
5		X	X		X	X		X	X					X	X		X	G	
6	X	X	X1		X	X		X1						X	X	X	X	G	
7		X	X		X	X		X		X				X	X	X3	X	G	
8		X	X		X	X1		X		X				X1	X		X	G	
9		X	X1		X	X	X	X		X				X	X		X	G	
10		X	X		X	X		X		X				X	X	X	X	G	
11		X	X		X			X1				X		X	X		X	G	
12		X			X	X		X	X	X			X	X			X	G	
13		X	X		X	X		X		X				X	X		X	G	
14	X	X	X		X			X1						X	X		X	G	
15	X	X			X			X		X		X		X	X		X	G	1
16	X	X			X			X		X				X	X		X	G	
17	X	X			X			X		X				X	X		X	G	
18		X	X		X			X		X	X2	X			X	X2	X	G	
19	X	X			X			X		X	X	X		X	X		X	G	
20		X	X	X	X	X		X		X				X1	X			G	
21		X	X1	X	X	X		X		X					X		X	G	
22	X		X1	X1	X	X		X				X		X	X	X1		G	
23			X2		X	X		X				X		X	X	X	X	G	
24		X	X		X	X		X						X	X	X	X1	G	
25		X	X	X	X	X		X						X1	X			G	1
26		X	X1	X2	X	X		X						X	X			G	
27		X	X	X	X	X		X1						X2	X			G	
28		X	X1	X1	X	X		X1						X1	X			G	
29		X	X	X1	X	X		X1	X1					X1	X	X1		G	
30		X	X	X	X	X1		X	X					X	X			G	
31	X	X	X2	X1	X	X1				X				X	X	X1		G	
32	X	X	X	X	X						X			X	X	X1		G	
33		X	X1	X	X	X		X		X				X	X	X1		G	
34		X	X	X	X	X		X		X1p				X1	X	X		G	
35		X	X	X	X	X		X		X				X	X	X		G	
36	X	X	X1	X	X1	X							X	X	X	X		G	
37	X	X	X	X	X	X							X	X	X	X		G	
38		X	X1	X	X	X		X		X1p				X	X	X		G	
39		X	X1	X1	X1	X		X		X				X	X	X		G	
40		X	X1	X1	X	X		X		X				X	X	X		G	

1919/20

Southern League position: 2nd out of 22 in Division 1
Manager: Harry Kent

New league opponents: Newport County, Swansea Town

Home-and-away league doubles
For – 8 (Brentford, Luton Town, Merthyr Town, Millwall, Northampton Town, Reading, Swansea Town, Swindon Town)
Against – 2 (Exeter City, Norwich City)

Divisional changes at end of season: The division became Division 3 of the Football League; Cardiff City to Division 2; Grimsby Town from Division 2

All Matches: Won 26, Drew 6, Lost 11, Goals 69-43

Highest Score: 6 (Match 32)

		HOME					AWAY					
	Pl	W	D	L	For	Ag	W	D	L	For	Ag	Pts
Portsmouth	42	13	6	2	48	14	10	6	5	25	13	58
WATFORD	42	15	3	3	39	12	11	3	7	30	30	58
Crystal Palace	42	15	5	1	44	15	7	7	7	25	28	56
Cardiff City	42	15	3	3	44	14	3	14	4	26	29	53
Plymouth Argyle	42	13	5	3	36	8	7	5	9	21	21	50
Queens Park Rangers	42	12	7	2	34	13	6	3	12	28	37	46
Reading	42	11	5	5	30	14	5	8	8	21	29	45
Southampton	42	13	4	4	51	22	5	4	12	21	41	44
Swansea Town	42	11	6	4	28	14	5	7	9	25	31	43
Exeter City	42	14	3	4	44	22	3	6	12	13	29	43
Southend United	42	10	8	3	32	18	3	9	9	14	30	43
Norwich City	42	13	3	5	43	18	3	5	13	18	39	41
Swindon Town	42	13	3	5	45	26	4	3	14	20	42	41
Millwall	42	10	7	4	32	15	4	5	12	20	34	40
Brentford	42	11	5	5	35	21	4	5	12	17	38	40
Brighton & Hove Albion	42	11	5	5	43	28	3	3	15	17	44	36
Bristol Rovers	42	10	7	4	43	29	1	6	14	18	49	35
Newport County	42	10	6	5	30	18	3	1	17	15	52	33
Northampton Town	42	9	4	8	35	40	4	5	12	29	63	33
Luton Town	42	7	7	7	29	28	3	3	15	22	48	30
Merthyr Town	42	7	6	8	30	31	2	5	14	17	47	29
Gillingham	42	7	5	9	24	23	3	2	16	10	51	27

No	DATE			COMPETITION	OPPONENTS	HOME	AWAY	ATTENDANCE
1	August	Sat	30	Southern League, Division 1	Gillingham		D 0-0	6,000
2	September	Mon	1	Southern League, Division 1	Northampton Town		W 2-1	4,000
3		Sat	6	Southern League, Division 1	CRYSTAL PALACE	4-1 W		6,000
4		Mon	8	Southern League, Division 1	NORTHAMPTON TOWN	3-2 W		3,000
5		Thu	11	Southern League, Division 1	Newport County		W 1-0	4,000
6		Sat	13	Southern League, Division 1	Swansea Town		W 1-0	9,000
7		Sat	20	Southern League, Division 1	SOUTHEND UNITED	1-1 D		6,043
8	October	Sat	4	Southern League, Division 1	NORWICH CITY	0-1 L		5,000
9		Sat	11	Southern League, Division 1	CARDIFF CITY	0-0 D		4,000
10		Sat	18	Southern League, Division 1	BRENTFORD	1-0 W		5,000
11		Sat	25	Southern League, Division 1	Queens Park Rangers		L 0-3	12,000
12	November	Sat	1	Southern League, Division 1	MERTHYR TOWN	5-0 W		4,000
13		Sat	8	Southern League, Division 1	Swindon Town		W 2-1	8,000
14		Sat	15	Southern League, Division 1	PLYMOUTH ARGYLE	3-0 W		6,000
15		Sat	22	Southern League, Division 1	Millwall		W 2-0	10,000
16		Wed	26	Southern League, Division 1	EXETER CITY	0-1 L		4,000
17		Sat	29	Southern League, Division 1	BRISTOL ROVERS	1-0 W		5,000
18	December	Sat	6	Southern League, Division 1	Brighton & Hove Albion		L 2-3	8,000
19		Sat	13	Southern League, Division 1	READING	3-1 W		6,000
20		Sat	20	FA Cup, 6th Qualifying Round	Southend United		L 0-1	5,000
21		Thu	25	Southern League, Division 1	PORTSMOUTH	0-1 L		8,000
22		Fri	26	Southern League, Division 1	Portsmouth		W 2-1	23,791
23		Sat	27	Southern League, Division 1	Southampton		L 1-5	10,000
24	January	Sat	3	Southern League, Division 1	GILLINGHAM	2-1 W		4,000
25		Sat	17	Southern League, Division 1	Crystal Palace		L 1-2	10,000
26		Sat	24	Southern League, Division 1	SWANSEA TOWN	1-0 W		6,000
27		Sat	31	Southern League, Division 1	Southend United		L 1-4	4,000
28	February	Sat	7	Southern League, Division 1	Exeter City		L 0-3	6,000
29		Sat	14	Southern League, Division 1	Norwich City		L 0-1	10,000
30		Sat	28	Southern League, Division 1	Brentford		W 3-0	10,000
31	March	Sat	6	Southern League, Division 1	QUEENS PARK RANGERS	1-0 W		8,500
32		Sat	13	Southern League, Division 1	Merthyr Town		W 6-3	5,000
33		Sat	20	Southern League, Division 1	SWINDON TOWN	3-1 W		6,000
34		Wed	24	Southern League, Division 1	NEWPORT COUNTY	0-0 D		3,000
35		Sat	27	Southern League, Division 1	Plymouth Argyle		D 1-1	10,000
36	April	Fri	2	Southern League, Division 1	LUTON TOWN	4-2 W		10,000
37		Sat	3	Southern League, Division 1	MILLWALL	1-0 W		7,000
38		Mon	5	Southern League, Division 1	Luton Town		W 2-1	13,000
39		Wed	14	Southern League, Division 1	Cardiff City		W 1-0	11,000
40		Sat	17	Southern League, Division 1	BRIGHTON & HOVE ALBION	3-0 W		6,000
41		Mon	19	Southern League, Division 1	Bristol Rovers		D 0-0	5,000
42		Sat	24	Southern League, Division 1	Reading		W 2-1	10,000
43	May	Sat	1	Southern League, Division 1	SOUTHAMPTON	3-0 W		7,000

League ever-presents: None
Most appearances in total: C.W. White & R.G. Williams 42 out of 43   **Most goals in total:** G.W.N. Edmonds 19
Hat-tricks: G.W.N. Edmonds (Match 3, and 5 goals Match 32), C.W. White (Match 12), P.M. Ronald (Match 14)
Penalty goals: G.W.N. Edmonds 2, V.F. Gregory 1   **Sent off:** None
Full international appearance(s) this season: None

Match	Ashmole, W.G.	Barnes, E.	Barnshaw, R.J.	Bassett, E.J.	Bradshaw, J.H.	Edmonds, G.W.N.	Gladwin, C.E.	Gregory, F.J.	Gregory, V.F.	Grimsdell, E.F.	Hoddinott, F.	Horsman, F.	Lewis, T.	Markland, W.A.	Ronald, P.M.	Toone, G.	Waterall, T.	White, C.W.	Wilkinson, F.	Williams, R.G.	Own goal
Apps	1	1	35	37	1	36	12	37	34	5	13	32	1	13	35	13	39	41	35	41	
Subs																					
Goals			3	6		19			2		7				10		5	15	1		1
Apps			1	1		1		1	1			1			1	1	1	1		1	
Subs																					
Goals																					
1			X	X		X	X	X				X			X		X	X	X	G	
2			X	X			X	X	X1			X			X		X1	X	X	G	
3				X1		X3p	X	X	X			X			X		X	X	X	G	
4				X		X	X	X				X			X	X	X1	X2		G	
5			X	X		X1p	X	X				X			X		X	X		G	
6			X	X		X1	X	X				X			X		X	X		G	
7			X	X		X	X	X				X			X1		X	X		G	
8			X	X		X	X	X				X			X		X	X		G	
9			X	X	X		X	X		X	X			X			X	X		G	
10			X	X		X1	X	X			X			X		X	X	X		G	
11			X				X	X			X			X	X	X	X	X	X	G	
12			X1	X		X1	X	X			X				X		X	X3	X	G	
13			X	X		X	X	X1			X				X		X	X	X1	G	
14			X	X		X	X	X			X				X3		X	X	X	G	
15			X	X		X1	X	X			X				X		X	X1	X	G	
16			X	X		X	X	X			X					X	X	X	X	G	
17			X	X		X	X	X			X					X	X1	X	X	G	
18			X	X				X	X1p	X1	X				X		X	X	X	G	
19			X	X1			X	X		X	X				X1		X	X	X	G	
20			X	X			X	X	X		X				X		X	X	X	G	
21			X	X			X	X	X		X				X		X		X	G	
22			X	X			X	X				X			X1		X	X1	X	G	
23			X	X			X	X	X	X1	X						X	X		G	
24			X	X		X1	X						X	X	X		X	X1	X	G	
25			X	X1			X	X	X			X					X	X	X	G	
26			X	X			X	X	X			X			X1		X	X	X	G	
27			X	X1			X	X	X			X			X		X	X		G	
28	X		X					X	X		X	X			X		X	X		G	
29		G	X					X	X			X			X	X	X	X	X		
30			X	X			X	X	X			X		X	X2		X1	X		G	
31			X1	X			X	X	X			X					X	X	X	G	
32			X	X		X5	X	X						X	X		X1	X	X	G	
33			X1				X	X	X	X	X						X	X1	X	G	
34			X				X	X	X	X	X						X	X	X	G	
35				X1			X	X	X			X			X	X	X	X	X	G	
36			X	X			X		X	X2	X						X1	X	X	G	1
37			X	X			X	X	X	X1	X						X	X	X	G	
38			X	X		X1	X	X		X	X						X	X1	X	G	
39			X	X		X1	X					X			X	X	X	X	X	G	
40				X		X1	X	X				X			X1	X	X	X1	X	G	
41				X		X	X	X				X			X	X	X	X	X	G	
42				X		X1	X	X				X			X	X	X	X1	X	G	
43				X1		X1	X	X				X			X	X	X	X1	X	G	

1920/21

Football League position: 6th out of 22 in Division 3
Manager: Harry Kent

New league opponents: Grimsby Town

Home-and-away league doubles
For – 3 (Brighton & Hove Albion, Newport County, Northampton Town)
Against – 1 (Swindon Town)

Divisional changes at end of season: Crystal Palace to Division 2; Grimsby Town to Division 3 (North); Aberdare Athletic & Charlton Athletic elected; the division became Division 3 (South)

All Matches: Won 21, Drew 8, Lost 15, Goals 63-48

Highest Score: 7 (Match 6)

		HOME					AWAY					
	Pl	W	D	L	For	Ag	W	D	L	For	Ag	Pts
Crystal Palace	42	15	4	2	45	17	9	7	5	25	17	59
Southampton	42	14	5	2	46	10	5	11	5	18	18	54
Queens Park Rangers	42	14	4	3	38	11	8	5	8	23	21	53
Swindon Town	42	14	5	2	51	17	7	5	9	22	32	52
Swansea Town	42	9	10	2	32	19	9	5	7	24	26	51
WATFORD	42	14	4	3	40	15	6	4	11	19	29	48
Millwall	42	11	5	5	25	8	7	6	8	17	22	47
Merthyr Town	42	13	5	3	46	20	2	10	9	14	29	45
Luton Town	42	14	6	1	51	15	2	6	13	10	41	44
Bristol Rovers	42	15	3	3	51	22	3	4	14	17	35	43
Plymouth Argyle	42	10	7	4	25	13	1	14	6	10	21	43
Portsmouth	42	10	8	3	28	14	2	7	12	18	34	39
Grimsby Town	42	12	5	4	32	16	3	4	14	17	43	39
Northampton Town	42	11	4	6	32	23	4	4	13	27	52	38
Newport County	42	8	5	8	20	23	6	4	11	23	41	37
Norwich City	42	9	10	2	31	14	1	6	14	13	39	36
Southend United	42	13	2	6	32	20	1	6	14	12	41	36
Brighton & Hove Albion	42	11	8	2	28	20	3	2	16	14	41	36
Exeter City	42	9	7	5	27	15	4	3	14	16	37	35
Reading	42	8	4	9	26	22	4	3	14	16	37	31
Brentford	42	7	9	5	27	23	2	3	16	15	44	30
Gillingham	42	6	9	6	19	24	2	3	16	15	50	28

No	DATE			COMPETITION	OPPONENTS	HOME	AWAY	ATTENDANCE
1	August	Sat	28	Football League, Division 3	Queens Park Rangers		W 2-1	21,000
2	September	Thu	2	Football League, Division 3	Swansea Town		L 1-2	12,000
3		Sat	4	Football League, Division 3	QUEENS PARK RANGERS	0-2 L		10,466
4		Wed	8	Football League, Division 3	SWANSEA TOWN	3-0 W		6,000
5		Sat	11	Football League, Division 3	Northampton Town		W 1-0	7,000
6		Sat	18	Football League, Division 3	NORTHAMPTON TOWN	7-1 W		6,000
7		Sat	25	Football League, Division 3	SOUTHEND UNITED	3-0 W		8,000
8	October	Sat	2	Football League, Division 3	Southend United		L 1-4	8,290
9		Sat	9	Football League, Division 3	Merthyr Town		L 0-2	15,000
10		Sat	16	Football League, Division 3	MERTHYR TOWN	1-0 W		7,000
11		Sat	23	Football League, Division 3	Plymouth Argyle		W 2-0	20,000
12		Sat	30	Football League, Division 3	PLYMOUTH ARGYLE	1-1 D		9,000
13	November	Sat	6	Football League, Division 3	Exeter City		W 2-1	6,000
14		Sat	13	Football League, Division 3	EXETER CITY	0-0 D		7,000
15		Sat	20	Football League, Division 3	Millwall		L 0-1	15,000
16		Sat	27	Football League, Division 3	MILLWALL	1-0 W		7,000
17	December	Sat	4	Football League, Division 3	Newport County		W 2-0	6,000
18		Sat	11	Football League, Division 3	NEWPORT COUNTY	5-1 W		6,000
19		Sat	25	Football League, Division 3	PORTSMOUTH	3-2 W		9,000
20		Mon	27	Football League, Division 3	Portsmouth		L 0-1	25,173
21	January	Sat	1	Football League, Division 3	GILLINGHAM	3-1 W		4,000
22		Sat	8	FA Cup, 1st Round	EXETER CITY	3-0 W		9,612
23		Sat	15	Football League, Division 3	SOUTHAMPTON	0-0 D		8,000
24		Sat	22	Football League, Division 3	Southampton		L 1-4	15,000
25		Sat	29	FA Cup, 2nd Round	Preston North End		L 1-4	22,000
26	February	Sat	5	Football League, Division 3	SWINDON TOWN	0-1 L		7,000
27		Sat	12	Football League, Division 3	READING	1-2 L		6,000
28		Sat	19	Football League, Division 3	Reading		D 0-0	6,000
29		Sat	26	Football League, Division 3	BRISTOL ROVERS	2-1 W		6,000
30	March	Sat	5	Football League, Division 3	Bristol Rovers		L 0-2	12,000
31		Sat	12	Football League, Division 3	BRENTFORD	1-0 W		5,000
32		Wed	16	Football League, Division 3	Gillingham		D 1-1	5,000
33		Sat	19	Football League, Division 3	Brentford		L 0-1	6,000
34		Fri	25	Football League, Division 3	LUTON TOWN	1-0 W		11,772
35		Sat	26	Football League, Division 3	Norwich City		D 1-1	8,000
36		Mon	28	Football League, Division 3	Luton Town		L 0-1	12,908
37	April	Sat	2	Football League, Division 3	NORWICH CITY	2-0 W		5,000
38		Sat	9	Football League, Division 3	Crystal Palace		D 2-2	14,000
39		Sat	16	Football League, Division 3	CRYSTAL PALACE	1-1 D		8,000
40		Wed	20	Football League, Division 3	Swindon Town		L 0-2	7,000
41		Sat	23	Football League, Division 3	Brighton & Hove Albion		W 3-0	10,000
42		Sat	30	Football League, Division 3	BRIGHTON & HOVE ALBION	1-0 W		5,000
43	May	Mon	2	Football League, Division 3	Grimsby Town		L 0-3	10,000
44		Sat	7	Football League, Division 3	GRIMSBY TOWN	4-2 W		5,000

League ever-presents: G. Toone
Most appearances in total: G. Toone 44 out of 44   **Most goals in total:** F. Hoddinott 25
Hat-tricks: None   **Penalty goals:** F. Hoddinott 6, J. Short 2
Sent off: None
Full international appearance(s) this season: F. Hoddinott (Wales)

	Bacon, E.F.	Barnshaw, R.J.	Bassett, E.J.	Carter, W.	Coles, W.T.	Cutts, G.H.	Gregory, F.J.	Hoddinott, F.	Horsman, F.	Johnson, J.	Mummery, A.E.P.	Ronald, P.M.	Short, J.	Slade, R.	Smith, F.W.	Toone, G.	Wallington, E.E.	Waterall, T.	White, C.W.	Wilkinson, F.	Williams, R.G.	Wright, A.	Own goal
Apps	12	12	33	18	1	1	21	39	38	19	5	29	13	9	11	42	9	36	35	37	41	1	
Subs																							
Goals		1	3				1	22				10	7		1		1	4	8			1	
Apps	2	2					2	2	2			2				2		2	2	2	2		
Subs																							
Goals								3										1					

	Bacon	Barnshaw	Bassett	Carter	Coles	Cutts	Gregory	Hoddinott	Horsman	Johnson	Mummery	Ronald	Short	Slade	Smith	Toone	Wallington	Waterall	White	Wilkinson	Williams	Wright	Own goal
1	X		X				X	X	X			X1				X		X	X1	X	G		
2	X		X				X	X	X			X1				X		X	X	X	G		
3		X	X				X	X	X			X				X		X	X	X	G		
4	X		X				X	X2p	X			X1				X		X	X	X	G		
5	X		X				X	X	X			X				X		X	X1	X	G		
6	X		X2				X	X2#	X			X2				X		X	X1	X	G		
7		X	X	X			X	X1	X			X1				X		X	X1	X	G		
8		X	X	X			X	X1	X			X				X		X	X	X	G		
9		X	X	X				X	X	X		X				X		X	X	X	G		
10		X	X					X	X	X		X				X		X1	X	X	G	X	
11		X	X				X	X2	X			X				X		X	X	X	G		
12		X	X				X1	X	X			X				X		X	X	X	G		
13	X		X					X1p	X	X		X1				X		X	X	X	G		
14	X		X	X				X	X	X		X				X		X	X		G		
15	X		X	X				X	X	X		X				X		X	X		G		
16		X1	X					X	X	X		X	X			X		X		X	G		
17		X	X	X				X2	X	X		X	X			X		X			G		
18		X	X1	X				X2p	X	X		X1	X1			X		X			G		
19		X	X					X2p	X	X		X	X1			X		X		X	G		
20		X	X					X	X	X		X	X			X		X		X	G		
21		X	X					X1	X	X		X1				X		X	X1	X	G		
22		X	X					X2	X	X		X				X		X1	X	X	G		
23		X	X					X	X	X		X				X		X	X	X	G		
24		X	X					X1		X		X		X		X		X	X	X	G		
25		X	X					X1	X	X		X				X		X	X	X	G		
26		X	X					X		X	X	X		X		X			X	X	G		
27	X		X							X	X	X1p	X			X			X	X	G		
28	X		X		X			X	X	X		X	X			X			X		G		
29			X				X	X	X	X		X	X1			X		X		X	G		1
30			X				X	X	X	X	X	X	X			X				X	G		
31		X	X					X1	X		X		X	X		X				X	G		
32				X				X	X					X	X1	X	X	X	X	X	G		
33			X	X				X	X		X			X	X	X			X	X	G		
34			X	X				X1	X					X	X	X		X	X	X	G		
35			X	X				X1	X					X	X	X		X	X	X	G		
36			X	X				X						X	X	X		X	X	X	G		
37			X				X	X						X	X	X	X	X1	X1	X	G		
38			X				X	X	X					X	X	X	X	X1	X1	X	G		
39			X				X	X	X					X	X	X1	X	X	X	X	G		
40	X				G		X		X				X	X	X	X	X	X	X	X	G		
41	X		X				X		X			X1	X2p			X	X	X	X	X	G		
42			X				X	X1	X					X	X	X	X	X	X	X	G		
43			X				X	X	X					X	X	X	X	X	X	X	G		
44			X				X	X1	X			X1				X	X	X1	X1	X	G		

1921/22

Football League position: 7th out of 22 in Division 3 (South)
Manager: Harry Kent

New league opponents: Aberdare Athletic, Charlton Athletic

Home-and-away league doubles
For – 2 (Merthyr Town, Southend United)
Against – 2 (Plymouth Argyle, Portsmouth)

Divisional changes at end of season: Southampton to Division 2; Bristol City from Division 2

All Matches: Won 14, Drew 18, Lost 12, Goals 56-50

Highest Score: 4 (Matches 24, 25, 29, 36 & 42)

		HOME						AWAY					
	PJ	W	D	L	For	Ag	W	D	L	For	Ag	Pts
Southampton	42	14	7	0	50	8	9	8	4	18	13	61
Plymouth Argyle	42	17	4	0	43	4	8	7	6	20	20	61
Portsmouth	42	13	5	3	38	18	5	12	4	24	21	53
Luton Town	42	16	2	3	47	9	6	6	9	17	26	52
Queens Park Rangers	42	13	7	1	36	12	5	6	10	17	32	49
Swindon Town	42	10	7	4	40	21	6	6	9	32	39	45
Watford	42	9	9	3	34	21	4	9	8	20	27	44
Aberdare Athletic	42	11	6	4	38	18	6	4	11	19	33	44
Brentford	42	15	2	4	41	17	1	9	11	11	26	43
Swansea Town	42	11	8	2	40	19	2	7	12	10	28	41
Merthyr Town	42	14	2	5	33	15	3	4	14	12	41	40
Millwall	42	6	13	2	22	10	4	5	12	12	32	38
Reading	42	10	5	6	28	15	4	5	12	12	32	38
Bristol Rovers	42	8	8	5	32	24	5	2	13	20	43	38
Norwich City	42	8	10	3	29	17	4	3	14	21	45	37
Charlton Athletic	42	10	6	5	28	15	3	5	13	15	37	37
Northampton Town	42	13	3	5	30	17	0	8	13	17	54	37
Gillingham	42	11	4	6	36	20	3	4	14	11	40	36
Brighton & Hove Albion	42	9	6	6	33	19	4	3	14	12	32	35
Newport County	42	8	7	6	22	18	5	3	13	22	43	34
Exeter City	42	7	5	9	22	29	4	7	10	16	30	34
Southend United	42	7	5	9	23	23	1	6	14	11	51	27

No	DATE			COMPETITION	OPPONENTS	HOME	AWAY	ATTENDANCE
1	August	Sat	27	Football League, Division 3 (South)	SWANSEA TOWN	0-0 D		7,000
2		Wed	31	Football League, Division 3 (South)	MILLWALL	0-1 L		5,000
3	September	Sat	3	Football League, Division 3 (South)	Swansea Town		L 0-3	15,000
4		Mon	5	Football League, Division 3 (South)	Millwall		D 0-0	7,000
5		Sat	10	Football League, Division 3 (South)	Brentford		D 1-1	12,000
6		Sat	17	Football League, Division 3 (South)	BRENTFORD	0-0 D		7,000
7		Sat	24	Football League, Division 3 (South)	Aberdare Athletic		L 0-3	10,000
8	October	Sat	1	Football League, Division 3 (South)	ABERDARE ATHLETIC	3-0 W		6,000
9		Sat	8	Football League, Division 3 (South)	BRIGHTON & HOVE ALBION	1-0 W		5,000
10		Sat	15	Football League, Division 3 (South)	Brighton & Hove Albion		D 1-1	10,000
11		Sat	22	Football League, Division 3 (South)	SOUTHAMPTON	1-1 D		6,000
12		Sat	29	Football League, Division 3 (South)	Southampton		L 0-2	11,000
13	November	Sat	5	Football League, Division 3 (South)	CHARLTON ATHLETIC	2-2 D		6,000
14		Sat	12	Football League, Division 3 (South)	Charlton Athletic		L 0-1	7,000
15		Sat	19	Football League, Division 3 (South)	Northampton Town		L 0-1	6,000
16	December	Sat	3	Football League, Division 3 (South)	QUEENS PARK RANGERS	2-2 D		5,000
17		Sat	10	Football League, Division 3 (South)	Queens Park Rangers		D 1-1	15,000
18		Sat	17	Football League, Division 3 (South)	EXETER CITY	0-0 D		5,000
19		Sat	24	Football League, Division 3 (South)	Exeter City		W 3-1	5,000
20		Mon	26	Football League, Division 3 (South)	READING	2-2 D		8,000
21		Tue	27	Football League, Division 3 (South)	Reading		L 1-2	13,000
22		Sat	31	Football League, Division 3 (South)	Norwich City		D 1-1	10,000
23	January	Sat	7	FA Cup, 1st Round	Blackpool		W 2-1	10,121
24		Sat	14	Football League, Division 3 (South)	NORWICH CITY	4-2 W		4,000
25		Sat	21	Football League, Division 3 (South)	SOUTHEND UNITED	4-1 W		4,000
26		Sat	28	FA Cup, 2nd Round	Tottenham Hotspur		L 0-1	47,660
27	February	Sat	4	Football League, Division 3 (South)	PORTSMOUTH	0-3 L		4,000
28		Sat	11	Football League, Division 3 (South)	Portsmouth		L 0-2	12,000
29		Sat	18	Football League, Division 3 (South)	MERTHYR TOWN	4-1 W		5,000
30		Sat	25	Football League, Division 3 (South)	Merthyr Town		W 2-1	5,000
31	March	Sat	4	Football League, Division 3 (South)	PLYMOUTH ARGYLE	0-1 L		5,000
32		Sat	11	Football League, Division 3 (South)	Plymouth Argyle		L 0-3	14,000
33		Sat	18	Football League, Division 3 (South)	Newport County		D 0-0	6,000
34		Sat	25	Football League, Division 3 (South)	NEWPORT COUNTY	1-0 W		5,000
35	April	Sat	1	Football League, Division 3 (South)	Luton Town		D 1-1	7,000
36		Sat	8	Football League, Division 3 (South)	LUTON TOWN	4-1 W		7,000
37		Fri	14	Football League, Division 3 (South)	NORTHAMPTON TOWN	2-2 D		9,000
38		Sat	15	Football League, Division 3 (South)	Swindon Town		W 3-0	5,000
39		Mon	17	Football League, Division 3 (South)	BRISTOL ROVERS	1-0 W		8,000
40		Tue	18	Football League, Division 3 (South)	Bristol Rovers		D 1-1	8,000
41		Sat	22	Football League, Division 3 (South)	SWINDON TOWN	2-2 D		4,000
42		Wed	26	Football League, Division 3 (South)	Southend United		W 4-1	1,500
43		Sat	29	Football League, Division 3 (South)	GILLINGHAM	1-0 W		5,000
44	May	Sat	6	Football League, Division 3 (South)	Gillingham		D 1-1	6,000

The following match was abandoned after 83 minutes, owing to fog:

	November	Sat	26	Football League, Division 3 (South)	NORTHAMPTON TOWN	1-2		5,000

League ever-presents: G. Toone
Most appearances in total: G. Toone 44 out of 44   **Most goals in total:** F. Pagnam 17
Hat-tricks: F.W. Smith (Match 42)   **Penalty goals:** F. Pagnam 2
Sent off: None
Full international appearance(s) this season: None

	Bagshaw, J.J. //	Barnard, C. //	Barnes, G.H.	Bellamy, H.	Carter, W.	Coutanche, W.J.	Cutts, G.H.	Gregory, F.J.	Hamilton, J.E. //	Horsman, F.	Johnson, J.	Marshall, W.	Mummery, A.E.P.	Pagnam, F.	Savage, H. //	Shawcroft, E. //	Short, J. //	Slade, R.	Smith, F.W.	Strain, J.	Toone, G.	Wallington, E.E.	White, C.W.	Wilkinson, J.T.	Williams, R.G.	Own goal
Apps	14	2	1	21	30	4	2	32	2	21	25	1	12	25	7	1	8	2	35	26	42	38	39	32	40	
Subs																										
Goals		1	1	2						1			2	15	1				12	1		4	7	6		1
Apps (cup)				2				2			2			2					2	2	2	2	2	2	2	
Subs (cup)																										
Goals (cup)														2												
1	X			X				X	X	X							X				X	X	X	X	G	
2	X			X				X	X		X						X		X			X	X	X	G	
3	X			X				X	X								X		X		X	X	X	X	G	
4	X			X			X			X			X				X				X	X	X	X	G	
5	X			X1				X		X			X				X				X	X	X	X	G	
6	X			X				X		X			X				X				X	X	X	X	G	
7	X			X				X		X			X				X				X	X	X	X	G	
8	X			X1	X			X		X									X		X	X1	X1	X	G	
9	X			X	X			X		X									X		X	X	X	X1	G	
10	X			X	X			X		X									X		X	X	X	X1	G	
11	X			X	X			X		X									X1		X	X	X	X	G	
12	X			X	X			X		X									X		X	X	X	X	G	
13	X	X1		X				X		X									X1		X	X	X	X	G	
14		X		X	X			X		X			X						X		X		X	X	G	
15	X			X				X		X			X					X	X		X	X	X	X	G	
16				X				X			X1		X						X	X	X	X	X	X1	G	
17				X				X			X					X			X	X	X	X	X	X1	G	
18				X				X			X			X					X	X	X	X	X	X	G	
19				X		G		X			X			X					X1	X	X1	X1	X			
20				X					X	X	X			X					X	X	X	X	X1		G	
21				X				X	X		X			X1					X	X	X			X	G	
22				X	X	G		X			X			X					X1	X	X	X	X	X		
23				X				X			X			X2					X	X	X	X	X	X	G	
24				X	X						X			X2p					X	X	X	X1	X1	X	G	
25				X	X						X			X1					X	X	X	X	X1	X2	G	
26				X				X			X			X					X	X	X	X	X	X	G	
27				X	X						X			X					X	X	X	X	X	X	G	
28				X						X				X			X		X	X	X	X	X	X	G	
29				X						X				X2			X		X1	X1	X	X	X	X	G	
30				X				X		X				X1					X	X	X	X1	X	X	G	
31				X				X		X		X		X					X	X	X	X	X	X	G	
32				X				X		X				X					X	X	X	X	X	X	G	
33			X	X				X		X				X						X	X	X	X	X	G	
34			X	X				X		X				X1	X					X	X	X	X		G	
35				X				X		X				X	X				X1	X	X	X	X		G	
36				X				X		X				X2					X1	X	X	X	X	X	G	1
37				X				X		X				X1					X1	X	X	X	X	X	G	
38				X				X		X			X1	X1p	X				X1	X	X	X			G	
39				X				X		X			X	X	X				X	X	X	X1			G	
40			X	X						X	X		X1	X	X				X	X	X				G	
41			X	X				X		X				X1	X1				X	X	X		X		G	
42		X1						X		X			X	X					X3	X	X	X	X		G	
43			X					X		X			X	X1					X	X	X	X	X		G	
44			X					X		X			X	X1					X	X	X	X	X		G	
(cup)	X			X				X			X			X		X1			X			X	X	X	X	G	

1922/23

Football League position: 10th out of 22 in Division 3 (South)
Manager: Harry Kent

New league opponents: None

Home-and-away league doubles
For – 4 (Exeter City, Gillingham, Luton Town, Newport County)
Against – 2 (Brighton & Hove Albion, Portsmouth)

Divisional changes at end of season: Bristol City to Division 2; Bournemouth & Boscombe Athletic elected

All Matches: Won 17, Drew 12, Lost 16, Goals 61-59

Highest Score: 6 (Match 35)

		HOME					AWAY					
	Pl	W	D	L	For	Ag	W	D	L	For	Ag	Pts
Bristol City	42	16	4	1	43	13	8	7	6	23	27	59
Plymouth Argyle	42	18	3	0	47	6	5	4	12	14	23	53
Swansea Town	42	13	6	2	46	14	9	3	9	32	31	53
Brighton & Hove Albion	42	15	3	3	39	13	5	8	8	13	21	51
Luton Town	42	14	4	3	47	18	7	3	11	21	31	49
Millwall	42	9	10	2	27	13	5	8	8	18	27	46
Portsmouth	42	10	5	6	34	20	9	3	9	24	32	46
Northampton Town	42	13	6	2	40	17	4	5	12	14	27	45
Swindon Town	42	14	4	3	41	17	3	7	11	21	39	45
Watford	42	10	6	5	35	23	7	4	10	22	31	44
Queens Park Rangers	42	10	4	7	34	24	6	6	9	20	25	42
Charlton Athletic	42	11	6	4	33	14	3	8	10	22	37	42
Bristol Rovers	42	7	9	5	25	19	6	7	8	10	17	42
Brentford	42	9	4	8	27	23	4	8	9	14	28	38
Southend United	42	10	6	5	35	18	2	7	12	14	36	37
Gillingham	42	13	4	4	38	18	2	3	16	13	41	37
Merthyr Town	42	10	4	7	27	17	1	10	10	12	31	36
Norwich City	42	8	7	6	29	26	5	3	13	22	45	36
Reading	42	9	8	4	24	15	1	6	14	12	40	37
Exeter City	42	10	4	7	27	18	3	3	15	20	66	33
Aberdare Athletic	42	6	8	7	25	23	3	3	15	17	47	29
Newport County	42	8	6	7	28	21	0	5	16	12	49	27

No	DATE			COMPETITION	OPPONENTS	HOME	AWAY	ATTENDANCE
1	August	Sat	26	Football League, Division 3 (South)	Queens Park Rangers		W 2-1	20,000
2		Wed	30	Football League, Division 3 (South)	MILLWALL	0-0 D		8,618
3	September	Sat	2	Football League, Division 3 (South)	QUEENS PARK RANGERS	0-3 L		10,783
4		Mon	4	Football League, Division 3 (South)	Millwall		L 1-5	12,000
5		Sat	9	Football League, Division 3 (South)	Northampton Town		D 1-1	8,000
6		Wed	13	Football League, Division 3 (South)	Bristol Rovers		W 2-1	10,000
7		Sat	16	Football League, Division 3 (South)	NORTHAMPTON TOWN	0-0 D		9,000
8		Sat	23	Football League, Division 3 (South)	Exeter City		W 2-1	5,000
9		Sat	30	Football League, Division 3 (South)	EXETER CITY	4-0 W		7,000
10	October	Sat	7	Football League, Division 3 (South)	Merthyr Town		W 3-2	8,000
11		Sat	14	Football League, Division 3 (South)	MERTHYR TOWN	1-1 D		8,500
12		Sat	21	Football League, Division 3 (South)	Gillingham		W 4-1	6,000
13		Sat	28	Football League, Division 3 (South)	GILLINGHAM	5-2 W		7,000
14	November	Sat	4	Football League, Division 3 (South)	READING	1-0 W		7,000
15		Sat	11	Football League, Division 3 (South)	Reading		L 0-1	9,000
16		Sat	18	Football League, Division 3 (South)	LUTON TOWN	2-1 W		11,000
17		Sat	25	Football League, Division 3 (South)	Luton Town		W 1-0	11,500
18	December	Sat	9	Football League, Division 3 (South)	BRISTOL ROVERS	0-1 L		5,000
19		Sat	16	Football League, Division 3 (South)	PLYMOUTH ARGYLE	1-0 W		8,500
20		Sat	23	Football League, Division 3 (South)	Plymouth Argyle		L 0-1	10,000
21		Mon	25	Football League, Division 3 (South)	BRENTFORD	2-0 W		10,000
22		Tue	26	Football League, Division 3 (South)	Brentford		L 1-2	10,000
23		Sat	30	Football League, Division 3 (South)	Charlton Athletic		D 0-0	6,000
24	January	Sat	6	Football League, Division 3 (South)	CHARLTON ATHLETIC	2-2 D		7,000
25		Sat	13	FA Cup, 1st Round	Cardiff City		D 1-1	33,000
26		Wed	17	FA Cup, 1st Round replay	CARDIFF CITY (after extra time)	2-2 D		12,727
27		Sat	20	Football League, Division 3 (South)	Southend United		L 1-2	4,000
28		Mon	22	FA Cup, 1st Round, 2nd replay	Cardiff City (at Aston Villa)		(L 1-2)	15,000
29		Sat	27	Football League, Division 3 (South)	SOUTHEND UNITED	1-1 D		6,000
30	February	Sat	10	Football League, Division 3 (South)	BRIGHTON & HOVE ALBION	1-2 L		5,000
31		Sat	17	Football League, Division 3 (South)	Swindon Town		D 1-1	4,306
32		Wed	21	Football League, Division 3 (South)	Brighton & Hove Albion		L 0-3	5,000
33		Sat	24	Football League, Division 3 (South)	SWINDON TOWN	0-3 L		4,000
34	March	Sat	3	Football League, Division 3 (South)	Aberdare Athletic		L 1-3	6,000
35		Sat	10	Football League, Division 3 (South)	ABERDARE ATHLETIC	6-0 W		4,000
36		Sat	17	Football League, Division 3 (South)	SWANSEA TOWN	2-1 W		8,000
37		Sat	24	Football League, Division 3 (South)	Swansea Town		D 0-0	20,000
38		Fri	30	Football League, Division 3 (South)	NORWICH CITY	2-1 W		10,000
39		Sat	31	Football League, Division 3 (South)	NEWPORT COUNTY	2-1 W		7,000
40	April	Mon	2	Football League, Division 3 (South)	Norwich City		L 0-2	12,000
41		Sat	7	Football League, Division 3 (South)	Newport County		W 1-0	8,000
42		Sat	14	Football League, Division 3 (South)	BRISTOL CITY	1-1 D		7,600
43		Sat	21	Football League, Division 3 (South)	Bristol City		L 1-3	20,000
44		Sat	28	Football League, Division 3 (South)	PORTSMOUTH	2-3 L		4,000
45	May	Sat	5	Football League, Division 3 (South)	Portsmouth		L 0-1	8,000

League ever-presents: F. Pagnam, G. Toone
Most appearances in total: F. Pagnam & G. Toone 45 out of 45   **Most goals in total:** F. Pagnam 32 (including Division 3 [South]'s highest tally of 30)
Hat-tricks: F. Pagnam (Match 9, Match 12, Match 13 & Match 35)   **Penalty goals:** F. Pagnam 4
Sent off: None
Full international appearance(s) this season: None

	Barnes, G.H.	Bellamy, H.	Carter, W.	Coutanche, W.J.	Cutts, G.H.	Gregory, F.J.	Horsman, F.	Johnson, J.	Kirby, R.J.S.	Marshall, W.	Miller, H.E.J.	Miller, R.B.	Mummery, A.E.P.	Newman, R.T.	Pagnam, F.	Smith, F.W.	Stephenson, J.	Strain, J.	Toone, G.	Wallington, E.E.	White, C.W.	Wilkinson, J.T.	Williams, R.G.	Wilson, R.D.	Own goal
Apps	3	15	24	2	2	35	36	14	1	1	2	1	38	1	42	39	38	26	42	4	29	26	40	1	
Subs																									
Goals			3										4		30	8	3	2			5	1		1	
Apps		1	2		1	3	3						1		3	3	3	3	3		3	2	2		
Subs																									
Goals															2	1	1								
1			X			X	X								X1	X1		X	X	X	X	X	G		
2			X			X	X						X		X	X		X	X	X	X		G		
3		X	X			X	X						X		X	X		X	X	X	X		G		
4						X		X		X			X	X	X1	X			X	X	X		G		
5		X				X	X						X		X1	X	X		X		X	X	G		
6		X				X	X						X		X2p	X	X		X		X	X	G		
7		X				X	X		X				X		X	X	X		X		X		G		
8		X				X	X						X		X	X	X1		X		X1	X	G		
9		X				X	X						X		X3	X	X		X		X	X1	G		
10						X	X						X		X	X	X1	X1	X		X1	X	G		
11						X	X						X		X1	X	X		X		X	X	G		
12		X				X	X						X		X3	X1	X		X		X	X	G		
13		X				X	X				X		X		X3	X1	X		X		X1		G		
14		X				X	X				X		X		X1	X	X		X		X		G		
15		X	X				X					X	X		X	X	X		X		X		G		
16		X				X	X						X		X1	X	X	X	X		X		G		1
17		X				X	X						X		X1p	X	X	X	X		X		G		
18		X				X	X								X	X	X	X	X		X	X	G		
19		X				X	X								X1	X	X	X	X		X	X	G		
20		X				X	X								X	X	X	X	X		X	X	G		
21	X	X				X	X						X1		X1	X	X	X	X		X		G		
22	X	X				X	X						X1		X	X	X	X	X		X		G		
23		X				X	X						X		X	X	X	X	X				X	G	
24		X				X	X						X1		X1	X	X	X	X				X	G	
25		X				X	X								X1	X	X	X	X		X	X	G		
26		X				X	X								X1	X1	X	X	X		X	X	G		
27				X	G	X	X						X		X	X1	X		X		X	X			
28		X			G	X	X						X		X	X	X1	X	X		X				
29		X				X	X						X		X	X	X	X	X		X	X1	G		
30		X				X	X						X		X	X	X	X	X		X	X1	G		
31						X	X						X		X1	X	X	X	X		X	X	G		
32	X					X	X						X		X	X	X	X	X		X		G		
33			X			X	X	X					X		X		X		X		X	X	G		
34			X			X	X	X					X		X1	X	X		X		X	X	G		
35			X			X	X						X1		X3p	X2	X	X	X		X		G		
36			X				X	X					X		X2	X	X	X	X		X		G		
37			X			X		X					X		X	X	X		X		X	X	G		
38	X		X1				X	X					X		X1	X	X	X	X		X		G		
39			X				X	X					X		X	X2	X	X	X		X		G		
40			X				X	X					X		X	X	X	X	X		X		G		
41			X	G			X	X					X		X	X	X1	X	X		X				
42		X1					X	X					X		X	X	X	X	X		X		G		
43	X	X					X	X					X		X1p	X	X	X	X				G		
44		X1					X	X					X		X	X	X	X	X		X		G		
45		X					X	X					X		X	X	X	X	X		X		G		

1923/24

Football League position: 20th out of 22 in Division 3 (South)
Manager: Harry Kent

		HOME					AWAY					
	Pl	W	D	L	For	Ag	W	D	L	For	Ag	Pts
Portsmouth	42	15	3	3	57	11	9	8	4	30	19	59
Plymouth Argyle	42	13	6	2	46	15	10	3	8	24	19	55
Millwall	42	17	3	1	45	11	5	7	9	19	27	54
Swansea Town	42	18	2	1	39	10	4	6	11	21	38	52
Brighton & Hove Albion	42	16	4	1	56	12	5	5	11	12	25	51
Swindon Town	42	14	5	2	38	11	3	8	10	20	33	47
Luton Town	42	11	7	3	35	19	5	7	9	15	25	46
Northampton Town	42	14	3	4	40	15	3	8	10	24	32	45
Bristol Rovers	42	11	7	3	34	15	4	6	11	18	31	43
Newport County	42	15	4	2	39	15	2	5	14	17	49	43
Norwich City	42	13	5	3	45	18	3	3	15	15	41	40
Aberdare Athletic	42	9	9	3	35	18	3	5	13	10	40	38
Merthyr Town	42	11	8	2	33	19	0	8	13	12	46	38
Charlton Athletic	42	8	7	6	26	20	3	8	10	12	25	37
Gillingham	42	11	6	4	27	15	1	7	13	16	43	37
Exeter City	42	14	3	4	33	17	1	4	16	4	35	37
Brentford	42	9	8	4	33	21	5	0	16	21	50	36
Reading	42	12	2	7	35	20	1	7	13	16	37	35
Southend United	42	11	7	3	35	19	1	3	17	18	65	34
WATFORD	42	8	8	5	35	18	1	7	13	10	36	33
Bournemouth & Boscombe Ath	42	6	8	7	19	19	5	3	13	21	46	33
Queens Park Rangers	42	9	6	6	28	26	2	3	16	9	51	31

New league opponents: Bournemouth & Boscombe Athletic

Home-and-away league doubles
For – none
Against – 4 (Brentford, Plymouth Argyle, Portsmouth, Queens Park Rangers)

Divisional changes at end of season: Portsmouth to Division 2; Bristol City from Division 2

All Matches: Won 11, Drew 16, Lost 19, Goals 47-55

Highest Score: 8 (Match 24)

No	DATE			COMPETITION	OPPONENTS	HOME	AWAY	ATTENDANCE	
1	August	Sat	25	Football League, Division 3 (South)	READING	2-1 W		10,000	
2	September	Sat	1	Football League, Division 3 (South)	Reading	D 1-1			10,162
3		Wed	5	Football League, Division 3 (South)	BOURNEMOUTH & BOSCOMBE ATHLETIC	0-0 D		5,561	
4		Sat	8	Football League, Division 3 (South)	GILLINGHAM	1-1 D		7,000	
5		Mon	10	Football League, Division 3 (South)	Norwich City	D 0-0			8,000
6		Sat	15	Football League, Division 3 (South)	Gillingham	D 0-0			8,000
7		Wed	19	Football League, Division 3 (South)	Bournemouth & Boscombe Athletic	D 1-1			4,000
8		Sat	22	Football League, Division 3 (South)	QUEENS PARK RANGERS	0-2 L		9,000	
9		Sat	29	Football League, Division 3 (South)	Queens Park Rangers	L 1-2			12,000
10	October	Sat	6	Football League, Division 3 (South)	PLYMOUTH ARGYLE	0-1 L		8,000	
11		Sat	13	Football League, Division 3 (South)	Plymouth Argyle	L 0-1			10,000
12		Sat	20	Football League, Division 3 (South)	MERTHYR TOWN	4-0 W		6,000	
13		Sat	27	Football League, Division 3 (South)	Merthyr Town	L 1-2			5,000
14	November	Sat	3	Football League, Division 3 (South)	Luton Town	D 0-0			10,000
15		Sat	10	Football League, Division 3 (South)	LUTON TOWN	0-0 D		9,407	
16		Sat	17	Football League, Division 3 (South)	CHARLTON ATHLETIC	1-0 W		5,000	
17		Sat	24	Football League, Division 3 (South)	Charlton Athletic	D 1-1			5,000
18	December	Sat	8	Football League, Division 3 (South)	NORWICH CITY	0-0 D		5,000	
19		Sat	15	Football League, Division 3 (South)	Swindon Town	D 0-0			5,250
20		Sat	22	Football League, Division 3 (South)	SWINDON TOWN	0-0 D		4,000	
21		Tue	25	Football League, Division 3 (South)	Swansea Town	L 0-1			10,000
22		Wed	26	Football League, Division 3 (South)	SWANSEA TOWN	2-2 D		9,000	
23		Sat	29	Football League, Division 3 (South)	Newport County	L 0-1			8,000
24	January	Sat	5	Football League, Division 3 (South)	NEWPORT COUNTY	8-2 W		4,500	
25		Sat	12	FA Cup, 1st Round	Middlesbrough		W 1-0		24,194
26		Sat	19	Football League, Division 3 (South)	MILLWALL	1-1 D		7,000	
27		Sat	26	Football League, Division 3 (South)	Millwall	L 0-2			16,000
28	February	Sat	2	FA Cup, 2nd Round	Exeter City	D 0-0			11,150
29		Wed	6	FA Cup, 2nd Round replay	EXETER CITY	1-0 W		9,234	
30		Sat	9	Football League, Division 3 (South)	Aberdare Athletic	L 0-4			5,000
31		Sat	16	Football League, Division 3 (South)	SOUTHEND UNITED	4-1 W		5,217	
32		Sat	23	FA Cup, 3rd Round	NEWCASTLE UNITED	0-1 L		23,444	
33	March	Sat	1	Football League, Division 3 (South)	EXETER CITY	4-1 W		4,482	
34		Sat	8	Football League, Division 3 (South)	Exeter City	L 0-1			6,000
35		Sat	15	Football League, Division 3 (South)	Portsmouth	L 0-4			12,000
36		Wed	19	Football League, Division 3 (South)	Southend United	L 0-3			7,114
37		Sat	22	Football League, Division 3 (South)	PORTSMOUTH	2-3 L		5,500	
38		Sat	29	Football League, Division 3 (South)	Brentford	L 1-4			6,500
39	April	Sat	5	Football League, Division 3 (South)	BRENTFORD	0-1 L		4,500	
40		Sat	12	Football League, Division 3 (South)	Bristol Rovers	L 2-4			5,000
41		Fri	18	Football League, Division 3 (South)	ABERDARE ATHLETIC	2-0 W		5,517	
42		Sat	19	Football League, Division 3 (South)	BRISTOL ROVERS	4-0 W		4,933	
43		Mon	21	Football League, Division 3 (South)	NORTHAMPTON TOWN	0-2 L		6,342	
44		Tue	22	Football League, Division 3 (South)	Northampton Town	W 2-1			6,000
45		Sat	26	Football League, Division 3 (South)	Brighton & Hove Albion	L 0-3			5,000
46	May	Sat	3	Football League, Division 3 (South)	BRIGHTON & HOVE ALBION	0-0 D		4,000	

League ever-presents: None
Most appearances in total: J. Stephenson 44 out of 46   **Most goals in total:** A.E.P. Mummery 12
Hat-tricks: A.E.P. Mummery (5 goals, Match 24), F. Pagnam (Match 33)   **Penalty goals:** J. Stephenson 1
Sent off: J. Johnson (Match 9)   **Full international appearance(s) this season:** None
(In Match 35, two of the opponents' goals were conceded after G. Toone had replaced the injured R.G. Williams as goalkeeper.)

Totals

	Anstiss, H.A.	Barnes, G.H.	Carter, W.	Dewick, L.F.	Eggleton, J.A.E.	Foxall, A.T.	Foxall, F.H.	Gregory, F.J.	Horsman, F.	Johnson, J.	Lacey, R.W.J.	Mummery, A.E.P.	Pagnam, F.	Poole, W.A.	Slade, R.	Smith, F.W.	Stephenson, J.	Strain, J.	Toone, G.	White, C.W.	White, V.H.	Wilkinson, J.T.	Williams, R.G.	Own goal
Apps	18	1	28	3	15	3	32	35	5	36	3	37	22	27	11	21	40	19	39	18	7	3	39	
Subs																								
Goals	5				1	1	1			1		12	5	6		2	3	2		3	1			1
Apps	4		1		4		3	4		4		4	3	1			4	3	4	1			4	
Subs																								
Goals													1				1							

Match appearances

Match	Anstiss, H.A.	Barnes, G.H.	Carter, W.	Dewick, L.F.	Eggleton, J.A.E.	Foxall, A.T.	Foxall, F.H.	Gregory, F.J.	Horsman, F.	Johnson, J.	Lacey, R.W.J.	Mummery, A.E.P.	Pagnam, F.	Poole, W.A.	Slade, R.	Smith, F.W.	Stephenson, J.	Strain, J.	Toone, G.	White, C.W.	White, V.H.	Wilkinson, J.T.	Williams, R.G.	Own goal
1	X1		X				X1	X		X		X	X			X	X		X				G	
2	X1		X				X	X		X		X	X			X	X		X				G	
3	X		X				X	X		X		X	X			X		X	X				G	
4			X					X		X		X	X			X	X		X	X1	X		G	
5	X		X					X		X		X				X	X		X	X	X		G	
6	X		X					X		X		X		X		X	X		X	X			G	
7			X					X		X		X		X1		X	X		X	X		X	G	
8			X					X		X		X		X		X	X		X	X			G	
9	X		X				X1	X		X				X		X	X		X	X			G	
10	X		X					X		X			X			X	X		X	X			G	
11							X	X		X		X	X		X	X	X		X	X			G	
12							X	X	X		X1	X	X1		X		X2		X	X			G	
13							X	X		X	X	X	X1		X		X		X	X			G	
14			X				X		X	X		X				X	X		X	X			G	
15			X				X		X	X		X				X	X		X	X	X		G	
16					X		X			X		X	X			X	X1		X			X	G	
17						X1	X	X		X		X	X			X	X		X			X	G	
18			X					X		X	X	X	X	X		X			X				G	
19			X					X		X		X	X	X		X			X	X			G	
20			X					X		X		X	X	X		X			X	X			G	
21	X		X					X		X		X		X		X			X				G	
22	X		X					X		X		X1		X		X			X				G	1
23	X		X					X		X		X		X		X	X		X				G	
24	X2		X1					X		X		X5	X			X	X		X				G	
25	X		X					X		X		X		X			X1p	X	X				G	
26	X		X					X		X		X		X		X	X1		X				G	
27	X		X					X	X	X		X		X		X			X				G	
28	X		X					X		X		X		X		X	X		X				G	
29	X		X					X		X		X	X1			X	X		X				G	
30	X							X		X		X		X	X	X	X		X		X		G	
31	X		X		X			X		X		X2	X1			X			X	X1			G	
32	X		X		X					X		X	X			X			X	X			G	
33	X1		X		X		X			X		X	X3			X			X				G	
34	X		X		X		X			X		X				X			X				G	
35	X		X		X		X			X		X				X			X				G	
36			X	G			X	X		X		X	X		X	X			X					
37			X	G				X		X		X	X1			X	X					X1		
38		X	X	G	X			X		X		X1	X				X			X				
39			X					X		X		X	X	X		X	X		X				G	
40								X		X		X1	X	X1		X	X	X	X		X		G	
41			X					X		X		X	X1	X	X1	X	X		X				G	
42			X					X		X		X2		X1	X	X1	X	X	X				G	
43			X					X		X		X		X	X	X	X	X	X				G	
44			X		X					X		X		X	X	X	X	X1	X	X1	X		G	
45			X						X			X		X	X	X	X	X	X				G	
46			X						X			X		X	X	X	X	X	X				G	

- 71 -

1924/25

Football League position: 11th out of 22 in Division 3 (South)
Manager: Harry Kent

New league opponents: None

Home-and-away league doubles
For – 3 (Merthyr Town, Millwall, Swindon Town)
Against – 4 (Brighton & Hove Albion, Newport County, Norwich City, Swansea Town)

Divisional changes at end of season: Swansea Town to Division 2; Crystal Palace from Division 2

All Matches: Won 17, Drew 10, Lost 17, Goals 42-52

Highest Score: 4 (Match 5)

	HOME						AWAY					
	Pl	W	D	L	For	Ag	W	D	L	For	Ag	Pts
Swansea Town	42	17	4	0	51	12	6	7	8	17	23	57
Plymouth Argyle	42	17	3	1	55	12	6	7	8	22	26	56
Bristol City	42	14	5	2	40	10	8	4	9	20	31	53
Swindon Town	42	17	2	2	51	13	3	9	9	15	25	51
Millwall	42	12	5	4	35	14	6	8	7	23	24	49
Newport County	42	13	6	2	35	12	7	3	11	27	30	49
Exeter City	42	13	4	4	37	19	6	5	10	22	29	47
Brighton & Hove Albion	42	14	3	4	43	17	5	5	11	16	28	46
Northampton Town	42	12	3	6	34	18	8	3	10	17	26	46
Southend United	42	14	1	6	34	18	5	4	12	17	43	43
WATFORD	42	12	3	6	22	20	5	6	10	16	27	43
Norwich City	42	10	8	3	39	18	4	5	12	14	33	40
Gillingham	42	11	8	2	25	11	2	6	13	10	33	40
Reading	42	9	6	6	28	15	5	4	12	9	23	38
Charlton Athletic	42	12	6	3	31	13	1	6	14	15	35	38
Luton Town	42	9	10	2	34	15	1	7	13	15	42	37
Bristol Rovers	42	10	5	6	26	13	2	8	11	16	36	37
Aberdare Athletic	42	13	4	4	40	21	1	5	15	14	46	37
Queens Park Rangers	42	10	6	5	28	19	4	2	15	14	44	36
Bournemouth & Boscombe Ath	42	8	6	7	20	17	5	2	14	20	41	34
Brentford	42	8	7	6	28	26	1	0	20	10	65	25
Merthyr Town	42	8	3	10	24	27	0	2	19	11	50	21

No	DATE			COMPETITION	OPPONENTS	HOME	AWAY	ATTENDANCE	
1	August	Sat	30	Football League, Division 3 (South)	NORTHAMPTON TOWN	1-0 W		9,500	
2	September	Wed	3	Football League, Division 3 (South)	Queens Park Rangers		D 0-0		9,000
3		Sat	6	Football League, Division 3 (South)	Gillingham		D 0-0		7,000
4		Wed	10	Football League, Division 3 (South)	QUEENS PARK RANGERS	1-0 W		7,500	
5		Sat	13	Football League, Division 3 (South)	Southend United		W 4-0		8,000
6		Thu	18	Football League, Division 3 (South)	Charlton Athletic		D 1-1		5,000
7		Sat	20	Football League, Division 3 (South)	NEWPORT COUNTY	0-5 L		7,000	
8		Sat	27	Football League, Division 3 (South)	Bristol Rovers		L 0-2		12,000
9	October	Sat	4	Football League, Division 3 (South)	EXETER CITY	3-0 W		7,000	
10		Sat	11	Football League, Division 3 (South)	Swansea Town		L 1-3		14,000
11		Sat	18	Football League, Division 3 (South)	READING	1-0 W		7,000	
12		Sat	25	Football League, Division 3 (South)	BOURNEMOUTH & BOSCOMBE ATHLETIC	2-1 W		5,000	
13	November	Sat	1	Football League, Division 3 (South)	Brighton & Hove Albion		L 0-2		3,000
14		Sat	8	Football League, Division 3 (South)	PLYMOUTH ARGYLE	1-0 W		8,000	
15		Sat	15	Football League, Division 3 (South)	Bristol City		D 1-1		10,000
16		Sat	22	Football League, Division 3 (South)	SWINDON TOWN	1-0 W		7,000	
17		Sat	29	Football League, Division 3 (South)	Aberdare Athletic		L 0-2		4,000
18	December	Sat	6	Football League, Division 3 (South)	Norwich City		L 1-2		6,000
19		Sat	13	Football League, Division 3 (South)	Brentford		D 0-0		4,000
20		Sat	20	Football League, Division 3 (South)	MILLWALL	1-0 W		6,000	
21		Thu	25	Football League, Division 3 (South)	LUTON TOWN	1-1 D		9,000	
22		Fri	26	Football League, Division 3 (South)	Luton Town		W 3-0		13,000
23		Sat	27	Football League, Division 3 (South)	Northampton Town		D 1-1		2,603
24	January	Sat	3	Football League, Division 3 (South)	GILLINGHAM	1-2 L		5,000	
25		Sat	10	FA Cup, 1st Round	BRIGHTON & HOVE ALBION	1-1 D		12,574	
26		Wed	14	FA Cup, 1st Round replay	Brighton & Hove Albion (after extra time)		L 3-4		10,500
27		Sat	17	Football League, Division 3 (South)	SOUTHEND UNITED	0-3 L		5,000	
28		Sat	24	Football League, Division 3 (South)	Newport County		L 0-3		8,000
29		Sat	31	Football League, Division 3 (South)	BRISTOL ROVERS	1-0 W		5,000	
30	February	Sat	7	Football League, Division 3 (South)	Exeter City		L 0-4		6,000
31		Sat	14	Football League, Division 3 (South)	SWANSEA TOWN	1-3 L		6,000	
32		Sat	21	Football League, Division 3 (South)	Reading		L 0-3		5,504
33		Sat	28	Football League, Division 3 (South)	Bournemouth & Boscombe Athletic		L 1-2		5,000
34	March	Sat	7	Football League, Division 3 (South)	BRIGHTON & HOVE ALBION	0-1 L		5,000	
35		Sat	14	Football League, Division 3 (South)	Plymouth Argyle		L 0-1		15,000
36		Sat	21	Football League, Division 3 (South)	BRISTOL CITY	1-0 W		5,000	
37		Sat	28	Football League, Division 3 (South)	Swindon Town		W 1-0		6,173
38	April	Sat	4	Football League, Division 3 (South)	ABERDARE ATHLETIC	0-0 D		5,000	
39		Fri	10	Football League, Division 3 (South)	MERTHYR TOWN	3-1 W		7,000	
40		Sat	11	Football League, Division 3 (South)	NORWICH CITY	0-2 L		6,000	
41		Tue	14	Football League, Division 3 (South)	Merthyr Town		W 1-0		5,000
42		Sat	18	Football League, Division 3 (South)	BRENTFORD	3-1 W		4,000	
43		Sat	25	Football League, Division 3 (South)	Millwall		W 1-0		10,000
44	May	Sat	2	Football League, Division 3 (South)	CHARLTON ATHLETIC	0-0 D		4,000	

League ever-presents: F.W. Smith
Most appearances in total: F.W. Smith 44 out of 44   **Most goals in total:** L.T.A. Andrews & F. Pagnam 7
Hat-tricks: F. Pagnam (Match 42)   **Penalty goals:** None
Sent off: None
Full international appearance(s) this season: None

Season totals

	Andrews, L.T.A. //	Baker, J.S.	Bell, J.	Carter, W.	Colledge, E. //	Crussell, J.F. //	Darvill, A.R. //	Dewick, L.F. //	Eggleton, J.A.E.	Francis, A. //	Furr, V.R. //	Gregory, F.J.	Lee, J. //	Mummery, A.E.P.	Pagnam, F.	Papworth, J.M.	Poole, W.A. //	Prior, G.	Slade, R.	Smith, F.W.	Stephenson, J.	Strain, J.	White, C.W. //	Williams, R.G.	Worrall, J.E. //
Apps	38	6	18	24	1	1	1	4	20	1	1	20	8	23	27	14	15	24	37	42	41	41	13	38	4
Subs																									
Goals	6	1	6	1					1					4	6	5	2			2	3		1		
Apps	2		1									1		2	2			2	2	2	2	2	2	2	
Subs																									
Goals	1														1			1					1		

Match appearances

Match	Andrews	Baker	Bell	Carter	Colledge	Crussell	Darvill	Dewick	Eggleton	Francis	Furr	Gregory	Lee	Mummery	Pagnam	Papworth	Poole	Prior	Slade	Smith	Stephenson	Strain	White	Williams	Worrall
1	X		X1	X					X			X	X						X	X	X	X		G	
2	X		X	X				G	X			X	X						X	X	X	X			
3	X		X						X			X	X	X					X	X	X	X		G	
4	X		X1	X				G	X	X		X	X						X	X	X				
5	X1		X2	X				G	X			X	X						X	X	X1	X			
6	X		X	X				G	X			X	X						X	X	X1	X			
7	X		X	X					X			X	X						X	X	X	X		G	
8	X		X	X	X				X						X				X	X	X	X		G	
9	X1		X	X1					X						X1		X		X	X	X	X		G	
10	X		X1	X					X						X		X		X	X	X	X		G	
11	X		X	X					X						X			X		X	X1	X		G	
12	X		X1	X					X						X		X1			X	X	X		G	
13	X		X	X					X						X		X			X	X	X		G	
14	X			X					X					X	X		X			X	X	X1		G	
15	X1			X					X						X		X			X	X	X	X	G	
16	X		X	X					X					X1			X			X	X	X	X	G	
17	X			X					X					X			X	X		X	X	X	X	G	
18	X			X					X					X	X		X			X	X	X1	X	G	
19	X			X					X					X	X		X			X	X	X	X	G	
20	X			X										X	X1		X			X	X	X	X	G	
21	X		X	X											X	X1		X		X	X	X	X	G	
22	X2		X	X											X1			X		X	X	X	X	G	
23	X1		X	X											X			X		X	X	X	X	G	
24	X			X					X		X	X		X1	X			X		X		X	X	G	
25	X		X											X	X			X	X	X	X	X	X1	G	
26	X1												X	X	X1			X	X	X	X	X	X	G	
27	X	X													X		X	X		X	X	X	X	G	
28	X			X											X	X				X	X	X	X	G	
29	X	X											X	X1	X			X		X	X	X	X	G	
30	X	X					X							X	X			X		X	X	X	X	G	
31	X													X1	X	X		X		X	X	X	X	G	X
32	X			X										X	X			X		X	X	X	X	G	
33	X								X1						X	X	X	X		X	X	X	X	G	
34									X					X	X	X		X		X	X	X	X	G	
35									X					X	X	X		X		X	X	X	X	G	
36	X								X					X		X1		X		X	X	X	X	G	X
37	X								X					X		X1		X		X	X	X	X	G	X
38	X								X					X		X		X		X	X	X	X	G	
39	X								X					X		X2	X	X		X	X	X	X1	G	
40	X								X					X		X		X		X	X	X	X	G	X
41		X1							X					X	X	X		X		X	X	X	X	G	
42		X							X					X	X3	X		X		X	X	X	X	G	
43	X	X							X						X	X1	X	X		X	X	X	X	G	
44	X				X				X						X	X		X		X	X	X	X	G	

1925/26

Football League position: 15th out of 22 in Division 3 (South)
Manager: Harry Kent

New league opponents: None

Home-and-away league doubles
For – 1 (Gillingham)
Against – 3 (Millwall, Plymouth Argyle, Reading)

Divisional changes at end of season: Reading to Division 2; Coventry City from Division 3 (North)

All Matches: Won 16, Drew 10, Lost 19, Goals 78-93

Highest Score: 6 (Match 35)

		HOME					AWAY					
	PJ	W	D	L	For	Ag	W	D	L	For	Ag	Pts
Reading	42	16	5	0	49	16	7	6	8	28	36	57
Plymouth Argyle	42	16	2	3	71	33	8	6	7	36	34	56
Millwall	42	14	6	1	52	12	7	5	9	21	27	53
Bristol City	42	14	3	4	42	15	7	6	8	30	36	51
Brighton & Hove Albion	42	12	4	5	47	33	7	5	9	37	40	47
Swindon Town	42	16	2	3	48	22	4	4	13	21	42	46
Luton Town	42	16	4	1	60	25	2	3	16	20	50	43
Bournemouth & Boscombe Ath	42	10	5	6	44	30	7	4	10	31	61	43
Aberdare Athletic	42	11	6	4	50	24	6	2	13	24	42	42
Gillingham	42	11	4	6	36	19	6	4	11	17	30	42
Southend United	42	13	2	6	50	20	6	2	13	28	53	42
Northampton Town	42	13	3	5	47	26	4	4	13	35	54	41
Crystal Palace	42	16	1	4	50	21	3	2	16	25	58	41
Merthyr Town	42	13	3	5	51	25	1	8	12	18	50	39
WATFORD	42	12	5	4	47	26	3	4	14	26	63	39
Norwich City	42	11	5	5	35	26	4	4	13	23	47	39
Newport County	42	11	5	5	39	27	3	5	13	25	47	38
Brentford	42	12	4	5	44	32	4	2	15	25	62	38
Bristol Rovers	42	9	4	8	44	28	6	2	13	22	41	36
Exeter City	42	13	2	6	54	25	2	3	16	18	45	35
Charlton Athletic	42	9	7	5	32	23	2	6	13	16	45	35
Queens Park Rangers	42	5	7	9	23	32	1	2	18	14	52	21

No	DATE			COMPETITION	OPPONENTS	HOME	AWAY	ATTENDANCE	
1	August	Sat	29	Football League, Division 3 (South)	ABERDARE ATHLETIC	2-0 W		8,695	
2		Mon	31	Football League, Division 3 (South)	Norwich City		D 1-1		9,660
3	September	Sat	5	Football League, Division 3 (South)	Brighton & Hove Albion		L 1-3		12,110
4		Wed	9	Football League, Division 3 (South)	NORWICH CITY	3-1 W		5,603	
5		Sat	12	Football League, Division 3 (South)	LUTON TOWN	2-0 W		13,035	
6		Wed	16	Football League, Division 3 (South)	Southend United		W 1-0		4,799
7		Sat	19	Football League, Division 3 (South)	BRENTFORD	2-2 D		4,771	
8		Wed	23	Football League, Division 3 (South)	SOUTHEND UNITED	1-4 L		4,780	
9		Sat	26	Football League, Division 3 (South)	Crystal Palace		L 0-4		14,065
10	October	Sat	3	Football League, Division 3 (South)	BRISTOL CITY	2-2 D		8,038	
11		Sat	10	Football League, Division 3 (South)	Plymouth Argyle		L 1-2		14,953
12		Sat	17	Football League, Division 3 (South)	Queens Park Rangers		L 0-2		10,711
13		Sat	24	Football League, Division 3 (South)	BRISTOL ROVERS	2-1 W		6,242	
14		Sat	31	Football League, Division 3 (South)	Merthyr Town		L 1-4		5,379
15	November	Sat	7	Football League, Division 3 (South)	NEWPORT COUNTY	5-1 W		5,393	
16		Sat	14	Football League, Division 3 (South)	Reading		L 1-4		9,775
17		Sat	21	Football League, Division 3 (South)	BOURNEMOUTH & BOSCOMBE ATHLETIC	0-0 D		5,909	
18		Sat	28	FA Cup, 1st Round	Brighton & Hove Albion		D 1-1		11,503
19	December	Wed	2	FA Cup, 1st Round replay	BRIGHTON & HOVE ALBION	2-0 W		5,601	
20		Sat	5	Football League, Division 3 (South)	GILLINGHAM	3-1 W		4,540	
21		Sat	12	FA Cup, 2nd Round	Swansea Town		L 2-3		18,000
22		Sat	19	Football League, Division 3 (South)	EXETER CITY	3-1 W		5,274	
23		Fri	25	Football League, Division 3 (South)	NORTHAMPTON TOWN	3-2 W		7,771	
24		Sat	26	Football League, Division 3 (South)	Northampton Town		D 2-2		12,335
25	January	Sat	2	Football League, Division 3 (South)	Aberdare Athletic		L 1-8		2,774
26		Sat	16	Football League, Division 3 (South)	BRIGHTON & HOVE ALBION	3-3 D		3,647	
27		Sat	23	Football League, Division 3 (South)	Luton Town		L 0-5		7,233
28		Sat	30	Football League, Division 3 (South)	Brentford		L 3-4		7,711
29	February	Sat	6	Football League, Division 3 (South)	CRYSTAL PALACE	3-0 W		6,693	
30		Sat	13	Football League, Division 3 (South)	Bristol City		L 0-1		14,628
31		Sat	20	Football League, Division 3 (South)	PLYMOUTH ARGYLE	0-1 L		9,749	
32		Thu	25	Football League, Division 3 (South)	Charlton Athletic		D 1-1		3,630
33		Sat	27	Football League, Division 3 (South)	QUEENS PARK RANGERS	3-1 W		6,578	
34	March	Sat	6	Football League, Division 3 (South)	Bristol Rovers		L 1-2		5,359
35		Sat	13	Football League, Division 3 (South)	MERTHYR TOWN	6-1 W		5,716	
36		Sat	20	Football League, Division 3 (South)	Newport County		D 3-3		5,282
37		Sat	27	Football League, Division 3 (South)	READING	0-1 L		9,805	
38	April	Fri	2	Football League, Division 3 (South)	Millwall		L 0-3		19,937
39		Sat	3	Football League, Division 3 (South)	Bournemouth & Boscombe Athletic		W 4-3		5,748
40		Mon	5	Football League, Division 3 (South)	MILLWALL	0-1 L		11,903	
41		Sat	10	Football League, Division 3 (South)	CHARLTON ATHLETIC	1-1 D		4,973	
42		Sat	17	Football League, Division 3 (South)	Gillingham		W 1-0		4,979
43		Wed	21	Football League, Division 3 (South)	Swindon Town		L 3-5		2,668
44		Sat	24	Football League, Division 3 (South)	SWINDON TOWN	3-2 W		4,823	
45	May	Sat	1	Football League, Division 3 (South)	Exeter City		L 1-6		5,671

League ever-presents: F.W. Smith, R.G. Williams
Most appearances in total: F.W. Smith & R.G. Williams 45 out of 45   **Most goals in total:** J. Swan 22
Hat-tricks: J. Swan (Match 15), F. Pagnam (Match 35)   **Penalty goals:** J. Swan 1
Sent off: None
Full international appearance(s) this season: None

	Baker, J.S. //	Bell, J.	Carter, W. //	Eggleton, J.A.E. //	Foster, C.J.	Gregory, F.J. //	Harris, J. //	McCulloch, R.G.//	Morris, H.	Mummery, A.E.P. //	Pagnam, F.	Papworth, J.M. //	Prior, G.	Slade, R.	Smith, E.E.	Smith, F.W.	Stephenson, J.	Strain, J.	Swan, J.	Williams, R.G. //	Own goal
Apps	3	2	2	13	38	25	29	14	5	4	27	13	23	36	29	42	40	39	36	42	
Subs																					
Goals	1				15		5	2		1	11	7			1	2	6		21	1	
Apps						3	3				3		3	3	3	3	3	3	3		
Subs																					
Goals											2		2						1		
1				X	X	X	X	X			X	X				X1	X1	X		G	
2				X		X	X	X1	X		X	X				X	X	X		G	
3			X	X	X	X				X	X1	X				X	X	X		G	
4					X1					X	X2				X	X	X	X	X	G	
5					X1	X				X	X				X	X	X	X	X1	G	
6					X				X	X1	X				X	X	X	X	X	G	
7					X		X				X1				X	X	X1	X	X	G	
8			X		X			X1			X				X	X	X	X		G	
9					X			X			X				X	X	X	X	X	G	
10					X			X			X2		X		X	X	X	X	X	G	
11					X	X		X			X				X	X	X	X	X1	G	
12					X	X		X			X				X	X	X	X		G	
13	X1				X	X	X1	X					X		X	X	X		X	G	
14	X				X	X	X1	X					X		X	X	X		X	G	
15					X1	X		X			X1				X	X	X	X	X3	G	
16					X	X		X			X				X	X	X	X	X1	G	
17			X	X	X	X		X					X		X	X	X			G	
18						X	X				X1		X	X	X	X	X	X	X	G	
19						X	X				X		X1	X	X	X	X	X	X1	G	
20			X	X					X		X1							X	X2	G	
21						X	X				X1		X1	X	X	X	X	X	X	G	
22					X2	X	X				X			X	X	X	X	X	X1	G	
23					X2	X	X				X			X	X	X	X1	X	X	G	
24					X		X				X1			X	X	X	X	X	X1	G	
25					X1		X				X			X	X	X	X	X	X	G	
26		X			X		X1				X1			X	X	X	X1	X	X	G	
27		X			X		X				X			X	X	X	X	X	X	G	
28				X	X1	X					X1		X			X	X	X		G	
29					X	X1	X				X		X	X		X	X2	X	X	G	
30					X	X	X				X		X	X		X	X	X	X	G	
31					X	X	X				X		X	X		X	X	X	X	G	
32					X	X1	X				X		X	X		X	X	X	X	G	
33					X	X1	X				X		X	X		X	X	X	X2	G	
34					X	X	X				X		X	X		X	X1	X	X	G	1
35					X	X1	X				X3		X	X		X	X	X	X2	G	
36					X		X	X1			X1		X	X		X	X	X	X1	G	
37					X		X				X		X	X		X	X	X	X	G	
38					X	X	X				X			X	X	X	X	X	X	G	
39					X1	X	X				X1			X	X	X	X	X	X2	G	
40					X	X	X				X			X	X	X	X	X		G	
41					X	X	X			X	X				X	X	X1	X	X	G	
42					X	X	X				X				X	X	X	X	X1	G	
43					X	X	X			X	X2			X	X1	X		X	X	G	
44					X1	X	X1				X			X	X	X	X	X	X1	G	
45	X				X	X	X				X			X		X	X	X	X1p	G	

1926/27

Football League position: 21st out of 22 in Division 3 (South)
Manager: Fred Pagnam

		HOME					AWAY					
	Pl	W	D	L	For	Ag	W	D	L	For	Ag	Pts
Bristol City	42	19	1	1	71	24	8	7	6	33	30	62
Plymouth Argyle	42	17	4	0	52	14	8	6	7	43	47	60
Millwall	42	16	2	3	55	19	7	8	6	34	32	56
Brighton & Hove Albion	42	15	4	2	61	24	6	7	8	18	26	53
Swindon Town	42	16	3	2	64	31	5	6	10	36	54	51
Crystal Palace	42	12	6	3	57	33	6	3	12	27	48	45
Bournemouth & Boscombe Ath	42	13	2	6	49	24	5	6	10	29	42	44
Luton Town	42	12	9	0	48	19	3	5	13	20	47	44
Newport County	42	15	4	2	40	20	4	2	15	17	51	44
Bristol Rovers	42	12	4	5	46	28	4	5	12	32	52	41
Brentford	42	10	9	2	46	20	3	5	13	24	41	40
Exeter City	42	14	4	3	46	18	1	6	14	30	45	40
Charlton Athletic	42	13	5	3	44	22	3	3	15	16	39	40
Queens Park Rangers	42	9	8	4	41	27	6	1	14	24	44	39
Coventry City	42	11	4	6	44	33	4	3	14	27	53	37
Norwich City	42	10	5	6	41	25	2	6	13	18	46	35
Merthyr Town	42	11	5	5	42	25	2	4	15	21	55	35
Northampton Town	42	13	4	4	36	23	2	1	18	23	64	35
Southend United	42	11	5	5	42	25	2	3	16	20	52	34
Gillingham	42	10	5	6	36	26	1	5	15	18	46	32
WATFORD	42	9	6	6	36	27	3	2	16	21	60	32
Aberdare Athletic	42	8	2	11	38	48	1	5	15	24	53	25

New league opponents: None

Home-and-away league doubles
For - none
Against – 4 (Bournemouth & Boscombe Athletic, Bristol City, Millwall, Plymouth Argyle)

Divisional changes at end of season: Bristol City to Division 2; Walsall from Division 3 (North); Torquay United elected in place of Aberdare Athletic

All Matches: Won 13, Drew 8, Lost 23, Goals 67-89

Highest Score: 10 (Match 17)

No	DATE			COMPETITION	OPPONENTS	HOME	AWAY	ATTENDANCE	
1	August	Sat	28	Football League, Division 3 (South)	CHARLTON ATHLETIC	1-0 W		11,555	
2	September	Wed	1	Football League, Division 3 (South)	COVENTRY CITY	1-0 W		6,461	
3		Sat	4	Football League, Division 3 (South)	Bristol City		L 0-5		14,962
4		Wed	8	Football League, Division 3 (South)	Crystal Palace		W 1-0		12,350
5		Sat	11	Football League, Division 3 (South)	BOURNEMOUTH & BOSCOMBE ATHLETIC	1-2 L		8,968	
6		Wed	15	Football League, Division 3 (South)	CRYSTAL PALACE	1-2 L		7,000	
7		Sat	18	Football League, Division 3 (South)	Plymouth Argyle		L 0-4		10,106
8		Sat	25	Football League, Division 3 (South)	NEWPORT COUNTY	0-0 D		7,720	
9	October	Sat	2	Football League, Division 3 (South)	Aberdare Athletic		L 2-3		2,379
10		Sat	9	Football League, Division 3 (South)	GILLINGHAM	4-0 W		6,010	
11		Sat	16	Football League, Division 3 (South)	NORTHAMPTON TOWN	4-0 W		8,022	
12		Sat	23	Football League, Division 3 (South)	Brighton & Hove Albion		L 1-4		10,043
13		Sat	30	Football League, Division 3 (South)	LUTON TOWN	2-1 W		12,199	
14	November	Sat	6	Football League, Division 3 (South)	Southend United		L 0-2		7,109
15		Sat	13	Football League, Division 3 (South)	MERTHYR TOWN	4-1 W		2,844	
16		Sat	20	Football League, Division 3 (South)	Exeter City		L 0-2		5,943
17		Sat	27	FA Cup, 1st Round	LOWESTOFT TOWN	10-1 W		6,800	
18	December	Sat	4	Football League, Division 3 (South)	Bristol Rovers		W 2-0		5,484
19		Sat	11	FA Cup, 2nd Round	BRIGHTON & HOVE ALBION	0-1 L		15,499	
20		Sat	18	Football League, Division 3 (South)	Brentford		L 0-3		7,631
21		Sat	25	Football League, Division 3 (South)	Queens Park Rangers		W 4-2		11,893
22		Mon	27	Football League, Division 3 (South)	QUEENS PARK RANGERS	1-2 L		13,004	
23		Tue	28	Football League, Division 3 (South)	MILLWALL	2-4 L		6,382	
24	January	Sat	1	Football League, Division 3 (South)	Coventry City		L 1-5		10,500
25		Sat	8	Football League, Division 3 (South)	SWINDON TOWN	2-2 D		6,438	
26		Sat	15	Football League, Division 3 (South)	Charlton Athletic		L 1-2		7,676
27		Sat	22	Football League, Division 3 (South)	BRISTOL CITY	0-1 L		3,987	
28		Sat	29	Football League, Division 3 (South)	Bournemouth & Boscombe Athletic		L 0-6		3,864
29	February	Sat	5	Football League, Division 3 (South)	PLYMOUTH ARGYLE	1-4 L		6,360	
30		Sat	12	Football League, Division 3 (South)	Newport County		L 1-2		4,291
31		Sat	19	Football League, Division 3 (South)	ABERDARE ATHLETIC	2-2 D		5,144	
32		Sat	26	Football League, Division 3 (South)	Gillingham		L 0-3		3,909
33	March	Sat	5	Football League, Division 3 (South)	Northampton Town		L 2-3		5,829
34		Sat	12	Football League, Division 3 (South)	BRIGHTON & HOVE ALBION	1-0 W		6,598	
35		Sat	19	Football League, Division 3 (South)	Luton Town		D 2-2		10,561
36		Sat	26	Football League, Division 3 (South)	SOUTHEND UNITED	4-2 W		5,127	
37	April	Sat	2	Football League, Division 3 (South)	Merthyr Town		D 1-1		1,262
38		Sat	9	Football League, Division 3 (South)	EXETER CITY	1-0 W		3,731	
39		Fri	15	Football League, Division 3 (South)	NORWICH CITY	1-1 D		7,785	
40		Sat	16	Football League, Division 3 (South)	Swindon Town		L 2-4		5,274
41		Mon	18	Football League, Division 3 (South)	Norwich City		L 0-4		11,371
42		Sat	23	Football League, Division 3 (South)	BRISTOL ROVERS	3-3 D		4,447	
43		Sat	30	Football League, Division 3 (South)	Millwall		L 1-3		8,664
44	May	Sat	7	Football League, Division 3 (South)	BRENTFORD	0-0 D		4,999	

League ever-presents: None
Most appearances in total: G. Prior 39 out of 44 **Most goals in total:** G.W.N. Edmonds 13
Hat-tricks: G.W.N. Edmonds (Match 10), J. Swan (Match 17), J. Warner (Match 17) **Penalty goals:** A. Daniels 1, G.H. Russell 1
Sent off: None
Full international appearance(s) this season: None

	Broad, J. //	Daniels, A.	Edmonds, G.W.N. //	Fletcher, E. //	Foster, C.J.	Leaver, J.	McCrae, J.C.F. //	Maxwell, J.F. //	Morris, H.	North, E.J. //	Packham, F.W. //	Pagnam, F. //	Prior, G.	Rand, J.E. //	Roberts, J. //	Russell, D.P. //	Russell, G.H. //	Slade, R.	Smith, E.E. //	Smith, F.W.	Stephenson, J. //	Strain, J. //	Swan, J. //	Warner, J.	Wilkinson, G.G.	Woodward, A.	Woodward, J.H. //	Yates, W.	Own goal
Apps	1	28	22	23	17	24	2	4	18	6	5	1	37	6	20	7	12	12	21	29	36	27	18	32	6	13	2	33	
Subs																													
Goals	1	4	12		6	3		1	2						5		1			2	3	1	6	8	2				
Apps	1	2	1	2									2						2	2	2	2	2	2				2	
Subs																													
Goals		1	1	1																			3	3					1
1		X		X		X	X			X			X			G				X	X		X1	X					
2		X		X		X1				X			X			G				X	X	X	X	X					
3		X				X							X			G	X	X		X	X	X	X	X					
4		X			X	X							X			G			X	X	X	X	X1	X					
5		X1				X				X			X			G			X	X	X	X	X	X					
6		X	X1			X			X				X			G			X	X		X	X	X					
7		X	X			X	X				X		X			G				X		X	X	X					
8		X	X								X		X	X	X		X		X	X		X					G		
9		X1									X		X	X	X		X		X	X		X	X1				G		
10		X	X3					X					X				X		X	X	X	X		X1				G	
11		X	X					X1									X1p	X	X	X1	X	X		X1				G	
12		X	X1	X				X									X		X	X	X	X		X				G	
13		X	X1	X									X						X	X	X	X	X	X1				G	
14		X	X	X									X						X	X	X	X	X	X				G	
15		X	X2	X									X	X					X	X	X1	X	X1					G	
16		X	X	X	X								X	X					X	X	X	X						G	
17		X1	X1	X1									X						X	X	X	X	X3	X3				G	1
18	X1	X		X									X						X	X	X	X	X	X1				G	
19	X	X		X									X						X	X	X	X	X	X				G	
20		X		X				X					X						X	X	X	X	X	X				G	
21			X2	X									X		X				X	X	X	X	X1	X1				G	
22			X	X		X							X		X				X		X	X	X1	X				G	
23			X1	X									X		X				X		X	X	X	X1		X		G	
24		X1p		X		X							X		X			X			X		X	X		X		G	
25			X	X									X		X2		X		X		X	X	X	X				G	
26		X	X	X					X				X		X				X		X1	X		X				G	
27		X	X	X					X						X		X		X		X	X		X				G	
28		X	X	X	X				X								X		X	X	X			X				G	
29		X1	X	X	X				X								X			X	X			X		X		G	
30		X		X		X				X	X		X				X			X		X1		X				G	
31		X	X			X				X			X				X			X	X	X		X2				G	
32				X	X	X			X			X	X		X					X	X			X				G	
33				X	X	X			X1				X		X						X			X	X1	X		G	
34					X	X1			X				X		X			X			X			X	X	X		G	
35					X1	X			X				X		X1			X			X			X	X	X		G	
36					X2	X			X	X			X		X			X			X1				X1	X		G	
37					X	X			X				X		X			X		X1	X	X			X			G	
38					X	X			X				X		X1			X			X	X		X	X			G	
39			X1		X	X			X				X		X			X		X	X					X		G	
40			X		X1	X			X				X	X	X1			X			X					X		G	
41		X	X		X	X			X		X		X					X						X		X		G	
42		X		X	X1	X1			X1				X	X						X	X					X		G	
43				X	X1	X			X				X		X					X	X			X		X		G	
44		X			X	X			X				X		X			X		X	X					X		G	

1927/28

Football League position: 15th out of 22 in Division 3 (South)
Manager: Fred Pagnam

New league opponents: Torquay United, Walsall

Home-and-away league doubles
For – 2 (Coventry City, Gillingham)
Against – 3 (Millwall, Newport County, Swindon Town)

Divisional changes at end of season: Millwall to Division 2; Fulham from Division 2

All Matches: Won 14, Drew 10, Lost 19, Goals 69-80

Highest Score: 5 (Match 42)

		HOME					AWAY					
	Pl	W	D	L	For	Ag	W	D	L	For	Ag	Pts
Millwall	42	19	2	0	87	15	11	3	7	40	35	65
Northampton Town	42	17	3	1	67	23	6	6	9	35	41	55
Plymouth Argyle	42	17	2	2	60	19	6	5	10	25	35	53
Brighton & Hove Albion	42	14	4	3	51	24	5	6	10	30	45	48
Crystal Palace	42	15	3	3	46	23	3	9	9	33	49	48
Swindon Town	42	12	6	3	60	26	7	3	11	30	43	47
Southend United	42	14	2	5	48	19	6	4	11	32	45	46
Exeter City	42	11	6	4	49	27	6	6	9	21	33	46
Newport County	42	12	5	4	52	38	6	4	11	29	46	45
Queens Park Rangers	42	8	5	8	37	35	9	4	8	35	36	43
Charlton Athletic	42	12	5	4	34	27	3	8	10	26	43	43
Brentford	42	12	4	5	49	30	4	4	13	27	44	40
Luton Town	42	13	5	3	56	27	3	2	16	38	60	39
Bournemouth & Boscombe Ath	42	12	6	3	44	24	1	6	14	28	55	38
WATFORD	42	10	5	6	42	34	4	5	12	26	44	38
Gillingham	42	10	3	8	42	34	5	3	10	29	55	36
Norwich City	42	9	8	4	41	26	1	8	12	25	44	36
Walsall	42	9	6	6	52	35	3	3	15	23	66	33
Bristol Rovers	42	11	3	7	41	36	3	1	17	26	57	32
Coventry City	42	5	8	8	40	36	6	1	14	27	60	31
Merthyr Town	42	7	6	8	38	40	2	7	12	15	51	31
Torquay United	42	4	10	7	27	36	4	4	13	26	67	30

No	DATE			COMPETITION	OPPONENTS	HOME	AWAY	ATTENDANCE
1	August	Sat	27	Football League, Division 3 (South)	COVENTRY CITY	3-1 W		10,151
2		Mon	29	Football League, Division 3 (South)	Walsall		L 0-2	7,744
3	September	Sat	3	Football League, Division 3 (South)	Newport County		L 2-3	7,362
4		Wed	7	Football League, Division 3 (South)	WALSALL	4-0 W		6,459
5		Sat	10	Football League, Division 3 (South)	SWINDON TOWN	2-5 W		10,483
6		Sat	17	Football League, Division 3 (South)	Queens Park Rangers		L 1-2	13,951
7		Sat	24	Football League, Division 3 (South)	LUTON TOWN	1-0 W		12,903
8	October	Sat	1	Football League, Division 3 (South)	CHARLTON ATHLETIC	1-2 L		5,350
9		Sat	8	Football League, Division 3 (South)	Bristol Rovers		L 1-3	7,247
10		Sat	15	Football League, Division 3 (South)	PLYMOUTH ARGYLE	1-2 L		9,016
11		Sat	22	Football League, Division 3 (South)	Exeter City		D 3-3	5,750
12		Sat	29	Football League, Division 3 (South)	CRYSTAL PALACE	2-1 W		7,346
13	November	Sat	5	Football League, Division 3 (South)	Millwall		L 2-4	13,302
14		Sat	12	Football League, Division 3 (South)	TORQUAY UNITED	1-2 L		6,929
15		Sat	19	Football League, Division 3 (South)	Norwich City		D 1-1	6,049
16		Wed	30	FA Cup, 1st Round	BRIGHTON & HOVE ALBION	1-2 L		6,058
17	December	Sat	3	Football League, Division 3 (South)	Southend United		L 0-3	5,320
18		Sat	10	Football League, Division 3 (South)	Coventry City		W 3-2	7,448
19		Sat	17	Football League, Division 3 (South)	Bournemouth & Boscombe Athletic		L 0-1	3,798
20		Sat	24	Football League, Division 3 (South)	BRENTFORD	1-1 D		5,226
21		Tue	27	Football League, Division 3 (South)	Gillingham		W 3-0	3,310
22	January	Sat	7	Football League, Division 3 (South)	NEWPORT COUNTY	2-3 L		5,972
23		Sat	14	Football League, Division 3 (South)	BRIGHTON & HOVE ALBION	3-3 D		5,912
24		Sat	21	Football League, Division 3 (South)	Swindon Town		L 0-4	7,356
25		Sat	28	Football League, Division 3 (South)	QUEENS PARK RANGERS	3-3 D		5,597
26	February	Sat	4	Football League, Division 3 (South)	Luton Town		L 2-3	8,012
27		Sat	11	Football League, Division 3 (South)	Charlton Athletic		W 2-0	5,464
28		Sat	18	Football League, Division 3 (South)	BRISTOL ROVERS	2-1 W		7,246
29		Sat	25	Football League, Division 3 (South)	Plymouth Argyle		W 1-0	11,281
30	March	Sat	3	Football League, Division 3 (South)	EXETER CITY	3-2 W		7,951
31		Sat	10	Football League, Division 3 (South)	Crystal Palace		L 1-2	9,851
32		Sat	17	Football League, Division 3 (South)	MILLWALL	0-3 L		13,727
33		Sat	24	Football League, Division 3 (South)	Torquay United		D 1-1	3,750
34		Sat	31	Football League, Division 3 (South)	NORWICH CITY	2-0 W		4,412
35	April	Sat	7	Football League, Division 3 (South)	Brighton & Hove Albion		D 1-1	7,969
36		Mon	9	Football League, Division 3 (South)	MERTHYR TOWN	1-1 D		8,360
37		Tue	10	Football League, Division 3 (South)	Merthyr Town		L 1-3	2,590
38		Sat	14	Football League, Division 3 (South)	SOUTHEND UNITED	1-1 D		5,048
39		Wed	18	Football League, Division 3 (South)	NORTHAMPTON TOWN	2-0 W		4,221
40		Sat	21	Football League, Division 3 (South)	Northampton Town		L 0-5	6,255
41		Sat	28	Football League, Division 3 (South)	BOURNEMOUTH & BOSCOMBE ATHLETIC	2-0 W		5,102
42	May	Wed	2	Football League, Division 3 (South)	GILLINGHAM	5-3 W		3,645
43		Sat	5	Football League, Division 3 (South)	Brentford		D 1-1	4,775

League ever-presents: A. Daniels
Most appearances in total: A. Daniels 43 out of 43   **Most goals in total:** W. Sheppard 25
Hat-tricks: W. Sheppard (Match 21)   **Penalty goals:** W. Sheppard 3
Sent off: None
Full international appearance(s) this season: None

	Armstrong, W.B.	Daniels, A.	Davison, J.	Foster, C.J.	Fuller, E.W.	Groome, J.P.G.	Hewitt, J.T.	Hills, W.R.	Jewett, G.	Kirkpatrick, J.	Leaver, J.	Mingay, H.J.	Morris, H.	Parker, R.	Prior, G.	Sheppard, W.	Slade, R.	Smith, F.W.	Vanner, H.J.	Warner, J.	Wilbourn, H.	Wilkinson, G.G.	Woodward, A.	Yates, J.	Yates, W.	Own goal
Apps	1	42	32	15	34	16	28	28	24	9	11	2	27	13	36	40	8	31	1	36	2	3	9	2	12	
Subs																										
Goals		6		3	14			2					2	2		25		1		12					1	
Apps	1	1	1	1			1					1		1	1	1		1		1			1			
Subs																										
Goals														1												
1		X			X			X	X	X	X		X		X	X2				X1					G	
2		X			X			X	X	X	X		X		X	X				X					G	
3		X	X	X	X2			X	X		X		X		X	X									G	
4		X	X1		X	X1		X1			X				X	X1				X					G	
5		X	X		X			X			X				X	X1				X			X		G	1
6		X	X		X			X1			X		X		X	X	X	X		X					G	
7		X	X	X				X	X		X		X			X1	X	X		X					G	
8		X	X	X1	X			X			X				X	X	X	X		X					G	
9	X	X	X		X			X			X				X1	X	X	X		X					G	
10		X	X		X			X			X		X		X	X		X		X1					G	
11	X1		X					X		X			X		X	X1p				X1			X		G	
12	X1		X					X		X			X		X	X				X			X		G	
13		X	X1				G	X		X			X		X	X	X			X1			X			
14		X					G	X		X			X	X1	X	X	X			X			X			
15		X	X	X	X			X				G	X1		X	X1	X			X			X			
16		X	X	X	X			X				G	X1		X	X	X			X			X			
17		X	X				G	X		X	X				X	X	X			X						
18		X	X		X	X1	G	X	X				X		X	X1				X1						
19		X	X		X	X	G	X	X				X		X	X				X						
20		X	X		X		G	X	X				X	X	X	X1				X						
21		X	X		X	X	G	X	X				X		X	X3				X						
22		X	X		X	X2	G	X	X				X		X	X				X						
23		X	X		X	X1	G	X	X				X		X	X2	X			X						
24		X	X		X	X	G	X	X				X		X	X				X						
25		X	X		X		G	X	X				X	X	X	X2	X			X1						
26		X	X		X		G	X	X				X	X	X	X1	X			X1						
27		X	X		X		G	X	X				X		X	X1	X		X	X1						
28	X1				X		G	X					X	X1	X	X	X	X	X	X						
29		X	X		X	X1	G	X	X				X		X	X				X				X		
30		X	X		X	X1	G		X				X2		X	X				X				X		
31		X	X	X	X		G		X				X		X	X		X1		X	X					
32		X	X	X	X		X		X				X		X	X		X		X						
33		X	X		X		G	X					X	X	X	X		X		X1						
34	X1	X			X		G	X					X	X	X	X		X		X1	X					
35		X	X		X		G	X					X	X	X	X1		X		X						
36		X	X		X		G	X					X	X	X	X1		X		X						
37		X	X	X	X		G	X					X		X	X		X		X1						
38	X1	X			X		G	X					X		X	X		X		X		X				
39	X1	X	X	X			G						X		X	X1p	X	X		X		X				
40		X	X	X	X		G	X					X		X	X	X	X		X		X				
41		X	X	X	X	X2	G						X		X	X		X		X			X			
42		X	X		X	X2	G						X		X	X2p	X	X	X	X1			X			
43		X	X		X	X1	G						X		X	X		X		X			X			

1928/29

Football League position: 8th out of 22 in Division 3 (South)
Manager: Fred Pagnam

New league opponents: None

Home-and-away league doubles
For – 3 (Brentford, Newport County, Southend United)
Against – 1 (Torquay United)

Divisional changes at end of season: Charlton Athletic to Division 2; Clapton Orient from Division 2

All Matches: Won 22, Drew 10, Lost 14, Goals 88-80

Highest Score: 6 (Match 28)

	HOME						AWAY					
	Pl	W	D	L	For	Ag	W	D	L	For	Ag	Pts
Charlton Athletic	42	14	5	2	51	22	9	3	9	35	38	54
Crystal Palace	42	14	2	5	40	25	9	6	6	41	42	54
Northampton Town	42	14	6	1	68	23	6	6	9	28	34	52
Plymouth Argyle	42	14	6	1	51	13	6	6	9	32	38	52
Fulham	42	14	3	4	60	31	7	7	7	41	40	52
Queens Park Rangers	42	13	7	1	50	22	6	7	8	32	39	52
Luton Town	42	16	3	2	64	28	3	8	10	25	45	49
WATFORD	42	15	3	3	55	31	4	7	10	24	43	48
Bournemouth & Boscombe Ath	42	14	4	3	54	31	5	5	11	30	46	47
Swindon Town	42	12	5	4	48	27	3	8	10	27	45	43
Coventry City	42	9	6	6	35	23	5	8	8	27	34	42
Southend United	42	10	7	4	44	27	5	4	12	36	48	41
Brentford	42	11	4	6	34	21	3	6	12	22	39	38
Walsall	42	11	7	3	47	25	2	5	14	26	54	38
Brighton & Hove Albion	42	14	2	5	39	28	2	4	15	19	48	38
Newport County	42	8	6	7	37	28	5	3	13	32	58	35
Norwich City	42	12	3	6	49	29	2	3	16	20	52	34
Torquay United	42	10	3	8	46	36	4	3	14	20	48	34
Bristol Rovers	42	10	7	4	42	28	4	1	16	21	51	33
Merthyr Town	42	11	6	4	42	28	0	2	19	13	75	30
Exeter City	42	7	6	8	49	40	2	5	14	18	48	29
Gillingham	42	7	8	6	22	24	3	1	17	21	59	29

No	DATE			COMPETITION	OPPONENTS	HOME	AWAY	ATTENDANCE
1	August	Sat	25	Football League, Division 3 (South)	Crystal Palace		L 0-3	19,466
2		Mon	27	Football League, Division 3 (South)	Coventry City		D 1-1	11,686
3	September	Sat	1	Football League, Division 3 (South)	SWINDON TOWN	3-2 W		10,959
4		Wed	5	Football League, Division 3 (South)	COVENTRY CITY	4-2 W		7,953
5		Sat	8	Football League, Division 3 (South)	Torquay United		L 0-1	6,047
6		Sat	15	Football League, Division 3 (South)	GILLINGHAM	1-0 W		9,881
7		Sat	22	Football League, Division 3 (South)	Plymouth Argyle		L 0-2	10,728
8		Sat	29	Football League, Division 3 (South)	FULHAM	2-6 L		15,011
9	October	Sat	6	Football League, Division 3 (South)	Queens Park Rangers		L 2-3	18,263
10		Sat	13	Football League, Division 3 (South)	BRISTOL ROVERS	1-0 W		9,593
11		Sat	20	Football League, Division 3 (South)	LUTON TOWN	3-2 W		20,395
12		Sat	27	Football League, Division 3 (South)	Brentford		W 1-0	8,301
13	November	Sat	3	Football League, Division 3 (South)	BOURNEMOUTH & BOSCOMBE ATHLETIC	0-3 L		9,570
14		Sat	10	Football League, Division 3 (South)	Merthyr Town		L 1-2	2,047
15		Sat	17	Football League, Division 3 (South)	SOUTHEND UNITED	4-1 W		7,593
16		Sat	24	FA Cup, 1st Round	Leyton		W 2-0	5,500
17	December	Sat	1	Football League, Division 3 (South)	BRIGHTON & HOVE ALBION	2-1 W		9,256
18		Sat	8	FA Cup, 2nd Round	MERTHYR TOWN	2-0 W		10,662
19		Sat	15	Football League, Division 3 (South)	CHARLTON ATHLETIC	3-1 W		6,570
20		Sat	22	Football League, Division 3 (South)	Northampton Town		L 0-3	9,438
21		Tue	25	Football League, Division 3 (South)	Newport County		W 2-0	3,351
22		Wed	26	Football League, Division 3 (South)	NEWPORT COUNTY	3-0 W		9,463
23		Sat	29	Football League, Division 3 (South)	CRYSTAL PALACE	3-3 D		9,693
24	January	Sat	5	Football League, Division 3 (South)	Swindon Town		L 0-5	4,417
25		Sat	12	FA Cup, 3rd Round	PRESTON NORTH END	1-0 W		18,344
26		Sat	19	Football League, Division 3 (South)	TORQUAY UNITED	0-2 L		7,974
27		Sat	26	FA Cup, 4th Round	Bournemouth & Boscombe Athletic		L 4-6	13,311
28	February	Sat	2	Football League, Division 3 (South)	PLYMOUTH ARGYLE	6-3 W		5,296
29		Sat	9	Football League, Division 3 (South)	Fulham		W 3-2	19,430
30		Sat	16	Football League, Division 3 (South)	QUEENS PARK RANGERS	4-1 W		7,185
31		Sat	23	Football League, Division 3 (South)	Bristol Rovers		D 1-1	6,958
32	March	Sat	2	Football League, Division 3 (South)	Luton Town		D 2-2	15,199
33		Sat	9	Football League, Division 3 (South)	BRENTFORD	2-0 W		10,453
34		Sat	16	Football League, Division 3 (South)	Bournemouth & Boscombe Athletic		D 3-3	4,326
35		Sat	23	Football League, Division 3 (South)	MERTHYR TOWN	4-0 W		8,297
36		Fri	29	Football League, Division 3 (South)	WALSALL	4-1 W		11,636
37		Sat	30	Football League, Division 3 (South)	Southend United		W 3-1	7,688
38	April	Mon	1	Football League, Division 3 (South)	Walsall		L 0-4	4,961
39		Sat	6	Football League, Division 3 (South)	EXETER CITY	3-0 W		8,842
40		Wed	10	Football League, Division 3 (South)	Exeter City		D 2-2	2,259
41		Sat	13	Football League, Division 3 (South)	Brighton & Hove Albion		D 1-1	5,682
42		Sat	20	Football League, Division 3 (South)	NORWICH CITY	2-2 D		9,405
43		Wed	24	Football League, Division 3 (South)	Gillingham		D 0-0	2,217
44		Sat	27	Football League, Division 3 (South)	Charlton Athletic		L 0-2	15,791
45	May	Thu	2	Football League, Division 3 (South)	Norwich City		L 2-5	6,732
46		Sat	4	Football League, Division 3 (South)	NORTHAMPTON TOWN	1-1 D		10,926

League ever-presents: None
Most appearances in total: J.T. Hewitt & G. Prior 44 out of 46   **Most goals in total:** F.C. McPherson 35
Hat-tricks: F.C. McPherson (Match 15, Match 29 & Match 36), T.A. Barnett (Match 28)   **Penalty goals:** F.C. McPherson 7
Sent off: J. Davison (Match 1), F. Barson (Match 8)
Full international appearance(s) this season: None

	Barnett, T.A.	Barson, F. //	Brelsford, B.	Brown, W.	Chapman, W.	Cowan, R.	Daniels, A.	Davison, J.	Fuller, E.W. //	Groome, J.P.G. //	Hewitt, J.T.	Hills, W.R. //	Holland, P.B.	Jewett, G. //	McBain, N.	McPherson, F.C.	Moule, A.S. //	Prior, G.	Sheppard, W.	Slade, R.	Smith, F.W.	Vanner, H.J. //	Warner, J.	Woodward, A.	Yates, W. //
Apps	32	10	18	11	38	5	38	25	21	1	40	2	11	5	27	33	11	40	38	1	20	1	12	20	2
Subs																									
Goals	12	1			2	1	6					1	2		2	33	4		12				2	1	
Apps	4			1	4		4	4	3		4		1		3	4		4	3		4			1	
Subs																									
Goals	5															2			2						
1		X			X		X	X			G			X				X	X		X		X	X	
2		X			X		X	X	X		G						X1	X	X		X		X		
3		X1			X		X1	X	X		G						X	X	X		X	X1			
4		X			X		X1	X	X								X2	X	X		X	X1		X	
5		X			X		X	X	X	X	G						X	X	X		X				
6	X	X	X		X		X	X			G						X1	X	X		X				
7	X	X	X		X		X	X			G						X	X		X	X		X		
8		X			X		X	X			G		X	X		X2		X	X		X				
9		X		X	X		X	X					X	X		X2p	X	X							G
10		X			X		X	X	X		G		X			X1	X	X			X				
11	X				X		X	X	X		G		X2	X			X	X1			X				
12	X1				X		X	X	X		G		X	X		X	X	X			X				
13	X				X		X	X	X		G		X			X		X	X		X			X	
14					X	X1	X	X			G		X			X		X	X		X		X		
15	X1			X	X		X	X			G					X3p		X	X		X				
16	X1			X	X		X	X			G				X	X1		X	X		X		X		
17	X			X	X		X	X			G				X	X2		X	X		X				
18	X1				X		X	X	X		G				X	X1		X	X		X				
19	X				X		X	X	X		G				X	X1		X	X2		X				
20	X				X		X	X	X		G		X		X	X		X	X		X				
21	X				X	X	X	X	X		G				X	X1		X	X1						
22	X1				X	X	X	X	X		G				X	X1		X	X1						
23	X			X	X1		X	X	X		G				X	X2p		X	X						
24	X			X	X		X	X	X		G				X	X		X	X						
25	X1				X		X	X	X		G				X	X		X	X		X				
26	X				X		X	X	X		G		X		X	X		X	X		X				
27	X2				X		X	X	X		G				X	X		X	X2		X				
28	X3	X			X		X		X		G				X	X1		X	X2		X				
29	X	X			X		X		X		G				X	X3		X	X		X				
30	X1	X			X		X1				G				X	X2p		X	X		X			X	
31	X	X			X		X				G				X	X1p		X	X		X			X	
32	X	X			X		X				G				X	X1p			X1					X	
33	X	X			X		X	X			G				X	X2		X	X					X	
34	X2	X			X		X				G				X	X1		X	X				X	X	
35	X1	X			X		X				G				X1	X		X	X2				X	X	
36	X	X			X		X1				G				X	X3p		X	X				X	X	
37	X	X			X1		X				G				X	X2		X	X				X	X	
38	X	X			X		X								X	X	X	X	X				X	G
39	X1	X			X		X1				G				X	X	X	X	X1				X		
40	X	X		X	X1		X				G				X	X1		X	X				X		
41	X	X		X	X		X				G				X	X1		X	X				X		
42		X			X		X				G	X			X1	X	X	X	X1				X		
43	X		X	X	X		X				G				X	X		X	X				X		
44	X		X	X	X		X				G				X	X		X	X				X		
45	X						X	X			G	X1			X	X		X	X				X	X1	
46	X1				X		X				G	X	X		X	X		X	X				X	X	

- 81 -

1929/30

Football League position: 15th out of 22 in Division 3 (South)
Manager: Neil McBain

		HOME					AWAY					
	Pl	W	D	L	For	Ag	W	D	L	For	Ag	Pts
Plymouth Argyle	42	18	3	0	63	12	12	5	4	35	26	68
Brentford	42	21	0	0	66	12	7	5	9	28	32	61
Queens Park Rangers	42	13	5	3	46	26	8	4	9	34	42	51
Northampton Town	42	14	6	1	53	20	7	2	12	29	38	50
Brighton & Hove Albion	42	16	2	3	54	20	5	6	10	33	43	50
Coventry City	42	14	3	4	54	25	5	6	10	34	48	47
Fulham	42	12	6	3	54	33	6	5	10	33	50	47
Norwich City	42	14	4	3	55	28	4	6	11	33	49	46
Crystal Palace	42	14	5	2	56	26	3	7	11	25	48	46
Bournemouth & Boscombe Ath	42	11	6	4	47	24	4	7	10	25	37	43
Southend United	42	11	6	4	41	19	4	7	10	28	40	43
Clapton Orient	42	10	8	3	38	21	4	5	12	17	41	41
Luton Town	42	13	4	4	42	25	1	8	12	22	53	40
Swindon Town	42	10	7	4	42	25	3	5	13	31	58	38
WATFORD	42	10	4	7	45	29	2	5	14	22	44	35
Exeter City	42	10	6	5	45	29	2	5	14	22	44	35
Walsall	42	10	7	4	42	24	3	4	14	26	54	34
Newport County	42	9	9	3	48	29	3	1	17	26	56	34
Torquay United	42	9	6	6	50	38	1	5	15	14	56	31
Bristol Rovers	42	11	3	7	45	31	0	5	16	22	62	30
Gillingham	42	9	5	7	38	28	2	3	16	13	52	30
Merthyr Town	42	5	6	10	39	49	1	3	17	21	86	21

New league opponents: Clapton Orient

Home-and-away league doubles
For – 5 (Bristol Rovers, Gillingham, Southend United, Swindon Town, Walsall)
Against – 6 (Brentford, Coventry City, Luton Town, Newport County, Northampton Town, Plymouth Argyle)

Divisional changes at end of season: Plymouth Argyle to Division 2; Notts County from Division 2; Thames elected in place of Merthyr Town

All Matches: Won 16, Drew 9, Lost 20, Goals 64-77

Highest Score: 4 (Matches 31, 39 & 43)

No	DATE			COMPETITION	OPPONENTS	HOME	AWAY	ATTENDANCE
1	August	Sat	31	Football League, Division 3 (South)	TORQUAY UNITED	2-0 W		11,558
2	September	Wed	4	Football League, Division 3 (South)	Brighton & Hove Albion		L 1-2	6,368
3		Sat	7	Football League, Division 3 (South)	Newport County		L 0-1	4,887
4		Sat	14	Football League, Division 3 (South)	LUTON TOWN	0-4 L		16,945
5		Wed	18	Football League, Division 3 (South)	BRIGHTON & HOVE ALBION	3-0 W		6,763
6		Sat	21	Football League, Division 3 (South)	COVENTRY CITY	1-3 L		10,048
7		Wed	25	Football League, Division 3 (South)	PLYMOUTH ARGYLE	0-2 L		7,015
8		Sat	28	Football League, Division 3 (South)	Clapton Orient		D 1-1	12,419
9	October	Sat	5	Football League, Division 3 (South)	BRENTFORD	1-2 L		10,814
10		Sat	12	Football League, Division 3 (South)	Bristol Rovers		W 2-1	6,978
11		Sat	19	Football League, Division 3 (South)	Bournemouth & Boscombe Athletic		L 2-3	8,040
12		Mon	26	Football League, Division 3 (South)	WALSALL	2-1 W		8,471
13	November	Sat	2	Football League, Division 3 (South)	Queens Park Rangers		D 0-0	12,774
14		Sat	9	Football League, Division 3 (South)	FULHAM	0-0 D		12,442
15		Sat	16	Football League, Division 3 (South)	Norwich City		L 1-3	5,555
16		Sat	23	Football League, Division 3 (South)	CRYSTAL PALACE	1-1 D		5,646
17		Sat	30	FA Cup, 1st Round	Ilford		W 3-0	8,000
18	December	Sat	7	Football League, Division 3 (South)	NORTHAMPTON TOWN	1-2 L		6,989
19		Sat	14	FA Cup, 2nd Round	PLYMOUTH ARGYLE	1-1 D		13,677
20		Wed	18	FA Cup, 2nd Round replay	Plymouth Argyle		L 0-3	18,575
21		Sat	21	Football League, Division 3 (South)	SOUTHEND UNITED	2-1 W		3,327
22		Wed	25	Football League, Division 3 (South)	Merthyr Town		D 2-2	1,127
23		Thu	26	Football League, Division 3 (South)	MERTHYR TOWN	2-3 L		10,975
24		Sat	28	Football League, Division 3 (South)	Torquay United		L 0-4	2,730
25	January	Sat	4	Football League, Division 3 (South)	NEWPORT COUNTY	2-3 L		5,851
26		Sat	11	Football League, Division 3 (South)	Gillingham		W 2-1	5,562
27		Sat	18	Football League, Division 3 (South)	Luton Town		L 0-2	9,920
28		Sat	25	Football League, Division 3 (South)	Coventry City		L 1-3	12,724
29	February	Sat	1	Football League, Division 3 (South)	CLAPTON ORIENT	3-0 W		6,842
30		Sat	8	Football League, Division 3 (South)	Brentford		L 0-5	11,356
31		Sat	15	Football League, Division 3 (South)	BRISTOL ROVERS	4-3 W		6,158
32		Wed	19	Football League, Division 3 (South)	Exeter City		L 0-1	3,101
33		Sat	22	Football League, Division 3 (South)	BOURNEMOUTH & BOSCOMBE ATHLETIC	0-0 D		5,580
34	March	Sat	1	Football League, Division 3 (South)	Walsall		W 2-1	4,913
35		Sat	8	Football League, Division 3 (South)	QUEENS PARK RANGERS	1-1 D		11,577
36		Sat	15	Football League, Division 3 (South)	Fulham		L 1-6	10,529
37		Sat	22	Football League, Division 3 (South)	NORWICH CITY	2-1 W		6,888
38		Sat	29	Football League, Division 3 (South)	Crystal Palace		D 1-1	12,310
39	April	Sat	5	Football League, Division 3 (South)	GILLINGHAM	4-1 W		4,787
40		Sat	12	Football League, Division 3 (South)	Northampton Town		L 0-2	6,134
41		Fri	18	Football League, Division 3 (South)	Swindon Town		W 3-1	4,656
42		Sat	19	Football League, Division 3 (South)	EXETER CITY	2-1 W		4,998
43		Mon	21	Football League, Division 3 (South)	SWINDON TOWN	4-1 W		9,272
44		Sat	26	Football League, Division 3 (South)	Southend United		W 3-1	4,495
45	May	Sat	3	Football League, Division 3 (South)	Plymouth Argyle		L 1-2	23,459

League ever-presents: None
Most appearances in total: J. Davison 40 out of 45   **Most goals in total:** F.C. McPherson 25
Hat-tricks: F.C. McPherson (Match 17), G.C. James (Match 39 & Match 44), T.A. Barnett (Match 43)   **Penalty goals:** F.C. McPherson 1
Sent off: None
Full international appearance(s) this season: None

	Barnett, T.A.	Blake, A.G.	Brelsford, B. //	Brown, W.	Chapman, W.	Cowan, R. //	Daniels, A. //	Davison, J.	Ferguson, J.J. //	Hewitt, J.T.	Holland, P.B.	James, G.C.	Lowe, H.P.	McBain, N.	McPherson, F.C.	McWilliams, R.	Miles, W.P.	Paton, J.A.J. //	Prior, G. //	Sheppard, W. //	Slade, R. //	Smith, A //	Smith, F.W.	Turner, J.A. //	Warner, J. //	Woodward, A.	Woolliscroft, A.
Apps	29	7	7	18	35	1	28	37	4	24	6	13	18	33	28	12	14	5	14	11	3	5	15	13	30	35	17
Subs																											
Goals	9		1		1							13	6	2	22	1	1									1	3
Apps	3				3		3	3						1	3	3		3			2			3		3	3
Subs																											
Goals															3												1
1	X				X		X			G				X	X2		X		X	X					X	X	
2	X				X		X			G				X	X1		X		X	X					X	X	
3	X				X						X			X	X		X		X	X		G			X	X	
4	X				X						X			X	X		X		X	X		G			X	X	
5	X			X	X		X	X			X			X	X2							G			X	X1	
6	X			X	X			X			X			X	X1				X			G			X	X	
7	X		X	X	X	X	X	X			X			X	X							G			X	X	
8	X		X1		X		X	X			X			X	X									G	X	X	
9	X		X		X		X	X						X1	X				X					G	X	X	
10	X	X			X		X	X						X	X2	X		X						G	X		
11	X	X			X		X	X						X	X2	X		X						G	X		
12	X	X			X		X	X						X	X2	X		X						G	X		
13	X	X			X		X	X						X	X	X		X						G	X		
14	X	X			X		X	X						X	X	X		X						G	X		
15	X1	X			X		X	X						X	X	X		X						G	X		
16	X	X			X		X	X						X	X1	X		X						G	X		
17	X				X		X	X						X	X3	X		X						G	X	X	
18	X				X		X	X						X	X1	X		X						G	X	X	
19	X				X		X	X							X	X		X			X			G	X	X	X1
20	X				X		X	X							X	X		X			X			G	X	X	
21					X		X			G		X			X1p	X1		X	X	X					X	X	
22					X		X	X		G		X			X2	X			X	X					X	X	
23							X	X	X	G		X			X2	X			X	X					X	X	
24	X			X			X	X		G		X				X			X				X		X	X	
25	X			X	X		X							X1	X1	X	X							G	X	X	
26	X1			X	X		X	X						X	X1									G	X	X	X
27	X			X	X		X	X						X	X									G	X	X	X
28					X			X		G			X1	X	X	X		X							X	X	
29				X	X			X		G			X1	X	X1	X									X	X	X1
30				X	X			X		G			X	X	X	X									X	X	X
31				X	X1			X		G			X1	X1	X	X							X		X		X1
32	X		X		X		X	X		G			X	X	X								X		X		
33	X		X		X		X	X		G		X	X	X									X		X		
34	X1		X		X		X	X		G		X1	X	X									X		X		
35			X		X		X	X		G		X	X1	X									X		X	X	
36					X		X	X	X	G		X1	X				X	X					X		X	X	
37			X				X	X		G		X2	X	X			X	X					X		X	X	
38			X				X	X		G		X	X1	X			X	X					X		X	X	
39			X	X	X		X			G		X3	X	X									X		X		X1
40			X	X	X		X			G		X	X	X									X		X	X	
41	X		X	X			X			G		X2	X				X1						X		X	X	
42	X2		X	X			X			G		X	X				X							X	X	X	X
43	X3		X	X			X			G		X1	X				X							X	X	X	X
44	X		X	X			X			G		X3					X							X	X	X	X
45	X1		X	X			X			G		X	X				X							X	X	X	X

1930/31

Football League position: 18th out of 22 in Division 3 (South)
Manager: Neil McBain

New league opponents: Notts County, Thames

Home-and-away league doubles
For – 1 (Newport County)
Against – 6 (Brentford, Clapton Orient, Crystal Palace, Exeter City, Notts County, Southend United)

Divisional changes at end of season: Notts County to Division 2; Walsall to Division 3 (North); Cardiff City & Reading from Division 2; Mansfield Town elected in place of Newport County

All Matches: Won 18, Drew 7, Lost 22, Goals 85-81

Highest Score: 6 (Matches 12 & 16)

		HOME					AWAY					
	Pl	W	D	L	For	Ag	W	D	L	For	Ag	Pts
Notts County	42	16	4	1	58	13	8	7	6	39	33	59
Crystal Palace	42	17	2	2	71	20	5	5	11	36	51	51
Brentford	42	14	3	4	62	30	8	3	10	28	34	50
Brighton & Hove Albion	42	13	5	3	45	20	4	10	7	23	33	49
Southend United	42	16	0	5	53	26	6	5	10	23	34	49
Northampton Town	42	10	6	5	37	20	8	6	7	40	39	48
Luton Town	42	15	3	3	61	17	4	5	12	15	34	46
Queens Park Rangers	42	15	0	6	57	23	5	3	13	25	52	43
Fulham	42	15	3	3	49	21	3	4	14	28	54	43
Bournemouth & Boscombe Ath	42	11	7	3	39	22	4	6	11	33	51	43
Torquay United	42	13	5	3	56	26	4	4	13	24	58	43
Swindon Town	42	15	5	1	68	29	1	5	15	21	60	42
Exeter City	42	12	6	3	55	35	5	1	15	29	55	41
Coventry City	42	11	4	6	55	28	5	5	11	20	37	41
Bristol Rovers	42	12	3	6	49	36	4	5	12	26	56	40
Gillingham	42	10	6	5	40	29	4	4	13	21	47	38
Walsall	42	9	5	7	44	38	5	4	12	34	57	37
WATFORD	42	9	4	8	41	29	5	3	13	31	46	35
Clapton Orient	42	12	3	6	47	33	2	4	15	16	58	35
Thames	42	12	5	4	34	20	1	3	17	20	73	34
Newport County	42	10	5	6	45	31	1	1	19	24	80	28
Norwich City	42	10	7	4	37	20	0	1	20	10	56	28

No	DATE			COMPETITION	OPPONENTS	HOME	AWAY	ATTENDANCE
1	August	Sat	30	Football League, Division 3 (South)	Fulham		L 2-3	14,124
2	September	Wed	3	Football League, Division 3 (South)	NORWICH CITY	2-2 D		7,217
3		Sat	6	Football League, Division 3 (South)	SWINDON TOWN	3-0 W		8,516
4		Thu	11	Football League, Division 3 (South)	Queens Park Rangers		W 3-2	8,114
5		Sat	13	Football League, Division 3 (South)	Bournemouth & Boscombe Athletic		D 1-1	6,055
6		Wed	17	Football League, Division 3 (South)	QUEENS PARK RANGERS	0-4 L		6,606
7		Sat	20	Football League, Division 3 (South)	LUTON TOWN	1-0 W		8,991
8		Sat	27	Football League, Division 3 (South)	NOTTS COUNTY	0-1 L		10,939
9	October	Sat	4	Football League, Division 3 (South)	Clapton Orient		L 0-4	5,784
10		Sat	11	Football League, Division 3 (South)	THAMES	1-0 W		7,705
11		Sat	18	Football League, Division 3 (South)	Bristol Rovers		W 5-1	8,733
12		Sat	25	Football League, Division 3 (South)	NEWPORT COUNTY	6-2 W		6,214
13	November	Sat	1	Football League, Division 3 (South)	Gillingham		L 2-4	3,717
14		Sat	8	Football League, Division 3 (South)	EXETER CITY	0-1 L		6,975
15		Sat	15	Football League, Division 3 (South)	Brighton & Hove Albion		L 0-1	6,034
16		Sat	22	Football League, Division 3 (South)	TORQUAY UNITED	6-0 W		4,950
17		Sat	29	FA Cup, 1st Round	Walthamstow Avenue		W 5-1	5,146
18	December	Sat	6	Football League, Division 3 (South)	BRENTFORD	1-3 L		6,775
19		Sat	13	FA Cup, 2nd Round	LUTON TOWN	3-1 W		17,770
20		Wed	17	Football League, Division 3 (South)	Crystal Palace		L 1-6	5,137
21		Sat	20	Football League, Division 3 (South)	SOUTHEND UNITED	1-3 L		5,750
22		Thu	25	Football League, Division 3 (South)	Walsall		D 2-2	6,842
23		Fri	26	Football League, Division 3 (South)	WALSALL	2-2 D		6,351
24		Sat	27	Football League, Division 3 (South)	FULHAM	2-2 D		7,248
25	January	Sat	3	Football League, Division 3 (South)	Swindon Town		L 1-2	3,958
26		Sat	10	FA Cup, 3rd Round	Oldham Athletic		W 3-1	7,080
27		Thu	15	Football League, Division 3 (South)	Northampton Town		W 3-2	3,902
28		Sat	17	Football League, Division 3 (South)	BOURNEMOUTH & BOSCOMBE ATHLETIC	2-0 W		6,790
29		Sat	24	FA Cup, 4th Round	BRIGHTON & HOVE ALBION	2-0 W		22,740
30		Wed	28	Football League, Division 3 (South)	Luton Town		L 1-4	3,603
31		Sat	31	Football League, Division 3 (South)	Notts County		L 0-1	11,705
32	February	Sat	7	Football League, Division 3 (South)	CLAPTON ORIENT	1-2 L		6,378
33		Sat	14	FA Cup, 5th Round	Birmingham		L 0-3	49,757
34		Mon	16	Football League, Division 3 (South)	Thames		L 2-3	853
35		Sat	21	Football League, Division 3 (South)	BRISTOL ROVERS	2-2 D		6,185
36		Sat	28	Football League, Division 3 (South)	Newport County		W 2-0	2,310
37	March	Sat	7	Football League, Division 3 (South)	GILLINGHAM	1-0 W		3,665
38		Sat	14	Football League, Division 3 (South)	Exeter City		L 1-2	5,211
39		Sat	21	Football League, Division 3 (South)	BRIGHTON & HOVE ALBION	5-0 W		5,441
40		Sat	28	Football League, Division 3 (South)	Torquay United		L 1-3	3,547
41	April	Fri	3	Football League, Division 3 (South)	COVENTRY CITY	4-1 W		5,541
42		Sat	4	Football League, Division 3 (South)	NORTHAMPTON TOWN	1-2 L		8,157
43		Tue	7	Football League, Division 3 (South)	Coventry City		D 2-2	7,565
44		Sat	11	Football League, Division 3 (South)	Brentford		L 1-2	8,163
45		Sat	18	Football League, Division 3 (South)	CRYSTAL PALACE	0-2 L		5,377
46		Sat	25	Football League, Division 3 (South)	Southend United		L 0-1	3,459
47	May	Sat	2	Football League, Division 3 (South)	Norwich City		W 1-0	5,394

League ever-presents: None
Most appearances in total: T.A. Barnett 43 out of 47   **Most goals in total:** G.C. James 31
Hat-tricks: G.C. James (Match 4, Match 11 & Match 17), R.N. White (Match 12), T.A. Barnett (4 goals, Match 16)   **Penalty goals:** J. Davison 1, N. McBain 1
Sent off: None   **Full international appearance(s) this season:** None
(In Match 45, one of the opponents' goals was conceded after J. Davison had replaced the injured T. Holland as goalkeeper.)

Summary totals (two competitions). The player columns run: Barnett T.A., Blake A.G., Brown W., Chapman W., Clement A.E., Davies W., Davison J., Gay J.M., Hewitt J.T., Holland P.B., Holland T., James G.C., Lewis D.J., Lindsay T., Lowe H.P., McBain N., McWilliams R., Miller P.S., Pick W.E., Reynolds J.W., Smith F.W., Smith G., Smith J.K., Tracey C., Walker A., White R.N., Wilson W., Woodward A., Woolliscroft A.

	Bar	Bla	Bro	Cha	Cle	Dav W	Dav J	Gay	Hew	Hol P	Hol T	Jam	Lew	Lin	Low	McB	McW	Mil	Pic	Rey	Sm F	Sm G	Sm J	Tra	Wal	Whi	Wil	Woo	Wls
Apps	38	20	31	36	14	1	33	4	12	4	30	29	1	7	10	25	10	14	23	6	34	1	1	3	2	11	1	38	23
Subs																													
Goals	19			1			2				1	24			2	1		1	5					1		9		4	2
Apps	5	1	5	4			4	1	2		3	5		2	1	5		2	3		5					4		4	3
Subs																													
Goals	2											7	1					1											2

Match-by-match appearances (X = appearance, number = goals scored, G = goalkeeper, p = penalty):

Match	Bar	Bla	Bro	Cha	Cle	Dav W	Dav J	Gay	Hew	Hol P	Hol T	Jam	Lew	Lin	Low	McB	McW	Mil	Pic	Rey	Sm F	Sm G	Sm J	Tra	Wal	Whi	Wil	Woo	Wls
1	X		X	X			X				G	X2				X	X				X							X	X
2	X1		X	X			X				G	X1				X	X				X							X	X
3	X1	X		X			X			X	G	X1				X	X				X								X1
4	X			X			X			X	G	X3				X	X				X							X	X
5	X			X			X			X1	G				X	X	X				X							X	X
6	X		X				X			X	G				X	X	X				X							X	X
7	X			X	X		X				G	X1				X	X			X								X	X
8	X			X	X		X				G	X				X	X				X							X	X
9	X	X		X	X		X				G	X					X				X							X	X
10	X1			X	X		X				G	X				X		X						X				X	
11	X2			X	X		X	G				X3				X		X						X				X	
12	X		X1	X			X1p	G						X		X					X					X3		X1	X
13	X			X	X		X	G				X2		X		X					X							X	X
14	X			X	X		X	G				X		X		X					X							X	X
15	X		X		X		X		G			X		X		X					X							X	X
16	X4		X		X		X		G			X1		X		X					X							X	X1
17	X		X	X			X		G			X3	X1			X					X							X	X1
18	X		X	X			X		G			X1	X			X					X							X	X
19	X1		X	X			X		G			X1	X			X					X							X	X1
20	X		X	X			X		G			X1	X			X					X							X	X
21	X		X	X			X		G			X1				X			X		X							X	X
22	X		X	X				X	G			X						X	X2		X				X			X	
23	X1		X	X				X	G			X						X	X		X				X			X1	
24			X	X			X		G					X	X1p	X1		X1	X		X				X			X	
25	X		X	X			X		G			X1				X		X	X		X							X	
26	X1	X	X	X			X		G			X1				X		X1	X		X							X	
27		X	X	X	X						G	X2			X1	X		X	X		X							X	
28	X	X	X	X			X				G	X1				X		X			X				X1			X	
29	X		X				X				G	X2			X	X		X	X		X							X	
30	X1	X	X		X						G	X			X	X		X	X									X	
31		X	X								G	X			X	X	X	X	X		X							X	
32	X		X	X			X	G				X1				X			X		X							X	
33	X		X	X			X				G	X				X			X		X							X	X
34	X1	X	X	X							G	X1	X			X			X		X							X	X
35	X	X	X	X							G	X1				X			X		X							X1	X
36	X2	X	X	X							G	X				X			X		X							X	X
37	X	X	X	X							G	X				X				X1	X							X	X
38	X	X	X	X							G				X	X			X		X					X1		X	
39	X1	X	X	X							G				X	X			X	X1	X					X2	X1		
40	X1	X	X	X							G				X	X			X		X					X		X	
41	X1	X	X	X			X1				G				X1	X			X		X					X1		X	
42	X	X	X	X							G					X		X	X		X					X1		X	
43	X1	X	X	X							G					X		X	X1		X					X		X	
44	X1	X	X	X	X						G					X		X	X		X					X		X	
45	X	X	X	X							G					X			X		X					X		X	X
46	X	X	X	X			X									X			X		X					X		X	X
47		X	X	X		X		G											X		X	X	X			X1	X		

- 85 -

1931/32

Football League position: 11th out of 22 in Division 3 (South)
Manager: Neil McBain

New league opponents: Mansfield Town

Home-and-away league doubles
For – 4 (Gillingham, Luton Town, Thames, Torquay United)
Against – 1 (Crystal Palace)

Divisional changes at end of season: Fulham to Division 2; Mansfield Town to Division 3 (North); Thames did not seek re-election; Bristol City from Division 2; Aldershot and Newport County elected

All Matches: Won 24, Drew 10, Lost 16, Goals 97-91

Highest Score: 6 (Match 3)

No	DATE			COMPETITION	OPPONENTS	HOME	AWAY	ATTENDANCE
1	August	Sat	29	Football League, Division 3 (South)	CLAPTON ORIENT	2-1 W		10,430
2	September	Wed	2	Football League, Division 3 (South)	Swindon Town		L 1-4	5,534
3		Sat	5	Football League, Division 3 (South)	Torquay United		W 6-3	4,559
4		Mon	7	Football League, Division 3 (South)	Mansfield Town		L 2-3	8,662
5		Sat	12	Football League, Division 3 (South)	BRISTOL ROVERS	5-2 W		4,797
6		Wed	16	Football League, Division 3 (South)	MANSFIELD TOWN	4-1 W		7,309
7		Sat	19	Football League, Division 3 (South)	Queens Park Rangers		D 4-4	16,497
8		Sat	26	Football League, Division 3 (South)	BOURNEMOUTH & BOSCOMBE ATHLETIC	4-2 W		11,008
9	October	Sat	3	Football League, Division 3 (South)	Crystal Palace		L 1-2	20,953
10		Sat	10	Football League, Division 3 (South)	GILLINGHAM	2-0 W		10,079
11		Sat	17	Football League, Division 3 (South)	Luton Town		W 1-0	14,765
12		Sat	24	Football League, Division 3 (South)	CARDIFF CITY	3-0 W		11,526
13		Sat	31	Football League, Division 3 (South)	Northampton Town		D 1-1	5,927
14	November	Sat	7	Football League, Division 3 (South)	READING	3-2 W		11,007
15		Sat	14	Football League, Division 3 (South)	Southend United		L 0-3	10,692
16		Sat	21	Football League, Division 3 (South)	FULHAM	3-1 W		14,133
17		Sat	28	FA Cup, 1st Round	Thames		D 2-2	4,460
18	December	Wed	2	FA Cup, 1st Round replay	THAMES (after extra time)	2-1 W		5,569
19		Sat	5	Football League, Division 3 (South)	Brentford		1-4 L	12,086
20		Sat	12	FA Cup, 2nd Round	Gainsborough Trinity		W 5-2	4,545
21		Wed	16	Football League, Division 3 (South)	Exeter City		L 0-2	2,470
22		Sat	19	Football League, Division 3 (South)	COVENTRY CITY	2-0 W		7,559
23		Fri	25	Football League, Division 3 (South)	NORWICH CITY	1-1 D		10,002
24		Sat	26	Football League, Division 3 (South)	Norwich City		L 1-4	17,164
25	January	Sat	2	Football League, Division 3 (South)	Clapton Orient		D 2-2	4,701
26		Sat	9	FA Cup, 3rd Round	FULHAM	1-1 D		15,978
27		Thu	14	FA Cup, 3rd Round replay	Fulham		W 3-0	23,113
28		Sat	16	Football League, Division 3 (South)	TORQUAY UNITED	1-0 W		9,335
29		Mon	18	Football League, Division 3 (South)	Thames		W 2-1	1,031
30		Sat	23	FA Cup, 4th Round	BRISTOL CITY	2-1 W		19,369
31		Wed	27	Football League, Division 3 (South)	Bristol Rovers		L 2-3	3,852
32		Sat	30	Football League, Division 3 (South)	QUEENS PARK RANGERS	2-2 D		12,286
33	February	Sat	6	Football League, Division 3 (South)	Bournemouth & Boscombe Athletic		D 3-3	5,083
34		Sat	13	FA Cup, 5th Round	BRADFORD	1-0 W		23,457
35		Wed	17	Football League, Division 3 (South)	CRYSTAL PALACE	1-2 L		4,584
36		Sat	20	Football League, Division 3 (South)	Gillingham		W 1-0	5,712
37		Sat	27	FA Cup, 6th Round	Newcastle United		L 0-5	57,879
38	March	Sat	5	Football League, Division 3 (South)	Cardiff City		L 1-2	10,019
39		Sat	12	Football League, Division 3 (South)	NORTHAMPTON TOWN	1-2 L		7,600
40		Sat	19	Football League, Division 3 (South)	Reading		L 1-2	11,266
41		Fri	25	Football League, Division 3 (South)	Brighton & Hove Albion		L 1-2	10,528
42		Sat	26	Football League, Division 3 (South)	SOUTHEND UNITED	1-1 D		8,409
43		Mon	28	Football League, Division 3 (South)	BRIGHTON & HOVE ALBION	2-2 D		7,012
44	April	Sat	2	Football League, Division 3 (South)	Fulham		L 0-5	22,592
45		Sat	9	Football League, Division 3 (South)	THAMES	3-2 W		2,765
46		Wed	13	Football League, Division 3 (South)	LUTON TOWN	3-1 W		4,635
47		Sat	16	Football League, Division 3 (South)	Brentford		W 2-1	6,723
48		Sat	23	Football League, Division 3 (South)	EXETER CITY	1-0 W		4,604
49		Sat	30	Football League, Division 3 (South)	Coventry City		L 0-5	12,799
50	May	Sat	7	Football League, Division 3 (South)	SWINDON TOWN	4-1 W		4,645

League ever-presents: W. Brown, H.P. Lowe
Most appearances in total: W. Brown & H.P. Lowe 50 out of 50   **Most goals in total:** G.C. James 26
Hat-tricks: G.C. James (Match 3 & Match 5), T.A. Barnett (Match 8)   **Penalty goals:** M.T. O'Brien 3
Sent off: None
Full international appearance(s) this season: M.T. O'Brien (Republic of Ireland)

	Barnes, J.B.	Barnett, T.A.	Brown, W.	Chapman, W.	Davison, J. //	Ellis, F.C. //	Holland, T. //	James, G.C.	Le May, F.J.S. //	Lewis, D.J.	Lowe, H.P.	O'Brien, M.T. //	Pick, W.E. //	Richards, D.	Rutherford, J.	Stokes, A.	Thurley, A. //	Trotter, J.	White, R.N. //	Woodward, A.	Woolliscroft, A.	Own goal
Apps	39	41	42	38	8	30	32	31	4	6	42	34	3	28	10	34	4	2	9	24	1	
Subs																						
Goals	5	16		4		1		25			17	2					1	7	1	1	1	
Apps	7	8	8	8		7	8	4			8	8	1	8		4			4	5		
Subs																						
Goals		3						1			6	1							4	1		

#	Barnes	Barnett	Brown	Chapman	Davison	Ellis	Holland	James	Le May	Lewis	Lowe	O'Brien	Pick	Richards	Rutherford	Stokes	Thurley	Trotter	White	Woodward	Woolliscroft	Own goal
1		X1	X	X		X	G				X	X	X	X		X			X1			
2		X	X	X		X	G				X	X	X	X		X			X1			
3	X	X1	X	X	X	X	G	X3			X2	X				X						
4	X	X	X	X	X	X	G	X2			X	X				X						
5	X1	X1	X	X	X	X	G	X3			X	X				X						
6		X1	X	X	X	X	G	X2			X1	X	X			X						
7	X	X1	X	X1	X	X	G	X			X2	X				X						
8	X	X3	X	X	X	X	G	X1			X	X				X						
9	X	X	X	X	X	X	G	X			X1	X				X						
10	X1	X	X	X	X	X	G	X1			X	X				X						
11	X	X	X	X		X	G	X1			X	X		X		X						
12	X	X	X	X		X1	G	X1			X1	X		X		X						
13	X	X	X	X1		X	G	X			X	X		X		X						
14	X1	X	X	X		X	G				X1	X		X		X			X1			
15	X	X	X	X		X	G				X	X		X		X						
16	X	X	X	X		X	G				X1	X		X		X			X2			
17	X	X	X	X		X	G				X	X		X		X			X2			
18		X1	X	X		X	G				X1	X	X	X		X			X			
19	X	X1	X	X		X	G				X	X		X		X			X			
20	X	X1	X	X		X	G				X2	X		X		X			X2			
21	X	X	X	X		X	G				X	X		X		X			X			
22	X	X	X	X			G				X	X		X		X	X1		X1			
23	X	X	X	X			G				X	X1p		X		X	X		X			
24	X	X1	X	X							X	X		X	G	X			X	X		
25	X	X	X						X		X	X		X	G	X			X2	X		
26	X	X	X	X			G				X	X		X		X			X	X1		
27	X	X	X	X		X	G	X			X2	X1p				X				X		
28	X	X	X	X		X	G	X1			X	X				X				X		
29	X	X	X				G	X1	X		X	X1p				X				X		
30	X	X1	X	X		X	G	X			X1	X				X				X		
31	X	X1	X	X		X	G	X1			X	X				X				X		
32	X	X1	X	X		X	G	X1			X	X				X				X		
33	X	X1	X	X		X	G	X1			X	X				X				X		1
34	X	X	X	X		X	G	X1			X	X				X				X		
35	X	X1	X	X		X	G	X			X	X				X				X		
36	X1	X	X	X		X	G	X1			X	X				X				X		
37	X	X	X	X		X	G	X			X	X				X				X		
38	X	X1	X			X	G	X	X		X	X				X				X		
39	X	X	X					X	X		X1	X			G	X				X		
40	X	X1	X	X						X	X	X			G	X				X		
41	X	X	X	X						X	X				G	X	X			X		
42	X	X	X	X						X	X1				G	X	X			X		
43	X	X	X	X						X	X2				G	X	X			X		
44	X	X	X	X						X	X				G	X	X			X		
45	X	X	X	X1		X				X	X1				G	X				X		
46	X	X	X	X1		X	G	X1			X1			X		X				X		
47	X	X	X	X		X	G	X1			X1			X		X				X		
48	X	X	X	X			G	X1			X	X		X		X				X		
49	X	X	X	X			G	X			X	X		X		X				X		
50	X1		X	X				X1			X1			X	G	X				X	X1	

1932/33

Football League position: 11th out of 22 in Division 3 (South)
Manager: Neil McBain

	HOME					AWAY					
	Pl	W	D	L	For	Ag	W	D	L	For	Ag	Pts
Brentford	42	15	4	2	45	19	11	6	4	45	30	62
Exeter City	42	17	2	2	57	13	7	8	6	31	35	58
Norwich City	42	16	3	2	49	17	6	10	5	39	38	57
Reading	42	14	5	2	68	30	5	8	8	35	41	51
Crystal Palace	42	14	4	3	51	21	5	4	12	27	43	46
Coventry City	42	16	1	4	75	24	3	5	13	31	53	44
Gillingham	42	14	4	3	54	24	4	4	13	18	37	44
Northampton Town	42	16	5	0	54	11	2	3	16	22	55	44
Bristol Rovers	42	13	5	3	38	22	2	9	10	23	34	44
Torquay United	42	12	7	2	51	26	4	5	12	21	41	44
WATFORD	42	11	8	2	37	22	5	4	12	29	41	44
Brighton & Hove Albion	42	13	3	5	42	20	4	5	12	24	45	42
Southend United	42	11	5	5	39	27	4	6	11	26	55	41
Luton Town	42	12	8	1	60	32	1	5	15	18	46	39
Bristol City	42	11	5	5	59	37	1	8	12	24	53	37
Queens Park Rangers	42	9	8	4	48	32	4	3	14	24	55	37
Aldershot	42	11	6	4	37	21	2	4	15	24	51	36
Bournemouth & Boscombe Ath	42	10	7	4	44	27	2	5	14	16	54	36
Cardiff City	42	12	4	5	48	30	0	3	18	21	69	31
Clapton Orient	42	7	8	6	39	35	1	5	15	20	58	29
Newport County	42	9	4	8	42	42	2	3	16	19	63	29
Swindon Town	42	7	9	5	36	29	2	2	17	24	76	29

New league opponents: Aldershot

Home-and-away league doubles
For – 3 (Bristol City, Coventry City, Crystal Palace)
Against – 1 (Brighton & Hove Albion)

Divisional changes at end of season: Brentford to Division 2; Charlton Athletic from Division 2

All Matches: Won 16, Drew 13, Lost 15, Goals 67-66

Highest Score: 4 (Matches 11 & 16)

No	DATE			COMPETITION	OPPONENTS	HOME	AWAY	ATTENDANCE
1	August	Sat	27	Football League, Division 3 (South)	Norwich City		W 2-1	13,477
2		Wed	31	Football League, Division 3 (South)	READING	1-1 D		10,109
3	September	Sat	3	Football League, Division 3 (South)	BRIGHTON & HOVE ALBION	0-4 L		7,995
4		Wed	7	Football League, Division 3 (South)	Reading		L 0-2	11,220
5		Sat	10	Football League, Division 3 (South)	Bristol Rovers		L 0-2	7,961
6		Sat	17	Football League, Division 3 (South)	ALDERSHOT	2-0 W		8,572
7		Sat	24	Football League, Division 3 (South)	Queens Park Rangers		L 1-2	10,653
8	October	Sat	1	Football League, Division 3 (South)	SOUTHEND UNITED	2-2 D		6,019
9		Sat	8	Football League, Division 3 (South)	Crystal Palace		W 3-0	12,095
10		Sat	15	Football League, Division 3 (South)	GILLINGHAM	2-0 W		8,128
11		Sat	22	Football League, Division 3 (South)	LUTON TOWN	4-1 W		12,130
12		Sat	29	Football League, Division 3 (South)	Exeter City		L 2-5	5,171
13	November	Sat	5	Football League, Division 3 (South)	TORQUAY UNITED	0-0 D		7,910
14		Sat	12	Football League, Division 3 (South)	Brentford		L 1-2	14,661
15		Sat	19	Football League, Division 3 (South)	COVENTRY CITY	3-1 W		6,208
16	December	Sat	3	Football League, Division 3 (South)	NORTHAMPTON TOWN	4-0 W		7,571
17		Sat	10	Football League, Division 3 (South)	Clapton Orient		L 0-2	4,562
18		Sat	17	Football League, Division 3 (South)	SWINDON TOWN	2-2 D		6,794
19		Sat	24	Football League, Division 3 (South)	Bournemouth & Boscombe Athletic		D 2-2	4,078
20		Mon	26	Football League, Division 3 (South)	Newport County		L 0-2	5,044
21		Tue	27	Football League, Division 3 (South)	NEWPORT COUNTY	3-2 W		9,131
22		Sat	31	Football League, Division 3 (South)	NORWICH CITY	1-2 L		6,975
23	January	Sat	7	Football League, Division 3 (South)	Brighton & Hove Albion		L 0-3	6,516
24		Sat	14	FA Cup, 3rd Round	SOUTHEND UNITED	1-1 D		11,403
25		Wed	18	FA Cup, 3rd Round replay	Southend United		L 0-2	8,036
26		Sat	21	Football League, Division 3 (South)	BRISTOL ROVERS	3-1 W		4,202
27		Wed	25	Football League, Division 3 (South)	Bristol City		W 3-2	2,402
28	February	Wed	1	Football League, Division 3 (South)	Aldershot		L 1-2	2,049
29		Sat	4	Football League, Division 3 (South)	QUEENS PARK RANGERS	2-2 D		6,055
30		Sat	11	Football League, Division 3 (South)	Southend United		L 1-2	5,048
31		Sat	18	Football League, Division 3 (South)	CRYSTAL PALACE	1-0 W		5,425
32		Sat	25	Football League, Division 3 (South)	Gillingham		D 3-3	4,208
33	March	Sat	11	Football League, Division 3 (South)	EXETER CITY	0-0 D		7,368
34		Sat	18	Football League, Division 3 (South)	Torquay United		L 2-3	3,241
35		Sat	25	Football League, Division 3 (South)	BRENTFORD	1-1 D		10,057
36	April	Sat	1	Football League, Division 3 (South)	Coventry City		W 3-1	11,333
37		Sat	8	Football League, Division 3 (South)	BRISTOL CITY	1-0 W		5,791
38		Fri	14	Football League, Division 3 (South)	Cardiff City		D 1-1	9,451
39		Sat	15	Football League, Division 3 (South)	Northampton Town		0-0 D	6,197
40		Mon	17	Football League, Division 3 (South)	CARDIFF CITY	2-1 W		7,713
41		Sat	22	Football League, Division 3 (South)	CLAPTON ORIENT	1-1 D		5,156
42		Wed	26	Football League, Division 3 (South)	Luton Town		L 2-3	4,140
43		Sat	29	Football League, Division 3 (South)	Swindon Town		W 2-1	2,955
44	May	Sat	6	Football League, Division 3 (South)	BOURNEMOUTH & BOSCOMBE ATHLETIC	2-1 W		3,938

League ever-presents: None
Most appearances in total: W. Findlay & A. Woodward 43 out of 44   **Most goals in total:** W.H.C. Lane 22
Hat-tricks: W.H.C. Lane (Match 32)   **Penalty goals:** M.T. O'Brien 3
Sent off: None
Full international appearance(s) this season: None

	Barnes, J.B.	Barnett, T.A.	Blake, A.G.	Brown, W.	Carter, J.H.	Chapman, W.	Davies, W.	Findlay, W.	Hufton, A.E.	Inglis, W.J.	Ison, E.	James, G.C.	Lane, W.H.C.	Lewis, D.J.	Lowe, H.P.	Moran, J.	O'Brien, M.T.	Richards, D.	Rutherford, J.	Slater, T.A.	Stokes, A.	Trotter, J.	Weeks, G.B.	Woodward, A.	Woolliscroft, A.	Own goal
Apps	36	26	1	38	3	39	6	41	2	12	3	10	36	3	27	35	27	7	21	19	4	2	1	41	22	
Subs																										
Goals	6	7			1	1	2				1	5	22		9		3							8	1	
Apps	1			2		2	1	2				2	2		1	2	2		1	1				2	1	
Subs																										
Goals												1														
1		X		X		X		X			X1		X		X		X		G				X	X		1
2		X		X		X		X		X			X1		X		X	X	G					X		
3		X		X		X		X		X			X				X	X	G					X	X	
4	X			X		X		X		X			X			X			G		X			X	X	
5	X			X		X		X		X			X			X			G		X			X	X	
6	X			X		X		X				X1	X1		X		X		G					X	X	
7	X			X		X		X				X	X		X1	X	X		G					X		
8	X			X		X		X					X1		X	X	X		G					X	X1	
9	X			X		X		X					X2		X	X	X1p		G					X	X	
10	X			X		X		X					X		X2	X	X		G					X	X	
11	X			X		X		X					X2		X1	X	X		G					X	X1	
12	X			X		X		X					X		X1	X	X		G					X	X1	
13	X			X		X		X	G				X		X	X	X							X	X	
14	X			X		X		X	G				X		X	X	X							X	X1	
15	X1			X		X		X					X		X	X	X1p		G					X	X	
16		X1		X	X1	X					X1		X1		X		X		G					X		
17		X		X		X	X	X					X		X		X		G					X	X	
18		X		X		X		X					X1		X		X		G					X	X1	
19	X			X			X1	X				X	X	X	X1				G					X		
20	X			X			X	X				X	X	X	X				G					X		
21	X			X			X	X				X2	X1	X	X				G					X		
22	X	X		X		X		X				X1			X		X	X	G					X		
23	X	X		X		X		X				X			X	X	X		G					X		
24				X		X	X	X				X1	X		X		X		G					X	X	
25	X			X		X		X				X	X		X	X	X			G				X		
26	X1			X		X		X				X	X			X	X1p			G				X	X1	
27	X	X		X		X		X					X1		X	X				G				X	X2	
28	X	X		X		X		X					X1		X	X				G				X	X	
29	X	X1				X		X					X1		X	X	X			G				X	X	
30	X	X1				X		X					X		X	X	X			G				X	X	
31	X	X				X		X					X1		X	X	X			G				X	X	
32	X	X				X		X					X3		X		X			G	X			X	X	
33	X	X	X			X		X					X		X					G	X			X		
34	X	X1	X		X1	X		X				X			X	X				G	X			X		
35	X1	X		X		X		X		X			X		X	X				G				X		
36	X1	X		X		X				X			X1		X1	X				G	X			X		
37	X	X		X		X	X			X			X1		X	X				G				X		
38	X	X		X	X1	X		X		X					X	X				G				X		
39	X	X		X	X	X		X		X					X	X				G				X		
40	X1	X		X	X	X		X		X					X1	X				G				X		
41	X1	X		X		X		X		X			X		X	X				G				X		
42	X	X1		X		X		X		X			X1		X	X				G				X		
43	X	X1		X		X		X		X			X1		X	X				G				X		
44	X	X1	X	X		X		X		X			X		X1	X				G						

1933/34

Football League position: 15th out of 22 in Division 3 (South)

Manager: Neil McBain

New league opponents: None

Home-and-away league doubles
For – 3 (Clapton Orient, Newport County, Torquay United)
Against – 5 (Bournemouth & Boscombe Athletic, Cardiff City, Charlton Athletic, Luton Town, Norwich City)

Divisional changes at end of season: Norwich City to Division 2; Millwall from Division 2

All Matches: Won 15, Drew 7, Lost 22, Goals 73-70

Highest Score: 6 (Match 19)

		HOME					AWAY					
	Pl	W	D	L	For	Ag	W	D	L	For	Ag	Pts
Norwich City	42	16	4	1	55	19	9	7	5	33	30	61
Coventry City	42	16	3	2	70	22	5	9	7	30	32	54
Reading	42	17	4	0	60	13	4	8	9	22	37	54
Queens Park Rangers	42	17	2	2	42	17	4		10	28	39	54
Charlton Athletic	42	14	5	2	53	27	8	3	10	30	29	52
Luton Town	42	14	3	4	55	28	7	7	7	28	33	52
Bristol Rovers	42	14	4	3	49	21	6	7	8	28	26	51
Swindon Town	42	13	5	3	42	25	4	6	11	22	43	45
Exeter City	42	12	5	4	43	19	4	6	11	25	38	43
Brighton & Hove Albion	42	12	7	2	47	18	3	6	12	21	42	43
Clapton Orient	42	14	4	3	60	25	2	6	13	15	44	42
Crystal Palace	42	11	6	4	40	25	5	3	13	31	42	41
Northampton Town	42	10	6	5	45	32	4	6	11	26	46	40
Aldershot	42	8	6	7	28	27	6	6	10	24	44	38
WATFORD	42	12	4	5	43	16	3	3	15	28	47	37
Southend United	42	9	6	6	32	27	3	4	14	19	47	34
Gillingham	42	8	8	5	49	41	3	3	15	26	55	33
Newport County	42	6	6	9	25	23	2	8	11	24	47	33
Bristol City	42	7	8	6	33	22	3	5	13	25	63	33
Torquay United	42	10	4	7	32	28	3	3	15	21	65	33
Bournemouth & Boscombe Ath	42	7	7	7	41	37	2	2	17	19	65	27
Cardiff City	42	6	4	11	32	43	3	2	16	25	62	24

No	DATE			COMPETITION	OPPONENTS	HOME	AWAY	ATTENDANCE	
1	August	Sat	26	Football League, Division 3 (South)	CARDIFF CITY	1-2 L		11,561	
2		Wed	30	Football League, Division 3 (South)	Bournemouth & Boscombe Athletic		L 2-3		6,772
3	September	Sat	2	Football League, Division 3 (South)	Exeter City		L 1-3		6,943
4		Wed	6	Football League, Division 3 (South)	BOURNEMOUTH & BOSCOMBE ATHLETIC	1-2 L		5,913	
5		Sat	9	Football League, Division 3 (South)	GILLINGHAM	2-1 W		8,267	
6		Sat	16	Football League, Division 3 (South)	Crystal Palace		L 3-4		14,542
7		Sat	23	Football League, Division 3 (South)	BRISTOL ROVERS	0-0 D		6,725	
8		Sat	30	Football League, Division 3 (South)	Southend United		D 1-1		6,799
9	October	Sat	7	Football League, Division 3 (South)	COVENTRY CITY	3-3 D		8,847	
10		Sat	14	Football League, Division 3 (South)	Reading		L 1-6		9,000
11		Sat	21	Football League, Division 3 (South)	Luton Town		L 1-2		10.674
12		Sat	28	Football League, Division 3 (South)	NORTHAMPTON TOWN	2-0 W		7,027	
13	November	Sat	4	Football League, Division 3 (South)	Torquay United		W 3-1		3.078
14		Sat	11	Football League, Division 3 (South)	QUEENS PARK RANGERS	0-0 D		14,299	
15		Sat	18	Football League, Division 3 (South)	Newport County		W 3-0		5,301
16		Sat	25	FA Cup, 1st Round	READING	0-3 L		14,892	
17	December	Sat	2	Football League, Division 3 (South)	Bristol City		L 0-1		7,744
18		Sat	16	Football League, Division 3 (South)	Swindon Town		L 0-1		6,603
19		Wed	20	Football League, Division 3 (South)	CLAPTON ORIENT	6-0 W		1,309	
20		Sat	23	Football League, Division 3 (South)	BRIGHTON & HOVE ALBION	2-0 W		5,346	
21		Mon	25	Football League, Division 3 (South)	CHARLTON ATHLETIC	0-1 L		9,400	
22		Tue	26	Football League, Division 3 (South)	Charlton Athletic		L 3-4		11,719
23		Sat	30	Football League, Division 3 (South)	Cardiff City		L 1-4		6,010
24	January	Sat	6	Football League, Division 3 (South)	EXETER CITY	2-0 W		5,122	
25		Sat	13	Football League, Division 3 (South)	NORWICH CITY	1-3 L		7,209	
26		Sat	20	Football League, Division 3 (South)	Gillingham		D 3-3		4,614
27		Wed	31	Football League, Division 3 (South)	CRYSTAL PALACE	3-1 W		2,391	
28	February	Sat	3	Football League, Division 3 (South)	Bristol Rovers		L 0-1		9,362
29		Sat	10	Football League, Division 3 (South)	SOUTHEND UNITED	2-1 W		5,984	
30		Sat	17	Football League, Division 3 (South)	Coventry City		L 0-2		13,614
31		Wed	21	Division 3 (South) Cup, 2nd Round	Exeter City		L 2-4		3,000
32		Sat	24	Football League, Division 3 (South)	READING	2-0 W		5,600	
33	March	Sat	3	Football League, Division 3 (South)	LUTON TOWN	0-1 L		10,204	
34		Sat	10	Football League, Division 3 (South)	Northampton Town		L 0-1		4,756
35		Sat	17	Football League, Division 3 (South)	TORQUAY UNITED	5-0 W		4,380	
36		Sat	24	Football League, Division 3 (South)	Queens Park Rangers		D 0-0		8,205
37		Fri	30	Football League, Division 3 (South)	Aldershot		L 2-3		5,756
38		Sat	31	Football League, Division 3 (South)	NEWPORT COUNTY	3-0 W		5,675	
39	April	Mon	2	Football League, Division 3 (South)	ALDERSHOT	3-0 W		6,653	
40		Sat	7	Football League, Division 3 (South)	Norwich City		L 1-3		12,095
41		Sat	14	Football League, Division 3 (South)	BRISTOL CITY	1-1 D		3,549	
42		Sat	21	Football League, Division 3 (South)	Clapton Orient		W 3-2		10,073
43		Sat	28	Football League, Division 3 (South)	SWINDON TOWN	4-0 W		3,179	
44	May	Sat	5	Football League, Division 3 (South)	Brighton & Hove Albion		L 0-2		4,692

League ever-presents: None   **Most apperances in total:** A. Woodward 43 out of 44   **Most goals in total:** T.A. Barnett 17
Hat-tricks: W.H.C. Lane (Match 19)   **Penalty goals:** W. Davies 1, H.P. Lowe 1
Sent off: None   **Full international appearance(s) this season:** None
(In Match 9, one of the opponents' goals was conceded after A. Woodward had replaced the injured T.A. Slater as goalkeeper. In identical circumstances in Match 10, Woodward conceded four goals.)

Player key (columns, left to right): Armstrong, J.H. | Barnett, T.A. | Brown, W. | Carter, J.H. | Chapman, W. | Davies, T. | Davies, W. | Devan, W.G. | Elkes, A.J. | Ewington, C. | Findlay, W. | Haywood, N.S.C. | Irvine, R. | Lane, W.H.C. | Lewis, D.J. | Lowe, H.P. | McHugh, J. | McLaren, J. | McPherson, F.C. | Moran, J. | Ritchie, A.W. | Scott, H. | Searle, F.B. | Slater, T.A. | Woodward, A. | Own goals

	Arm	Bar	Bro	Car	Cha	DaT	DaW	Dev	Elk	Ewi	Fin	Hay	Irv	Lan	Lew	Low	McH	McL	McP	Mor	Rit	Sco	Sea	Sla	Woo	OG
Apps	33	41	27	10	24	5	23	10	9	3	37	1	22	36	23	11	2	30	11	31	17	1	4	10	41	
Subs																										
Goals		17		4	1		11	1	1		2		2	13		5			4		3				5	2
Apps	2	1	1		2	1	1	1		1		1	1	1	1		2		2			1		2		
Subs																										
Goals													1												1	

#	Arm	Bar	Bro	Car	Cha	DaT	DaW	Dev	Elk	Ewi	Fin	Hay	Irv	Lan	Lew	Low	McH	McL	McP	Mor	Rit	Sco	Sea	Sla	Woo	OG
1		X1	X						X		X			X					X	X	X	X		G	X	
2		X	X						X1		X		X	X1					X	X	X			G	X	
3		X	X						X		X		X	X					X1	X	X			G	X	
4		X	X						X		X		X	X					X1	X	X			G	X	
5		X	X	X1					X		X		X	X					X	X				G	X1	
6		X1	X	X					X		X		X	X2					X	X				G	X	
7		X	X	X			X		X		X		X							X				G	X	
8		X1	X	X			X		X		X		X	X						X				G	X	
9		X2	X	X			X		X		X		X	X1						X				G	X	
10	X	X1	X				X	X			X		X	X						X				G	X	
11	X	X	X		X						X		X1	X			G			X	X				X	
12	X	X	X	X	X		X				X							G		X			X		X2	
13	X	X2	X	X	X		X				X							G		X			X		X1	
14	X	X	X	X	X		X				X							G		X			X		X	
15	X	X1		X		X					X			X1				G		X	X1		X			
16	X	X	X		X		X				X							G		X			X		X	
17	X	X			X						X		X	X	X			G		X	X				X	
18	X	X		X	X	X	X							X	X			G		X					X	
19	X	X2		X1	X						X			X3	X			G		X	X				X	
20	X	X1		X1	X						X			X	X			G		X	X				X	
21	X	X		X	X						X			X	X			G		X	X				X	
22	X	X		X	X		X				X			X2	X			G		X					X	1
23	X	X		X	X		X1p				X			X	X			G		X					X	
24	X	X		X1	X		X1				X			X	X			G		X					X	
25	X	X		X1	X		X				X			X	X			G		X					X	
26	X	X			X		X2				X		X1	X	X			G		X					X	
27	X	X1			X		X				X		X	X1	X			G		X					X1	
28	X	X			X		X				X		X	X	X			G		X					X	
29	X	X1			X		X1				X		X	X	X			G		X					X	
30	X	X			X		X				X		X	X	X			G		X					X	
31	X				X		X				X		X1	X	X	X		G		X					X1	
32	X	X	X				X				X1		X	X1				G		X	X				X	
33	X	X	X				X						X	X				G		X	X				X	
34	X		X	X			X							X	X	X		G			X				X	
35	X	X2	X		X		X				X1			X	X	X1		G							X	1
36	X	X	X		X		X							X	X	X		G							X	
37	X	X	X				X1							X	X	X		G			X1				X	
38	X	X1	X				X1							X	X	X1		G			X				X	
39	X	X	X				X1							X2	X	X		G			X				X	
40	X	X	X				X							X	X	X1		G			X				X	
41	X	X	X				X							X	X	X		G			X1				X	
42	X	X	X				X2	X			X			X		X1p		G			X				X	
43	X	X	X				X1	X			X					X1	G	X2			X				X	
44	X	X	X				X	X			X			X		X		G			X				X	

1934/35

Football League position: 6th out of 22 in Division 3 (South)

Manager: Neil McBain

New league opponents: None

Home-and-away league doubles
For – 5 (Bournemouth & Boscombe Athletic, Gillingham, Newport County, Southend United, Torquay United)
Against – 2 (Brighton & Hove Albion, Cardiff City)

Divisional changes at end of season: Charlton Athletic to Division 2; Notts County from Division 2

All Matches: Won 23, Drew 13, Lost 16, Goals 91-58

Highest Score: 7 (Matches 21 & 24)

		HOME						AWAY					
	Pl	W	D	L	For	Ag	W	D	L	For	Ag	Pts
Charlton Athletic	42	17	2	2	62	20	10	5	6	41	32	61
Reading	42	16	5	0	59	23	5	6	10	30	42	53
Coventry City	42	14	5	2	56	14	7	4	10	30	36	51
Luton Town	42	12	7	2	60	23	7	5	9	32	37	50
Crystal Palace	42	15	3	3	51	14	4	7	10	35	50	48
WATFORD	42	14	2	5	53	19	5	7	9	23	30	47
Northampton Town	42	14	4	3	40	21	5	4	12	25	46	46
Bristol Rovers	42	14	6	1	54	27	3	4	14	19	50	44
Brighton & Hove Albion	42	15	4	2	51	16	2	5	14	18	46	43
Torquay United	42	15	2	4	60	22	3	4	14	21	53	42
Exeter City	42	11	5	5	48	29	5	4	12	22	46	41
Millwall	42	11	4	6	33	26	6	3	12	24	36	41
Queens Park Rangers	42	14	6	1	49	22	2	3	16	14	50	41
Clapton Orient	42	13	3	5	47	21	2	7	12	18	44	40
Bristol City	42	14	3	4	37	18	1	6	14	15	50	39
Swindon Town	42	11	7	3	45	22	2	5	14	22	56	38
Bournemouth & Boscombe Ath	42	10	5	6	36	26	5	2	14	18	45	37
Aldershot	42	12	6	3	35	20	1	4	16	15	55	36
Cardiff City	42	11	6	4	46	27	2	3	16	20	55	35
Gillingham	42	10	7	4	36	25	1	6	14	19	50	35
Southend United	42	10	4	7	40	29	1	5	15	25	49	31
Newport County	42	7	4	10	36	40	1	3	17	18	72	25

No	DATE			COMPETITION	OPPONENTS	HOME	AWAY		ATTENDANCE
1	August	Sat	25	Football League, Division 3 (South)	Bristol City		L 1-3		14,041
2		Wed	29	Football League, Division 3 (South)	BRIGHTON & HOVE ALBION	0-1 L			5,660
3	September	Sat	1	Football League, Division 3 (South)	MILLWALL	2-3 L			9,062
4		Wed	5	Football League, Division 3 (South)	Brighton & Hove Albion		L 0-2		6,557
5		Sat	8	Football League, Division 3 (South)	Coventry City		D 1-1		21,044
6		Sat	15	Football League, Division 3 (South)	CLAPTON ORIENT	5-0 W			7,455
7		Sat	22	Football League, Division 3 (South)	Gillingham		W 2-1		4,404
8		Sat	29	Football League, Division 3 (South)	READING	1-0 W			8,499
9	October	Sat	6	Football League, Division 3 (South)	Northampton Town		L 0-1		5,534
10		Sat	13	Football League, Division 3 (South)	BOURNEMOUTH & BOSCOMBE ATHLETIC	3-1 W			6,999
11		Sat	20	Football League, Division 3 (South)	CARDIFF CITY	1-3 L			7,844
12		Wed	24	Division 3 (South) Cup, 2nd Round	BRISTOL CITY	4-1 W			1,623
13		Sat	27	Football League, Division 3 (South)	Aldershot		D 0-0		3,572
14	November	Sat	3	Football League, Division 3 (South)	SOUTHEND UNITED	3-1 W			6,596
15		Sat	10	Football League, Division 3 (South)	Luton Town		D 2-2		11,260
16		Sat	17	Football League, Division 3 (South)	QUEENS PARK RANGERS	2-0 W			8,066
17		Sat	24	FA Cup, 1st Round	CORINTHIANS	2-0 W			12,712
18	December	Sat	1	Football League, Division 3 (South)	CHARLTON ATHLETIC	2-0 W			6,994
19		Sat	8	FA Cup, 2nd Round	WALSALL	1-1 D			12,786
20		Thu	13	FA Cup, 2nd Round replay	Walsall (after extra time)		L 0-1		8,924
21		Sat	15	Football League, Division 3 (South)	SWINDON TOWN	7-4 W			3,990
22		Sat	22	Football League, Division 3 (South)	Torquay United		W 3-1		2,489
23		Tue	25	Football League, Division 3 (South)	Newport County		W 1-0		7,290
24		Wed	26	Football League, Division 3 (South)	NEWPORT COUNTY	7-0 W			11,695
25		Sat	29	Football League, Division 3 (South)	BRISTOL CITY	4-0 W			8,814
26	January	Sat	5	Football League, Division 3 (South)	Millwall		D 0-0		13,423
27		Sat	12	Football League, Division 3 (South)	Crystal Palace		D 0-0		11,288
28		Sat	19	Football League, Division 3 (South)	COVENTRY CITY	2-0 W			13,615
29		Sat	26	Football League, Division 3 (South)	Clapton Orient		D 1-1		8,783
30	February	Sat	2	Football League, Division 3 (South)	GILLINGHAM	3-1 W			9,622
31		Sat	9	Football League, Division 3 (South)	Reading		L 2-3		12,895
32		Wed	13	Division 3 (South) Cup, 3rd Round	QUEENS PARK RANGERS	1-1 D			3,000
33		Sat	16	Football League, Division 3 (South)	NORTHAMPTON TOWN	1-1 D			9,442
34		Sat	23	Football League, Division 3 (South)	Bournemouth & Boscombe Athletic		W 2-1		6,768
35		Thu	28	Div 3 (South) Cup, 3rd Round replay	Queens Park Rangers		D 1-1		
36	March	Sat	2	Football League, Division 3 (South)	Cardiff City		L 1-2		9,247
37		Sat	9	Football League, Division 3 (South)	ALDERSHOT	0-1 L			4,854
38		Thu	14	Div 3 (South) Cup, 3rd Round, 2nd replay	Queens Park Rangers (after extra time)		W 2-0		
39		Sat	16	Football League, Division 3 (South)	Southend United		W 2-0		7,055
40		Sat	23	Football League, Division 3 (South)	LUTON TOWN	2-2 D			10,828
41		Thu	28	Division 3 (South) Cup, Semi-Final	Coventry City		D 0-0		2,500
42		Sat	30	Football League, Division 3 (South)	Queens Park Rangers		L 1-2		6,732
43	April	Wed	3	Div 3 (South) Cup, Semi-Final replay	COVENTRY CITY	2-1 W			2,057
44		Sat	6	Football League, Division 3 (South)	CRYSTAL PALACE	2-0 W			6,588
45		Sat	13	Football League, Division 3 (South)	Charlton Athletic		L 2-5		18,395
46		Mon	15	Division 3 (South) Cup, Final	Bristol Rovers (at Millwall)	(L 2-3)			1,500
47		Fri	19	Football League, Division 3 (South)	EXETER CITY	0-1 L			7,119
48		Sat	20	Football League, Division 3 (South)	BRISTOL ROVERS	3-0 W			4,260
49		Mon	22	Football League, Division 3 (South)	Exeter City		D 1-1		8,241
50		Tue	23	Football League, Division 3 (South)	Bristol Rovers		L 0-2		6,280
51		Sat	27	Football League, Division 3 (South)	Swindon Town		L 1-2		3,396
52	May	Sat	4	Football League, Division 3 (South)	TORQUAY UNITED	3-0 W			4,409

League ever-presents: None
Most appearances in total: J. McLaren 51 out of 52   **Most goals in total:** W.H.C. Lane 35
Hat-tricks: W.H.C. Lane (Match 12 & Match 21)   **Penalty goals:** J. Poxton 2, W. Findlay 1, F.C. McPherson 1
Sent off: T. Davies (Match 27)
Full international appearance(s) this season: None

	Armstrong, J.H.	Barnett, T.A.	Brown, W.	Carter, J.H.	Davies, T.	Davies, W.	Devan, W.G.	Ewington, C.	Findlay, W.	Jackson, W.	Lane, W.H.C.	Lewis, D.J.	Lowe, H.P.	McHugh, J.	McLaren, J.	McPherson, F.C.	Moran, J.	O'Brien, R.V.	Poxton, J.	Rattray, C.R.	Reed, A.G.	Woodward, A.
Apps	19	35	37	2	26	27	23	5	37	4	38	12	12	1	41	6	30	21	23	19	3	41
Subs																						
Goals		12		2	1	5	6		4	1	27		2			1		6	9			
Apps	7	5	10	2	7	6	1		5		8	3	6		10	4	7	8	3	7	2	9
Subs																						
Goals				1							8					2		2	1	1		

Match	Armstrong	Barnett	Brown	Carter	Davies,T	Davies,W	Devan	Ewington	Findlay	Jackson	Lane	Lewis	Lowe	McHugh	McLaren	McPherson	Moran	O'Brien	Poxton	Rattray	Reed	Woodward
1	X	X1	X			X			X			X	X		G	X			X			X
2	X	X	X		X	X			X			X	X		G	X			X			X
3	X	X						X	X		X2				G		X	X	X	X		X
4	X	X	X						X		X				G		X	X	X	X		X
5	X	X	X						X		X				G		X	X	X1	X		X
6	X	X1	X						X		X2				G		X	X	X2p	X		X
7	X	X1	X						X		X1				G		X	X	X	X		X
8	X	X1	X						X		X				G		X	X	X	X		X
9	X	X	X						X		X				G		X	X	X	X		X
10	X	X	X						X		X1				G		X	X1	X1p	X		X
11	X	X	X						X		X				G		X	X	X1	X		X
12	X	X	X						X		X3	X			G		X		X1	X		X
13	X	X	X						X		X	X			G		X		X1	X		X
14	X	X1	X						X		X1	X			G		X		X1	X		X
15	X	X	X						X		X1				G		X	X1	X1	X		X
16	X	X	X	X					X						G		X	X1	X1	X		X
17	X	X	X	X					X						G		X	X1	X	X1		X
18	X	X	X	X2					X						G		X	X	X	X		X
19	X	X	X1						X						G		X	X	X	X		X
20		X	X		X	X			X		X				G		X	X		X		X
21		X1	X		X	X1	X1		X1		X3			G			X			X		X
22		X1	X		X	X1	X1		X		X				G		X			X		X
23		X	X	X	X	X			X		X1				G		X			X		X
24		X2	X		X	X1	X2		X		X2				G		X			X		X
25		X1	X		X	X	X		X1p		X				G		X		X2			X
26		X	X		X	X	X		X		X				G		X		X			X
27		X	X		X	X	X		X		X				G		X		X			X
28		X	X		X	X	X		X		X1				G		X		X			X
29		X	X		X	X	X		X1	X	X				G		X		X			X
30		X	X		X	X	X		X	X1	X2				G		X		X			X
31		X	X		X	X			X1	X	X1				G		X				X	X
32		X	X		X	X			X1	X					G				X	X	X	X
33		X	X		X	X1			X	X	X				G		X					X
34		X	X		X1	X	X		X		X1				G		X		X			X
35			X		X				X		X1	X	X		G	X		X	X	X		X
36		X1	X		X	X	X		X		X	X			G			X				X
37		X	X		X	X	X		X		X	X			G			X				X
38	X		X		X	X					X2	X	X		G			X		X	X	
39			X		X	X	X1		X		X1	X	X		G			X		X		X
40			X		X	X	X		X		X1	X	X1		G			X		X		X
41	X		X		X	X					X		X		G	X	X	X				X
42			X		X	X	X		X		X1		X		G	X	X					X
43	X		X		X	X					X		X		G	X2p	X	X				X
44		X	X		X	X			X		X2				G	X	X	X				X
45		X	X		X	X1			X		X				G	X1	X	X				X
46	X		X		X	X					X1		X		G	X	X	X1				X
47		X	X		X				X		X	X	X		G	X				X		X
48	X				X	X	X	X			X2	X	X		G			X1				X
49	X				X	X	X	X			X1	X	X		G			X				X
50	X				X	X	X	X			X	X	X		G			X				X
51					X	X	X	X			X	X	X1		G			X			X	X
52		X1	X		X	X	X				X	X			G			X2			X	X

1935/36

Football League position: 5th out of 22 in Division 3 (South)
Manager: Neil McBain

New league opponents: None

Home-and-away league doubles
For – 4 (Cardiff City, Crystal Palace, Exeter City, Swindon Town)
Against – 1 (Luton Town)

Divisional changes at end of season: Coventry City to Division 2; Walsall from Division 3 (North)

All Matches: Won 23, Drew 10, Lost 15, Goals 94-66

Highest Score: 6 (Match 31)

	HOME					AWAY					
	Pl	W	D	L	For	Ag	W	D	L	For	Ag	Pts
Coventry City	42	19	1	1	75	12	5	8	8	27	33	57
Luton Town	42	13	6	2	56	20	9	6	6	25	25	56
Reading	42	18	0	3	52	20	8	2	11	35	42	54
Queens Park Rangers	42	14	4	3	55	19	8	5	8	29	34	53
WATFORD	42	12	3	6	47	29	8	6	7	33	25	49
Crystal Palace	42	15	4	2	64	20	7	1	13	32	54	49
Brighton & Hove Albion	42	13	4	4	48	25	5	4	12	22	38	44
Bournemouth & Boscombe Ath	42	9	6	6	36	26	7	5	9	24	30	43
Notts County	42	10	5	6	40	25	5	7	9	20	32	42
Torquay United	42	14	3	4	41	27	2	5	14	21	35	41
Aldershot	42	9	8	4	33	21	5	6	10	24	40	40
Millwall	42	9	6	6	29	21	5	4	12	25	50	40
Bristol City	42	11	5	5	32	21	4	5	12	16	38	40
Clapton Orient	42	13	2	6	34	15	3	4	14	21	46	38
Northampton Town	42	12	5	4	38	24	3	3	15	24	66	38
Gillingham	42	9	5	7	34	25	5	4	12	32	52	37
Bristol Rovers	42	11	6	4	48	31	3	3	15	21	64	37
Southend United	42	8	7	6	38	21	5	3	13	23	41	36
Swindon Town	42	10	5	6	43	33	4	3	14	21	40	36
Cardiff City	42	11	5	5	37	23	2	5	14	23	50	36
Newport County	42	8	4	9	36	44	3	5	13	24	67	31
Exeter City	42	7	5	9	38	41	1	6	14	21	52	27

No	DATE			COMPETITION	OPPONENTS	HOME	AWAY	ATTENDANCE	
1	August	Sat	31	Football League, Division 3 (South)	BRISTOL CITY	0-2 L		12,204	
2	September	Wed	4	Football League, Division 3 (South)	Exeter City		W 3-1		8,157
3		Sat	7	Football League, Division 3 (South)	Millwall		D 0-0		16,434
4		Wed	11	Football League, Division 3 (South)	EXETER CITY	1-0 W		8,490	
5		Sat	14	Football League, Division 3 (South)	TORQUAY UNITED	2-2 D		9,907	
6		Wed	18	Football League, Division 3 (South)	Brighton & Hove Albion		L 1-2		4,831
7		Sat	21	Football League, Division 3 (South)	Aldershot		D 1-1		4,350
8		Wed	25	Division 3 (South) Cup, 1st Round	Notts County		L 1-2		5,000
9		Sat	28	Football League, Division 3 (South)	SWINDON TOWN	2-1 W		8,846	
10	October	Sat	5	Football League, Division 3 (South)	Coventry City		L 0-2		17,786
11		Sat	12	Football League, Division 3 (South)	NEWPORT COUNTY	2-5 L		8,110	
12		Sat	19	Football League, Division 3 (South)	Bristol Rovers		W 1-0		7,111
13		Sat	26	Football League, Division 3 (South)	CLAPTON ORIENT	1-1 D		8,199	
14	November	Sat	2	Football League, Division 3 (South)	Southend United		D 1-1		7,667
15		Sat	9	Football League, Division 3 (South)	LUTON TOWN	1-3 L		14,906	
16		Sat	16	Football League, Division 3 (South)	Crystal Palace		W 2-1		9,376
17		Sat	23	Football League, Division 3 (South)	READING	4-2 W		10,723	
18		Sat	30	FA Cup, 1st Round	Nunhead		W 4-2		4,200
19	December	Sat	7	Football League, Division 3 (South)	GILLINGHAM	1-2 L		3,914	
20		Sat	14	FA Cup, 2nd Round	Rotherham United		D 1-1		12,700
21		Wed	18	FA Cup, 2nd Round replay	ROTHERHAM UNITED	1-0 W		5,218	
22		Sat	21	Football League, Division 3 (South)	NORTHAMPTON TOWN	4-1 W		4,759	
23		Wed	25	Football League, Division 3 (South)	Queens Park Rangers		L 1-3		14,573
24		Thu	26	Football League, Division 3 (South)	QUEENS PARK RANGERS	2-1 W		14,251	
25	January	Sat	4	Football League, Division 3 (South)	MILLWALL	2-1 W		7,539	
26		Sat	11	FA Cup, 3rd Round	Southall		W 4-1		14,095
27		Wed	15	Football League, Division 3 (South)	Cardiff City		W 2-0		3,765
28		Sat	18	Football League, Division 3 (South)	Torquay United		L 1-2		3,382
29		Sat	25	FA Cup, 4th Round	Leicester City		L 3-6		32,650
30		Wed	29	Football League, Division 3 (South)	ALDERSHOT	0-0 D		1,867	
31	February	Sat	1	Football League, Division 3 (South)	Swindon Town		W 6-1		5,341
32		Sat	8	Football League, Division 3 (South)	COVENTRY CITY	5-0 W		11,679	
33		Sat	15	Football League, Division 3 (South)	Newport County		5-0 W		5,405
34		Sat	22	Football League, Division 3 (South)	BRISTOL ROVERS	1-2 L		5,213	
35		Sat	29	Football League, Division 3 (South)	Luton Town		L 1-2		13,226
36	March	Sat	7	Football League, Division 3 (South)	BOURNEMOUTH & BOSCOMBE ATHLETIC	4-1 W		6,541	
37		Sat	14	Football League, Division 3 (South)	Clapton Orient		W 2-0		8,768
38		Sat	21	Football League, Division 3 (South)	CRYSTAL PALACE	3-2 W		10,432	
39		Sat	28	Football League, Division 3 (South)	Reading		L 0-3		9,541
40	April	Wed	1	Football League, Division 3 (South)	Bristol City		D 2-2		3,412
41		Sat	4	Football League, Division 3 (South)	CARDIFF CITY	4-0 W		5,165	
42		Fri	10	Football League, Division 3 (South)	NOTTS COUNTY	1-2 L		10,191	
43		Sat	11	Football League, Division 3 (South)	Gillingham		D 0-0		4,920
44		Mon	13	Football League, Division 3 (South)	Notts County		W 2-0		6,343
45		Sat	18	Football League, Division 3 (South)	SOUTHEND UNITED	5-0 W		6,467	
46		Wed	22	Football League, Division 3 (South)	Bournemouth & Boscombe Athletic		D 2-2		3,630
47		Sat	25	Football League, Division 3 (South)	Northampton Town		L 0-2		4,109
48	May	Sat	2	Football League, Division 3 (South)	BRIGHTON & HOVE ALBION	2-1 W		5,685	

League ever-presents: A. Woodward
Most appearances in total: A. Woodward 48 out of 48   **Most goals in total:** T.A. Barnett 17
Hat-tricks: T.A. Barnett (Match 26), F.C. McPherson (Match 29), L. Fletcher (Match 31), W.G. Devan (Match 32), T.C. Walters (Match 41 & Match 45)
Penalty goals: F.C. McPherson 3   **Sent off:** None
Full international appearance(s) this season: None

	Armstrong, J.H.	Barnett, T.A.	Brown, W.	Davies, T.	Davies, W.	Devan, W.G.	Ewington, C.	Findlay, W.	Fletcher, L.	Goodier, E.	Harris, W.T.	Jones, O.H.	Jones, T.J.	Lane, W.H.C.	Lewis, D.J.	McHugh, J.	McLaren, J.	McPherson, F.C.	Moran, J.	Morgan, E.	O'Brien, R.V.	Reed, A.G.	Walters, T.C.	Woodward, A.	Wright, N.	Own goals
Apps	16	34	16	23	29	28	1	13	15	1	3	8	21	14	38	4	30	16	4	26	37	5	17	42	21	
Subs																										
Goals		13		2	8	14			9				1	6			7			1	1	1	11	2	3	2
Apps	4	5	2	1	6	4		5	5				2	1	6	2	4	1		1	5	1		6	5	
Subs																										
Goals		4				1			3					1				3						2		
1			X	X		X				X			X	X	X		G				X			X	X	
2	X	X2	X			X							X	X			G			X	X1			X	X	
3	X	X	X			X							X	X			G			X	X			X	X	
4	X	X	X			X							X	X1			G			X	X			X	X	
5	X	X	X			X							X	X1			G			X	X			X	X1	
6	X		X		X1	X							X	X	X		G				X			X	X	
7	X		X			X							X	X	X		G				X			X	X1	
8		X		X	X	X							X1	X			G				X	X		X	X	
9	X		X		X1								X	X1	X		G				X	X		X	X	
10	X	X	X										X	X	X		G				X	X		X	X	
11	X	X	X			X							X	X	X		G	X1						X	X	
12			X	X		X							X	X	X		G				X		X1	X	X	
13			X	X		X							X	X	X		G				X		X1	X	X	
14		X	X		X							X		X		G				X		X1	X	X	
15			X	X	X								X	X1	X		G						X	X	X	
16		X1	X	X									X	X1	X		G			X				X	X	
17		X2	X	X				X	X				X1		X		G							X	X1	
18		X1	X	X				X	X1				X		X		G							X	X2	
19			X	X1			X	X	X				X		X		G							X	X	
20	X	X		X	X			X	X1						X		G			X				X	X	
21	X	X		X	X1			X	X						X		G			X				X	X	
22	X	X1		X	X1				X2						X		G			X	X			X	X	
23	X	X		X	X				X						X		G			X	X			X	X	1
24	X	X		X1	X				X						X		G			X	X			X1	X	
25	X	X		X	X				X1						X	G				X	X			X1	X	
26	X	X3		X	X				X1						X	G				X	X			X	X	
27	X	X		X	X1				X						X			X1		X	X			X		
28	X	X		X	X				X1						X			X		X	X			X		
29	X	X			X			X	X				X		X			X3p		X				X		
30	X	X			X				X				X		X	G		X		X	X			X		
31		X2	X1	X	X				X3			G			X					X	X1			X		
32		X	X	X	X3				X1			G			X					X1	X			X		
33		X1	X	X	X1				X1			G			X			X2		X	X			X		
34		X	X	X	X1				X			G			X			X		X	X			X		
35		X	X	X	X1				X			G			X			X		X	X			X		
36		X	X	X2	X1				X			G			X			X1p		X	X			X		
37		X1	X	X1	X							G			X			X		X	X	X	X	X		
38		X2	X	X	X							G			X			X1p		X	X	X	X	X		
39		X	X	X	X										X	G	X			X	X	X	X	X	X	
40		X	X1	X	X										X	G	X			X	X	X	X	X	X1	
41		X	X	X	X1										X	G	X			X	X	X	X3	X	X	
42		X	X	X	X										X	G	X			X	X	X	X	X	X	1
43		X	X	X	X								X		X		G			X	X	X	X	X		
44		X1	X	X	X1								X		X		G			X	X	X	X	X		
45		X	X	X1	X1								X		X		G			X	X	X	X3	X		
46		X		X	X						X				X		G			X	X	X	X1	X1	X	
47		X		X	X						X				X		G			X	X	X	X	X	X	
48		X		X2	X						X				X		G			X	X	X	X	X	X	

- 95 -

1936/37

Football League position: 4th out of 22 in Division 3 (South)
Manager: Neil McBain

New league opponents: None

Home-and-away league doubles
For – 5 (Bristol Rovers, Newport County, Northampton Town, Queens Park Rangers, Torquay United)
Against – 2 (Luton Town, Notts County)

Divisional changes at end of season: Luton Town to Division 2; Mansfield Town from Division 3 (North)

All Matches: Won 22, Drew 12, Lost 13, Goals 95-66

Highest Score: 7 (Match 43)

		HOME					AWAY					
	Pl	W	D	L	For	Ag	W	D	L	For	Ag	Pts
Luton Town	42	19	1	1	69	16	8	3	10	34	37	58
Notts County	42	15	3	3	44	23	8	7	6	30	29	56
Brighton & Hove Albion	42	15	5	1	49	16	9	0	12	25	27	53
WATFORD	42	14	4	3	53	21	5	7	9	32	39	49
Reading	42	14	5	2	53	23	5	6	10	23	37	49
Bournemouth & Boscombe Ath	42	17	3	1	45	20	3	6	12	20	39	49
Northampton Town	42	15	4	2	56	22	5	2	14	29	46	46
Millwall	42	12	4	5	43	24	6	9	6	21	30	46
Queens Park Rangers	42	12	2	7	51	24	6	7	8	22	28	45
Southend United	42	10	8	3	49	23	7	3	11	29	44	45
Gillingham	42	14	5	2	36	18	4	3	14	16	48	44
Clapton Orient	42	10	8	3	39	17	5	5	11	20	33	43
Swindon Town	42	12	4	5	52	24	2	7	12	23	49	39
Crystal Palace	42	11	7	3	45	20	2	5	14	17	41	38
Bristol Rovers	42	14	3	4	49	20	2	1	18	22	60	36
Bristol City	42	13	3	5	42	20	2	3	16	16	50	36
Walsall	42	11	3	7	38	34	2	7	12	25	51	36
Cardiff City	42	10	5	6	35	24	4	2	15	19	63	35
Newport County	42	7	7	7	37	28	5	3	13	30	70	34
Torquay United	42	9	5	7	42	32	2	5	14	15	48	32
Exeter City	42	9	5	7	36	37	1	7	13	23	51	32
Aldershot	42	5	6	10	29	29	2	3	16	21	60	23

No	Date			Competition	Opponents	Home	Away	Attendance
1	August	Sat	29	Football League, Division 3 (South)	Newport County		W 3-1	10,267
2	September	Wed	2	Football League, Division 3 (South)	Southend United		D 1-1	7,372
3		Sat	5	Football League, Division 3 (South)	GILLINGHAM	6-1 W		9,055
4		Wed	9	Football League, Division 3 (South)	SOUTHEND UNITED	1-3 L		9,356
5		Sat	12	Football League, Division 3 (South)	Aldershot		D 2-2	3,960
6		Sat	19	Football League, Division 3 (South)	SWINDON TOWN	2-2 D		9,665
7		Wed	23	Football League, Division 3 (South)	BOURNEMOUTH & BOSCOMBE ATHLETIC	4-0 W		5,168
8		Sat	26	Football League, Division 3 (South)	Millwall		L 1-2	21,228
9	October	Thu	1	Division 3 (South) Cup, 1st Round	Newport County		W 4-1	3,000
10		Sat	3	Football League, Division 3 (South)	BRISTOL ROVERS	3-0 W		9,768
11		Sat	10	Football League, Division 3 (South)	Northampton Town		W 1-0	8,958
12		Sat	17	Football League, Division 3 (South)	Luton Town		L 1-4	20,955
13		Sat	24	Football League, Division 3 (South)	CARDIFF CITY	2-0 W		14,015
14		Wed	28	Division 3 (South) Cup, 2nd Round	GILLINGHAM	3-2 W		2,000
15		Sat	31	Football League, Division 3 (South)	Crystal Palace		L 0-2	7,707
16	November	Sat	7	Football League, Division 3 (South)	EXETER CITY	1-1 D		7,363
17		Wed	11	Division 3 (South) Cup, 3rd Round	Bristol Rovers		W 1-0	1,000
18		Sat	14	Football League, Division 3 (South)	Reading		L 0-3	9,188
19		Sat	21	Football League, Division 3 (South)	QUEENS PARK RANGERS	2-0 W		12,349
20		Sat	28	FA Cup, 1st Round	Ipswich Town		L 1-2	18,229
21	December	Sat	5	Football League, Division 3 (South)	TORQUAY UNITED	4-0 W		5,866
22		Sat	12	Football League, Division 3 (South)	Notts County		L 1-2	8,187
23		Sat	19	Football League, Division 3 (South)	CLAPTON ORIENT	2-1 W		6,312
24		Fri	25	Football League, Division 3 (South)	Brighton & Hove Albion		D 1-1	14,923
25		Sat	26	Football League, Division 3 (South)	NEWPORT COUNTY	3-0 W		8,140
26		Mon	28	Football League, Division 3 (South)	BRIGHTON & HOVE ALBION	1-0 W		6,055
27	January	Sat	2	Football League, Division 3 (South)	Gillingham		L 1-2	8,320
28		Sat	9	Football League, Division 3 (South)	ALDERSHOT	5-3 W		7,089
29		Sat	16	Football League, Division 3 (South)	Bristol City		D 2-2	7,653
30		Sat	23	Football League, Division 3 (South)	Swindon Town		D 1-1	5,277
31	February	Wed	3	Football League, Division 3 (South)	MILLWALL	2-2 D		4,268
32		Sat	6	Football League, Division 3 (South)	Bristol Rovers		W 1-0	7,776
33		Sat	13	Football League, Division 3 (South)	NORTHAMPTON TOWN	4-1 W		10,430
34		Sat	20	Football League, Division 3 (South)	LUTON TOWN	1-3 L		27,632
35		Sat	27	Football League, Division 3 (South)	Cardiff City		D 2-2	6,283
36	March	Sat	6	Football League, Division 3 (South)	CRYSTAL PALACE	3-1 W		7,671
37		Sat	13	Football League, Division 3 (South)	Exeter City		L 1-2	6,043
38		Sat	20	Football League, Division 3 (South)	READING	6-1 W		8,101
39		Fri	26	Football League, Division 3 (South)	Walsall		L 1-3	3,691
40		Sat	27	Football League, Division 3 (South)	Queens Park Rangers		W 2-1	12,945
41		Mon	29	Football League, Division 3 (South)	WALSALL	0-0 D		10,117
42	April	Sat	3	Football League, Division 3 (South)	BRISTOL CITY	1-0 W		6,372
43		Sat	10	Football League, Division 3 (South)	Torquay United		W 7-4	2,277
44		Sat	17	Football League, Division 3 (South)	NOTTS COUNTY	0-2 L		10,586
45		Sat	24	Football League, Division 3 (South)	Clapton Orient		D 1-1	5,716
46		Mon	26	Division 3 (South) Cup, Semi-Final	Notts County (see below)		D 1-1	1,000
47	May	Sat	1	Football League, Division 3 (South)	Bournemouth & Boscombe Athletic		L 2-3	5,110

The unfinished Division 3 (South) Cup competition was continued the following season

League ever-presents: W. Davies, E. Morgan
Most appearances in total: E. Morgan 47 out of 47   **Most goals in total:** T.A. Barnett 20
Hat-tricks: W.Davies (4 goals, Match 3), L. Fletcher (Match 36)   **Penalty goals:** W. Davies 5
Sent off: None
Full international appearance(s) this season: None

	Armstrong, J.H.	Barnett, T.A.	Davies, T.	Davies, W.	Devan, W.G.	Ewington, C.	Fisher, P.	Fletcher, L.	Hurst, S.C.	Jones, T.J.	Lewis, D.J.	Lewis, T.G.	Lynch, T.J.	McHugh, J.	McLaren, J.	Morgan, E.	O'Brien, R.V.	Reed, A.G.	Tinklin, H.F.	Walters, T.C.	Williams, W.L.	Woodward, A.	Own goals
Apps	36	41	4	42	25	3	3	21	29	15	5	7	2	6	34	42	41	39	8	25	1	33	
Subs																							
Goals	1	19		11	11		1	13	12	2						1	4			7		3	
Apps	5	5	1	4	5			3	3	1		4		1	4	5	5	4	2	2		1	
Subs																							
Goals		1		4	1			1	2											1			
1		X1		X	X	X1					X				G	X	X	X		X		X	1
2		X		X	X					X	X				G	X	X	X		X1		X	
3		X		X4p	X				X1	X					G	X	X	X		X1		X	
4		X1		X	X					X	X				G	X	X	X		X		X	
5				X	X	X	X1	X1		X					G	X	X	X				X	
6		X		X		X	X	X1							G	X	X	X		X1		X	
7	X	X1		X	X1	X		X2							G	X	X	X		X			
8	X	X1		X	X			X			X				G	X	X	X		X			
9	X	X		X1	X1			X1			X				G	X	X	X		X1			
10	X	X		X1p	X2			X							G	X	X	X		X		X	
11	X	X		X	X			X1							G	X	X	X		X		X	
12	X	X1		X	X										G	X	X	X	X	X		X	
13	X	X1		X	X										G	X	X	X	X	X		X	1
14	X	X1		X1p	X			X1			X				G	X	X	X					
15	X	X		X				X							G	X	X	X		X		X	
16	X1	X		X					X	X					G	X	X	X				X	
17	X	X		X				X1		X	X				G	X	X	X					
18	X	X		X	X			X							G	X	X	X	X			X	
19	X	X		X1	X				X						G	X	X1					X	
20	X	X		X1p	X				X	X					G	X	X					X	
21	X	X2		X	X2			X							G	X	X	X				X	
22	X	X		X	X1			X							G	X	X	X	X			X	
23	X	X		X1											G	X	X1	X	X	X	X	X	
24	X	X		X	X			X1						G		X	X	X		X		X	
25	X	X		X	X			X1						G		X	X	X1		X1		X	
26	X	X1		X	X			X						G		X	X	X		X		X	
27	X	X	X	X	X1			X					G			X	X	X				X	
28	X	X2		X	X1			X1					G			X	X	X1		X		X	
29	X	X		X	X1			X1						G		X	X	X		X		X	
30	X	X1		X	X			X						G		X	X	X		X		X	
31	X	X		X1p	X			X1						G		X	X	X		X		X	
32	X	X		X				X1	X	X					G	X	X	X				X	
33	X	X		X				X2	X1	X1					G	X	X	X				X	
34	X	X		X				X1	X	X					G	X	X	X				X	
35	X	X1		X					X	X					G	X	X1	X				X	
36	X	X		X				X3		X					G	X	X	X				X	
37	X	X		X				X1		X					G	X	X	X				X	
38	X	X2		X1				X2	X1	X	X				G	X	X					X	
39	X	X		X				X	X	X	X				G	X	X	X				X	1
40	X	X1		X				X1	X	X	X				G	X	X	X				X	
41	X	X		X				X	X	X		X			G	X	X	X					
42	X	X1		X				X	X	X		X			G	X	X	X					
43	X	X2		X2	X1			X	X			X			G	X	X	X		X2			
44	X	X	X	X	X			X	X			X		G		X	X			X			
45	X	X	X	X				X	X	X		X		G		X	X			X1			
46	X	X	X	X1	X			X	X			X		G		X	X			X			
47	X	X	X	X	X1			X1	X			X		G		X	X			X			

1937/38

Football League position: 4th out of 22 in Division 3 (South)
Manager: Bill Findlay

New league opponents: None

Home-and-away league doubles
For – 5 (Bristol Rovers, Mansfield Town, Notts County, Swindon Town, Torquay United)
Against – 2 (Crystal Palace, Northampton Town)

Divisional changes at end of season: Millwall to Division 2; Port Vale from Division 3 (North); Ipswich Town elected in place of Gillingham

All Matches: Won 27, Drew 14, Lost 12, Goals 101-57

Highest Score: 8 (Match 6)

		HOME					AWAY					
	Pl	W	D	L	For	Ag	W	D	L	For	Ag	Pts
Millwall	42	15	3	3	53	15	8	7	6	30	22	56
Bristol City	42	14	6	1	37	13	7	7	7	31	27	55
Queens Park Rangers	42	15	3	3	44	17	7	6	8	36	30	53
WATFORD	42	14	4	3	50	15	7	7	7	23	28	53
Brighton & Hove Albion	42	15	3	3	40	16	6	6	9	24	28	51
Reading	42	17	2	2	44	21	3	9	9	27	42	51
Crystal Palace	42	14	4	3	45	17	4	8	9	22	30	48
Swindon Town	42	12	4	5	33	19	5	6	10	16	30	44
Northampton Town	42	12	4	5	30	19	5	5	11	21	38	43
Cardiff City	42	13	7	1	57	22	2	5	14	10	32	42
Notts County	42	10	6	5	29	17	6	3	12	21	33	41
Southend United	42	12	5	4	43	23	3	5	13	27	45	40
Bournemouth & Boscombe Ath	42	8	10	3	36	20	6	2	13	20	37	40
Mansfield Town	42	12	5	4	46	26	3	4	14	16	41	39
Bristol Rovers	42	10	7	4	28	20	3	6	12	18	41	39
Newport County	42	9	9	3	43	20	2	6	13	12	37	38
Exeter City	42	10	4	7	37	32	3	8	10	20	38	38
Aldershot	42	11	4	6	23	14	4	1	16	16	45	33
Clapton Orient	42	10	7	4	27	19	3	0	18	15	42	33
Torquay United	42	7	5	9	22	28	2	7	12	16	45	30
Walsall	42	10	4	7	34	37	1	3	17	18	51	29
Gillingham	42	9	5	7	25	25	1	1	19	11	52	26

No	DATE			COMPETITION	OPPONENTS	HOME	AWAY	ATTENDANCE
1	August	Sat	28	Football League, Division 3 (South)	BRISTOL ROVERS	4-0 W		11,544
2	September	Wed	1	Football League, Division 3 (South)	BRISTOL CITY	3-1 W		7,733
3		Sat	4	Football League, Division 3 (South)	Gillingham		D 0-0	8,408
4		Wed	8	Football League, Division 3 (South)	Bristol City		L 1-3	10,259
5		Sat	11	Football League, Division 3 (South)	EXETER CITY	0-0 D		9,109
6		Mon	13	Div 3 (South) Cup, 1936/37 Semi-Final replay	NOTTS COUNTY	8-3 W		1,065
7		Wed	15	Football League, Division 3 (South)	Crystal Palace		L 1-4	6,391
8		Sat	18	Football League, Division 3 (South)	Swindon Town		W 2-0	12,169
9		Sat	25	Football League, Division 3 (South)	ALDERSHOT	5-1 W		8,585
10		Wed	29	Div 3 (South) Cup, 1936/37 Final, 1st Leg	MILLWALL	2-2 D		2,714
11	October	Sat	2	Football League, Division 3 (South)	Millwall		D 1-1	32,385
12		Sat	9	Football League, Division 3 (South)	READING	4-0 W		12,247
13		Sat	16	Football League, Division 3 (South)	NORTHAMPTON TOWN	1-3 L		11,100
14		Mon	18	Div 3 (South) Cup, 1936/37 Final, 2nd Leg	MILLWALL (Trophy shared)		D 1-1	3,396
15		Thu	21	Division 3 (South) Cup, 1st Round	Newport County		D 2-2	1,000
16		Sat	23	Football League, Division 3 (South)	Walsall		L 1-3	4,815
17		Wed	27	Div 3 (South) Cup, 1st Round replay	NEWPORT COUNTY	4-0 W		261
18		Sat	30	Football League, Division 3 (South)	CARDIFF CITY	4-0 W		11,183
19	November	Sat	6	Football League, Division 3 (South)	Bournemouth & Boscombe Athletic		D 0-0	6,412
20		Wed	10	Division 3 (South) Cup, 2nd Round	Notts County		W 2-0	1,000
21		Sat	13	Football League, Division 3 (South)	BRIGHTON & HOVE ALBION	1-1 D		9,281
22		Sat	20	Football League, Division 3 (South)	Queens Park Rangers		L 0-2	12,533
23		Sat	27	FA Cup, 1st Round	CHELTENHAM TOWN	3-0 W		8,149
24	December	Sat	4	Football League, Division 3 (South)	Clapton Orient		D 1-1	6,485
25		Sat	11	FA Cup, 2nd Round	WALSALL	3-0 W		10,303
26		Sat	18	Football League, Division 3 (South)	Mansfield Town		W 1-0	5,274
27		Sat	25	Football League, Division 3 (South)	NEWPORT COUNTY	3-0 W		7,473
28		Mon	27	Football League, Division 3 (South)	Newport County		D 0-0	13,820
29		Tue	28	Football League, Division 3 (South)	TORQUAY UNITED	4-0 W		5,138
30	January	Sat	1	Football League, Division 3 (South)	Bristol Rovers		W 2-0	9,670
31		Sat	8	FA Cup, 3rd Round	Sunderland		L 0-1	35,713
32		Sat	15	Football League, Division 3 (South)	GILLINGHAM	1-1 D		7,843
33		Wed	19	Football League, Division 3 (South)	SOUTHEND UNITED	3-1 W		4,524
34		Sat	22	Football League, Division 3 (South)	Exeter City		W 2-1	7,001
35		Sat	29	Football League, Division 3 (South)	SWINDON TOWN	4-0 W		11,343
36	February	Sat	5	Football League, Division 3 (South)	Aldershot		L 0-1	7,289
37		Sat	12	Football League, Division 3 (South)	MILLWALL	1-1 D		13,816
38		Sat	19	Football League, Division 3 (South)	Reading		L 1-4	12,560
39		Sat	26	Football League, Division 3 (South)	Northampton Town		L 2-3	7,085
40		Mon	28	Division 3 (South) Cup, 3rd Round	Queens Park Rangers		W 3-2	2,095
41	March	Sat	5	Football League, Division 3 (South)	WALSALL	2-1 W		9,575
42		Sat	12	Football League, Division 3 (South)	Cardiff City		D 1-1	25,349
43		Wed	16	Division 3 (South) Cup, Semi-Final	Reading		L 0-3	2,107
44		Sat	19	Football League, Division 3 (South)	BOURNEMOUTH & BOSCOMBE ATHLETIC	0-2 L		10,294
45		Sat	26	Football League, Division 3 (South)	Brighton & Hove Albion		W 2-1	14,781
46	April	Sat	2	Football League, Division 3 (South)	QUEENS PARK RANGERS	3-1 W		20,456
47		Sat	9	Football League, Division 3 (South)	Southend United		D 2-2	6,760
48		Fri	15	Football League, Division 3 (South)	NOTTS COUNTY	2-0 W		14,984
49		Sat	16	Football League, Division 3 (South)	CLAPTON ORIENT	2-0 W		11,943
50		Mon	18	Football League, Division 3 (South)	Notts County		W 2-1	8,789
51		Sat	23	Football League, Division 3 (South)	Torquay United		W 1-0	3,986
52		Sat	30	Football League, Division 3 (South)	MANSFIELD TOWN	2-0 W		9,222
53	May	Sat	7	Football League, Division 3 (South)	CRYSTAL PALACE	1-2 L		13,713

Summary statistics (top block). Columns in player order:

	Armstrong, J.H.	Barnett, T.A.	Black, W.	Brown, J.	Davies, W.	Devan, W.G.	Evans, D.R.	Fletcher, L.	Gallimore, L.	Hawkins, H.	Hetherington, J.A.	Johnson, G.A.	Jones, T.J.	Laing, D.B.P.	Lewis, D.J.	Lewis, T.G.	McHugh, J.	McLaren, J.	Morgan, E.	O'Brien, R.V.	Ovenstone, D.	Reed, A.G.	Robinson, R.	Walters, T.C.	Wipfler, C.J.	Woodward, A.	Own goals
Apps	42	42	16	6	7	4	16		30	5	3	22	40	15	6	5	3	39	37	42	1	37	2	15	12	15	
Subs																											
Goals		9	3	2	2	1	5					8	14	5		2			6	1				6	5		4
Apps	7	7	4	3	2		5	1	7	4		2	7	4	3	4	3	8	11	11	1	8	5	7	4	3	
Subs																											
Goals		3	4	1			3					1	2	1		4			2					6	1		

Match-by-match appearances and goals:

#	Arm	Bar	Bla	Bro	Dav	Dev	Eva	Fle	Gal	Haw	Het	Joh	Jon	Lai	LeD	LeT	McH	McL	Mor	OBr	Ove	Ree	Rob	Wal	Wip	Woo	OG
1	X	X2	X		X								X1					G	X	X		X			X	X	1
2	X	X	X	X1	X								X2					G	X	X		X				X	
3	X	X	X	X									X					G	X	X		X				X	
4	X	X	X		X	X1							X					G	X	X		X				X	
5	X	X	X		X					X			X		X			G	X	X		X					
6	X	X2	X4		X					X			X1					G	X1	X		X				X	
7	X	X	X	X1						X			X					G	X	X		X				X	
8	X	X	X1		X		X						X1		X			G	X	X		X					
9	X	X1	X			X	X						X2		X			G	X	X		X					2
10	X		X				X2						X		X	X		G	X	X	X	X					
11	X	X	X1	X			X						X		X			G	X	X		X					
12	X	X	X1	X1			X1						X		X			G	X1p	X		X					
13	X	X	X	X1			X								X			G	X	X	X	X					
14	X	X	X				X		X	X								G	X	X		X		X1			
15		X	X				X		X									G	X	X		X		X2	X	X	
16	X	X	X				X		X									G	X1p	X		X		X	X		
17		X		X1	X				X							X2	G		X1p	X		X		X	X	X	
18	X	X2			X				X				X			X2	G		X	X					X	X	
19	X	X			X				X				X			X	G		X	X					X	X	
20	X			X			X1		X				X			X1	G		X	X					X		
21	X	X		X					X				X			X	G		X	X				X1	X		
22	X	X							X				X	X		X		G	X	X		X	X				
23	X	X					X		X				X1			X1		G	X	X		X		X1			
24	X	X							X				X	X	X1	X		G	X	X		X		X			
25	X	X1							X				X1	X	X			G	X	X		X		X1			
26	X	X							X				X	X	X			G	X	X		X		X1			
27	X	X							X				X1	X	X2			G	X	X		X		X			
28	X	X							X				X	X	X			G	X	X		X		X			
29	X	X2							X				X	X	X1			G	X	X		X		X1		X	
30	X	X							X				X1	X				G	X	X		X		X1			
31	X	X							X				X	X	X			G	X	X		X		X			
32	X	X							X				X	X1	X			G	X	X		X		X			
33	X	X1							X				X1	X1	X			G	X	X		X		X			
34	X	X							X				X1	X	X			G	X	X		X		X1			
35	X	X							X				X1	X				G	X1p	X		X		X2			
36	X	X							X				X	X				G	X	X		X		X			
37	X	X							X				X	X1				G	X	X		X		X			
38	X	X							X				X	X	X			G	X1	X		X		X			
39	X	X							X		X		X					G	X	X1		X		X		X1	
40			X						X				X	X1	X			G	X	X		X		X	X	X2	
41	X	X							X	X	X		X1					G	X1	X		X		X			
42	X	X1	X						X	X	X		X					G	X	X		X		X			
43		X						X	X				X					G	X	X				X	X	X	X
44	X	X	X				X		X				X					G	X	X		X		X			
45	X	X	X				X		X			X1	X1					G	X	X		X		X			
46	X	X	X				X1					X1	X					G	X1p	X		X		X			
47	X	X					X		X			X	X1	X1				G	X	X		X				X	
48	X	X					X		X			X	X					G	X	X		X		X		X2	
49	X	X					X2		X			X	X					G		X		X		X	X	X	
50	X	X					X		X			X	X1					G		X		X		X	X1	X	
51	X	X					X		X			X	X1					G		X		X		X	X	X	
52	X	X					X1		X			X1	X					G		X		X		X	X	X	
53	X	X					X		X			X	X					G		X		X		X	X	X	1

1938/39

Football League position: 4th out of 22 in Division 3 (South)
Manager: Bill Findlay

New league opponents: Ipswich Town, Port Vale

Home-and-away league doubles
For – 2 (Exeter City, Port Vale)
Against – none

Divisional changes at end of season: Newport County to Division 2; Norwich City from Division 2

All Matches: Won 19, Drew 12, Lost 15, Goals 70-65

Highest Score: 4 (Matches 5, 15, 18, 19, 21, 25 & 30)

	Pl	HOME					AWAY					Pts
		W	D	L	For	Ag	W	D	L	For	Ag	
Newport County	42	15	4	2	37	16	7	7	7	21	29	55
Crystal Palace	42	15	4	2	49	18	5	8	8	22	34	52
Brighton & Hove Albion	42	14	5	2	43	14	5	6	10	25	35	49
WATFORD	42	14	6	1	44	15	4	5	12	18	36	46
Reading	42	12	6	3	46	23	4	8	9	23	36	46
Queens Park Rangers	42	10	8	3	44	15	5	6	10	24	34	44
Ipswich Town	42	14	3	4	46	21	2	9	10	16	31	44
Bristol City	42	14	5	2	42	19	2	7	12	19	44	44
Swindon Town	42	15	4	2	53	25	3	4	14	19	52	44
Aldershot	42	13	6	2	31	15	3	6	12	22	51	44
Notts County	42	12	6	3	36	16	5	3	13	23	38	43
Southend United	42	14	5	2	38	13	2	4	15	23	51	41
Cardiff City	42	12	1	8	40	28	3	10	8	21	37	41
Exeter City	42	9	9	3	40	32	4	5	12	25	50	40
Bournemouth & Boscombe Ath	42	10	8	3	38	22	3	5	13	14	36	39
Mansfield Town	42	13	5	3	41	20	2	7	12	11	43	39
Northampton Town	42	10	5	6	36	23	4	4	13	16	35	38
Port Vale	42	10	5	6	36	23	4	4	13	16	35	37
Torquay United	42	7	5	9	27	28	4	10	7	27	42	37
Clapton Orient	42	10	9	2	40	16	1	4	16	13	39	35
Walsall	42	9	6	6	47	23	2	5	14	21	46	33
Bristol Rovers	42	8	8	5	30	17	2	5	14	25	44	33

No	DATE			COMPETITION	OPPONENTS	HOME	AWAY	ATTENDANCE	
1	August	Sat	27	Football League, Division 3 (South)	BRISTOL CITY	2-2 D		11,386	
2		Mon	29	Football League, Division 3 (South)	Northampton Town		L 0-2		10,784
3	September	Sat	3	Football League, Division 3 (South)	Crystal Palace		L 0-2		18,910
4		Thu	8	Football League, Division 3 (South)	Newport County		L 0-1		8,500
5		Sat	10	Football League, Division 3 (South)	WALSALL	4-2 W		8,270	
6		Wed	14	Football League, Division 3 (South)	NEWPORT COUNTY	1-1 D		5,310	
7		Sat	17	Football League, Division 3 (South)	PORT VALE	2-0 W		9,503	
8		Sat	24	Football League, Division 3 (South)	Swindon Town		L 0-3		12,941
9	October	Sat	1	Football League, Division 3 (South)	TORQUAY UNITED	0-0 D		8,247	
10		Sat	8	Football League, Division 3 (South)	Clapton Orient		D 0-0		8,919
11		Sat	15	Football League, Division 3 (South)	Mansfield Town		D 0-0		6,491
12		Sat	22	Football League, Division 3 (South)	BOURNEMOUTH & BOSCOMBE ATHLETIC	1-0 W		8,818	
13		Wed	26	Division 3 (South) Cup, 1st Round	Reading		L 1-5		
14		Sat	29	Football League, Division 3 (South)	Southend United		L 0-3		6,385
15	November	Sat	5	Football League, Division 3 (South)	EXETER CITY	4-2 W		7,256	
16		Sat	12	Football League, Division 3 (South)	Cardiff City		L 3-5		11,646
17		Sat	19	Football League, Division 3 (South)	IPSWICH TOWN	0-0 D		8,636	
18		Sat	26	FA Cup, 1st Round	NORTHAMPTON TOWN	4-1 W		9,946	
19	December	Sat	3	Football League, Division 3 (South)	BRISTOL ROVERS	4-1 W		6,603	
20		Sat	10	FA Cup, 2nd Round	Scunthorpe & Lindsey United		W 2-1		11,390
21		Sat	17	Football League, Division 3 (South)	QUEENS PARK RANGERS	4-1 W		11,254	
22		Sat	24	Football League, Division 3 (South)	Bristol City		L 0-2		7,127
23		Mon	26	Football League, Division 3 (South)	NOTTS COUNTY	0-1 L		2,522	
24		Tue	27	Football League, Division 3 (South)	Notts County		W 3-0		21,208
25		Sat	31	Football League, Division 3 (South)	CRYSTAL PALACE	4-1 W		9,853	
26	January	Sat	7	FA Cup, 3rd Round	Tottenham Hotspur		L 1-7		34,896
27		Wed	11	Football League, Division 3 (South)	Reading		L 2-3		4,420
28		Sat	14	Football League, Division 3 (South)	Walsall		L 0-2		10,002
29		Sat	21	Football League, Division 3 (South)	Port Vale		W 2-1		5,204
30		Sat	28	Football League, Division 3 (South)	SWINDON TOWN	4-1 W		7,450	
31	February	Sat	4	Football League, Division 3 (South)	Torquay United		L 1-2		4,373
32		Sat	11	Football League, Division 3 (South)	CLAPTON ORIENT	1-0 W		8,884	
33		Sat	18	Football League, Division 3 (South)	MANSFIELD TOWN	2-0 W		7,254	
34		Sat	25	Football League, Division 3 (South)	Bournemouth & Boscombe Athletic		D 1-1		3,677
35	March	Sat	4	Football League, Division 3 (South)	SOUTHEND UNITED	3-0 W		5,708	
36		Sat	11	Football League, Division 3 (South)	Exeter City		W 3-1		5,150
37		Sat	18	Football League, Division 3 (South)	CARDIFF CITY	1-0 W		6,714	
38		Sat	25	Football League, Division 3 (South)	Ipswich Town		L 1-5		11,450
39	April	Sat	1	Football League, Division 3 (South)	READING	3-1 W		6,073	
40		Fri	7	Football League, Division 3 (South)	Aldershot		D 1-1		6,987
41		Sat	8	Football League, Division 3 (South)	Bristol Rovers		D 1-1		7,755
42		Mon	10	Football League, Division 3 (South)	ALDERSHOT	1-1 D		8,771	
43		Sat	15	Football League, Division 3 (South)	BRIGHTON & HOVE ALBION	1-1 D		6,339	
44		Sat	22	Football League, Division 3 (South)	Queens Park Rangers		L 0-1		7,364
45		Wed	26	Football League, Division 3 (South)	Brighton & Hove Albion		D 0-0		2,260
46		Sat	29	Football League, Division 3 (South)	NORTHAMPTON TOWN	2-0 W		3,465	

League ever-presents: T.J. Jones, A.G. Reed
Most appearances in total: T.J. Jones & A.G. Reed 46 out of 46   **Most goals in total:** W.L. Dunderdale 21
Hat-tricks: W.L. Dunderdale (Match 36)   **Penalty goals:** None
Sent off: None
Full international appearance(s) this season: None

	Armstrong, J.H.	Barnett, T.A.	Dabbs, B.E.	Davies, W.	Dunderdale, W.L.	Evans, D.R.	Gallimore, L.	Hetherington, J.A.	Johnson, G.A.	Johnson, G.E.	Jones, D.O.E.	Jones, T.J.	Lewis, D.J.	Lewis, T.G.	McHugh, J.	McLaren, J.	Morgan, E.	O'Brien, R.V.	Reed, A.G.	Wipfler, C.J.	Woodward, A.	Own goals
Apps	41	36	3	40	30	31	26	5	1	1	2	42	17	13	22	20	3	38	42	10	39	
Subs																						
Goals	1	11		3	19	6		1				6		9						2	2	2
Apps	4	4		4	3	4	4					4		1		4		4	4		4	
Subs																						
Goals		1		1	2	2						2										
1	X	X		X1	X1		X					X				G	X	X	X	X		
2	X			X	X		X	X				X	X			G	X		X	X		
3	X			X	X		X					X				G	X	X	X	X		
4	X	X		X	X		X					X				G		X	X	X	X	
5	X			X	X2		X	X				X				G		X	X	X1	X	
6	X1			X	X		X	X				X				G		X	X	X	X	
7	X		X	X1	X		X		X		X	X				G		X	X1		X	
8	X		X	X	X		X	X			X	X				G		X		X		
9	X		X	X	X		X	X				X				G		X	X	X		
10	X	X		X	X		X					X				G		X	X	X	X	
11	X	X		X	X		X					X				G		X	X	X		
12	X	X		X	X		X					X		X1		G		X	X		X	
13	X	X		X	X1		X					X		X		G		X	X		X	
14	X	X		X	X		X					X		X		G		X	X		X	
15	X	X1			X2		X					X		X1		G		X	X		X	
16	X	X1		X	X2		X					X				G		X	X		X	
17		X		X	X		X	X				X				G		X	X		X	
18	X	X1		X1	X		X					X1				G		X	X		X	
19	X	X1		X	X1		X					X1				G		X	X		X1	
20	X	X		X	X1		X					X1				G		X	X		X	
21	X	X1		X	X1		X1					X				G		X	X		X	1
22	X	X		X	X		X					X				G		X	X		X	
23	X	X		X	X		X					X				G		X	X		X	
24	X	X1		X	X1		X					X				G		X	X		X	1
25	X	X		X2	X1		X					X1				G		X	X		X	
26	X	X		X	X1		X					X				G		X	X		X	
27	X	X		X	X1		X					X1			G			X	X		X	
28	X	X		X	X		X					X			G			X	X		X	
29	X	X		X	X2		X					X			G			X	X		X	
30	X	X1		X	X1		X					X1			G			X	X		X1	
31	X	X1		X	X		X					X	X		G			X	X		X	
32	X	X1		X	X		X					X	X		G			X	X		X	
33	X	X		X	X1		X					X1	X		G			X	X		X	
34	X	X		X	X		X1					X	X		G			X	X		X	
35	X	X2		X	X1		X					X	X		G			X	X		X	
36	X	X		X	X3		X					X	X		G			X	X		X	
37	X	X		X			X					X	X	X1	G			X	X		X	
38	X	X		X		X1						X	X	X	G			X	X		X	
39	X	X1		X		X						X	X	X2	G			X	X		X	
40	X	X		X		X						X	X	X1	G			X	X		X	
41	X	X		X		X						X	X	X1	G			X	X		X	
42	X	X		X		X						X	X	X1	G			X	X		X	
43	X	X		X		X						X	X	X1	G			X	X		X	
44	X	X		X		X						X	X	X	G			X	X		X	
45	X	X		X		X						X	X	X	G			X	X		X	
46	X	X		X		X1						X1	X	X	G			X	X		X	

1946/47

Football League position: 16th out of 22 in Division 3 (South)   **Manager:** Bill Findlay (Matches 1-34), Jack Bray (Matches 35-46)

		HOME					AWAY					
	Pl	W	D	L	For	Ag	W	D	L	For	Ag	Pts
Cardiff City	42	18	3	0	60	11	12	3	6	33	19	66
Queens Park Rangers	42	15	2	4	42	15	8	9	4	32	25	57
Bristol City	42	13	4	4	56	20	7	7	7	38	36	51
Swindon Town	42	15	4	2	56	25	4	7	10	28	48	49
Walsall	42	11	6	4	42	25	6	6	9	32	34	46
Ipswich Town	42	15	5	1	53	33	1	5	9	7	28	32	46
Bournemouth & Boscombe Ath	42	12	4	5	43	20	6	4	11	29	34	44
Southend United	42	9	7	5	38	22	8	3	10	33	38	44
Reading	42	11	6	4	53	30	5	5	11	30	44	43
Port Vale	42	14	4	3	51	28	3	5	13	17	35	43
Torquay United	42	11	5	5	33	23	4	7	10	19	38	42
Notts County	42	11	4	6	35	19	4	6	11	28	44	40
Northampton Town	42	11	5	5	46	33	4	5	12	26	42	40
Bristol Rovers	42	9	6	6	34	26	7	2	12	25	43	40
Exeter City	42	11	4	6	37	27	4	3	14	23	42	39
WATFORD	42	11	4	6	39	27	6	1	14	22	49	39
Brighton & Hove Albion	42	8	7	6	31	35	1	5	11	23	37	38
Crystal Palace	42	9	7	5	29	19	4	4	13	20	43	37
Leyton Orient	42	10	5	6	40	28	2	3	16	14	47	32
Aldershot	42	6	7	8	25	26	4	5	12	23	52	32
Norwich City	42	6	3	12	38	48	4	5	12	26	52	28
Mansfield Town	42	8	5	8	31	38	1	5	15	17	58	28

New league opponents: None

Home-and-away league doubles
For – 3 (Aldershot, Bristol Rovers, Reading)
Against – 2 (Mansfield Town, Queens Park Rangers)

Divisional changes at end of season: Cardiff City to Division 2; Mansfield Town to Division 3 (North); Newport County & Swansea Town from Division 2

All Matches: Won 18, Drew 7, Lost 21, Goals 65-80

Highest Score: 4 (Matches 4, 13, 23 & 24)

(NB Clapton Orient changed its name to Leyton Orient in October 1946)

No	DATE			COMPETITION	OPPONENTS	HOME	AWAY	ATTENDANCE
1	August	Sat	31	Football League, Division 3 (South)	Queens Park Rangers		L 1-2	19,446
2	September	Wed	4	Football League, Division 3 (South)	MANSFIELD TOWN	1-2 L		4,219
3		Sat	7	Football League, Division 3 (South)	CLAPTON ORIENT	3-1 W		9,093
4		Mon	9	Football League, Division 3 (South)	Bristol Rovers		W 4-3	11,838
5		Sat	14	Football League, Division 3 (South)	Ipswich Town		L 0-2	14,418
6		Wed	18	Football League, Division 3 (South)	BRISTOL ROVERS	1-0 W		4,904
7		Sat	21	Football League, Division 3 (South)	NOTTS COUNTY	2-2 D		10,100
8		Sat	28	Football League, Division 3 (South)	WALSALL	0-2 L		9,235
9	October	Sat	5	Football League, Division 3 (South)	Reading		W 3-2	11,680
10		Wed	9	Football League, Division 3 (South)	Mansfield Town		L 0-2	5,218
11		Sat	12	Football League, Division 3 (South)	CRYSTAL PALACE	1-0 W		9,904
12		Sat	19	Football League, Division 3 (South)	Northampton Town		L 1-4	9,976
13		Sat	26	Football League, Division 3 (South)	ALDERSHOT	4-1 W		5,937
14	November	Sat	2	Football League, Division 3 (South)	Brighton & Hove Albion		D 1-1	9,458
15		Sat	9	Football League, Division 3 (South)	EXETER CITY	3-1 W		7,032
16		Sat	16	Football League, Division 3 (South)	Port Vale		L 0-3	9,539
17		Sat	23	Football League, Division 3 (South)	BRISTOL CITY	2-3 L		11,415
18		Sat	30	FA Cup, 1st Round	Wellington Town		D 1-1	7,500
19	December	Wed	4	FA Cup, 1st Round replay	WELLINGTON TOWN	1-0 W		6,159
20		Sat	7	Football League, Division 3 (South)	BOURNEMOUTH & BOSCOMBE ATHLETIC	0-2 L		5,981
21		Sat	14	FA Cup, 2nd Round	PORT VALE	1-1 D		8,499
22		Mon	16	FA Cup, 2nd Round replay	Port Vale		L 1-2	7,342
23		Sat	21	Football League, Division 3 (South)	NORWICH CITY	4-1 W		3,078
24		Wed	25	Football League, Division 3 (South)	SOUTHEND UNITED	4-0 W		6,849
25		Thu	26	Football League, Division 3 (South)	Southend United		L 0-5	15,254
26		Sat	28	Football League, Division 3 (South)	QUEENS PARK RANGERS	0-2 L		18,610
27	January	Sat	4	Football League, Division 3 (South)	Leyton Orient		L 1-3	9,126
28		Sat	11	Football League, Division 3 (South)	Swindon Town		L 0-5	13,981
29		Sat	18	Football League, Division 3 (South)	IPSWICH TOWN	2-0 W		8,185
30		Sat	25	Football League, Division 3 (South)	Notts County		L 1-4	9,511
31	February	Sat	1	Football League, Division 3 (South)	Walsall		W 3-1	6,222
32		Sat	8	Football League, Division 3 (South)	READING	2-1 W		4,317
33		Sat	15	Football League, Division 3 (South)	Crystal Palace		L 0-2	10,779
34	March	Sat	15	Football League, Division 3 (South)	Exeter City		L 0-1	4,919
35		Sat	22	Football League, Division 3 (South)	PORT VALE	2-0 W		6,370
36		Sat	29	Football League, Division 3 (South)	Bristol City		W 2-1	13,700
37	April	Fri	4	Football League, Division 3 (South)	TORQUAY UNITED	3-3 D		8,923
38		Sat	5	Football League, Division 3 (South)	SWINDON TOWN	1-1 D		9,992
39		Mon	7	Football League, Division 3 (South)	Torquay United		L 0-2	5,643
40		Sat	12	Football League, Division 3 (South)	Bournemouth & Boscombe Athletic		W 1-0	11,452
41		Sat	19	Football League, Division 3 (South)	CARDIFF CITY	2-0 W		20,030
42		Sat	26	Football League, Division 3 (South)	Norwich City		L 2-4	15,077
43	May	Sat	3	Football League, Division 3 (South)	Cardiff City		L 0-1	30,368
44		Sat	10	Football League, Division 3 (South)	NORTHAMPTON TOWN	1-1 D		5,655
45		Sat	17	Football League, Division 3 (South)	Aldershot		W 2-1	4,208
46		Sat	24	Football League, Division 3 (South)	BRIGHTON & HOVE ALBION	1-4 L		5,376

League ever-presents: A.L. Farnen, L. Morgan
Most appearances in total: A.L. Farnen & L. Morgan 46 out of 46   **Most goals in total:** D.R. Evans 19
Hat-tricks: D.R. Evans (Match 24)   **Penalty goals:** R. Ross 5
Sent off: None   **Full international appearance(s) this season:** None
(In Match 20, both the opponents' goals were conceded after R. Gray had replaced the injured T. Rigg as goalkeeper)

	Beckett, W.	Birse, C.D.V.	Chase, C.T.	Davies, W.	Drinkwater, C.J.	Dunderdale, W.L.	Early, M.	Evans, D.R.	Farnen, A.L.	Gallimore, L.	Gibson, F.A.	Gillespie, P.	Gray, R.	Harper, J.J.	Harris, W.T.	Hopkinson, S.	Malpass, S.T.	Morgan, L.	Rigg, T.	Robertson, L.V.	Ross, R.	Thompson, W.	Usher, J.A.G.	Weir, J.	Williams, K.	Wipfler, C.J.	Young, G.	Own goal
Apps	7	7	14	38	1	30	5	35	42	8	1	6	16	32	31	1	18	42	32	6	33	9	7	1	2	13	25	
Subs																												
Goals	1		1	6		13	1	18							6					2	6		2			1	3	1
Apps	2	2		4		3		4	4			1	4	3	4			4	2		2	2	1			2		
Subs																												
Goals	1					2		1																				
1				X		X	X	X	X				X					X	G	X1	X						X	
2				X			X	X1	X	X			X					X	G	X	X						X	
3				X			X	X1	X				X					X	G	X1	X1p						X	
4				X		X1		X1	X	X				X				X	G	X			X1				X1	
5				X		X		X	X				X					X		X	X	G					X	
6	X			X				X1	X	X	X		X					X	G	X	X							
7	X1			X1		X	X		X				X					X	G	X							X	
8	X			X		X	X	X	X				X					X	G	X							X	
9				X		X2		X1	X					X	X			X	G	X						X	X	
10				X		X		X	X					X	X			X	G	X						X	X	
11				X				X1	X					X	X			X	G	X			X			X	X	
12				X				X	X					X	X			X	G	X1p			X			X	X	
13				X				X2	X				X	X	X			X	G	X1p			X1				X	
14		X		X				X	X				X	X	X1			X	G	X			X					
15				X		X1		X	X				X	X	X1			X	G	X1p							X	
16				X		X		X	X				X	X	X			X	G	X							X	
17				X		X		X1	X				X	X	X1			X	G	X							X	
18	X			X		X1		X	X				X	X	X			X	G	X								
19		X		X		X1		X	X				X	X	X			X	G	X								
20		X	X	X				X	X				X	X	X			X	G			X					X	
21	X1	X		X				X	X				X	X	X			X				G				X		
22		X		X		X		X1	X			X	X	X				X				G	X			X		
23		X		X		X2		X	X			X	X	X				X				G			1	X1		
24		X		X		X1		X3	X			X	X	X				X				G				X		
25				X		X		X	X			X	X	X				X				G		X		X	X	
26				X		X		X	X			X	X	X				X		X		G	X			X		
27	X		X			X1		X	X			X	X	X				X				G				X		
28		X			X			X	X			X	X	X				X				G				X	X	
29	X		X	X1		X1			X				X	X			X	X		X		G				X		
30	X		X	X		X1			X				X	X			X	X		X		G				X		
31		X	X	X1		X1			X					X	X		X	X	G	X						X		
32		X	X1	X1		X		X	X					X	X		X	X	G	X						X		
33		X	X	X		X		X	X					X	X		X	X	G	X						X		
34		X	X			X		X	X					X	X		X	X	G	X					X			
35		X	X1	X1				X	X					X	X		X	X	G	X					X			
36		X	X	X2			X	X	X					X	X		X	X	G	X								
37		X1	X	X		X		X1	X					X	X		X	X	G	X1p								
38	X		X	X				X	X					X	X1		X	X	G	X								
39			X	X				X	X					X	X		X	X	G	X			X					
40		X		X		X		X1	X					X	X		X	X	G								X	
41		X		X1		X		X	X					X	X1		X	X	G								X	
42		X		X1		X		X	X					X	X		X	X	G								X1	
43				X		X		X	X					X	X		X	X	G	X							X	
44				X		X		X	X					X	X		X	X	G	X1							X	
45				X		X		X2	X					X			X	X	G	X						X	X	
46				X		X		X	X					X	X	X	X	X	G	X							X1	

1947/48

Football League position: 15th out of 22 in Division 3 (South) **Manager:** Jack Bray (Matches 1-25), Eddie Hapgood (Matches 31-44)

New league opponents: None

Home-and-away league doubles
For – 1 (Leyton Orient)
Against – 2 (Queens Park Rangers, Reading)

Divisional changes at end of season: Queens Park Rangers to Division 2; Millwall from Division 2

All Matches: Won 14, Drew 11, Lost 19, Goals 58-83

Highest Score: 4 (Matches 4 & 41)

	HOME						AWAY					
	Pl	W	D	L	For	Ag	W	D	L	For	Ag	Pts
Queens Park Rangers	42	16	3	2	44	17	10	6	5	30	20	61
Bournemouth & Boscombe Ath	42	13	5	3	42	13	11	4	6	34	22	57
Walsall	42	13	5	3	37	12	8	4	9	33	28	51
Ipswich Town	42	16	1	4	42	18	7	2	12	25	43	49
Swansea Town	42	14	6	1	48	14	4	6	11	22	38	48
Notts County	42	12	4	5	44	27	7	4	10	24	32	46
Bristol City	42	11	4	6	47	26	7	3	11	30	39	43
Port Vale	42	14	4	3	48	18	2	7	12	15	36	43
Southend United	42	11	8	2	32	16	4	5	12	19	42	43
Reading	42	10	5	6	37	28	5	6	10	19	30	41
Exeter City	42	11	6	4	34	22	4	5	12	21	41	41
Newport County	42	9	8	4	38	28	5	5	11	23	45	41
Crystal Palace	42	12	5	4	32	14	1	8	12	17	35	39
Northampton Town	42	10	5	6	35	32	4	6	11	23	44	39
WATFORD	42	6	9	6	31	37	8	4	9	26	42	38
Swindon Town	42	6	6	9	21	20	4	6	11	20	26	36
Leyton Orient	42	8	5	8	31	32	5	5	11	20	41	36
Torquay United	42	7	6	8	40	29	4	7	10	23	33	35
Aldershot	42	5	10	6	22	26	5	5	11	23	41	35
Bristol Rovers	42	7	3	11	39	34	6	5	10	32	41	34
Norwich City	42	8	3	10	33	34	5	5	11	28	42	34
Brighton & Hove Albion	42	8	4	9	26	31	3	8	10	17	42	34

No	DATE			COMPETITION	OPPONENTS	HOME	AWAY	ATTENDANCE
1	August	Sat	23	Football League, Division 3 (South)	BRIGHTON & HOVE ALBION	2-3 L		9,787
2		Thu	28	Football League, Division 3 (South)	Swansea Town		L 0-3	23,037
3		Sat	30	Football League, Division 3 (South)	Norwich City		L 0-1	20,233
4	September	Wed	3	Football League, Division 3 (South)	SWANSEA TOWN	4-1 W		7,674
5		Sat	6	Football League, Division 3 (South)	BRISTOL ROVERS	3-2 W		10,315
6		Wed	10	Football League, Division 3 (South)	PORT VALE	1-1 D		8,802
7		Sat	13	Football League, Division 3 (South)	Northampton Town		W 1-0	7,817
8		Mon	15	Football League, Division 3 (South)	Port Vale		L 0-7	12,236
9		Sat	20	Football League, Division 3 (South)	ALDERSHOT	1-2 L		9,257
10		Sat	27	Football League, Division 3 (South)	Crystal Palace		W 2-1	16,764
11	October	Sat	4	Football League, Division 3 (South)	TORQUAY UNITED	2-2 D		9,946
12		Sat	11	Football League, Division 3 (South)	Bournemouth & Boscombe Athletic		D 1-1	18,541
13		Sat	18	Football League, Division 3 (South)	IPSWICH TOWN	2-3 L		10,716
14		Sat	25	Football League, Division 3 (South)	Bristol City		W 2-1	31,087
15	November	Sat	1	Football League, Division 3 (South)	READING	0-1 L		11,196
16		Sat	8	Football League, Division 3 (South)	Walsall		L 0-2	18,004
17		Sat	15	Football League, Division 3 (South)	LEYTON ORIENT	2-1 W		8,942
18		Sat	22	Football League, Division 3 (South)	Exeter City		L 1-3	9,623
19		Sat	29	FA Cup, 1st Round (after extra time)	TORQUAY UNITED	1-1 D		9,172
20	December	Sat	6	FA Cup, 1st Round replay	Torquay United		L 0-3	8,000
21		Fri	26	Football League, Division 3 (South)	QUEENS PARK RANGERS	0-1 L		22,406
22		Sat	27	Football League, Division 3 (South)	Queens Park Rangers		L 1-5	18,005
23	January	Sat	3	Football League, Division 3 (South)	NORWICH CITY	2-2 D		7,400
24		Sat	10	Football League, Division 3 (South)	NEWPORT COUNTY	1-2 L		7,427
25		Sat	17	Football League, Division 3 (South)	Bristol Rovers		L 0-3	12,864
26		Sat	24	Football League, Division 3 (South)	Southend United		D 1-1	8,178
27		Sat	31	Football League, Division 3 (South)	NORTHAMPTON TOWN	1-1 D		18,834
28	February	Sat	7	Football League, Division 3 (South)	Aldershot		D 1-1	6,462
29		Sat	14	Football League, Division 3 (South)	CRYSTAL PALACE	0-5 L		14,767
30		Sat	21	Football League, Division 3 (South)	Torquay United		W 1-0	4,494
31		Sat	28	Football League, Division 3 (South)	BOURNEMOUTH & BOSCOMBE ATHLETIC	0-3 L		15,778
32	March	Sat	6	Football League, Division 3 (South)	Ipswich Town		W 3-1	11,644
33		Sat	13	Football League, Division 3 (South)	BRISTOL CITY	1-1 D		13,262
34		Sat	20	Football League, Division 3 (South)	Reading		L 0-2	11,502
35		Fri	26	Football League, Division 3 (South)	Swindon Town		L 0-3	15,000
36		Sat	27	Football League, Division 3 (South)	WALSALL	2-0 W		12,824
37		Mon	29	Football League, Division 3 (South)	SWINDON TOWN	1-0 W		13,925
38	April	Sat	3	Football League, Division 3 (South)	Leyton Orient		W 2-0	13,483
39		Wed	7	Football League, Division 3 (South)	NOTTS COUNTY	1-3 L		12,532
40		Sat	10	Football League, Division 3 (South)	EXETER CITY	3-1 W		10,867
41		Sat	17	Football League, Division 3 (South)	Newport County		W 4-3	8,971
42		Sat	24	Football League, Division 3 (South)	SOUTHEND UNITED	2-2 D		9,964
43		Wed	28	Football League, Division 3 (South)	Brighton & Hove Albion		W 3-1	9,402
44	May	Sat	1	Football League, Division 3 (South)	Notts County		D 3-3	23,076

League ever-presents: None
Most appearances in total: W.T. Harris 43 out of 44   **Most goals in total:** W. Davies 11
Hat-tricks: None   **Penalty goals:** A.W. Hicklin 1
Sent off: None
Full international appearance(s) this season: None

	Calvert, J.W.H.	Chase, C.T.	Cheney, D.	Davies, G.G.	Davies, W.	Dunderdale, W.L.	Eggleston, T.	Evans, D.R.	Farnen, A.L.	Fisher, K.D.W.	Gray, M.	Harper, J.J.	Harris, W.T.	Hartley, T.W.	Hicklin, A.W.	Hunt, G.H.	Jones, B.J.	Lunn, G.	Malpass, S.T.	Morgan, L.	Nolan, P.	Osborne, J	Paton, T.G.	Rigg, T.	Smith, J.T.	Surtees, H.	Thomas, D.W.J.	Usher, J.A.G.	Woodroffe, L.C.	Young, G.	Own goal
Apps	5	2	18	1	36	14	18	6	27	9	10	16	41	6	21	11	25	5	12	8	22	16	8	36	10	13	18	16	19	13	
Subs																															
Goals			5		11	2		1			3	1		1	5							6	8	1		1	7	1	1	2	1
Apps				2	1							2	2		2		2	2						2	2	2		2		1	
Subs																															
Goals																													1		

	Calvert	Chase	Cheney	Davies,G.G.	Davies,W.	Dunderdale	Eggleston	Evans	Farnen	Fisher	Gray	Harper	Harris	Hartley	Hicklin	Hunt	Jones	Lunn	Malpass	Morgan	Nolan	Osborne	Paton	Rigg	Smith	Surtees	Thomas	Usher	Woodroffe	Young	O.g.
1					X			X	X	X	X2					X	X							G	X				X		
2					X	X		X			X	X	X				X	X						G	X				X		
3					X	X					X	X	X				X	X						G	X				X		
4					X2			X1	X			X	X		X1		X							G	X	X				X	
5					X			X	X			X	X		X1		X							G	X	X1				X1	
6					X			X	X			X	X		X1		X							G	X	X				X	
7					X1						X	X	X		X	X	X							G	X	X				X	
8					X						X	X	X		X	X	X							G	X	X				X	
9			G		X	X1					X		X	X		X		X								X			X		
10					X1	X					X		X		X		X				X1			G		X			X	X	
11					X	X					X		X		X		X				X2			G		X			X	X	
12					X	X					X		X		X	X	X				X1			G		X			X	X	
13					X	X1							X		X1p	X	X				X			G	X	X			X	X	
14					X1	X							X		X	X	X				X			G		X			X	X1	
15					X	X							X		X	X	X				X			G		X			X	X	
16					X						X	X	X			X	X				X			G		X			X	X	
17					X						X1	X	X		X	X	X				X1			G		X			X		
18					X1								X		X	X	X				X			G	X	X			X	X	
19					X							X	X		X	X	X				X			G	X	X			X1	X	
20					X	X						X	X		X	X	X				X			G	X	X			X		
21					X	X						X	X		X	X	X				X			G					X	X	
22		X			X	X						X	X		X	X	X							G					X1		
23		X			X1	X						X1	X		X	X		X			X			G					X		
24					X1			X	X			X	X		X		X							G					X	X	
25						X		X	X			X	X		X		X							G					X	X	
26					X	X			X			X	X		X1		X							G					X	X	
27	G		X1		X		X						X			X	X			X	X					X			X		
28	G		X		X								X	X	X	X	X			X	X						X1				
29	G		X		X								X	X		X	X			X	X					X			X		
30	G		X		X						X		X	X1			X			X	X					X			X		
31	G		X		X						X		X	X			X			X	X					X			X		
32			X1		X						X		X				X			X	X	X1		G	X1			X	X1	X	
33			X1		X				X		X		X				X			X	X	X		G		X	X		X		
34			X		X				X		X		X				X			X	X	X		G		X	X		X		
35			X		X				X		X		X		X		X			X	X			G		X			X		
36			X		X				X		X		X				X			X1	X1			G		X			X		
37			X		X				X		X	X	X			X					X			G		X		X	X		1
38			X		X				X		X	X	X			X					X			G		X2		X	X		
39			X		X				X		X	X	X			X					X1			G		X		X	X		
40			X1		X1				X		X	X	X			X					X1			G		X		X	X		
41			X1		X				X		X	X	X			X					X2			G		X		X1	X		
42			X		X1				X		X	X	X			X					X			G				X1	X		
43			X		X				X		X	X	X			X					X2			G				X1	X		
44			X		X1				X		X	X	X			X					X1			G		X		X1			

1948/49

Football League position: 17th out of 22 in Division 3 (South)

Manager: Eddie Hapgood

		HOME					AWAY					
	Pl	W	D	L	For	Ag	W	D	L	For	Ag	Pts
Swansea Town	42	20	1	0	60	11	7	7	7	27	23	62
Reading	42	17	1	3	48	18	8	4	9	29	32	55
Bournemouth & Boscombe Ath	42	15	2	4	42	17	6	8	7	27	31	52
Swindon Town	42	11	9	1	38	20	7	6	8	26	36	51
Bristol Rovers	42	13	5	3	42	23	6	5	10	19	28	48
Brighton & Hove Albion	42	11	5	5	32	26	4	13	4	23	29	48
Ipswich Town	42	14	3	4	53	30	4	6	11	25	47	45
Millwall	42	12	7	2	42	23	5	4	12	21	41	45
Torquay United	42	12	5	4	45	26	5	6	10	20	44	45
Norwich City	42	11	6	4	32	10	5	6	10	35	39	44
Notts County	42	15	3	3	68	19	4	2	15	34	49	43
Exeter City	42	12	5	4	45	26	3	5	13	18	50	40
Port Vale	42	11	3	7	32	21	3	8	10	19	33	39
Walsall	42	9	5	7	34	28	6	3	12	22	36	38
Newport County	42	8	6	7	41	35	6	3	12	27	57	37
Bristol City	42	8	9	4	28	24	3	5	13	16	38	36
WATFORD	42	6	9	6	24	21	4	6	11	17	33	35
Southend United	42	5	10	6	18	18	4	6	11	23	28	34
Leyton Orient	42	9	6	6	36	29	2	6	13	22	51	34
Northampton Town	42	9	6	6	33	20	3	3	15	18	42	33
Aldershot	42	6	5	10	26	29	5	6	10	22	30	33
Crystal Palace	42	7	8	6	27	27	1	3	17	11	49	27

New league opponents: None

Home-and-away league doubles
For – 1 (Walsall)
Against – 3 (Bournemouth & Boscombe Athletic, Exeter City, Swindon Town)

Divisional changes at end of season: Swansea Town to Division 2; Nottingham Forest from Division 2

All Matches: Won 10, Drew 15, Lost 18, Goals 42-56

Highest Score: 4 (Matches 3 & 21)

No	DATE			COMPETITION	OPPONENTS	HOME	AWAY	ATTENDANCE
1	August	Sat	21	Football League, Division 3 (South)	Swansea Town		L 0-2	12,107
2		Wed	25	Football League, Division 3 (South)	NEWPORT COUNTY	2-2 D		10,568
3		Sat	28	Football League, Division 3 (South)	READING	4-1 W		14,534
4	September	Thu	2	Football League, Division 3 (South)	Newport County		D 1-1	4,662
5		Sat	4	Football League, Division 3 (South)	Crystal Palace		L 1-3	16,003
6		Wed	8	Football League, Division 3 (South)	TORQUAY UNITED	1-1 D		10,149
7		Sat	11	Football League, Division 3 (South)	ALDERSHOT	0-1 L		12,253
8		Wed	15	Football League, Division 3 (South)	Torquay United		L 1-3	7,555
9		Sat	18	Football League, Division 3 (South)	BOURNEMOUTH & BOSCOMBE ATHLETIC	0-1 L		12,895
10		Sat	25	Football League, Division 3 (South)	Ipswich Town		W 2-1	15,060
11		Wed	29	Football League, Division 3 (South)	MILLWALL	1-1 D		10,224
12	October	Sat	2	Football League, Division 3 (South)	NOTTS COUNTY	1-1 D		22,612
13		Sat	9	Football League, Division 3 (South)	Brighton & Hove Albion		D 0-0	15,299
14		Sat	16	Football League, Division 3 (South)	SOUTHEND UNITED	0-0 D		13,254
15		Sat	23	Football League, Division 3 (South)	Swindon Town		L 0-1	14,663
16		Sat	30	Football League, Division 3 (South)	LEYTON ORIENT	2-1 W		13,256
17	November	Sat	6	Football League, Division 3 (South)	Exeter City		L 1-2	7,939
18		Sat	13	Football League, Division 3 (South)	BRISTOL CITY	1-1 D		12,360
19		Sat	20	Football League, Division 3 (South)	Northampton Town		D 1-1	8,437
20	December	Sat	4	FA Cup, 1st Round	Leytonstone		L 1-2	6,000
21		Sat	18	Football League, Division 3 (South)	SWANSEA TOWN	4-2 W		11,469
22		Sat	25	Football League, Division 3 (South)	Bristol Rovers		L 1-3	14,367
23		Mon	27	Football League, Division 3 (South)	BRISTOL ROVERS	0-0 D		11,949
24	January	Sat	1	Football League, Division 3 (South)	Reading		L 1-3	8,051
25		Sat	8	Football League, Division 3 (South)	Port Vale		L 1-3	8,613
26		Sat	15	Football League, Division 3 (South)	CRYSTAL PALACE	2-0 W		7,410
27		Sat	22	Football League, Division 3 (South)	Aldershot		D 0-0	6,406
28		Sat	29	Football League, Division 3 (South)	NORWICH CITY	1-1 D		10,129
29	February	Sat	5	Football League, Division 3 (South)	Bournemouth & Boscombe Athletic		L 1-2	13,216
30		Sat	19	Football League, Division 3 (South)	IPSWICH TOWN	1-2 L		10,930
31		Sat	26	Football League, Division 3 (South)	Notts County		L 0-4	32,069
32	March	Sat	5	Football League, Division 3 (South)	BRIGHTON & HOVE ALBION	0-0 D		8,665
33		Sat	12	Football League, Division 3 (South)	Southend United		W 1-0	8,312
34		Sat	19	Football League, Division 3 (South)	SWINDON TOWN	0-3 L		8,830
35		Sat	26	Football League, Division 3 (South)	Leyton Orient		L 0-1	8,479
36	April	Sat	2	Football League, Division 3 (South)	EXETER CITY	0-1 L		7,611
37		Sat	9	Football League, Division 3 (South)	Bristol City		D 1-1	11,902
38		Fri	15	Football League, Division 3 (South)	WALSALL	2-0 W		9,360
39		Sat	16	Football League, Division 3 (South)	NORTHAMPTON TOWN	0-1 L		9,609
40		Mon	18	Football League, Division 3 (South)	Walsall		W 1-0	7,167
41		Sat	23	Football League, Division 3 (South)	Norwich City		W 1-0	16,509
42		Sat	30	Football League, Division 3 (South)	PORT VALE	2-1 W		6,316
43	May	Sat	7	Football League, Division 3 (South)	Millwall		D 2-2	16,585

The following match was abandoned after 63 minutes, owing to fog:						=========	=========	=========
	November	Sat	27	FA Cup, 1st Round	Leytonstone		1-1	7,300

League ever-presents: None
Most appearances in total: D.W.J. Thomas 39 out of 43   Most goals in total: D.W.J. Thomas 14
Hat-tricks: None   Penalty goals: W. Davies 3
Sent off: B. Ratcliffe (Match 8)   Full international appearance(s) this season: None
(In Match 5, two of the opponents' goals were conceded after W.T. Harris had replaced the injured T. Rigg as goalkeeper)

Summary

	Bates, W.H.	Cumner, R.H.	Davies, G.G.	Davies, W.	Drury, G.B.	Eggleston, T.	Farnen, A.L.	Fisher, K.D.W.	Harper, J.J.	Harris, W.T.	High, S.W.	Hunt, G.H.	Jones, B.J.	Lesslie, K.G.	Malpass, S.T.	Morton, G.D.	Nolan, P.	Oliver, H.S.	Osborne, J.	Paton, T.G.	Ratcliffe, B.	Rigg, T.	Ritchie, R.	Surtees, H.	Thomas, D.W.J.	Woodroffe, L.C.	Young, G.	Own goals
Apps	13	35	8	27	33	32	8	28	18	19	7	12	1	7	11	22	2	35	18	26	24	12	1	1	38	19	5	
Subs																												
Goals	1	5		7	3					3				1					5						14		2	
Apps			1	1	1					1				1				1	1	1	1	1			1			
Subs																												
Goals														1														

Match-by-match

Match	Bates, W.H.	Cumner, R.H.	Davies, G.G.	Davies, W.	Drury, G.B.	Eggleston, T.	Farnen, A.L.	Fisher, K.D.W.	Harper, J.J.	Harris, W.T.	High, S.W.	Hunt, G.H.	Jones, B.J.	Lesslie, K.G.	Malpass, S.T.	Morton, G.D.	Nolan, P.	Oliver, H.S.	Osborne, J.	Paton, T.G.	Ratcliffe, B.	Rigg, T.	Ritchie, R.	Surtees, H.	Thomas, D.W.J.	Woodroffe, L.C.	Young, G.	Own goals
1		X		X	X	X				X								X	X		X	G			X	X		
2		X		X1p	X	X				X					X						X	G			X1	X		
3		X1		X		X				X				X1	X				X1		X	G			X1			
4		X		X		X				X				X	X				X		X			X	X1			
5		X		X	X	X				X				X	X				X1		X	G			X			
6		X	G	X	X	X				X				X	X				X1		X				X			
7		X	G	X		X				X				X	X		X	X	X		X							
8		X	G	X	X	X				X			X	X					X1		X		X					
9		X	G	X	X	X				X				X				X	X		X							
10		X	G	X	X	X				X								X	X1		X		X		X			1
11		X		X	X	X				X								X	X		X	G			X1			
12		X		X	X	X				X								X	X		X	G			X1			
13		X		X	X	X				X								X	X		X	G			X			
14		X	G	X	X	X	X			X								X	X		X				X			
15		X	G	X	X	X				X								X	X		X				X			
16		X	G	X1		X		X		X								X	X		X				X1			
17		X1		X	X	X				X							G	X	X		X				X			
18		X1		X	X	X				X								X	X		X	G			X			
19		X		X	X	X				X	X1							X	X		X				X	X		
20				X	X	X				X				X1				X	X		X	X	G		X			
21	X	X1		X1	X		X								X			X			X	G			X2	X		
22	X	X		X	X		X								X			X			X	G			X1	X		
23	X	X		X	X	X	X								X	G		X							X	X		
24	X	X		X	X	X	X								X	G		X							X1	X		
25	X	X			X		X								X	G		X					X	X	X1		X	
26		X		X	X			X	X	X2						G		X					X		X		X	
27		X		X	X			X	X	X						G		X					X		X		X	
28	X			X	X			X	X	X						G		X					X		X		X	1
29	X			X	X	X		X	X	X						G		X							X1		X	
30	X1			X	X			X	X	X	X					G	X	X							X			
31	X		X	X	X			X		X						G		X		X					X			
32	X			X	X			X	X			X				G		X		X					X	X		
33	X			X1	X	X		X	X							G		X		X					X	X		
34	X			X	X			X	X			X				G		X		X					X	X		
35	X	X		X		X			X			X				G		X							X	X		
36		X		X				X	X			X				G		X		X				X	X	X		
37		X		X1	X			X	X			X				G		X		X					X	X		
38		X		X	X1			X	X			X				G		X		X					X1	X		
39		X			X			X	X			X				G		X	X	X					X	X		
40		X		X	X			X	X			X				G		X		X					X1	X		
41		X		X1p	X			X	X			X				G		X		X					X	X		
42		X		X2p	X			X	X			X				G		X		X					X	X		
43		X1		X1	X			X	X			X				G		X		X					X	X		
		X		X		X			X	X						X1		X	X	X	X	G			X			

1949/50

Football League position: 6th out of 22 in Division 3 (South) **Manager:** Eddie Hapgood (Matches 1–37), Ron Gray (Matches 38–47)

New league opponents: Nottingham Forest

Home-and-away league doubles
For – 3 (Aldershot, Bristol City, Nottingham Forest)
Against – 2 (Exeter City, Port Vale)

Divisional changes at end of season: Notts County to Division 2; Plymouth Argyle from Division 2; Colchester United & Gillingham elected to increase the division to one of 24 clubs

All Matches: Won 19, Drew 14, Lost 14, Goals 56-39

Highest Score: 6 (Matches 21 & 26)

		HOME					AWAY					
	Pl	W	D	L	For	Ag	W	D	L	For	Ag	Pts
Notts County	42	17	3	1	60	12	8	5	8	35	38	58
Northampton Town	42	12	6	3	43	21	8	5	8	29	29	51
Southend United	42	15	4	2	43	15	4	9	8	23	33	51
Nottingham Forest	42	11	0	3	37	15	7	9	5	30	24	49
Torquay United	42	13	6	2	40	23	6	4	11	26	40	48
WATFORD	42	10	6	5	26	15	6	7	8	19	22	45
Crystal Palace	42	12	5	4	35	21	3	9	9	20	33	44
Brighton & Hove Albion	42	9	8	4	32	24	7	4	10	25	45	44
Bristol Rovers	42	12	5	4	34	18	7	0	14	17	33	43
Reading	42	15	2	4	48	21	2	6	13	22	43	42
Norwich City	42	11	5	5	44	21	5	5	11	21	42	42
Bournemouth & Boscombe Ath	42	11	6	4	38	19	5	4	12	19	37	42
Port Vale	42	12	6	3	33	13	3	5	13	14	29	41
Swindon Town	42	9	7	5	41	30	6	4	11	18	32	41
Bristol City	42	12	4	5	38	19	3	6	12	22	42	40
Exeter City	42	9	8	4	37	27	5	3	13	26	48	39
Ipswich Town	42	9	6	6	36	36	3	5	13	21	50	35
Leyton Orient	42	10	6	5	37	24	2	5	14	16	35	35
Walsall	42	8	5	5	37	25	1	8	12	24	37	34
Aldershot	42	10	5	6	30	16	3	3	15	18	44	34
Newport County	42	11	5	5	50	34	2	3	16	17	64	34
Millwall	42	11	1	9	39	29	3	3	15	16	34	32

No	DATE			COMPETITION	OPPONENTS	HOME	AWAY	ATTENDANCE
1	August	Sat	20	Football League, Division 3 (South)	Leyton Orient		D 0-0	16,522
2		Thu	25	Football League, Division 3 (South)	READING	1-1 D		12,671
3		Sat	27	Football League, Division 3 (South)	EXETER CITY	1-2 L		11,869
4		Wed	31	Football League, Division 3 (South)	Reading		L 0-1	15,460
5	September	Sat	3	Football League, Division 3 (South)	Ipswich Town		D 1-1	14,410
6		Wed	7	Football League, Division 3 (South)	Bournemouth & Boscombe Athletic		D 0-0	16,318
7		Sat	10	Football League, Division 3 (South)	Port Vale		0-2 L	11,583
8		Thu	15	Football League, Division 3 (South)	BOURNEMOUTH & BOSCOMBE ATHLETIC	4-1 W		7,564
9		Sat	17	Football League, Division 3 (South)	Notts County		L 0-1	33,962
10		Sat	24	Football League, Division 3 (South)	SOUTHEND UNITED	1-0 W		11,244
11	October	Sat	1	Football League, Division 3 (South)	Bristol Rovers		W 2-0	14,906
12		Sat	8	Football League, Division 3 (South)	Swindon Town		W 1-0	14,298
13		Sat	15	Football League, Division 3 (South)	TORQUAY UNITED	1-0 W		13,133
14		Sat	22	Football League, Division 3 (South)	Aldershot		W 1-0	7,932
15		Sat	29	Football League, Division 3 (South)	NOTTINGHAM FOREST	1-0 W		17,467
16	November	Sat	5	Football League, Division 3 (South)	Northampton Town		D 0-0	9,783
17		Sat	12	Football League, Division 3 (South)	NORWICH CITY	0-0 D		16,065
18		Sat	19	Football League, Division 3 (South)	Newport County		D 3-3	11,884
19		Sat	26	FA Cup, 1st Round	Bromley		W 2-1	8,750
20	December	Sat	3	Football League, Division 3 (South)	Brighton & Hove Albion		L 1-2	9,775
21		Sat	10	FA Cup, 2nd Round	NETHERFIELD	6-0 W		15,545
22		Sat	17	Football League, Division 3 (South)	LEYTON ORIENT	2-1 W		9,500
23		Sat	24	Football League, Division 3 (South)	Exeter City		L 1-3	7,565
24		Mon	26	Football League, Division 3 (South)	Crystal Palace		L 0-2	15,056
25		Tue	27	Football League, Division 3 (South)	CRYSTAL PALACE	0-0 D		16,985
26		Sat	31	Football League, Division 3 (South)	IPSWICH TOWN	6-0 W		10,638
27	January	Sat	7	FA Cup, 3rd Round	PRESTON NORTH END	2-2 D		25,019
28		Wed	11	FA Cup, 3rd Round replay	Preston North End		W 1-0	27,000
29		Sat	14	Football League, Division 3 (South)	Port Vale		L 0-2	17,429
30		Sat	21	Football League, Division 3 (South)	NOTTS COUNTY	2-1 W		17,611
31		Sat	28	FA Cup, 4th Round	MANCHESTER UNITED	0-1 L		32,384
32	February	Sat	4	Football League, Division 3 (South)	Southend United		D 1-1	11,736
33		Sat	11	Football League, Division 3 (South)	WALSALL	3-0 W		10,984
34		Sat	18	Football League, Division 3 (South)	BRISTOL ROVERS	0-2 L		14,591
35		Sat	25	Football League, Division 3 (South)	SWINDON TOWN	1-2 L		11,214
36	March	Sat	4	Football League, Division 3 (South)	Torquay United		L 1-2	8,556
37		Sat	11	Football League, Division 3 (South)	ALDERSHOT	1-0 W		10,981
38		Sat	18	Football League, Division 3 (South)	Nottingham Forest		W 1-0	17,288
39		Sat	25	Football League, Division 3 (South)	NORTHAMPTON TOWN	0-0 D		13,630
40	April	Sat	1	Football League, Division 3 (South)	Norwich City		L 1-2	20,014
41		Fri	7	Football League, Division 3 (South)	Millwall		W 3-1	26,158
42		Sat	8	Football League, Division 3 (South)	NEWPORT COUNTY	0-1 L		11,729
43		Mon	10	Football League, Division 3 (South)	MILLWALL	0-0 D		7,199
44		Sat	15	Football League, Division 3 (South)	Bristol City		W 1-0	12,394
45		Thu	20	Football League, Division 3 (South)	BRISTOL CITY	2-0 W		8,977
46		Sat	22	Football League, Division 3 (South)	BRIGHTON & HOVE ALBION	0-0 D		10,845
47		Sat	29	Football League, Division 3 (South)	Walsall		D 1-1	4,017

League ever-presents: T.G. Brown, J.J. Harper, G.D. Morton, T.G. Paton, D.W.J. Thomas
Most appearances in total: T.G. Brown, J.J. Harper, G.D. Morton, T.G. Paton & D.W.J. Thomas 47 out of 47   **Most goals in total:** D.W.J. Thomas 21
Hat-tricks: None   **Penalty goals:** H.S. Oliver 2
Sent off: None
Full international appearance(s) this season: None

	Brown, T.G.	Cunner, R.H.	Davies, W.	Day, A.	Drury, G.B.	Eggleston, T.	Fisher, K.D.W.	Harper, J.J.	Hartburn, J.	Hunt, G.H.	Jackett, F.	Jones, T.	Morton, G.D.	Nolan, P.	Oliver, H.S.	Paton, T.G.	Pilkington, L.	Stockley, K.S.	Thomas, D.W.J.	Woodroffe, L.C.	Worthington, E.S.	Own goals
Apps	42	23	7	4	2	35	34	42	34	12	2	15	42	3	37	42	3	1	42	17	23	
Subs																						
Goals	5	2	3	1		1			6			2							17	3	4	1
Apps	5	4	2			5	3	5	4			1	5		5	5		1	5		5	
Subs																						
Goals	1								2			1			2				4		1	
1	X	X			X	X		X		X			G		X	X			X	X		
2	X	X				X		X		X			G		X	X			X	X	X1	
3	X	X				X		X		X			G		X	X			X	X1	X	
4	X		X				X	X		X		X	G		X	X			X	X		
5	X			X1			X	X	X	X			G		X	X			X	X		
6	X		X				X	X	X	X			G		X	X			X	X		
7	X		X				X	X	X	X			G		X	X			X	X		
8	X1						X	X	X	X			G		X	X			X2	X1	X	
9	X						X	X	X	X			G		X	X			X	X		
10	X						X	X	X			X	G		X	X			X1		X	
11	X					X	X	X	X			X	G			X			X2		X	
12	X					X	X	X	X			X1	G			X			X		X	
13	X					X	X	X	X			X	G		X	X			X1		X	
14	X					X	X	X	X			X1	G		X	X			X		X	
15	X					X	X	X	X1			X	G		X	X			X		X	
16	X					X	X	X	X			X	G		X	X			X		X	
17	X					X	X	X	X			X	G		X	X			X		X	
18	X					X	X	X	X1			X	G		X	X			X2		X	
19	X					X	X	X	X1			X1	G		X	X			X		X	
20	X					X	X	X	X			X	G		X	X			X1		X	
21	X1	X				X	X	X	X1				G		X1p	X			X2		X	1
22	X	X1				X	X	X	X				G		X	X			X		X1	
23	X	X1			X	X		X	X				G		X	X			X		X	
24	X	X				X		X	X		X		G		X	X			X		X	
25	X	X				X		X	X		X		G		X	X			X		X	
26	X1	X				X		X	X1				G		X	X		X	X2		X2	
27	X	X				X		X	X				G		X1p	X		X	X1		X	
28	X	X	X			X		X	X				G		X	X			X1		X	
29	X	X	X			X		X	X			X	G		X	X			X			
30	X	X	X1			X	X	X				X	G	X		X			X			1
31	X	X	X			X	X	X					G		X	X			X		X	
32	X1	X	X			X	X	X					G		X	X			X		X	
33	X	X	X1			X	X	X					G		X	X			X2		X	
34	X	X	X			X	X	X					G		X	X			X		X	
35	X	X				X	X	X					G	X		X			X1	X		
36	X	X				X	X	X					G	X		X			X1	X		
37	X1	X				X	X	X				X	G		X	X			X			
38	X					X	X	X	X1			X	G		X	X			X	X		
39	X					X	X	X	X				G		X	X	X		X	X		
40	X	X				X	X	X					G		X	X			X1	X		
41	X1	X				X	X	X					G		X	X			X1	X1		
42	X	X				X	X	X					G		X	X			X	X		
43	X					X	X	X	X				G		X	X			X	X	X	
44	X	X	X1			X	X	X					G		X	X			X			
45	X	X				X1	X	X	X1				G		X	X	X		X			
46	X	X	X			X	X	X					G		X	X			X			
47	X	X				X	X	X	X1				G		X	X	X		X			

1950/51

Football League position: 23rd out of 24 in Division 3 (South)
Manager: Ron Gray

New league opponents: Colchester United

Home-and-away league doubles
For – 1 (Leyton Orient)
Against – 7 (Bristol City, Ipswich Town, Northampton Town, Norwich City, Southend United, Swindon Town, Walsall)

Divisional changes at end of season: Nottingham Forest to Division 2; Shrewsbury Town from Division 3 (North)

All Matches: Won 9, Drew 11, Lost 27, Goals 54-90

Highest Score: 5 (Match 7)

	HOME					AWAY					
	Pl	W	D	L	For	Ag	W	D	L	For	Ag	Pts
Nottingham Forest	46	16	6	1	57	17	14	4	5	53	23	70
Norwich City	46	16	6	1	42	14	9	8	6	40	31	64
Reading	46	15	6	2	57	17	6	9	8	31	36	57
Plymouth Argyle	46	16	5	2	54	19	8	4	11	31	36	57
Millwall	46	15	6	2	52	23	8	4	11	28	34	56
Bristol Rovers	46	15	7	1	46	18	5	8	10	18	24	55
Southend United	46	15	4	4	64	27	6	6	11	28	42	52
Ipswich Town	46	15	4	4	48	24	8	2	13	21	34	52
Bristol City	46	15	4	4	41	25	5	7	11	23	34	51
Bournemouth & Boscombe Ath	46	17	5	1	49	16	5	2	16	16	41	51
Newport County	46	13	4	6	48	25	6	5	12	29	45	47
Port Vale	46	13	6	4	43	24	3	7	13	25	44	45
Brighton & Hove Albion	46	11	8	4	51	31	2	9	12	20	48	43
Exeter City	46	11	4	8	33	30	7	2	14	29	55	42
Walsall	46	12	4	7	32	20	3	6	14	20	42	40
Colchester United	46	12	5	6	43	25	2	4	17	20	51	40
Swindon Town	46	15	4	4	38	17	3	0	20	17	50	40
Aldershot	46	11	8	4	37	20	4	2	17	19	68	40
Leyton Orient	46	13	2	8	36	28	2	6	15	17	47	38
Torquay United	46	13	2	8	47	39	1	7	15	17	42	37
Northampton Town	46	8	9	6	39	30	2	7	14	16	37	36
Gillingham	46	10	7	6	41	30	3	2	18	28	71	35
WATFORD	46	8	5	10	29	30	2	1	16	25	60	29
Crystal Palace	46	6	5	12	18	39	2	6	15	15	45	27

No	DATE			COMPETITION	OPPONENTS	HOME	AWAY	ATTENDANCE
1	August	Sat	19	Football League, Division 3 (South)	Southend United		L 1-5	15,446
2		Thu	24	Football League, Division 3 (South)	READING	3-1 W		13,174
3		Sat	26	Football League, Division 3 (South)	EXETER CITY	1-2 L		12,203
4		Wed	30	Football League, Division 3 (South)	Reading		L 0-1	13,295
5	September	Sat	2	Football League, Division 3 (South)	Bournemouth & Boscombe Athletic		D 3-3	15,899
6		Thu	7	Football League, Division 3 (South)	NEWPORT COUNTY	0-2 L		9,451
7		Sat	9	Football League, Division 3 (South)	GILLINGHAM	5-0 W		10,529
8		Thu	14	Football League, Division 3 (South)	Newport County		D 2-2	12,116
9		Sat	16	Football League, Division 3 (South)	Bristol City		L 0-3	17,645
10		Sat	23	Football League, Division 3 (South)	MILLWALL	0-0 D		18,074
11		Sat	30	Football League, Division 3 (South)	BRIGHTON & HOVE ALBION	1-1 D		9,611
12	October	Sat	7	Football League, Division 3 (South)	Norwich City		L 1-3	24,623
13		Sat	14	Football League, Division 3 (South)	NORTHAMPTON TOWN	0-1 L		14,409
14		Sat	21	Football League, Division 3 (South)	Port Vale		L 1-2	12,112
15		Sat	28	Football League, Division 3 (South)	NOTTINGHAM FOREST	1-1 D		14,699
16	November	Sat	4	Football League, Division 3 (South)	Torquay United		L 2-3	6,897
17		Sat	11	Football League, Division 3 (South)	ALDERSHOT	1-2 L		10,212
18		Sat	18	Football League, Division 3 (South)	Swindon Town		L 2-3	8,177
19		Sat	25	FA Cup, 1st Round	Norwich City		L 0-2	21,527
20	December	Sat	9	Football League, Division 3 (South)	CRYSTAL PALACE	1-0 W		7,987
21		Sat	16	Football League, Division 3 (South)	SOUTHEND UNITED	1-3 L		5,910
22		Sat	23	Football League, Division 3 (South)	Exeter City		D 3-3	7,252
23		Mon	25	Football League, Division 3 (South)	LEYTON ORIENT	2-0 W		7,983
24		Tue	26	Football League, Division 3 (South)	Leyton Orient		W 2-1	9,827
25		Sat	30	Football League, Division 3 (South)	BOURNEMOUTH & BOSCOMBE ATHLETIC	2-1 W		9,616
26	January	Wed	10	Football League, Division 3 (South)	Plymouth Argyle		L 1-3	6,887
27		Sat	13	Football League, Division 3 (South)	Gillingham		L 1-3	10,038
28		Sat	20	Football League, Division 3 (South)	BRISTOL CITY	1-2 L		9,032
29		Sat	27	Football League, Division 3 (South)	PLYMOUTH ARGYLE	1-1 D		9,631
30	February	Sat	3	Football League, Division 3 (South)	Millwall		L 0-4	11,373
31		Sat	10	Football League, Division 3 (South)	COLCHESTER UNITED	2-0 W		9,122
32		Sat	17	Football League, Division 3 (South)	Brighton & Hove Albion		D 1-1	7,534
33		Sat	24	Football League, Division 3 (South)	NORWICH CITY	0-2 L		13,293
34	March	Sat	3	Football League, Division 3 (South)	Northampton Town		L 0-6	9,136
35		Sat	10	Football League, Division 3 (South)	PORT VALE	2-0 W		6,610
36		Sat	17	Football League, Division 3 (South)	Nottingham Forest		L 1-2	14,866
37		Fri	23	Football League, Division 3 (South)	IPSWICH TOWN	0-2 L		7,596
38		Sat	24	Football League, Division 3 (South)	TORQUAY UNITED	2-2 D		7,073
39		Mon	26	Football League, Division 3 (South)	Ipswich Town		L 1-2	13,490
40		Sat	31	Football League, Division 3 (South)	Aldershot		D 1-1	5,558
41	April	Sat	6	Football League, Division 3 (South)	SWINDON TOWN	1-2 L		3,658
42		Sat	14	Football League, Division 3 (South)	Colchester United		L 1-4	8,073
43		Thu	19	Football League, Division 3 (South)	Walsall		L 0-1	9,070
44		Sat	21	Football League, Division 3 (South)	BRISTOL ROVERS	1-0 W		6,135
45		Mon	23	Football League, Division 3 (South)	Bristol Rovers		L 0-3	10,735
46		Sat	28	Football League, Division 3 (South)	Crystal Palace		D 1-1	5,238
47	May	Sat	5	Football League, Division 3 (South)	WALSALL	1-3 L		5,147

League ever-presents: None
Most appearances in total: T. Eggleston 44 out of 47   **Most goals in total:** J. Hartburn 13
Hat-tricks: None   **Penalty goals:** J. Hartburn 4, H.S. Oliver 2
Sent off: None
Full international appearance(s) this season: None

	Brown, T.G.	Carpenter, T.A.E.	Case, N.	Collins, A.N.	Cumner, R.H.	Daly, R.G.	Dudley, R.A.	Eggleston, T.	Fisher, K.D.W.	Garbutt, R.H.	Harper, J.J.	Hartburn, J.	Jones, B.J.	Jones, W.M.	Kelly, J.	Laing, R.S.	McCrystal D.	Morton, G.D.	Nolan, P.	Oliver, H.S.	Paton, T.G.	Pilkington, L.	Small, D.	Thomas, D.W.J.	Thompson, C.A.	Varty, T.H.	Wilson, J.T.	Woodroffe, L.C.	Worthington, E.S.
Apps	28	4	10	6	4	3	1	43	35	22	37	32	21	10	9	40	1	41	9	32	40	2	4	7	12	34	10	8	1
Subs																													
Goals	3		4						2	8		13		1		7			1	2				1	5	5		2	
Apps						1			1	1	1	1	1	1				1							1			1	1
Subs																													
Goals																													

#	Brown	Carpenter	Case	Collins	Cumner	Daly	Dudley	Eggleston	Fisher	Garbutt	Harper	Hartburn	Jones B	Jones W	Kelly	Laing	McCrystal	Morton	Nolan	Oliver	Paton	Pilkington	Small	Thomas	Thompson	Varty	Wilson	Woodroffe	Worthington
1	X						X		X		X	X				X1	G			X	X			X					X
2	X			X					X	X1	X	X1				X		G		X1p	X			X					
3	X			X					X		X	X1				X		G		X	X			X					
4									X	X	X	X				X		G		X	X		X	X					
5					X				X	X	X1	X				X1		G		X	X					X1			
6					X				X	X	X	X				X		G		X	X					X			
7									X	X	X1	X	X1			X2		G	X1	X	X					X			
8									X	X	X	X1				X1		G	X	X	X					X			
9									X	X	X	X				X		G	X	X	X			X		X			
10									X	X	X	X				X		G	X	X	X					X			
11	X								X	X	X1	X				X		G		X	X					X			
12	X								X	X	X	X1				X		G		X	X					X			
13	X								X	X	X	X				X		G		X	X			X				X	
14				X					X	X1	X	X	X					G		X						X		X	
15				X					X	X1	X	X	X					G								X		X	
16				X					X	X	X	X	X			X		G								X		X2	
17				X					X	X	X	X	X1p			X		G			X					X		X	
18		G				X			X	X	X1	X	X1p	X	X	X					X					X			
19				X					X	X	X	X	X	X				G								X		X	X
20				X					X	X	X	X	X1	X				G								X		X	
21			X	X	X				X	X	X	X	X1p	X		X		G								X			
22	X	X1							X	X		X1	X			X		G		X	X					X1			
23	X		X						X	X	X	X1	X			X1		G			X					X			
24	X		X						X	X	X	X	X			X		G			X					X2			
25	X		X						X	X	X	X2p	X			X		G			X					X			
26	X	X1							X	X	X	X	X			X		G			X					X			
27	X	X1							X	X		X	X			X		G		X	X	X				X			
28	X1		X						X	X		X	X			X		G		X	X					X			
29	X1								X		X	X	X			X		G		X	X					X			
30	X								X		X	X	X			X		G		X	X					X			
31	X								X		X1	X	X			X		G		X	X					X1	X		
32	X								X		X1	X				X		G		X	X					X	X		
33	X								X		X	X	X			X		G		X	X					X			
34	X								X		X	X			X	X		G		X	X					X			
35	X								X	X1	X			X	X	X		G		X1p	X					X			
36	X										X	X			X	X		G		X	X					X	X1	X	
37	X										X			X	X	X		G		X	X					X	X		
38	X	G									X			X	X	X				X	X					X2	X	X	
39		X1							X		X	X				X		G		X	X					X	X	X	
40	X								X		X	X			X	X1		G	X	X						X			
41	X1								X		X	X				X		G	X	X						X			
42	X								X			X				X		G	X	X	X					X1		X	X
43	X								X	X		X		X	X	X		G			X					X	X	X	
44		G							X	X			X	X	X	X					X				X	X1		X	
45		G							X	X			X	X	X	X					X		X			X		X	
46	X								X				X	X	X			G		X	X		X	X		X1		X	
47			X						X				X	X1				G		X	X		X	X		X	X	X	

- 111 -

1951/52

Football League position: 21st out of 24 in Division 3 (South)
Manager: Haydn Green (Matches 6-48)

New league opponents: Shrewsbury Town

Home-and-away league doubles
For – 2 (Bristol City, Shrewsbury Town)
Against – 4 (Colchester United, Millwall, Plymouth Argyle, Torquay United)

Divisional changes at end of season: Plymouth Argyle to Division 2; Port Vale to Division 3 (North); Coventry City & Queens Park Rangers from Division 2

All Matches: Won 14, Drew 10, Lost 24, Goals 63-83

Highest Score: 5 (Matches 13 & 19)

	HOME					AWAY					
	Pl	W	D	L	For Ag	W	D	L	For Ag	Pts
Plymouth Argyle	46	19	3	1	70 19	10	5	8	37 34	66
Reading	46	19	2	2	73 23	10	1	12	39 37	61
Norwich City	46	18	1	4	55 15	8	8	7	34 35	61
Millwall	46	16	5	2	46 21	7	7	9	28 32	58
Brighton & Hove Albion	46	15	4	4	57 24	9	6	8	30 39	58
Newport County	46	13	7	3	45 26	8	5	10	32 50	54
Bristol Rovers	46	14	5	4	60 20	6	7	10	29 33	52
Northampton Town	46	17	1	5	65 31	5	4	14	28 43	49
Southend United	46	16	6	1	56 17	3	4	16	19 49	48
Colchester United	46	12	7	4	32 22	5	5	13	24 55	46
Torquay United	46	10	3	10	53 42	7	7	9	33 56	44
Aldershot	46	11	4	8	40 27	7	4	12	38 62	44
Port Vale	46	11	11	1	33 16	3	4	16	17 50	43
Bournemouth & Boscombe Ath	46	11	4	8	42 30	5	6	12	27 45	42
Bristol City	46	13	6	4	44 26	2	6	15	14 43	42
Swindon Town	46	9	9	5	29 22	5	5	13	22 46	42
Ipswich Town	46	12	4	7	45 31	4	5	14	18 43	41
Leyton Orient	46	12	5	6	39 26	4	4	15	16 42	41
Crystal Palace	46	9	7	7	32 28	6	2	15	29 52	39
Shrewsbury Town	46	11	3	9	35 29	2	7	14	27 57	36
Watford	46	7	7	9	34 37	6	3	14	23 44	36
Gillingham	46	10	7	6	47 31	1	6	16	24 50	35
Exeter City	46	10	4	9	40 36	3	5	15	25 50	35
Walsall	46	11	3	9	38 31	2	2	19	17 63	31

No	DATE			COMPETITION	OPPONENTS	HOME	AWAY	ATTENDANCE
1	August	Sat	18	Football League, Division 3 (South)	Shrewsbury Town		W 3-2	12,417
2		Thur	23	Football League, Division 3 (South)	LEYTON ORIENT	0-1 L		12,137
3		Sat	25	Football League, Division 3 (South)	ALDERSHOT	2-2 D		10,362
4		Wed	29	Football League, Division 3 (South)	Leyton Orient		D 0-0	11,664
5	September	Sat	1	Football League, Division 3 (South)	Port Vale		D 1-1	11,790
6		Thu	6	Football League, Division 3 (South)	SWINDON TOWN	1-7 L		9,808
7		Sat	8	Football League, Division 3 (South)	Bristol Rovers		W 1-0	20,561
8		Wed	12	Football League, Division 3 (South)	Swindon Town		W 1-0	11,828
9		Sat	15	Football League, Division 3 (South)	PLYMOUTH ARGYLE	1-3 L		9,017
10		Sat	22	Football League, Division 3 (South)	Norwich City		L 0-3	25,123
11		Sat	29	Football League, Division 3 (South)	EXETER CITY	1-1 D		10,310
12	October	Sat	6	Football League, Division 3 (South)	READING	3-1 W		12,472
13		Sat	13	Football League, Division 3 (South)	Newport County		W 5-2	9,636
14		Sat	20	Football League, Division 3 (South)	SOUTHEND UNITED	0-0 D		14,128
15		Sat	27	Football League, Division 3 (South)	Bournemouth & Boscombe Athletic		D 0-0	11,609
16	November	Sat	3	Football League, Division 3 (South)	MILLWALL	1-2 L		17,053
17		Sat	10	Football League, Division 3 (South)	Brighton & Hove Albion		L 1-4	18,203
18		Sat	17	Football League, Division 3 (South)	GILLINGHAM	2-2 D		10,771
19		Sat	24	FA Cup, 1st Round	Aylesbury United		W 5-0	8,000
20	December	Sat	1	Football League, Division 3 (South)	IPSWICH TOWN	1-1 D		10,829
21		Sat	8	Football League, Division 3 (South)	Bristol City		W 3-1	8,511
22		Sat	15	FA Cup, 2nd Round	HARTLEPOOLS UNITED	1-2 L		15,179
23		Sat	22	Football League, Division 3 (South)	Aldershot		L 0-2	4,986
24		Tue	25	Football League, Division 3 (South)	NORTHAMPTON TOWN	2-4 L		7,847
25		Wed	26	Football League, Division 3 (South)	Northampton Town		W 4-1	18,295
26		Sat	29	Football League, Division 3 (South)	PORT VALE	2-0 W		9,023
27	January	Sat	5	Football League, Division 3 (South)	BRISTOL ROVERS	0-3 L		10,947
28		Sat	12	Football League, Division 3 (South)	SHREWSBURY TOWN	4-1 W		7,784
29		Wed	16	Football League, Division 3 (South)	COLCHESTER UNITED	0-1 L		3,528
30		Sat	19	Football League, Division 3 (South)	Plymouth Argyle		L 1-3	20,381
31		Sat	26	Football League, Division 3 (South)	NORWICH CITY	1-1 D		10,040
32	February	Sat	2	Football League, Division 3 (South)	Walsall		L 1-3	6,581
33		Sat	9	Football League, Division 3 (South)	Exeter City		L 0-3	9,597
34		Sat	16	Football League, Division 3 (South)	Reading		L 1-4	15,261
35		Sat	23	Football League, Division 3 (South)	WALSALL	2-0 W		8,909
36	March	Sat	1	Football League, Division 3 (South)	NEWPORT COUNTY	1-1 D		9,553
37		Sat	8	Football League, Division 3 (South)	Southend United		L 1-5	8,779
38		Sat	15	Football League, Division 3 (South)	BOURNEMOUTH & BOSCOMBE ATHLETIC	1-2 L		7,207
39		Sat	22	Football League, Division 3 (South)	Millwall		L 0-1	19,669
40	April	Thu	3	Football League, Division 3 (South)	BRIGHTON & HOVE ALBION	3-1 W		4,488
41		Sat	5	Football League, Division 3 (South)	Gillingham		L 0-1	9,578
42		Fri	11	Football League, Division 3 (South)	CRYSTAL PALACE	2-0 W		10,273
43		Sat	12	Football League, Division 3 (South)	TORQUAY UNITED	1-2 L		8,452
44		Mon	14	Football League, Division 3 (South)	Crystal Palace		L 0-2	12,093
45		Sat	19	Football League, Division 3 (South)	Ipswich Town		L 0-3	8,901
46		Wed	23	Football League, Division 3 (South)	Torquay United		L 0-2	5,686
47		Sat	26	Football League, Division 3 (South)	BRISTOL CITY	3-1 W		6,078
48	May	Sat	3	Football League, Division 3 (South)	Colchester United		L 0-1	6,128

League ever-presents: None
Most appearances in total: T. Eggleston & B.J. Jones 46 out of 48   **Most goals in total:** C.L. Thompson 25
Hat-tricks: C.L. Thompson (Match 13 & Match 25)   **Penalty goals:** T.G. Brown 1, W.M. Jones 1
Sent off: None
Full international appearance(s) this season: None

Season totals

Player	Apps	Subs	Goals	Sub Goals
Adams, L.E.	1			
Brown, T.G.	27		2	
Collins, A.N.	38	2	2	
Cook, R.K.	40	2	6	1
Day, B.J.	3			
Eastway, R.J.	12	2		
Eggleston, T.	44	2	5	
Ephgrave, G.A.	4			
Evans, B.R.	2		1	
Haigh, G.	29	2	5	2
Harper, I.R.	3			
Harper, J.J.	14			
Jackett, F.	11			
Jones, B.J.	44			
Jones, W.M.	17	2	6	
Kelly, J.	16	1	1	
Laing, R.S.	20		1	
Maskell, D.	5			
Meadows, J.A.	18	2	1	
Morton, G.D.	2			
Nolan, P.	13			
Oliver, H.S.	18			
Paton, T.G.	25	2		
Saphin, R.F.E.	39	2		
Small, D.	1			
Steiner, G.G.	3			
Thompson, G.A.	41	2	22	3
Underwood, E.D.	1			
Wilson, J.T.	15	1	3	
Own goals			2	

Match-by-match appearances and goals

Match	Adams	Brown	Collins	Cook	Day	Eastway	Eggleston	Ephgrave	Evans	Haigh	Harper, I.R.	Harper, J.J.	Jackett	Jones, B.J.	Jones, W.M.	Kelly	Laing	Maskell	Meadows	Morton	Nolan	Oliver	Paton	Saphin	Small	Steiner	Thompson	Underwood	Wilson	Own goals
1				X1			X	X1	X					X			X					X	X	G			X1		X	
2			X				X	X	X					X			X					X	X	G			X		X	
3				X1			X		X			X	X	X1			X					X	X	G			X			
4			X				X		X					X	X	X	X					X	X	G			X			
5			X	X	X				X					X	X	X1						X	X	G			X			
6		X	X	X			X	G						X	X	X						X	X				X1			
7		X	X				X	G						X	X	X						X					X1			
8			X	X1			X	G						X	X	X		X				X					X			
9			X	X			X	G						X	X	X		X				X					X1			
10				X			X							X	X	X		X		X		X		G					X	
11		X1		X			X			X				X	X			X						G					X	
12			X	X1			X			X1				X	X1	X					G	X					X			
13			X	X			X			X				X	X1	X					G	X					X3			1
14			X	X			X							X	X	X	X						X	G			X			
15			X	X			X							X	X	X		X					X	G			X			
16			X	X			X							X	X	X			X1			X	X	G			X			
17		X	X	X			X1						X	X		X			X				X	G			X			
18			X	X		X	X2			X				X								X	X	G			X	X		
19			X	X1		X	X			X2				X					X				X	G			X2	X		
20			X	X		X	X							X			X	X					X	G			X1	X		
21			X	X		X	X			X1				X	X								X	G			X2			
22			X	X		X	X			X				X	X								X	G			X1			
23			X	X		X	X			X				X	X								X	G			X			
24		X	X	X		X	X			X1				X									X	G			X1			
25		X	X	X1		X	X			X				X									X	G			X3			
26		X	X	X		X	X1			X1				X									X	G			X			
27		X	X	X		X	X							X									X	G			X			
28		X	X				X			X				X	X2p		X						X	G			X2			
29		X					X			X				X	X		X	X					X	G	X		X			
30		X	X	X			X1			X				X			X	X					X	G			X			
31		X	X	X			X			X				X			X	X					X	G			X1			
32		X	X	X			X			X				X	X1		X						X	G			X			
33		X	X	X			X							X	X		X		X				X	G			X			
34		X	X	X1	X	X						X		X	X		X						X	G						
35	X	X	X	X	X		X							X	X								X	G			X2			
36		X	X1	X			X					X		X	X		X						X	G			X			
37		X	X	X			X					X		X	X		X						X	G			X1	G		
38		X	X	X	X		X							X	X		X1						X	G					X	
39			X	X			X				X	X	X	X									X	G			X		X	
40	X1p	X		X			X				X	X	X	X									X	G					X2	
41		X	X				X				X	X	X	X									X	G			X		X	
42		X	X				X			X				X								X	X	G			X1		X1	
43		X	X				X				X	X1		X	X		X						X	G			X		X	
44		X					X				X	X		X	X		X			X				G			X		X	
45		X					X				X				X			X					X	G		X	X	X		
46		X			X	X	X								X			X				X		G		X	X	X		
47	X1	X	X		X	X	X							X			X					X		G			X1			1
48		X	X				X							X			X					X		G		X	X			

1952/53

Football League position: 10th out of 24 in Division 3 (South) **Manager:** Haydn Green (Matches 1-13), Len Goulden (Matches 18-49)

	HOME					AWAY					
	Pl	W	D	L	For	Ag	W	D	L	For	Ag	Pts
Bristol Rovers	46	17	4	2	55	19	9	8	6	37	27	64
Millwall	46	14	7	2	46	16	10	7	6	36	28	62
Northampton Town	46	18	4	1	75	30	8	6	9	34	40	62
Norwich City	46	16	6	1	56	17	9	4	10	43	38	60
Bristol City	46	13	8	2	62	28	9	7	7	33	33	59
Coventry City	46	15	5	3	52	22	4	7	12	25	40	50
Brighton & Hove Albion	46	12	6	5	48	30	7	6	10	33	45	50
Southend United	46	15	5	3	41	21	3	8	12	28	53	49
Bournemouth & Boscombe Ath	46	15	3	5	49	23	4	6	13	25	46	47
WATFORD	46	12	8	3	39	21	3	9	11	23	42	47
Reading	46	17	3	3	53	18	2	5	16	16	46	46
Torquay United	46	15	4	4	61	28	3	5	15	26	60	45
Crystal Palace	46	12	7	4	40	26	3	6	14	26	56	43
Leyton Orient	46	12	7	4	52	28	4	3	16	16	45	42
Newport County	46	12	4	7	43	34	4	6	13	27	48	42
Ipswich Town	46	10	7	6	34	28	3	8	12	26	46	40
Exeter City	46	11	8	4	40	24	2	6	15	21	47	40
Swindon Town	46	9	5	9	38	33	5	7	11	26	46	40
Aldershot	46	8	8	7	36	29	4	7	12	25	48	39
Queens Park Rangers	46	9	9	5	37	34	3	6	14	24	48	39
Gillingham	46	10	7	6	30	26	2	8	13	25	48	39
Colchester United	46	9	9	5	40	29	3	5	15	19	47	38
Shrewsbury Town	46	11	5	7	38	35	1	7	15	30	56	36
Walsall	46	5	9	9	35	46	2	1	20	21	72	24

New league opponents: None

Home-and-away league doubles
For - none
Against – none

Divisional changes at end of season: Bristol Rovers to Division 2; Southampton from Division 2

All Matches: Won 16, Drew 18, Lost 15, Goals 66-66

Highest Score: 4 (Match 1)

No	DATE			COMPETITION	OPPONENTS	HOME	AWAY	ATTENDANCE
1	August	Sat	23	Football League, Division 3 (South)	BRISTOL CITY	4-1 W		22,409
2		Mon	25	Football League, Division 3 (South)	Queens Park Rangers		D 2-2	23,007
3		Sat	30	Football League, Division 3 (South)	Torquay United		D 2-2	8,965
4	September	Thu	4	Football League, Division 3 (South)	QUEENS PARK RANGERS	1-1 D		22,875
5		Sat	6	Football League, Division 3 (South)	NORTHAMPTON TOWN	2-1 W		21,959
6		Thu	11	Football League, Division 3 (South)	Shrewsbury Town		L 1-3	9,314
7		Sat	13	Football League, Division 3 (South)	Leyton Orient		L 0-2	16,148
8		Thu	18	Football League, Division 3 (South)	SHREWSBURY TOWN	1-1 D		12,962
9		Sat	20	Football League, Division 3 (South)	IPSWICH TOWN	1-0 W		17,240
10		Thu	25	Football League, Division 3 (South)	BRISTOL ROVERS	2-3 L		13,228
11		Sat	27	Football League, Division 3 (South)	Reading		L 0-3	14,899
12		Tue	30	Football League, Division 3 (South)	Southend United		L 0-1	5,499
13	October	Sat	4	Football League, Division 3 (South)	BOURNEMOUTH & BOSCOMBE ATHLETIC	3-0 W		15,389
14		Sat	11	Football League, Division 3 (South)	SWINDON TOWN	2-1 W		16,541
15		Sat	18	Football League, Division 3 (South)	Aldershot		W 2-1	8,650
16		Sat	25	Football League, Division 3 (South)	COLCHESTER UNITED	2-0 W		15,166
17	November	Sat	1	Football League, Division 3 (South)	Norwich City		L 2-5	23,919
18		Sat	8	Football League, Division 3 (South)	COVENTRY CITY	1-1 D		16,027
19		Sat	15	Football League, Division 3 (South)	Exeter City		1-1 D	10,097
20		Sat	22	FA Cup, 1st Round	Leytonstone		W 2-0	7,560
21		Sat	29	Football League, Division 3 (South)	Millwall		D 1-1	18,029
22	December	Sat	6	FA Cup, 2nd Round	Walthamstow Avenue		D 1-1	8,571
23		Wed	10	FA Cup, 2nd Round replay	WALTHAMSTOW AVENUE (after extra time)	1-2 L		7,841
24		Sat	13	Football League, Division 3 (South)	Walsall		D 0-0	3,251
25		Sat	20	Football League, Division 3 (South)	Bristol City		L 1-5	11,741
26		Fri	26	Football League, Division 3 (South)	CRYSTAL PALACE	2-0 W		12,422
27	January	Sat	3	Football League, Division 3 (South)	TORQUAY UNITED	1-1 D		11,470
28		Sat	10	Football League, Division 3 (South)	WALSALL	3-0 W		11,457
29		Wed	14	Football League, Division 3 (South)	BRIGHTON & HOVE ALBION	2-3 L		4,555
30		Sat	17	Football League, Division 3 (South)	Northampton Town		L 1-4	13,054
31		Sat	24	Football League, Division 3 (South)	LEYTON ORIENT	1-0 W		11,343
32		Sat	31	Football League, Division 3 (South)	Brighton & Hove Albion		W 2-1	13,360
33	February	Sat	7	Football League, Division 3 (South)	Ipswich Town		D 1-1	8,177
34		Sat	14	Football League, Division 3 (South)	READING	2-1 W		8,356
35		Sat	21	Football League, Division 3 (South)	Bournemouth & Boscombe Athletic		L 1-4	9,320
36		Sat	28	Football League, Division 3 (South)	Swindon Town		D 0-0	8,081
37	March	Sat	7	Football League, Division 3 (South)	ALDERSHOT	1-1 D		11,650
38		Sat	14	Football League, Division 3 (South)	Colchester United		D 1-1	6,657
39		Sat	21	Football League, Division 3 (South)	NORWICH CITY	3-2 W		15,697
40		Sat	28	Football League, Division 3 (South)	Coventry City		L 0-1	8,059
41	April	Fri	3	Football League, Division 3 (South)	Newport County		D 1-1	9,319
42		Sat	4	Football League, Division 3 (South)	EXETER CITY	3-1 W		12,751
43		Mon	6	Football League, Division 3 (South)	NEWPORT COUNTY	0-1 L		11,455
44		Sat	11	Football League, Division 3 (South)	Bristol Rovers		W 3-0	22,614
45		Thu	16	Football League, Division 3 (South)	GILLINGHAM	0-0 D		8,322
46		Sat	18	Football League, Division 3 (South)	MILLWALL	1-1 D		17,688
47		Thu	23	Football League, Division 3 (South)	SOUTHEND UNITED	1-1 D		10,642
48		Sat	25	Football League, Division 3 (South)	Gillingham		L 1-2	10,507
49		Wed	29	Football League, Division 3 (South)	Crystal Palace		L 0-1	6,020

League ever-presents: A.N. Collins
Most appearances in total: A.N. Collins 49 out of 49   **Most goals in total:** J.A. Meadows 13
Hat-tricks: None   **Penalty goals:** J.D. Bowie 2, J.A. Meadows 2
Sent off: None
Full international appearance(s) this season: None

	Bowie, J.D.	Brown, T.G.	Collins, A.N.	Cook, R.K. //	Croker, P.H.I. //	Eggleston, T. //	Evans, H. //	Gallogly, C. //	Jackett, F. //	Jones, B.J.	Kelly, J.	Meadows, J.A.	Mitchell, F.R.	Nolan, P.	Paterson, T.	Paton, J.	Phipps, H.J.	Reid, M.J. //	Saphin, R.F.E.	Thompson, C.A. //	Underwood, E.D.	Own goals
Apps	32	5	46	13	23	5	7	35	1	38	36	26	38	8	29	33	41	19	17	25	29	
Subs																						
Goals	11		6	2			2				1	12			6	2		8		9		3
Apps			3	1	3					3	3	2	3	3	3	3				3	3	
Subs																						
Goals			1									1								2		
1	X1		X		X	X		X					X		X	X1	X		G	X2		
2	X		X		X	X		X					X		X	X	X		G	X2		
3	X1		X		X			X					X		X1	X	X		G	X		
4	X		X	X	X	X		X					X		X1	X	X		G			
5	X1		X	X	X	X		X					X		X		X		G	X1		
6			X	X	X			X		X			X		X	X	X		G	X1		
7	X		X	X	X			X		X			X		X		X		G	X		
8	X	X	X		X			X		X			X1				X		G	X		
9	X	X	X					X		X	X		X1				X		G	X		
10	X		X	X				X		X	X		X1	X			X		G	X1		
11	X	X	X		X			X		X			X			X	X		G	X		
12	X		X		X			X		X		X	X			X	X		G	X		
13	X		X1		X			X		X			X			X1	X		G	X		1
14	X1p		X		X			X		X			X			X	X		G	X1		
15	X1		X		X					X	X		X			X	X		G	X		1
16	X1		X	X	X					X	X		X			X	X		G	X		
17		X1	X	X	X					X	X		X		X	X1	X		G	X		
18		X	X1	X						X	X		X		X	X	X			X	G	
19		X1	X	X						X	X		X		X	X	X			X	G	
20		X	X	X						X	X		X		X	X	X			X2	G	
21		X	X	X						X	X		X		X	X	X			X1	G	
22		X	X		X					X	X	X1	X		X	X	X			X	G	
23		X1	X		X					X	X	X	X		X	X	X			X	G	
24		X	X		X					X	X	X	X		X	X		X		X	G	
25		X	X		X					X	X	X1	X	X		X	X			X	G	
26		X	X				X1	X		X	X	X	X			X	X	X1			G	
27		X	X				X	X		X	X	X	X			X	X	X1			G	
28		X	X				X	X		X	X	X2p	X			X	X	X1			G	
29		X	X				X1	X		X	X	X1	X			X	X	X1			G	
30		X	X				X	X		X	X	X	X			X	X	X1			G	
31		X	X				X	X		X	X	X1p	X			X	X	X			G	
32		X1	X				X	X		X	X1	X	X			X	X			X	G	
33	X		X					X		X	X	X1	X			X	X	X			G	
34	X		X1					X		X	X	X			X	X	X	X1			G	
35	X1		X					X		X	X	X	X		X	X	X				G	
36	X		X					X		X	X	X	X	X	X						G	
37	X		X					X		X	X	X	X	X		X		X1			G	
38	X		X					X		X	X	X1	X	X	X			X			G	
39	X1p		X					X		X	X	X1	X			X	X	X1			G	
40	X		X					X		X	X	X			X	X	X	X			G	
41	X		X1					X		X	X	X			X	X	X	X			G	
42	X		X					X		X	X	X2			X	X	X	X1			G	
43	X		X					X		X	X	X			X	X	X	X			G	
44	X2		X					X		X	X	X1			X	X	X			X	G	
45	X		X					X	X	X	X	X				X	X			X	G	
46	X1		X					X		X	X	X	X			X	X			X	G	
47	X		X		X					X	X	X1	X			X	X	X			G	
48	X	X	X		X					X	X	X	X			X	X			G		1
49	X	X	X		X					X	X		X		X	X	X			X	G	

1953/54

Football League position: 4th out of 24 in Division 3 (South)
Manager: Len Goulden

New league opponents: None

Home-and-away league doubles
For – 3 (Coventry City, Gillingham, Newport County)
Against – 2 (Exeter City, Norwich City)

Divisional changes at end of season: Ipswich Town to Division 2; Brentford from Division 2

All Matches: Won 21, Drew 10, Lost 16, Goals 85-72

Highest Score: 6 (Matches 8 & 22)

		HOME					AWAY					
	Pl	W	D	L	For	Ag	W	D	L	For	Ag	Pts
Ipswich Town	46	15	5	3	47	19	12	5	6	35	32	64
Brighton & Hove Albion	46	17	3	3	57	31	9	6	8	29	30	61
Bristol City	46	18	3	2	59	18	7	3	13	29	48	56
WATFORD	46	16	3	4	52	23	5	7	11	33	46	52
Northampton Town	46	18	4	1	63	18	2	7	14	19	37	51
Southampton	46	17	5	1	51	22	5	2	16	25	41	51
Norwich City	46	13	5	5	43	28	7	6	10	30	38	51
Reading	46	14	3	6	57	33	6	6	11	29	40	49
Exeter City	46	12	2	9	39	22	8	6	9	29	36	48
Gillingham	46	14	3	6	37	22	5	7	11	24	44	48
Leyton Orient	46	14	5	4	48	26	4	6	13	31	47	47
Millwall	46	15	3	5	44	24	4	6	13	30	53	47
Torquay United	46	10	10	3	48	33	7	2	14	33	55	46
Coventry City	46	14	4	5	36	15	4	4	15	25	41	45
Newport County	46	14	4	5	42	28	5	2	16	19	53	44
Southend United	46	15	2	6	46	22	3	5	13	23	49	43
Aldershot	46	11	5	7	45	31	6	4	13	29	55	43
Queens Park Rangers	46	10	5	8	32	25	6	5	12	28	43	42
Bournemouth & Boscombe Ath	46	11	6	6	32	20	3	16	20	43	42	
Swindon Town	46	13	5	5	48	21	2	5	16	19	49	40
Shrewsbury Town	46	12	8	3	48	34	2	4	17	17	42	40
Crystal Palace	46	11	7	5	41	30	3	5	15	19	56	40
Colchester United	46	7	9	5	34	29	3	3	17	15	49	30
Walsall	46	8	5	10	22	27	1	3	19	18	60	26

No	DATE			COMPETITION	OPPONENTS	HOME	AWAY	ATTENDANCE
1	August	Wed	19	Football League, Division 3 (South)	Southampton	L 0-2		16,754
2		Sat	22	Football League, Division 3 (South)	Shrewsbury Town	L 4-6		12,080
3		Mon	24	Football League, Division 3 (South)	Millwall	L 0-1		18,321
4		Sat	29	Football League, Division 3 (South)	TORQUAY UNITED	3-1 W		11,166
5	September	Tue	1	Football League, Division 3 (South)	MILLWALL	2-1 W		13,997
6		Sat	5	Football League, Division 3 (South)	Northampton Town	L 1-4		13,827
7		Wed	9	Football League, Division 3 (South)	Reading	L 1-4		12,671
8		Sat	12	Football League, Division 3 (South)	GILLINGHAM	6-1 W		12,929
9		Tue	15	Football League, Division 3 (South)	READING	3-0 W		12,729
10		Sat	19	Football League, Division 3 (South)	Coventry City		W 1-0	13,752
11		Wed	23	Football League, Division 3 (South)	Brighton & Hove Albion		D 3-3	14,557
12		Sat	26	Football League, Division 3 (South)	BOURNEMOUTH & BOSCOMBE ATHLETIC	2-3 L		17,233
13		Tue	29	Football League, Division 3 (South)	BRIGHTON & HOVE ALBION	1-1 D		9,560
14	October	Sat	3	Football League, Division 3 (South)	Ipswich Town		L 0-1	15,406
15		Sat	10	Football League, Division 3 (South)	Newport County		W 1-0	5,959
16		Sat	17	Football League, Division 3 (South)	NORWICH CITY	1-3 L		15,116
17		Sat	24	Football League, Division 3 (South)	Queens Park Rangers		W 4-0	15,434
18		Sat	31	Football League, Division 3 (South)	SOUTHAMPTON	2-0 W		13,157
19	November	Sat	7	Football League, Division 3 (South)	Colchester United		D 2-2	6,905
20		Sat	14	Football League, Division 3 (South)	CRYSTAL PALACE	4-1 W		14,547
21		Sat	21	FA Cup, 1st Round	Nuneaton Borough	L 0-3		12,665
22		Sat	28	Football League, Division 3 (South)	ALDERSHOT	6-1 W		12,685
23	December	Sat	5	Football League, Division 3 (South)	Swindon Town		D 2-2	8,769
24		Sat	19	Football League, Division 3 (South)	SHREWSBURY TOWN	3-1 W		10,194
25		Fri	25	Football League, Division 3 (South)	SOUTHEND UNITED	2-2 D		12,002
26		Sat	26	Football League, Division 3 (South)	Southend United		L 0-3	7,545
27	January	Sat	2	Football League, Division 3 (South)	Torquay United		D 2-2	7,629
28		Sat	16	Football League, Division 3 (South)	NORTHAMPTON TOWN	1-1 D		13,134
29		Sat	23	Football League, Division 3 (South)	Gillingham		W 3-2	9,547
30	February	Sat	6	Football League, Division 3 (South)	COVENTRY CITY	1-0 W		10,125
31		Sat	13	Football League, Division 3 (South)	Bournemouth & Boscombe Athletic		3-1 W	8,514
32		Wed	24	Football League, Division 3 (South)	WALSALL	3-1 W		4,358
33		Sat	27	Football League, Division 3 (South)	NEWPORT COUNTY	1-0 W		13,428
34	March	Wed	3	Football League, Division 3 (South)	IPSWICH TOWN	1-0 W		7,418
35		Sat	6	Football League, Division 3 (South)	Norwich City		L 1-4	14,349
36		Sat	13	Football League, Division 3 (South)	BRISTOL CITY	2-0 W		13,048
37		Sat	20	Football League, Division 3 (South)	Aldershot		L 1-3	5,943
38		Sat	27	Football League, Division 3 (South)	COLCHESTER UNITED	3-0 W		11,246
39	April	Sat	3	Football League, Division 3 (South)	Crystal Palace		D 1-1	9,477
40		Sat	10	Football League, Division 3 (South)	SWINDON TOWN	2-1 W		11,634
41		Fri	16	Football League, Division 3 (South)	EXETER CITY	0-2 L		14,861
42		Sat	17	Football League, Division 3 (South)	Walsall		D 0-0	7,154
43		Mon	19	Football League, Division 3 (South)	Exeter City		L 1-2	8,939
44		Thu	22	Football League, Division 3 (South)	Leyton Orient		D 1-1	7,095
45		Sat	24	Football League, Division 3 (South)	QUEENS PARK RANGERS	0-2 L		12,431
46		Tue	27	Football League, Division 3 (South)	Bristol City		L 1-2	10,765
47		Fri	30	Football League, Division 3 (South)	LEYTON ORIENT	3-1 W		6,078

League ever-presents: D.G. Bewley
Most appearances in total: D.G. Bewley 47 out of 47   **Most goals in total:** H.R. Brown 21
Hat-tricks: J.D. Bowie (Match 2)   **Penalty goals:** J.D. Bowie 10
Sent off: F.R. Mitchell (Match 26)
Full international appearance(s) this season: None

	Adams, C.J.	Bennett, E.E.	Bewley, D.G.	Bowie, J.D.	Brown, H.R.	Brown, T.G.	Cook, M.	Gallogly, C.	Hapgood, E.A.	Jones, B.J.	Kelly, J.	Meadows, J.A.	Mitchell, F.R.	Nolan, P.	Oelofse, R.J.G.	Paterson, T.	Paton, J.	Phipps, H.J.	Saphin, R.F.E.	Shipwright, W.K.	Smith, E.W.A.	Underwood, E.D.	Wilson, J.T.	Own goals
Apps	11	23	46	43	36	6	44	12	1	29	44	8	40	31	15	13	37	6	1	2	28	22	8	
Subs																								
Goals	1			20	21	1	9				1	2		1		1	11				8		5	4
Apps			1	1	1		1			1	1		1	1			1					1	1	
Subs																								
Goals							1																	
1			X	X	X		X				X	X	X		X		X	X				G		
2			X	X3p	X1		X				X	X	X		X		X	X				G		
3			X	X	X	X	X			X	X		X		X		X					G		
4			X	X1p		X1	X				X		X			X1	X					G	X	
5			X	X			X				X	X1	X			X	X					G	X1	
6			X	X			X				X	X	X			X1	X					G	X	
7			X	X1			X	X			X	X	X	X			X					G	X	
8			X	X2p	X2		X			X	X		X	X		X	X					G		2
9			X	X1	X1		X			X	X		X	X	X1		X					G		
10			X	X	X		X1			X	X		X	X		X	X					G		
11			X	X1	X2		X			X	X		X	X		X	X					G		
12			X	X	X		X1			X	X		X	X	X	X1						G		
13			X	X	X	X	X1			X	X		X	X			X					G		
14			X	X	X		X			X	X		X	X			X					G		
15			X	X	X1	X	X			X	X		X	X			X					G		
16			X	X	X1	X	X			X	X		X	X	X	X						G		
17			X	X1p	X1		X			X	X		X	X			X1				X	G		1
18			X	X	X1		X			X	X		X	X			X				X1	G		
19			X	X1	X		X			X	X		X	X1			X				X	G		
20			X	X	X1		X			X	X		X	X			X1					G	X2	
21			X	X	X		X			X	X		X	X			X					G	X	
22			X	X2p	X2		X2			X	X		X		X		X				X	G		
23			X	X1p	X		X			X	X		X		X		X1				X	G		
24		G	X	X	X		X			X	X		X		X		X1				X2			
25		G	X	X	X2		X			X	X		X		X		X				X			
26		G	X	X			X			X	X	X	X		X		X				X			
27		G	X	X1p	X		X			X	X		X		X		X			X1				
28		G	X	X1p	X		X			X	X		X		X		X				X			
29		G	X	X	X1		X			X	X			X	X	X	X1				X1			
30			X	X1p	X		X			X	X		X		X		X			G	X			
31		G	X	X	X		X1			X	X			X	X	X	X1				X1			
32		G	X	X	X		X1			X	X		X	X			X1				X1			
33		G	X	X1p	X		X			X	X		X	X			X				X			
34		G	X	X	X		X			X	X		X	X			X1				X			
35		G	X	X	X1		X			X	X		X	X			X				X			
36		G	X	X1	X1		X			X	X		X	X			X				X			
37	X	G	X	X	X1		X			X	X		X		X								X	
38	X1	G	X	X	X1		X1	X			X		X		X						X			
39	X	G	X	X	X		X	X		X1		X	X								X			
40	X	G	X	X1	X1		X	X			X		X								X			
41	X	G	X	X	X		X	X			X		X								X			
42	X	G	X	X	X		X	X			X		X								X			
43	X	G	X	X			X1	X			X		X				X				X			
44	X	G	X	X			X				X1	X	X	X			X				X			
45	X	G	X				X				X	X	X	X	X				X		X			
46	X	G	X				X	X			X			X		X			X		X1		X	
47	X	G	X				X	X			X			X		X			X		X2		X2	1

1954/55

Football League position: 7th out of 24 in Division 3 (South)
Manager: Len Goulden

New league opponents: None

Home-and-away league doubles
For – 3 (Colchester United, Newport County, Walsall)
Against – 1 (Bristol City)

Divisional changes at end of season: Bristol City to Division 2; Ipswich Town from Division 2

All Matches: Won 20, Drew 15, Lost 15, Goals 80-67

Highest Score: 7 (Match 6)

	HOME					AWAY					
	Pl	W	D	L	For	Ag	W	D	L	For	Ag	Pts
Bristol City	46	17	4	2	62	22	13	6	4	39	25	70
Leyton Orient	46	16	2	5	48	20	10	7	6	41	27	61
Southampton	46	16	6	1	49	19	8	5	10	26	32	59
Gillingham	46	12	8	3	41	28	8	7	8	36	38	55
Millwall	46	14	6	3	44	25	6	5	12	28	43	51
Brighton & Hove Albion	46	14	4	5	47	27	6	6	11	29	36	50
WATFORD	46	11	9	3	45	26	7	5	11	26	36	50
Torquay United	46	12	6	5	51	39	6	6	11	31	43	48
Coventry City	46	15	5	3	50	26	3	6	14	17	33	47
Southend United	46	13	5	5	48	28	4	7	12	35	52	46
Brentford	46	11	6	6	44	36	5	8	10	38	46	46
Norwich City	46	13	5	5	40	23	5	5	13	20	37	46
Northampton Town	46	13	5	5	47	27	6	3	14	26	54	46
Aldershot	46	12	6	5	44	23	4	7	12	31	48	45
Queens Park Rangers	46	13	7	3	46	25	2	7	14	23	50	44
Shrewsbury Town	46	14	5	4	49	24	2	5	16	21	54	42
Bournemouth & Boscombe Ath	46	7	8	8	32	29	5	10	8	25	36	42
Reading	46	7	10	6	32	26	6	5	12	33	47	41
Newport County	46	8	8	7	32	29	3	8	12	28	44	38
Crystal Palace	46	9	11	3	32	24	2	5	16	20	56	38
Swindon Town	46	10	8	5	30	19	1	7	15	16	45	37
Exeter City	46	9	7	7	30	31	2	8	13	17	42	37
Walsall	46	9	6	8	49	36	1	8	14	26	50	34
Colchester United	46	7	6	10	33	40	2	7	14	20	51	31

No	DATE			COMPETITION	OPPONENTS	HOME	AWAY	ATTENDANCE
1	August	Sat	21	Football League, Division 3 (South)	Queens Park Rangers		L 1-2	19,617
2		Tue	24	Football League, Division 3 (South)	SWINDON TOWN	3-0 W		10,841
3		Sat	28	Football League, Division 3 (South)	NEWPORT COUNTY	3-2 W		15,696
4	September	Wed	1	Football League, Division 3 (South)	Swindon Town		1-6 L	10,279
5		Sat	4	Football League, Division 3 (South)	Exeter City		D 0-0	9,304
6		Tue	7	Football League, Division 3 (South)	CRYSTAL PALACE	7-1 W		11,861
7		Sat	11	Football League, Division 3 (South)	COLCHESTER UNITED	2-0 W		14,488
8		Wed	15	Football League, Division 3 (South)	Crystal Palace		D 1-1	9,549
9		Sat	18	Football League, Division 3 (South)	Norwich City		L 1-3	20,953
10		Tue	21	Football League, Division 3 (South)	NORTHAMPTON TOWN	1-1 D		10,692
11		Sat	25	Football League, Division 3 (South)	SOUTHEND UNITED	1-1 D		14,968
12		Thu	30	Football League, Division 3 (South)	Northampton Town		W 1-0	4,128
13	October	Sat	2	Football League, Division 3 (South)	Aldershot		L 0-3	7,669
14		Sat	9	Football League, Division 3 (South)	LEYTON ORIENT	1-3 L		17,544
15		Sat	16	Football League, Division 3 (South)	Gillingham		W 1-0	10,232
16		Sat	23	Football League, Division 3 (South)	READING	1-3 L		12,738
17		Sat	30	Football League, Division 3 (South)	Coventry City		L 2-3	14,143
18	November	Sat	6	Football League, Division 3 (South)	WALSALL	4-0 W		6,928
19		Sat	13	Football League, Division 3 (South)	Bristol City		L 0-1	21,690
20		Sat	20	FA Cup, 1st Round	Corby Town	W 2-0		6,783
21		Sat	27	Football League, Division 3 (South)	Brighton & Hove Albion		L 1-3	10,359
22	December	Sat	4	Football League, Division 3 (South)	BRENTFORD	2-2 D		10,438
23		Sat	11	FA Cup, 2nd Round	Carlisle United		D 2-2	13,576
24		Wed	15	FA Cup, 2nd Round replay	CARLISLE UNITED	4-1 W		5,500
25		Sat	18	Football League, Division 3 (South)	QUEENS PARK RANGERS	1-1 D		11,427
26		Sat	25	Football League, Division 3 (South)	Bournemouth & Boscombe Athletic		D 1-1	9,897
27		Mon	27	Football League, Division 3 (South)	BOURNEMOUTH & BOSCOMBE ATHLETIC	1-0 W		15,202
28	January	Sat	1	Football League, Division 3 (South)	Newport County		W 2-0	7,132
29		Sat	8	FA Cup, 3rd Round	DONCASTER ROVERS	1-2 L		17,130
30		Sat	22	Football League, Division 3 (South)	Colchester United		W 3-1	4,729
31		Sat	29	Football League, Division 3 (South)	Millwall		L 0-1	14,969
32	February	Sat	5	Football League, Division 3 (South)	NORWICH CITY	2-2 D		10,456
33		Sat	12	Football League, Division 3 (South)	Southend United		W 3-1	6,188
34		Sat	19	Football League, Division 3 (South)	ALDERSHOT	0-0 D		6,066
35		Sat	26	Football League, Division 3 (South)	Leyton Orient		W 1-0	17,476
36	March	Sat	5	Football League, Division 3 (South)	GILLINGHAM	1-1 D		9,298
37		Sat	12	Football League, Division 3 (South)	Reading		D 1-1	9,184
38		Sat	19	Football League, Division 3 (South)	COVENTRY CITY	1-0 W		8,956
39		Sat	26	Football League, Division 3 (South)	Walsall		W 1-0	4,011
40		Wed	30	Football League, Division 3 (South)	MILLWALL	5-3 W		4,992
41	April	Sat	2	Football League, Division 3 (South)	BRISTOL CITY	0-2 L		15,850
42		Fri	8	Football League, Division 3 (South)	SOUTHAMPTON	2-1 W		13,473
43		Sat	9	Football League, Division 3 (South)	Torquay United		D 2-2	6,113
44		Mon	11	Football League, Division 3 (South)	Southampton		L 0-2	10,178
45		Sat	16	Football League, Division 3 (South)	BRIGHTON & HOVE ALBION	0-0 D		8,746
46		Mon	18	Football League, Division 3 (South)	Shrewsbury Town		L 1-2	6,804
47		Sat	23	Football League, Division 3 (South)	Brentford		L 2-3	9,394
48		Tue	26	Football League, Division 3 (South)	TORQUAY UNITED	4-1 W		5,129
49		Sat	30	Football League, Division 3 (South)	SHREWSBURY TOWN	2-1 W		7,787
50	May	Fri	6	Football League, Division 3 (South)	EXETER CITY	1-1 D		4,775

League ever-presents: E.E. Bennett, D.G. Bewley, M. Cook
Most appearances in total: E.E. Bennett, D.G. Bewley & M. Cook 50 out of 50   **Most goals in total:** M. Cook 31
Hat-tricks: H.R. Brown (Match 6), M. Cook (Match 18, & 4 goals Match 40)   **Penalty goals:** J.A. Meadows 3, J.D. Bowie 1
Sent off: H.R. Brown (Match 36)
Full international appearance(s) this season: None

	Adams, C.J.	Bateman, C.	Bennett, E.E.	Bewley, D.G.	Bowie, J.D.	Brown, H.R.	Catleugh, G.C.	Cook, M.	Cooke, W.H.	Hernon, J.	Kelly, J.	Meadows, J.A.	Mitchell, F.R.	Nolan, P.	Paterson, T.	Paton, J.	Roberts, T.	Shipwright, W.K.	Smith, E.W.A.	Smith, L.	Walker, P.M.	Walker, R.W.	Wilson, J.T.	Own goals
Apps	41	29	46	46	40	31	20	46	10	16	14	33	41	3	3	14	1	42	10	7	6	3	4	
Subs																								
Goals	3			1	7	13	2	26		4	1	4				4			4					2
Apps	4	4	4	4	3	1		4				4	4			3		4	4		1			
Subs																								
Goals	1				1			5										1			1			
1	X		G	X	X	X1		X	X	X	X		X							X				
2	X		G	X	X	X1		X1	X	X	X1		X	X										
3	X		G	X	X	X1		X	X1	X			X	X										1
4	X		G	X	X	X		X1	X	X	X		X	X										
5	X		G	X	X	X		X	X	X	X		X					X						
6	X		G	X	X1	X3		X2	X	X1	X	X						X						
7	X		G	X	X1	X		X1	X	X	X		X					X						
8	X		G	X	X	X		X1	X	X	X		X					X						
9	X		G	X	X	X		X1	X	X	X		X					X						
10	X		G	X	X	X1	X	X	X				X					X						
11	X		G	X	X			X					X					X		X				
12			G	X	X1p	X	X	X					X			X		X		X				
13			G	X	X	X	X	X					X			X		X		X				
14			G	X	X	X1		X					X			X		X	X	X				
15	X	X	G	X	X1			X				X	X					X	X			X		
16	X	X	G	X	X			X				X	X					X	X1			X		
17	X	X	G	X	X			X1				X	X					X	X1					
18	X	X	G	X	X			X3				X	X					X	X					1
19	X	X	G	X				X				X	X					X	X					
20	X	X	G	X				X				X	X					X	X1			X1		
21	X	X	G	X				X				X			X	X1		X	X		X			
22	X		G	X				X				X			X	X1	X	X	X1					
23	X	X	G	X				X2				X	X			X		X	X		X			
24	X1	X	G	X	X1			X2				X	X			X		X	X		X			
25	X	X	G	X				X1				X	X		X	X		X			X			
26	X	X	G	X	X	X1		X				X	X			X		X	X					
27	X	X	G	X	X	X		X				X	X			X		X	X					
28	X	X	G	X1	X	X		X				X	X					X	X1					
29	X	X	G	X	X	X		X1				X	X					X	X					
30	X1	X	G	X	X			X1				X	X			X1		X	X					
31	X	X	G	X	X		X	X				X	X			X		X						
32	X	X	G	X	X			X				X	X			X1		X						
33	X1	X	G	X	X	X1	X	X1				X						X					X	
34	X	X	G	X	X	X	X	X				X						X					X	
35	X	X	G	X	X			X1				X	X					X			X			
36	X	X	G	X	X			X		X		X1p	X					X			X			
37	X1	X	G	X	X	X	X	X				X						X					X	
38	X	X	G	X	X	X1	X	X				X	X					X						
39	X	X	G	X	X1		X	X				X	X					X			X			
40	X	X	G	X	X	X1	X	X4				X	X					X						
41	X	X	G	X	X	X	X	X				X	X					X						
42	X	X	G	X	X1	X	X	X				X1p	X					X						
43	X	X	G	X	X	X	X2	X				X	X					X						
44	X		G	X		X	X	X		X		X	X					X		X				
45	X	X	G	X	X			X		X		X	X					X			X			
46	X		G	X		X	X	X		X		X1p	X					X		X	X			
47	X1	X	G	X	X	X1		X		X		X	X					X						
48		X	G	X		X	X1	X2		X1		X	X					X				X		
49	X	X	G	X		X	X	X1		X1		X	X					X						
50		X	G	X	X		X	X		X		X1	X					X		X				

1955/56

Football League position: 21st out of 24 in Division 3 (South) **Manager:** Len Goulden (Matches 1-15 & 34-49), Johnny Paton (Matches 16-33)

		HOME					AWAY					
	Pl	W	D	L	For	Ag	W	D	L	For	Ag	Pts
Leyton Orient	46	18	3	2	76	20	11	5	7	30	29	66
Brighton & Hove Albion	46	20	2	1	73	16	9	5	9	39	34	65
Ipswich Town	46	16	6	1	59	28	9	8	6	47	32	64
Southend United	46	16	4	3	58	25	5	7	11	30	55	53
Torquay United	46	11	10	2	48	21	9	2	12	38	42	52
Brentford	46	11	8	4	40	30	8	6	9	29	36	52
Norwich City	46	15	4	4	56	31	4	9	10	30	51	51
Coventry City	46	16	4	3	54	20	4	5	14	19	40	49
Bournemouth & Boscombe Ath	46	13	6	4	39	14	6	4	13	24	37	48
Gillingham	46	12	3	8	38	28	7	7	9	31	43	48
Northampton Town	46	14	3	6	44	27	6	4	13	23	44	47
Colchester United	46	14	4	5	56	37	4	7	12	20	44	47
Shrewsbury Town	46	12	9	2	47	21	5	3	15	22	45	46
Southampton	46	13	6	4	60	30	5	2	16	31	51	44
Aldershot	46	9	9	5	36	33	3	7	13	34	57	40
Exeter City	46	10	6	7	39	30	5	4	14	19	47	40
Reading	46	10	2	11	40	37	5	7	11	30	42	39
Queens Park Rangers	46	12	6	5	43	28	2	4	15	23	54	39
Newport County	46	12	2	9	32	26	3	7	13	26	53	39
Walsall	46	13	5	5	43	28	2	3	18	25	56	38
WATFORD	46	8	5	10	31	39	5	6	12	21	46	37
Millwall	46	13	4	6	56	31	2	2	19	27	69	36
Crystal Palace	46	7	3	13	27	32	5	7	11	27	51	34
Swindon Town	46	4	10	9	18	22	4	4	15	16	56	30

New league opponents: None

Home-and-away league doubles
For - none
Against – 4 (Bournemouth & Boscombe Athletic, Gillingham, Leyton Orient, Queens Park Rangers)

Divisional changes at end of season: Leyton Orient to Division 2; Plymouth Argyle from Division 2

All Matches: Won 14, Drew 11, Lost 24, Goals 61-97

Highest Score: 5 (Match 21)

No	DATE			COMPETITION	OPPONENTS	HOME	AWAY	ATTENDANCE	
1	August	Sat	20	Football League, Division 3 (South)	MILLWALL	4-2 W		15,486	
2		Tue	23	Football League, Division 3 (South)	COVENTRY CITY	2-1 W		13,590	
3		Sat	27	Football League, Division 3 (South)	Gillingham		L 0-3		11,227
4		Mon	29	Football League, Division 3 (South)	Coventry City		L 0-3		18,053
5	September	Sat	3	Football League, Division 3 (South)	BOURNEMOUTH & BOSCOMBE ATHLETIC	0-2 L		12,684	
6		Tue	6	Football League, Division 3 (South)	READING	1-0 W		8,558	
7		Sat	10	Football League, Division 3 (South)	Norwich City		L 1-4		16,323
8		Wed	14	Football League, Division 3 (South)	Reading		L 1-6		5,288
9		Sat	17	Football League, Division 3 (South)	COLCHESTER UNITED	1-1 D		9,129	
10		Mon	19	Football League, Division 3 (South)	Brentford		D 0-0		6,870
11		Sat	24	Football League, Division 3 (South)	Leyton Orient		L 1-3		16,943
12		Tue	27	Football League, Division 3 (South)	SOUTHEND UNITED	3-2 W		5,989	
13	October	Sat	1	Football League, Division 3 (South)	EXETER CITY	2-3 L		10,275	
14		Sat	8	Football League, Division 3 (South)	Crystal Palace		W 2-1		13,993
15		Sat	15	Football League, Division 3 (South)	BRIGHTON & HOVE ALBION	1-3 L		10,126	
16		Sat	22	Football League, Division 3 (South)	Southampton		L 0-2		11,305
17		Tue	25	Southern Floodlight Cup, 1st Round	ALDERSHOT	2-6 L		3,800	
18		Sat	29	Football League, Division 3 (South)	SHREWSBURY TOWN	3-4 L		7,714	
19	November	Sat	5	Football League, Division 3 (South)	Ipswich Town		D 0-0		16,194
20		Sat	12	Football League, Division 3 (South)	WALSALL	4-2 W		8,460	
21		Sat	19	FA Cup, 1st Round	RAMSGATE ATHLETIC	5-3 W		12,743	
22		Sat	26	Football League, Division 3 (South)	NEWPORT COUNTY	1-1 D		7,818	
23	December	Sat	3	Football League, Division 3 (South)	Swindon Town		D 0-0		7,258
24		Sat	10	FA Cup, 2nd Round	Bedford Town		L 2-3		13,150
25		Sat	17	Football League, Division 3 (South)	Millwall		D 1-1		4,405
26		Sat	24	Football League, Division 3 (South)	GILLINGHAM	0-1 L		5,091	
27		Mon	26	Football League, Division 3 (South)	NORTHAMPTON TOWN	2-2 W		7,041	
28		Tue	27	Football League, Division 3 (South)	Northampton Town		W 3-1		13,758
29		Sat	31	Football League, Division 3 (South)	Bournemouth & Boscombe Athletic		L 0-4		6,290
30	January	Sat	14	Football League, Division 3 (South)	NORWICH CITY	1-1 D		6,522	
31		Sat	21	Football League, Division 3 (South)	Colchester United		L 1-4		7,699
32		Sat	28	Football League, Division 3 (South)	QUEENS PARK RANGERS	0-1 L		5,784	
33	February	Sat	4	Football League, Division 3 (South)	LEYTON ORIENT	0-4 L		7,468	
34		Sat	11	Football League, Division 3 (South)	Exeter City		W 2-1		4,207
35		Sat	18	Football League, Division 3 (South)	CRYSTAL PALACE	0-2 L		4,865	
36		Sat	25	Football League, Division 3 (South)	Brighton & Hove Albion		W 3-2		16,590
37		Wed	29	Football League, Division 3 (South)	Torquay United		L 1-4		3,184
38	March	Sat	3	Football League, Division 3 (South)	SOUTHAMPTON	1-0 W		4,926	
39		Sat	10	Football League, Division 3 (South)	Shrewsbury Town		D 0-0		8,238
40		Sat	17	Football League, Division 3 (South)	IPSWICH TOWN	0-2 L		9,450	
41		Sat	24	Football League, Division 3 (South)	Walsall		L 1-2		10,879
42		Fri	30	Football League, Division 3 (South)	ALDERSHOT	1-1 D		8,074	
43		Sat	31	Football League, Division 3 (South)	TORQUAY UNITED	2-1 W		6,752	
44	April	Mon	2	Football League, Division 3 (South)	Aldershot		D 1-1		6,277
45		Sat	7	Football League, Division 3 (South)	Newport County		W 1-0		3,933
46		Sat	14	Football League, Division 3 (South)	SWINDON TOWN	2-1 W		3,505	
47		Sat	21	Football League, Division 3 (South)	Queens Park Rangers		L 2-3		7,564
48		Wed	25	Football League, Division 3 (South)	Southend United		L 0-1		6,680
49		Sat	28	Football League, Division 3 (South)	BRENTFORD	0-2 L		7,192	

League ever-presents: None
Most appearances in total: M. Cook 48 out of 49   Most goals in total: L. Graham 16
Hat-tricks: L. Graham (Match 21)   Penalty goals: L. Graham 2, J.A. Meadows 1
Sent off: None   Full international appearance(s) this season: None
(In Match 8, four of the opponents' goals were conceded by M. Cook (1) and E. Bateman (3), who had spells in goal after E.E. Bennett had been injured.)

Appearance / goal summary

	Adams, C.J.	Atkinson, B.H.	Bateman, C.	Bateman, E.	Bennett, E.E.	Bewley, D.G.	Bowie, D.G.	Brown, H.R.	Bunce, F.	Catleugh, G.C.	Cook, M.	Gooch, J.A.G.	Graham, L.	Hernon, J.	King, T.H.	Lock, F.W.	Marden, R.J.	Meadows, J.A.	Mitchell, F.R.	Pygall, D.A.	Shaw, A.	Shipwright, W.K.	Smith, R.	Walker, P.M.	Wilson, J.T.	Own goals
Apps	23	16	19	21	12	21	10	29	10	24	45	14	44	27	20	34	26	24	38	1	3	23	2	15	5	
Subs																										
Goals	1						1	2	1	3	13		13	6			6	1				1	3	1		
Apps	3		2	1	1	2	2	2	1		3		2	3	2	3		1	2			1	1		1	
Subs																										
Goals								1	1		2		3	1										1		

Match-by-match appearances

Match	Adams	Atkinson	Bateman,C	Bateman,E	Bennett	Bewley	Bowie	Brown	Bunce	Catleugh	Cook	Gooch	Graham	Hernon	King	Lock	Marden	Meadows	Mitchell	Pygall	Shaw	Shipwright	Smith	Walker	Wilson	Own goals
1					G	X	X1	X			X1		X1			X	X1	X	X			X				
2		X			G	X	X				X2		X			X	X	X	X			X				
3		X			G	X	X				X		X			X	X	X	X			X				
4		X			G	X	X				X		X			X	X	X	X			X				
5	X				G	X	X				X		X			X		X	X			X		X		
6	X				G						X		X1	X		X		X	X			X		X		
7			X	X	G	X					X		X			X	X1	X				X				
8		X		X	G	X					X1		X	X		X	X	X				X				
9		X	X			X				X	X		X		G	X	X1	X				X				
10		X	X			X				X	X		X		G	X	X	X				X				
11	X	X				X	X				X1		X		G	X	X				X					
12	X1	X				X					X2		X	X	G	X	X				X					
13	X	X				X					X		X1p	X1	G	X	X				X					
14	X	X				X					X1		X	X1	G	X	X					X				
15	X	X				X					X1		X	X1	G	X	X					X				
16	X					X		X			X		X		G		X	X				X	X			
17	X							X			X1		X1		G	X		X				X	X		X	
18		X						X1	X1		X		X1	X	G	X		X				X	X			
19	X	X	X								X		X	X	G	X						X	X	X		
20	X	X	X	X							X		X2	X1	G	X						X				1
21	X	X	X	X							X1		X3	X1	G	X						X				
22	X	X	X	G		X					X		X	X1		X						X				
23	X	X	X	G		X					X		X	X		X						X				
24	X		X	G		X	X	X			X		X1	X								X				1
25	X		X	X		X	X	X			X1		X		G	X						X				
26	X		X	X		X	X	X		X	X		X		G	X						X				
27	X	X		X		X		X			X2		X		G							X				
28		X	X	X						X	X1		X1	X1	G	X						X		X		
29		X	X	X						X	X		X	X	G	X						X		X		
30		X	X	X				X1		X	X		X	X	G							X		X		
31		X	X	X				X1		X	X		X	X	G							X		X		
32		X	X	X				X		X	X		X	X	G							X		X		
33		X	X	X				X		X	X		X		G							X		X		
34	X	X		G				X		X	X		X	X1		X	X					X		X		X1
35	X	X		G				X		X	X		X	X		X	X					X		X		
36								X	X	X	X	G	X1p	X			X	X				X		X	X2	
37								X	X	X	X	G	X	X			X	X				X		X	X1	
38								X	X	X	X1	G	X	X			X	X				X		X	X	
39								X	X	X	X	G	X	X			X	X				X		X	X	
40								X	X	X	X	G	X	X			X	X				X		X		
41	X							X		X	X	G	X1				X	X				X		X	X	
42	X							X		X	X	G	X				X	X1	X	X		X		X		
43	X							X	X	X		G	X				X	X1	X1p	X		X		X		
44								X	X	X1	X		X	X			X	X	X			X		X		
45	X						X	X		X	X	G	X				X1	X	X			X		X		
46	X						X	X		X1	X	G	X1					X	X	X		X		X		
47	X						X	X		X1	X	G	X1					X	X	X		X		X		
48	X						X	X	X	X	X	G	X					X	X			X		X		
49	X						X	X	X	X	X	G		X			X	X	X			X		X		

1956/57

Football League position: 11th out of 24 in Division 3 (South)
Manager: Neil McBain

New league opponents: None

Home-and-away league doubles
For – 3 (Coventry City, Northampton Town, Reading)
Against – 3 (Queens Park Rangers, Shrewsbury Town, Swindon Town)

Divisional changes at end of season: Ipswich Town to Division 2; Port Vale from Division 2

All Matches: Won 20, Drew 11, Lost 20, Goals 88-85

Highest Score: 6 (Match 23)

	HOME					AWAY					
	Pl	W	D	L	For	Ag	W	D	L	For	Ag	Pts
Ipswich Town	46	18	3	2	72	20	7	6	10	29	34	59
Torquay United	46	19	4	0	71	18	5	7	11	18	46	59
Colchester United	46	15	8	0	49	19	7	6	10	35	37	58
Southampton	46	15	4	4	48	20	7	6	10	28	32	54
Bournemouth & Boscombe Ath	46	15	7	1	57	20	4	7	12	31	42	52
Brighton & Hove Albion	46	15	6	2	59	26	4	8	11	27	39	52
Southend United	46	14	3	6	42	20	4	9	10	31	45	48
Brentford	46	12	9	2	55	29	4	7	12	23	47	48
Shrewsbury Town	46	11	9	3	45	24	4	9	10	27	55	48
Queens Park Rangers	46	12	7	4	42	21	6	4	13	19	39	47
WATFORD	46	11	6	6	44	32	7	4	12	28	43	46
Newport County	46	15	5	3	49	22	3	4	16	17	51	45
Reading	46	13	4	6	44	30	5	5	13	36	51	45
Northampton Town	46	15	5	3	49	22	3	4	16	17	51	45
Walsall	46	11	7	5	49	25	5	5	13	31	49	44
Coventry City	46	12	5	6	52	36	4	7	12	22	48	44
Millwall	46	13	7	3	46	29	3	5	15	18	55	44
Plymouth Argyle	46	10	8	5	38	31	6	3	14	30	42	43
Aldershot	46	11	5	7	43	35	4	7	12	36	57	42
Crystal Palace	46	7	10	6	31	28	4	8	11	31	47	40
Exeter City	46	8	8	7	37	29	4	5	14	24	50	37
Gillingham	46	7	8	8	29	29	5	5	13	25	56	37
Swindon Town	46	12	3	8	43	33	3	3	17	23	63	36
Norwich City	46	7	5	11	33	37	1	10	12	28	57	31

No	DATE			COMPETITION	OPPONENTS	HOME	AWAY	ATTENDANCE
1	August	Sat	18	Football League, Division 3 (South)	Gillingham		W 3-0	9,934
2		Tue	21	Football League, Division 3 (South)	BRIGHTON & HOVE ALBION	2-1 W		12,909
3		Sat	25	Football League, Division 3 (South)	SWINDON TOWN	3-4 L		10,944
4		Wed	29	Football League, Division 3 (South)	Brighton & Hove Albion		D 2-2	13,274
5	September	Sat	1	Football League, Division 3 (South)	Brentford		W 5-1	18,760
6		Tue	4	Football League, Division 3 (South)	TORQUAY UNITED	4-1 W		15,360
7		Sat	8	Football League, Division 3 (South)	ALDERSHOT	3-0 W		15,648
8		Wed	12	Football League, Division 3 (South)	Torquay United		L 0-3	8,319
9		Sat	15	Football League, Division 3 (South)	Newport County		L 0-3	11,547
10		Tue	18	Football League, Division 3 (South)	MILLWALL	2-0 W		15,124
11		Sat	22	Football League, Division 3 (South)	Shrewsbury Town		L 0-1	9,352
12		Mon	24	Football League, Division 3 (South)	Millwall		D 1-1	13,978
13		Sat	29	Football League, Division 3 (South)	WALSALL	1-0 W		11,344
14	October	Sat	6	Football League, Division 3 (South)	PLYMOUTH ARGYLE	0-1 L		11,601
15		Tue	9	Southern Floodlight Cup, 1st Round	CHARLTON ATHLETIC	2-2 D		5,527
16		Sat	13	Football League, Division 3 (South)	Queens Park Rangers		L 1-3	14,170
17		Sat	20	Football League, Division 3 (South)	NORTHAMPTON TOWN	2-1 W		9,906
18		Tue	23	Southern Floodlight Cup, 1st Round replay	Charlton Athletic (played at Millwall)		W 4-1	1,634
19		Sat	27	Football League, Division 3 (South)	Southend United		L 0-2	9,367
20	November	Sat	3	Football League, Division 3 (South)	CRYSTAL PALACE	1-4 L		8,785
21		Wed	7	Southern Floodlight Cup, 2nd Round	Luton Town		L 3-4	3,935
22		Sat	10	Football League, Division 3 (South)	Exeter City		W 2-1	7,491
23		Sat	17	FA Cup, 1st Round	Newport (Isle of Wight)		W 6-0	5,100
24		Sat	24	Football League, Division 3 (South)	Coventry City		W 2-0	10,705
25	December	Sat	1	Football League, Division 3 (South)	NORWICH CITY	3-3 D		9,538
26		Sat	8	FA Cup, 2nd Round	IPSWICH TOWN	1-3 L		13,993
27		Sat	15	Football League, Division 3 (South)	GILLINGHAM	2-3 L		3,684
28		Sat	22	Football League, Division 3 (South)	Swindon Town		L 0-2	6,312
29		Tue	25	Football League, Division 3 (South)	IPSWICH TOWN	2-1 W		4,544
30		Wed	26	Football League, Division 3 (South)	Ipswich Town		L 1-4	11,352
31		Sat	29	Football League, Division 3 (South)	BRENTFORD	1-1 D		8,416
32	January	Sat	12	Football League, Division 3 (South)	Aldershot		L 1-3	4,308
33		Sat	19	Football League, Division 3 (South)	NEWPORT COUNTY	5-0 W		7,676
34	February	Sat	2	Football League, Division 3 (South)	SHREWSBURY TOWN	2-3 L		8,214
35		Sat	9	Football League, Division 3 (South)	Walsall		L 0-2	14,758
36		Sat	16	Football League, Division 3 (South)	Plymouth Argyle		D 3-3	13,335
37		Sat	23	Football League, Division 3 (South)	QUEENS PARK RANGERS	2-4 L		4,428
38	March	Sat	2	Football League, Division 3 (South)	Northampton Town		W 2-1	9,309
39		Sat	9	Football League, Division 3 (South)	COLCHESTER UNITED	0-0 D		10,505
40		Sat	16	Football League, Division 3 (South)	Crystal Palace		D 0-0	8,830
41		Sat	23	Football League, Division 3 (South)	EXETER CITY	1-1 D		7,404
42		Tue	26	Football League, Division 3 (South)	BOURNEMOUTH & BOSCOMBE ATHLETIC	1-1 D		7,090
43		Sat	30	Football League, Division 3 (South)	Southampton		L 1-3	11,992
44	April	Sat	6	Football League, Division 3 (South)	COVENTRY CITY	1-0 W		5,587
45		Sat	13	Football League, Division 3 (South)	Norwich City		W 2-1	10,207
46		Fri	19	Football League, Division 3 (South)	READING	1-0 W		8,356
47		Sat	20	Football League, Division 3 (South)	SOUTHEND UNITED	1-1 D		7,715
48		Mon	22	Football League, Division 3 (South)	Reading		W 2-1	6,555
49		Sat	27	Football League, Division 3 (South)	SOUTHAMPTON	4-2 W		7,279
50		Mon	29	Football League, Division 3 (South)	Colchester United		L 0-2	9,226
51	May	Fri	3	Football League, Division 3 (South)	Bournemouth & Boscombe Athletic		L 0-4	7,522

League ever-presents: G.C. Catleugh, M. Cook, W.K. Shipwright, P.M. Walker
Most appearances in total: G.C. Catleugh, M. Cook, W.K. Shipwright & P.M. Walker 51 out of 51   **Most goals in total:** L. Graham 17
Hat-tricks: None   **Penalty goals:** J.A. Meadows 2
Sent off: None
Full international appearance(s) this season: None

	Allen, D.S.	Anderson, T.C.	Atkinson, B.H.	Barber, W.G.	Bateman, E.	Beament, R.J.	Brown, H.R.	Bunce, F.	Catleugh, G.C.	Cook, M.	Gooch, J.A.G.	Graham, L.	Harrop, J.	Lock, F.W.	McMillan, T.P.	Marden, R.J.	Meadows, J.A.	Mitchell, F.R.	Reid, J.	Shipwright, W.K.	Strain, J.H.	Underwood, E.D.	Walker, P.M.	Wilson, J.T.	Woodison, A.G.
Apps	6	19	4	2	2	1	37	2	46	46	29	43	38	8	11	15	42	36	1	46	3	16	46	7	
Subs																									
Goals	1	5					4		4	12		13			1	3	5	12		1			10	1	
Apps	4		1		1		2		5	5	2	4	5		2	1	4	5		5		3	5		1
Subs																									
Goals									1	4		4			1	1	3						2		
1							X		X	X1	G	X1	X			X1	X	X		X			X		
2							X		X	X1	G	X	X			X	X1p	X		X			X		
3			X1						X	X	G	X	X			X	X1p	X		X			X		
4							X		X	X	G	X1	X			X	X1	X		X			X		
5							X		X	X1	G	X	X			X2	X2	X		X			X		
6							X		X	X2	G	X	X			X1	X1	X		X			X		
7							X		X	X1	G	X1	X			X1	X	X		X			X		
8							X		X	X	G	X	X			X	X	X		X			X		
9							X		X	X		X	X			X	X	X		X		G	X		
10							X		X	X1		X1	X			X	X	X		X		G	X		
11							X		X	X		X	X			X	X	X		X		G	X		
12							X		X	X		X	X			X1	X	X		X		G	X		
13							X		X	X		X	X			X	X	X		X		G	X1		
14							X		X	X		X	X			X	X	X		X		G	X		
15									X	X1		X	X		X	X1		X		X		G	X		
16							X		X	X1	G		X			X		X		X			X		
17	X			X					X1	X	G	X1	X			X		X		X			X		
18	X			X					X1	X1	G	X1	X			X1		X		X			X		
19	X			X					X	X		X	X			X		X		X			X		
20	X	X							X	X	G	X	X			X		X		X			X1		
21	X								X	X		X			X1	X1		X		X		G	X1		X
22	X1		X						X	X	G	X1	X			X		X		X			X		
23	X		X						X	X2	G	X2	X			X1		X		X			X1		
24	X		X						X	X1	G	X1	X			X		X		X			X		
25	X		X						X	X1	G	X1	X			X1		X		X			X		
26	X						X		X	X		X1	X			X		X		X		G	X		
27							X	X	X	X		X1	X			X1		X		X		G	X		
28							X	X	X	X		X	X		X			X		X			X		
29							X		X	X	G	X	X				X	X	X1	X			X1		
30							X		X	X		X	X		X		X	X		X		G	X1		
31							X		X	X		X	X		X1		X	X		X		G	X		
32		X					X		X1	X		X	X			X	X	X		X		G	X		
33		X1					X		X	X		X1	X			X1	X	X		X		G	X2		
34		X1					X		X	X1	G	X	X			X	X	X		X			X		
35		X					X		X	X	X	X	X			X	X	X		X			X		
36		X					X		X1	X	X	X	X			X1	X	X		X			X1		
37		X					X1		X	X	G		X			X		X		X			X	X1	
38		X1					X		X	X1	G		X			X		X		X			X	X	
39		X					X		X	X	G		X			X		X		X			X	X	
40		X					X		X	X	X	X	X					X		X			X	X	
41		X					X1		X	X	G	X	X					X		X			X	X	
42		X							X	X	G	X1	X					X		X	X		X	X	
43		X							X	X	G	X	X					X		X	X		X1	X	
44		X							X	X		X1	X		X	X		X		X	X	G	X1		
45		X	X						X	X		X			X	X1		X		X		G	X1		
46		X1	X						X	X		X			X	X		X		X		G	X		
47		X							X	X		X			X	X		X		X		G	X1		
48		X1							X	X1		X		X	X			X		X		G	X		
49		X					X1		X	X	G	X		X1	X1	X1				X			X		
50		X	X						X	X	G	X		X	X					X			X		
51			X			G	X		X	X		X		X	X	X				X			X		

1957/58

Football League position: 16th out of 24 in Division 3 (South)

Manager: Neil McBain

		HOME					AWAY					
	Pl	W	D	L	For	Ag	W	D	L	For	Ag	Pts
Brighton & Hove Albion	46	13	6	4	52	30	11	6	6	36	34	60
Brentford	46	15	5	3	52	24	9	5	9	30	32	58
Plymouth Argyle	46	17	4	2	43	17	8	4	11	24	31	58
Swindon Town	46	14	7	2	47	16	7	8	8	32	34	57
Reading	46	14	5	4	52	23	7	8	8	27	28	55
Southampton	46	16	3	4	78	31	6	7	10	34	41	54
Southend United	46	14	5	4	56	26	7	7	9	34	32	54
Norwich City	46	11	9	3	41	28	8	6	9	34	42	53
Bournemouth & Boscombe Ath	46	16	5	2	54	24	5	4	14	27	50	51
Queens Park Rangers	46	15	6	2	40	14	3	8	12	24	51	51
Newport County	46	12	6	5	40	24	5	8	10	33	43	48
Colchester United	46	13	5	5	45	27	4	8	11	32	52	47
Northampton Town	46	13	1	9	60	33	6	5	12	27	46	44
Crystal Palace	46	12	5	6	46	30	3	8	12	24	42	43
Port Vale	46	12	6	5	49	24	4	4	15	18	34	42
WATFORD	46	9	8	6	34	24	4	8	11	25	50	42
Shrewsbury Town	46	10	6	7	29	25	5	4	14	20	46	40
Aldershot	46	7	9	7	31	34	5	7	11	28	55	40
Coventry City	46	10	9	4	41	34	3	4	16	20	57	39
Walsall	46	10	7	6	37	24	4	2	17	24	51	37
Torquay United	46	9	7	7	33	34	2	6	15	16	40	35
Gillingham	46	12	5	6	33	24	1	4	18	19	57	35
Millwall	46	6	6	11	37	36	5	3	26	25	53	31
Exeter City	46	10	4	9	37	35	1	5	17	20	64	31

New league opponents: None

Home-and-away league doubles

For – 2 (Exeter City, Millwall)

Against – 3 (Brighton & Hove Albion, Plymouth Argyle, Port Vale)

Divisional changes at end of season: Brighton & Hove Albion to Division 2; the remainder of the top-half clubs joined their Division 3 (North) counterparts, and Notts County & Doncaster Rovers from Division 2, to form a new Division 3; Watford and the other clubs which finished in the bottom half of each third division combined to form a new Division 4.

All Matches: Won 15, Drew 16, Lost 19, Goals 69-87

Highest Score: 5 (Match 25)

No	DATE			COMPETITION	OPPONENTS	HOME	AWAY	ATTENDANCE
1	August	Sat	24	Football League, Division 3 (South)	Bournemouth & Boscombe Athletic		L 1-2	16,615
2		Tue	27	Football League, Division 3 (South)	SWINDON TOWN	0-0 D		12,109
3		Sat	31	Football League, Division 3 (South)	WALSALL	1-1 D		9,952
4	September	Wed	4	Football League, Division 3 (South)	Swindon Town		D 0-0	10,519
5		Sat	7	Football League, Division 3 (South)	Coventry City		D 2-2	13,401
6		Wed	11	Football League, Division 3 (South)	Torquay United		L 0-1	6,314
7		Sat	14	Football League, Division 3 (South)	SHREWSBURY TOWN	3-0 W		9,446
8		Tue	17	Football League, Division 3 (South)	TORQUAY UNITED	1-0 W		7,183
9		Sat	21	Football League, Division 3 (South)	Reading		D 1-1	13,240
10		Tue	24	Football League, Division 3 (South)	BRENTFORD	4-1 W		7,031
11		Sat	28	Football League, Division 3 (South)	NORTHAMPTON TOWN	0-2 L		11,579
12	October	Tue	1	Football League, Division 3 (South)	Brentford		D 0-0	10,880
13		Sat	5	Football League, Division 3 (South)	Millwall		W 3-2	17,440
14		Sat	12	Football League, Division 3 (South)	ALDERSHOT	1-3 L		10,782
15		Tue	15	Football League, Division 3 (South)	COLCHESTER UNITED	1-1 D		6,771
16		Sat	19	Football League, Division 3 (South)	Plymouth Argyle		L 1-2	17,901
17		Tue	22	Southern Floodlight Cup, 1st Round	CRYSTAL PALACE	4-1 W		2,370
18		Sat	26	Football League, Division 3 (South)	PORT VALE	0-2 L		9,513
19	November	Sat	2	Football League, Division 3 (South)	Newport County		L 1-2	8,212
20		Sat	9	Football League, Division 3 (South)	SOUTHAMPTON	3-0 W		7,920
21		Tue	12	Southern Floodlight Cup, 2nd Round	FULHAM	4-2 W		4,927
22		Sat	16	FA Cup, 1st Round	Plymouth Argyle		L 2-6	20,875
23		Sat	23	Football League, Division 3 (South)	SOUTHEND UNITED	1-1 D		7,838
24		Sat	30	Football League, Division 3 (South)	Queens Park Rangers		L 0-3	10,104
25	December	Sat	7	Football League, Division 3 (South)	EXETER CITY	5-4 W	.	4,371
26		Sat	14	Football League, Division 3 (South)	Gillingham		D 1-1	7,996
27		Sat	21	Football League, Division 3 (South)	BOURNEMOUTH & BOSCOMBE ATHLETIC	1-1 D		5,877
28		Thu	26	Football League, Division 3 (South)	Colchester United		L 0-4	9,379
29		Sat	28	Football League, Division 3 (South)	Walsall		W 3-1	8,943
30	January	Sat	11	Football League, Division 3 (South)	COVENTRY CITY	1-0 W		5,962
31		Sat	18	Football League, Division 3 (South)	Shrewsbury Town		D 1-1	5,418
32	February	Sat	1	Football League, Division 3 (South)	READING	1-1 D		8,090
33		Sat	8	Football League, Division 3 (South)	Northampton Town		W 3-2	8,370
34		Sat	15	Football League, Division 3 (South)	MILLWALL	3-0 W		10,474
35		Sat	22	Football League, Division 3 (South)	Aldershot		D 2-2	4,503
36	March	Sat	1	Football League, Division 3 (South)	PLYMOUTH ARGYLE	0-2 L		10,588
37		Sat	8	Football League, Division 3 (South)	Port Vale		L 0-5	8,565
38		Sat	15	Football League, Division 3 (South)	NEWPORT COUNTY	2-2 D		7,109
39		Sat	22	Football League, Division 3 (South)	Southend United		L 1-2	9,883
40		Tue	25	Football League, Division 3 (South)	CRYSTAL PALACE	2-1 W		4,304
41		Sat	29	Football League, Division 3 (South)	GILLINGHAM	3-0 W		6,375
42		Mon	31	Southern Floodlight Cup, Semi-Final	PORTSMOUTH	0-1 L		4,466
43	April	Fri	4	Football League, Division 3 (South)	NORWICH CITY	1-4 L		10,931
44		Sat	5	Football League, Division 3 (South)	Southampton		L 0-5	11,832
45		Mon	7	Football League, Division 3 (South)	Norwich City		D 1-1	29,807
46		Sat	12	Football League, Division 3 (South)	QUEENS PARK RANGERS	0-0 D		8,022
47		Sat	19	Football League, Division 3 (South)	Exeter City		W 2-1	5,230
48		Wed	23	Football League, Division 3 (South)	Crystal Palace		L 2-4	10,139
49		Sat	26	Football League, Division 3 (South)	BRIGHTON & HOVE ALBION	0-1 L		8,307
50		Wed	30	Football League, Division 3 (South)	Brighton & Hove Albion		L 0-6	31,038

League ever-presents: None
Most appearances in total: G.C. Catleugh 49 out of 50   **Most goals in total:** T.P. McMillan 11
Hat-tricks: T.P. McMillan (Match 13 & Match 25)   **Penalty goals:** J.A. Meadows 4
Sent off: C.R. Billington (Match 1)
Full international appearance(s) this season: None

	Anderson, T.C.	Barber, W.G.	Bateman, C. //	Bell, R.M.	Billington, C.R.	Brown, H.R. //	Catleugh, G.C.	Chung, C.	Collins, A.N. //	Collins, R.M.	Cook, M. //	Curran, J. //	Devine, W.	Graham, L. //	Harrop, J.	Howfield, R.M.	McMillan, T.P.	McNeice, V.	Meadows, J.A.	Pygall, D.A.	Shipwright, W.K.	Walker, P.M.	Woodison, A.G. //	Own goal
Apps	33	18	2	33	14	9	45	41	17	16	27	30	11	3	29	27	22	25	32	9	24	39		
Subs																								
Goals	7			1			2	7	1		8		3			5	10		5			9		1
Apps	2	3		1	3			4	2	1	1	3	3	1		3	3	1	1	4	1	2	4	1
Subs																								
Goals	2								1		2					1	1		2			1		
1		X		X	X	X	X	X	X		X1	G		X							X			
2		X		X	X	X	X	X	X		X	G		X							X			
3		X		X	X		X	X	X		X1	G		X							X	X		
4	X	X		X	X		X	X	X		X	G				X					X			
5	X1	X		X	X		X1	X	X		X	G									X	X		
6	X	X		X	X		X	X	X		X	G									X	X		
7	X	X		X	X		X		X1	X1	X1	G									X	X		
8	X	X		X	X		X1	X	X		X	G									X	X		
9	X	X		X		X	X	X1	X		X	G									X	X		
10	X	X		X		X	X	X2	X		X1	G									X	X1		
11	X	X		X			X	X	X		X	G									X	X		
12	X			X			X	X	X		X	G							X		X	X		
13	X			X			X	X	X		X	G					X3		X		X			
14	X1			X			X	X	X		X	G					X		X		X			
15	X1	X		X			X	X	X		X	G					X				X			
16	X	X		X			X	X	X		X	G					X		X			X1		
17	X2	X		X			X		X1		X	G					X1	X	X			X		
18	X	X		X			X	X			X	G					X	X	X			X		
19	X	X		X				X	X1		X	G				X	X				X	X		
20		X		X				X			X2	G				X	X		X1			X		
21		X		X				X	X		X1	G				X	X1		X1		X	X1		
22		X		X				X	X		X1	G				X	X		X1		X	X		
23		X		X				X	X		X	G				X	X		X1p		X	X		
24	X	X	X	X				X	X		X	G				X	X				X	X		
25			X	X				X	X		X	G				X	X3	X	X			X2		
26				X				X	X		X1	G				X	X	X	X		X	X		
27				X				X	X		X	G				X	X	X	X		X	X1		
28				X				X	X		X	G				X	X	X	X		X	X		
29				X				X	X		X1	G				X	X1	X1	X		X	X		
30	X			X				X	X			G				X	X1	X	X		X	X		
31	X			X				X	X1		X	G				X		X	X		X	X		
32	X			X				X	X				G			X	X1	X				X2		
33	X			X				X	X1				G			X	X	X	X			X2		
34	X			X				X	X				G			X	X1	X1	X1p			X		
35	X			X1				X	X				G			X	X1	X1	X			X		
36	X			X				X	X				G			X	X	X	X			X		
37	X			X				X	X				G			X	X	X	X	X		X		
38	X1			X				X	X				G			X	X1	X	X			X		
39	X			X				X					G	X1		X	X	X	X			X		
40	X1			X				X					G	X		X	X1	X				X		
41	X1			X				X					G	X		X	X	X	X1p			X		1
42	X			X				X					G	X		X	X	X	X			X	X	
43	X			X				X	X				G			X	X	X	X			X1		
44	X			X				X					G			X	X	X	X			X		
45	X			X				X					G	X1		X	X	X	X	X		X		
46	X			X				X					G	X		X	X	X	X			X		
47	X1			X				X	X				G	X		X	X	X	X	X		X1		
48				X				X	X				G	X1		X	X	X	X	X1p		X		
49				X				X	X				G	X		X	X	X	X	X		X		
50	X			X				X	X				G	X			X	X	X	X		X		

Football League position: 15th out of 24 in Division 4 **Manager:** Neil McBain (Matches 1-35), Ron Burgess (Matches 36-51)

		HOME					AWAY					
	Pl	W	D	L	For	Ag	W	D	L	For	Ag	Pts
Port Vale	46	14	6	3	62	30	12	6	5	48	28	64
Coventry City	46	18	4	1	50	11	6	8	9	34	36	60
York City	46	12	10	1	37	17	9	8	6	36	35	60
Shrewsbury Town	46	15	5	3	59	24	9	5	9	42	39	58
Exeter City	46	16	4	3	55	24	7	7	9	32	37	57
Walsall	46	13	5	5	56	25	8	5	10	39	39	52
Crystal Palace	46	12	8	3	54	27	8	4	11	36	44	52
Northampton Town	46	14	5	4	48	25	7	4	12	37	53	51
Millwall	46	13	6	4	46	23	7	4	12	30	46	50
Carlisle United	46	11	6	6	37	30	8	6	9	25	35	50
Gillingham	46	14	6	3	53	27	6	3	14	29	50	49
Torquay United	46	11	5	7	45	32	5	7	11	33	45	44
Chester	46	10	5	8	39	33	6	7	10	33	51	44
Bradford (Park Avenue)	46	15	1	7	51	29	3	6	14	28	48	43
WATFORD	46	10	6	7	46	36	6	4	13	35	43	42
Darlington	46	7	8	8	37	36	6	8	9	29	32	42
Workington	46	9	10	4	40	32	3	7	13	23	46	41
Crewe Alexandra	46	11	5	7	52	32	4	5	14	18	50	40
Hartlepools United	46	11	8	4	50	41	4	6	13	24	47	40
Gateshead	46	11	3	9	33	30	5	5	13	25	55	40
Oldham Athletic	46	15	0	8	39	29	1	4	18	20	55	36
Aldershot	46	8	4	11	37	45	6	3	14	26	52	35
Barrow	46	6	6	11	34	45	3	6	16	17	59	28
Southport	46	7	8	8	26	25	0	4	19	15	61	26

New league opponents: Barrow, Carlisle United, Chester, Crewe Alexandra, Darlington Gateshead, Hartlepools United, Oldham Athletic, Southport, Workington, York City

Home-and-away league doubles
For – 2 (Oldham Athletic, Southport)
Against – 3 (Coventry City, Shrewsbury Town, Walsall)

Divisional changes at end of season: Port Vale, Coventry City, York City & Shrewsbury Town to Division 3; Stockport County, Doncaster Rovers, Notts County & Rochdale from Division 3

All Matches: Won 17, Drew 12, Lost 22, Goals 86-85

Highest Score: 5 (Matches 1, 17 & 19)

No		DATE		COMPETITION	OPPONENTS	HOME	AWAY	ATTENDANCE	
1	August	Sat	23	Football League, Division 4	SOUTHPORT	5-1 W		10,101	
2		Tue	26	Football League, Division 4	PORT VALE	0-2 L		11,948	
3		Sat	30	Football League, Division 4	Torquay United		W 3-2		7,265
4	September	Mon	1	Football League, Division 4	Port Vale		W 3-1		10,517
5		Sat	6	Football League, Division 4	CREWE ALEXANDRA	0-1 L		10,563	
6		Tue	9	Football League, Division 4	CRYSTAL PALACE	2-2 D		10,327	
7		Sat	13	Football League, Division 4	Northampton Town		L 1-2		11,106
8		Wed	17	Football League, Division 4	Crystal Palace		L 0-3		16,034
9		Sat	20	Football League, Division 4	WORKINGTON	3-0 W		8,393	
10		Sat	27	Football League, Division 4	York City		D 0-0		8,603
11	October	Wed	1	Football League, Division 4	Chester		L 1-2		4,578
12		Sat	4	Football League, Division 4	BRADFORD (PARK AVENUE)	2-1 W		6,661	
13		Wed	8	Football League, Division 4	Darlington		D 1-1		2,737
14		Sat	11	Football League, Division 4	MILLWALL	1-1 D		10,972	
15		Tue	14	Football League, Division 4	CHESTER	4-2 W		7,046	
16		Sat	18	Football League, Division 4	Aldershot		D 0-0		4,680
17		Sat	25	Football League, Division 4	GATESHEAD	5-1 W		14,156	
18		Mon	27	Southern Floodlight Cup, 1st Round	Southampton		D 0-0		5,240
19	November	Sat	1	Football League, Division 4	Oldham Athletic		W 5-3		6,441
20		Tue	4	Southern Floodlight Cup, 1st Round replay	SOUTHAMPTON	2-3 L		8,328	
21		Sat	8	Football League, Division 4	BARROW	1-1 D		12,794	
22		Sat	15	FA Cup, 1st Round	READING	1-1 D		17,663	
23		Wed	19	FA Cup, 1st Round replay	Reading		W 2-0		22,164
24		Sat	22	Football League, Division 4	GILLINGHAM	2-2 D		10,369	
25		Sat	29	Football League, Division 4	Exeter City		L 0-3		8,866
26	December	Sat	6	FA Cup, 2nd Round	Torquay United		L 0-2		7,690
27		Sat	13	Football League, Division 4	Shrewsbury Town		L 2-4		4,275
28		Sat	20	Football League, Division 4	Southport		W 3-0		2,244
29		Fri	26	Football League, Division 4	Walsall		L 2-3		10,324
30		Sat	27	Football League, Division 4	WALSALL	1-2 L		11,933	
31	January	Sat	3	Football League, Division 4	TORQUAY UNITED	1-2 L		7,459	
32		Sat	17	Football League, Division 4	Crewe Alexandra		W 3-1		4,434
33		Sat	24	Football League, Division 4	COVENTRY CITY	1-4 L		8,918	
34		Sat	31	Football League, Division 4	NORTHAMPTON TOWN	3-1 W		6,200	
35	February	Sat	7	Football League, Division 4	Workington		L 1-3		4,991
36		Sat	14	Football League, Division 4	YORK CITY	2-3 L		5,799	
37		Sat	21	Football League, Division 4	Bradford (Park Avenue)		D 1-1		6,304
38		Sat	28	Football League, Division 4	Millwall		L 1-4		11,003
39	March	Sat	7	Football League, Division 4	ALDERSHOT	2-1 W		4,182	
40		Sat	14	Football League, Division 4	Gateshead		L 0-1		3,331
41		Mon	16	Football League, Division 4	Carlisle United		L 0-2		4,924
42		Sat	21	Football League, Division 4	OLDHAM ATHLETIC	2-1 W		5,188	
43		Fri	27	Football League, Division 4	Hartlepools United		L 3-4		6,460
44		Sat	28	Football League, Division 4	Barrow		W 4-0		4,597
45		Mon	30	Football League, Division 4	HARTLEPOOLS UNITED	4-1 W		6,480	
46	April	Sat	4	Football League, Division 4	CARLISLE UNITED	2-2 D		7,219	
47		Sat	11	Football League, Division 4	Gillingham		L 1-2		6,205
48		Sat	18	Football League, Division 4	EXETER CITY	2-1 W		4,845	
49		Tue	21	Football League, Division 4	DARLINGTON	0-0 D		5,689	
50		Sat	25	Football League, Division 4	Coventry City		L 0-1		13,434
51	May	Thu	7	Football League, Division 4	SHREWSBURY TOWN	1-4 L		5,580	

The following match was abandoned after 74 minutes, owing to floodlight failure:

	April	Tue	28	Football League, Division 4	SHREWSBURY TOWN	2-5		5,326	

League ever-presents: G.C. Catleugh
Most appearances in total: G.C. Catleugh 51 out of 51   **Most goals in total:** P.J. Gordon 13
Hat-tricks: C. Chung (Match 9)   **Penalty goals:** J.A. Meadows 3, R.M. Howfield 1
Sent off: None
Full international appearance(s) this season: None

Summary (player columns in order: Barber W.G., Bell R.M., Benning M.D., Bunce F., Catleugh G.C., Chung C., Collins R.M., Devine W., Fleming G.K., Gavin J.T., Gordon P.J., Harrop J., Hartle B., Holton C.C., Howfield R.M., McNeice V., Meadows J.A., Shipwright W.K., Smith W.A., Storer P.R., Walker P.M.):

	Bar	Bell	Ben	Bun	Cat	Chu	Col	Dev	Fle	Gav	Gor	Har	Hart	Hol	How	McN	Mea	Shi	Smi	Sto	Wal
Apps	2	40	3	21	46	28	27	19	24	43	39	40	5	30	20	33	38	9	10	9	20
Subs																					
Goals		1		7	2	6		3	10	12	13		1	9	4		5			5	3
Apps		5		5	5		5		4	5	5	4		5		5	5	1			1
Subs																					
Goals				1	1					1				1			1				

Match grid:

Match	Bar	Bell	Ben	Bun	Cat	Chu	Col	Dev	Fle	Gav	Gor	Har	Hart	Hol	How	McN	Mea	Shi	Smi	Sto	Wal	OG
1		X		X	X	X	G	X1		X	X	X				X	X1				X2	1
2		X		X	X	X	G	X		X	X	X				X	X				X	
3		X		X	X	X	G	X		X1	X	X				X	X				X2	
4		X		X	X	X	G	X		X2	X	X				X1	X		X		X	
5		X		X	X	X	G	X		X	X	X				X	X				X	
6		X		X	X	X	G	X		X1	X	X		X1		X	X				X	
7		X		X	X1	X	G	X		X	X	X				X	X				X	
8		X		X	X	X	G	X		X	X	X				X	X				X	
9		X		X	X3		G			X	X	X				X	X				X	
10		X		X	X		G			X	X	X				X	X				X	
11		X		X	X1		G			X	X	X				X	X				X	
12		X		X	X					X	X	X2		X		X	X				X	
13		X		X	X		G			X	X	X1		X		X	X				X	
14		X					G	X		X1	X	X		X		X	X				X	
15		X		X	X			X		X2	X1	X1		X		X	X				X	
16		X		X	X		G			X	X	X		X		X	X				X	
17		X		X2	X		G			X	X1	X1		X		X	X					1
18		X		X	X		G			X	X			X		X	X	X			X	
19		X		X1	X		G			X	X1	X1		X2		X	X					
20		X		X1	X		G			X	X	X	X	X1		X	X					
21		X		X	X		G			X1	X	X	X	X		X	X					
22		X		X	X		G			X	X	X	X	X		X	X1p					
23		X		X	X1		G			X	X1	X	X	X		X	X					
24		X		X1	X1		G			X	X	X	X	X		X	X					
25		X		X	X		G			X	X	X	X	X		X	X					
26		X		X	X		G			X	X	X	X	X		X	X					
27		X			X	X	G			X	X	X	X	X2		X						
28		X			X	X	G			X1	X	X	X1	X		X			X			1
29		X			X	X	G			X1	X	X1	X	X		X			X			
30		X			X	X	G			X	X1	X	X	X	X							
31		X		X	X	X1				X	X			X	X	X	X	G				
32		X		X	X	X			G		X1			X2	X	X	X	X				
33		X		X	X	X			G		X1			X	X	X	X	X				
34		X		X	X	X				X	X	X		X2	X		X1		G			
35		X		X	X	X				X	X1	X		X	X		X		G			
36			X	X	X2			X			X			X	X	X	X		G			
37	X		X	X	X	X					X			X1	X	X	X		G			
38	X		X	X	X	X					X			X	X1	X	X		G			
39				X	X	X				X1	X1	X		X	X	X	X		G			
40		X		X	X	X				X	X	X		X	X	X			G			
41		X			X			X		X	X	X		X	X	X			G			
42		X		X1				X		X	X	X	X1	X		X			G		X	
43		X			X			X		X2	X	X	X	X		X				G	X1	
44	X1				X			X		X1	X1	X	X	X			X1p			G	X	
45		X			X			X		X1	X	X2	X	X			X1p			G	X	
46		X			X			X2		X	X	X	X	X			X			G	X	
47		X			X			X		X	X1	X	X	X		X				G	X	
48		X1		X	X	X		X			X			X	X1	X				G	X	
49	X	X		X	X	X		X			X			X	X					G	X	
50				X	X	X		X			X			X	X	X				G	X	
51				X	X	X		X			X		X	X	X1p	X				G	X	
				X	X			X			X			X	X	X	X1p			G	X1	

Football League position: 4th out of 24 in Division 4 – promoted to Division 3
Manager: Ron Burgess

New league opponents: Doncaster Rovers, Rochdale, Stockport County

Home-and-away league doubles
For – 6 (Chester, Crewe Alexandra, Darlington, Gateshead, Northampton Town, Workington)
Against – 2 (Doncaster Rovers, Torquay United)

Promoted with Watford: Walsall, Notts County, Torquay United

All Matches: Won 28, Drew 11, Lost 15, Goals 107-76

Highest Score: 7 (Match 15)

		HOME					AWAY					
	Pl	W	D	L	For	Ag	W	D	L	For	Ag	Pts
Walsall	46	14	5	4	57	33	14	4	5	45	27	65
Notts County	46	19	1	3	66	27	7	7	9	41	42	60
Torquay United	46	17	3	3	56	27	9	5	9	28	31	60
WATFORD	46	17	2	4	62	28	7	7	9	30	39	57
Millwall	46	12	8	3	54	28	6	9	8	30	33	53
Northampton Town	46	13	6	4	50	22	9	3	11	35	41	53
Gillingham	46	17	4	2	47	21	4	6	13	27	48	52
Crystal Palace	46	12	6	5	61	27	7	6	10	23	37	50
Exeter City	46	13	7	3	50	30	6	4	13	30	40	49
Stockport County	46	15	6	2	35	10	4	5	14	23	44	49
Bradford (Park Avenue)	46	12	10	1	48	25	5	5	13	22	43	49
Rochdale	46	15	4	4	46	19	3	6	14	19	41	46
Aldershot	46	14	5	4	50	22	4	4	15	27	52	45
Crewe Alexandra	46	14	3	6	51	31	4	6	13	28	57	45
Darlington	46	11	6	6	40	30	6	3	14	23	43	43
Workington	46	10	8	5	41	20	4	6	13	27	40	42
Doncaster Rovers	46	13	3	7	40	23	3	7	13	29	53	42
Barrow	46	11	8	4	52	29	4	3	16	25	58	41
Carlisle United	46	9	6	8	28	28	6	5	12	23	38	41
Chester	46	10	8	5	37	26	4	4	15	22	51	40
Southport	46	9	7	7	30	32	1	7	15	18	60	34
Gateshead	46	12	3	8	37	27	0	6	17	21	59	33
Oldham Athletic	46	5	7	11	20	30	5	5	13	21	53	28
Hartlepools United	46	9	2	12	40	41	1	5	17	19	68	27

No	DATE			COMPETITION	OPPONENTS	HOME	AWAY	ATTENDANCE
1	August	Sat	22	Football League, Division 4	STOCKPORT COUNTY	0-0 D		9,849
2		Mon	24	Football League, Division 4	Bradford (Park Avenue)		D 1-1	8,052
3		Sat	29	Football League, Division 4	Exeter City		L 0-2	8,323
4	September	Tue	1	Football League, Division 4	BRADFORD (PARK AVENUE)	1-0 W		8,801
5		Sat	5	Football League, Division 4	Doncaster Rovers		L 0-1	7,108
6		Wed	9	Football League, Division 4	Crewe Alexandra		W 3-1	10,432
7		Sat	12	Football League, Division 4	OLDHAM ATHLETIC	6-0 W		8,751
8		Tue	15	Football League, Division 4	CREWE ALEXANDRA	2-0 W		10,867
9		Sat	19	Football League, Division 4	Carlisle United		L 0-1	7,005
10		Wed	23	Football League, Division 4	Crystal Palace		L 1-8	21,938
11		Sat	26	Football League, Division 4	NOTTS COUNTY	4-2 W		10,131
12		Tue	29	Football League, Division 4	CRYSTAL PALACE	4-2 W		14,881
13	October	Sat	3	Football League, Division 4	Walsall		W 4-3	12,689
14		Sat	10	Football League, Division 4	TORQUAY UNITED	0-1 L		11,991
15		Tue	13	Football League, Division 4	HARTLEPOOLS UNITED	7-2 W		11,183
16		Sat	17	Football League, Division 4	Millwall		D 2-2	19,298
17		Sat	24	Football League, Division 4	SOUTHPORT	2-1 W		12,028
18		Sat	31	Football League, Division 4	Gillingham		L 0-2	7,308
19	November	Tue	3	Southern Floodlight Cup, 2nd Round	LEYTON ORIENT	0-2 L		4,064
20		Sat	7	Football League, Division 4	BARROW	2-0 W		8,564
21		Sat	14	FA Cup, 1st Round	Cheltenham Town		D 0-0	5,200
22		Tue	17	FA Cup, 1st Round replay	CHELTENHAM TOWN	3-0 W		11,520
23		Sat	21	Football League, Division 4	DARLINGTON	2-1 W		10,018
24		Sat	28	Football League, Division 4	Gateshead		W 3-1	2,473
25	December	Sat	5	FA Cup, 2nd Round	WYCOMBE WANDERERS	5-1 W		23,907
26		Sat	12	Football League, Division 4	WORKINGTON	3-2 W		7,815
27		Sat	19	Football League, Division 4	Stockport County		L 0-4	4,259
28		Mon	28	Football League, Division 4	Northampton Town		W 2-1	8,359
29	January	Sat	2	Football League, Division 4	EXETER CITY	5-2 W		9,045
30		Sat	9	FA Cup, 3rd Round	BIRMINGHAM CITY	2-1 W		31,314
31		Sat	16	Football League, Division 4	DONCASTER ROVERS	1-2 L		9,153
32		Sat	23	Football League, Division 4	Oldham Athletic		D 0-0	4,065
33		Sat	30	FA Cup, 4th Round	Southampton		D 2-2	28,169
34	February	Tue	2	FA Cup, 4th Round replay	SOUTHAMPTON	1-0 W		28,154
35		Sat	6	Football League, Division 4	CARLISLE UNITED	3-1 W		12,242
36		Sat	13	Football League, Division 4	Notts County		L 1-2	18,423
37		Sat	20	FA Cup, 5th Round	Sheffield United		L 2-3	40,124
38		Sat	27	Football League, Division 4	Torquay United		L 1-2	6,974
39	March	Tue	1	Football League, Division 4	NORTHAMPTON TOWN	3-1 W		13,024
40		Sat	5	Football League, Division 4	MILLWALL	0-2 L		17,317
41		Sat	12	Football League, Division 4	Southport		D 1-1	3,446
42		Wed	16	Football League, Division 4	Aldershot		D 2-2	9,010
43		Sat	19	Football League, Division 4	GILLINGHAM	3-1 W		12,550
44		Wed	23	Football League, Division 4	Hartlepools United		D 0-0	1,989
45		Sat	26	Football League, Division 4	Barrow		L 1-2	4,850
46	April	Sat	2	Football League, Division 4	ALDERSHOT	1-3 L		12,328
47		Sat	9	Football League, Division 4	Darlington		W 3-0	4,149
48		Fri	15	Football League, Division 4	CHESTER	4-2 W		13,948
49		Sat	16	Football League, Division 4	GATESHEAD	5-0 W		13,495
50		Mon	18	Football League, Division 4	Chester		W 1-0	5,962
51		Sat	23	Football League, Division 4	Rochdale		D 3-3	4,371
52		Tue	26	Football League, Division 4	ROCHDALE	2-1 W		17,774
53		Sat	30	Football League, Division 4	Workington		W 1-0	3,175
54	May	Tue	3	Football League, Division 4	WALSALL	2-2 D		20,641

The following match was abandoned after 48 minutes, owing to a waterlogged pitch:

	December	Sat	26	Football League, Division 4	NORTHAMPTON TOWN	1-0		8,836

League ever-presents: None
Most appearances in total: C.C. Holton 53 out of 54   **Most goals in total:** C.C. Holton 48 (including the Football League's highest tally of 42)
Hat-tricks: C.C. Holton (Match 13, Match 15, Match 48 & Match 49), E.D.H. Uphill (Match 22)   **Penalty goals:** C.C. Holton 10, E.D.H. Uphill 3
Sent off: None
Full international appearance(s) this season: None

	Barber, W.G. //	Bell, R.M.	Benning, M.D.	Bunce, F.	Catleugh, G.C.	Chung, C.	Fairbrother, J. //	Fleming, G.K. //	Gordon, P.J. //	Gregory, A.C.	Harrop, J. //	Hartle, B. //	Holton, C.C.	Linton, J.	McNeice, V.	Meadows, J.A. //	Nicholas, K.W.	Porter, A.	Price, J.D. //	Pygall, D.A.	Sanchez, J.	Uphill, E.D.H.	Walker, P.M.	Warn, K.D. //	Own goal
Apps	3	24	45	24	41	37		3	4	13	4	34	45	43	38	1	43	10	22	1	8	44	16	3	
Subs																									
Goals			4	3		1				4		6	42									30	2		
Apps		4	7	8	8	8	1	1	1			1	6	8	8		8	7	4			8			
Subs																									
Goals												1	6		1							6		1	
1			X	X	X	X	X						X	G	X		X		X			X			
2			X	X			X	X					X	G	X		X		X			X1p	X		
3			X		X	X			X				X	G	X		X		X			X	X		
4			X	X	X	X						X	X1	G	X		X		X				X		
5			X	X	X	X						X	X1	G	X		X		X				X		
6			X	X	X	X						X	X1	G	X		X		X			X2			
7			X1	X	X	X1						X1	X2	G	X		X		X			X1			
8			X	X	X	X						X	X1	G	X		X		X			X1			
9			X	X	X	X						X	X	G	X		X		X			X			
10			X	X	X	X					X	X	X1	G	X		X		X			X			
11			X	X	X	X						X1	X1	G	X		X		X			X2p			
12			X	X	X	X						X1	X2	G	X		X		X			X1			
13			X	X	X	X						X	X3	G	X		X		X			X1			
14			X	X	X	X					X	X	X	G	X		X		X			X			
15			X	X2	X	X						X	X3	G	X		X		X			X2			
16			X	X	X	X						X	X2	G	X		X		X			X			
17			X	X	X	X						X	X2	G	X		X		X			X			
18			X	X	X	X					X	X	X	G	X		X		X			X			
19			X	X	X	X	X		X		X		X	G	X		X					X			
20			X	X	X	X						X	X1	G	X		X		X			X1			
21			X	X	X	X						X	X	G	X		X		X			X			
22			X	X	X	X	X					X	X	G	X		X		X			X3			
23			X	X	X	X	X					X	X	G	X		X		X			X2			
24			X1	X	X	X						X	X2#	G	X		X		X			X			
25			X	X	X	X						X	X2p	G	X1		X		X			X2			
26			X		X	X						X1	X1	G	X		X		X			X1	X		
27		X	X		X	X						X	X	G	X		X					X	X		
28		X	X		X	X						X	X	G	X		X					X2			
29		X	X		X	X						X1	X2p	G	X		X					X2			
30		X	X	X	X	X						X	X1	G	X		X					X1			
31		X	X		X							X	X	G	X	X	X					X1	X		
32		X	X		X							X	X	G	X		X	X				X	X		
33		X	X	X	X	X						X	X1	G	X		X					X			1
34		X	X	X	X	X						X1	X	G	X		X					X			
35		X	X	X1	X	X						X	X1p	G	X		X					X1			
36		X	X		X	X						X	X1	G	X		X					X			
37		X	X	X	X	X						X	X2	G	X		X					X			
38		X	X1		X						X	X	X	G	X		X	X				X			
39		X	X		X	X			X			X	X1p	G	X		X					X2			
40		X	X		X	X			X			X	X	G	X		X					X			
41		X	X	X	X	X						X1	X	G	X		X					X			
42		X	X		X	X				X		X	X2	G	X		X					X			
43		X	X		X	X				X		X	X1	G	X		X					X2			
44		X	X		X	X				X		X	X	G	X		X					X			
45		X	X		X	X				X		X	X1	G	X		X					X			
46		X	X		X	X				X1		X	X	G	X		X					X			
47	X	X	X								X1		X1	G			X	X			X	X1	X		
48	X	X	X								X		X3p	G			X	X			X	X1	X		
49		X	X1			X					X1		X3#				X	X			X	X	X	G	
50		X	X							X			X				X	X			X	X	X	G	
51	X	X	X								X		X				X	X		X	X	X2p	X1	G	
52		X	X		X					X			X1	G			X	X			X	X1			
53		X	X		X					X			X1	G			X	X			X	X			
54		X	X		X					X			X1p	G			X	X			X	X	X1		
		X	X	X	X	X						X	X1p	G	X		X					X			

1960/61

Football League position: 4th out of 24 in Division 3
Manager: Ron Burgess

New league opponents: Barnsley, Bradford City, Bury, Chesterfield, Halifax Town, Hull City, Tranmere Rovers

Home-and-away league doubles
For – 3 (Coventry City, Grimsby Town, Swindon Town)
Against – 2 (Bristol City, Queens Park Rangers)

Divisional changes at end of season: Bury & Walsall to Division 2; Tranmere Rovers, Bradford City, Colchester United & Chesterfield to Division 4; Portsmouth & Lincoln City from Division 2; Peterborough United, Crystal Palace, Northampton Town & Bradford (Park Avenue) from Division 4

All Matches: Won 22, Drew 14, Lost 16, Goals 92-80

Highest Score: 7 (Match 48)

	Pl	HOME					AWAY					Pts
		W	D	L	For	Ag	W	D	L	For	Ag	
Bury	46	18	3	2	62	17	12	5	6	46	28	68
Walsall	46	19	4	0	62	20	9	2	12	36	40	62
Queens Park Rangers	46	18	4	1	58	23	7	6	10	35	37	60
WATFORD	46	12	7	4	52	27	8	5	10	33	45	52
Notts County	46	16	3	4	52	24	5	6	12	30	53	51
Grimsby Town	46	14	4	5	48	32	6	6	11	29	37	50
Port Vale	46	15	3	5	63	30	2	12	9	33	49	49
Barnsley	46	15	5	3	56	30	6	2	15	27	50	49
Halifax Town	46	14	7	2	42	22	2	10	11	29	56	49
Shrewsbury Town	46	15	3	5	54	26	2	9	12	29	49	46
Hull City	46	13	6	4	51	28	4	6	13	22	45	46
Torquay United	46	8	12	3	37	26	6	5	12	38	57	45
Newport County	46	12	7	4	51	30	5	4	14	30	60	45
Bristol City	46	15	4	4	50	19	2	6	15	20	49	44
Coventry City	46	14	6	3	54	25	2	6	15	26	58	44
Swindon Town	46	13	6	4	41	16	1	9	13	21	39	43
Brentford	46	10	9	4	41	28	3	8	12	15	42	43
Reading	46	13	5	5	48	29	1	7	15	24	54	40
Bournemouth & Boscombe Ath	46	8	12	3	34	29	7	3	13	24	54	40
Southend United	46	10	8	5	38	26	4	3	16	22	50	39
Tranmere Rovers	46	11	5	7	53	39	4	3	16	19	54	38
Bradford City	46	8	8	7	37	36	3	6	14	28	51	36
Colchester United	46	8	5	10	40	44	3	6	14	28	51	36
Chesterfield	46	9	6	8	42	29	1	6	16	25	58	32

No	DATE			COMPETITION	OPPONENTS	HOME	AWAY	ATTENDANCE
1	August	Sat	20	Football League, Division 3	NOTTS COUNTY	2-2 D		16,218
2		Tue	23	Football League, Division 3	Brentford		L 1-2	16,673
3		Sat	27	Football League, Division 3	Tranmere Rovers		W 2-0	7,649
4		Tue	30	Football League, Division 3	BRENTFORD	6-1 W		17,883
5	September	Sat	3	Football League, Division 3	HALIFAX TOWN	4-3 W		13,853
6		Mon	5	Football League, Division 3	Port Vale		L 0-3	15,175
7		Sat	10	Football League, Division 3	Shrewsbury Town		D 2-2	6,437
8		Tue	13	Football League, Division 3	PORT VALE	0-0 D		16,719
9		Sat	17	Football League, Division 3	WALSALL	2-0 W		14,586
10		Tue	20	Football League, Division 3	SWINDON TOWN	1-0 W		14,480
11		Sat	24	Football League, Division 3	Bury		W 2-0	9,462
12		Wed	28	Football League, Division 3	Swindon Town		W 2-1	15,811
13	October	Sat	1	Football League, Division 3	CHESTERFIELD	3-1 W		15,085
14		Mon	3	Football League, Division 3	Southend United		L 1-6	11,476
15		Sat	8	Football League, Division 3	Bradford City		D 2-2	4,572
16		Tue	11	Football League Cup, 1st Round	DERBY COUNTY	2-5 L		10,936
17		Sat	15	Football League, Division 3	BARNSLEY	1-2 L		14,045
18		Sat	29	Football League, Division 3	COLCHESTER UNITED	2-2 D		13,024
19	November	Sat	5	FA Cup, 1st Round	BRENTFORD	2-2 D		18,716
20		Tue	8	FA Cup, 1st Round replay	Brentford		W 2-0	21,000
21		Sat	12	Football League, Division 3	HULL CITY	2-2 D		13,746
22		Sat	19	Football League, Division 3	Reading		D 1-1	11,554
23		Sat	26	FA Cup, 2nd Round	Crystal Palace		D 0-0	33,699
24		Tue	29	FA Cup, 2nd Round replay	CRYSTAL PALACE	1-0 W		28,483
25	December	Sat	10	Football League, Division 3	QUEENS PARK RANGERS	0-3 L		15,546
26		Sat	17	Football League, Division 3	Notts County		L 1-3	10,262
27		Fri	23	Football League, Division 3	Torquay United		D 2-2	6,419
28		Tue	27	Football League, Division 3	TORQUAY UNITED	3-0 W		16,275
29		Sat	31	Football League, Division 3	TRANMERE ROVERS	2-2 D		12,613
30	January	Sat	7	FA Cup, 3rd Round	Rotherham United		L 0-1	14,854
31		Sat	14	Football League, Division 3	Halifax Town		D 0-0	5,293
32		Sat	21	Football League, Division 3	SHREWSBURY TOWN	3-1 W		10,027
33		Sat	28	Football League, Division 3	Grimsby Town		W 3-1	6,469
34	February	Sat	4	Football League, Division 3	Walsall		L 2-5	10,465
35		Sat	11	Football League, Division 3	BURY	1-1 D		12,996
36		Sat	18	Football League, Division 3	Chesterfield		L 0-2	4,433
37		Sat	25	Football League, Division 3	BRISTOL CITY	0-1 L		7,680
38	March	Mon	6	Football League, Division 3	Newport County		L 1-5	5,208
39		Sat	11	Football League, Division 3	NEWPORT COUNTY	4-1 W		9,157
40		Tue	14	Football League, Division 3	Bristol City		L 1-4	11,892
41		Sat	18	Football League, Division 3	Colchester United		W 4-1	4,648
42		Wed	22	Football League, Division 3	Barnsley		W 1-0	3,627
43		Sat	25	Football League, Division 3	GRIMSBY TOWN	2-0 W		10,384
44		Fri	31	Football League, Division 3	Bournemouth & Boscombe Athletic		W 1-0	11,424
45	April	Sat	1	Football League, Division 3	Hull City		L 2-3	7,267
46		Mon	3	Football League, Division 3	BOURNEMOUTH & BOSCOMBE ATHLETIC	0-1 L		8,311
47		Sat	8	Football League, Division 3	READING	2-0 W		10,247
48		Tue	11	Football League, Division 3	COVENTRY CITY	7-2 W		10,501
49		Fri	14	Football League, Division 3	Coventry City		W 1-0	10,437
50		Sat	22	Football League, Division 3	BRADFORD CITY	2-2 D		9,371
51		Tue	25	Football League, Division 3	SOUTHEND UNITED	3-0 W		7,089
52		Sat	29	Football League, Division 3	Queens Park Rangers		L 1-2	10,181

League ever-presents: None
Most appearances in total: R.M. Bell 51 out of 52   **Most goals in total:** C.C. Holton 34
Hat-tricks: F. Bunce (Match 4), C.C. Holton (Match 4)   **Penalty goals:** C.C. Holton 7
Sent off: None   **Full international appearance(s) this season:** None
(In Match 14, five of the opponents' goals were conceded after C.C. Holton had replaced the injured E.D. Underwood as goalkeeper.)

	Barnes, P.	Bell, R.M.	Benning, M.D.	Bunce, F.	Catleugh, G.C.	Chung, C.	Crisp, R.J.	Fairbrother, J.	Gregory, A.C.	Harmer, T.C.	Heard, D.M. //	Holton, C.C.	Lawson, N. //	Linton, J.	McNeice, V.	Meldrum, C.	Nicholas, K.W.	Porter, A.	Pygall, D.A. //	Sanchez, J. //	Smith, J. //	Underwood, E.D.	Uphill, E.D.H. //	Walker, P.M.	Own goal
Apps	6	45	37	43	14	37	7	11	12	30		42		22	40	9	38	28	9	11	20	24	7	14	
Subs																									
Goals			6	16		1	1	3	1	3		32			3	1	2				8		7	1	
Apps		6	6	5	1	5		2	1	5	1	6	1	6	6	1	4	6			3			1	
Subs																									
Goals			1	2						2		2													
1	X	X	X			X			X			X		G			X	X			X2	X			
2	X	X	X			X			X			X1		G			X	X			X	X			
3	X	X	X			X				X1		X		G			X	X			X	X			1
4	X	X	X	X3		X						X3		G			X	X			X	X			
5	X	X	X	X1		X						X2		G			X	X			X1	X			
6	X	X	X	X		X						X		G			X	X			X	X			
7		X	X	X1								X1			X		X	X			X	G	X		
8		X	X	X		X						X			X			X	X	X		G			
9		X	X	X		X						X1			X			X	X	X1		G			
10		X	X	X		X						X			X		X1	X	X	X		G			
11		X	X1	X		X						X			X		X1	X	X	X		G			
12		X	X	X		X						X1			X			X	X	X1		G			
13		X	X	X		X						X1			X			X	X	X2		G			
14		X	X	X		X						X			X			X	X	X1		G			
15		X	X	X		X						X1		G	X			X	X1	X	X				
16	X	X		X				X1	X		X	X1	X	G			X			X					
17		X	X	X		X						X1		G	X			X	X	X	X				
18		X	X	X1					X	X		X1		G	X			X		X					
19	X	X	X1	X						X		X1		G	X			X	X		X				
20	X	X1	X	X					X1	X		X		G	X			X	X						
21		X	X	X		X			X			X2		G	X			X	X						
22		X	X	X		X			X1			X		G	X			X	X						
23	X	X	X	X					X			X		G	X			X	X		X				
24	X	X	X1	X					X			X		G	X			X	X		X				
25		X	X	X		X			X			X		G	X			X	X		X				
26		X	X	X		X			X			X1		G	X			X	X		X				
27		X1	X	X	X			X		X				G	X	X		X1						X	
28		X	X2	X				X1		X				G	X	X		X						X	
29		X2	X	X					X	X				G	X	X		X						X	
30	X	X	X	X					X	X		X		G	X	X		X						X	
31		X	X						X	X		X		G	X	X	X	X						X	
32	X	X	X2						X	X		X1		G	X	X		X						X	
33	X	X	X						X	X		X2		G	X	X		X						X1	
34	X	X	X						X	X		X2#		G	X	X		X						X	
35	X	X	X						X	X		X1p		G	X	X		X						X	
36	X	X	X			X			X	X		X		G	X	X		X			X				
37	X		X					X	X	X		X			X			X					X	G	
38	X	X						X	X	X		X1p			X			X						G	
39	X	X	X1							X		X1			X			X	X				X2	G	
40	X	X	X	X						X		X			X			X					X1	G	
41	X	X	X1	X	X					X		X			X		X2				X		X1	G	
42	X		X	X	X	X				X		X			X			X		X1				G	
43	X		X1	X	X	X				X		X1p			X			X	X					G	
44	X		X	X	X	X				X1		X			X			X	X					G	
45	X		X	X	X	X1				X		X			X			X	X					G	
46	X		X	X	X	X				X		X			X			X	X					G	
47	X	X1	X	X			X	X	X			X1p			X			X						G	
48	X		X2				X1	X	X1			X1			X			X					X2	G	
49	X		X	X			X	X	X			X1p			X			X					X	G	
50	X		X	X			X	X	X1			X1			X			X					X	G	
51	X	X	X2	X		X		X	X			X1			X			X						G	
52	X	X1	X	X		X		X	X			X			X			X						G	

1961/62

Football League position: 17th out of 24 in Division 3
Manager: Ron Burgess

New league opponents: Lincoln City, Peterborough United

Home-and-away league doubles
For – 3 (Port Vale, Queens Park Rangers, Torquay United)
Against – 2 (Coventry City, Peterborough United)

Divisional changes at end of season: Portsmouth and Grimsby Town to Division 2; Torquay United, Lincoln City, Brentford and Newport County to Division 3; Bristol Rovers and Brighton & Hove Albion from Division 2; Millwall, Colchester United, Wrexham and Carlisle United from Division 4

All Matches: Won 18, Drew 15, Lost 21, Goals 81-85

Highest Score: 4 (Matches 5 & 36)

	HOME					AWAY					
	Pl	W	D	L	For	Ag	W	D	L	For	Ag	Pts
Portsmouth	46	15	6	2	48	23	12	5	6	39	24	65
Grimsby Town	46	18	3	2	49	18	10	3	10	31	38	62
Bournemouth & Boscombe Ath	46	14	8	1	42	18	7	9	7	27	27	59
Queens Park Rangers	46	15	3	5	65	31	9	8	6	46	42	59
Peterborough United	46	16	0	7	60	38	10	6	7	47	44	58
Bristol City	46	15	3	5	56	27	8	5	10	38	45	54
Reading	46	14	5	4	46	24	8	4	11	31	42	53
Northampton Town	46	12	6	5	52	24	8	5	10	33	33	51
Swindon Town	46	11	8	4	48	26	6	7	10	30	45	49
Hull City	46	15	2	6	43	20	5	6	12	24	34	48
Bradford (Park Avenue)	46	13	5	5	47	27	7	2	14	33	51	47
Port Vale	46	12	4	7	41	23	5	7	11	24	43	45
Notts County	46	14	5	4	44	23	3	4	16	23	51	43
Coventry City	46	11	6	6	38	26	5	5	13	26	45	43
Crystal Palace	46	8	8	7	50	41	6	6	11	33	39	42
Southend United	46	10	7	6	31	26	3	9	11	26	43	42
WATFORD	46	10	9	4	37	26	4	4	15	26	48	41
Halifax Town	46	9	5	9	34	35	6	5	12	28	49	40
Shrewsbury Town	46	8	7	8	46	37	5	5	13	27	47	38
Barnsley	46	9	6	8	45	41	4	6	13	26	54	38
Torquay United	46	9	4	10	48	44	6	2	15	28	56	36
Lincoln City	46	4	10	9	31	43	5	7	11	26	44	35
Brentford	46	11	3	9	34	29	2	3	18	19	64	34
Newport County	46	6	5	12	29	38	1	3	19	17	64	22

No	DATE			COMPETITION	OPPONENTS	HOME	AWAY	ATTENDANCE
1	August	Sat	19	Football League, Division 3	NORTHAMPTON TOWN	0-0 D		16,849
2		Tue	22	Football League, Division 3	PETERBOROUGH UNITED	2-3 L		20,889
3		Sat	26	Football League, Division 3	LINCOLN CITY	3-3 D		12,790
4		Mon	28	Football League, Division 3	Peterborough United		L 3-4	18,078
5	September	Sat	2	Football League, Division 3	Torquay United		W 4-3	6,246
6		Tue	5	Football League, Division 3	SHREWSBURY TOWN	1-1 D		15,562
7		Sat	9	Football League, Division 3	SWINDON TOWN	2-0 W		10,339
8		Mon	11	Football League Cup, 1st Round	HALIFAX TOWN	3-0 W		6,298
9		Sat	16	Football League, Division 3	Halifax Town		L 0-2	5,666
10		Thu	21	Football League, Division 3	Hull City		L 0-1	14,376
11		Sat	23	Football League, Division 3	QUEENS PARK RANGERS	3-2 W		15,555
12		Tue	26	Football League, Division 3	HULL CITY	1-1 D		12,406
13		Sat	30	Football League, Division 3	Barnsley		L 0-3	5,602
14	October	Tue	3	Football League, Division 3	CRYSTAL PALACE	3-2 W		14,228
15		Sat	7	Football League, Division 3	Port Vale		W 3-1	10,120
16		Wed	11	Football League, Division 3	Crystal Palace		D 1-1	23,390
17		Sat	14	Football League, Division 3	BRISTOL CITY	1-1 D		11,860
18		Mon	16	Football League Cup, 2nd Round	READING	3-1 W		6,420
19		Wed	18	Football League, Division 3	Shrewsbury Town		L 1-5	5,711
20		Sat	21	Football League, Division 3	Southend United		W 1-0	9,399
21		Sat	28	Football League, Division 3	NOTTS COUNTY	3-1 W		10,086
22	November	Sat	4	FA Cup, 1st Round	Southend United		W 2-0	12,375
23		Sat	11	Football League, Division 3	BRENTFORD	2-1 W		8,356
24		Wed	15	Football League Cup, 3rd Round	York City		D 1-1	8,508
25		Fri	17	Football League, Division 3	Reading		L 2-3	11,578
26		Tue	21	Football Lge Cup, 3rd Round replay	YORK CITY (after extra time)	2-2 D		7,095
27		Sat	25	FA Cup, 2nd Round	Romford		W 3-1	12,110
28	December	Sat	2	Football League, Division 3	Bradford (Park Avenue)		D 1-1	8,948
29		Mon	4	Football Lge Cup, 3rd Round, 2nd replay	York City		L 2-3	7,019
30		Sat	9	Football League, Division 3	GRIMSBY TOWN	2-1 W		8,917
31		Sat	16	Football League, Division 3	Northampton Town		L 0-2	12,590
32		Sat	23	Football League, Division 3	Lincoln City		D 0-0	4,286
33		Tue	26	Football League, Division 3	BOURNEMOUTH & BOSCOMBE ATHLETIC	0-0 D		9,441
34		Sat	30	Football League, Division 3	Bournemouth & Boscombe Athletic		L 1-4	8,383
35	January	Sat	6	FA Cup, 3rd Round	Preston North End		L 2-3	16,518
36		Sat	13	Football League, Division 3	TORQUAY UNITED	4-1 W		7,832
37		Sat	20	Football League, Division 3	Swindon Town		L 1-3	7,688
38		Sat	27	Football League, Division 3	NEWPORT COUNTY	3-1 W		8,183
39	February	Sat	3	Football League, Division 3	HALIFAX TOWN	0-0 D		7,237
40		Sat	10	Football League, Division 3	Queens Park Rangers		W 2-1	11,142
41		Sat	17	Football League, Division 3	BARNSLEY	3-1 W		7,826
42		Sat	24	Football League, Division 3	PORT VALE	2-0 W		7,778
43	March	Sat	3	Football League, Division 3	Bristol City		L 1-2	11,712
44		Fri	9	Football League, Division 3	SOUTHEND UNITED	1-3 L		8,245
45		Mon	12	Football League, Division 3	Coventry City		L 0-1	7,233
46		Sat	17	Football League, Division 3	Notts County		L 0-1	6,987
47		Fri	23	Football League, Division 3	COVENTRY CITY	0-1 L		5,611
48		Fri	30	Football League, Division 3	Brentford		L 1-3	6,450
49	April	Fri	6	Football League, Division 3	READING	1-1 D		4,961
50		Sat	14	Football League, Division 3	Newport County		D 0-0	2,346
51		Fri	20	Football League, Division 3	PORTSMOUTH	0-0 D		12,689
52		Sat	21	Football League, Division 3	BRADFORD (PARK AVENUE)	0-2 L		6,360
53		Mon	23	Football League, Division 3	Portsmouth		L 1-2	18,169
54		Sat	28	Football League, Division 3	Grimsby Town		L 3-5	14,299

League ever-presents: E.D. Underwood
Most appearances in total: E.D. Underwood 53 out of 54   **Most goals in total:** R.J. Crisp 13
Hat-tricks: T.J. Williams (Match 5)   **Penalty goals:** A.C. Gregory 1, T.C. Harmer 1
Sent off: None
Full international appearance(s) this season: None

	Barnes, P.	Bell, R.M.	Benning, M.D.	Brown, R.H.	Bunce, F.	Catleugh, G.C.	Chung, C.	Crisp, R.J.	Day, R.A.	Fairbrother, J.	Gregory, A.C.	Harmer, T.C.	Harris, G.A.	Holton, C.C.	Linton, J.	McNeice, V.	Mancini, T.J.	Meldrum, C.	Nicholas, K.W.	Porter, A.	Ryden, J.J.	Stokes, A.F.	Underwood, E.D.	Walker, P.M.	Williams, T.J.	Own goals
Apps	4	40	18	21	44	22	11	34	1	15	36	33	1	3		41	2	17	31	20	24	14	46	16	12	
Subs																										
Goals		4	6	7	2	2		10		10	3	3		1			1	1	2			3		3	6	2
Apps		7	6	2	7	7	1	7		2	6	6			1	6	1	6	2	2	2	2	7	6	2	
Subs																										
Goals				1	4			3		1	2	1							1			1		3	1	

#	Barnes	Bell	Benning	Brown	Bunce	Catleugh	Chung	Crisp	Day	Fairbrother	Gregory	Harmer	Harris	Holton	Linton	McNeice	Mancini	Meldrum	Nicholas	Porter	Ryden	Stokes	Underwood	Walker	Williams	Own
1		X	X		X						X			X		X			X	X	X	X	G			
2		X1			X						X	X		X1		X			X	X	X	X	G			
3			X		X2						X	X		X		X			X	X1	X	X	G			
4					X	X		X2			X					X			X	X	X	X	G	X1		
5		X			X			X			X					X			X	X	X	X1	G		X3	
6		X			X			X1			X					X			X	X	X	X	G		X	
7		X			X			X			X					X			X	X	X	X	G		X1	1
8		X			X1			X			X					X	X		X	X	X1		G		X1	
9		X			X			X			X					X			X	X	X	X	G		X	
10		X			X			X			X					X			X	X	X	X	G		X	
11		X			X					X2						X			X	X	X1	X	G	X	X	
12		X			X			X				X	X			X			X				G	X1	X	
13		X			X			X				X	X			X			X				G	X		
14		X	X1		X1			X				X1	X			X		X					G	X		
15		X	X		X1			X				X2	X			X		X					G	X		
16		X			X			X				X	X			X		X					G	X		1
17		X			X			X				X	X			X		X					G	X1		
18		X			X2	X		X1				X				X	X	X		X			G	X		
19		X	X1		X	X		X				X				X		X		X	X		G			
20		X			X			X				X				X		X		X	X1	X	G			
21		X	X		X1	X		X1			X1	X	X			X		X					G			
22		X	X		X	X		X			X	X2	X			X		X					G			
23		X	X		X	X1		X			X1	X	X			X		X					G			
24		X	X		X	X		X			X1	X	X		G	X		X							X	
25		X	X1		X	X		X			X	X1				X		X					G		X	
26		X	X		X			X			X	X				X		X					G		X2	X
27		X	X	X1	X1	X		X			X	X1p				X		X					G		X	
28		X	X	X1	X			X			X	X				X		X					G		X	
29		X	X	X	X		X	X1			X	X							X	X			G		X1	
30		X	X	X1	X			X			X	X				X		X					G		X1	
31		X	X	X	X			X			X	X				X		X					G		X	
32		X	X	X	X			X			X	X				X		X					G		X	
33		X	X	X	X			X			X	X				X		X					G		X	
34		X	X1	X	X	X		X			X	X				X		X					G		X	
35		X	X	X	X			X			X1	X				X		X1					G		X	
36		X	X	X1	X			X2			X1	X				X		X					G		X	
37		X	X	X	X	X	X	X			X1					X		X					G			
38		X	X1	X	X	X		X1			X1					X		X					G			
39		X		X	X	X		X			X	X	X			X		X					G			
40		X		X	X	X1		X1			X	X	X			X		X					G			
41		X	X1	X	X			X1		X1p	X					X		X					G			
42		X		X	X			X1		X	X					X		X					G		X1	
43		X		X	X			X		X1	X					X		X					G		X	
44		X		X1	X			X		X	X					X		X					G		X	
45		X			X	X	X	X	X	X	X					X				X			G			
46		X			X	X	X	X		X	X					X				X	X		G			
47		X			X	X		X		X	X					X				X	X		G			
48	X	X			X			X		X1	X					X				X	X		G			
49	X	X			X	X		X		X	X1									X	X		G			
50	X	X			X			X			X					X				X	X		G			
51		X			X	X	X				X	X				X				X	X	X	G			
52	X				X	X	X					X	X			X				X	X		G			
53					X	X1	X				X	X					X	X	X	X	X		G			
54					X1	X	X1				X	X1					X	X	X	X	X		G			

1962/63

Football League position: 17th out of 24 in Division 3
Manager: Ron Burgess

New league opponents: Wrexham

Home-and-away league doubles
For – 3 (Brighton & Hove Albion, Halifax Town, Notts County)
Against – 4 (Bournemouth & Boscombe Athletic, Bristol Rovers, Millwall, Peterborough United)

Divisional changes at end of season: Northampton Town and Swindon Town to Division 2; Bradford (Park Avenue), Brighton & Hove Albion, Carlisle United and Halifax Town to Division 4; Walsall and Luton Town from Division 2; Brentford, Oldham Athletic, Crewe Alexandra and Mansfield Town from Division 4

All Matches: Won 20, Drew 9, Lost 23, Goals 92-93

Highest Score: 6 (Match 9)

		HOME					AWAY					
	Pl	W	D	L	For	Ag	W	D	L	For	Ag	Pts
Northampton Town	46	16	6	1	64	19	10	4	9	45	41	62
Swindon Town	46	18	2	3	60	22	4	12	7	27	34	58
Port Vale	46	16	4	3	47	25	7	4	12	25	33	54
Coventry City	46	14	6	3	54	28	4	11	8	29	41	53
Bournemouth & Boscombe Ath	46	11	12	0	39	16	7	4	12	24	30	52
Peterborough United	46	11	5	7	48	33	9	6	8	45	42	51
Notts County	46	15	3	5	46	29	4	10	9	27	45	51
Southend United	46	11	7	5	38	24	8	5	10	37	53	50
Wrexham	46	14	6	3	54	27	6	3	14	30	56	49
Hull City	46	12	6	5	40	22	7	4	12	34	47	48
Crystal Palace	46	10	7	6	38	22	7	6	10	30	36	47
Colchester United	46	11	6	6	41	35	7	5	11	32	58	47
Queens Park Rangers	46	9	6	8	44	36	8	5	10	41	40	45
Bristol City	46	10	9	4	54	38	6	4	13	46	54	45
Shrewsbury Town	46	13	4	6	57	41	3	8	12	26	40	44
Millwall	46	11	6	6	50	32	4	7	12	32	55	43
WATFORD	46	12	3	8	55	46	5	4	14	27	53	41
Barnsley	46	12	6	5	39	28	3	5	15	24	46	41
Bristol Rovers	46	11	8	4	45	29	4	3	16	25	59	41
Reading	46	13	4	6	51	30	3	4	16	23	48	40
Bradford (Park Avenue)	46	10	9	4	43	36	4	3	16	36	51	40
Brighton & Hove Albion	46	7	6	10	28	38	5	6	12	30	46	36
Carlisle United	46	12	4	7	41	37	1	5	17	20	52	35
Halifax Town	46	8	3	12	41	51	1	9	13	23	55	30

No	DATE			COMPETITION	OPPONENTS	HOME	AWAY	ATTENDANCE
1	August	Sat	18	Football League, Division 3	SOUTHEND UNITED	3-1 W		11,487
2		Thu	23	Football League, Division 3	Notts County		W 3-1	6,121
3		Sat	25	Football League, Division 3	Millwall		L 0-6	16,125
4		Tue	28	Football League, Division 3	NOTTS COUNTY	4-0 W		11,423
5	September	Sat	1	Football League, Division 3	SHREWSBURY TOWN	4-3 W		10,601
6		Tue	4	Football League, Division 3	Coventry City		L 1-3	16,287
7		Thu	6	Football League Cup, 1st Round	COLCHESTER UNITED	1-2 L		4,730
8		Sat	8	Football League, Division 3	Port Vale		W 3-1	11,108
9		Tue	11	Football League, Division 3	COVENTRY CITY	6-1 W		10,277
10		Sat	15	Football League, Division 3	READING	4-0 W		13,281
11		Wed	19	Football League, Division 3	Bournemouth & Boscombe Athletic		L 0-1	11,493
12		Sat	22	Football League, Division 3	Bristol City		D 3-3	13,426
13		Tue	25	Football League, Division 3	BOURNEMOUTH & BOSCOMBE ATHLETIC	0-1 L		16,016
14		Sat	29	Football League, Division 3	BRIGHTON & HOVE ALBION	2-0 W		11,826
15	October	Tue	2	Football League, Division 3	BRADFORD (PARK AVENUE)	3-2 W		12,136
16		Sat	6	Football League, Division 3	Swindon Town		L 1-3	13,988
17		Wed	10	Football League, Division 3	Bradford (Park Avenue)		L 0-1	6,492
18		Sat	13	Football League, Division 3	PETERBOROUGH UNITED	2-3 L		13,606
19		Sat	20	Football League, Division 3	Barnsley		L 1-4	7,793
20		Sat	27	Football League, Division 3	NORTHAMPTON TOWN	4-2 W		19,015
21	November	Sat	3	FA Cup, 1st Round	POOLE TOWN	2-2 D		12,545
22		Tue	6	FA Cup, 1st Round replay	Poole Town		W 2-1	6,575
23		Sat	10	Football League, Division 3	HULL CITY	4-2 W		7,518
24		Sat	17	Football League, Division 3	Crystal Palace		W 1-0	10,716
25		Sat	24	FA Cup, 2nd Round	Southend United		W 2-0	16,892
26	December	Sat	1	Football League, Division 3	Halifax Town		W 3-1	3,090
27		Sat	8	Football League, Division 3	BRISTOL ROVERS	0-1 L		7,837
28		Sat	15	Football League, Division 3	Southend United		D 1-1	9,252
29		Wed	26	Football League, Division 3	Carlisle United		L 1-2	5,497
30		Sat	29	Football League, Division 3	CARLISLE UNITED	5-1 W		8,397
31	February	Wed	20	FA Cup, 3rd Round	ROTHERHAM UNITED	2-0 W		5,165
32		Sat	23	Football League, Division 3	SWINDON TOWN	3-3 D		11,338
33		Wed	27	FA Cup, 4th Round	Southampton		L 1-3	13,336
34	March	Sat	2	Football League, Division 3	Peterborough United		L 0-4	12,692
35		Tue	12	Football League, Division 3	BARNSLEY	0-0 D		6,717
36		Sat	16	Football League, Division 3	Northampton Town		L 0-1	12,230
37		Sat	23	Football League, Division 3	QUEENS PARK RANGERS	2-5 L		10,597
38		Tue	26	Football League, Division 3	BRISTOL CITY	1-4 L		5,972
39		Sat	30	Football League, Division 3	Hull City		L 0-1	5,462
40	April	Wed	3	Football League, Division 3	Reading		D 0-0	5,684
41		Sat	6	Football League, Division 3	CRYSTAL PALACE	1-4 L		8,471
42		Tue	9	Football League, Division 3	WREXHAM	3-1 W		5,301
43		Sat	13	Football League, Division 3	Wrexham		D 0-0	7,127
44		Mon	15	Football League, Division 3	COLCHESTER UNITED	1-1 D		6,693
45		Tue	16	Football League, Division 3	Colchester United		L 2-3	5,315
46		Sat	20	Football League, Division 3	HALIFAX TOWN	2-1 W		3,688
47		Sat	27	Football League, Division 3	Bristol Rovers		L 1-3	7,806
48		Tue	30	Football League, Division 3	MILLWALL	0-2 L		6,278
49	May	Sat	4	Football League, Division 3	Brighton & Hove Albion		W 4-1	9,392
50		Sat	11	Football League, Division 3	Shrewsbury Town		L 0-3	4,069
51		Mon	13	Football League, Division 3	Queens Park Rangers		D 2-2	5,040
52		Sat	18	Football League, Division 3	PORT VALE	1-2 L		5,955

The following matches were abandoned after 67 minutes (owing to fog) and at half-time (waterlogged pitch), respectively:

	December	Sat	22	Football League, Division 3	MILLWALL	2-1		10,967
	March	Sat	9	Football League, Division 3	BARNSLEY	0-1		4,039

League ever-presents: D. Ward
Most appearances in total: D. Ward 52 out of 52   **Most goals in total:** D. Ward 30 (including Division 3's highest tally of 29)
Hat-tricks: D. Ward (Match 30)   **Penalty goals:** None
Sent off: R.M. Howfield (Match 20)
Full international appearance(s) this season: None

	Bell, R.M.	Brown, R.H. //	Bunce, F. //	Catleugh, G.C.	Chung, C.	Crisp, R.J.	Fairbrother, J. //	Fraser, J.W.	Gregory, A.C.	Harris, G.A.	Howfield, R.M.	Jennings, P.A. //	Jones, B.E. //	Larkin, B.P.	Linton, J. //	Livesey, C.E.	McNeice, V.	Mancini, T.J. //	Meldrum C. //	Nicholas, K.W.	Owen, B.E.	Porter, A. //	Underwood, E.D.//	Ward, D.	Woods, D.J. //	Own goal
Apps	37	7	6	4	26	8	14	14	38	36	38	2	2	36	6	19	43	6	6	44	3	14	38	46	13	
Subs																										
Goals		4			4		6	2	4	12	11			1		3				1		2		29	2	1
Apps	6		1		6		1	5	5	6	5			4	2	3	5	1	1	5			4	6		
Subs																										
Goals					2			1	1	3	2													1		
1			X				X2		X		X			X		X	X			X			G	X1		
2			X				X2		X		X			X		X	X		X1	X			G	X		
3			X				X		X		X			X		X	X			X			G	X		
4							X1		X	X	X1			X		X	X			X			G	X2		
5							X		X1	X1	X1			X		X	X			X			G	X1		
6							X		X	X1	X			X		X	X			X			G	X		
7	X				X		X	X1	X	X				X		G	X			X				X		
8	X	X2						X	X1	X				X			X			X			G	X		
9	X	X1						X1	X	X2	X			X			X			X			G	X2		
10	X	X						X	X	X	X1			X			X			X			G	X2		1
11	X	X						X	X	X	X			X			X			X			G	X		
12	X							X	X	X	X1	X1	G				X			X				X1		
13	X							X	X	X	X	X	G				X			X				X		
14	X					X		X	X	X2	X					X				X		X	G	X		
15	X		X			X			X	X	X2					X				X		X	G	X1		
16	X		X	X					X	X1	X			X		X				X			G	X		
17	X		X	X					X	X	X			X		X				X			G	X		
18	X						X1		X	X1				X		X				X		X	G	X	X	
19	X						X		X					X		X	X			X			G	X1	X	
20	X						X		X	X1	X1			X			X			X			G	X	X1	
21	X		X				X1		X	X	X1			X			X			X			G	X		
22	X						X	X	X1	X1	X			X			X			X			G	X		
23	X						X1		X	X	X			X			X			X			G	X2	X1	
24	X						X		X	X1	X			X			X			X			G	X	X	
25	X						X1	X	X	X1				X		X	X			X			G	X		
26	X						X		X	X	X1			X			X			X			G	X2	X	
27	X						X		X	X	X			X			X			X			G	X	X	
28	X						X		X	X	X					X	X			X			G	X	X1	
29	X						X		X	X	X					X1	X			X			G	X	X	
30	X						X		X1	X	X1			X		X	X			X			G	X3		
31	X						X		X	X	X1			X1		X	X			X			G	X		
32	X						X1		X	X	X1					X	X1			X			G	X		
33	X						X		X	X	X				G	X	X			X				X1		
34	X						X		X	X	X				G	X	X			X		X		X		
35	X						X		X	X	X					X	X			X			G	X	X	
36	X						X		X		X			X		X	X			X			G	X	X	
37	X						X		X	X	X			X		X	X			X			G	X2		
38	X			X			X		X	X	X1			X					X	X			G	X		
39			X	X	X				X	X				X	G	X	X			X				X		
40			X	X		X			X	X				X	G	X	X			X				X		
41			X	X		X			X	X				X	G	X	X							X1		
42	X			X		X1			X1	X				X		X	X			X			G	X1		
43	X			X		X			X	X				X		X	X			X			G	X		
44	X			X		X			X1	X				X		X	X			X			G	X		
45	X					X		X1	X1	X				X		X	X			X			G	X		
46	X	X1			X				X	X				X		X	X			X			G	X1		
47	X	X			X					X				X		X	X			X			G	X1	X	
48	X	X			X					X				X		X	X			X			G	X	X	
49	X			X1					X		X			X					X	X		X2		G	X1	
50	X			X					X	X				X		X	X			X		X	G	X		
51	X					X			X	X		G	X			X	X			X		X		X2		
52	X					X			X	X		G	X			X1	X			X		X		X		
	X			X1					X	X	X				X1	X				X			G	X	X	
	X			X					X	X	X					X	X			X		X	G	X	X	

1963/64

Football League position: 3rd out of 24 in Division 3

Manager: Bill McGarry

		HOME					AWAY					
	Pl	W	D	L	For	Ag	W	D	L	For	Ag	Pts
Coventry City	46	14	7	2	62	32	8	9	6	36	29	60
Crystal Palace	46	17	4	2	38	14	6	10	7	35	37	60
WATFORD	46	16	6	1	57	28	7	6	10	22	31	58
Bournemouth & Boscombe Ath	46	17	4	2	47	15	7	4	12	32	43	56
Bristol City	46	13	7	3	52	24	7	8	8	32	40	55
Reading	46	15	5	3	49	26	6	5	12	30	36	52
Mansfield Town	46	15	8	0	51	20	5	3	15	25	42	51
Hull City	46	11	9	3	45	27	5	8	10	28	41	49
Oldham Athletic	46	13	3	7	44	35	7	5	11	29	35	48
Peterborough United	46	13	6	4	52	27	5	5	13	23	43	47
Shrewsbury Town	46	13	6	4	43	19	5	5	13	30	61	47
Bristol Rovers	46	9	6	8	52	34	10	2	11	39	45	46
Port Vale	46	13	6	4	35	13	3	8	12	18	36	46
Southend United	46	9	10	4	42	26	6	5	12	35	52	45
Queens Park Rangers	46	13	4	6	47	34	5	5	13	29	44	45
Brentford	46	11	4	8	54	36	4	10	9	33	44	44
Colchester United	46	10	8	5	45	26	2	11	10	25	42	43
Luton Town	46	12	2	9	42	41	4	8	11	22	39	42
Walsall	46	7	9	7	34	35	6	5	12	25	41	40
Barnsley	46	9	9	5	34	29	3	6	14	34	65	39
Millwall	46	9	4	10	33	29	5	2	12	20	38	38
Crewe Alexandra	46	10	5	8	29	26	1	7	15	21	51	34
Wrexham	46	9	4	10	50	42	4	2	17	25	65	32
Notts County	46	7	8	8	29	26	2	1	20	16	66	27

New league opponents: None

Home-and-away league doubles
For – 4 (Bristol Rovers, Crewe Alexandra, Notts County, Walsall)
Against – none

Divisional changes at end of season: Coventry City & Crystal Palace to Division 2; Millwall, Crewe Alexandra, Wrexham & Notts County to Division 4; Grimsby Town & Scunthorpe United from Division 2; Gillingham, Carlisle United, Workington & Exeter City from Division 4

All Matches: Won 24, Drew 13, Lost 13, Goals 83-65

Highest Score: 5 (Match 29)

No	DATE			COMPETITION	OPPONENTS	HOME	AWAY	ATTENDANCE	
1	August	Sat	24	Football League, Division 3	HULL CITY	3-3 D		9,251	
2		Mon	26	Football League, Division 3	Millwall		W 3-0		13,021
3		Sat	31	Football League, Division 3	Bournemouth & Boscombe Athletic		L 0-2		10,701
4	September	Wed	4	Football League Cup, 1st Round	Mansfield Town		L 1-2	7,975	
5		Sat	7	Football League, Division 3	WREXHAM	4-2 W		8,181	
6		Tue	10	Football League, Division 3	MILLWALL	2-2 D		11,020	
7		Sat	14	Football League, Division 3	Queens Park Rangers		L 0-1		10,829
8		Tue	17	Football League, Division 3	Barnsley		D 0-0		6,348
9		Sat	21	Football League, Division 3	BRISTOL ROVERS	3-2 W		8,193	
10		Sat	28	Football League, Division 3	Oldham Athletic		L 0-1		14,560
11	October	Tue	1	Football League, Division 3	BARNSLEY	2-1 W		5,612	
12		Sat	5	Football League, Division 3	PETERBOROUGH UNITED	1-2 L		10,543	
13		Wed	9	Football League, Division 3	Crystal Palace		L 0-2		16,913
14		Sat	12	Football League, Division 3	Notts County		W 2-1		6,887
15		Tue	15	Football League, Division 3	CRYSTAL PALACE	3-1 W		9,595	
16		Sat	19	Football League, Division 3	LUTON TOWN	2-0 W		13,239	
17		Mon	21	Football League, Division 3	Southend United		L 0-3		9,785
18		Sat	26	Football League, Division 3	Coventry City		D 2-2		25,910
19		Tue	29	Football League, Division 3	SOUTHEND UNITED	3-1 W		9,253	
20	November	Sat	2	Football League, Division 3	MANSFIELD TOWN	3-0 W		9,138	
21		Sat	9	Football League, Division 3	Brentford		W 2-1		17,094
22		Sat	16	FA Cup, 1st Round	Peterborough United		D 1-1		15,163
23		Tue	19	FA Cup, 1st Round replay	PETERBOROUGH UNITED (after extra time)	2-1 W		15,081	
24		Sat	23	Football League, Division 3	Bristol City		L 0-2		9,962
25		Sat	30	Football League, Division 3	PORT VALE	1-1 D		9,890	
26	December	Sat	7	FA Cup, 2nd Round	Newport County		L 0-2		5,353
27		Sat	14	Football League, Division 3	Hull City		D 2-2		8,011
28		Sat	21	Football League, Division 3	BOURNEMOUTH & BOSCOMBE ATHLETIC	3-0 W		7,459	
29		Thu	26	Football League, Division 3	WALSALL	5-3 W		11,048	
30		Sat	28	Football League, Division 3	Walsall		W 3-1		6,296
31	January	Sat	4	Football League, Division 3	SHREWSBURY TOWN	2-1 W		9,115	
32		Sat	11	Football League, Division 3	Wrexham		L 1-3		8,757
33		Sat	18	Football League, Division 3	QUEENS PARK RANGERS	3-1 W		11,550	
34		Sat	25	Football League, Division 3	Reading		L 0-2		9,763
35	February	Sat	1	Football League, Division 3	Bristol Rovers		W 2-1		10,698
36		Sat	8	Football League, Division 3	OLDHAM ATHLETIC	2-1 W		12,993	
37		Sat	15	Football League, Division 3	Peterborough United		W 1-0		9,225
38		Sat	22	Football League, Division 3	NOTTS COUNTY	2-0 W		11,370	
39		Sat	29	Football League, Division 3	Crewe Alexandra		W 1-0		4,866
40	March	Sat	7	Football League, Division 3	COVENTRY CITY	1-1 D		23,410	
41		Sat	21	Football League, Division 3	CREWE ALEXANDRA	4-1 W		10,279	
42		Fri	27	Football League, Division 3	COLCHESTER UNITED	3-1 W		18,393	
43		Sat	28	Football League, Division 3	Shrewsbury Town		L 0-3		5,173
44		Tue	31	Football League, Division 3	Colchester United		D 1-1		6,477
45	April	Sat	4	Football League, Division 3	BRISTOL CITY	2-2 D		9,907	
46		Mon	6	Football League, Division 3	Mansfield Town		D 1-1		11,779
47		Sat	11	Football League, Division 3	Port Vale		D 0-0		7,688
48		Sat	18	Football League, Division 3	READING	1-0 W		14,397	
49		Tue	21	Football League, Division 3	BRENTFORD	2-2 D		19,381	
50		Sat	25	Football League, Division 3	Luton Town		L 1-2		19,799

League ever-presents: G.A. Harris, P.A. Jennings
Most appearances in total: G.A. Harris & P.A. Jennings 50 out of 50   **Most goals in total:** C.E. Livesey 25
Hat-tricks: None   **Penalty goals:** G.A. Harris 2, C. Chung 1
Sent off: None
Full international appearance(s) this season: P.A. Jennings (Northern Ireland)

	Bell, R.M.	Burgess, E.R.C.	Catleugh, G.C.	Chung, C.	Crisp, R.J.	Fraser, J.W. //	Gregory, A.C. //	Harris, G.A.	Howfield, R.M. //	Jennings, P.A. //	Jones, B.R.	Larkin, B.P.	Livesey, C.E. //	McAnearney, J.	McCready, T. //	McNeice, V. //	Mancini, T.J.	Nicholas, K.W.	Oliver, K	Owen, B.E.	Spelman, R.E.	Ward, D. //	Welbourne, D.
Apps	40	1	23	26	26	10	8	46	7	46	24	10	45	25	1	11	19	26	44	4	32	13	19
Subs																							
Goals			1	1	1		2	16	2			1	23	8					19	1	2	2	
Apps	4		3	1	4			4	1	4		3	4		2	1	3	2	3		3	1	1
Subs																							
Goals													2						2				
1	X		X	X				X	X	G			X2			X		X	X1		X		
2	X		X	X				X1	X	G			X1			X		X	X		X	X1	
3	X		X	X				X	X	G			X			X		X	X		X		
4	X		X		X			X	X	G	X		X1			X		X			X		
5	X		X					X1		G	X		X2			X		X	X		X1	X	
6	X		X1p					X		G	X		X1			X		X	X		X		
7	X		X			X		X		G			X			X		X	X		X		
8	X		X					X		G	X		X				X	X	X		X		
9	X		X					X1		G	X		X				X	X	X1		X	X1	
10	X		X					X		G	X		X				X	X	X		X		
11	X				X	X1		X		G			X1				X	X	X		X		
12	X				X	X	X1	X		G			X				X	X	X		X		
13	X				X	X	X	X		G			X				X	X	X		X		
14	X		X		X	X1	X1	X	X	G							X	X	X		X		
15	X				X	X	X	X	X1	G			X1				X	X	X1				
16	X				X	X	X	X1	X1	G			X				X	X	X				
17	X				X	X	X	X		G			X				X	X	X				
18	X	X			X			X2		G	X		X				X	X	X		X		
19	X	X			X			X		G	X		X2				X	X	X1		X		
20	X	X			X			X		G	X1		X1				X	X	X1		X		
21	X	X			X			X2		G	X		X				X	X	X		X		
22	X	X			X			X		G	X		X				X	X	X1		X		
23	X	X			X			X		G	X		X1		X		X		X1		X		
24	X	X						X		G			X	X	X		X		X1		X		X
25	X	X						X		G	X		X	X			X		X1		X		X
26	X	X			X			X		G			X		X		X		X		X		X
27	X	X				X		X		G	X		X	X1			X		X1				X
28	X	X						X		G	X		X1	X1			X		X1		X		X
29	X	X						X		G	X		X2	X1			X		X2		X		X
30	X	X						X		G	X		X	X2		X			X1		X		X
31	X	X						X		G	X		X1	X1		X			X		X		X
32	X	X						X		G	X		X1	X		X			X		X		X
33	X	X						X1		G	X		X	X		X			X2		X		X
34	X	X						X		G	X		X	X		X			X		X		X
35	X		X	X	X			X		G	X		X2	X					X				X
36	X		X	X	X			X1		G	X		X1	X					X				X
37	X		X	X	X1	X		X		G			X	X				X	X				X
38	X		X	X	X			X		G	X		X	X1					X1				X
39	X		X	X	X			X		G	X		X	X					X1				X
40	X		X	X	X			X		G	X		X	X					X1				X
41	X		X	X				X		G	X		X2	X					X1		X1		X
42	X		X	X1				X1p		G	X		X	X					X1		X		X
43	X		X	X				X		G	X		X	X					X		X		X
44		X	X	X	X			X		G	X		X1	X					X		X		X
45	X		X	X	X			X1p		G	X		X1	X					X		X		X
46		X	X	X	X			X		G	X		X	X				X			X1	X	X
47			X	X	X			X		G	X		X	X				X			X	X	X
48		X	X					X1		G	X		X	X				X			X	X	X
49		X	X	X				X		G	X		X	X1				X			X1	X	X
50			X	X				X1		G	X		X	X				X			X	X	X

1964/65

Football League position: 9th out of 24 in Division 3
Manager: Bill McGarry (Matches 1-12), Ken Furphy (Matches 22-49)

New league opponents: Scunthorpe United

Home-and-away league doubles
For – 4 (Luton Town, Scunthorpe United, Southend United, Walsall)
Against – 1 (Gillingham)

Divisional changes at end of season: Carlisle United and Bristol City to Division 2; Luton Town, Port Vale, Colchester United and Barnsley to Division 4; Swindon Town and Swansea Town from Division 2; Brighton & Hove Albion, Millwall, York City and Oxford United from Division 4

All Matches: Won 17, Drew 17, Lost 15, Goals 75-71

Highest Score: 5 (Matches 34 & 46)

		HOME					AWAY					
	Pl	W	D	L	For	Ag	W	D	L	For	Ag	Pts
Carlisle United	46	14	5	4	46	24	11	5	7	30	29	60
Bristol City	46	14	6	3	53	18	10	5	8	39	37	59
Mansfield Town	46	17	4	2	61	23	7	7	9	34	38	59
Hull City	46	14	6	3	51	25	9	6	8	40	32	58
Brentford	46	18	4	1	55	18	6	5	12	28	37	57
Bristol Rovers	46	14	7	2	52	21	6	8	9	30	37	55
Gillingham	46	16	5	2	45	13	7	4	12	25	37	55
Peterborough United	46	16	3	4	61	33	6	4	13	24	41	51
WATFORD	46	13	8	2	45	21	4	8	11	26	43	50
Grimsby Town	46	11	10	2	37	21	5	7	11	31	46	49
Bournemouth & Boscombe Ath	46	12	4	7	40	24	6	7	10	32	39	47
Southend United	46	14	4	5	48	24	5	4	14	30	47	46
Reading	46	12	8	3	45	26	4	6	13	25	44	46
Queens Park Rangers	46	15	5	3	48	22	2	5	16	24	57	46
Workington	46	11	7	5	30	22	6	5	12	28	47	46
Shrewsbury Town	46	10	6	7	46	36	5	6	12	34	46	42
Exeter City	46	8	7	8	33	27	4	10	9	18	25	41
Scunthorpe United	46	9	8	6	42	27	5	4	14	23	45	40
Walsall	46	9	4	10	34	36	6	3	14	21	44	37
Oldham Athletic	46	10	3	10	40	39	3	7	13	21	44	36
Luton Town	46	6	8	9	32	36	5	3	15	19	58	33
Port Vale	46	7	6	10	27	33	2	8	13	14	43	32
Colchester United	46	7	6	10	30	34	4	2	16	20	55	30
Barnsley	46	8	5	10	33	31	1	6	16	21	59	29

No	DATE			COMPETITION	OPPONENTS	HOME	AWAY	ATTENDANCE
1	August	Sat	22	Football League, Division 3	HULL CITY	2-1 W		9,586
2		Tue	25	Football League, Division 3	Workington		L 0-2	7,245
3		Sat	29	Football League, Division 3	Gillingham		L 2-5	11,508
4	September	Sat	5	Football League, Division 3	BRISTOL CITY	2-2 D		9,418
5		Tue	8	Football League, Division 3	Carlisle United		D 1-1	8,817
6		Fri	11	Football League, Division 3	Queens Park Rangers		D 2-2	8,833
7		Thu	17	Football League, Division 3	CARLISLE UNITED	0-0 D		9,387
8		Sat	19	Football League, Division 3	SHREWSBURY TOWN	2-2 D		7,741
9		Tue	22	Football League Cup, 2nd Round	PORTSMOUTH	2-2 D		5,248
10		Sat	26	Football League, Division 3	Reading		L 2-6	8,584
11		Tue	29	Football League, Division 3	WALSALL	3-0 W		7,003
12	October	Sat	3	Football League, Division 3	SOUTHEND UNITED	2-1 W		8,402
13		Tue	6	Football League, Division 3	Walsall		W 4-0	4,463
14		Sat	10	Football League, Division 3	MANSFIELD TOWN	3-1 W		8,044
15		Mon	12	Football Lge Cup, 2nd Round replay	Portsmouth (after extra time)		L 1-2	8,404
16		Sat	17	Football League, Division 3	Grimsby Town		L 0-1	6,876
17		Tue	20	Football League, Division 3	Barnsley		L 0-4	4,756
18		Sat	24	Football League, Division 3	PETERBOROUGH UNITED	1-1 D		8,159
19		Mon	26	Football League, Division 3	Port Vale		D 2-2	5,271
20		Sat	31	Football League, Division 3	Bournemouth & Boscombe Athletic		D 0-0	9,579
21	November	Sat	7	Football League, Division 3	EXETER CITY	1-0 W		7,818
22		Sat	14	FA Cup, 1st Round	Reading		L 1-3	9,940
23		Sat	21	Football League, Division 3	BRISTOL ROVERS	1-1 D		9,130
24		Sat	28	Football League, Division 3	Brentford		L 1-5	12,950
25	December	Sat	12	Football League, Division 3	Hull City		D 1-1	6,165
26		Sat	19	Football League, Division 3	GILLINGHAM	1-2 L		6,412
27		Sat	26	Football League, Division 3	Luton Town		W 4-2	11,070
28		Mon	28	Football League, Division 3	LUTON TOWN	2-0 W		6,867
29	January	Sat	2	Football League, Division 3	Bristol City		D 1-1	10,758
30		Sat	16	Football League, Division 3	QUEENS PARK RANGERS	0-2 L		7,526
31		Sat	23	Football League, Division 3	Shrewsbury Town		D 2-2	6,778
32		Wed	27	Football League, Division 3	Oldham Athletic		L 0-2	5,730
33		Sat	30	Football League, Division 3	COLCHESTER UNITED	3-0 W		5,770
34	February	Sat	6	Football League, Division 3	READING	5-1 W		6,655
35		Sat	13	Football League, Division 3	Southend United		W 1-0	7,314
36		Sat	20	Football League, Division 3	Mansfield Town		L 0-3	6,180
37		Sat	27	Football League, Division 3	GRIMSBY TOWN	1-1 D		6,931
38	March	Sat	6	Football League, Division 3	Colchester United		D 0-0	3,385
39		Mon	8	Football League, Division 3	WORKINGTON	3-2 W		5,366
40		Sat	13	Football League, Division 3	BOURNEMOUTH & BOSCOMBE ATHLETIC	2-0 W		6,814
41		Tue	16	Football League, Division 3	BARNSLEY	1-1 D		6,078
42		Sat	20	Football League, Division 3	Exeter City		L 0-1	5,161
43		Sat	27	Football League, Division 3	OLDHAM ATHLETIC	3-2 W		5,329
44	April	Sat	3	Football League, Division 3	Bristol Rovers		L 0-1	6,894
45		Sat	10	Football League, Division 3	BRENTFORD	1-1 D		7,373
46		Fri	16	Football League, Division 3	SCUNTHORPE UNITED	5-0 W		7,140
47		Sat	17	Football League, Division 3	Peterborough United		L 1-2	7,924
48		Tue	20	Football League, Division 3	Scunthorpe United		W 2-0	3,420
49		Sat	24	Football League, Division 3	PORT VALE	1-0 W		7,627

League ever-presents: None
Most appearances in total: D. Welbourne 45 out of 49   **Most goals in total:** G.A. Harris 21
Hat-tricks: G.A. Harris (Match 27), J. McAnearney (Match 46)   **Penalty goals:** G.A. Harris 3
Sent off: None
Full international appearance(s) this season: None

	Anderson, T.C. //	Bell, R.M.	Bond, D.J.T.	Burgess, E.R.C. //	Carr, D.	Catleugh, G.C. //	Chung, C. //	Cowen, J.M.	Crisp, R.J. //	French, G.E.	Furphy, K.	George, F.R. //	George, R.S. //	Goy, P.J. //	Harris, G.A.	Houghton, W.G.	Jones, B.R.	Larkin, B.P.	McAnearney, J.	Mancini, T.J.	Nicholas, K.W. //	Oliver, K.	Owen, B.E.	Pate, A.M.	Saunders, R.	Spelman, R.E. //	Welbourne, D.	Williams, J.R.	Own goals
Apps	20	9	18	2	6	8	14	9	14	4	21	10	4	27	42	26	25	3	39	32	16	14	33	5	38	8	43	16	
Subs																													
Goals	2		1		1				2						19	1	1	1	10			7	4		17	1	1		3
Apps		2	1			1	2		1			1	3	2	1	3	1	2	2	1	2	2			2	1	2	1	
Subs																													
Goals															2				1						1				
1							X		X					G	X	X	X	X1	X1		X		X				X		
2							X		X					G	X		X	X	X		X	X	X				X		
3			X		X	X								G	X2#		X		X		X	X	X				X		
4		X			X	X				G					X		X		X		X		X		X2		X		
5		X			X	X	X			G					X		X		X		X	X1	X				X		
6		X			X	X			X	G					X		X		X			X1	X				X1		
7		X			X	X			X					G	X		X		X			X	X				X		
8		X				X			X	X				G	X		X		X			X1	X				X		1
9	X	X				X			X					G	X2p	X	X					X			X	X		X	
10		X							X		G				X	X	X		X		X				X1	X1			
11		X	X						X		G				X1				X		X				X2	X	X		
12		X	X						X1		G				X		X1		X		X	X			X2		X		
13		X				X			X		G				X1		X		X		X1	X			X2		X		
14		X				X			X		G				X		X		X2		X	X			X1		X		
15		X				X			X					G	X		X		X		X				X	X	X	X1	
16		X				X			X					G	X		X		X		X				X		X		
17			X			X			X					G	X		X		X		X				X		X		
18			X1						X					G	X		X		X		X				X	X	X		
19									X				X	G	X				X1		X	X1	X		X		X		
20									X				X	G	X				X		X	X	X		X		X		
21													X	G		X	X		X		X	X	X1		X		X		
22							X						X	G		X	X		X	X	X1	X	X				X		
23									X					G	X	X	X		X	X		X1			X	X	X		
24									X					G	X	X	X		X	X		X1			X	X	X		
25			X						X					G	X	X	X1		X	X					X	X	X		
26	X								X					G	X	X			X		X				X1	X	X	X	
27	X			X		X			X					G	X3	X			X1				X		X		X	X	
28	X			X		X			X					G	X	X			X				X		X	X1		X1	
29	X					X			X					G	X	X			X				X		X	X	X	X	
30	X					X			X					G	X	X			X				X		X	X	X	X	
31	X1					X			X		G				X1	X			X				X		X	X	X	X	
32	X					X			X					G	X	X			X				X		X	X	X	X	
33	X		X						X					G	X1	X1				X			X		X	X	X	X	1
34	X1		X						X					G	X1	X				X			X1		X2		X	X	
35	X		X						X					G	X1	X				X			X		X		X	X	
36			X		X				X					G	X	X				X			X		X		X	X	
37	X		X						X		G				X1	X				X			X		X		X	X	
38	X								X					G	X	X	X		X				X		X		X	X	
39	X								X					G	X1	X			X1	X			X		X	X1	X	X	
40	X		X					G	X						X1	X			X				X		X		X	X	1
41			X					G	X		X				X1	X			X	X			X		X		X	X	
42	X							G	X						X	X	X		X	X			X		X		X	X	
43	X		X		X			G							X	X			X			X1	X		X2		X	X	
44			X					G	X						X	X	X		X				X		X	X	X		
45			X					G	X						X1		X		X	X			X		X	X	X	X	
46	X		X					G	X						X1		X		X3	X			X1		X	X	X		
47	X		X			X1		G	X						X		X		X				X		X	X	X		
48	X					X			X1					G	X1	X	X		X	X			X		X		X		
49	X					X		G	X						X1	X	X		X	X			X		X		X		

1965/66

Football League position: 12th out of 24 in Division 3
Manager: Ken Furphy

New league opponents: Oxford United

Home-and-away league doubles
For – 3 (Exeter City, Oldham Athletic, Swindon Town)
Against – 4 (Brighton & Hove Albion, Swansea Town, Walsall, Workington)

Divisional changes at end of season: Hull City & Millwall to Division 2; Southend United, Exeter City, Brentford & York City to Division 4; Middlesbrough & Leyton Orient from Division 2; Doncaster Rovers, Darlington, Torquay United & Colchester United from Division 4

All Matches: Won 18, Drew 13, Lost 18, Goals 61-56

Highest Score: 5 (Match 17)

			HOME					AWAY				
	Pl	W	D	L	For	Ag	W	D	L	For	Ag	Pts
Hull City	46	19	2	2	64	24	12	5	6	45	38	69
Millwall	46	19	4	0	47	13	8	7	8	29	30	65
Queens Park Rangers	46	16	3	4	62	29	8	6	9	33	36	57
Scunthorpe United	46	9	8	6	44	34	12	3	8	36	33	53
Workington	46	13	6	4	38	18	6	8	9	29	39	52
Gillingham	46	14	4	5	33	19	8	4	11	29	35	52
Swindon Town	46	11	8	4	43	18	8	5	10	31	30	51
Reading	46	13	5	5	36	19	6	8	9	34	44	51
Walsall	46	13	7	3	48	21	7	3	13	29	43	50
Shrewsbury Town	46	13	7	3	48	22	6	4	13	25	42	49
Grimsby Town	46	15	6	2	47	25	2	7	14	21	37	47
WATFORD	46	12	4	7	33	19	5	9	9	22	32	47
Peterborough United	46	13	6	4	50	26	4	6	13	30	40	46
Oxford United	46	11	3	9	38	33	8	5	10	32	41	46
Brighton & Hove Albion	46	11	4	8	48	28	3	7	13	19	37	43
Bristol Rovers	46	11	10	2	38	15	3	4	16	26	49	42
Swansea Town	46	11	4	5	61	37	1	7	15	20	59	41
Bournemouth & Boscombe Ath	46	9	8	6	24	19	4	4	15	14	37	38
Mansfield Town	46	10	5	8	31	36	5	3	15	28	53	38
Oldham Athletic	46	8	7	8	34	33	4	6	13	21	48	37
Southend United	46	15	1	7	43	28	1	3	19	11	55	36
Exeter City	46	9	6	8	36	28	3	5	15	17	51	35
Brentford	46	9	4	10	34	30	1	8	14	14	39	32
York City	46	5	7	11	30	44	1	2	17	23	62	27

No	DATE			COMPETITION	OPPONENTS	HOME	AWAY	ATTENDANCE
1	August	Sat	21	Football League, Division 3	Reading		W 2-1	11,899
2		Tue	24	Football League, Division 3	HULL CITY	1-1 D		10,648
3		Sat	28	Football League, Division 3	EXETER CITY	3-0 W		10,580
4	September	Sat	4	Football League, Division 3	Peterborough United		D 2-2	10,431
5		Sat	11	Football League, Division 3	MILLWALL	0-1 L		12,039
6		Tue	14	Football League, Division 3	MANSFIELD TOWN	2-1 W		11,521
7		Sat	18	Football League, Division 3	Gillingham		D 2-2	7,884
8		Wed	22	Football League Cup, 2nd Round	Rotherham United		L 0-2	9,051
9		Sat	25	Football League, Division 3	OLDHAM ATHLETIC	4-0 W		8,880
10	October	Sat	2	Football League, Division 3	SWINDON TOWN	2-0 W		11,432
11		Mon	4	Football League, Division 3	Mansfield Town		D 2-2	8,479
12		Sat	9	Football League, Division 3	Grimsby Town		L 1-2	6,759
13		Sat	16	Football League, Division 3	BRENTFORD	1-1 D		12,339
14		Sat	23	Football League, Division 3	Bristol Rovers		D 1-1	8,826
15		Sat	30	Football League, Division 3	YORK CITY	3-2 W		8,641
16	November	Sat	6	Football League, Division 3	Oxford United		W 2-1	12,756
17		Sat	13	FA Cup, 1st Round	Corinthian-Casuals		W 5-1	7,309
18		Sat	20	Football League, Division 3	Walsall		L 0-3	7,264
19		Wed	24	Football League, Division 3	Hull City		L 1-3	15,511
20		Sat	27	Football League, Division 3	WORKINGTON	1-2 L		6,508
21	December	Sat	4	FA Cup, 2nd Round	Southend United		L 1-2	10,412
22		Sat	11	Football League, Division 3	SOUTHEND UNITED	4-1 W		5,923
23		Mon	27	Football League, Division 3	Brighton & Hove Albion		L 0-2	19,104
24	January	Sat	1	Football League, Division 3	GRIMSBY TOWN	1-1 D		7,022
25		Sat	8	Football League, Division 3	Swansea Town		L 2-4	7,359
26		Sat	15	Football League, Division 3	BRISTOL ROVERS	2-0 W		4,681
27		Fri	21	Football League, Division 3	York City		L 0-1	3,889
28		Sat	29	Football League, Division 3	READING	1-2 L		6,941
29	February	Sat	5	Football League, Division 3	Exeter City		W 2-1	4,773
30		Tue	15	Football League, Division 3	Queens Park Rangers		D 1-1	8,185
31		Sat	19	Football League, Division 3	PETERBOROUGH UNITED	1-0 W		6,409
32		Sat	26	Football League, Division 3	Millwall		D 0-0	16,424
33	March	Sat	5	Football League, Division 3	QUEENS PARK RANGERS	1-2 L		11,600
34		Sat	12	Football League, Division 3	GILLINGHAM	1-0 W		5,141
35		Fri	18	Football League, Division 3	Oldham Athletic		W 1-0	10,389
36		Tue	22	Football League, Division 3	BRIGHTON & HOVE ALBION	0-1 L		6,116
37		Sat	26	Football League, Division 3	Swindon Town		W 1-0	10,584
38	April	Sat	2	Football League, Division 3	OXFORD UNITED	1-1 D		6,029
39		Fri	8	Football League, Division 3	SHREWSBURY TOWN	1-0 W		7,290
40		Sat	9	Football League, Division 3	Bournemouth & Boscombe Athletic		L 0-2	7,316
41		Mon	11	Football League, Division 3	Shrewsbury Town		D 0-0	4,062
42		Sat	16	Football League, Division 3	WALSALL	0-1 L		4,715
43		Sat	23	Football League, Division 3	Workington		L 0-1	2,358
44		Tue	26	Football League, Division 3	SCUNTHORPE UNITED	2-1 W		4,072
45		Sat	30	Football League, Division 3	BOURNEMOUTH & BOSCOMBE ATHLETIC	1-0 W		4,517
46	May	Fri	6	Football League, Division 3	Southend United		L 0-1	5,572
47		Tue	10	Football League, Division 3	Brentford		D 1-1	5,550
48		Fri	13	Football League, Division 3	SWANSEA TOWN	0-1 L		3,952
49		Tue	17	Football League, Division 3	Scunthorpe United		D 1-1	3,738

	Anderson, T.C.	Bond, D.J.T.	Brace, S.C.	Carr, D.	Furphy, K.	Garvey, B.	Harris, G.A.	Holton, C.C.	Houghton, W.G.	Hugo, R.V.	Jones, B.R.	Lomas, C.I.	McAnearney, J.	Mancini, T.J.	Melling, T.	Owen, B.E.	Pate, A.M.	Saunders, R.	Scullion, S.M.A.	Slater, R.	Welbourne, D.	Williams, A.	Williams, J.R.	Own goals
Apps	1	44	16	4	19	35	37	24	22	24	38	6	19	7	1	33	8	1	19	46	46	41	15	
Subs					+2		+1			+1	+1	+1	+2	+1			+1					+1		
Goals		7	4	2			8	12	1	6			1			3		1	2		2	4		2
Apps		3	2		2	1	3	3	2	1	3			2		3				3	3	2		
Subs																								
Goals			2						1							2					1			
1		X		X2	X	X	X	X		X						X				G	X	X		
2	X	X1	X		X	X	X	X		X										G	X	X		
3		X					X1	X	X	X1	X								X1	G	X	X		
4		X1		X	X	X	X	R	S1	X						X				G	X	X		
5		X			X	X	X			X	X					X	X			G	X	X		
6		X1				X	X	X1		X	X					X	X			G	X	X		
7		X				X	X	X1		X1	X			S		X	R			G	X	X		
8		X		X	X	X	X			X	X			X		X				G	X			
9		X	X		X	X	X1	X2			X			X		X1				G	X			
10		X	X		X	X	X2				X			X		X				G	X	X		
11		X	X		X	X	X1				X			X		X				G	X	X		1
12		X	X			X	X1	X			X			X		X				G	X	X		
13		X	X1			X	X	X	X		X					X				G	X	X		
14		X	X1	S		X	X	X	X							X				G	X	R		
15		X	X	X			X1	X2	X		X					X				G	X	X		
16		X	X1			X	X				X					X1				G	X	X		
17		X	X2			X	X	X			X					X2				G	X1	X		
18		X	X			X	X	X			X					X				G	X	X		
19		X	X				X1	X	X	X	X			S		R				G	X	X		
20		X	X1			X	X				X			X		X	X			G	X	X		
21		X	X			X	X	X1			X					X				G	X	X		
22		X1		S		X	X1	X1	X1	X	X			R		X				G	X			
23		R	X			X	X	X	X	X						X				G	X		S	
24		X				X	X	X1	X	X	X					X	X			G	X		X	
25		X				X	X	X	X	X	X1	X				X1	X			G	X			
26		X				X	X1	X		X1	X					X				G	X	X	X	
27		X	X			X	X			X	X					X				G	X	X	X	
28		X1				X	X	X			X		X			X				G	X	X	X	
29		X		X	X						X		X			X			X1	G	X	X	X	1
30		X		R	X			X1				S	X			X			X	G	X	X	X	
31		X			X	S		R			X		X1			X			X	G	X	X	X	
32		X		X	X	X					X					X			X	G	X	X	X	
33		X		X	X	X					X					X			X	G	X	X1	X	
34		X		X	X				X	X			X			X			X	G	X	X1	X	
35		X1		X	X				X	X			X			X			X	G	X	X	X	
36		X		X	X	X					S		X			X			X	G	X	X	R	
37		X	X	X	X						X		X	X		X			X	G	X	X1		
38		X	X	X	X						X		X	X		X			X	G	X	X1		
39		X		X	X	X					X		X	X		X			X	G	X1	X		
40			X	X	X				X		R		X			X	S		X	G	X	X		
41		X		X	X	X			X	X						X			X	G	X	X		
42		X		X	X	X			X	X						X			X	G	X	X		
43		X			X			X			X					X	X		X	G	X	X		
44		X			X		X1	X	X		X					X1				G	X	X		
45		X1			X		X	X	X	X	X					X				G	X	X		
46		X			X		X	X	X	X	X					X				G	X	X	X	
47		X		X	X	X1		X			X					X				G	X	X		
48		X		X	X			X			X					X			X	G	X1	X		
49		X		X	X			R			S			X	X	X				G	X1	X	X	

1966/67

Football League position: 3rd out of 24 in Division 3
Manager: Ken Furphy

New league opponents: Middlesbrough

Home-and-away league doubles
For – 5 (Bristol Rovers, Grimsby Town, Swindon Town, Walsall, Workington)
Against – 2 (Mansfield Town, Scunthorpe United)

Divisional changes at end of season: Queens Park Rangers & Middlesbrough to Division 2; Swansea Town, Darlington, Doncaster Rovers & Workington to Division 4; Northampton Town & Bury from Division 2; Stockport County, Southport, Barrow & Tranmere Rovers from Division 4

All Matches: Won 22, Drew 16, Lost 14, Goals 68-53

Highest Score: 4 (Matches 28 & 33)

		HOME					AWAY					
	Pl	W	D	L	For	Ag	W	D	L	For	Ag	Pts
Queens Park Rangers	46	18	4	1	66	15	8	11	4	37	23	67
Middlesbrough	46	16	3	4	51	20	7	6	10	36	44	55
WATFORD	46	15	5	3	39	17	5	9	9	22	29	54
Reading	46	13	7	3	45	20	9	2	12	31	37	53
Bristol Rovers	46	13	8	2	47	28	7	5	11	29	39	53
Shrewsbury Town	46	15	5	3	48	24	5	7	11	29	38	52
Torquay United	46	17	3	3	57	20	4	6	13	16	34	51
Swindon Town	46	14	5	4	53	21	6	5	12	28	38	50
Mansfield Town	46	12	4	7	48	37	8	5	10	36	42	49
Oldham Athletic	46	15	4	4	51	16	4	6	13	29	47	48
Gillingham	46	11	9	3	36	18	4	7	12	22	44	46
Walsall	46	12	8	3	37	16	4	2	15	28	56	46
Colchester United	46	14	3	6	52	30	3	7	13	24	43	44
Leyton Orient	46	10	9	4	36	27	3	9	11	22	44	44
Peterborough United	46	12	4	7	40	31	2	11	10	26	40	43
Oxford United	46	10	8	5	41	29	5	5	13	20	37	43
Grimsby Town	46	13	5	5	46	23	4	4	15	15	45	43
Scunthorpe United	46	10	9	4	36	29	3	7	13	24	43	42
Brighton & Hove Albion	46	10	8	5	37	27	3	7	13	24	44	41
Bournemouth & Boscombe Ath	46	8	10	5	24	24	4	7	12	15	33	41
Swansea Town	46	9	9	5	50	30	3	6	14	35	59	39
Darlington	46	8	7	8	26	28	5	4	14	21	53	37
Doncaster Rovers	46	11	6	6	40	40	1	2	20	18	77	32
Workington	46	9	3	11	35	35	3	4	16	20	54	31

No	DATE			COMPETITION	OPPONENTS	HOME AWAY	ATTENDANCE
1	August	Sat	20	Football League, Division 3	Darlington	L 0-1	9,342
2		Tue	23	Football League Cup, 1st Round	READING	1-1 D	5,144
3		Sat	27	Football League, Division 3	QUEENS PARK RANGERS	1-0 W	9,860
4		Mon	29	Football Lge Cup, 1st Round replay	Reading	L 0-1	5,600
5	September	Sat	3	Football League, Division 3	Colchester United	L 1-2	4,232
6		Tue	6	Football League, Division 3	SHREWSBURY TOWN	1-0 W	5,474
7		Sat	10	Football League, Division 3	Swindon Town	W 2-1	9,999
8		Sat	17	Football League, Division 3	READING	1-0 W	6,615
9		Fri	23	Football League, Division 3	Doncaster Rovers	D 0-0	13,040
10		Mon	26	Football League, Division 3	Shrewsbury Town	D 1-1	4,774
11	October	Sat	1	Football League, Division 3	MANSFIELD TOWN	0-1 L	5,219
12		Sat	8	Football League, Division 3	MIDDLESBROUGH	2-0 W	6,677
13		Sat	15	Football League, Division 3	Swansea Town	D 2-2	5,843
14		Mon	17	Football League, Division 3	Peterborough United	D 2-2	7,402
15		Sat	22	Football League, Division 3	BOURNEMOUTH & BOSCOMBE ATHLETIC	3-0 W	7,718
16		Sat	29	Football League, Division 3	Leyton Orient	D 1-1	5,741
17	November	Sat	5	Football League, Division 3	GILLINGHAM	1-1 D	5,874
18		Sat	12	Football League, Division 3	Workington	W 2-1	1,947
19		Tue	15	Football League, Division 3	PETERBOROUGH UNITED	3-1 W	6,080
20		Sat	19	Football League, Division 3	SCUNTHORPE UNITED	0-1 L	7,084
21		Sat	26	FA Cup, 1st Round	SOUTHEND UNITED	1-0 W	8,797
22	December	Sat	3	Football League, Division 3	OXFORD UNITED	2-0 W	6,414
23		Sat	10	Football League, Division 3	Bristol Rovers	W 3-0	8,227
24		Wed	14	Football League, Division 3	Torquay United	L 0-1	4,277
25		Sat	17	Football League, Division 3	DARLINGTON	2-0 W	6,640
26		Mon	26	Football League, Division 3	TORQUAY UNITED	2-1 W	6,225
27		Sat	31	Football League, Division 3	Queens Park Rangers	L 1-4	17,703
28	January	Sat	7	FA Cup, 2nd Round	Enfield	W 4-2	7,623
29		Sat	14	Football League, Division 3	SWINDON TOWN	2-0 W	17,056
30		Sat	21	Football League, Division 3	Reading	D 1-1	8,827
31		Sat	28	FA Cup, 3rd Round	LIVERPOOL	0-0 D	33,553
32	February	Wed	1	FA Cup, 3rd Round replay	Liverpool	L 1-3	54,451
33		Sat	4	Football League, Division 3	DONCASTER ROVERS	4-1 W	11,747
34		Sat	11	Football League, Division 3	Mansfield Town	L 1-2	11,291
35		Sat	18	Football League, Division 3	WALSALL	2-1 W	11,344
36		Sat	25	Football League, Division 3	Middlesbrough	L 0-3	22,059
37	March	Fri	3	Football League, Division 3	SWANSEA TOWN	1-1 D	10,109
38		Sat	11	Football League, Division 3	Walsall	W 1-0	7,772
39		Sat	18	Football League, Division 3	Bournemouth & Boscombe Athletic	D 0-0	5,243
40		Fri	24	Football League, Division 3	BRIGHTON & HOVE ALBION	1-1 D	15,614
41		Sat	25	Football League, Division 3	LEYTON ORIENT	1-3 L	10,280
42		Mon	27	Football League, Division 3	Brighton & Hove Albion	L 0-1	13,640
43	April	Sat	1	Football League, Division 3	Gillingham	L 1-4	6,016
44		Sat	8	Football League, Division 3	WORKINGTON	2-1 W	5,190
45		Wed	12	Football League, Division 3	Grimsby Town	W 2-0	4,417
46		Fri	14	Football League, Division 3	Scunthorpe United	L 0-1	4,927
47		Sat	22	Football League, Division 3	OLDHAM ATHLETIC	2-2 D	8,132
48		Tue	25	Football League, Division 3	GRIMSBY TOWN	3-1 W	8,902
49		Sat	29	Football League, Division 3	Oxford United	D 0-0	10,126
50	May	Sat	6	Football League, Division 3	BRISTOL ROVERS	3-1 W	17,530
51		Tue	9	Football League, Division 3	COLCHESTER UNITED	0-0 D	20,072
52		Sat	13	Football League, Division 3	Oldham Athletic	D 1-1	5,803

League ever-presents: K. Eddy, D. Welbourne
Most appearances in total: K. Eddy & D. Welbourne 52 out of 52   **Most goals in total:** T.G. Garbett 18
Hat-tricks: None   **Penalty goals:** None   **Sent off:** None
Full international appearance(s) this season: None
(In Match 36, substitute M.J. Block replaced R. Slater when the latter was injured, but K. Eddy took over as the goalkeeper and conceded the last two goals)

	Block, M.J.	Bond, D.J.T.	Clarke, C.E.	Cowen, J.M.	Eddy, K.	Farrall, A.	Furie, J.P.	Furphy, K.	Garbett, T.G.	Garvey, B.	Jones, B.R.	Lawton, J.M.	Low, A.R.	McAnearney, J.	Melling, T.	Owen, B.E.	Pate, A.M.	Scullion, S.M.A.	Slater, R.	Smith, A.	Walley, J.T.	Welbourne, D.	Williams, A.	Williams, J.R.	Own goals
Apps	11	31	1	8	46	35	0	44	41	45	3	5	11	1	22	17	1	39	38	3	14	46	2	42	
Subs	+2		+1			+1						+1			+1			+1							
Goals	2	9			1	6		1	17				2		5	4		5			1	6		2	
Apps		6			6	6		4	5	6	2				6	1		6	6			6	2	4	
Subs																									
Goals		1				3			1						2										
1		X	X		X	X			X	X					X			X	G			X		X	
2		X1			X	X			X	X					X	X		X	G			X		X	
3		X			X	X			X	X				X	X			X1	G			X		X	
4		X			X	X			X	X	X				X			X	G			X		X	
5		X			X	X		X	X1	X					X			X	G			X		X	
6		X1			X	X		X	X	X					X			X	G			X		X	
7		X			X	X		X	X1	X					X1			X	G			X		X	
8		X			X	X		X	X1	X					X			X	G			X		X	
9		X	S		X	X			X	R					X			X	G	X		X		X	
10		X1			X	X		X	X	X	X				X			X	G			X			
11		X			X	X		X	X	X					X			X	G			X		X	
12	X	X			X	X1		X	X1	X					X			X	G			X		X	
13	X1	X1			X	X		X	X	X					S	R			G			X		X	
14		X			X	X		X	X1	X					X			X	G			X1		X	
15		X1			X	X		X	X	X					X	X2			G			X		X	
16		X			X	X		X	X1	X					X			X	G			X		X	
17		X			X	X		X	X	X					X1			X	G			X		X	
18		X1			X	X		X	X	X					X1			X	G			X		X	
19		X			X	X		X	X1	X					X			X1	G			X1		X	
20		X			X	X		X	X	X					X			X	G			X		X	
21		X			X	X1		X	X	X					X			X	G			X		X	
22	X1	X			X	X		X	X1	X						X			G			X		X	
23	X	X1			X	X2		X	X	X						X			G			X		X	
24	X	X			X	X		X	X	X						X			G			X		X	
25	X	X1			X	X		X	X1	X						X		X	G			X			
26	R	X			X			X	X	X					X1	X1		S	G			X1		X	
27		X			X			X	X	X					X			X	G			X1		X	
28		X			X	X2		X	X1	X					X1			X	G			X		X	
29		X1			X	X		X	X1	X					X			X	G			X		X	
30	S	X			X	X		X	X	X					X1			X	G			X		R	
31		X			X	X		X	X	X					X			X	G			X		X	
32		X			X	X		X	X	X					X1			X	G			X		X	
33		X1			X	X		X	X2	X					X			X1	G			X		X	
34		X			X	X		X	X	X					X			X	G			X1		X	
35	X	X			X	X		X	X1				X					X	G			X		X	1
36	S	X			X	X		X	X	X			X					X	GR			X		X	
37		X		G	X	X1		X	X	X			X					X				X		X	
38	X			G	X			X	X1	X			X			X		X				X		X	
39				G	X			X	X	X	X		X					X		X		X		X	
40				G	X			X	X	X	X		X					X		X		X1		X	
41				G	X		S	X	X1	X			R			X		X				X		X	
42	X			G	X	X		X	X	X								X			X	X	X	X	
43				G	X	X		X	X		X							X		X	X1		X	X	
44				G	X			X	X	X					X1			X			X	X		X	1
45					X	X1		X	X	X					X1			X	G		X	X		X	
46					X	R		X	X	X					S			X	G		X	X		X	
47	X				X			X1	X1	X			X					X	G		X	X		X	
48					X1			X	X	X			X					X	G		X	X1		X	
49					X			X	X	X			X					X	G		X	X		X	
50					X			X	X1	X			X		X1			X	G		X	X		X	
51					X			X	X	X			X		X			X	G		X	X		X	
52					X	X1		X	X	X					X	X			G		X	X		X	

1967/68

Football League position: 6th out of 24 in Division 3
Manager: Ken Furphy

		HOME					AWAY					
	PJ	W	D	L	For	Ag	W	D	L	For	Ag	Pts
Oxford United	46	18	3	2	49	20	4	10	9	20	27	57
Bury	46	19	3	1	64	24	5	5	13	27	42	56
Shrewsbury Town	46	14	6	3	42	17	6	9	8	19	32	55
Torquay United	46	14	6	3	42	17	6	5	12	20	39	53
Reading	46	15	5	3	43	17	6	4	13	27	43	51
WATFORD	46	15	3	5	59	20	6	5	12	15	30	50
Walsall	46	12	7	4	47	22	7	5	11	27	39	50
Barrow	46	14	6	3	43	13	7	2	14	22	41	50
Peterborough United	46	14	4	5	46	23	6	6	11	33	44	50
Swindon Town	46	13	8	2	51	16	3	9	11	23	35	49
Brighton & Hove Albion	46	11	8	4	31	14	5	8	10	26	41	48
Gillingham	46	13	6	4	35	19	5	6	12	24	44	48
Bournemouth & Boscombe Ath	46	13	7	3	39	17	3	8	12	17	34	47
Stockport County	46	16	5	2	49	22	3	4	16	21	53	47
Southport	46	13	6	4	35	22	4	6	13	30	43	46
Bristol Rovers	46	14	3	6	42	25	3	6	14	30	53	43
Oldham Athletic	46	11	3	9	37	32	7	4	12	23	33	43
Northampton Town	46	11	8	4	37	22	3	6	14	21	41	42
Orient	46	10	6	7	27	24	2	11	10	19	38	41
Tranmere Rovers	46	10	6	7	39	28	4	5	14	23	46	39
Mansfield Town	46	7	6	10	39	38	5	7	11	12	38	37
Grimsby Town	46	10	7	6	33	21	4	2	17	19	48	37
Colchester United	46	6	8	9	29	40	3	7	13	21	47	33
Scunthorpe United	46	8	9	6	36	33	2	3	18	20	53	32

New league opponents: None

Home-and-away league doubles
For – 3 (Bristol Rovers, Grimsby Town, Tranmere Rovers)
Against – 2 (Oldham Athletic, Southport)

Divisional changes at end of season: Oxford United & Bury to Division 2; Peterborough United (relegated for financial irregularities), Grimsby Town, Colchester United & Scunthorpe United to Division 4; Rotherham United & Plymouth Argyle from Division 2; Luton Town, Barnsley, Hartlepools United & Crewe Alexandra from Division 4

All Matches: Won 24, Drew 10, Lost 19, Goals 81-55

Highest Score: 7 (Match 25)

No	DATE			COMPETITION	OPPONENTS	HOME AWAY		ATTENDANCE
1	August	Sat	19	Football League, Division 3	WALSALL	1-2 L		8,861
2		Tue	22	Football League Cup 1st Round	Bournemouth & Boscombe Athletic		D 1-1	6,573
3		Sat	26	Football League, Division 3	Southport		L 0-2	5,151
4		Tue	29	Football Lge Cup, 1st Round replay	BOURNEMOUTH & BOSCOMBE ATH (after extra time)	0-0 D		6,502
5	September	Sat	2	Football League, Division 3	SCUNTHORPE UNITED	4-0 W		6,670
6		Mon	4	Football League, Division 3	Peterborough United		L 1-5	9,460
7		Wed	6	Football Lge Cup, 1st Round, 2nd replay	Bournemouth & Boscombe Athletic (at Swindon Town)	(W 2-1)		2,720
8		Sat	9	Football League, Division 3	Oldham Athletic		L 0-2	5,678
9		Wed	13	Football League Cup, 2nd Round	Stoke City		L 0-2	10,126
10		Sat	16	Football League, Division 3	BRISTOL ROVERS	4-0 W		7,500
11		Sat	23	Football League, Division 3	Barrow		D 0-0	7,442
12		Tue	26	Football League, Division 3	PETERBOROUGH UNITED	4-1 W		9,930
13		Sat	30	Football League, Division 3	OXFORD UNITED	2-0 W		11,091
14	October	Mon	2	Football League, Division 3	Colchester United		L 1-2	6,420
15		Sat	7	Football League, Division 3	ORIENT	1-1 D		9,900
16		Fri	13	Football League, Division 3	Tranmere Rovers		W 2-1	9.795
17		Sat	21	Football League, Division 3	STOCKPORT COUNTY	5-0 W		8,486
18		Tue	24	Football League, Division 3	COLCHESTER UNITED	1-1 D		10,669
19		Sat	28	Football League, Division 3	Brighton & Hove Albion		L 0-1	12,806
20	November	Sat	4	Football League, Division 3	SHREWSBURY TOWN	2-0 W		6,939
21		Sat	11	Football League, Division 3	Swindon Town		L 0-2	13,147
22		Tue	14	Football League, Division 3	Scunthorpe United		D 1-1	3,270
23		Sat	18	Football League, Division 3	READING	3-0 W		10,800
24		Sat	25	Football League, Division 3	Torquay United		L 0-1	7,444
25	December	Sat	2	Football League, Division 3	GRIMSBY TOWN	7-1 W		9,074
26		Sat	9	FA Cup, 1st Round	Lowestoft Town		W 1-0	5,454
27		Sat	16	Football League, Division 3	Walsall		D 1-1	9,409
28		Sat	23	Football League, Division 3	SOUTHPORT	0-1 L		11,012
29		Tue	26	Football League, Division 3	Bournemouth & Boscombe Athletic		W 1-0	7,125
30		Sat	30	Football League, Division 3	BOURNEMOUTH & BOSCOMBE ATHLETIC	0-2 L		9,643
31	January	Sat	6	FA Cup, 2nd Round	HEREFORD UNITED	3-0 W		14,759
32		Tue	16	Football League, Division 3	OLDHAM ATHLETIC	1-2 L		12,531
33		Sat	20	Football League, Division 3	Bristol Rovers		W 2-0	7,702
34		Sat	27	FA Cup, 3rd Round	SHEFFIELD UNITED	0-1 L		23,461
35	February	Sat	3	Football League, Division 3	BARROW	3-2 W		8,238
36		Sat	10	Football League, Division 3	Oxford United		L 0-1	7,470
37		Sat	17	Football League, Division 3	BURY	1-1 D		9,017
38		Sat	24	Football League, Division 3	Orient		W 1-0	5,425
39	March	Fri	1	Football League, Division 3	TRANMERE ROVERS	3-2 W		7,850
40		Sat	9	Football League, Division 3	Mansfield Town		W 2-1	6,629
41		Fri	15	Football League, Division 3	Stockport County		L 0-2	6,687
42		Tue	19	Football League, Division 3	MANSFIELD TOWN	1-2 L		7,324
43		Sat	23	Football League, Division 3	BRIGHTON & HOVE ALBION	4-0 W		6,384
44		Sat	30	Football League, Division 3	Shrewsbury Town		L 1-3	6,435
45	April	Sat	6	Football League, Division 3	SWINDON TOWN	2-0 W		7,569
46		Fri	12	Football League, Division 3	NORTHAMPTON TOWN	5-1 W		9,917
47		Sat	13	Football League, Division 3	Reading		L 0-2	7,943
48		Tue	16	Football League, Division 3	Northampton Town		D 1-1	6,732
49		Sat	20	Football League, Division 3	TORQUAY UNITED	2-1 W		9,632
50		Wed	24	Football League, Division 3	Gillingham		D 0-0	4,890
51		Sat	27	Football League, Division 3	Grimsby Town		W 1-0	2,832
52	May	Sat	4	Football League, Division 3	GILLINGHAM	3-0 W		7,973
53		Sat	11	Football League, Division 3	Bury		L 0-2	12,749

League ever-presents: B. Garvey, S.M.A. Scullion, R. Slater, D. Welbourne, J.R. Williams
Most appearances in total: B. Garvey, S.M.A. Scullion, R. Slater & J.R. Williams 53 out of 53   **Most goals in total:** J.B. Dyson 15
Hat-tricks: A.W. Currie (Match 12 & Match 25), T.G. Garbett (Match 23), J.B. Dyson (4 goals, Match 46)   **Penalty goals:** K. Eddy 3
Sent off: J. Hamilton (Match 24)
Full international appearance(s) this season: None

	Currie, A.W.	Dyson, J.B.	Eddy, K.	Farrall, A.	Furphy, K.	Garbett, T.G.	Garvey, B.	Hale, R.	Hamilton, J.	Irvin, D.V.	Lawton, J.M.	Lewis, B.	Low, A.R.	Owen, B.E.	Rivers, A.D.	Scullion, S.M.A.	Slater, R.	Walley, J.T.	Welbourne, D.	Williams, J.R.	Own goal
Apps	17	20	37	12	11	43	46	41	7	0	5	14	8	18	0	46	46	43	46	46	
Subs	+1			+1	+4					+1	+2	+2	+1		+2	+2			+1		
Goals	9	15	2	2		14	2	6	2	1	1	4	1	1		9		1	3		1
Apps	2		6	2	4	7	7	7	3			2	2		2	7	7	6	6	7	
Subs	+1										+1				+1						
Goals			1					2				2				1		1			
1			X	S		X	X	X1	X					R		X	G	X	X	X	
2			X	R		X	X	X	X					S		X1	G	X	X	X	
3			X	X		X	X	X	R			S				X	G	X	X	X	
4			X	R		X	X	X	X			S				X	G	X	X	X	
5			X		X	X	X1	X2			X					X1	G		X	X	
6			X		X	X	X	X	X		X					X	G		X1	X	
7			X		X	X	X	X	X		X2					X	G		X	X	
8			X		X	X	X	X	R		X					X	G	S	X	X	
9	S		X	R		X	X	X				X				X	G	X	X	X	
10	X2		X			X1	X	X				X				X1	G	X	X	X	
11	X		X			X	X	X				X				X	G	X	X	X	
12	X3		X			X	X	X				X				X	G	X1	X	X	
13	X1		X			X	X	X				X				X1	G	X	X	X	
14	X		X			X1	X	X	S			R				X	G	X	X	X	
15	X		X			X	X	X1					X			X	G	X	X	X	
16			R			X1	X	X			X			X	S	X1	G	X	X	X	
17	X			X1		X1	X	X			S1			R		X2	G	X	X	X	
18	X			X		X	X1	X			X					X	G	X	X	X	
19	R			X		X	X	X						X	S	X	G	X	X	X	
20	X			X1		X	X	X				X				X	G	X	X	X	
21	R			X		X	X	X			S					X	G	X	X	X	
22	X			X		X	X	X				X				X1	G	X	X	X	
23	X			X		X3	X	X				X				X	G	X	X	X	
24	R			X	S	X	X	X	X							X	G	X	X	X	
25	X3			X		X2	X	X2				X				X	G	X	X	X	
26	X			X		X	X	X				X				X1	G	X	X	X	
27		X				X1	X	X				X	X			X	G	X	X	X	
28	X		X			X	X	X				X				X	G	X	X	X	
29			X	X	S	X	X1	X						R		X	G	X	X	X	
30	S		X	R		X	X	X	X							X	G	X	X	X	
31	X	X1p		X	X	X	X2					X				X	G	X	X	X	
32	X	X		X1	X	X						X				X	G	X	X	X	
33		X2	X			X	X	X				X				X	G	X	X	X	
34		X				X	X	X			X	X				X	G	X	X	X	
35	X1	X				X	X	X	S		R2					X	G	X	X	X	
36	X	X				X	X	X				X				X	G	X	X	X	
37	X	X		X		X	X					X				X	G	X	X	X	1
38	X	X		X		X	X	R			S1					X	G	X	X	X	
39	X1	X1p		X	X1	X						X				X	G	X	X	X	
40	X1	X		X	X1	X						X				X	G	X	X	X	
41	X	X		X	X	X						X				X	G	X	X	X	
42	X1	X		X	X	X							R		S	X	G	X	X	X	
43	X2	X		X	X	X						X				X	G	X	X2	X	
44	X	X			X	X	X	R	S1							X	G	X	X	X	
45	X1	X1p				X	X	X				X				X	G	X	X	X	
46		X4	X			X	X	X				X				X1	G	X	X	X	
47	X	X		S		X	X						R			X	G	X	X	X	
48	X	X				X	X	X1				X				X	G	X	X	X	
49	X1	X				X	X	X				X1				X	G	X	X	X	
50	X	X					X	X			X	X				X	G	X	X	X	
51	X	X					X	X			X1	X				X	G	X	X	X	
52	X1	X			X1	X	X					X				X1	G	X	X	X	
53	R	X			S	X	X					X				X	G	X	X	X	

1968/69

Football League position: 1st out of 24 in Division 3 – promoted to Division 2
Manager: Ken Furphy

				HOME					AWAY				
	Pl	W	D	L	For	Ag	W	D	L	For	Ag	Pts
WATFORD	46	16	5	2	35	7	11	5	7	39	27	64
Swindon Town	46	18	4	1	38	7	9	6	8	33	28	64
Luton Town	46	20	3	0	57	14	5	8	10	17	24	61
Bournemouth & Boscombe Ath	46	16	2	5	41	17	5	7	11	19	28	51
Plymouth Argyle	46	10	8	5	34	25	7	7	9	19	24	49
Torquay United	46	13	4	6	35	18	5	8	10	19	28	48
Tranmere Rovers	46	12	3	8	36	31	7	7	9	34	37	48
Southport	46	14	8	1	52	20	3	5	15	19	44	47
Stockport County	46	14	5	4	49	25	2	9	12	18	43	46
Barnsley	46	13	6	4	37	21	3	8	12	21	42	46
Rotherham United	46	12	6	5	40	21	4	7	12	16	29	45
Brighton & Hove Albion	46	12	7	4	49	21	4	6	13	23	44	45
Walsall	46	10	9	4	34	18	4	7	12	16	31	44
Reading	46	13	3	7	41	25	2	10	11	26	41	43
Mansfield Town	46	14	5	4	37	18	2	6	15	21	44	43
Bristol Rovers	46	12	6	5	41	27	4	5	14	22	44	43
Shrewsbury Town	46	11	8	4	28	17	5	5	13	23	50	43
Orient	46	10	8	5	31	19	4	6	13	20	39	42
Barrow	46	11	6	6	30	23	6	2	15	26	52	42
Gillingham	46	10	10	3	35	20	3	5	15	19	43	41
Northampton Town	46	9	8	6	37	30	5	4	14	17	31	40
Hartlepool	46	6	12	5	25	29	4	7	12	15	41	39
Crewe Alexandra	46	11	4	8	40	31	2	5	16	12	45	35
Oldham Athletic	46	9	6	8	33	27	4	3	16	17	56	35

New league opponents: Rotherham United

Home-and-away league doubles
For – 10 (Barrow, Bournemouth & Boscombe Athletic, Brighton & Hove Albion, Crewe Alexandra, Gillingham, Oldham Athletic, Plymouth Argyle, Reading, Rotherham United, Tranmere Rovers)
Against – 2 (Barnsley, Stockport County)

Promoted with Watford: Swindon Town

All Matches: Won 30, Drew 11, Lost 11, Goals 82-40

Highest Score: 5 (Matches 28 & 33)

No	DATE			COMPETITION	OPPONENTS	HOME	AWAY	ATTENDANCE
1	August	Sat	10	Football League, Division 3	Bristol Rovers	D 1-1		8,077
2		Wed	14	Football League Cup, 1st Round	Luton Town		L 0-3	20,167
3		Sat	17	Football League, Division 3	SHREWSBURY TOWN	2-0 W		9,574
4		Tue	27	Football League, Division 3	WALSALL	0-0 D		9,403
5		Sat	31	Football League, Division 3	STOCKPORT COUNTY	0-1 L		8,517
6	September	Sat	7	Football League, Division 3	SWINDON TOWN	0-0 D		8,709
7		Tue	10	Football League, Division 3	Northampton Town		L 0-2	6,824
8		Fri	13	Football League, Division 3	Reading		W 1-0	11,926
9		Mon	16	Football League, Division 3	Hartlepool		L 1-2	5,140
10		Sat	21	Football League, Division 3	BOURNEMOUTH & BOSCOMBE ATHLETIC	1-0 W		7,688
11		Sat	28	Football League, Division 3	Crewe Alexandra		W 3-2	5,740
12	October	Sat	5	Football League, Division 3	LUTON TOWN	1-0 W		22,133
13		Tue	8	Football League, Division 3	Walsall		D 0-0	6,074
14		Sat	12	Football League, Division 3	Oldham Athletic		W 3-0	4,019
15		Sat	19	Football League, Division 3	BARROW	4-0 W		10,639
16		Sat	26	Football League, Division 3	Brighton & Hove Albion		W 1-0	8,335
17	November	Sat	2	Football League, Division 3	GILLINGHAM	2-1 W		11,625
18		Mon	4	Football League, Division 3	BARNSLEY	1-2 L		10,612
19		Sat	9	Football League, Division 3	Orient		D 1-1	6,525
20		Sat	16	FA Cup, 1st Round	Cheltenham Town		W 4-0	5,800
21		Sat	23	Football League, Division 3	Rotherham United		W 2-0	9,013
22		Sat	30	Football League, Division 3	TORQUAY UNITED	0-0 D		11,172
23	December	Sat	7	FA Cup, 2nd Round	BRENTFORD	1-0 W		12,871
24		Sat	14	Football League, Division 3	OLDHAM ATHLETIC	2-0 W		6,950
25		Sat	21	Football League, Division 3	Barrow		W 4-1	4,553
26		Sat	28	Football League, Division 3	BRIGHTON & HOVE ALBION	1-0 W		12,536
27	January	Sat	4	FA Cup, 3rd Round	PORT VALE	2-0 W		14,076
28		Sat	11	Football League, Division 3	Gillingham		W 5-0	6,641
29		Sat	18	Football League, Division 3	ORIENT	0-0 D		13,328
30		Sat	25	FA Cup, 4th Round	Manchester United		D 1-1	63,498
31		Fri	31	Football League, Division 3	Tranmere Rovers		W 3-0	6,802
32	February	Mon	3	FA Cup, 4th Round replay	MANCHESTER UNITED	0-2 L		34,099
33		Sat	8	Football League, Division 3	ROTHERHAM UNITED	5-1 W		10,681
34		Sat	15	Football League, Division 3	Torquay United		L 1-2	7,043
35		Sat	22	Football League, Division 3	MANSFIELD TOWN	2-1 W		13,347
36	March	Sat	1	Football League, Division 3	BRISTOL ROVERS	1-0 W		13,454
37		Mon	3	Football League, Division 3	Southport		D 1-1	4,075
38		Sat	8	Football League, Division 3	Shrewsbury Town		D 1-1	6,507
39		Tue	11	Football League, Division 3	TRANMERE ROVERS	3-1 W		13,335
40		Fri	14	Football League, Division 3	NORTHAMPTON TOWN	3-0 W		16,549
41		Fri	21	Football League, Division 3	Stockport County		L 2-4	7,029
42		Sat	29	Football League, Division 3	Swindon Town		W 1-0	28,898
43	April	Tue	1	Football League, Division 3	SOUTHPORT	1-0 W		18,685
44		Sat	5	Football League, Division 3	CREWE ALEXANDRA	4-0 W		19,112
45		Mon	7	Football League, Division 3	HARTLEPOOL	0-0 D		20,771
46		Tue	8	Football League, Division 3	Plymouth Argyle		W 2-1	16,203
47		Sat	12	Football League, Division 3	Bournemouth & Boscombe Athletic		W 3-1	10,574
48		Tue	15	Football League, Division 3	PLYMOUTH ARGYLE	1-0 W		22,515
49		Sat	19	Football League, Division 3	READING	1-0 W		20,923
50		Tue	22	Football League, Division 3	Barnsley		L 2-3	6,555
51		Wed	30	Football League, Division 3	Luton Town		L 1-2	25,234
52	May	Mon	5	Football League, Division 3	Mansfield Town		L 0-3	8,754

The following match was abandoned after 62 minutes, owing to snow:

	February	Wed	19	Football League, Division 3	Luton Town		1-1	21,143

	Dyson, J.B. //	Eddy, K.	Endean, B.	Garbett, T.G.	Garvey, B.	Green, H.R.	Hale, R.	Lees, W.J.	Lewis, B.	Low, A.R. //	Owen, B.E.	Packer, M.D.	Scullion, S.M.A.	Sinclair, R.	Slater, R.	Walker, M.S.G.	Walley, J.T.	Welbourne, D.	Williams, J.R.	Own goals
Apps	18	46	28	39	33	12	39	14	10	6	30	1	42	6	4	42	46	46	44	
Subs			+2	+1		+7	+1	+3	+6	+1	+1		+1	+2						
Goals	4	8	18	10		5	1	3	3	1	4		6	2			4	2	3	
Apps	2	6	5	6	4	1	6		1		5		6		1	5	6	6	6	
Subs				+1							+1									
Goals		1	2	2		1					2									

Match	Dyson	Eddy	Endean	Garbett	Garvey	Green	Hale	Lees	Lewis	Low	Owen	Packer	Scullion	Sinclair	Slater	Walker	Walley	Welbourne	Williams	Own goals
1	X	X			X		X	R	X1		S		X		G		X	X	X	
2	X	X		X	X		X		R		S		X		G		X	X	X	
3	X1	X1p		X	X	X			X				X		G		X	X	X	
4	X	X		X	X	S		X					X		G		X	X	R	
5	X	X		X	X	R					S		X	X	G		X	X		
6	X	X		X	X	S			X		R		X			G	X	X	X	
7	X	X		X	X	X			X		R		S			G	X	X	X	
8	X	X		X1	X				X	X	X		X			G	X	X	X	
9	R	X	S	X	X				X	X			X			G	X	X	X	1
10	X1	X		X	X	X			X				X			G	X	X	X	
11	X	X1p		X	X	X			X				X2			G	X	X	X	
12	X	X		X	X	X		X1					X			G	X	X	X	
13	X	X		X	X	X					X		X			G	X	X	X	
14	X1	X	R2	X		X			S	X	X		X			G	X	X	X	
15	X1	X		X1	X	X					X1		X			G	X1	X	X	
16	X	X	S	X1	X	X					R		X			G	X	X	X	
17	X	X2		X	X	X					X		X			G	X	X	X	
18	R	X		X	X	X			S		X1		X			G	X	X	X	
19		X1	X	X	S	X					R		X			G	X	X	X	
20	X1p	X1	X1	X		X1					X		X			G	X	X	X	
21		X	X	X		X		S			R		X1			G	X	X	X	1
22		X	X	X		X					X		X			G	X	X	X	
23	X	X	X	X1		X					X		X			G	X	X	X	
24	X	X	X2	X		X					X		X			G	X	X	X	
25		X1	X2	X1	X	X					X		X			G	X	X	X	
26		X	X	X	S1	X					R		X			G	X	X	X	
27		X	X1	X	X	X					X		X1			G	X	X	X	
28		X	X3	X	X	S1					X1		X			G	X	X	X	
29		X	X	X	X	S	R				X		X			G	X	X	X	
30		X	R	X	X	S					X		X1			G	X	X	X	
31		X	X	X2	X	X					X		X			G	X1	X	X	
32		X	X	X		X	X				X		X			G	X	X	X	
33		X	R1		X	X	X1	S2			X		X			G	X1	X	X	
34		X	X1		X	R	X	S			X		X			G	X	X	X	
35		X	X1		X1	X	X	X	S		R		X			G	X	X	X	
36		X	X		X1	X	X				X		X			G	X	X	X	
37		X	X1	X	X	X					X		X			G	X	X	X	
38		X	X1	X	X	X	X	X			X					G	X	X		
39		X	X1	X	X	X		X1			X		X			G	X1	X	X	
40	X2p	X	X1	X		X					X		X			G	X	X	X	
41		X	X	R		X		X1					X	S		G	X	X1	X	
42		X	X1	X		X	X	X					X			G	X	X	X	
43		X	X		S	X	X	R					X			G	X	X1	X	
44		X	X2	X	X1	X	X						X1			G	X	X	X	
45		X	X		X	R	X	X	S				X			G	X	X	X	
46		X		X	X	X	X	S1			R			X1		G	X	X	X	
47		X1	X1		S	X	X	X			R		X			G	X	X	X	1
48		X	X		X	X					X		X	X1		G	X	X	X	
49		X	R		X	X	X	S					X1	X		G	X	X	X	
50		X	X1		X	X	X	X1					X	X		G	X	X	X	
51		X	X	S		X	X				R		X1	X		G	X	X	X	
52		X	X	X	X	X		X					R	S		G	X	X	X	
		X	X1			X	X	X			X		X			G	X	X	X	

1969/70

Football League position: 19th out of 22 in Division 2
Manager: Ken Furphy

New league opponents: Aston Villa, Birmingham City, Backburn Rovers, Blackpool, Bolton Wanderers, Huddersfield Town, Leicester City, Preston North End, Sheffield United

Home-and-away league doubles
For – 1 (Aston Villa)
Against – 4 (Blackburn Rovers, Carlisle United, Middlesbrough, Queens Park Rangers)

Divisional changes at end of season: Huddersfield Town & Blackpool to Division 1; Aston Villa & Preston North End to Division 3; Sunderland & Sheffield Wednesday from Division 1; Orient & Luton Town from Division 3

All Matches: Won 14, Drew 13, Lost 23, Goals 54-69

Highest Score: 4 (Match 17)

		HOME					AWAY					
	Pl	W	D	L	For	Ag	W	D	L	For	Ag	Pts
Huddersfield Town	42	14	6	1	36	10	10	6	5	32	27	60
Blackpool	42	10	9	2	25	16	10	4	7	31	29	53
Leicester City	42	12	6	3	37	22	7	7	7	27	28	51
Middlesbrough	42	15	4	2	36	14	5	6	10	19	31	50
Swindon Town	42	13	7	1	35	17	4	9	8	22	30	50
Sheffield United	42	16	2	3	50	16	3	12	23	28	49
Cardiff City	42	12	7	2	38	14	6	6	9	23	27	49
Blackburn Rovers	42	15	2	4	42	19	5	5	11	12	31	47
Queens Park Rangers	42	13	5	3	47	24	4	6	11	19	33	45
Millwall	42	14	4	3	38	18	1	10	10	18	38	44
Norwich City	42	13	5	3	37	14	3	6	12	12	32	43
Carlisle United	42	10	6	5	39	28	4	7	10	19	28	41
Hull City	42	11	6	4	43	28	4	5	12	29	42	41
Bristol City	42	11	7	3	37	13	2	6	13	17	37	39
Oxford United	42	9	9	3	23	13	3	6	12	12	29	39
Bolton Wanderers	42	9	6	6	31	23	3	6	12	23	38	36
Portsmouth	42	11	3	7	39	35	5	5	11	27	45	35
Birmingham City	42	9	7	5	33	22	2	4	15	18	56	33
WATFORD	42	6	8	7	26	21	3	5	13	18	36	31
Charlton Athletic	42	7	8	6	23	28	0	9	12	12	48	31
Aston Villa	42	7	8	6	23	21	1	5	15	13	41	29
Preston North End	42	7	6	8	31	28	1	6	14	12	35	28

No	DATE			COMPETITION	OPPONENTS	HOME	AWAY	ATTENDANCE
1	August	Sat	9	Football League, Division 2	Bristol City		L 0-1	19,346
2		Wed	13	Football League Cup, 1st Round	LINCOLN CITY	2-1 W		10,086
3		Sat	16	Football League, Division 2	BOLTON WANDERERS	0-0 D		15,975
4		Wed	20	Football League, Division 2	QUEENS PARK RANGERS	0-1 L		27,968
5		Sat	23	Football League, Division 2	Charlton Athletic		D 0-0	15,971
6		Mon	25	Football League, Division 2	Preston North End		L 0-3	10,041
7		Sat	30	Football League, Division 2	SHEFFIELD UNITED	1-2 L		16,221
8	September	Wed	3	Football League Cup, 2nd Round	LIVERPOOL	1-2 L		21,149
9		Sat	6	Football League, Division 2	Oxford United		L 1-2	12,620
10		Sat	13	Football League, Division 2	ASTON VILLA	3-0 W		19,341
11		Wed	17	Football League, Division 2	HUDDERSFIELD TOWN	1-1 D		17,548
12		Sat	20	Football League, Division 2	Blackpool		W 3-0	14,859
13		Sat	27	Football League, Division 2	BLACKBURN ROVERS	0-2 L		18,478
14	October	Sat	4	Football League, Division 2	Leicester City		L 1-3	25,422
15		Wed	8	Football League, Division 2	Bolton Wanderers		W 3-2	7,140
16		Sat	11	Football League, Division 2	CARLISLE UNITED	1-2 L		16,125
17		Sat	18	Football League, Division 2	PORTSMOUTH	4-0 W		15,657
18		Sat	25	Football League, Division 2	Middlesbrough		L 1-3	15,344
19	November	Sat	1	Football League, Division 2	BIRMINGHAM CITY	2-3 L		17,436
20		Sat	8	Football League, Division 2	Millwall		L 0-1	12,776
21		Tue	11	Football League, Division 2	Queens Park Rangers		L 1-2	19,719
22		Sat	15	Football League, Division 2	SWINDON TOWN	0-0 D		15,432
23		Sat	22	Football League, Division 2	Hull City		D 1-1	9,146
24	December	Sat	6	Football League, Division 2	Cardiff City		L 1-3	15,058
25		Sat	13	Football League, Division 2	Aston Villa		W 2-0	20,161
26		Sat	20	Football League, Division 2	OXFORD UNITED	2-0 W		10,091
27		Fri	26	Football League, Division 2	CHARLTON ATHLETIC	1-1 D		19,947
28		Sat	27	Football League, Division 2	Sheffield United		D 1-1	21,992
29	January	Sat	3	FA Cup, 3rd Round	Bolton Wanderers		W 2-1	22,447
30		Sat	10	Football League, Division 2	BLACKPOOL	0-1 L		12,069
31		Sat	17	Football League, Division 2	Blackburn Rovers		L 0-1	8,441
32		Sat	24	FA Cup, 4th Round	STOKE CITY	1-0 W		23,354
33		Sat	31	Football League, Division 2	LEICESTER CITY	2-1 W		19,898
34	February	Sat	7	FA Cup, 5th Round	GILLINGHAM	2-1 W		25,868
35		Tue	10	Football League, Division 2	Carlisle United		L 0-5	7,660
36		Sat	14	Football League, Division 2	BRISTOL CITY	2-0 W		12,744
37		Sat	21	FA Cup, 6th Round	LIVERPOOL	1-0 W		34,047
38		Tue	24	Football League, Division 2	MILLWALL	1-1 D		20,612
39		Sat	28	Football League, Division 2	Birmingham City		D 0-0	22,796
40	March	Fri	6	Football League, Division 2	HULL CITY	1-1 D		15,470
41		Sat	14	FA Cup, Semi-Final	Chelsea (at Tottenham Hotspur)		(L 1-5)	55,209
42		Sat	21	Football League, Division 2	CARDIFF CITY	2-1 W		17,152
43		Fri	27	Football League, Division 2	MIDDLESBROUGH	2-3 L		22,486
44		Sat	28	Football League, Division 2	Swindon Town		L 0-1	22,597
45	April	Wed	1	Football League, Division 2	Portsmouth		L 1-3	10,900
46		Sat	4	Football League, Division 2	PRESTON NORTH END	0-0 D		15,236
47		Tue	7	Football League, Division 2	NORWICH CITY	1-1 D		15,789
48		Fri	10	FA Cup, 3rd/4th–place play-off	Manchester United (at Arsenal)		(L 0-2)	15,105
49		Tue	14	Football League, Division 2	Huddersfield Town		L 1-3	27,916
50		Sat	18	Football League, Division 2	Norwich City		D 1-1	16,202

League ever-presents: S.M.A. Scullion (including one substitute appearance), M.S.G. Walker, D Welbourne & J.R. Williams
Most appearances in total: D. Welbourne & J.R. Williams 50 out of 50 **Most goals in total:** B. Endean 14
Hat-tricks: None **Penalty goals:** K. Eddy 6, R. Lugg 1, M.D. Packer 1
Sent off: None
Full international appearance(s) this season: None

	Eddy, K.	Endean, B.	Franks, C.J.	Garbett, T.G.	Garvey, B. //	Green, H.R. //	Hale, R. //	Jennings, W.J.	Lees, W.J.	Lewis, B. //	Lugg, R.	Owen, B.E. //	Packer, M.D.	Scullion, S.M.A.	Sinclair, R.	Slater, R. //	Walker, M.S.G.	Walley, J.T.	Welbourne, D.	Williams, J.R.	Own goals
Apps	36	38	11	30	20	7	15		28	17	22	10	13	41	7		42	41	42	42	
Subs			+2	+1	+1	+4	+2			+3		+2	+6	+1	+6						
Goals	6	10	1	4		3				2	3		2	5				6	1		1
Apps	6	7	3	7	2	0	1	1	8	3	5	2	3	7	1	1	7	8	8	8	
Subs					+1	+1	+1														
Goals	1	4	1	1							2			1							
1	X			X	X	X	X		X	R				X	S		G		X	X	
2	X	X1					X		X	X				X1	X		G	X	X	X	
3	X	R		S			X		X	X				X	X		G	X	X	X	
4	X	X				S	X		R	X				X	X		G	X	X	X	
5	X			X	X	X	X			X				X			G	X	X	X	
6	X			X	X	X	X			R		S		X			G	X	X	X	
7	X1p	X		X	X				X			R		X	S		G	X	X	X	
8	X1p	X		X	X	S			R	X				X		G		X	X	X	
9	X	X1		X	X	S			X					R	X		G	X	X	X	
10	X1	X	X	X	X					X				X			G	X1	X	X	1
11	X	X1	X	R	X					X			S	X			G	X	X	X	
12	X	X	X1		X					X				X2	X		G	X	X	X	
13	X	X	X		X					X			S	X	R		G	X	X	X	
14	X	X1	X		X		S			R			X	X			G	X	X	X	
15	X	X1			X	R1	X			S1			X	X			G	X	X	X	
16	X	X			X	X	X			S			R1	X			G	X	X	X	
17	X1p	R				X2	X		X			X		X	S		G	X1	X	X	
18	X1p	X				R	X		X			X		X	S		G	X	X	X	
19	X1p	X				S	X		X			R		X	X		G	X1	X	X	
20	X	X		X	X		S		X			R		X			G	X	X	X	
21	X	X1		X	X		X		X					X			G	X	X	X	
22	X	X		X	X		X				X			X			G	X	X	X	
23	X	R			X		X			X	X1			X	S		G	X	X	X	
24	X			X	X		R			X1	X		S	X			G	X	X	X	
25	X	X1		X1					X	R	X			X	S		G	X	X	X	
26	X	X1		X					X	S	X			X	R		G	X1	X	X	
27	X	X		X					X	X	X1		S	R			G	X	X	X	
28	X	R1		X					X	X	X		S	X			G	X	X	X	
29	X	X2		X			S		R	X	X		X				G	X	X	X	
30	X	X		X	X	S				X	X			R			G	X	X	X	
31	X	X		X	X					R	X		X	S			G	X	X	X	
32	X	X	X1	X					X		X			X			G	X	X	X	
33	X1p	X1	X	X					X		X			X			G	X	X	X	
34	X	X	X	X					X		X2			X			G	X	X	X	
35	R	X	X	X					X		X		S	X			G	X	X	X	
36		X		X1					X		X1p	X	X	X			G	X	X	X	
37		X1		X					X		X	X	X	X			G	X	X	X	
38		X		X	S				X		X	X	R	X			G	X	X1	X	
39		X		X					X		X	X	X	X			G	X	X	X	
40		X		X					X		X	X	X1p	X			G	X	X	X	
41		X		X1	S				X		X	R	X	X			G	X	X	X	
42	X	X1		X					X		X		X	X			G	X1	X	X	
43	X	R	S	X1					X		X		X	X			G	X1	X	X	
44	X	X	R						X		X	S	X	X			G	X	X	X	
45		X	S	X					X		X	R	X	X1			G	X	X	X	
46		X	X	X					X		X		X	X			G	X	X	X	
47	X	X	X	X1					X		X			X			G	X	X	X	
48	X		X	X	X			X	X					X			G	X	X	X	
49	X	X	X	X	X				X					X1			G	X	X	X	
50	X	X		X			X		X		X			X1			G	X	X	X	

1970/71

Football League position: 18th out of 22 in Division 2
Manager: Ken Furphy

New league opponents: Sheffield Wednesday, Sunderland

Home-and-away league doubles
For – 1 (Blackburn Rovers)
Against – 4 (Bristol City, Hull City, Luton Town, Millwall)

Divisional changes at end of season: Leicester City & Sheffield United to Division 1;
Blackburn Rovers & Bolton Wanderers to Division 3; Burnley & Blackpool from Division 1;
Preston North End & Fulham from Division 3

All Matches: Won 12, Drew 14, Lost 21, Goals 49-67

Highest Score: 5 (Match 25)

No	DATE			COMPETITION	OPPONENTS	HOME	AWAY	ATTENDANCE
1	August	Sat	15	Football League, Division 2	BLACKBURN ROVERS	2-1 W		15,589
2		Wed	19	Football League Cup, 1st Round	PETERBOROUGH UNITED	2-0 W		9,757
3		Sat	22	Football League, Division 2	Sunderland	D 3-3		16,228
4		Sat	29	Football League, Division 2	HULL CITY	1-2 L		17,034
5	September	Tue	1	Football League, Division 2	Swindon Town	D 1-1		16,176
6		Sat	5	Football League, Division 2	Queens Park Rangers	D 1-1		18,656
7		Tue	8	Football League Cup, 2nd Round	Swindon Town	L 2-4		13,271
8		Sat	12	Football League, Division 2	CARLISLE UNITED	0-0 D		10,462
9		Sat	19	Football League, Division 2	Oxford United	L 1-2		13,270
10		Sat	26	Football League, Division 2	SHEFFIELD UNITED	0-0 D		15,891
11		Wed	30	Football League, Division 2	NORWICH CITY	2-0 W		14,163
12	October	Sat	3	Football League, Division 2	Portsmouth	L 0-5		15,712
13		Sat	10	Football League, Division 2	CARDIFF CITY	0-1 L		16,244
14		Sat	17	Football League, Division 2	Blackburn Rovers	W 3-2		7,331
15		Mon	19	Football League, Division 2	Millwall	L 0-3		11,988
16		Sat	24	Football League, Division 2	BIRMINGHAM CITY	2-1 W		14,707
17		Sat	31	Football League, Division 2	Middlesbrough	D 2-2		16,018
18	November	Sat	7	Football League, Division 2	LEICESTER CITY	0-1 L		17,107
19		Sat	14	Football League, Division 2	Bristol City	L 0-3		11,100
20		Sat	21	Football League, Division 2	Orient	D 1-1		8,797
21		Sat	28	Football League, Division 2	BOLTON WANDERERS	1-1 D		12,020
22	December	Sat	5	Football League, Division 2	Sheffield Wednesday	L 1-2		12,139
23		Sat	12	Football League, Division 2	LUTON TOWN	0-1 L		24,381
24		Sat	19	Football League, Division 2	SUNDERLAND	1-1 D		12,739
25	January	Wed	6	FA Cup, 3rd Round	READING	5-0 W		13,206
26		Sat	9	Football League, Division 2	Norwich City	L 1-2		12,711
27		Sat	16	Football League, Division 2	MILLWALL	0-4 L		14,072
28		Sat	23	FA Cup, 4th Round	Oxford United	D 1-1		17,843
29		Wed	27	FA Cup, 4th Round replay	OXFORD UNITED	1-2 L		19,200
30		Sat	30	Football League, Division 2	Bolton Wanderers	W 1-0		9,940
31	February	Sat	6	Football League, Division 2	SHEFFIELD WEDNESDAY	3-0 W		12,841
32		Sat	13	Football League, Division 2	Luton Town	L 0-1		20,137
33		Sat	20	Football League, Division 2	ORIENT	0-0 D		14,336
34		Fri	26	Football League, Division 2	MIDDLESBROUGH	1-0 W		14,112
35	March	Tue	2	Football League, Division 2	Charlton Athletic	W 2-1		10,415
36		Sat	6	Football League, Division 2	Birmingham City	L 0-2		27,605
37		Sat	13	Football League, Division 2	BRISTOL CITY	0-3 L		12,288
38		Sat	20	Football League, Division 2	Leicester City	D 1-1		24,817
39		Sat	27	Football League, Division 2	QUEENS PARK RANGERS	1-2 L		16,625
40	April	Sat	3	Football League, Division 2	Hull City	L 0-1		17,199
41		Fri	9	Football League, Division 2	PORTSMOUTH	0-0 D		12,826
42		Sat	10	Football League, Division 2	CHARLTON ATHLETIC	1-1 D		12,867
43		Tue	13	Football League, Division 2	Carlisle United	L 1-2		9,484
44		Sat	17	Football League, Division 2	Cardiff City	W 1-0		26,536
45		Sat	24	Football League, Division 2	OXFORD UNITED	2-1 W		10,211
46		Wed	28	Football League, Division 2	SWINDON TOWN	1-2 L		10,793
47	May	Sat	1	Football League, Division 2	Sheffield United	L 0-3		38,857

League ever-presents: None
Most appearances in total: T.G. Garbett 46 (including two substitute appearances) out of 47   **Most goals in total:** R.G. Wigg 17
Hat-tricks: B. Endean (Match 25)   **Penalty goals:** K. Eddy 4
Sent off: None
Full international appearance(s) this season: J.T. Walley (Wales)

	Butler, D.	Eddy, K.	Edmonds, D.J.	Endean, B. //	Farley, J.D.	Franks, C.J.	Garbett, T.G.	Jennings, W.J.	Lees, W.J.	Lugg, R.	Packer, M.D.	Pearce, J. //	Scullion, S.M.A.	Sinclair, R.	Walker, M.S.G.	Walley, J.T.	Welbourne, D.	Wigg, R.G.	Williams, J.R.	Woods, C.M.P.	Own goal
Apps	25	34	11	6	11	9	39	9	38	15	17	0	30	18	31	41	32	40	27	29	
Subs		+1		+3		+5	+2	+1		+3	+4	+1	+5	+1			+3			+2	
Goals		3			1	2	1	2	1				3	1		5	2	13		3	1
Apps	3	5		3			5		5	1	0		5	2	5	4	4	5	5	3	
Subs				+1							+2										
Goals		1		3									2					4		1	
1		X					X		X				X	X	G	X2	X	X	X	X	
2		X	S				X		X				X	R	G	X	X	X1	X	X1	
3		X					X		X1	S			X	R	G	X1	X	X1	X	X	
4		X				S	X						X	R	G	X	X	X	X	X1	
5		X	X						X	X			X		G	X	X	X1	X	X	
6		X	R			S			X	X			X		G	X	X	X1	X	X	
7		X					X		X	X			X1		G	X	X	X1	X	X	
8		X	S				X		X	R			X		G	X	X	X	X	X	
9		X					X		X	X	S		R		G	X	X	X1	X	X	
10		X					X		X	X			X		G	X	X	X	X	X	
11		X1p	S				X		X	X			X		G	X	X	R1	X	X	
12		X					X	R	X	S			X		G	X	X	X	X	X	
13		X					X		X	X	S		X		G	X	X	X	X	R	
14		X					X	X	X	X			X	S	G	X	X1	R2		X	
15		X	X						X	X			X		G	X	X			X	
16		X1p				X	X		X				X		G	X	X		X	X1	
17		X				R	X		X	S	X		X2		G	X	X		X	X	
18		X				S	X		X	R			X		G	X	X		X	X	
19		X	X			S			X				X		G	X	X		X	R	
20	X	X					X		X				X	X	G	X			X1	X	
21	X	X					X		X				X	X	G	X1			X	X	
22	X	X					X1		X	S	X		X	X	G	X			X	R	
23	X	X					X		X	R	X		X		G	X	S		X	R	
24	X	X1p	S				X		X	X			X		G	X			X	R	
25	X	X1p	X3				X		X				X1		G	X			X	X	
26	X		X	X	X	X	X	X	S				R		G	X			X1	X	
27	X	X	X		S	X	X		R				X		G	X			X	X	
28	X	X	X				X		X		S		R		G	X	X		X1	X	
29	X	X	X				X		X		S		R	X	G				X1	X	
30	X		G	X	S	X	X	R					X			X	X1		X	X	
31	X		G	X		X	X2	X					S	X1		X	X		R	X	
32	X		G	R		X	X	X					S	X		X	X		X	X	
33	X		G	X		X	X	X					S	X		X	R		X	X	
34	X	S	G	X		X	R	X						X		X	X		X1	X	
35	X	R	G	X1		X							S1	X		X	X		X	X	
36	X	X	G	X		X	S	R			X					X	X		X	X	
37	X	X	G	R		X	X						X			X	X		X	X	S
38	X		G	X		X	X	X					X			X1	X		X	X	
39	X		X				X	X					X		G	X	X		X1	X	
40	X	X	R			X	X	X			X		X		G		X			S	
41	X	X			S	X		X			X		X	X	G	X		R		X	
42	X	X				X	X				X	S	R		G	X	X	X		X	1
43	X	X				X1	X				X	S	R		G	X	X			X	
44	X	X				X	X						X		G	X	X		X	X1	
45	X	X				X1	X						X		G	X	X		X1	X	
46	X	X	G			X	X	X			X		X			R	S	X1		X	
47	X	X	G			X	X	X	R		X		X			X	S			X	

- 151 -

1971/72

Football League position: 22nd out of 22 in Division 2 – relegated to Division 3
Manager: George Kirby

New league opponents: Burnley

Home-and-away league doubles
For – none
Against - 10 (Birmingham City, Bristol City, Carlisle United, Charlton Athletic, Fulham, Hull City, Middlesbrough, Millwall, Orient, Queens Park Rangers)

Relegated with Watford: Charlton Athletic

All Matches: Won 7, Drew 10, Lost 30, Goals 30-82

Highest Score: 2 (Matches 2, 6, 20, 21, 22 & 41)

		HOME					AWAY					
	Pl	W	D	L	For	Ag	W	D	L	For	Ag	Pts
Norwich City	42	13	8	0	40	16	8	7	6	20	20	57
Birmingham City	42	15	6	0	46	14	4	12	5	14	17	56
Millwall	42	14	7	0	38	17	5	10	6	26	29	55
Queens Park Rangers	42	16	4	1	39	3	4	10	7	18	19	54
Sunderland	42	11	7	3	42	24	6	9	6	25	33	50
Blackpool	42	12	6	3	43	16	8	1	12	27	34	47
Burnley	42	13	4	4	43	22	7	2	12	27	33	46
Bristol City	42	14	3	4	43	22	4	7	10	18	27	46
Middlesbrough	42	16	4	1	31	11	3	4	14	19	37	46
Carlisle United	42	12	6	3	38	22	5	3	13	23	35	43
Swindon Town	42	10	6	5	29	16	5	6	10	18	31	42
Hull City	42	10	6	5	33	21	4	4	13	16	32	38
Luton Town	42	7	8	6	25	24	3	10	8	18	24	38
Sheffield Wednesday	42	11	7	3	33	22	2	5	14	18	36	38
Oxford United	42	10	8	3	28	17	2	6	13	15	38	38
Portsmouth	42	9	7	5	31	26	3	6	12	28	42	37
Orient	42	12	4	5	32	19	2	5	14	18	42	37
Preston North End	42	11	4	6	32	21	1	8	12	20	37	36
Cardiff City	42	9	7	5	37	25	1	7	13	19	44	34
Fulham	42	10	7	4	29	20	2	3	16	16	48	34
Charlton Athletic	42	9	7	5	33	25	3	2	16	22	52	33
WATFORD	42	5	5	11	15	25	0	4	17	9	50	19

No	DATE			COMPETITION	OPPONENTS	HOME	AWAY	ATTENDANCE
1	August	Sat	14	Football League, Division 2	Fulham		L 0-3	13,560
2		Wed	18	Football League Cup, 1st Round	NORTHAMPTON TOWN	2-0 W		7,663
3		Sat	21	Football League, Division 2	SUNDERLAND	1-1 D		11,283
4		Sat	28	Football League, Division 2	Charlton Athletic		L 0-2	11,966
5	September	Wed	1	Football League, Division 2	SWINDON TOWN	0-0 D		10,580
6		Sat	4	Football League, Division 2	CARDIFF CITY	2-2 D		10,233
7		Tue	7	Football League Cup, 2nd Round	Stockport County	W 1-0		4,001
8		Sat	11	Football League, Division 2	Carlisle United		L 0-2	9,745
9		Sat	18	Football League, Division 2	BLACKPOOL	1-0 W		10,594
10		Sat	25	Football League, Division 2	Queens Park Rangers		L 0-3	15,698
11		Tue	28	Football League, Division 2	Birmingham City		L 1-4	28,095
12	October	Sat	2	Football League, Division 2	PORTSMOUTH	1-0 W		11,633
13		Wed	6	Football League Cup, 3rd Round	PRESTON NORTH END	1-1 D		8,853
14		Sat	9	Football League, Division 2	Bristol City		L 1-2	18,100
15		Mon	11	Football Lge Cup, 3rd Round replay	Preston North End		L 1-2	12,436
16		Sat	16	Football League, Division 2	FULHAM	1-2 L		9,303
17		Wed	20	Football League, Division 2	HULL CITY	1-2 L		7,983
18		Sat	23	Football League, Division 2	Middlesbrough		L 1-2	19,947
19		Sat	30	Football League, Division 2	SHEFFIELD WEDNESDAY	1-1 D		11,314
20	November	Sat	6	Football League, Division 2	Millwall		L 2-3	13,812
21		Sat	13	Football League, Division 2	LUTON TOWN	2-1 W		14,000
22		Sat	20	Football League, Division 2	BURNLEY	2-1 W		11,538
23		Sat	27	Football League, Division 2	Preston North End		L 0-2	11,318
24	December	Sat	4	Football League, Division 2	ORIENT	0-1 L		9,518
25		Sat	11	Football League, Division 2	Norwich City		D 1-1	20,227
26		Sat	18	Football League, Division 2	Cardiff City		L 0-2	11,092
27		Mon	27	Football League, Division 2	OXFORD UNITED	0-1 L		14,270
28	January	Sat	1	Football League, Division 2	Blackpool		L 0-5	10,745
29		Sat	8	Football League, Division 2	CHARLTON ATHLETIC	0-3 L		9,218
30		.Sat	15	FA Cup, 3rd Round	NOTTS COUNTY	1-4 L		13,448
31		Sat	22	Football League, Division 2	BIRMINGHAM CITY	0-1 L		10,884
32		Sat	29	Football League, Division 2	Hull City		L 0-4	10,546
33	February	Sat	12	Football League, Division 2	MIDDLESBROUGH	0-1 L		8,109
34		Sat	19	Football League, Division 2	Sheffield Wednesday		L 1-2	13,842
35		Sat	26	Football League, Division 2	MILLWALL	0-1 L		14,575
36	March	Sat	4	Football League, Division 2	Luton Town		D 0-0	10,816
37		Sat	11	Football League, Division 2	BRISTOL CITY	0-2 L		5,384
38		Sat	25	Football League, Division 2	CARLISLE UNITED	1-2 L		6,004
39		Fri	31	Football League, Division 2	QUEENS PARK RANGERS	0-2 L		14,719
40	April	Sat	1	Football League, Division 2	Oxford United		D 0-0	6,604
41		Mon	3	Football League, Division 2	Portsmouth		D 2-2	7,909
42		Sat	8	Football League, Division 2	Burnley		L 0-3	8,695
43		Sat	15	Football League, Division 2	PRESTON NORTH END	1-0 W		5,507
44		Mon	17	Football League, Division 2	Sunderland		L 0-5	8,981
45		Sat	22	Football League, Division 2	Orient		L 0-1	7,244
46		Tue	25	Football League, Division 2	Swindon Town		L 0-2	9,009
47		Sat	29	Football League, Division 2	NORWICH CITY	1-1 D		22,421

League ever-presents: None
Most appearances in total: K. Eddy 45 out of 47   **Most goals in total:** K. Eddy 7
Hat-tricks: None   **Penalty goals:** K. Eddy 1
Sent off: None
Full international appearance(s) this season: None

	Baxter, W.A.	Butler, D.	Eddy, K.	Edmonds, D.J.	Farley, J.D.	Franks, C.J.	Garbett, T.G.	Jennings, W.J.	Kenning, M.J.	Lees, W.J.	Lindsay, J.Y.	Lugg, R.	McGettigan, L.	Morrissey, P.J.	Packer, M.D.	Rankin, A.G.	Rowan, B.	Sinclair, R.	Walker, M.S.G.	Walker, P.G.	Walley, J.T.	Watt, J.G.	Welbourne, D.	Wigg, R.G.	Williams, J.R.	Woodfield, D.	Woods, C.M.P.
Apps	11	33	40	4	14	34	4	14	15	24	36	14	23	12	8	19	8	1	19	2	17	0	24	36	38	1	11
Subs					+4	+5		+2	+1	+1		+5	+2				+4	+2		+1	+1	+1	+2	+3	+1		
Goals			6		3				1		2		3	1									2	4	2		
Apps	1	4	5		2	3	1	1	1	4	4	2	4		2	1	1		4	1	3		2	3	5		1
Subs						+2																		+2			
Goals			1						1	1									1				2				

	Baxter	Butler	Eddy	Edmonds	Farley	Franks	Garbett	Jennings	Kenning	Lees	Lindsay	Lugg	McGettigan	Morrissey	Packer	Rankin	Rowan	Sinclair	Walker M.S.G.	Walker P.G.	Walley	Watt	Welbourne	Wigg	Williams	Woodfield	Woods
1		X	X		S	X				X	R		X						G		X			X	X		X
2		X	X		S	X				X	R		X						G	X1				X1	X		X
3		X	X					X	R	X			X					S	G		X			X1	X		X
4		X	X			X	R			X		S	X						G		X			X	X		X
5		X		X		X				X	X		X						G		X		X	X	X		
6		X		X			X			X	X		X1						G		X		X1	X	X		
7		X	X1		R		S			X	X		X						G		X			X	X		X
8		X	X		R		S			X	X		X						G		X			X	X		
9		X	X1		S					X	X		X						G		X			X	R		X
10		X	X		S					X	X		X						G		X			X	X	R	
11		X	X			X					R		S		X1				G		X			X	X		X
12		X	X			X					X		S		X				G		X			X	X	X1	R
13		X	X			X					X1	X	X						G		X			X	X		X
14	X	X	X			X					X	X1	X						G	S				R	X		X
15	X	X	X			X					X	X	X1	R	X				G					S	X		
16	X	X	X	G	X1						X	X	X								X			X	X		X
17		X	X	G		X					X		X			R					X		X1	S	X	X	
18		X	X	G	X	X					X		X			X	S				R			X1			
19		X	X1	G	X	X	S				X		X			X	X				R			X			
20	X	X	X		X	X1					X1					R		S	G		X			X	X		
21	X	X	X1		X	X1					X								G		X			X	X		
22	X	X	X	R	X						X	X		S1			G				X			X1	X		
23	X	X	X	R	X						X		S			X	G				X			X	X		
24	X	X	X		X						X	X	X				G	S			X			R	X		
25	X	R	X		X						X	X	S	X1		G	X							X	X		
26	X		X		X			S			X	X	X	X		G	X							R	X		
27	X		X		S	X					X	X	X	R		G	X							X	X		
28	X		X		S					X	X		X			G	X				X			R	X		X
29		X		S						X	X	R	X			G	X				X			X	X		
30		X		X	X		X	X	X					X	G	R				X				S1	X		
31		X		X			X	X	X	R		X			X	G	X				S			X	X		
32		X		X			X	X		X	X	X	X			G	X							X	X		
33		X		X			R	X	X	X	X					G	X						S	X			
34		X		X			R	X	X	X	X					G	S				X			X	X1		
35		X	X	S	X					X	X	X	X			G							R	X	X		
36		X	X		X					X	X	X	X			G							X	X	X		
37		X	X		X			S		X	X	R	X			G							X	X	X		
38		X	X	S	X			X	X1		R	X				G							X	X	X		
39		X	X		X			X	X	S	X	X				G							X	R			
40		X	X		X			X	X		X					G							X	X	X		
41		X	X2p		X			X	R	X	X					G	X						S		X	X	
42		X	X		X			X	X		X	R				G	S						X	X	X		
43		X	X1	X	X			X	X		X		R			G							X	S	X		
44		X	X	X	X			R	X		X	X				G							X	S	X		
45		X	X	X	X			X	X		R	S			X	G							X	X			
46		R	X	X	X			X	X		X				X	G							X	X	S		
47			X	X	X			X	R	X	X					G						S		X	X1	X	

1972/73

Football League position: 19th out of 24 in Division 3
Manager: George Kirby

New league opponents: None

Home-and-away league doubles
For – 1 (Walsall)
Against – 2 (Grimsby Town, Swansea City)

Divisional changes at end of season: Bolton and Notts County to Division 2; Rotherham United, Brentford, Swansea City and Scunthorpe United to Division 4; Huddersfield Town and Brighton & Hove Albion from Division 2; Southport, Hereford United, Cambridge United and Aldershot from Division 4

All Matches: Won 14, Drew 17, Lost 19, Goals 49-53

Highest Score: 5 (Match 37)

	HOME						AWAY					
	Pl	W	D	L	For	Ag	W	D	L	For	Ag	Pts
Bolton Wanderers	46	18	4	1	44	9	7	7	9	29	30	61
Notts County	46	17	4	2	40	12	6	7	10	27	35	57
Blackburn Rovers	46	12	8	3	34	16	8	7	8	23	31	55
Oldham Athletic	46	12	7	4	40	18	7	9	7	32	36	54
Bristol Rovers	46	17	4	2	55	20	3	9	11	22	36	53
Port Vale	46	15	6	2	41	21	6	5	12	15	48	53
AFC Bournemouth	46	14	6	3	44	16	3	10	10	22	39	50
Plymouth Argyle	46	14	3	6	43	26	6	7	10	31	40	50
Grimsby Town	46	16	2	5	45	18	4	6	13	22	43	48
Tranmere Rovers	46	12	8	3	38	17	3	8	12	18	35	46
Charlton Athletic	46	12	7	4	46	24	5	4	14	23	43	45
Wrexham	46	11	9	3	39	23	3	8	12	16	31	45
Rochdale	46	8	8	7	22	26	6	9	8	26	28	45
Southend United	46	13	6	4	40	14	4	4	15	21	40	44
Shrewsbury Town	46	10	10	3	31	21	5	4	14	15	33	44
Chesterfield	46	13	4	6	37	22	4	5	14	20	39	43
Walsall	46	14	3	6	37	26	4	4	15	19	40	43
York City	46	8	10	5	24	14	5	5	13	18	32	41
WATFORD	46	11	8	4	32	23	1	9	13	11	25	41
Halifax Town	46	9	8	6	29	23	4	7	12	14	30	41
Rotherham United	46	12	4	7	34	27	5	3	15	17	38	41
Brentford	46	12	5	6	33	18	3	2	18	18	51	37
Swansea City	46	11	5	7	37	29	3	4	16	14	44	37
Scunthorpe United	46	8	7	8	18	25	2	3	18	15	47	30

No	DATE			COMPETITION	OPPONENTS	HOME	AWAY	ATTENDANCE
1	August	Sat	12	Football League, Division 3	TRANMERE ROVERS	1-0 W		6,473
2		Wed	16	Football League Cup, 1st Round	Orient		L 0-2	5,193
3		Sat	19	Football League, Division 3	Wrexham		L 0-1	5,645
4		Sat	26	Football League, Division 3	AFC BOURNEMOUTH	3-2 W		8,373
5		Tue	29	Football League, Division 3	Shrewsbury Town		D 0-0	2,919
6	September	Sat	2	Football League, Division 3	Grimsby Town		L 0-2	8,790
7		Sat	9	Football League, Division 3	OLDHAM ATHLETIC	2-1 W		6,161
8		Sat	16	Football League, Division 3	Blackburn Rovers		D 0-0	6,484
9		Mon	18	Football League, Division 3	York City		D 0-0	3,066
10		Sat	23	Football League, Division 3	NOTTS COUNTY	1-0 W		8,363
11		Wed	27	Football League, Division 3	ROTHERHAM UNITED	1-1 D		7,769
12		Sat	30	Football League, Division 3	Charlton Athletic		L 1-2	7,304
13	October	Sat	7	Football League, Division 3	Rochdale		L 0-1	3,871
14		Tue	10	Football League, Division 3	PORT VALE	1-1 D		5,556
15		Sat	14	Football League, Division 3	SOUTHEND UNITED	1-0 W		7,860
16		Sat	21	Football League, Division 3	Chesterfield		D 0-0	6,843
17		Tue	24	Football League, Division 3	Halifax Town		D 1-1	2,046
18		Sat	28	Football League, Division 3	BRISTOL ROVERS	2-1 W		8,391
19	November	Sat	4	Football League, Division 3	Rotherham United		L 0-1	4,055
20		Sat	11	Football League, Division 3	YORK CITY	2-2 D		6,864
21		Sat	18	FA Cup, 1st Round	GUILDFORD CITY	4-2 W		7,041
22		Sat	25	Football League, Division 3	Walsall		W 3-1	4,718
23	December	Sat	2	Football League, Division 3	BOLTON WANDERERS	2-1 W		7,349
24		Sat	9	FA Cup, 2nd Round	ALDERSHOT	2-0 W		8,956
25		Sat	23	Football League, Division 3	PLYMOUTH ARGYLE	3-2 W		7,750
26		Tue	26	Football League, Division 3	Notts County		L 0-1	9,282
27	January	Sat	6	Football League, Division 3	AFC Bournemouth		L 0-3	11,841
28		Sat	13	FA Cup, 3rd Round	SHEFFIELD UNITED	0-1 L		15,676
29		Sat	20	Football League, Division 3	GRIMSBY TOWN	1-2 L		6,064
30		Sat	27	Football League, Division 3	Oldham Athletic		L 1-2	9,303
31	February	Sat	3	Football League, Division 3	Port Vale		L 0-1	3,987
32		Sat	10	Football League, Division 3	BLACKBURN ROVERS	1-3 L		7,217
33		Fri	16	Football League, Division 3	Tranmere Rovers		L 0-1	5,401
34		Sat	24	Football League, Division 3	SWANSEA CITY	0-1 L		6,051
35		Tue	27	Football League, Division 3	Swansea City		L 1-2	4,052
36	March	Fri	2	Football League, Division 3	ROCHDALE	0-0 D		5,338
37		Tue	6	Football League, Division 3	SCUNTHORPE UNITED	5-1 W		4,578
38		Fri	9	Football League, Division 3	Southend United		D 0-0	6,394
39		Wed	14	Football League, Division 3	WREXHAM	0-0 D		5,663
40		Sat	17	Football League, Division 3	CHESTERFIELD	0-0 D		5,788
41		Mon	19	Football League, Division 3	Brentford		D 1-1	8,232
42		Sat	24	Football League, Division 3	Bristol Rovers		L 1-2	6,798
43		Wed	28	Football League, Division 3	HALIFAX TOWN	2-1 W		5,202
44		Sat	31	Football League, Division 3	WALSALL	1-0 W		5,327
45	April	Sat	7	Football League, Division 3	Bolton Wanderers		D 1-1	17,252
46		Sat	14	Football League, Division 3	BRENTFORD	2-2 D		7,813
47		Fri	20	Football League, Division 3	CHARLTON ATHLETIC	1-1 D		9,241
48		Sat	21	Football League, Division 3	Scunthorpe United		L 0-1	1,544
49		Mon	23	Football League, Division 3	Plymouth Argyle		D 1-1	9,722
50		Sat	28	Football League, Division 3	SHREWSBURY TOWN	0-1 L		6,026

League ever-presents: C.J. Franks (including one substitute appearance)
Most appearances in total: C.J. Franks 50 (including one substitute appearance) out of 50   **Most goals in total:** P.J. Morrissey 10
Hat-tricks: None   **Penalty goals:** M.J. Kenning 1, J.Y. Lindsay 1, P.J. Morrissey 1
Sent off: None
Full international appearance(s) this season: None

	Bond, D.J.T.	Butler, D.	Craker, L.D.	Farley, J.D.	Franks, C.J. //	Jenkins, R.A.	Jennings, W.J.	Keen, M.T.	Kenning, M.J. //	Lees, W.J.	Lindsay, J.Y.	McGettigan, L.	McGovern, M.J. //	Markham, L.S.	Mercer, K.	Morrissey, P.J.	Packer, M.D. //	Rankin, A.G.	Walker, M.S.G. //	Welbourne, D.	Wigg, R.G. //	Williams, J.R.	Woodfield, D.	Own goals
Apps	3	43	17	38	45	22	10	44	20	38	15	11	4	7	0	37	18	43	3	42	15	23	8	
Subs				+2	+1	+4	+9		+5			+2		+5	+1	+3	+1			+1	+3			
Goals			2	3	2	2	5	3	1		6			1		10				3	3		2	
Apps		4		4	4	2		4	2	3	1		1			4	2	3	1	3	2	3	1	
Subs																				+1	+1			
Goals		1		1					1	1										1	1			
1		X		X	X			X	X	X	X1					X		G		X	X			
2		X	X	X				X			X	X				R			G	S	X	X	X	
3		X	X	S				X			X	X				X			G	X	X	R		
4		X		X	X1			X		X	X1			X1		X		G		X	X			
5		X		R	X			X	S	X		X		X		X		G		X	X	X		
6		X		X	X			X	S	X		X		X		X		G		R	X	X		
7		X		X	X			X		X	X2	S		X		R	X	G		X				
8		X		X	X			X	X	R	X			X		S	X	G		X				
9		X		X	X			X	X		X			X		X	G			X		X		
10		X		X1	X			X	X	X	X			S		X		G		X	R			
11		X		X	X			X	X	X	R	S				X		G		X	X1			
12		X		X1	X			X	X	X	X					X		G		X	X			
13		X		X	X			X	R	X	X			S		X		G		X	X			
14		X		X	X			X	X	X	X	R		S		X		G		X1				
15		X		X	X			X	S	X	X1p	R		X		X		G		X				
16		X		X	X			X	R	X	X			S		X		G		X		X		
17		X		X	X			X	X	X1				X		R		G		X	S	X		
18		X		X	X			X	S		R			X1				G		X	X	X	X	1
19		X		X	X			X		X	X	R		X				G		S	R	X		
20		X		X	X	S		X1		X		R		X				G		X	X1	X		
21	X1			X	X			X	X1p	X			X			X		G		X1	X1			
22		X		X	X	X		X1	X	X			X2					G		X		X		
23		X		X1	X	X	S	X	R	X			X					G		X		X		1
24		X		X1	X	X		X		X1			X			X	X	G		X		X		
25		R		X	X1	X	S	X		X			X2	X		X		G		X		X		
26		X		X	X			X		X			X	X		X		G		X		X		
27		X		X	X	X	S	X	X	R			X			X		G		X		X		
28		X		X	X	X		X	R	X			X			X		G		X	S	X		
29		X		X	X	S	X	X	X			X1				X		G		R		X		
30		X			X	X		X	R	X			X	X		X	X		G	X1	S	X		
31			R	X	X	X	S	X		X						X			G	X	X	X		
32		X		X	X	X	S	X					X1p	R		X		G		X		X	X	
33				X	X	R	X	X		X			S	X		X		G		X	X	X		
34	X			X	X	R	X		X	X			S	X		X	X	G		X				
35	X	X	X1	X	X	S		X			X			R	X	X		G		X				
36	X	X	X	R	X			X			X			X	X	X		G		X	S			
37		X	X	X	S2		X		X			R		X2		X	X1	G		X				
38		X	X	X	X			X	S	R				X		X		G		X		X		
39	R	X	X	X	X	S		X	X					X		X		G		X		X		
40		X	X	X	X			X	X					X		X		G		X		X		
41		X	X		X	X	S	X	R1			X				X		G		X		X		
42		R	X		X	X	X1	X				X				X	S	G		X		X		
43			X	R	X	S	X	X1	X	X						X		G		X1		X		
44		X	X		X	X	X1	X	X	R						X		G		X		X		
45		X	X		X	X	X1	X			X					X		G		X		X		
46		X	X	S	X	X	X2	X		X			R			X		G		X		X		
47		X	X1	X	X	X	X	X	X							X		G		X				
48		X	X	X	X			X		X	X			S		X		G		X				
49		X	X		X	X	R	X		X			S1			X		G		X				
50		X	X	S	X	X	R	X		X			X			X		G		X				

- *155* -

1973/74

Football League position: 7th out of 24 in Division 3
Manager: Mike Keen

New league opponents: Cambridge United, Hereford United

Home-and-away league doubles
For – 4 (Brighton & Hove Albion, Port Vale, Rochdale, Southend United)
Against – 1 (Plymouth Argyle)

Divisional changes at end of season: Oldham Athletic, Bristol Rovers & York City to Division 2; Cambridge United, Shrewsbury Town, Southport & Rochdale to Division 4; Crystal Palace, Preston North End & Swindon Town from Division 2; Peterborough United, Gillingham, Colchester United & Bury from Division 4

All Matches: Won 20, Drew 13, Lost 17, Goals 69-62

Highest Score: 4 (Matches 32, 39 & 40)

		HOME					AWAY					
	Pl	W	D	L	For	Ag	W	D	L	For	Ag	Pts
Oldham Athletic	46	13	6	4	50	23	12	6	5	33	24	62
Bristol Rovers	46	15	6	2	37	15	7	11	5	28	18	61
York City	46	13	8	2	37	15	8	11	4	30	23	61
Wrexham	46	15	6	2	44	15	7	6	10	19	28	56
Chesterfield	46	14	6	3	31	16	7	8	8	24	26	56
Grimsby Town	46	14	6	3	48	21	4	9	10	19	29	51
WATFORD	46	12	6	5	34	21	7	6	10	30	35	50
Aldershot	46	13	6	4	47	22	6	5	12	18	30	49
Halifax Town	46	9	11	3	23	15	5	10	8	25	36	49
Huddersfield Town	46	14	5	4	37	16	3	8	12	19	39	47
AFC Bournemouth	46	11	5	7	25	23	5	10	8	29	35	47
Southend United	46	10	7	6	40	30	6	7	10	22	32	46
Blackburn Rovers	46	13	4	6	38	21	5	6	12	24	43	46
Charlton Athletic	46	13	5	5	43	29	6	3	14	23	44	46
Walsall	46	11	7	5	37	19	5	6	12	20	29	45
Tranmere Rovers	46	10	8	5	31	15	5	11	7	19	29	45
Plymouth Argyle	46	13	6	4	37	17	4	4	15	22	37	44
Hereford United	46	10	5	8	31	25	4	10	9	22	32	43
Brighton & Hove Albion	46	10	3	10	31	31	6	8	9	21	27	43
Port Vale	46	12	6	5	37	23	2	8	13	15	35	42
Cambridge United	46	11	7	5	36	27	2	2	19	12	54	35
Shrewsbury Town	46	7	7	9	24	24	3	4	16	17	38	31
Southport	46	4	14	5	19	20	2	2	19	16	62	28
Rochdale	46	1	12	10	24	38	1	5	17	14	56	21

No	DATE			COMPETITION	OPPONENTS	HOME	AWAY	ATTENDANCE
1	August	Sat	25	Football League, Division 3	HUDDERSFIELD TOWN	1-1 D		6,246
2		Wed	29	Football League Cup, 1st Round	Reading		D 2-2	6,279
3		Fri	31	Football League, Division 3	Southend United		W 3-2	7,508
4	September	Wed	5	Football Lge Cup, 1st Round replay	READING (after extra time)	2-3 L		7,872
5		Sat	8	Football League, Division 3	OLDHAM ATHLETIC	0-1 L		6,635
6		Wed	12	Football League, Division 3	WREXHAM	2-0 W		5,998
7		Sat	15	Football League, Division 3	Hereford United		D 1-1	8,634
8		Wed	19	Football League, Division 3	Cambridge United		L 2-3	5,090
9		Sat	22	Football League, Division 3	YORK CITY	1-1 D		6,452
10		Sat	29	Football League, Division 3	Brighton & Hove Albion		W 1-0	7,645
11	October	Wed	3	Football League, Division 3	CAMBRIDGE UNITED	3-0 W		6,470
12		Sat	6	Football League, Division 3	BRISTOL ROVERS	0-0 D		10,202
13		Sat	13	Football League, Division 3	Chesterfield		L 1-3	4,912
14		Sat	20	Football League, Division 3	PLYMOUTH ARGYLE	0-3 L		6,905
15		Mon	22	Football League, Division 3	Wrexham		L 0-1	5,055
16		Sat	27	Football League, Division 3	AFC Bournemouth		L 0-1	7,422
17	November	Sat	3	Football League, Division 3	ALDERSHOT	2-1 W		6,264
18		Sat	10	Football League, Division 3	Rochdale		W 3-1	1,459
19		Mon	12	Football League, Division 3	HALIFAX TOWN	0-0 D		5,358
20		Sat	17	Football League, Division 3	Blackburn Rovers		L 0-5	8,851
21		Sat	24	FA Cup, 1st Round	CHELMSFORD CITY	1-0 W		6,555
22	December	Sat	8	Football League, Division 3	CHARLTON ATHLETIC	1-3 L		6,366
23		Sat	15	FA Cup, 2nd Round	AFC BOURNEMOUTH	0-1 L		5,884
24		Sat	22	Football League, Division 3	BRIGHTON & HOVE ALBION	1-0 W		5,909
25		Wed	26	Football League, Division 3	Shrewsbury Town		L 2-3	3,875
26		Sat	29	Football League, Division 3	Oldham Athletic		W 3-0	6,714
27	January	Tue	1	Football League, Division 3	SOUTHEND UNITED	1-0 W		8,195
28		Sat	5	Football League, Division 3	Southport		D 1-1	1,689
29		Sat	12	Football League, Division 3	HEREFORD UNITED	2-1 W		7,479
30		Sat	19	Football League, Division 3	Huddersfield Town		W 2-1	6,301
31		Sat	26	Football League, Division 3	WALSALL	1-3 L		7,149
32	February	Sat	2	Football League, Division 3	TRANMERE ROVERS	4-2 W		5,454
33		Sun	10	Football League, Division 3	York City		D 2-2	7,104
34		Sat	16	Football League, Division 3	CHESTERFIELD	2-1 W		7,683
35		Sat	23	Football League, Division 3	Bristol Rovers		L 0-1	14,069
36	March	Sat	2	Football League, Division 3	SHREWSBURY TOWN	1-0 W		5,860
37		Sat	9	Football League, Division 3	AFC BOURNEMOUTH	1-1 D		7,616
38		Sat	16	Football League, Division 3	Plymouth Argyle		L 0-2	7,336
39		Sat	23	Football League, Division 3	ROCHDALE	4-0 W		5,616
40		Wed	27	Football League, Division 3	SOUTHPORT	4-0 W		5,850
41		Sat	30	Football League, Division 3	Aldershot		L 0-1	5,596
42	April	Tue	2	Football League, Division 3	Walsall		L 2-2	3,799
43		Sat	6	Football League, Division 3	Halifax Town		D 0-0	1,366
44		Mon	8	Football League, Division 3	Tranmere Rovers		L 0-1	3,497
45		Sat	13	Football League, Division 3	BLACKBURN ROVERS	0-0 D		7,175
46		Tue	16	Football League, Division 3	Port Vale		W 2-1	3,056
47		Sat	20	Football League, Division 3	Charlton Athletic		W 3-1	4,146
48		Wed	24	Football League, Division 3	PORT VALE	2-1 W		5,883
49		Sat	27	Football League, Division 3	GRIMSBY TOWN	1-2 L		7,002
50		Mon	29	Football League, Division 3	Grimsby Town		D 2-2	8,813

League ever-presents: D.J.T. Bond, D. Butler
Most appearances in total: D.J.T. Bond & D. Butler 50 out of 50   **Most goals in total:** W.J. Jennings 29 (including Division 3's highest tally of 26)
Hat-tricks: W.J. Jennings (Match 3 & Match 32), P.J. Morrissey (Match 26)   **Penalty goals:** S.M.A. Scullion 2, P.J. Morrissey 1
Sent off: None
Full international appearance(s) this season: None

	Bond, D.J.T.	Butler, D.	Craker, L.D.	Dalrymple, M.O. //	Farley, J.D. //	Jenkins, R.A.	Jennings, W.J.	Keen, M.T.	Lees, W.J.	Lindsay, J.Y. //	McGettigan, L.	Markham, L.S.	Morgan, I.A. //	Morrissey, P.J.	Rankin, A.G.	Scullion, S.M.A.	Walsh, J.T.	Welbourne, D. //	Williams, J.R.	Woodfield, D. //
Apps	46	46	18	5	34	22	44	44	42	13	1	6	15	37	41	28	1	18	40	5
Subs			+5		+2	+2	+1	+1		+1			+1	+1			+1	+1	+1	+1
Goals	2	1			4	4	26		2	4		1	1	12		7				
Apps	4	4	1		3	0	3	3	4	3		1	2	4	4	1		4	3	
Subs			+1		+1	+2														
Goals							3	1						1						
1	X	X			X		X1	X	R	X				X	G			X	X	S
2	X	X			R	S	X1	X1	X	X				X	G			X	X	
3	X	X			X		X3	X	X	X				X	G			X	X	
4	X	X			X	X	X2	X	X	X				R	G			X	X	
5	X	X	S				X	R	X	X	X			X	G			X	X	
6	R	X	S		X		X1	X	X	X				X1	G			X	X	
7	X	X			X		X	X	X1	X				X	G			X	X	
8	X	X			X		X	X	X2		X				G			X	X	
9	X	X			X		X	X	X	X				X1	G			X	X	
10	X	X			X		X	X	X	X				X1	G			X		X
11	X	X1			X		X1	X	X	X				X1	G			X		X
12	X	X			R		X	X	X	X		S	S	X	G			X		X
13	X	X				X	X1	X	X	R		X			G			X	S	X
14	X	X			S		X	X	X	R		X		X	G				X	X
15	X	X	S		X		X	X	X		S	X		R	G			X	X	
16	X	X			X	S	X	X	X					X	G			X	R	
17	X	X	R		X	X	S		X				X1	X1	G			X	X	
18	X	X			X1	R	X	X	X	S2				X	G			X	X	
19	X	X			X		X	X	X	X				X	G			X	X	
20	X	X			X		X	X	X					X	G			X	X	
21	X	X	S		R		X		X	X		X	X	X1	G			X		
22	X	X	X		X			S	R			X	X	X1	G	X		X		
23	X	X	X		S			X	X					R	X	G	X		X	X
24	X	X	X				X1	X	X					X	G	X			X	
25	X1	X	X				X1	X	X					X	G	X			X	
26	X	X	X				X	X	X				X	X3p	G	X			X	
27	X	X	X				X1	X	X					X	G	X			X	
28	X	X	X				X1	X	X					X	G	X			X	
29	X	X	X		S		X2	X	X					X	G	X			R	
30	X	X	X				X1	X	X					X1	G	X	X		X	
31	X1	X	X				X	X	X					X	R	G	X	S	X	
32	X	X	X		X1	X	X3	X	X							G	X		X	
33	X	X	X		X	X1	X1	X	X							G	X		X	
34	X	X	X		X	X	X1	X				X1				G	X		X	
35	X	X	X		X	X	X	X				X				G	X		X	
36	X	X	X		X	X	X	X				X			G	X1p	X		X	
37	X	X	X		X	X	X1	X				R			S	G	X		X	
38	X	X	R		X	S	X	X	X					X	G	X			X	
39	X	X			X	X2	X	X	X					X1	G	X1			X	
40	X	X	X		X1	X	X2	X	X					X	G	R1			X	
41	X	X			X	X	X	X	X					X	G	X			X	
42	X	X			X	X	X2	X	X					X	G	X			X	
43	X	X	S		X	R	X	X	X					X	G	X			X	
44	X	X			X	X	X	X	X					X	G	X			X	
45	X	X			X	X	X	X	X					X	G	X			X	
46	X	X		G	X	X	X	X						X1		R1		S	X	
47	X	X		G	X1	X	X1	X	X					X		X1			X	
48	X	X		G	X	X1	X	X	X1					X		X			X	
49	X	X	S	G	X	X1	X	X						R		X			X	
50	X	X	X	G	X	X	X	X								X2p			X	

- 157 -

1974/75

Football League position: 23rd out of 24 in Division 3 – relegated to Division 4
Manager: Mike Keen

		HOME					AWAY					
	Pl	W	D	L	For	Ag	W	D	L	For	Ag	Pts
Blackburn Rovers	46	15	7	1	40	16	7	9	7	28	29	60
Plymouth Argyle	46	16	5	2	38	19	8	6	9	41	39	59
Charlton Athletic	46	15	5	3	51	29	7	6	10	25	32	55
Swindon Town	46	18	3	2	43	17	3	8	12	21	41	53
Crystal Palace	46	14	8	1	48	22	4	7	12	18	35	51
Port Vale	46	15	6	2	37	19	3	9	11	24	35	51
Peterborough United	46	10	9	4	24	19	9	3	11	23	36	50
Walsall	46	15	5	3	46	13	3	8	12	21	39	49
Preston North End	46	16	5	2	42	19	3	6	14	21	37	49
Gillingham	46	14	6	3	43	23	3	8	12	22	37	48
Colchester United	46	13	7	3	45	22	4	6	13	25	41	47
Hereford United	46	14	6	3	42	21	2	8	13	22	45	46
Wrexham	46	10	8	5	41	23	5	7	11	24	32	45
Bury	46	13	6	4	38	17	3	6	14	15	33	44
Chesterfield	46	11	7	5	37	25	5	5	13	25	41	44
Grimsby Town	46	12	8	3	35	19	3	5	15	20	45	43
Halifax Town	46	11	8	4	33	17	3	5	15	15	40	41
Southend United	46	11	9	3	32	17	2	7	14	14	34	42
Brighton & Hove Albion	46	14	7	2	38	21	2	3	18	18	43	42
Aldershot *	46	13	5	5	40	21	1	6	16	13	42	38
AFC Bournemouth	46	9	6	8	27	25	4	6	13	17	33	38
Tranmere Rovers	46	12	4	7	39	21	2	5	16	16	36	37
WATFORD	46	9	7	7	30	31	1	10	12	22	44	37
Huddersfield Town	46	9	6	8	32	29	2	4	17	15	47	32

* One point deducted for fielding an unregistered player

New league opponents: None

Home-and-away league doubles
For - none
Against – 5 (Charlton Athletic, Crystal Palace, Peterborough United, Walsall, Wrexham)

Relegated with Watford: AFC Bournemouth, Tranmere Rovers, Huddersfield Town

All Matches: Won 10, Drew 18, Lost 21, Goals 54-82

Highest Score: 4 (Match 18)

No	DATE			COMPETITION	OPPONENTS	HOME	AWAY	ATTENDANCE
1	August	Sat	17	Football League, Division 3	Colchester United		D 1-1	5,715
2		Wed	21	Football League Cup, 1st Round	CRYSTAL PALACE	1-1 D		10,733
3		Sat	24	Football League, Division 3	PRESTON NORTH END	3-2 W		8,918
4		Tue	27	Football Lge Cup, 1st Round replay	Crystal Palace		L 1-5	12,180
5		Sat	31	Football League, Division 3	Huddersfield Town		L 1-3	5,007
6	September	Wed	4	Football League, Division 3	Hereford United		W 1-0	7,357
7		Sat	7	Football League, Division 3	HALIFAX TOWN	2-2 D		6,050
8		Sat	14	Football League, Division 3	Brighton & Hove Albion		L 0-2	11,606
9		Tue	17	Football League, Division 3	Grimsby Town		D 2-2	5,003
10		Sat	21	Football League, Division 3	SOUTHEND UNITED	2-0 W		6,955
11		Wed	25	Football League, Division 3	GILLINGHAM	0-0 D		6,268
12		Sat	28	Football League, Division 3	Swindon Town		D 2-2	6,326
13	October	Wed	2	Football League, Division 3	HEREFORD UNITED	1-1 D		5,572
14		Sat	5	Football League, Division 3	BURY	2-1 W		6,522
15		Sat	12	Football League, Division 3	Peterborough United		L 0-1	9,747
16		Sat	19	Football League, Division 3	AFC Bournemouth		1-0 W	7,361
17		Tue	22	Football League, Division 3	Charlton Athletic		L 1-4	7,118
18		Sat	26	Football League, Division 3	Chesterfield		D 4-4	3,933
19	November	Sat	2	Football League, Division 3	ALDERSHOT	1-1 D		6,535
20		Wed	6	Football League, Division 3	CHARLTON ATHLETIC	0-2 L		6,710
21		Sat	9	Football League, Division 3	Plymouth Argyle		D 1-1	8,063
22		Sat	16	Football League, Division 3	PORT VALE	3-2 W		6,659
23		Sat	23	FA Cup, 1st Round	COLCHESTER UNITED	0-1 L		8,228
24		Sat	30	Football League, Division 3	Blackburn Rovers		D 0-0	10,247
25	December	Sat	7	Football League, Division 3	CRYSTAL PALACE	1-2 L		11,635
26		Sat	21	Football League, Division 3	Wrexham		L 1-5	4,128
27		Thu	26	Football League, Division 3	BRIGHTON & HOVE ALBION	1-1 D		6,492
28		Sat	28	Football League, Division 3	Tranmere Rovers		D 2-2	2,497
29	January	Sat	4	Football League, Division 3	GRIMSBY TOWN	3-2 W		5,668
30		Sat	11	Football League, Division 3	Crystal Palace		L 0-1	17,055
31		Sat	18	Football League, Division 3	BLACKBURN ROVERS	0-0 D		5,828
32	February	Sat	1	Football League, Division 3	PLYMOUTH ARGYLE	1-3 L		8,583
33		Sat	8	Football League, Division 3	Aldershot		L 1-3	4,776
34		Wed	19	Football League, Division 3	Walsall		L 0-2	7,177
35		Sat	22	Football League, Division 3	Port Vale		D 0-0	4,164
36		Fri	28	Football League, Division 3	HUDDERSFIELD TOWN	1-0 W		4,828
37	March	Sat	8	Football League, Division 3	Gillingham		L 1-2	7,281
38		Sat	15	Football League, Division 3	SWINDON TOWN	1-0 W		5,523
39		Wed	19	Football League, Division 3	COLCHESTER UNITED	1-2 L		3,941
40		Sat	22	Football League, Division 3	Halifax Town		L 0-2	1,872
41		Fri	28	Football League, Division 3	Southend United		D 0-0	5,924
42		Sat	29	Football League, Division 3	WREXHAM	1-2 L		4,549
43	April	Sat	5	Football League, Division 3	CHESTERFIELD	2-2 D		4,339
44		Sat	12	Football League, Division 3	Bury		L 0-1	4,514
45		Mon	14	Football League, Division 3	TRANMERE ROVERS	1-0 W		4,390
46		Sat	19	Football League, Division 3	PETERBOROUGH UNITED	0-3 L		5,785
47		Tue	22	Football League, Division 3	Preston North End		D 2-2	5,819
48		Sat	26	Football League, Division 3	AFC Bournemouth		L 2-4	4,867
49		Tue	29	Football League, Division 3	WALSALL	2-3 L		9,472

League ever-presents: K.G.A. Goodeve, A.G. Rankin
Most appearances in total: K.G.A. Goodeve & A.G. Rankin 49 out of 49   **Most goals in total:** R.A. Jenkins 11
Hat-tricks: None   **Penalty goals:** S.M.A. Scullion (4)
Sent off: B.A. Greenhalgh (Match 44)
Full international appearance(s) this season: None

	Bond, D.J.T.	Bristow, G.A.	Butler, D.	Craker, L.D.	Downes, R.D.	Garner, A.H.	Goodeve, K.G.A.	Greenhalgh, B.A.	How, T.A.	Jenkins, R.A.	Jennings, W.J.	Joslyn, R.D.W.	Keen, M.T.	Lees, W.J.	McGettigan, L.	Markham, L.S.	Mayes, A.K.	Mercer, K.	Morrissey, P.J.	Rankin, A.G.	Scullion, S.M.A.	Walsh, J.T.	Williams, J.R.
Apps	41	0	19	16	43	13	46	12	11	31	3	27	36	20	5	9	18	11	15	46	35	11	38
Subs		+2		+1						+1			+1		+6	+5	+4	+4	+2				
Goals	4		1	1	3	2	4	1		11		2	2	3		1	2	1	4		10		
Apps	3		2	3	3		3			1	2		3	1	1	0	1		2	3	2		3
Subs										+1						+1							
Goals										1									1				
1	X		X	X	X		X			X			X						X	G	X1		X
2	X		X	X	X		X			X			X						X1	G	X		X
3	X2		X	X	X		X			X			X						X1	G	X		X
4	X		X	X	X		X			S	X1		X						R	G	X		X
5	X		X		X		X			X1	X		X	X					X	G	X		X
6	X		X		X		X			R1			X	X		S			X	G	X		X
7	X		R		X		X			X1			X	X		S			X	G	X1		X
8	X		X	R	X		X			X			X	X		S			X	G	X		X
9	X		X		X		X			X1			X	X		S			X1	G	R		X
10	X		X	X	X					X1			X	X1					X	G	X		X
11	X		X	X	X		X			X			X	X					X	G	X		X
12	X		X	X	X		X			X1			X	X					X1	G	X		X
13	X		X	X	X		X			X			X	X					X	G	X1p		X
14	X		R	X1	X		X						X	X		S		X1		G	X		X
15	X		X	X	X		X			X			X	X	X			R	S	G			X
16	X		X	X	X		X			X1			X	X	X		X			G			X
17	X		X	X1	X		X						X	X	X			R	S	G			X
18	X		S	X	X		X			X1			X1	X					X1	G	R1	X	X
19	X		X	X	X		X			X			X	X1					X	G		X	X
20	X		X	R	X		X			X			X	X		S			X	G	X	X	X
21	X		R		X		X			X			X	X		X		S1	X	G		X	X
22	X		X		X		X			X1	X		X	X1	X		X1			G			X
23	X		X	X	X		R						X	X	X	S	X			G			X
24	X		X	X	X		X					X	X				X			G			X
25	X		X	X	X		X					X1	X	R		S	X			G			X
26	X	S	X	X	X		X					X1	X				X			G	R		X
27	X			X1	X		X					X	R			S	X			G	X		X
28	X	S		X	X		X1			X1			X				X		R	G	X		X
29	X			X	X1		X1			X1			X				X			G	X		X
30	X			R	X		X			X			X				X	S		G	X		X
31	X				X		X		X	R			X				X	S		G	X		X
32	X				X		X1		X				X	S			X	R	X	G	X		X
33	X1				X		X					X	X	X			X	X		G	X		X
34	X				X	X	X		X	X			X	R				S		G	X	X	
35	X				X	X	X		X				X	X				X		G	X	X	
36	X				X	X	X						X	X				X		G	X1p	X	
37	R				X	X1	X		X				X	X				S	X	G	X	X	
38	X		X		X1	X	X						X						X	G	X	X	
39	X		X		X	X	X						X					S	X	G	X1	R	
40	X		X		X	R	X						X					S	X	G	X	X	
41			X		X		X					X	X				X	X		G			X
42			X		X	X	X					X	X1				X	X		G			X
43		X1	X		X	X1	X					X	X				X	X		G			X
44		R	X		X	X	X	X				X	X				S		X	G	X		X
45			X		X	X	X	X				X	X				S		X	G	X1p		X
46	X		X		X	X	X	X				X	R				S		X	G	X		X
47	X1		X		X	X	X	X				X	R				S			G	X1		X
48	X		X		X	X	X	X				X	R				S1			G	X1		X
49	X		X		X	X1	X	S				X	R						R	G	X1p		X

1975/76

Football League position: 8th out of 24 in Division 4

Manager: Mike Keen

New league opponents: None

Home-and-away league doubles
For – 6 (Doncaster Rovers, Exeter City, Newport County, Scunthorpe United, Southport, Workington)
Against – 3 (Huddersfield Town, Lincoln City, Northampton Town)

Divisional changes at end of season: Lincoln City, Northampton Town, Reading & Tranmere Rovers to Division 3; Aldershot, Colchester United, Southend United & Halifax Town from Division 3

All Matches: Won 23, Drew 7, Lost 20, Goals 65-67

Highest Score: 3 (Matches 25, 35, 39, 40, 45 & 49)

		HOME						AWAY					
	Pl	W	D	L	For	Ag	W	D	L	For	Ag	Pts
Lincoln City	46	21	2	0	71	15	11	8	4	40	24	74
Northampton Town	46	18	5	0	62	20	11	5	7	25	20	68
Reading	46	19	3	1	42	9	5	9	9	28	42	60
Tranmere Rovers	46	18	3	2	61	16	6	7	10	28	39	58
Huddersfield Town	46	11	6	6	28	17	10	8	5	28	24	56
AFC Bournemouth	46	15	5	3	39	16	5	7	11	18	32	52
Exeter City	46	13	7	3	37	17	5	7	11	19	30	50
WATFORD	46	16	4	3	38	18	6	2	15	24	44	50
Torquay United	46	12	6	5	31	24	6	8	9	24	39	50
Doncaster Rovers	46	10	6	7	42	31	9	5	9	33	38	49
Swansea City	46	14	8	1	51	21	2	7	14	15	36	47
Barnsley	46	12	8	3	34	16	2	8	13	18	32	44
Cambridge United	46	7	10	6	36	28	7	5	11	22	34	43
Hartlepool	46	10	6	7	37	29	6	4	13	25	49	42
Rochdale	46	7	11	5	27	23	5	7	11	13	31	42
Crewe Alexandra	46	10	7	6	36	21	3	8	12	22	36	41
Bradford City	46	9	7	7	35	26	3	10	10	28	39	41
Brentford	46	12	7	4	37	18	2	6	15	19	42	41
Scunthorpe United	46	11	3	9	31	24	3	7	13	19	35	38
Darlington	46	11	7	5	30	14	3	3	17	18	43	38
Stockport County	46	8	7	8	23	23	5	5	9	22	45	38
Newport County	46	8	7	8	35	33	5	2	16	22	57	35
Southport	46	6	6	11	27	31	2	4	17	14	46	26
Workington	46	5	4	14	19	43	2	3	18	11	44	21

No	DATE			COMPETITION	OPPONENTS	HOME	AWAY	ATTENDANCE
1	August	Sat	16	Football League, Division 4	Barnsley		L 0-1	3,690
2		Tue	19	Football Lge Cup, 1st Round, 1st Leg	NORTHAMPTON TOWN	2-0 W		3,368
3		Sat	23	Football League, Division 4	HUDDERSFIELD TOWN	0-2 L		4,500
4		Wed	27	Football Lge Cup, 1st Round, 2nd Leg	Northampton Town		D 1-1	4,255
5		Sat	30	Football League, Division 4	Darlington		L 0-1	2,988
6	September	Sat	6	Football League, Division 4	HARTLEPOOL	2-1 W		3,598
7		Tue	9	Football League Cup, 2nd Round	TOTTENHAM HOTSPUR	0-1 L		14,997
8		Sat	13	Football League, Division 4	Reading		L 0-3	5,521
9		Sat	20	Football League, Division 4	DONCASTER ROVERS	2-1 W		4,228
10		Tue	23	Football League, Division 4	Cambridge United		L 1-4	3,234
11		Sat	27	Football League, Division 4	Bradford City		L 0-1	2,308
12	October	Sat	4	Football League, Division 4	STOCKPORT COUNTY	1-1 D		4,143
13		Sat	11	Football League, Division 4	WORKINGTON	2-0 W		3,872
14		Sat	18	Football League, Division 4	Rochdale		L 1-2	1,528
15		Tue	21	Football League, Division 4	SCUNTHORPE UNITED	1-0 W		3,581
16		Sat	25	Football League, Division 4	CREWE ALEXANDRA	2-1 W		4,262
17	November	Sat	1	Football League, Division 4	Northampton Town		L 0-3	6,656
18		Tue	4	Football League, Division 4	Southport		W 2-1	1,046
19		Sat	8	Football League, Division 4	AFC BOURNEMOUTH	1-1 D		4,714
20		Sat	15	Football League, Division 4	Brentford		L 0-1	6,930
21		Sat	22	FA Cup, 1st Round	BRIGHTON & HOVE ALBION	0-3 L		9,283
22		Fri	28	Football League, Division 4	Tranmere Rovers		L 0-3	3,473
23	December	Sat	6	Football League, Division 4	LINCOLN CITY	1-3 L		4,178
24		Fri	12	Football League, Division 4	Stockport County		D 2-2	5,055
25		Sat	20	Football League, Division 4	NEWPORT COUNTY	3-1 W		3,271
26		Fri	26	Football League, Division 4	Swansea City		L 2-4	4,091
27		Sat	27	Football League, Division 4	EXETER CITY	2-0 W		5,055
28	January	Sat	3	Football League, Division 4	Torquay United		L 0-1	2,515
29		Sat	10	Football League, Division 4	DARLINGTON	2-0 W		3,865
30		Sat	17	Football League, Division 4	Doncaster Rovers		W 2-1	5,845
31		Sat	24	Football League, Division 4	READING	2-1 W		6,644
32	February	Sat	7	Football League, Division 4	SOUTHPORT	2-0 W		4,334
33		Tue	10	Football League, Division 4	Scunthorpe United		W 1-0	2,200
34		Sat	14	Football League, Division 4	AFC Bournemouth		L 1-4	4,897
35		Sat	21	Football League, Division 4	BRENTFORD	3-2 W		6,223
36		Tue	24	Football League, Division 4	CAMBRIDGE UNITED	1-0 W		4,888
37	March	Wed	3	Football League, Division 4	Crewe Alexandra		D 2-2	2,068
38		Sat	6	Football League, Division 4	NORTHAMPTON TOWN	0-1 L		7,389
39		Sat	13	Football League, Division 4	Workington		W 3-1	1,209
40		Tue	16	Football League, Division 4	ROCHDALE	3-0 W		3,886
41		Sat	20	Football League, Division 4	TRANMERE ROVERS	2-2 D		5,449
42		Fri	26	Football League, Division 4	Lincoln City		L 1-5	8,798
43		Wed	31	Football League, Division 4	Newport County		W 2-0	1,092
44	April	Sat	3	Football League, Division 4	BARNSLEY	1-0 W		4,203
45		Tue	6	Football League, Division 4	BRADFORD CITY	3-0 W		3,745
46		Sat	10	Football League, Division 4	Hartlepool		L 1-2	1,993
47		Fri	16	Football League, Division 4	TORQUAY UNITED	0-0 D		5,436
48		Sat	17	Football League, Division 4	SWANSEA CITY	2-1 W		4,536
49		Mon	19	Football League, Division 4	Exeter City		W 3-1	2,489
50		Sat	24	Football League, Division 4	Huddersfield Town		L 0-1	3,787

League ever-presents: None
Most appearances in total: A.G. Rankin 47 out of 50   **Most goals in total:** R.A. Jenkins 19
Hat-tricks: K. Mercer (Match 49)   **Penalty goals:** D.J.T. Bond 5, S.M.A. Scullion 1
Sent off: None
Full international appearance(s) this season: None

	Akers, V.D. //	Blissett, L.L.	Bond, D.J.T.	Bristow, G.A.	Butler, D. //	Coffill, P.T.	Downes, R.D.	Garner, A.H.	Gibbs, P.L.	Goodeve, K.G.A. //	Greenhalgh, B.A. //	Horsfield, A.	How, T.A.	Jenkins, R.A.	Joslyn, R.D.W.	Lees, W.J.	McCarthy, K.J.	Mayes, A.K.	Mercer, K.	Rankin, A.G.	Scullion, S.M.A. //	Walsh, J.T.
Apps	22	1	39	18	2	29	28	43	3	21	5	41	32	39	16	16	28	11	12	43	24	33
Subs		+2	+1	+2		+1	+2				+1		+1	+1	+3	+2		+3	+11			
Goals		1	10			3	2					12	1	19		1	1		10			2
Apps	4		4		1		3	3		3	2	1	3	4	4	2		2	1	4	2	1
Subs											+1							+1				
Goals							1			1	1											
1	X		X			X	X			X	X		X	X	X				X	G		
2	X		X			X1	X			X	X1		X	X	X				X	G		
3	X		X			X	X			X	X		X	X	R			X	S	G		
4	X		X			X	X			X1	X		X	X	X				X	G		
5	X		X			X	X			X	R		X	X	X	S			X	G		
6	X	X1		X		X				X				X	X	X			X1	G		X
7	X	X		R		X				X				X	X	X		S	X	G		X
8	R		X	X		X				X		X		S	X	X			X	G		R
9	X		X				X	X		X		X1		X1	X					G	X	X
10	X		X				R	X		X		X		X1	S	X				G	X	X
11	X		X				X	X		X		X		X	X				X	G		X
12	X		X		X		X			X			R	X1	X				S	G	X	X
13	X	X1				R	S	X		X		X		X	X					G	X1p	X
14	X		X				X	X		X		X		X1	X					G	X	X
15	X		X				X	X		X		X		X1	X					G	X	X
16	R		X				X	X		X		X1		X	X1	S				G	X	X
17	X		R				X	X		X		X		X	S	X				G	X	X
18	X							X		X		X1	X	X1	X			X		G	X	X
19	X		X					X		X		X		X1			R	S		G	X	X
20	X		X					X		X		X		X		X	S		X	G	X	R
21	X		X							X		S	X	X	X	X	X			G	X	R
22	X					X	X			R		X	X	X	X		X	S		G		
23	X					X						X	X	X1	X		X			G	X	
24	X					X				S		R1	X	X1	X		X			G	X	
25	X					X						X1	X	X2	X	X	X			G	X	
26	X	S				X						X1	X1	X	X	X				G	R	
27			X2p	X			X	X		X		X	X	X			X			G		
28			X	X	S		X	X		X		X	X	R			X			G	X	
29			X	X			X	X		X		X1	X	X			X			G	X1	
30			X	X			X			X		X2	X	X			X			G	X	X
31			X	X			R	X		X		X1	X	X1			X		S	G	X	X
32			X	X			X	X		X		X	X	X			R		S2	G	X	X
33			X1	X			X	X		X		R	X	X			X			G	X	X
34			X1p	X			X	X		X		R	X	X			X			G	X	X
35			X	X		R	X1	X		X1		X		X			X			G		X
36			X	X		X1		X		X		X		X			X			G		X
37			X2#	X		X	X	X		X		X		X			X			G		X
38			X	R		X	X	X		X		X		X			X		S	G		X
39			X	X		X	X					X	X	X2			R	S	X1	G		X
40			X	X		X	R					X		X	X2				X1	G		X
41			X	X		X1	X	X				X		R1			X			G	S	X
42			X			X	X	X				X		X		X	X		X1	G		X
43			X	S		R	X1	X				X		X1			X		X	G		X
44	S		X1p			R	X	X				X		X			X		X	G		X
45	S		X1			X	R	X				X		X1			X		X1	G		X
46			X	X		X	X	X				X		X		S	X		X1	G		R
47			X	X		R	X	X				X		S			X	X	X	G	X	X
48	X1		X			X1	S	X	G	X		X						X	R		X	X
49			X			X	X	X	G			X		X			X		X3		X	X
50			S			X	R	X	G			X		X			X	X	X			X

- 161 -

1976/77

Football League position: 7th out of 24 in Division 4
Manager: Mike Keen (Matches 1–47)

	HOME						AWAY					
	Pl	W	D	L	For	Ag	W	D	L	For	Ag	Pts
Cambridge United	46	16	5	2	57	18	10	8	5	30	22	65
Exeter City	46	17	5	1	40	13	8	7	8	30	33	62
Colchester United	46	19	2	2	51	14	6	7	10	26	29	59
Bradford City	46	16	7	0	51	18	6	10	7	33	59	59
Swansea City	46	18	3	2	60	30	7	5	11	32	38	58
Barnsley	46	16	5	2	45	18	7	4	12	17	21	55
WATFORD	46	15	7	1	46	13	8	3	12	21	37	51
Doncaster Rovers	46	16	2	5	47	25	5	7	11	24	40	51
Huddersfield Town	46	15	5	3	36	15	4	7	12	24	34	50
Southend United	46	11	9	3	35	19	4	10	9	17	26	49
Darlington	46	13	5	5	37	25	5	8	10	22	39	49
Crewe Alexandra	46	10	6	1	36	15	3	5	15	11	45	49
AFC Bournemouth	46	13	8	2	39	13	2	10	11	15	31	48
Stockport County	46	10	10	3	29	19	3	14	20	40		48
Brentford	46	14	3	6	48	27	4	4	15	29	49	43
Torquay United	46	12	5	6	33	22	5	4	14	26	43	43
Aldershot	46	10	8	5	29	19	6	3	14	20	40	43
Rochdale	46	8	7	8	32	25	5	5	13	18	34	38
Newport County	46	11	6	6	33	21	3	4	16	9	37	38
Scunthorpe United	46	11	6	6	32	24	2	5	16	17	49	36
Halifax Town	46	11	6	6	36	18	0	8	15	11	40	36
Hartlepool	46	8	9	6	30	20	2	3	18	17	53	32
Southport	46	3	12	8	17	28	0	7	16	16	49	25
Workington	46	3	7	13	23	42	1	4	18	18	60	19

New league opponents: None

Home-and-away league doubles
For – 3 (Southport, Swansea City, Workington)
Against – 1 (Brentford)

Divisional changes at end of season: Cambridge United, Exeter City, Colchester United & Bradford City to Division 3; Reading, Northampton Town, Grimsby Town & York City from Division 3; Wimbledon elected in place of Workington

All Matches: Won 22, Drew 16, Lost 15, Goals 80-60

Highest Score: 5 (Match 42)

No	DATE			COMPETITION	OPPONENTS	HOME	AWAY	ATTENDANCE
1	August	Sat	14	Football Lge Cup, 1st Round, 1st Leg	BRENTFORD	1-1 D		4,827
2		Tue	17	Football Lge Cup, 1st Round, 2nd Leg	Brentford		W 2-0	5,540
3		Sat	21	Football League, Division 4	Southend United		L 1-2	5,267
4		Tue	24	Football League, Division 4	HARTLEPOOL	4-0 W		4,667
5		Sat	28	Football League, Division 4	SCUNTHORPE UNITED	2-1 W		5,001
6		Tue	31	Football League Cup, 2nd Round	Crystal Palace		W 3-1	14,105
7	September	Sat	4	Football League, Division 4	Cambridge United		L 0-4	4,403
8		Sat	11	Football League, Division 4	COLCHESTER UNITED	2-1 W		5,386
9		Sat	18	Football League, Division 4	Rochdale		L 1-3	1,760
10		Tue	21	Football League Cup, 3rd Round	Sheffield Wednesday		L 1-3	15,787
11		Sat	25	Football League, Division 4	EXETER CITY	4-1 W		5,079
12	October	Sat	2	Football League, Division 4	HALIFAX TOWN	0-0 D		4,353
13		Sat	9	Football League, Division 4	Crewe Alexandra		L 0-2	2,684
14		Sat	16	Football League, Division 4	AFC BOURNEMOUTH	1-1 D		5,697
15		Sat	23	Football League, Division 4	Workington		W 1-0	1,623
16		Tue	26	Football League, Division 4	Huddersfield Town		D 2-2	5,299
17		Sat	30	Football League, Division 4	BARNSLEY	1-0 W		5,313
18	November	Tue	2	Football League, Division 4	ALDERSHOT	1-1 D		5,228
19		Sat	6	Football League, Division 4	Torquay United		L 1-3	2,593
20		Sat	20	FA Cup, 1st Round	Gillingham		W 1-0	6,818
21		Sat	27	Football League, Division 4	Bradford City		D 0-0	4,316
22	December	Sat	4	Football League, Division 4	SWANSEA CITY	2-0 W		4,595
23		Sat	11	FA Cup, 2nd Round	Hillingdon Borough		W 3-2	5,042
24		Sat	18	Football League, Division 4	Darlington		D 0-0	2,887
25		Mon	27	Football League, Division 4	STOCKPORT COUNTY	1-1 D		8,229
26	January	Sat	1	Football League, Division 4	TORQUAY UNITED	4-0 W		6,824
27		Sat	8	FA Cup, 3rd Round	Northwich Victoria		L 2-3	8,989
28		Tue	11	Football League, Division 4	NEWPORT COUNTY	2-0 W		4,600
29		Sat	15	Football League, Division 4	Hartlepool		L 0-1	2,391
30		Sat	22	Football League, Division 4	SOUTHEND UNITED	1-1 D		6,994
31		Sat	29	Football League, Division 4	Southport		W 3-1	1,443
32	February	Sat	5	Football League, Division 4	Scunthorpe United		D 0-0	3,201
33		Sat	12	Football League, Division 4	CAMBRIDGE UNITED	2-0 W		8,417
34		Sat	19	Football League, Division 4	Colchester United		L 0-1	5,628
35		Sat	26	Football League, Division 4	ROCHDALE	3-1 W		6,331
36	March	Sat	5	Football League, Division 4	Exeter City		D 2-2	5,867
37		Wed	9	Football League, Division 4	Barnsley		D 1-1	7,429
38		Sat	12	Football League, Division 4	Halifax Town		D 1-1	1,902
39		Sat	19	Football League, Division 4	CREWE ALEXANDRA	3-1 W		6,399
40		Wed	23	Football League, Division 4	Brentford		L 0-3	7,600
41		Sat	26	Football League, Division 4	AFC Bournemouth		L 1-2	4,445
42		Tue	29	Football League, Division 4	DONCASTER ROVERS	5-1 W		5,476
43	April	Sat	2	Football League, Division 4	WORKINGTON	2-0 W		6,487
44		Sat	9	Football League, Division 4	BRENTFORD	0-1 L		9,382
45		Mon	11	Football League, Division 4	Stockport County		D 2-2	2,536
46		Tue	12	Football League, Division 4	Aldershot		L 1-2	4,043
47		Sat	16	Football League, Division 4	HUDDERSFIELD TOWN	2-0 W		6,181
48		Tue	19	Football League, Division 4	SOUTHPORT	2-0 W		5,814
49		Sat	23	Football League, Division 4	Doncaster Rovers		L 0-1	4,476
50		Sat	30	Football League, Division 4	BRADFORD CITY	1-1 D		6,147
51	May	Tue	3	Football League, Division 4	Newport County		L 0-3	2,218
52		Sat	7	Football League, Division 4	Swansea City		W 4-1	11,084
53		Sat	14	Football League, Division 4	DARLINGTON	1-1 D		6,142

League ever-presents: A.H. Garner, K. Mercer
Most appearances in total: A.H. Garner 53 out of 53   **Most goals in total:** K. Mercer 25
Hat-tricks: R.A. Jenkins (Match 4)   **Penalty goals:** D.J.T. Bond 4
Sent off: A.J. Geidmintis (Match 41 & Match 47), A.K. Mayes (Match 47)
Full international appearance(s) this season: None

	Blissett, L.L.	Bond, D.J.T.	Bristow, G.A.	Coffill, P.T.	Craker, L.D.	Downes, R.D.	Eades, T.G.	Garner, A.H.	Geidmintis, A.J.	Gibbs, P.L.	Horsfield, A.	How, T.A.	Jenkins, R.A.	Joslyn, R.D.W.	McCarthy, K.J.	Mayes, A.K.	Mercer, K.	Poole, R.J.	Pritchett, K.B.	Rankin, A.G.	Sherwood, S.	Walley, J.T.	Walsh, J.T.	Own goal
Apps	1	44	0	23	9	35	4	46	32	1	37	16	22	37	6	40	46	3	32	37	8	12	15	
Subs	+3		+1	+4					+1				+13		+1	+3		+4				+1	+2	
Goals		5		2	1	2		2			4		10	3		14	22	1						1
Apps		6		3	1	6		7	6		4	4	3	7	2	4	4	2	3	7		4	4	
Subs				+1									+1			+1	+2							
Goals		3		1									1	2		3	3							

Match	Blissett	Bond	Bristow	Coffill	Craker	Downes	Eades	Garner	Geidmintis	Gibbs	Horsfield	How	Jenkins	Joslyn	McCarthy	Mayes	Mercer	Poole	Pritchett	Rankin	Sherwood	Walley	Walsh	Own goal
1		X1		X		X		X			X	X	X	X	R		S			G		X	X	
2				X				X	X		X		X1	X	X		X1			G		X	X	
3		X		X	X		S				X	X	R	X			X1			G		X	X	
4		X	X	X		X					X		X3	R			S	X1		G		X	X	
5		X	X	X		X				R	X			X1		S1	X			G		X	X	
6		X	S	X		X		X			X			X1		X2		R		G		X	X	
7	S	X		R		X		X	X	G	X			X		X	X					X	X	
8		R	X	X				X1			X			X		X1	X	S		G		X	X	
9	S		X								X			X1	R	X	X	X		G		X	X	
10		X			X			X	R		X			X1		X	S	X		G		X	X	
11		X1p	S	X	X	X					X			X1		X1	X	R1		G			X	
12		X		X	X	X					X			X		X	X	X		G			X	
13		X		X	R	X					X			X		X	X	S		G			X	
14				X	X	X	X1						X	X		X	X			G			X	
15		X			X			X			X		X	X		X	X1			G				
16		X			X1			X	X		X1			X		X	X			G				
17		X			X			X	X		X		R	X1	X	S	X			G				
18		X		S	X			X	X		X			X		X	X1	R		G			X	
19	X	S			R			X	X		X			X		X	X	X1	X	G				
20		X			X	X		X	X		X			X			X1		X	G				
21		X			X	X		X	X		X					S	X	R	X	G				
22		X	R		X	X		X			X						X1	X1	S	G				
23		X1p		X1		R		X	X		X			S		X	X	X1	X	G				
24		X		X		X		X	X		X			S	R	X	X		X	G				
25		X		X1		R		X	X		X			S	S	X	X		X	G				
26		X1	R		X			X	X		X1			X		X	S1	X1	X	G				
27		X1	R		X			X	X		X			X	X		S	X1	X	G				
28		X1	R		X			X	X		X			S	X		X	X1	X	G				
29		X			X			X	X		X			S	X		X	X	X	G	R			
30		X	X		X			X	X		X			S			X1	R	X	G				
31		X	R		X			X	X		X			S			X2	X1	X	G				
32		X	X		X			X	X		X						X	X	X	G				
33		X	R		X			X	X		X			S1	X		X	X1	X	G				
34		X	R		X			X	X		X			S	X		X	X	X	G				
35		X1p			X			X	X		X			X	X		X	X2	X	G				
36		X			X			X	X		X			X	X		X1	X1	X	G				
37		X			X			X	X		X			X	X		X	X1	X	G				
38		R			X1			X	X		X			X	X		X	X	X	G	S			
39		X			S1			X	X		X		X1	R			X1	X	X	G				
40		X			X			X	X		X			X			X	X1	X	G			X	
41		X						X	X		X		X1	X		X	X	R	X	G		S	X	
42		X1p			X1			X	X		X		X2				X	X1	X	G		S	X	
43	S	X			X			X	X		X1		X				X	R1	X	G				
44		R			X			X	X		X		X		X		X	X	X	G	S	X	X	
45		X	R		X			X	X		X			S			X1	X1	X	G		X		
46		X	R		X			X	X				S				X	X1	X		G	X		
47		X	X		X			X	X								X	X2	X		G	X		
48		X	X		X			X			X	X	S1				R	X1	X		G	X		
49		X			R			X			X		S				X	X	X		G	X		
50		X	X		X			X			X		X	X				X1	X		G		X	
51		X	X		X			X			X		X	X				X	X		G		X	
52		X			X			X			X	X	X1	X			X2	R1	X		G	S		
53	X	X		S	X			X			X	X		R			X	X	X		G			1

1977/78

Football League position: 1st out of 24 in Division 4 – promoted to Division 3
Manager: Graham Taylor

New league opponents: Wimbledon

Home-and-away league doubles
For – 10 (AFC Bournemouth, Doncaster Rovers, Hartlepool United, Northampton Town, Reading, Rochdale, Scunthorpe United, Stockport County, Torquay United, Wimbledon)
Against – none

Promoted with Watford: Southend United, Swansea City, Brentford

All Matches: Won 35, Drew 11, Lost 8, Goals 98-43

Highest Score: 6 (Match 35)

		HOME					AWAY					
	Pl	W	D	L	For	Ag	W	D	L	For	Ag	Pts
WATFORD	46	18	4	1	44	14	12	7	4	41	24	71
Southend United	46	15	5	3	46	18	10	5	8	20	21	60
Swansea City	46	16	5	2	54	17	7	5	11	33	30	56
Brentford	46	15	6	2	50	17	8		9	36	37	56
Aldershot	46	15	8	0	45	16	4	8	11	22	31	54
Grimsby Town	46	14	6	3	30	15	7	5	11	27	36	53
Barnsley	46	15	4	4	44	20	3	10	10	17	29	50
Reading	46	12	7	4	33	23	6	7	10	22	29	50
Torquay United	46	12	6	5	43	25	4	9	10	14	31	47
Northampton Town	46	9	8	6	32	30	8	5	10	31	38	47
Huddersfield Town	46	13	5	5	41	21	2	10	11	22	34	45
Doncaster Rovers	46	11	8	4	37	26	3	3	17	17	55	45
Wimbledon	46	8	11	4	39	26	6	5	12	27	41	44
Scunthorpe United	46	12	6	5	31	14	2	10	11	19	41	44
Crewe Alexandra	46	11	8	4	34	25	4	6	13	16	44	44
Newport County	46	14	6	3	43	22	2	5	16	22	51	43
AFC Bournemouth	46	12	6	5	28	20	2	9	12	13	31	43
Stockport County	46	14	4	5	41	19	2	6	15	15	37	42
Darlington	46	10	8	5	31	22	4	5	14	21	37	41
Halifax Town	46	7	10	6	28	23	3	11	9	24	39	41
Hartlepool United	46	12	4	7	34	29	3	3	17	17	55	37
York City	46	8	7	8	27	31	4	5	14	23	38	36
Southport	46	5	13	5	30	32	1	6	16	24	44	31
Rochdale	46	8	6	9	29	28	0	2	21	14	57	24

No	DATE			COMPETITION	OPPONENTS	HOME	AWAY	ATTENDANCE
1	August	Sat	13	Football Lge Cup, 1st Round, 1st Leg	READING	2-1 W		5,722
2		Wed	17	Football Lge Cup, 1st Round, 2nd Leg	Reading		L 0-1	4,533
3		Sat	20	Football League, Division 4	Stockport County		W 3-1	3,056
4		Tue	23	Football Lge Cup, 1st Round replay	READING	5-0 W		7,082
5		Sat	27	Football League, Division 4	YORK CITY	1-3 L		7,620
6		Tue	30	Football League Cup, 2nd Round	Grimsby Town		W 2-1	4,345
7	September	Sat	3	Football League, Division 4	Doncaster Rovers		W 1-0	2,963
8		Tue	6	Football League, Division 4	GRIMSBY TOWN	1-0 W		6,850
9		Sat	10	Football League, Division 4	HUDDERSFIELD TOWN	2-0 W		7,852
10		Wed	14	Football League, Division 4	Reading		W 3-1	4,862
11		Sat	17	Football League, Division 4	Barnsley		L 0-1	6,443
12		Sat	24	Football League, Division 4	DARLINGTON	2-1 W		7,632
13		Tue	27	Football League, Division 4	AFC BOURNEMOUTH	2-1 W		8,191
14	October	Sat	1	Football League, Division 4	Rochdale		W 3-2	1,278
15		Mon	3	Football League, Division 4	Brentford		W 3-0	14,500
16		Sat	8	Football League, Division 4	SWANSEA CITY	2-1 W		10,232
17		Sat	15	Football League, Division 4	Aldershot		L 0-1	8,059
18		Sat	22	Football League, Division 4	NEWPORT COUNTY	2-0 W		10,749
19		Tue	25	Football League Cup, 3rd Round	West Bromwich Albion		L 0-1	22,140
20		Sat	29	Football League, Division 4	CREWE ALEXANDRA	5-2 W		10,871
21	November	Sat	5	Football League, Division 4	Hartlepool United		W 2-1	3,121
22		Sat	12	Football League, Division 4	SCUNTHORPE UNITED	4-1 W		10,565
23		Sat	19	Football League, Division 4	Southend United		L 0-1	10,919
24		Sat	26	FA Cup, 1st Round	HENDON	2-0 W		11,825
25	December	Sat	3	Football League, Division 4	HALIFAX TOWN	1-1 D		9,329
26		Sat	10	Football League, Division 4	Southport		D 2-2	1,727
27		Sat	17	FA Cup, 2nd Round	COLCHESTER UNITED	2-0 W		11,907
28		Mon	26	Football League, Division 4	NORTHAMPTON TOWN	3-0 W		15,056
29		Tue	27	Football League, Division 4	Torquay United		W 3-2	6,228
30		Sat	31	Football League, Division 4	Wimbledon		W 3-1	7,324
31	January	Mon	2	Football League, Division 4	HARTLEPOOL UNITED	1-0 W		16,866
32		Sat	7	FA Cup, 3rd Round	West Ham United		L 0-1	36,475
33		Fri	13	Football League, Division 4	STOCKPORT COUNTY	1-0 W		12,754
34		Sat	21	Football League, Division 4	York City		W 4-0	3,831
35		Sat	28	Football League, Division 4	DONCASTER ROVERS	6-0 W		11,816
36	February	Sat	11	Football League, Division 4	BARNSLEY	0-0 D		13,216
37		Sat	25	Football League, Division 4	ROCHDALE	1-0 W		10,139
38	March	Fri	3	Football League, Division 4	Swansea City	D 3-3		15,000
39		Tue	7	Football League, Division 4	READING	1-0 W		11,439
40		Sat	11	Football League, Division 4	ALDERSHOT	1-0 W		12,641
41		Tue	14	Football League, Division 4	Huddersfield Town		L 0-1	6,603
42		Fri	17	Football League, Division 4	Newport County		D 2-2	8,409
43		Fri	24	Football League, Division 4	Crewe Alexandra		D 2-2	4,652
44		Sat	25	Football League, Division 4	TORQUAY UNITED	1-0 W		10,491
45		Tue	28	Football League, Division 4	Northampton Town		W 2-0	8,041
46	April	Sat	1	Football League, Division 4	WIMBLEDON	2-0 W		11,212
47		Tue	4	Football League, Division 4	AFC Bournemouth		W 2-1	6,532
48		Sat	8	Football League, Division 4	Scunthorpe United		W 1-0	5,202
49		Tue	11	Football League, Division 4	Grimsby Town		D 1-1	7,189
50		Sat	15	Football League, Division 4	SOUTHEND UNITED	1-1 D		18,947
51		Tue	18	Football League, Division 4	Darlington		D 0-0	2,407
52		Sat	22	Football League, Division 4	Halifax Town		D 1-1	3,542
53		Tue	25	Football League, Division 4	BRENTFORD	1-1 D		16,544
54		Sat	29	Football League, Division 4	SOUTHPORT	3-2 W		10,089

League ever-presents: R.D. Downes (including two substitute appearances), A.H. Garner
Most appearances in total: R.D. Downes (including three substitute appearances) & A.H. Garner 54 out of 54   **Most goals in total:** R.A. Jenkins 18
Hat-tricks: K. Mercer (Match 20), A.K. Mayes (Match 34)   **Penalty goals:** S. Ellis 4, K.B. Pritchett 4
Sent off: I.R. Bolton (Match 49)
Full international appearance(s) this season: None

Summary totals (top block):

	Allder, D.S.	Blissett, L.L.	Bolton, I.R.	Bond, D.J.T.	Booth, D.	Coffill, P.T.	Downes, R.D.	Ellis, S.	Garner, A.H.	Geidmintis, A.J.	How, T.A.	Jenkins, R.A.	Joslyn, R.D.W.	McCarthy, K.J.	McClenaghan, A.	Mayes, A.K.	Mercer, K.	Pollard, B.E.	Pritchett, K.B.	Rankin, A.G.	Sherwood, S.	Svarc, R.L.	Walsh, J.T.
Apps	1	17	44	5	31	4	44	27	46	16	18	38	43	1	2	36	17	24	45	30	16	1	0
Subs		+16				+2	+2	+1								+5	+2	+2					+2
Goals		6	6		1		9	4	7		1	16	4			15	9	3	4				
Apps		3	8	2	3	1	7	6	8	6	1	7	7			5	7	1	8	2	6		
Subs						+1	+1									+3	+1						
Goals			1			1	1	1	1			2	1			1	4		1				

Match-by-match grid (X = start, R = substituted, S = substitute used, G = goalkeeper, numerals = goals, p = penalty, # = sent off):

Match	Allder	Blissett	Bolton	Bond	Booth	Coffill	Downes	Ellis	Garner	Geidmintis	How	Jenkins	Joslyn	McCarthy	McClenaghan	Mayes	Mercer	Pollard	Pritchett	Rankin	Sherwood	Svarc	Walsh
1			X	X		X	X	X	X	X						X	X2		X	G			
2			X	X		S	X	X	X			R	X			X	X		X	G			
3			X	R		S	X1p	X	X			X2	X			X	X		X	G			
4			X			X1	X1p	X	X			X	X1			X1	X		X1	G			
5			X	R		S	X	X	X			X	X			X1	X		X	G			
6			X1			S	X	X	X	X		X1	X			X	R		X	G			
7			X			S	X	X	X	X		X1	X			X	R		X	G			
8		X1	X			R	X	X	X	X		X	X			S			X	G			
9		X	X			R	X	X	X	X		X2	X			S			X	G			
10		X1	X			R	X	X	X	X		X	X			S2			X	G			
11		X	X				X	X	X	X		R	X			X			X	G		S	
12		X1	X			S	X	X1p	X	X					X	X			X	G		R	
13		X	X1			X1	X	X	X	R			X			X			X	G		S	
14	R	X	X				X	X	X		X	X1				X1	S1		X	G			
15			X				X	X1	X		X	X1	X			X1	X		X		G		
16			X				X1	X	X		X	X	X			X	X1		X		G		
17		S	X				X	X	X		X	X	X			R	X		X		G		
18		S	X				X1	X	X		X	X	X			R	X1		X		G		
19	X	X					X	X	X		X	R				S	X		X	G			
20	X	X					X1	X	X1		X	X	X				X3		X	G			
21	X	X			X		X	X	X1			X	X				X1		X	G			
22	X	X			X		X	X	X			X2	X				X2		X	G			
23	S	X			X		R	X	X			X	X				X	X	X	G			
24	R	X			X		X	X	X1			X	X			S	X1		X	G			
25		X			X		X	X	X1			X	X				X	X	X	G			
26		X			X		R	X	X			X1	X			S	X	X1	X	G			
27		X			X		X	X	X			X1	X			S	R1	X	X	G			
28		X			X		X1	X	X			X	X			X1		X1	X	G			
29	S	X1			X		X	X	X			X	X			X2		R	X	G			
30	S	X			X		X1	X	X			X1	R			X1		X		G			
31	S	X1			X		X	X	X			X	X			X		R	X	G			
32	X	X			X		R	X	X			X	X			X		S	X	G			
33		X			X		X	X	X1			X	X			X		X	X		G		
34	X1	X			X		X	X	X			X	X			X3		X	X		G		
35	S	X1			X		X1	R	X1			X1	X2			X		X	X		G		
36	S	X			X		X		X		X	R	X			X		X	X		G		
37		X			X		X		X			X	X1			X	X		X		G		
38	S	X1			X		R		X			X	X1			X1		X	X		G		
39	X	X			X		X	S	X1		R					X		X	X		G		
40	S	X			X		X1	X	X			X				X		R	X		G		
41	S	X			X		X	X	X			X	X			X		R	X		G		
42	X	X			X		X1	X	X			X1				X			X		G		
43	R	X			X		X	X1p	X			X1	X			X		S	X		G		
44		X			X		X	X	X1			X	X			X			X		G		
45	S	X1			X		X	R	X			X	X			X1			X		G		
46	S	X		R			X		X		X	X				X1		X	X1p		G		
47		X			X		X1		X		X	X	X			X		X1	X		G		
48	S	X			X		X		X		X	X	X1			R		X	X		G		
49		X			X		X		X		R	X				X		S	X1p		G		
50	S				X		X		X		X	X1	X			X		X	R		G		
51	X	X			X		X		X		X	R	X			S			X		G		
52	S			X	X		X		X	X1			R	X	X	X			X		G		
53	X1	X	X	X	X		X		X	X						X	R	S	X		G		
54	X1	X	X	X	X		X		X						X	X		X	X2#		G		

1978/79

Football League position: 2nd out of 24 in Division 3 – promoted to Division 2
Manager: Graham Taylor

		HOME					AWAY					
	Pl	W	D	L	For	Ag	W	D	L	For	Ag	Pts
Shrewsbury Town	46	14	9	0	36	11	7	10	6	25	30	61
WATFORD	46	15	5	3	47	22	9	7	7	36	30	60
Swansea City	46	16	6	1	57	32	8	6	9	26	29	60
Gillingham	46	15	7	1	39	15	6	10	7	26	27	59
Swindon Town	46	17	2	4	44	14	8	5	10	30	38	57
Carlisle United	46	11	10	2	31	13	4	12	7	22	29	52
Colchester United	46	13	9	1	35	19	4	8	11	25	36	51
Hull City	46	12	9	2	36	14	7	2	14	30	47	49
Exeter City	46	14	6	3	38	18	3	9	11	23	38	49
Brentford	46	14	4	5	35	19	5	5	13	18	30	47
Oxford United	46	10	8	5	27	20	4	10	9	17	30	45
Blackpool	46	12	5	6	38	19	6	4	13	23	40	45
Southend United	46	11	6	6	30	17	4	9	10	21	32	45
Sheffield Wednesday	46	9	8	6	30	22	4	11	8	23	31	45
Plymouth Argyle	46	11	9	3	40	27	4	5	14	27	41	44
Chester	46	11	9	3	42	21	3	7	13	15	40	44
Rotherham United	46	13	3	7	30	23	4	7	12	19	32	44
Mansfield Town	46	7	11	5	30	24	5	8	10	21	24	43
Bury	46	6	11	6	35	32	5	9	9	24	33	42
Chesterfield	46	10	5	8	35	34	3	9	11	16	31	40
Peterborough United	46	8	7	8	26	24	3	7	13	18	39	36
Walsall	46	7	6	10	34	32	3	6	14	22	39	32
Tranmere Rovers	46	4	12	7	26	31	2	4	17	19	47	28
Lincoln City	46	5	7	11	26	38	2	4	17	15	50	25

New league opponents: None

Home-and-away league doubles
For – 5 (Chesterfield, Gillingham, Lincoln City, Sheffield Wednesday, Walsall)
Against – 1 (Swansea City)

Promoted with Watford: Shrewsbury Town, Swansea City

All Matches: Won 31, Drew 15, Lost 12, Goals 104-61

Highest Score: 5 (Matches 4 & 9)

No	DATE			COMPETITION	OPPONENTS	HOME	AWAY	ATTENDANCE
1	August	Sat	12	Football Lge Cup, 1st Round, 1st Leg	BRENTFORD	4-0 W		9,292
2		Tue	15	Football Lge Cup, 1st Round, 2nd Leg	Brentford		W 3-1	7,414
3		Sat	19	Football League, Division 3	Walsall		W 4-2	6,423
4		Tue	22	Football League, Division 3	BLACKPOOL	5-1 W		11,934
5		Sat	26	Football League, Division 3	PETERBOROUGH UNITED	1-2 L		12,156
6		Tue	29	Football League Cup, 2nd Round	NEWCASTLE UNITED	2-1 W		15,494
7	September	Sat	2	Football League, Division 3	Gillingham		W 3-2	8,248
8		Sat	9	Football League, Division 3	SWANSEA CITY	0-2 L		17,413
9		Wed	13	Football League, Division 3	Lincoln City		W 5-0	5,924
10		Sat	16	Football League, Division 3	Bury		W 2-1	4,102
11		Sat	23	Football League, Division 3	OXFORD UNITED	4-2 W		12,949
12		Tue	26	Football League, Division 3	Rotherham United		L 1-2	6,442
13		Sat	30	Football League, Division 3	TRANMERE ROVERS	4-0 W		10,753
14	October	Wed	4	Football League Cup, 3rd Round	Manchester United		W 2-1	40,534
15		Sat	7	Football League, Division 3	Chester		L 1-2	6,468
16		Sat	14	Football League, Division 3	BRENTFORD	2-0 W		15,180
17		Tue	17	Football League, Division 3	CARLISLE UNITED	2-1 W		12,444
18		Sat	21	Football League, Division 3	Chesterfield		W 2-0	7,800
19		Sat	28	Football League, Division 3	EXETER CITY	1-0 W		14,397
20	November	Sat	4	Football League, Division 3	Hull City		L 0-4	7,739
21		Wed	8	Football League Cup, 4th Round	Exeter City		W 2-0	14,746
22		Sat	11	Football League, Division 3	GILLINGHAM	1-0 W		13,941
23		Sat	18	Football League, Division 3	Peterborough United		W 1-0	8,048
24		Sat	25	FA Cup, 1st Round	DAGENHAM	3-0 W		11,551
25	December	Sat	2	Football League, Division 3	MANSFIELD TOWN	1-1 D		10,568
26		Sat	9	Football League, Division 3	Plymouth Argyle		D 1-1	11,907
27		Wed	13	Football League Cup, 5th Round	Stoke City		D 0-0	26,070
28		Sat	16	FA Cup, 2nd Round	SOUTHEND UNITED	1-1 D		13,377
29		Mon	18	FA Cup, 2nd Round replay	Southend United		L 0-1	15,463
30		Sat	23	Football League, Division 3	Colchester United		W 1-0	5,424
31		Tue	26	Football League, Division 3	SHREWSBURY TOWN	2-2 D		20,276
32		Sat	30	Football League, Division 3	SWINDON TOWN	2-0 W		15,486
33	January	Sat	6	Football League, Division 3	LINCOLN CITY	2-0 W		12,142
34		Tue	9	Football Lge Cup, 5th Round replay	STOKE CITY (after extra time)	3-1 W		21,455
35		Wed	17	Football Lge Cup, Semi-Final, 1st Leg	Nottingham Forest		L 1-3	32,438
36		Sat	20	Football League, Division 3	BURY	3-3 D		12,003
37		Sat	27	Football League, Division 3	Oxford United		D 1-1	10,310
38		Tue	30	Football Lge Cup, Semi-Final, 2nd Leg	NOTTINGHAM FOREST	0-0 D		27,656
39	February	Sat	3	Football League, Division 3	ROTHERHAM UNITED	2-2 D		12,805
40		Sat	10	Football League, Division 3	Tranmere Rovers		D 1-1	4,219
41		Sat	24	Football League, Division 3	Brentford		D 3-3	13,860
42	March	Sat	3	Football League, Division 3	CHESTERFIELD	2-0 W		12,352
43		Sat	10	Football League, Division 3	Exeter City		D 0-0	7.082
44		Tue	20	Football League, Division 3	Swansea City		L 2-3	19,850
45		Sat	24	Football League, Division 3	Blackpool		D 1-1	9,253
46		Tue	27	Football League, Division 3	WALSALL	3-1 W		11,891
47		Sat	31	Football League, Division 3	SHEFFIELD WEDNESDAY	1-0 W		16,239
48	April	Mon	2	Football League, Division 3	Southend United		L 0-1	11,406
49		Sat	7	Football League, Division 3	Mansfield Town		W 3-0	7,944
50		Fri	13	Football League, Division 3	COLCHESTER UNITED	0-3 L		17,903
51		Sat	14	Football League, Division 3	Shrewsbury Town		D 1-1	13,320
52		Tue	17	Football League, Division 3	SOUTHEND UNITED	2-0 W		15,835
53		Sat	21	Football League, Division 3	Swindon Town		L 0-2	16,397
54		Tue	24	Football League, Division 3	Carlisle United		L 0-1	7,141
55		Sat	28	Football League, Division 3	PLYMOUTH ARGYLE	2-2 D		14,816
56	May	Wed	2	Football League, Division 3	CHESTER	1-0 W		12,174
57		Sat	5	Football League, Division 3	Sheffield Wednesday		W 3-2	13,746
58		Mon	14	Football League, Division 3	HULL CITY	4-0 W		26,347

League ever-presents: R.A. Jenkins, J. Stirk
Most appearances in total: R.A. Jenkins & J. Stirk 58 out of 58   **Most goals in total:** R.A. Jenkins 37 (including the Football League's highest tally of 29)
Hat-tricks: R.A. Jenkins – (Match 4, 4 goals Match 11, & Match 24)   **Penalty goals:** I.R. Bolton 4, K.B. Pritchett 3, L.L. Blissett 1
Sent off: S.F. Sims (Match 44)
Full international appearance(s) this season: None

	Blissett, L.L.	Bolton, I.R.	Booth, D.	Cassells, K.B.	Downes, R.D.	Ellis, S.	Garner, A.H.	Harrison, S.J.	How, T.A.	Jenkins, R.A.	Joslyn, R.D.W.	Mayes, A.K.	Mercer, K.	Pollard, B.E.	Pritchett, K.B.	Rankin, A.G.	Sherwood, S.	Sims, S.F.	Stirk, J.	Train, R.
Apps	40	43	37	0	34	3	42	23		46	44	5	9	33	22	30	16	13	46	20
Subs	+1			+3	+3	+3					+1	+8	+5	+1				+1		+1
Goals	21	9			2		4			29	8		2	4	2			1		1
Apps	7	10	10	2	9		12	4	2	12	10	4	4	11	9	5	7		12	2
Subs	+1			+2							+2	+3	+1							
Goals	7	1			2					8	1	1			1					
1		X	X		X1		X			X2	X1	S	R	X	X	G			X	
2		X1	X		X1		X			X	X	X1		X	X	G			X	
3		X	R		X	X1	X1			X1	X1		X	X1		G			X	
4		X	X		X		X			X3	X1	S	X1	R		G			X	
5	S	X	X		X		X			X	X	R		X	X1p	G			X	
6	S2	X	X				X			X	R		X	X	X	G			X	
7	X1	X	X				X			X	X2			X	X	G			X	
8	X	X	X				X			X	X	S		X	X	G			R	
9	X2	R	X		X	S	X1			X1	X			X1		G			X	
10	X	X1	X		X	S	X			X1	X			X	R	G			X	
11	X1	X	X		X	S	X			X4	R			X		G			X	
12	X1	X	X		S	X	X	X		X				R		G			X	
13	X	X1p	X		X1		X	R		X2	X	S		X		G			X	
14	X2	X	X				X	X		X	X			X		G			X	
15	X1	X	X				X	X		X	X			X		G			X	
16	X1	X	X				X	X		X1	X			X		G			X	
17	X	X1	X				X	X		X	X			X1		G			X	
18	X1	X	X		R		X	X		X1	X	S		X		G			X	
19	X1	X	X				X	X		X	X		X	R	X	G			X	
20	X	X	X				X	X		X	R		X	S	X	G			X	
21	X	X	X				X			X	X1	S	X	R	X1p	G			X	
22	X	X	X				X			X	X1	X		X	X	G			X	
23	X1	X	X				X			X	X			X	X	G			X	
24		X		S	X		X	X		X3	X	X		R	X	G			X	
25	X	X	X	S	X		R			X	X		X			G			X	X1
26	X	X			X		X	X		X1	X		X			G			X	X
27	X	X	X				X			X	X			X	X	G			X	
28	R				X		X	X1		X		S		X	X	G			X	X
29		X	R		X		X	X	X	X	X	S		X	X	G			X	X
30		X			X		X	X		X1	X		X			G	X		X	X
31		X			X		X	X		X2	X	S	R			G	X		X	X
32	X2	X					X	X		X	X	R	S			G	X		X	X
33	X2	X					X	X		X	X			X	X	G	X		X	X
34	X2	X	X	S			X			X1	X	R		X	X	G			X	
35	X1	X	X	R			X			X	X	S		X	X	G			X	
36	X2	X					X	X		X1	X			X		G			X	X
37	X	X		S			X	X		X	X			R			G	X1	X	X
38	X	X	X		X		X	X		X	X		S	R		G			X	
39	X		X		X		X	X		X2	R		S			G	X		X	X
40	X1p				X		X	X		X	X			X		G	X		X	X
41	X1	X	X				X			X1	S			X	X1p	G	X		X	R
42	R	X1	X				X			X1		S	X	X	X	G			X	X
43		X	X		X		X			X		S	X	X	X	G			X	X
44	X	X1	X		R		X1			X		S	X	X	X	G			X	X
45	X	X	X		R		X1			X			X	X	X				X	S
46	X2	X	X				X1			X			X	X	X	G			X	
47	X	X	R				X			X	X		S	X1	X	G			X	X
48	X	X		S			X			X	X		R	X	X	G			X	X
49	R	X	X	S			X			X2	X1			X	X	G			X	X
50	X	X	R	S			X			X	X			X	X	G			X	
51	X	X1	X		X	X				X	X			X		G			X	
52	X	X1p	X				X			X	X1			X	X	G			X	
53	X	X	X		X		X			X	X		R	X		G	S		X	
54	X	X	X				X	X		X	X		S	R		G			X	
55	X	X					X	X		X	X1		X1				G		X	X
56	X	X1	X		X1		X	X		X	X		X				G		X	
57	X1	X1p	X		X		X	X		X	X1						G		X	X
58	X1	X1p	X				X	X		X	X1						G		X	X

1979/80

Football League position: 18th out of 22 in Division 2
Manager: Graham Taylor

	HOME					AWAY					
	Pl	W	D	L	For Ag	W	D	L	For	Ag	Pts
Leicester City	42	12	5	4	32 19	9	8	4	26	19	55
Sunderland	42	16	5	0	47 13	5	7	9	22	29	54
Birmingham City	42	14	5	2	37 16	7	6	8	21	22	53
Chelsea	42	14	3	4	34 16	9	4	8	32	36	53
Queens Park Rangers	42	10	9	2	46 25	8	4	9	29	28	49
Luton Town	42	9	10	2	36 17	7	7	7	30	28	49
West Ham United	42	13	2	6	37 21	7	5	9	17	22	47
Cambridge United	42	11	6	4	40 23	3	10	8	21	30	44
Newcastle United	42	13	6	2	35 19	2	8	11	18	30	44
Preston North End	42	8	10	3	30 23	4	9	8	26	29	43
Oldham Athletic	42	12	5	4	30 21	4	6	11	19	32	43
Swansea City	42	13	1	7	31 20	4	8	9	17	33	43
Shrewsbury Town	42	12	3	6	41 23	6	2	13	19	30	41
Orient	42	7	9	5	29 31	5	8	8	19	23	41
Cardiff City	42	11	4	6	21 16	5	4	12	20	32	40
Wrexham	42	13	2	6	26 15	3	4	14	34	38	38
Notts County	42	4	11	6	24 22	7	4	10	27	30	37
WATFORD	42	9	6	6	27 18	3	7	11	12	28	37
Bristol Rovers	42	9	8	4	33 23	2	5	14	17	41	35
Fulham	42	6	4	11	19 28	5	3	13	23	46	29
Burnley	42	5	9	7	19 23	1	6	14	20	50	27
Charlton Athletic	42	6	6	9	25 31	0	4	17	14	47	22

New league opponents: Chelsea, Newcastle United

Home-and-away league doubles
For – 2 (Newcastle United, Notts County)
Against – 5 (Chelsea, Leicester City, Luton Town, Orient, Shrewsbury Town)

Divisional changes at end of season: Leicester City, Sunderland & Birmingham City to Division 1; Fulham, Burnley & Charlton Athletic to Division 3; Bristol City, Derby County & Bolton Wanderers from Division 1; Grimsby Town, Blackburn Rovers & Sheffield Wednesday from Division 3

All Matches: Won 16, Drew 13, Lost 19, Goals 51-55

Highest Score: 4 (Matches 29, 46 & 48)

No	DATE			COMPETITION	OPPONENTS	HOME	AWAY	ATTENDANCE
1	August	Sat	11	Football Lge Cup, 1st Round, 1st Leg	Colchester United		L 0-2	4,638
2		Tue	14	Football Lge Cup, 1st Round, 2nd Leg	COLCHESTER UNITED	2-1 W		10,051
3		Sat	18	Football League, Division 2	Leicester City		L 0-2	15,772
4		Tue	21	Football League, Division 2	SWANSEA CITY	0-0 D		15,208
5		Sat	25	Football League, Division 2	Cambridge United		D 2-2	7,606
6	September	Sat	1	Football League, Division 2	WEST HAM UNITED	2-0 W		23,329
7		Sat	8	Football League, Division 2	Bristol Rovers		D 1-1	6,137
8		Sat	15	Football League, Division 2	CARDIFF CITY	1-1 D		13,741
9		Sat	22	Football League, Division 2	Chelsea		L 0-2	21,480
10		Sat	29	Football League, Division 2	CHARLTON ATHLETIC	2-1 W		13,598
11	October	Sat	6	Football League, Division 2	QUEENS PARK RANGERS	1-2 L		22,341
12		Tue	9	Football League, Division 2	Swansea City		L 0-1	15,185
13		Sat	13	Football League, Division 2	Orient		L 0-1	7,506
14		Sat	20	Football League, Division 2	NEWCASTLE UNITED	2-0 W		17,715
15		Sat	27	Football League, Division 2	Wrexham		L 0-3	9,442
16	November	Sat	3	Football League, Division 2	LEICESTER CITY	1-3 L		14,743
17		Sat	10	Football League, Division 2	Shrewsbury Town		L 0-1	8,150
18		Sat	17	Football League, Division 2	BIRMINGHAM CITY	1-0 W		14,378
19		Sat	24	Football League, Division 2	Fulham		D 0-0	10,126
20	December	Sat	1	Football League, Division 2	NOTTS COUNTY	2-1 W		12,023
21		Sat	8	Football League, Division 2	Burnley		L 0-1	8,559
22		Sat	15	Football League, Division 2	SUNDERLAND	1-1 D		13,965
23		Fri	21	Football League, Division 2	Preston North End		W 2-1	8,956
24		Wed	26	Football League, Division 2	LUTON TOWN	0-1 L		20,227
25		Sat	29	Football League, Division 2	CAMBRIDGE UNITED	0-0 D		13,481
26	January	Sat	5	FA Cup, 3rd Round	Queens Park Rangers		W 2-1	19,398
27		Sat	12	Football League, Division 2	West Ham United		D 1-1	23,553
28		Sat	19	Football League, Division 2	BRISTOL ROVERS	0-0 D		12,020
29		Sat	26	FA Cup, 4th Round	HARLOW TOWN	4-3 W		24,586
30	February	Sat	2	Football League, Division 2	Cardiff City		L 0-1	7,995
31		Sat	9	Football League, Division 2	CHELSEA	2-3 L		24,716
32		Sat	16	FA Cup, 5th Round	Wolverhampton Wanderers		W 3-0	32,881
33		Tue	19	Football League, Division 2	Oldham Athletic		D 1-1	7,530
34		Sat	23	Football League, Division 2	ORIENT	0-3 L		15,144
35		Tue	26	Football League, Division 2	Charlton Athletic		D 0-0	6,860
36	March	Sat	1	Football League, Division 2	Newcastle United		W 2-0	23,104
37		Sat	8	FA Cup, 6th Round	ARSENAL	1-2 L		28,000
38		Fri	14	Football League, Division 2	Queens Park Rangers		D 1-1	16,504
39		Tue	18	Football League, Division 2	WREXHAM	3-1 W		11,589
40		Sat	22	Football League, Division 2	SHREWSBURY TOWN	0-1 L		12,833
41		Sat	29	Football League, Division 2	Birmingham City		L 0-2	16,582
42	April	Sat	5	Football League, Division 2	Luton Town		L 0-1	12,783
43		Mon	7	Football League, Division 2	OLDHAM ATHLETIC	1-0 W		12,896
44		Wed	9	Football League, Division 2	PRESTON NORTH END	0-0 D		11,967
45		Sat	12	Football League, Division 2	Notts County		W 2-1	7,279
46		Sat	19	Football League, Division 2	FULHAM	4-0 W		15,898
47		Sat	26	Football League, Division 2	Sunderland		L 0-5	32,195
48	May	Sat	3	Football League, Division 2	BURNLEY	4-0 W		11,912

League ever-presents: L.L. Blissett (including two substitute appearances), R. Train
Most appearances in total: L.L. Blissett 48 (including two substitute appearances) out of 48   **Most goals in total:** L.L. Blissett (11)
Hat-tricks: None   **Penalty goals:** I.R. Bolton 4
Sent off: I.R. Bolton (Match 6)
Full international appearance(s) this season: None

Summary (League apps/subs/goals, then Cup apps/subs/goals):

	Blissett, L.L.	Bolton, I.R.	Booth, D.	Callaghan, N.J.	Cassells, K.B.	Downes, R.D.	Garner, A.H.	Harrison, S.J.	Henderson, M.R.	How, T.A.	Jackett, K.F.	Jenkins, R.A.	Joslyn, R.D.W.	Mercer, K.	Patching, M.	Pollard, B.E.	Poskett, M.	Pritchett, K.B.	Rankin, A.G.	Rostron, J.W.	Sherwood, S.	Sims, S.F.	Steele, E.G.	Stirk, J.	Terry, S.G.	Train, R.	Ward, J.P.	Own goal
Apps	40	39	29	1	5	8	10	35	28	13	1	22	11	14	14	11	13	7	10	31	4	34	28		2	42	10	
Subs	+2		+3		+2						+1	+1		+2	+1		+3	+3									+2	
Goals	10	4	2									5		2	1	1	3	2		3		2				1	2	1
Apps	6	6	4			2	2	6	4			5	2	0	3	0	3		1	4	1	6	4	2		4	1	
Subs														+1	+1	+1												
Goals	1	4												2		4						1						

Match appearances:

Match	Blissett, L.L.	Bolton, I.R.	Booth, D.	Callaghan, N.J.	Cassells, K.B.	Downes, R.D.	Garner, A.H.	Harrison, S.J.	Henderson, M.R.	How, T.A.	Jackett, K.F.	Jenkins, R.A.	Joslyn, R.D.W.	Mercer, K.	Patching, M.	Pollard, B.E.	Poskett, M.	Pritchett, K.B.	Rankin, A.G.	Rostron, J.W.	Sherwood, S.	Sims, S.F.	Steele, E.G.	Stirk, J.	Terry, S.G.	Train, R.	Ward, J.P.	Own goal
1	X	X	X			R	X	X				X	X	S					G			X		X				
2	X	X2p	R			X	X	X				X	X				S					G	X	X				
3	X	X						X		X		X	X	X		X						G	X			X		
4	X	X						X				X	X	X		X						G	X			X		
5	X1	X	S					X				X1	R	X		X						G	X			X		
6	X2	X	X			X		X				X	R	S								G	X			X		
7	X		X			X	X	X		X		X1	X									G	X			X		
8	X	X	X			X	X	X				X	X									G				X1		
9	X	X	X			X	X	X				X	R									G	X			X	S	
10	X	X1				R		X				X1	X	S								G	X			X	X	
11	X	X			S	R	X	X				X	X	X1								G	X			X		
12	X	X	S	X		X	X		R			X	X	X								G	X			X		
13	X	X		X		X	X					R	X		X		S					G	X			X		
14	X1	X	X		X			X		X		X1								G		X	X			X		
15	X		X		X		X	X		X		R								G		X	X		S	X		
16	X		X			X	X		X			X		X1								X	G	X		X		
17	X	X	X			X	X					X										X	G	X		X	X	
18	X	X	X			X	X					X										X	G	X		X	X1	
19	X	X	X			X	X					X					S					X	G	X		X	R	
20	X1	X1p	X			X	X					X				X						X	G	X		X		
21	X	X	X				X	X				X				R	S					X	G			X		
22	X	X	X1			X	X	X	X			X										X	G			X		
23	X	X						X	X			X1				X						X	G			X		
24	X	X				X		X	X			X				X						X	G			X		
25	X	X	S					X	X			X				R						X	G			X	X	
26	X	X1p	X					X	X			X					X1					X	G			X	X	
27	R	X						X	X			X					X1	S				X	G			X	X	
28	S	X	R					X	X			X					X	X				X	G			X	X	
29	X	X1						X	X			X					X2	X1				X	G			X		
30	X	X	X					X	X			X					X					X	G			X		
31	X1	X						X				X1					X	X	X			X	G			X		
32	X1	X						X	X			X					X	X2				X	G			X		
33	X	X1						X	X			X					X	X				X	G			X		
34	X	X	S					X	X			X					X	R				X	G			X		
35	X	X	X					X	X			X					X					X	G			X		
36	X	X	X					X	X			X1				X						X	G			X		1
37	X	X	X					R	X			X				S	X1					X	G			X		
38	X1	X	X					X	X			X					X					X	G			X		
39	X2	X	X					X	X			X					X1					X	G			X		
40	X	X	R					X	X			X				S	X					X	G			X		
41	X	X	X					X	X			R				S	X					X	G			X		
42	X	X	X					R	X			S				X	X					X	G			X		
43	X	X	X1					X				X				X	X		X			X	G			X		
44	X	X						X				X				R	S		X			X	G			X		
45	X1	X	X					X								X1	X		X			X	G			X	X	
46	X	X1p	X					X								X1	X		X	X1			G			X	X1	
47	X	X	R					X			S					X	X		X				G	X		X	X	
48	S	R		X				X			X					X	X2		X1	G		X1		X		X	X	

1980/81

Football League position: 9th out of 22 in Division 2
Manager: Graham Taylor

New league opponents: Derby County

Home-and-away league doubles
For – 2 (Notts County, Wrexham)
Against – 2 (Luton Town, West Ham United)

Divisional changes at end of season: West Ham United, Notts County & Swansea City to Division 1; Preston North End, Bristol City & Bristol Rovers to Division 3; Norwich City, Leicester City & Crystal Palace from Division 1; Rotherham United, Barnsley & Charlton Athletic from Division 3.

All Matches: Won 22, Drew 13, Lost 18, Goals 72-63

Highest Score: 7 (Match 8)

		HOME					AWAY					
	Pl	W	D	L	For	Ag	W	D	L	For	Ag	Pts
West Ham United	42	19	1	1	53	12	9	9	3	26	17	66
Notts County	42	10	8	3	26	15	8	9	4	23	23	53
Swansea City	42	12	5	4	39	19	6	9	6	25	25	50
Blackburn Rovers	42	12	8	1	28	7	4	10	7	14	22	50
Luton Town	42	10	6	5	35	23	8	6	7	26	23	48
Derby County	42	9	8	4	34	26	6	7	8	23	26	45
Grimsby Town	42	10	8	3	21	10	5	7	9	23	32	45
Queens Park Rangers	42	11	7	3	36	12	4	6	11	20	34	43
WATFORD	42	13	5	3	34	18	3	6	12	16	27	43
Sheffield Wednesday	42	14	4	3	38	14	3	4	14	15	28	42
Newcastle United	42	11	7	3	22	13	3	7	11	8	32	42
Chelsea	42	8	6	7	27	15	6	6	9	19	26	40
Cambridge United	42	13	1	7	36	23	4	5	12	17	42	40
Shrewsbury Town	42	9	7	5	33	22	2	10	9	13	25	39
Oldham Athletic	42	7	9	5	19	16	5	6	10	20	32	39
Wrexham	42	5	8	8	22	24	7	5	9	21	21	37
Orient	42	9	8	4	34	20	4	4	13	18	36	38
Bolton Wanderers	42	10	5	6	40	27	4	5	12	21	39	38
Cardiff City	42	7	7	7	23	24	5	5	11	21	36	36
Preston North End	42	8	7	6	28	26	3	7	11	13	36	36
Bristol City	42	6	10	5	19	15	1	6	14	10	36	30
Bristol Rovers	42	4	9	8	21	24	1	4	16	13	41	23

(This was the last season in which only two points were awarded for a win)

No	DATE			COMPETITION	OPPONENTS		HOME AWAY	ATTENDANCE
1	August	Sat	9	Football Lge Cup, 1st Round, 1st Leg	MILLWALL		2-1 W	9,050
2		Tue	12	Football Lge Cup, 1st Round, 2nd Leg	Millwall		W 2-0	5,210
3		Sat	16	Football League, Division 2	SWANSEA CITY		2-1 W	11,316
4		Tue	19	Football League, Division 2	Luton Town		L 0-1	13,887
5		Sat	23	Football League, Division 2	Cambridge United		L 1-3	6,546
6		Tue	26	Football Lge Cup, 2nd Round, 1st Leg	Southampton		L 0-4	16,659
7		Sat	30	Football League, Division 2	BRISTOL CITY		1-0 W	10,450
8	September	Tue	2	Football Lge Cup, 2nd Round, 2nd Leg	SOUTHAMPTON (after extra time)		7-1 W	15,992
9		Sat	6	Football League, Division 2	Shrewsbury Town		L 1-2	5,500
10		Sat	13	Football League, Division 2	PRESTON NORTH END		2-1 W	11,275
11		Sat	20	Football League, Division 2	West Ham United		L 2-3	24,288
12		Tue	23	Football League Cup, 3rd Round	Sheffield Wednesday		W 2-1	14,085
13		Sat	27	Football League, Division 2	CHELSEA		2-3 L	19,802
14	October	Sat	4	Football League, Division 2	Cardiff City		L 0-1	6,407
15		Tue	7	Football League, Division 2	DERBY COUNTY		1-1 D	11,703
16		Sat	11	Football League, Division 2	WREXHAM		1-0 W	10,694
17		Sat	18	Football League, Division 2	Grimsby Town		D 1-1	8,906
18		Sat	25	Football League, Division 2	OLDHAM ATHLETIC		2-1 W	10,853
19		Tue	28	Football League Cup, 4th Round	NOTTINGHAM FOREST		4-1 W	22,597
20	November	Sat	1	Football League, Division 2	Newcastle United		L 1-2	14,619
21		Tue	4	Football League, Division 2	Bristol Rovers		L 1-3	5,450
22		Sat	8	Football League, Division 2	BOLTON WANDERERS		3-1 W	11,296
23		Tue	11	Football League, Division 2	LUTON TOWN		0-1 L	16,939
24		Sat	22	Football League, Division 2	BLACKBURN ROVERS		1-1 D	13,436
25		Sat	29	Football League, Division 2	Sheffield Wednesday		L 0-1	14,761
26	December	Tue	2	Football League Cup, 5th Round	COVENTRY CITY		2-2 D	27,542
27		Sat	6	Football League, Division 2	NOTTS COUNTY		2-0 W	11,133
28		Tue	9	Football Lge Cup, 5th Round replay	Coventry City		L 0-5	30,348
29		Sat	13	Football League, Division 2	Derby County		D 1-1	16,464
30		Tue	16	Football League, Division 2	Swansea City		L 0-1	13,305
31		Sat	20	Football League, Division 2	GRIMSBY TOWN		3-1 W	10,209
32		Fri	26	Football League, Division 2	Orient		D 1-1	10,041
33		Sat	27	Football League, Division 2	QUEENS PARK RANGERS		1-1 D	22,911
34	January	Sat	3	FA Cup, 3rd Round	Colchester United		W 1-0	7,769
35		Sat	10	Football League, Division 2	Blackburn Rovers		D 0-0	9,466
36		Sat	17	Football League, Division 2	Bristol City		D 0-0	8,746
37		Sat	24	FA Cup, 4th Round	WOLVERHAMPTON WANDERERS		1-1 D	24,328
38		Tue	27	FA Cup, 4th Round replay	Wolverhampton Wanderers		L 1-2	30,854
39		Sat	31	Football League, Division 2	CAMBRIDGE UNITED		0-0 D	11,944
40	February	Sat	7	Football League, Division 2	Preston North End		L 1-2	5,107
41		Sat	14	Football League, Division 2	SHREWSBURY TOWN		1-0 W	11,034
42		Sat	21	Football League, Division 2	Chelsea		W 1-0	19,153
43		Sat	28	Football League, Division 2	WEST HAM UNITED		1-2 L	20,786
44	March	Sat	7	Football League, Division 2	CARDIFF CITY		4-2 W	10,014
45		Sat	21	Football League, Division 2	BRISTOL ROVERS		3-1 W	10,162
46		Sat	28	Football League, Division 2	Oldham Athletic		L 1-2	4,802
47	April	Sat	4	Football League, Division 2	NEWCASTLE UNITED		0-0 D	10,986
48		Sat	11	Football League, Division 2	Bolton Wanderers		L 1-2	8,461
49		Fri	17	Football League, Division 2	ORIENT		2-0 W	12,459
50		Sat	18	Football League, Division 2	Queens Park Rangers		D 0-0	10,571
51		Sat	25	Football League, Division 2	Notts County		W 2-1	10,345
52	May	Sat	2	Football League, Division 2	SHEFFIELD WEDNESDAY		2-1 W	12,351
53		Mon	4	Football League, Division 2	Wrexham		W 1-0	4,659

Most appearances in total: L.L. Blissett & K.F. Jackett (including one substitute appearance) 53 out of 53   **Most goals in total:** M. Poskett 21
Hat-tricks: R.A. Jenkins (Match 19)   **Penalty goals:** L.L. Blissett 3, I.R. Bolton 3
Sent off: None
Full international appearance(s) this season: G.J. Armstrong (Northern Ireland)

	Armstrong, G.J.	Blissett, L.L.	Bolton, I.R.	Callaghan, N.I.	Cassells, K.B. //	Harrison, S.J. //	Henderson, M.R.	Jackett, K.F.	Jenkins, R.A.	Patching, M.	Poskett, M.	Pritchett, K.B.	Rice, P.J.	Rostron, J.W.	Sherwood, S.	Sims, S.F.	Steele, E.G.	Taylor, L.	Terry, S.G.	Train, R.	Ward, J.P. //
Apps	24	42	21	18	1	24	18	42	20	6	40	9	25	24	22	37	20	23	5	29	12
Subs				+3	+1	+1	+1	+2				+4			+3			+1			+3
Goals	3	11	4	2			3	4	1		13	1				1		1		1	4
Apps	5	11	4	3	1	9	6	10	8	4	10		5	8	4	10	7	3	1	11	1
Subs				+2		+1	+1	+1			+1										+1
Goals	2	2	1	1				5	1		8					1				1	
1		X	X			R	X	S	X	X	X2		X			X	G			X	
2		X1	X	S			X	X	R	X	X		X			X1	G			X	
3		X	X				X	X	X	X	X2		X			X	G			X	
4		X	X				X	X	X	X	X		X			X	G			X	
5		X	X				X	X	X	X	X1		X			X	G			X	
6		X	X			X	X	R	S	X	X		X			X	G			X	
7		X	X				X	X	X1	X			X			X	G			X	
8		X	X1p	S1			X	X	X1	X1	X2		X			X	G			R1	
9	R	X			S		X	X	X1	X	X		X			X	G			X	
10		X	X1p	S			X	X	X1	R	X		X			X	G			X	
11		X	X	R		S	X1		X		X1		X			X	G			X	
12		X			X	X	X	X	X1		X1		X			X	G			X	
13		X	X1p	X1			X	X	X		X		X			X	G			X	
14		X		R			X	X	X		X	S	X			X	G			X	
15		X		R			X	X	X1		X	S	X			X	G			X	
16		X		R			X	X	X		X	S	X			X1	G			X	
17		X					X	X	X		X	X	R			X	G	X1			S
18		X2p					X	X	X		X	S	R			X	G	X			X
19		X1p					X	X	X	X3	X		X			X	G	X			X
20		X					X	X	X		X1		X			X	G	X			X
21		X		S	X	X	X	X1	X		X1		R			X	G	X			
22		X		X		X	X	X			X1			X1		X	G	X			X1
23		X		R		X	X	X	X		X			X		X	G	S		X	
24	X	X1					X		X	S	X		X	X		X	G	R		X	
25	R	X					X	S	X		X		X	X		X	G			X	
26	X1	X					X		X		X1		X	X		X	G			X	
27		X		X1			X		X	X1	X		X				G	X	X		
28	X	X		X			X		S	X	R		X		G			X	X		
29	X	X1		R			X		X		X		X		G		X	X	X	X	S
30	X	X		X			X		X	S	X		X		G	X		X		X	R
31	X1	X		R			X		X		X1		X		G	X		X1		X	
32	X	X1		X			X		X		X		X	X	G	X		X		X	
33	X	X					X		X		X		X	R	G	X		X		X	S1
34	X	X		X			X		X		X1		X		G	X		X		X	
35	X	X		X			X		X		X		X		G		X	X		X	
36	X	X		X			X		X		X		X		G	X		X		X	
37	X1	X		R			X		X		X		X		G	X		X		X	S
38	X	X				X			X	X	S1		X	R	G	X		X		X	
39	X	X					X		X	X	X		X		G	X		X		X	
40	X	X					X		X	R1	X		X	S	G	X		X		X	
41	X	X	X1	X					X		X	X	X		G	X		X			
42	X	X	X						X		X1	X	X		G	X		X		X	
43	X	X	X						X		X1	X	X		G	X		X		X	
44	X	X1	X						X		X2	X1	X		G	X		X		X	
45	X1	X1	X						X		X	X	X		G	X		X		X1	
46	X	X	X						X		X	X	X	S	G	X		X		R1	
47	X	X	X						X		X	X	X		G	X		X		X	
48	X1	X	X						X		X	R	X	S	G	X		X		X	
49	X	X	X1	S		X			X1		X		X		G	X		X	X	R	
50	X	X	X	X		X			X			X	X	X	G			X	X		
51	X	X2p	X	X		X			X		X		X		G	X		X			
52	X	X1	X	X					X		X1		X	X	G	X		X			
53	X	X1	X	X		X			X		X		X		G	X		X			

1981/82

Football League position: 2nd out of 22 in Division 2 – promoted to Division 1
Manager: Graham Taylor

		HOME					AWAY					
	Pl	W	D	L	For	Ag	W	D	L	For	Ag	Pts
Luton Town	42	16	3	2	48	19	9	10	2	38	27	88
WATFORD	42	13	6	2	46	16	10	5	6	30	26	80
Norwich City	42	14	3	4	41	19	8	2	11	23	31	71
Sheffield Wednesday	42	10	8	3	31	23	10	2	9	24	28	70
Queens Park Rangers	42	15	4	2	40	9	6	2	13	25	26	69
Barnsley	42	13	4	4	33	14	6	6	9	26	27	67
Rotherham United	42	13	5	3	42	19	7	2	12	24	35	67
Leicester City	42	12	5	4	31	19	6	7	8	25	29	66
Newcastle United	42	14	4	3	30	14	4	4	13	22	36	62
Blackburn Rovers	42	11	4	6	26	15	5	7	9	21	28	59
Oldham Athletic	42	9	9	3	28	23	6	5	10	22	28	59
Chelsea	42	10	5	6	37	30	5	7	9	23	30	57
Charlton Athletic	42	11	5	5	33	22	2	7	12	17	43	51
Cambridge United	42	11	4	6	31	19	2	5	14	17	34	48
Crystal Palace	42	9	2	10	25	26	4	7	10	9	19	48
Derby County	42	9	8	4	32	23	3	4	14	21	45	48
Grimsby Town	42	5	8	8	29	30	6	5	10	24	35	46
Shrewsbury Town	42	10	6	5	26	19	1	7	13	11	38	46
Bolton Wanderers	42	10	4	7	28	24	3	3	15	11	37	46
Cardiff City	42	9	2	10	28	32	3	6	12	17	29	44
Wrexham	42	9	4	8	22	22	2	7	12	18	34	44
Orient	42	6	8	7	23	24	4	1	16	13	37	39

New league opponents: None

Home-and-away league doubles
For – 6 (Blackburn Rovers, Chelsea, Orient, Rotherham United, Shrewsbury Town, Wrexham)
Against – none

Promoted with Watford: Luton Town , Norwich City

All Matches: Won 30, Drew 13, Lost 12, Goals 102-59

Highest Score: 6 (Match 33)

No	DATE			COMPETITION	OPPONENTS	HOME	AWAY	ATTENDANCE
1	August	Sat	15	League Group Cup, Preliminary Group	READING	4-1 W		4,049
2		Wed	19	League Group Cup, Preliminary Group	Oxford United		W 4-2	2,602
3		Sat	22	League Group Cup, Preliminary Group	Aldershot		D 1-1	2,469
4		Sat	29	Football League, Division 2	Newcastle United		W 1-0	19,376
5	September	Tue	1	Football League, Division 2	GRIMSBY TOWN	0-2 L		11,276
6		Sat	5	Football League, Division 2	OLDHAM ATHLETIC	1-1 D		9,018
7		Sat	12	Football League, Division 2	Chelsea		W 3-1	20,036
8		Sat	19	Football League, Division 2	ROTHERHAM UNITED	1-0 W		10,696
9		Tue	22	Football League, Division 2	Wrexham		W 1-0	3,911
10		Sat	26	Football League, Division 2	Luton Town		L 1-4	12,839
11	October	Sat	3	Football League, Division 2	BARNSLEY	3-1 W		10,827
12		Tue	6	Football Lge Cup, 2nd Round, 1st Leg	Grimsby Town		L 0-1	7,044
13		Sat	10	Football League, Division 2	ORIENT	3-0 W		10,136
14		Sat	17	Football League, Division 2	Cambridge United		W 2-1	7,239
15		Sat	24	Football League, Division 2	NORWICH CITY	3-0 W		14,463
16		Tue	27	Football Lge Cup, 2nd Round, 2nd Leg	GRIMSBY TOWN	3-1 W		13,213
17		Sat	31	Football League, Division 2	Shrewsbury Town		W 2-0	5,672
18	November	Sat	7	Football League, Division 2	Bolton Wanderers		L 0-2	7,066
19		Tue	10	Football League Cup, 3rd Round	LINCOLN CITY	2-2 D		12,198
20		Sat	14	Football League, Division 2	CARDIFF CITY	0-0 D		13,982
21		Sat	21	Football League, Division 2	BLACKBURN ROVERS	3-2 W		11,822
22		Wed	25	Football Lge Cup, 3rd Round replay	Lincoln City		W 3-2	8,773
23		Sat	28	Football League, Division 2	Sheffield Wednesday		L 1-3	15,990
24	December	Tue	1	Football League Cup, 4th Round	QUEENS PARK RANGERS	4-1 W		18,276
25		Sat	5	Football League, Division 2	CHARLTON ATHLETIC	2-2 D		12,186
26		Tue	8	League Group Cup, Quarter-Final	Burnley		L 1-2	2,658
27		Sat	12	Football League, Division 2	Leicester City		D 1-1	10,340
28	January	Sat	2	FA Cup, 3rd Round	MANCHESTER UNITED	1-0 W		26,104
29		Sat	9	Football League, Division 2	Oldham Athletic		D 1-1	7,409
30		Sat	16	Football League, Division 2	NEWCASTLE UNITED	2-3 L		12,489
31		Mon	18	Football League Cup, 5th Round	Ipswich Town		L 1-2	20,817
32		Sat	23	FA Cup, 4th Round	WEST HAM UNITED	2-0 W		27,004
33		Tue	26	Football League, Division 2	DERBY COUNTY	6-1 W		12,684
34		Sat	30	Football League, Division 2	Rotherham United		W 2-1	8,129
35	February	Sat	6	Football League, Division 2	CHELSEA	1-0 W		17,386
36		Tue	9	Football League, Division 2	Barnsley		D 0-0	17,070
37		Sat	13	FA Cup, 5th Round	Leicester City		L 0-2	27,991
38		Sat	20	Football League, Division 2	LUTON TOWN	1-1 D		22,798
39		Sat	27	Football League, Division 2	Orient		W 3-1	6,595
40	March	Sat	6	Football League, Division 2	CAMBRIDGE UNITED	0-0 D		12,361
41		Tue	9	Football League, Division 2	QUEENS PARK RANGERS	4-0 W		17,264
42		Sat	13	Football League, Division 2	Norwich City		L 2-4	15,534
43		Tue	16	Football League, Division 2	Grimsby Town		W 2-0	6,146
44		Sat	20	Football League, Division 2	SHREWSBURY TOWN	3-1 W		11,832
45		Sat	27	Football League, Division 2	BOLTON WANDERERS	3-0 W		12,963
46	April	Sat	3	Football League, Division 2	Cardiff City		L 0-2	6,734
47		Fri	9	Football League, Division 2	CRYSTAL PALACE	1-1 D		18,224
48		Mon	12	Football League, Division 2	Queens Park Rangers		D 0-0	22,091
49		Sat	17	Football League, Division 2	Blackburn Rovers		W 2-1	7,284
50		Sat	24	Football League, Division 2	SHEFFIELD WEDNESDAY	4-0 W		23,987
51		Tue	27	Football League, Division 2	Crystal Palace		W 3-0	12,355
52	May	Sat	1	Football League, Division 2	Charlton Athletic		D 1-1	9,747
53		Tue	4	Football League, Division 2	WREXHAM	2-0 W		20,028
54		Sat	8	Football League, Division 2	LEICESTER CITY	3-1 W		20,857
55		Sat	15	Football League, Division 2	Derby County		L 2-3	14,946

League ever-presents: I.R. Bolton, L. Taylor
Most appearances in total: I.R. Bolton 54 out of 55   **Most goals in total:** L.L. Blissett 25
Hat-tricks: None   **Penalty goals:** L.L. Blissett 10
Sent off: L.L. Blissett (Match 4)
Full international appearance(s) this season: G.J. Armstrong (Northern Ireland)

	Armstrong, G.J.	Barnes, J.C.B.	Blissett, L.L.	Bolton, I.R.	Callaghan, I.R. //	Donnellan, G. //	Franklin, P.L.	Gilligan, J.M.	Henderson, M.R. //	Jackett, K.F.	Jenkins, R.A.	Johnson, D.N.C.	Lohman, J.H.P.	Palmer, C.A.	Poskett, M. //	Pritchett, K.B.	Rice, P.J.	Rostron, J.W.	Sherwood, S.	Sims, S.F.	Steele, S.F.	Taylor, L.	Terry, S.G.	Train, R. //	Own goal
Apps	18	35	40	42	34			0	4	18	32	0	26		4	18	41	24	41	16	1	42	26		
Subs	+15	+1			+3			+1			+1	+1			+3			+3		+1					
Goals	7	13	19	5	5				2	13		2			1		2					4	2		1
Apps	9	8	13	12	12	0	0	1	5	9	6	0	4	1	3	9	10	3	12	6	1	11	7	1	
Subs	+2				+1	+1	+1	+1				+1						+3					+2		
Goals	3	1	6	1	3				1		1	2			2	1		1				2	1		
1	X		X1p	X	X1					X	R				X2		X	S	G	X		R	S		
2	X1		X1	X1	X1					X	X				X		X		G	X		X			
3	X		X	X	R	S			X1	X	X						X		G	X				X	
4	X		X	X	X1					X	X						X		G	X		X			
5	X		X	X	X					X	X						X	S	G	X		R			
6	X1	S	X	X	X					X						R	X	X	G	X		X			
7	X1	X		X	X1					X	X						X	X1	G	X		X			
8	X1	X		X	X					X	X						X		G	X		X			
9	X	X	X	X	X					X	X						X		G	X		X1			
10	X	X	X	X1	X					X	R					S	X		G	X		X			
11		X1	X	X	X			S		X1						R1	X	X	G	X		X			
12		X	X	X	X			S	X	X						X	X		G	R		X			
13	X	X2	X	X	X					X							X	X	G			X	X1		
14		X	X2	X	X					X	X						X	X	G			X	X		
15		X1	X1	X1	X					X	R					X	X	S	G			X	X		
16		X	X1	X	X					X	X2						X	X	G	X		X			
17	S	X1	R	X	X					X	X1						X	X	G			X	X		
18	S	X	X	X						X	R						X	X	G			X	X		
19	R	X	X1p	X	X					X1						X	X	S	G			X	X		
20		X	X		X					X						R	X	S	G			X	X		
21	S	R	X	X	X				X	X1	X2						X		G			X	X		
22	X		X	X	X					X	X					X1		X1	G			X	X1		
23	X1		X	X	X					X					S	X	X	R	G			X	X		
24	S1	R	X1	X	X					X	X						X	X	G			X2	X		
25			X	X	X					X	X		X1				X	X	G			X1	X		
26	X		X1		X	S			X			S	R	X		R		X		X	G	X			
27	S				X					X	R1		X				X	R	G			X	X		
28	S	X	X	X	X						X		X1				X	R	G			X	X		
29	S	X	X	X	X						X1		R				X	X	G			X	X		
30	S	X	X	X	X						X1		R				X	X	G			X	X1		
31	X	X1	X	X	R						X						X	X	G			X	X	S	
32	X1	X1	X	X	X1						R		X			X	X	S	G			X			
33	X2	X1	X1	X1	S1						X		X				R	X	G			X	X		
34	X	X1	X	X1	S					X			X				X	R	G			X	X		
35	X	X	X1p	X									X				X	X	G			X	X		
36	R	X	X	X	S								X				X	X	G			X	X		
37	R	X	X	X	S								X				X	X	G			X	X		
38	S	X	R	X	X								X				X	X1	G			X	X		
39	S	X	X2p	X	R						X1		X				X	X	G			X	X		
40	S	X	X	X									X				X	X	G			X	X		
41		X	X1	X	X						X1		X				X	X	G			X1	X		1
42	S	X1	X	X	R						X		X				X	X	G			X1	X		
43		X1	X	X							X1		X			X	X	X	G			X	X		
44	S	X	X2p	X							X1		X			R	X	X	G			X	X		
45	S	X	X2p	X							X		X1			X	X	R			G	X	X		
46	S	X	X	X							X		R			X	X	X	G			X	X		
47	S	X1	X	X	X						R		X			X	X	X	G			X	X		
48	X	X	X	R									X			S	X	X	G	X		X	X		
49	X	X	X1p	X	X1								X				X	X	G	S		X	R		
50		X1	X2	X	X1								X				X	X	G	X		X			
51	X1	R	X2#	X	X								S				X	X	G	X		X			
52	X		X	X	X								X1				X	X	G	X		X			
53		X	X	X									X2				X	X	G	X		X			
54	S	X2	X1	X	X								R				X	X	G	X		X			
55	X	X	X1p	X1	X						S		R				X	X	G			X	X		

Football League position: 2nd out of 22 in Division 1
Manager: Graham Taylor

	HOME					AWAY					
	Pl	W	D	L	For	Ag	W	D	L	For	Ag	Pts
Liverpool	42	16	4	1	55	16	8	6	7	32	21	82
WATFORD	42	16	2	3	49	20	6	3	12	25	37	71
Manchester United	42	14	7	0	39	10	5	6	10	17	28	70
Tottenham Hotspur	42	15	4	2	50	15	5	5	11	35		69
Nottingham Forest	42	12	5	4	34	18	8	4	9	28	32	69
Aston Villa	42	17	2	2	47	15	4	3	14	15	35	68
Everton	42	13	6	2	43	19	5	4	12	23	29	64
West Ham United	42	13	3	5	41	23	7	1	13	27	39	64
Ipswich Town	42	11	3	7	39	23	4	10	7	25	27	58
Arsenal	42	11	6	4	36	19	5	4	12	22	37	58
West Bromwich Albion	42	11	5	5	35	20	4	7	10	16	29	57
Southampton	42	11	5	5	36	22	4	7	10	18	36	57
Stoke City	42	13	4	4	34	21	3	5	13	19	43	57
Norwich City	42	10	6	5	29	17	3	4	14	19	42	48
Notts County	42	12	4	5	37	25	3	3	15	18	46	52
Sunderland	42	7	10	4	30	22	5	4	12	18	39	50
Birmingham City	42	9	7	5	29	24	3	7	11	11	31	50
Luton Town	42	7	7	7	34	33	5	6	10	31		49
Coventry City	42	10	5	6	29	17	3	4	14	19	42	48
Manchester City	42	9	5	7	26	23	4	3	14	21	47	47
Swansea City	42	10	4	7	32	29	0	7	14	19	40	41
Brighton & Hove Albion	42	8	7	6	25	22	1	6	14	13	46	40

New league opponents: Arsenal, Everton, Liverpool, Manchester City, Manchester United, West Bromwich Albion

Home-and-away league doubles
For – 4 (Arsenal, Southampton, Swansea City, West Bromwich Albion)
Against – 2 (Manchester United, Nottingham Forest)

Divisional changes at end of season: Manchester City, Swansea City and Brighton & Hove Albion to Division 2; Queens Park Rangers, Wolverhampton Wanderers and Leicester City from Division 2

All Matches: Won 29, Drew 6, Lost 18, Goals 100-80

Highest Score: 8 (Match 10)

No	DATE			COMPETITION	OPPONENTS	HOME	AWAY	ATTENDANCE
1	August	Sat	14	Football Lge Trophy, Preliminary Group	ORIENT	4-1 W		4,063
2		Tue	17	Football Lge Trophy, Preliminary Group	COLCHESTER UNITED	2-1 W		3,837
3		Sat	21	Football Lge Trophy, Preliminary Group	Southend United		W 4-1	2,447
4		Sat	28	Football League, Division 1	EVERTON	2-0 W		19,630
5		Tue	31	Football League, Division 1	Southampton		W 4-1	19,714
6	September	Sat	4	Football League, Division 1	Manchester City		L 0-1	29,617
7		Tue	7	Football League, Division 1	SWANSEA CITY	2-1 W		15,577
8		Sat	11	Football League, Division 1	WEST BROMWICH ALBION	3-0 W		17,639
9		Sat	18	Football League, Division 1	Nottingham Forest		L 0-2	16,550
10		Sat	25	Football League, Division 1	SUNDERLAND	8-0 W		16,816
11	October	Sat	2	Football League, Division 1	Birmingham City		D 1-1	13,870
12		Tue	5	Football Lge Cup, 2nd Round, 1st Leg	Bolton Wanderers		W 2-1	5,664
13		Sat	9	Football League, Division 1	NORWICH CITY	2-2 D		18,597
14		Sat	16	Football League, Division 1	Aston Villa		L 0-3	21,572
15		Sat	23	Football League, Division 1	COVENTRY CITY	0-0 D		17,334
16		Tue	26	Football Lge Cup, 2nd Round, 2nd Leg	BOLTON WANDERERS (after extra time)	2-1 W		11,520
17		Sat	30	Football League, Division 1	Notts County		L 2-3	9,171
18	November	Sat	6	Football League, Division 1	Tottenham Hotspur		W 1-0	42,215
19		Wed	10	Football League Cup, 3rd Round	Nottingham Forest		L 3-7	14,873
20		Sat	13	Football League, Division 1	STOKE CITY	1-0 W		18,713
21		Sat	20	Football League, Division 1	BRIGHTON & HOVE ALBION	4-1 W		16,586
22		Sat	27	Football League, Division 1	Arsenal		W 4-2	34,287
23	December	Sat	4	Football League, Division 1	MANCHESTER UNITED	0-1 L		25,669
24		Wed	8	Football Lge Trophy, Quarter-Final	Reading		L 3-5	3,517
25		Sat	11	Football League, Division 1	Liverpool		L 1-3	36,690
26		Sat	18	Football League, Division 1	IPSWICH TOWN	2-1 W		18,048
27		Mon	27	Football League, Division 1	Luton Town		L 0-1	21,145
28		Wed	29	Football League, Division 1	WEST HAM UNITED	2-1 W		24,870
29	January	Sat	1	Football League, Division 1	Brighton & Hove Albion		D 1-1	15,139
30		Mon	3	Football League, Division 1	MANCHESTER CITY	2-0 W		20,049
31		Sat	8	FA Cup, 3rd Round	PLYMOUTH ARGYLE	2-0 W		17,630
32		Sat	15	Football League, Division 1	Everton		L 0-1	19,233
33		Sat	22	Football League, Division 1	SOUTHAMPTON	2-0 W		17,169
34		Sat	29	FA Cup, 4th Round	FULHAM	1-1 D		24,574
35	February	Tue	1	FA Cup, 4th Round replay	Fulham		W 2-1	22,206
36		Sun	6	Football League, Division 1	Swansea City		W 3-1	14,461
37		Sat	19	FA Cup, 5th Round	Aston Villa		L 1-4	34,330
38		Sat	26	Football League, Division 1	ASTON VILLA	2-1 W		19,318
39	March	Wed	2	Football League, Division 1	Norwich City		L 0-3	16,662
40		Sat	5	Football League, Division 1	Coventry City		W 1-0	11,235
41		Sat	12	Football League, Division 1	NOTTS COUNTY	5-3 W		16,273
42		Sat	19	Football League, Division 1	TOTTENHAM HOTSPUR	0-1 L		27,373
43		Tue	22	Football League, Division 1	BIRMINGHAM CITY	2-1 W		14,229
44		Sat	26	Football League, Division 1	Stoke City		L 0-4	14,276
45	April	Sat	2	Football League, Division 1	West Ham United		L 1-2	22,647
46		Mon	4	Football League, Division 1	LUTON TOWN	5-2 W		20,120
47		Sat	9	Football League, Division 1	West Bromwich Albion		W 3-1	11,828
48		Sat	16	Football League, Division 1	NOTTINGHAM FOREST	1-3 L		17,537
49		Sat	23	Football League, Division 1	Manchester United		L 0-2	43,048
50		Sat	30	Football League, Division 1	ARSENAL	2-1 W		20,529
51	May	Mon	2	Football League, Division 1	Sunderland		D 2-2	13,971
52		Sat	7	Football League, Division 1	Ipswich Town		L 1-3	19,921
53		Sat	14	Football League, Division 1	LIVERPOOL	2-1 W		27,173

League ever-presents: J.C.B. Barnes, J.W. Rostron, S. Sherwood
Most appearances in total: J.C.B. Barnes 53 out of 53   **Most goals in total:** L.L. Blissett 33 (including the Football League's highest tally of 27)
Hat-tricks: L.L. Blissett (4 goals Match 10, & Match 41)   **Penalty goals:** L.L. Blissett 8
Sent off: None
Full international appearance(s) this season: G.J. Armstrong (Northern Ireland), J.C.B. Barnes (England), L.L. Blissett (England), K.F. Jackett (Wales)

	Armstrong, G.J.	Barnes, J.C.B.	Blissett, L.L.	Bolton, I.R.	Callaghan, N.I.	Franklin, P.L.	Gilligan, J.M.	Jackett, K.F.	Jenkins, R.A.	Jobson, R.I.	Johnson, D.N.C.	Lohman, J.H.P.	Palmer, C.A.	Patching, M.	Price, N.	Pritchett, K.B.	Rice, P.J.	Rostron, J.W.	Sherwood, S.	Sims, S.F.	Steele, E.G.	Sterling, W.R.	Taylor, L.	Terry, S.G.	Own goals
Apps	8	42	41	37	41	1	4	41	18	13	2	13		3			40	42	42	28		2	37	7	
Subs	+11							+2		+2	+6											+1	+2		
Goals	2	10	27		9		2	4	5	1		1		1			1	3					5	1	2
Apps	2	11	11	8	11		2	10	6	1	1	4	1	2	0	1	9	10	10	10	1		7	3	
Subs	+3				+1					+2	+2		+1	+1	+1										
Goals	2	3	6				1		6			3						1		1			1	1	1
1	X	X	X	R			S1	X	R2	S							X	X	G	X			X1		
2	S	X	X1		X			X	X1			X				S	R	X	G	X			R		
3	X1	X	X1p	X	R			X	X	S1		X				S	X		G	R					1
4	X1	X	X	X	R			X				X					X1	X	G				S		
5	X1	X	X	X	X2			X	X1			X					X	X	G						
6	X	X	X	X	X			X	X			R					X	X	G				S		
7	X	X	X1p	X	X1			X	R			S					X	X	G				X		
8	X	X	X2	X	X			X				X					X	X	G				X1		
9	X	X	X	X	X			X	S			R					X	X	G				X		
10		X	X4	X	X2			X	X2								X	X	G				X	X	
11	S	R	X1	X	X			X	X								X	X	G				X	X	
12	S1	X	X	X	X			X	X1								R	X	G				X	X	
13	S	X	X	X	X		X1	X				X						X	G				R	X1	
14	S	X	X	X	X			X	R			X						X	G				X	X	
15	R	X	X	X				X	S			X					X	X	G	X			X		
16		X	X1	S	X			X	X			R					X	X	G	X1			X		
17		X1	X1	X	X			X	X								X	X	G	X			X		
18		X	X	X	X			X	X								X	X	G	X			X1		
19		X	X	X	X			X	X2	S							X	X	G	R			X1		
20		X1	X	X	X		X	X									X	X	G	X			X		
21		X1	X2#	X	X		R	X		S							X	X	G	X			X1		
22		X2	X	X	X		X1	X									X	X	G	X			X		1
23		X	X	X	X		X	R		S							X	X	G	X			X		
24		X2	X1	X	X					X	X	X	X	S			R			X	G				
25		X	X	X	X			X	X								X	X1	G	X			X		
26		X		X	X		X	X1	X								X	X	G	X			X1		
27		X	X	X	X			X	X								X	X	G	X			X		
28		X	X	X	X			X1	X1								X	X	G	X			X		
29		X	X	X	X			X1	R			S					X	X	G	X			X		
30		X	X	X	X		X2	X									X	X	G	X			X		
31		X	X1	X	X		X	X									X	X1	G	X			X		
32		X	X	X	X			X	R			S					X	X	G	X			X		
33		X	X1	X	X		X	X									X	X	G	X			X		1
34		X	X	X	X		R	X				S1					X	X	G	X			X		
35		X1	X	X	X			X				X1					X	X	G	X			X		
36		X1	X2	X	X			X				X					X	X	G	X			X		
37	S	X	X1p	X	X			X				R					X	X	G	X			X		
38		X	X1	X	X			X		X							X	X1	G	X			X		
39	S	X	X	X	R			X		X							X	X	G	X			X		
40		X	X	X	X			X		X							X	X	G	X			X1		
41		X1	X3	X	X1			R		X		S					X	X	G	X			X		
42	S	X	X	X	X			X		R							X	X	G	X			X		
43	S	X	X2	X	X			X		R							X	X	G	X			X		
44	X	X	X	X	X			R				S					X	X	G	X			X		
45	S	X	X	X	X1					X		R					X	X	G	X			X		
46	S	X1	X2p	R1				X	X1			X					X	X	G				X	X	
47		X1	X	X	X1			X				X1					X	X	G				X	X	
48	S	X	X1p	X				X		X		R					X	X	G				X	X	
49		X	X	X				X		X	R						X	X	G	X		S	X		
50		X1	X1p	X	X			X		X							X	X	G	X			X		
51	S	X	X2	X	X			X			R	X					X	X	G				X		
52	S	X	X	X				X		R		X					X	X1	G	X		X			
53		X	X1	X	X			X		S				X1			X	X	G	R		X			

1983/84

Football League position: 11th out of 22 in Division 1
Manager: Graham Taylor

New league opponents: Wolverhampton Wanderers

Home-and-away league doubles
For – 2 (Notts County, Stoke City)
Against – 2 (Liverpool, Norwich City)

Divisional changes at end of season: Birmingham City, Notts County & Wolverhampton Wanderers to Division 2; Chelsea, Sheffield Wednesday & Newcastle United from Division 2

All Matches: Won 23, Drew 12, Lost 22, Goals 96-102

Highest Score: 5 (Matches 23 and 38)

	HOME					AWAY					
	Pl	W	D	L	For	Ag	W	D	L	For	Ag	Pts
Liverpool	42	14	5	2	50	12	8	9	4	23	20	80
Southampton	42	15	4	2	44	17	7	7	7	22	21	77
Nottingham Forest	42	14	4	3	47	17	8	4	9	29	28	74
Manchester United	42	14	3	4	43	18	6	11	4	28	23	74
Queens Park Rangers	42	14	4	3	37	12	8	3	10	30	25	73
Arsenal	42	10	5	6	41	29	8	4	9	33	31	63
Everton	42	9	9	3	21	12	7	5	9	23	30	62
Tottenham Hotspur	42	11	4	6	31	24	6	6	9	33	41	61
West Ham United	42	10	4	7	39	24	7	5	9	21	31	60
Aston Villa	42	14	3	4	34	22	3	6	12	25	39	60
WATFORD	42	9	7	5	36	31	7	2	12	32	46	57
Ipswich Town	42	11	4	6	34	23	4	4	13	21	34	53
Sunderland	42	8	9	4	26	18	5	4	12	16	35	52
Norwich City	42	9	8	4	34	20	3	7	11	14	29	51
Leicester City	42	11	5	5	40	30	2	7	12	25	38	51
Luton Town	42	7	5	9	30	33	7	4	10	23	38	51
West Bromwich Albion	42	10	4	7	30	25	4	5	12	18	37	51
Stoke City	42	11	4	6	30	23	2	7	12	14	40	50
Coventry City	42	8	5	8	33	33	5	6	10	24	44	50
Birmingham City	42	7	7	7	19	18	5	5	11	20	32	48
Notts County	42	6	7	8	31	36	4	4	13	19	36	41
Wolverhampton Wanderers	42	4	8	9	15	28	2	3	16	12	52	29

No	DATE			COMPETITION	OPPONENTS	HOME	AWAY	ATTENDANCE	
1	August	Sat	27	Football League, Division 1	COVENTRY CITY	2-3 L		15,551	
2		Tue	30	Football League, Division 1	IPSWICH TOWN	2-2 D		15,419	
3	September	Sat	3	Football League, Division 1	Birmingham City		L 0-2		11,931
4		Tue	6	Football League, Division 1	Queens Park Rangers		D 1-1		17,111
5		Sat	10	Football League, Division 1	NOTTS COUNTY	3-1 W		12,896	
6		Wed	14	UEFA Cup, 1st Round, 1st Leg	1FC Kaiserslautern		L 1-3		19,906
7		Sat	17	Football League, Division 1	Stoke City		W 4-0		12,691
8		Sat	24	Football League, Division 1	TOTTENHAM HOTSPUR	2-3 L		21,056	
9		Wed	28	UEFA Cup, 1st Round, 2nd Leg	1FC KAISERSLAUTERN	3-0 W		21,457	
10	October	Sat	1	Football League, Division 1	West Bromwich Albion		L 0-2		14,456
11		Tue	4	Football Lge Cup, 2nd Round, 1st Leg	Huddersfield Town		L 1-2		10,631
12		Sat	15	Football League, Division 1	NORWICH CITY	1-3 L		12,843	
13		Wed	19	UEFA Cup, 2nd Round, 1st Leg	LEVSKI SPARTAK	1-1 D		16,139	
14		Sat	22	Football League, Division 1	Everton		L 0-1		13,571
15		Tue	25	Football Lge Cup, 2nd Round, 2nd Leg	HUDDERSFIELD TOWN	2-2 D		13,006	
16		Fri	28	Football League, Division 1	WEST HAM UNITED	0-0 D		14,559	
17	November	Wed	2	UEFA Cup, 2nd Round, 2nd Leg	Levski Spartak (after extra time)		W 3-1		60,000
18		Sat	5	Football League, Division 1	LEICESTER CITY	3-3 D		14,487	
19		Sat	12	Football League, Division 1	Sunderland		L 0-3		15,407
20		Sat	19	Football League, Division 1	Manchester United		L 1-4		43,111
21		Wed	23	UEFA Cup, 3rd Round, 1st Leg	SPARTA PRAGUE	2-3 L		15,590	
22		Sat	26	Football League, Division 1	LUTON TOWN	1-2 L		17,791	
23	December	Sat	3	Football League, Division 1	Wolverhampton Wanderers		W 5-0		11,905
24		Wed	7	UEFA Cup, 3rd Round, 2nd Leg	Sparta Prague		L 0-4		38,000
25		Sat	10	Football League, Division 1	NOTTINGHAM FOREST	3-2 W		14,047	
26		Sat	17	Football League, Division 1	Arsenal		L 1-3		25,104
27		Mon	26	Football League, Division 1	ASTON VILLA	3-2 W		18,276	
28		Tue	27	Football League, Division 1	Southampton		L 0-1		20,659
29		Sat	31	Football League, Division 1	BIRMINGHAM CITY	1-0 W		14,403	
30	January	Mon	2	Football League, Division 1	Tottenham Hotspur		W 3-2		32,495
31		Sat	7	FA Cup, 3rd Round	Luton Town		D 2-2		15,007
32		Tue	10	FA Cup, 3rd Round replay	LUTON TOWN (after extra time)	4-3 W		20,586	
33		Sat	14	Football League, Division 1	Coventry City		W 2-1		13,307
34		Sat	21	Football League, Division 1	STOKE CITY	2-0 W		14,469	
35		Sat	28	FA Cup, 4th Round	Charlton Athletic		W 2-0		22,392
36	February	Wed	1	Football League, Division 1	Liverpool		L 0-3		20,746
37		Sat	4	Football League, Division 1	WEST BROMWICH ALBION	3-1 W		14,133	
38		Sat	11	Football League, Division 1	Notts County		W 5-3		8.078
39		Sat	18	FA Cup, 5th Round	BRIGHTON & HOVE ALBION	3-1 W		28,000	
40		Tue	21	Football League, Division 1	West Ham United		W 4-2		19,241
41		Sat	25	Football League, Division 1	EVERTON	4-4 D		16,892	
42	March	Sat	3	Football League, Division 1	Leicester City		L 1-4		13,295
43		Sat	10	FA Cup, 6th Round	Birmingham City		W 3-1		40,220
44		Sat	17	Football League, Division 1	QUEENS PARK RANGERS	1-0 W		18,797	
45		Tue	20	Football League, Division 1	SUNDERLAND	2-1 W		16,255	
46		Sat	24	Football League, Division 1	Ipswich Town		D 0-0		14,956
47		Sat	31	Football League, Division 1	LIVERPOOL	0-2 L		21,293	
48	April	Sat	7	Football League, Division 1	Norwich City		L 1-6		14,451
49		Sat	14	FA Cup, Semi-Final	Plymouth Argyle (at Aston Villa)	(W 1-0)		43,858	
50		Tue	17	Football League, Division 1	MANCHESTER UNITED	0-0 D		20,764	
51		Sat	21	Football League, Division 1	Aston Villa		L 1-2		16,110
52		Tue	24	Football League, Division 1	SOUTHAMPTON	1-1 D		16,755	
53		Sat	28	Football League, Division 1	Luton Town		W 2-1		12,594
54	May	Sat	5	Football League, Division 1	WOLVERHAMPTON WANDERERS	0-0 D		13,534	
55		Mon	7	Football League, Division 1	Nottingham Forest		L 1-5		13,732
56		Sat	12	Football League, Division 1	ARSENAL	2-1 W		22,486	
57		Sat	19	FA Cup, Final	Everton (at Wembley Stadium)		(L 0-2)		100,000

League ever-presents: None
Most appearances in total: N.I. Callaghan 56 out of 57   **Most goals in total:** M.J.G. Johnston 24
Hat-tricks: M.J.G. Johnston (Match 23)   **Penalty goals:** J.C.B. Barnes 1, N.I. Callaghan 1, M.J.G. Johnston 1
Sent off: S.G. Terry (Match 14), G.G. Reilly (Match 25), N. Price (Match 26), J.W. Rostron (Match 53)
Full international appearance(s) this season: J.C.B. Barnes (England), K.F. Jackett (Wales), M.J.G. Johnston (Scotland)

	Atkinson, P.G.	Bardsley, D.J.	Barnes, J.C.B.	Bolton, I.R.	Callaghan, N.I.	Cassidy, F.J.A.	Franklin, P.L.	Gibbs, N.J.	Gilligan, J.M.	Jackett, K.F.	Jobson, R.I.	Johnson, D.N.C.	Johnston, M.J.G.	Lohman, J.H.P.	Palmer, C.A.	Patching, M.	Porter, G.M.	Price, N.	Reilly, G.G.	Rice, P.J.	Richardson, I.P.	Rostron, J.W.	Sherwood, S.	Sims, S.F.	Sinnott, L.	Steele, E.G.	Sterling, W.R.	Taylor, L.	Terry, S.G.	Own goals
Apps	8	25	39	7	41		24	2	9	31	11	2	28	7	10	1	1	7	27	6	4	39	40	22	19	2	7	26	17	
Subs	+3			+1				+1	+3		+2		+1			+1	+1		+3					+1			+3	+1		
Goals			11		10				4		2		20	2	1				8		2	4	1			1		1	1	
Apps	0	7	15	4	15	0	10	2	4	13	7	2	7	1	6			4	8	0	6	14	14	8	2	1	0	8	7	
Subs	+2				+1				+1		+2	+1						+1	+1			+1			+1			+1		
Goals			5		2				3	1			4						4		3	3		1				1		
1			X1	X	X				X		S1		X						X			X	G	R				X	X	
2		X	X	X1	X								X1						X	X		X	G					X	X	
3		X		X	X					X	S		X		R				X	X		X	G						X	
4		X1		X	X					X	X		X		X							X	G	X						
5		X1		X	X			S		X	X		R	X1					X1			X	G	X						
6		X		X	X		X		X1	X	X		X	R					S			X	G	R					S	
7		X2		X	X					X	X1		X1	X					X			X	G						X	
8		X		X1p					S	X	X		X	X					R			X1	G		X				X	
9		X	X		X				X	X	X		X							X2	X	G							X	1
10		X	X	X	X				R	X	X		X						S	X	G			X					X	
11		X1	X	X	X				X	X			X					X	X	X		X		G			X		
12		X	S	X					X	X	R							X	X		X		X	G			X1	
13		R	X	X					X	X	X	S		X				R	X1	G	S						X	
14		X	X						X	X	X	X		X					X	G			X				X	
15		X		X			X		X1	R	X	X		X					S	X	G	X1						
16		X	X	X		X				X								X	G	X	X						
17		X	X	X1		X				X			X			X		X1	X1	G	X						
18		X	X	X1		X				X			X				X	X2	X	G	X						
19		X	X	X		X				X			X	X	X	X	X						X		
20		X		X1		X			X		X		X					X	G	X	X					X	
21		X		X		X	X	S1	R	S	R					X	X1	G	X				X		
22	X	X		X1		X			X		X				X	X	X	G	X					X	
23	X	X		X		X		X		X3		S	X	R2		X	G	X					X	
24		X		X	S	X	X		X	R			R			X	X	G	X		S			X	
25	X	X		X1	X		X		X		X1		X	X1		X	G	X					X	
26	X	X		X	X		X		X1		X	R		X	G	X	S				X	
27		X	X1	X	X		X2	X		X				X	G	X				X	
28	S	X	X	X	X		X		X		R		X	G	X				X	
29		X	X	X	X		X		X1		X		X	G	X				X	
30		X	X1p	X	X		X		X2		X		X	G	X				X	
31	X	X1	X	X		X		X1p		X		X	G	X				X	
32	X	X1	X1	X		X		X1		X1		X	G	X				X	
33	X	X	X	X		X		X		X1		X	G1	X				X	
34	X	X	X	X		X		X1		X1		X	G	X				X	
35	X	X	X	X		X		X1		X1		X	G	X				X	
36	S	X	X	X	X		X		R		X	G	X				X	
37	S	X	X	X	X	X2	X	R	X1		X	G	X					
38		X	R	X2		X		X1		X1		X	G				S	X	X	1
39	S	X	X	X	X		X1	X1	R1		X	G				X	X	
40	X	X	X2	X1	X		X		X1		X1	G	X				X	
41	X	X	X2	X	X		X		X1		X1	G	X				X	
42		X	X	R		X		X	X	X		X1	G	X		S	X	
43	X	X2	X	X	X		X		X		X	G				X1	X	
44	X	X	X	X		X	S		X	R	X1	G	X			X	X	
45	X	X	X	X		X		X2		X	G	X		R	S	X	
46	X	X	X	X	X		X		X	G	X			X	X	
47	R	X	X	X		X		X	S	X	X	G	X	
48	R	X	X	X		X		X1		X	S	X	X	X	
49		X	X	X		S	X		X	X1	X	G	X	X	R	
50		X	X	X	X		X		X	X	G	X	X	X	
51	X	X	X	R		X		S	X	X	G	X	X1	X	
52		X	X	X		X1		X	X	G	X	X	X	
53	X	X	R	X1		X1		X	X	G	X	S	X	X	
54	X		X	X	S	X		X	X	G	X	R	X	X	
55	X		X	X	X	X	X1		G	X	X	X	X	
56		X	X	S		X	X1		X	X1	R	G	X	X	X	
57	S	X	X		X		X		R	X		G	X	X	X	

1984/85

Football League position: 11th out of 22 in Division 1

Manager: Graham Taylor

	HOME					AWAY					
	Pl	W	D	L For Ag		W	D	L For Ag		Pts
Everton	42	16	3	2 58 17		12	3	6 30 26		90
Liverpool	42	12	4	5 36 19		10	7	4 32 16		77
Tottenham Hotspur	42	11	3	7 46 31		12	5	4 32 20		77
Manchester United	42	13	6	2 47 13		9	4	8 30 34		76
Southampton	42	13	4	4 29 18		6	7	8 27 29		68
Chelsea	42	13	3	5 38 20		5	9	7 25 28		66
Arsenal	42	14	5	2 37 14		5	4	12 24 35		66
Sheffield Wednesday	42	12	7	2 39 21		5	7	9 19 24		65
Nottingham Forest	42	13	4	4 35 18		6	3	12 21 30		64
Aston Villa	42	10	7	4 34 20		5	4	12 26 40		56
WATFORD	42	10	5	6 48 30		4	8	9 33 41		55
West Bromwich Albion	42	11	4	6 36 23		5	3	13 22 39		55
Luton Town	42	12	5	4 40 22		3	4	14 17 39		54
Newcastle United	42	11	4	6 33 26		2	9	10 22 44		52
Leicester City	42	10	4	7 39 25		5	2	14 26 48		51
West Ham United	42	7	8	6 27 23		6	4	11 24 45		51
Ipswich Town	42	8	7	6 27 20		5	4	12 19 37		50
Coventry City	42	11	3	7 29 22		4	2	15 18 42		50
Queens Park Rangers	42	11	6	4 41 30		2	5	14 12 42		50
Norwich City	42	9	6	6 28 24		4	4	13 18 40		49
Sunderland	42	7	6	8 20 26		3	4	14 20 36		40
Stoke City	42	3	3	15 18 41		0	5	16 6 50		17

New league opponents: None

Home-and-away league doubles
For – 1 (Stoke City)
Against – 3 (Coventry City, Everton, West Bromwich Albion)

Divisional changes at end of season: Norwich City, Sunderland & Stoke City to Division 2; Oxford United, Birmingham City & Manchester City from Division 2

All Matches: Won 19, Drew 15, Lost 18, Goals 102-79

Highest Score: 5 (Matches 28, 42, 50 and 51)

No	DATE			COMPETITION	OPPONENTS	HOME	AWAY	ATTENDANCE
1	August	Sat	25	Football League, Division 1	Manchester United		D 1-1	53,668
2		Tue	28	Football League, Division 1	QUEENS PARK RANGERS	1-1 D		23,165
3	September	Sat	1	Football League, Division 1	ARSENAL	3-4 L		21,320
4		Wed	5	Football League, Division 1	Leicester City		D 1-1	12,055
5		Sat	8	Football League, Division 1	West Ham United		L 0-2	20,377
6		Sat	15	Football League, Division 1	ASTON VILLA	3-3 D		16,440
7		Sat	22	Football League, Division 1	Norwich City		L 2-3	14,896
8		Tue	25	Football Lge Cup, 2nd Round, 1st Leg	CARDIFF CITY	3-1 W		12,884
9		Sat	29	Football League, Division 1	EVERTON	4-5 L		18,335
10	October	Sat	6	Football League, Division 1	COVENTRY CITY	0-1 L		15,184
11		Tue	9	Football Lge Cup, 2nd Round, 2nd Leg	Cardiff City		L 0-1	4,607
12		Sat	13	Football League, Division 1	Chelsea		W 3-2	25,340
13		Sat	20	Football League, Division 1	Luton Town		L 2-3	12,192
14		Sat	27	Football League, Division 1	NEWCASTLE UNITED	3-3 D		18,794
15		Wed	31	Football League Cup, 3rd Round	Leeds United		W 4-0	21,221
16	November	Sat	3	Football League, Division 1	Ipswich Town		D 3-3	15,680
17		Sat	10	Football League, Division 1	SUNDERLAND	3-1 W		18,953
18		Sat	17	Football League, Division 1	SHEFFIELD WEDNESDAY	1-0 W		18,338
19		Tue	20	Football League Cup, 4th Round	WEST BROMWICH ALBION	4-1 W		16,378
20		Sat	24	Football League, Division 1	Stoke City		W 3-1	10,564
21	December	Sat	1	Football League, Division 1	NOTTINGHAM FOREST	2-0 W		17,758
22		Sat	8	Football League, Division 1	West Bromwich Albion		L 1-2	13,581
23		Sat	15	Football League, Division 1	TOTTENHAM HOTSPUR	1-2 L		24,437
24		Sat	22	Football League, Division 1	Arsenal		D 1-1	31,302
25		Wed	26	Football League, Division 1	Southampton		W 2-1	19,754
26		Sat	29	Football League, Division 1	LEICESTER CITY	4-1 W		19,491
27	January	Tue	1	Football League, Division 1	Liverpool		D 1-1	27,073
28		Sat	5	FA Cup, 3rd Round	SHEFFIELD UNITED	5-0 W		17,604
29		Wed	23	Football League Cup, 5th Round	SUNDERLAND	0-1 L		22,591
30		Sat	26	FA Cup, 4th Round	Grimsby Town		W 3-1	12,989
31	February	Sat	2	Football League, Division 1	Everton		L 0-4	34,026
32		Sun	24	Football League, Division 1	Sheffield Wednesday		D 1-1	27,871
33	March	Sat	2	Football League, Division 1	Newcastle United		L 1-3	24,923
34		Mon	4	FA Cup, 5th Round	Luton Town		D 0-0	18,506
35		Wed	6	FA Cup, 5th Round replay	LUTON TOWN (after extra time)	2-2 D		19,867
36		Sat	9	FA Cup, 5th Round, 2nd replay	Luton Town		L 0-1	15,586
37		Tue	12	Football League, Division 1	Sunderland		D 1-1	22,375
38		Sat	16	Football League, Division 1	CHELSEA	1-3 L		16,318
39		Tue	19	Football League, Division 1	LUTON TOWN	3-0 W		14,185
40		Sat	23	Football League, Division 1	Coventry City		L 1-3	9,794
41		Sat	30	Football League, Division 1	Queens Park Rangers		L 0-2	12,771
42	April	Tue	2	Football League, Division 1	WEST HAM UNITED	5-0 W		17,389
43		Sat	6	Football League, Division 1	SOUTHAMPTON	1-1 D		17,456
44		Sat	13	Football League, Division 1	NORWICH CITY	2-0 W		15,262
45		Tue	16	Football League, Division 1	IPSWICH TOWN	3-1 W		16,074
46		Wed	24	Football League, Division 1	Aston Villa		D 1-1	11,493
47		Sat	27	Football League, Division 1	STOKE CITY	2-0 W		14,613
48	May	Sat	4	Football League, Division 1	Nottingham Forest		D 1-1	12,649
49		Tue	7	Football League, Division 1	WEST BROMWICH ALBION	0-2 L		14,074
50		Sat	11	Football League, Division 1	Tottenham Hotspur		W 5-1	23,167
51		Mon	13	Football League, Division 1	MANCHESTER UNITED	5-1 W		20,500
52		Fri	17	Football League, Division 1	Liverpool		L 3-4	29,130

League ever-presents: None
Most appearances in total: L.L. Blissett 51 (including three substitute appearances) out of 52   **Most goals in total:** L.L. Blissett 28
Hat-tricks: J.C.B. Barnes (Match 8), L.L. Blissett (4 goals - Match 28)   **Penalty goals:** L.L. Blissett 6
Sent off: None
Full international appearance(s) this season: J.C.B. Barnes (England), K.F. Jackett (Wales), M.J.G. Johnston (Scotland), J. McClelland (Northern Ireland)

	Bardsley, D.J.	Barnes, J.C.B.	Blissett, L.L.	Callaghan, N.I.	Coton, A.P.	Gibbs, N.J.	Gilligan, J.M.	Jackett, K.F.	Jobson, R.I.	Johnston, M.J.G.	Lohman, J.H.P.	McClelland J.	Porter, G.M.	Reilly, G.G.	Richardson, I.P.	Rostron, J.W.	Sherwood, S.	Simnott, L.	Sterling, W.R.	Taylor, L.	Terry, S.G.	West, C.	Own goals
Apps	17	40	38	36	33	11	5	35	2	9	5	29	5	19	1	38	9	29	13	38	38	12	
Subs		+3		+2		+1	+5	+1			+2		+4	+2					+1	+2	+1		
Goals		12	21	8				4	1	3		1		6		3		4	3	4	7	4	
Apps	3	7	10	7	7			4		8	1	3	7			5		10	3	9	7	9	10
Subs	+1			+1															+1				
Goals		3	7	2				2				1								1	3	2	
1	X	R	X	X1				X		X				S		X	G	X		X	X		
2	X		R	X				X		X				X1		X	G	X	S	X	X		
3	R	X	S1	X				X		X1				X		X	G	X		X	X	1	
4	X	X	S	X				X		X				R		X	G	X		X1	X		
5	X	X	X	X				X		X			S	R			G	X	X		X		
6	X	X1	X1	X			S	X		X1							G	X	R	X	X		
7	X	X	X	X				X		X1			X					X		X	X1		
8	X	X3	X	X				X		X				X		X	G			X	X		
9	X	X1	R	X1	G			X		X				X1				X	S	X	X	1	
10	X	X	S	X	G			X		X		R	X					X		X	X		
11	X	X	X	X	G									R				X	X	S	X		
12	X	X1	X	X	G		X	X1	X1									X	X	X			
13	X	X	X1	X	G		S	X	X					X1				X	X	R			
14	X	X	X2	X	G			X						X				X	X	X1	X		
15	X	X	X2		G		X1									X		X	X1		X		
16	X	X1	X2	X	G					X				X				X		X	X		
17	X	X	X	R	G					X1		X		X				X	X1	S	X1		
18		X1	X		G					X		X		X		X		X	X	X	X		
19		X	X1		G					X		X		X1		X		X	X	X1	X1		
20		X	X1		G	S				X		X		R1		X1		X	X	X	X		
21		X	X	X	G					X		X		X1		X		X	X1	X	X		
22		X1	X	X	G					X		X		S		X		X	R	X	X		
23		X	X	R	G					X		X		X		X		X	S	X	X1		
24		X	X	S	G					X	R	X		X		X		X		X1	X		
25		X	X2p	X	G		S				R	X		X		X		X		X	X		
26		X1	X		G		S				R	X		X1		X		X	X1	X	X1		
27		X	X1p		G		X	S				X		X		X		X	R	X	X		
28		X	X4p		G			X				X		X		X		X	X	X1	X		
29		X	X	S	G			X				X		X		X		X	R	X	X		
30			X2	X	G		X1	X				X				X		X	X	X	X		
31	X	X	X	X	G		R	X		S		X				X		X		X	X		
32		X	X	X1				X				X				X	G	X	X	X	X		
33	X	R	X	X						S		X1				X	G	X	X	X	X		
34			X	X			X	X		X	X	X				X	G	X	X	X	X		
35	S		X	X			X			X		X				X	G	X	R	X1	X1		
36		X	X	X	G					X		X				X		X	X	X	X		
37		X1	S	G						X	X	X	X		R	X		X	X	X	X		
38	X	X1	R	G			S			X	X	X	X			X		X		X	X		
39	X	X	X2p	X1	G		X	X		X						X				X	X		
40	R	X	X1	X	G			X		X		S				X				X	X		
41		X	R	G	X			X		X		S				X				X	X	X	
42		X1	X2	X	G			X		X						X			X1	X	X1		
43		X	X	G	X			X		X						X				X	X	X	
44		X1	X	X	G			X		X						X1				X	X	X	
45		X1	X	X	G			X		X						X1				X	X	X1	
46		X	X	X1	G			X		X		X				X			X	X		X	
47		X	X1p	X	G			X		X1		X				X			X	X			
48		X	X	X	G			X		X		X				X				X	X	X1	
49		X	X	X	G			X		X		X				X				X	X		
50		X1	X1p	X1	G	X		X		X		X				X				X	X	X1	1
51		X	R1	X2	G					X1		X	S			X			X	X	X	X1	
52		X1		X	G	X		X				X	X			X				X	X	X1	1

1985/86

Football League position: 12th out of 22 in Division 1
Manager: Graham Taylor

New league opponents: None

Home-and-away league doubles
For – 5 (Arsenal, Birmingham City, Chelsea, Coventry City, Manchester City)
Against – 4 (Everton, Liverpool, Luton Town, West Ham United)

Divisional changes at end of season: Ipswich Town, Birmingham City & West Bromwich Albion to Division 2; Norwich City, Charlton Athletic & Wimbledon from Division 2

All Matches: Won 21, Drew 15, Lost 17, Goals 87-72

Highest Score: 5 (Matches 3 and 53)

	HOME						AWAY					
	Pl	W	D	L	For	Ag	W	D	L	For	Ag	Pts
Liverpool	42	16	4	1	58	10	14	10	6	5	31	23	88
Everton	42	16	3	2	54	18	10	5	6	33	23	86
West Ham United	42	17	2	2	48	16	9	4	8	26	24	84
Manchester United	42	12	5	4	35	12	10	5	6	35	24	76
Sheffield Wednesday	42	13	6	2	36	23	8	4	9	27	31	73
Chelsea	42	12	4	5	32	27	8	7	6	25	29	71
Arsenal	42	13	5	3	29	15	7	4	10	20	32	69
Nottingham Forest	42	11	5	5	38	25	8	6	7	31	28	68
Luton Town	42	12	6	3	37	15	6	6	9	24	29	66
Tottenham Hotspur	42	12	2	7	47	25	7	6	8	27	27	65
Newcastle United	42	12	5	4	46	31	5	7	9	21	41	63
WATFORD	42	11	6	4	40	22	5	5	11	29	40	59
Queens Park Rangers	42	12	3	6	33	20	3	4	14	20	44	52
Southampton	42	10	6	5	32	18	2	4	15	19	44	46
Manchester City	42	7	7	7	25	26	4	5	12	18	31	45
Aston Villa	42	7	6	8	27	28	3	8	10	24	39	44
Coventry City	42	6	5	10	31	35	5	5	11	17	36	43
Oxford United	42	7	7	7	34	27	3	5	13	28	53	42
Leicester City	42	7	8	6	35	35	3	4	14	19	41	42
Ipswich Town	42	8	5	8	20	24	3	3	15	12	31	41
Birmingham City	42	5	2	14	13	25	3	3	15	17	48	29
West Bromwich Albion	42	3	8	10	21	36	1	4	16	14	53	24

No	DATE			COMPETITION	OPPONENTS	HOME	AWAY	ATTENDANCE
1	August	Sat	17	Football League, Division 1	Tottenham Hotspur		L 0-4	29,884
2		Tue	20	Football League, Division 1	BIRMINGHAM CITY	3-0 W		14,029
3		Sat	24	Football League, Division 1	WEST BROMWICH ALBION	5-1 W		13,599
4		Mon	26	Football League, Division 1	Sheffield Wednesday		L 1-2	21,962
5		Sat	31	Football League, Division 1	COVENTRY CITY	3-0 W		13,832
6	September	Wed	4	Football League, Division 1	Leicester City		D 2-2	9,672
7		Sat	7	Football League, Division 1	Liverpool		L 1-3	31,395
8		Sat	14	Football League, Division 1	QUEENS PARK RANGERS	2-0 W		16,167
9		Sat	21	Football League, Division 1	Nottingham Forest		L 2-3	12,921
10		Tue	24	Football Lge Cup, 2nd Round, 1st Leg	Crewe Alexandra		W 3-1	4,252
11		Sat	28	Football League, Division 1	CHELSEA	3-1 W		16,081
12	October	Sat	5	Football League, Division 1	Southampton		L 1-3	14,172
13		Tue	8	Football Lge Cup, 2nd Round, 2nd Leg	CREWE ALEXANDRA	3-2 W		11,538
14		Sat	12	Football League, Division 1	MANCHESTER CITY	3-2 W		15,559
15		Sat	19	Football League, Division 1	Everton		L 1-4	26,425
16		Sat	26	Football League, Division 1	OXFORD UNITED	2-2 D		16,448
17		Tue	29	Football League Cup, 3rd Round	QUEENS PARK RANGERS	0-1 L		16,826
18	November	Sat	2	Football League, Division 1	Newcastle United		D 1-1	20,649
19		Sat	9	Football League, Division 1	ASTON VILLA	1-1 D		14,085
20		Sat	16	Football League, Division 1	West Ham United		L 1-2	21,490
21		Sat	23	Football League, Division 1	LUTON TOWN	1-2 L		16,197
22		Sat	30	Football League, Division 1	Manchester United		D 1-1	42,181
23	December	Sat	7	Football League, Division 1	Birmingham City		W 2-1	7,043
24		Sat	14	Football League, Division 1	TOTTENHAM HOTSPUR	1-0 W		16,195
25		Sun	22	Football League, Division 1	West Bromwich Albion		L 1-3	11,092
26		Sat	28	Football League, Division 1	LEICESTER CITY	2-1 W		14,709
27	January	Wed	1	Football League, Division 1	Ipswich Town		D 0-0	15,922
28		Sat	4	FA Cup, 3rd Round	Coventry City		W 3-1	10,498
29		Sun	12	Football League, Division 1	LIVERPOOL	2-3 L		16,957
30		Sat	18	Football League, Division 1	Coventry City		W 2-0	7,499
31		Sat	25	FA Cup, 4th Round	Manchester City		D 1-1	31,632
32	February	Sat	1	Football League, Division 1	SHEFFIELD WEDNESDAY	2-1 W		13,144
33		Mon	3	FA Cup, 4th Round replay	MANCHESTER CITY (after extra time)	0-0 D		19,347
34		Thu	6	FA Cup, 4th Round, 2nd replay	Manchester City		W 3-1	27,260
35	March	Wed	5	FA Cup, 5th Round	BURY	1-1 D		13,316
36		Sat	8	FA Cup, 5th Round replay	Bury		W 3-0	7,501
37		Tue	11	FA Cup, 6th Round	Liverpool		D 0-0	36,775
38		Sat	15	Football League, Division 1	Manchester City		W 1-0	18,899
39		Mon	17	FA Cup, 6th Round replay	LIVERPOOL (after extra time)	1-2 L		28,097
40		Sat	22	Football League, Division 1	Queens Park Rangers		L 1-2	14,079
41		Sat	29	Football League, Division 1	IPSWICH TOWN	0-0 D		14,988
42		Mon	31	Football League, Division 1	Arsenal		W 2-0	19,599
43	April	Tue	1	Football League, Division 1	ARSENAL	3-0 W		18,410
44		Sat	5	Football League, Division 1	NEWCASTLE UNITED	4-1 W		14,704
45		Wed	9	Football League, Division 1	Oxford United		D 1-1	10,680
46		Sat	12	Football League, Division 1	Aston Villa		L 1-4	12,781
47		Tue	15	Football League, Division 1	EVERTON	0-2 L		18,960
48		Sat	19	Football League, Division 1	WEST HAM UNITED	0-2 L		16,696
49		Mon	21	Football League, Division 1	NOTTINGHAM FOREST	1-1 D		11,510
50		Sat	26	Football League, Division 1	Luton Town		L 2-3	11,810
51		Tue	29	Football League, Division 1	SOUTHAMPTON	1-1 D		11,868
52	May	Sat	3	Football League, Division 1	MANCHESTER UNITED	1-1 D		18,414
53		Mon	5	Football League, Division 1	Chelsea		W 5-1	12,017

League ever-presents: None
Most appearances in total: S.G. Terry 52 out of 53   **Most goals in total:** C. West 16
Hat-tricks: C. West (Match 3)   **Penalty goals:** K.F. Jackett 4
Sent off: None
Full international appearance(s) this season: M. Allen (Wales), J.C.B. Barnes (England), K.F. Jackett (Wales), J. McClelland (Northern Ireland)

	Allen, M.	Bardsley, D.J.	Barnes, J.C.B.	Blissett, L.L.	Callaghan, N.I.	Coton, A.P.	Franklin, P.L.	Gibbs, N.J.	Jackett, K.F.	Lohman, J.H.P. //	McClelland, J.	Porter, G.M.	Roberts, I.W.	Rostron, J.W.	Sherwood, S.	Sinnott, L.	Smillie, N.	Sterling, W.R.	Talbot, B.E.	Taylor, L. //	Terry, S.G.	West, C. //
Apps	10	10	39	20	21	40	4	40	41	0	31	7	1	29	2	18	10	23	41	1	41	33
Subs	+3	+3		+3	+2					+4		+1	+3	+1				+6	+1			
Goals	2	2	9	7	4			1	4	1	1	1		5		2	3	3	7		4	13
Apps	0		11	3	7	11		11	10	2	9	1		11		3	2	8	10	1	11	10
Subs	+3									+2	+1											+1
Goals			4	1	2				3					1			1	2			1	3
1			X	X	X	G		X	X		X			X					X		X	X
2			X2	X	X	G		X	X		X			X					X		X	X1
3			X	X	X	G		X	X		X			X					X1		X1	X3
4			X	X1	S	G		X	X		X			X				R	X		X	X
5			X	R	X	G		X	X		X			X1			S1		X		X	X1
6			X		X	G		X	X		X			X2			X		X		X	X
7			X	S	X	G		X	X		X			X				R	X		X	X
8			X	X1	X1	G		X	X		X			X					X		X	X
9			X	X	X1	G		X	X		X		S	X1					X		R	X
10			X	X1	X	G		X	X1		R		S	X1					X		X	X
11			X1	X1	X	G		X	X		X			X					X		X1	X1
12			X	X	X	G		X	X	S	X			X					X1		X	R
13			X1	X	X1	G		X	X	S	R			X					X		X1	X
14			X1	X1	X1	G		X	X		X					X			X		X	X
15			X	S	X	G		X	X1p		X					X			X	R	X	X
16			X	X1	X	G		X	X		X1					X			X		X	X
17			X	X	X	G		X	X	R	X					X			X	X	X	S
18			X	X	X	G		X	X		X					X			X		X	X1
19			X	R	X	G		X	X		X					X	X1		X		X	X
20	X	X	X			G			X		X	R				X	X	S	X1		X	
21	X	X	X			G			X		X	R				X	X	S	X	X1	X	
22			X	X		G		X	X		X					X	X	S	R		X	X1
23			X1			G	X	X	X		X				X	X	X1	R	X		X	X
24			X1			G		X	X	X	S				X	X	X	R	X		X	X
25			X			G		X	X	S	X				X	X	R	X1	X		X	X
26	S		X	R		G		X	X		X			X			X	X	X		X	X2
27	R		X		S	G		X	X		X			X			X	X	X		X	X
28			X		X	G		X	X1		X			X			X	X	X		X	X2
29			X		X	G	X	X	X1	S1	X			X			X	R	X			X
30			X2		R	G		X	X	S	X			X			X	X	X		X	X
31			X		X	G		X	X1p		X			X			X	X	X		X	X
32			X1		X	G		X	X		X			X			X	X	X		X	X1
33	S		X		X	G		X	X		X			X			R	X	X		X	X
34			X1			G		X	X	S	X			X			X1	X1	R		X	X
35			X1		X	G		X	X	X	X			X			X	X	X		X	X1
36	S		R		X1	G		X	X		X			X			X1	X	X		X	X1
37			X			G		X	X		X			X	X		X	X	X		X	X
38			X			G		X	X		X			X	X		X	X	X1		X	X
39	S		X1			G		X	X		X			X	X		X	R	X		X	X
40	S	X	X		X	G		X	X		X							X	X		X1	R
41		S	R		X	G		X	X		X			X			X	X	X		X	
42	X1	X	X1			G		X	X		X		S	X			R	X	X		X	
43	X1	X	X			G		X	X1p		X	X					X1		X		X	
44	X	X	X		X1	G		X	X		X	X1					X1		X1		X	
45	X	X	X			G		X	X		X1	R	S				X	X	X		X	
46	R	X	X			G		X	X		X		S				X1		X	X	X	
47	S	X	X			G	R	X	X		X						X	X	X		X	
48		X	X			G	R	X	X		X					S	X	X	X		X	X
49	R	X	X1		X	G		X	X		X						X	S	X		X	X
50	R	S	X			G		X	X1p		X					X1	X	X	X		X	X
51			X	S		G		X	X		X					X	R	X	X		X	X1
52			X	X1		G		X	X		X					X	X	X	X		X	X
53		S2	X	X		G		X	X		X					R		X	X2		X	X1

1986/87

Football League position: 9th out of 22 in Division 1
Manager: Graham Taylor

New league opponents: None

Home-and-away league doubles
For – 3 (Leicester City, Luton Town, Oxford United)
Against – 3 (Coventry City, Queens Park Rangers, Wimbledon)

Divisional changes at end of season: Leicester City, Manchester City & Aston Villa to Division 2; Derby County & Portsmouth from Division 2

All Matches: Won 23, Drew 12, Lost 18, Goals 86-71

Highest Score: 5 (Match 19)

		HOME					AWAY					
	Pl	W	D	L	For	Ag	W	D	L	For	Ag	Pts
Everton	42	16	4	1	49	11	10	4	7	27	20	86
Liverpool	42	15	3	3	43	16	8	5	8	29	26	77
Tottenham Hotspur	42	14	3	4	40	14	7	5	9	29	29	71
Arsenal	42	12	5	4	31	12	8	5	8	27	23	70
Norwich City	42	9	10	2	27	20	8	7	6	26	31	68
Wimbledon	42	11	5	5	32	22	8	4	9	25	28	66
Luton Town	42	14	5	2	29	13	4	7	10	18	32	66
Nottingham Forest	42	12	8	1	36	14	6	3	12	28	37	65
WATFORD	42	12	5	4	38	20	6	4	11	29	34	63
Coventry City	42	14	4	3	35	17	3	8	10	15	28	63
Manchester United	42	13	3	5	38	18	1	11	9	14	27	56
Southampton	42	11	5	5	44	24	3	5	13	25	44	52
Sheffield Wednesday	42	9	7	5	39	24	4	6	11	19	35	52
Chelsea	42	8	6	7	30	30	5	7	9	23	24	52
West Ham United	42	10	4	7	33	28	4	6	11	19	39	52
Queens Park Rangers	42	9	7	5	31	27	4	4	13	17	37	50
Newcastle United	42	10	4	7	33	29	2	7	12	14	36	47
Oxford United	42	8	8	5	30	25	3	5	13	14	44	46
Charlton Athletic	42	7	7	7	26	22	4	4	13	19	33	44
Leicester City	42	9	7	5	39	24	2	2	17	15	52	42
Manchester City	42	8	6	7	28	24	0	9	12	8	33	39
Aston Villa	42	7	7	7	25	25	1	5	15	20	54	36

No	DATE			COMPETITION	OPPONENTS	HOME	AWAY	ATTENDANCE
1	August	Sat	23	Football League, Division 1	OXFORD UNITED	3-0 W		16,960
2		Tue	26	Football League, Division 1	Queens Park Rangers		L 2-3	14,021
3		Sat	30	Football League, Division 1	Nottingham Forest		D 1-1	14,723
4	September	Sat	6	Football League, Division 1	WIMBLEDON	0-1 L		14,412
5		Sat	13	Football League, Division 1	Norwich City		W 3-1	15,487
6		Tue	16	Football League, Division 1	MANCHESTER UNITED	1-0 W		21,529
7		Sat	20	Football League, Division 1	SHEFFIELD WEDNESDAY	0-1 L		13,941
8		Tue	23	Football Lge Cup, 2nd Round, 1st Leg	ROCHDALE	1-1 D		9,670
9		Sat	27	Football League, Division 1	Coventry City		L 0-1	11,058
10	October	Sat	4	Football League, Division 1	WEST HAM UNITED	2-2 D		16,560
11		Tue	7	Football Lge Cup, 2nd Round, 2nd Leg	Rochdale		W 2-1	5,449
12		Sat	11	Football League, Division 1	Arsenal		L 1-3	24,076
13		Sat	18	Football League, Division 1	ASTON VILLA	4-2 W		16,420
14		Sat	25	Football League, Division 1	Everton		L 2-3	28,577
15		Wed	29	Football League Cup, 3rd Round	WEST HAM UNITED	2-3 L		17,523
16	November	Sat	1	Football League, Division 1	Chelsea		D 0-0	13,334
17		Sat	8	Football League, Division 1	CHARLTON ATHLETIC	4-1 W		14,358
18		Sat	15	Football League, Division 1	Newcastle United		D 2-2	23,645
19		Sat	22	Football League, Division 1	LEICESTER CITY	5-1 W		13,501
20		Wed	26	Full Members Cup, 3rd Round	Manchester City		L 0-1	6,393
21		Sat	29	Football League, Division 1	Southampton		L 1-3	14,537
22	December	Sat	6	Football League, Division 1	LIVERPOOL	2-0 W		23,171
23		Sat	13	Football League, Division 1	Tottenham Hotspur		L 1-2	23,137
24		Fri	19	Football League, Division 1	NORWICH CITY	1-1 D		12,900
25		Fri	26	Football League, Division 1	Luton Town		W 2-0	11,140
26		Sat	27	Football League, Division 1	NEWCASTLE UNITED	1-0 W		17,852
27	January	Thu	1	Football League, Division 1	MANCHESTER CITY	1-1 D		15,514
28		Sat	3	Football League, Division 1	Wimbledon		L 1-2	8,063
29		Sat	10	FA Cup, 3rd Round	MAIDSTONE UNITED	3-1 W		15,952
30		Sat	24	Football League, Division 1	Oxford United		W 3-1	9,710
31	February	Sun	1	FA Cup, 4th Round	CHELSEA	1-0 W		18,832
32		Sat	7	Football League, Division 1	NOTTINGHAM FOREST	1-1 D		15,227
33		Sat	14	Football League, Division 1	Manchester United		L 1-3	35,763
34		Sat	21	FA Cup, 5th Round	Walsall		D 1-1	15,621
35		Tue	24	FA Cup, 5th Round replay	WALSALL (after extra time)	4-4 D		20,350
36		Sat	28	Football League, Division 1	Sheffield Wednesday		W 1-0	20,530
37	March	Mon	2	FA Cup, 5th Round, 2nd replay	Walsall		W 1-0	15,897
38		Sun	8	Football League, Division 1	EVERTON	2-1 W		14,035
39		Sat	14	FA Cup, 6th Round	Arsenal		W 3-1	43,276
40		Sat	21	Football League, Division 1	ARSENAL	2-0 W		18,127
41		Wed	25	Football League, Division 1	Aston Villa		D 1-1	12,575
42		Sat	28	Football League, Division 1	West Ham United		L 0-1	16,485
43	April	Sat	4	Football League, Division 1	Charlton Athletic		L 3-4	4,958
44		Mon	6	Football League, Division 1	QUEENS PARK RANGERS	0-3 L		13,839
45		Sat	11	FA Cup, Semi-Final	Tottenham Hotspur (at Aston Villa)	(L 1-4)		46,151
46		Tue	14	Football League, Division 1	CHELSEA	3-1 W		14,108
47		Sat	18	Football League, Division 1	Manchester City		W 2-1	18,541
48		Tue	21	Football League, Division 1	LUTON TOWN	2-0 W		14,650
49		Sat	25	Football League, Division 1	Leicester City		W 2-1	9,448
50		Thur	30	Football League, Division 1	COVENTRY CITY	2-3 L		11,590
51	May	Sat	2	Football League, Division 1	SOUTHAMPTON	1-1 D		13,067
52		Mon	4	Football League, Division 1	Liverpool		L 0-1	40,150
53		Sat	9	Football League, Division 1	TOTTENHAM HOTSPUR	1-0 W		20,034

League ever-presents: None
Most appearances in total: J. McClelland 52 out of 53   **Most goals in total:** M.P. Falco 16
Hat-tricks: M.P. Falco (Match 13)   **Penalty goals:** K.F. Jackett 6, S.F. Sims 1
Sent off: A.P. Coton (Match 12)   **Full international appearance(s) this season:** J.C.B. Barnes (England), K.F. Jackett (Wales), J. McClelland (Northern Ireland)
(In Match 12, two of the opponents' goals were conceded after A.P. Coton had been sent off and replaced as goalkeeper by N.I. Callaghan.)

Summary (top rows — League then Cup competitions):

	Allen, M.	Bardsley, D.J.	Barnes, J.C.B.	Blissett, L.L.	Callaghan, N.I.	Coton, A.P.	Falco, M.P.	Franklin, P.L.	Gibbs, N.J.	Jackett, K.F.	McClelland, J.	Plumley, G.E.	Porter, G.M.	Pullan, C.J.	Richardson, K.	Roberts, I.W.	Rostron, J.W.	Sherwood, S.	Sims, S.F.	Sinnott, L.	Smillie, N.	Sterling, W.R.	Talbot, B.E.	Terry, S.G.	Own goals
Apps	1	41	37	35	17	31	33	3	14	32	41		22	0	39	2	39	11	19	5		17	5	18	
Subs	+3				+3			+1					+4	+1		+1				+5		+1	+2		
Goals		5	10	11	3		14			6	1		4		2	1	1		1			4	1	2	1
Apps	2	10	11	7	5	9	8		3	9	11	1	4		11	1	11	1	7	3	1	1	1	4	
Subs	+4												+3											+1	
Goals	2	2	4	4			2			3							1							1	

Match appearances:

Match	Allen	Bardsley	Barnes	Blissett	Callaghan	Coton	Falco	Franklin	Gibbs	Jackett	McClelland	Plumley	Porter	Pullan	Richardson	Roberts	Rostron	Sherwood	Sims	Sinnott	Smillie	Sterling	Talbot	Terry	O.g.
1		X1	R1	X1	S	G				X	X				X		X					X	X	X	
2		X	X1	X	S	G	R			X	X				X		X					X	X1	X	
3		X	X	X		G				X	X				X		X					X	X	X	
4		X	X	X		G	X			X	X				X		X					X			
5		X		X1	X	G	R			X	X				X1		X					X1	S		
6		X		X	X	G				X	X				X	S1	X					R	X	X	
7		X		X	X	G				X	X				X		X		X			R	X	X	
8	S	X	X		X	G				X	X				X	X	X1					R		X	
9		X	X	R	X	G				X	X				X		X					X	X	S	
10		X	X	X1	X1	G				X	X		S		X	R			X				X		
11		X	X1	X	X	G				X1	X				X		X			X			X		
12		X	R	X	X	G	X1			X	X				X		X			S			X		
13		X	X	X	X	G	X3			X1	X				X		X						X		
14		X	X	R	X		X			X1p					X		X	G	X	S			X		1
15	X	X1	X				X1p			X	X				X		X	G	X			X	X		
16		X	X			G	X			X	X				X		X					X	X	X	
17		X1	X	X1	X	G	X2			X	X				X		X					X			
18		X	X	X1	X	G	X			X1p	X				X		X					X			
19		X	X1	X	X1	G	X1			X1p	X		S		X		X1	R					X		
20		X	X	X		G	X			X	X		S		X	X	X							R	
21		X	X	R	X	G	X			X	X		S		X	X	X							X1	
22		X	X1		X	G	X			X	X1				X		X							X	
23		X	X		R	G	X1			X	X				X		X			S				X	
24		X	X1		X	G	R			X	X				X		X							X	
25		X	X			G	X			X	X				X1		X1		X					X	
26		X	X1		X	G	X			X	X				X		X		X						
27		X	X1		X	G	X			X	X				X		X		X						
28		X	X	X		X				X	X1				X		X		X					X	
29	S1	X	X		X	G	X2			X	X		R		X		X							X	
30		X	X1	X	X1	G	X1			X	X				X		X							X	
31	S	X	X	R1	X	G	X			X	X				X		X							X	
32		X	X1	X		G	X			X	X				X		X							X	
33		X	X	R		G	X		X1	X			S		X		X							X	
34	X1	X				G	X			X	X		X		X		X							X	
35	R		X2	X1		G	X			X	X1p		X			S	X							X	
36		X	X	X1		G	X			X	X				X		X					X		X	
37		X	X	X		G	X			R	X		S		X		X					X		X	1
38		X	X	X1		G	X1			S	X				X		X					X	R		
39		X	X1	X2		G	X			X					X		X					X			
40		X	X	X1		G	X			X	X1				X		X					X			
41	S	X	R	X		G	X1			X	X				X		X					X			
42		X		X		G	X			X	X		X		X		X					X			
43	S	R	X	X1			X1			X	X		X		X		X	G	X1p						
44		X	X		X		X						R		X		X	G	X	S		X			
45	S1	X	X		X		X		G	X			X		R	R								S	
46	X1	X	X1				X			X1			X		X		X	G						X	
47	X	X1	X				X			X			X		X		X	G	R			S1			
48		X	X1	X			X			X			X		X		X	G				X1			
49	X1	X	X				X			X			X		X		X	G				X1			
50		X	X	X			X2			X			X		X		X	G				X			
51		X	X	X					X	X					X		X	G				X		X1	
52	S	X	X	X			X		X	X	X				X		X	G				R			
53	R	X	X				X1p		X	X	X1p	X	X		X	S	X	G							

- 183 -

1987/88

Football League position: 20th out of 21 in Division 1 – relegated to Division 2
Manager: Dave Bassett (Matches 1-29), Steve Harrison (Matches 31-53)

New league opponents: None

Home-and-away league doubles
For – 2 (Arsenal, Wimbledon)
Against – 7 (Coventry City, Everton, Liverpool, Luton Town, Manchester United, Southampton, West Ham United)

Relegated with Watford: Chelsea, Portsmouth, Oxford United

All Matches: Won 13, Drew 15, Lost 25, Goals 54-67

Highest Score: 8 (Match 11)

		HOME					AWAY					
	Pl	W	D	L	For	Ag	W	D	L	For	Ag	Pts
Liverpool	40	15	5	0	49	9	11	7	2	38	15	90
Manchester United	40	14	5	1	41	17	9	7	4	30	21	81
Nottingham Forest	40	11	7	2	40	17	9	6	5	27	22	73
Everton	40	14	4	2	34	11	5	9	6	19	16	70
Queens Park Rangers	40	12	4	4	30	14	7	6	7	18	24	67
Arsenal	40	11	4	5	35	16	7	8	5	23	23	66
Wimbledon	40	8	9	3	32	20	6	6	8	26	27	57
Newcastle United	40	9	6	5	32	23	5	8	7	23	30	56
Luton Town	40	11	6	3	40	21	3	5	12	17	37	53
Coventry City	40	6	8	6	23	25	7	6	7	23	28	53
Sheffield Wednesday	40	10	2	8	27	30	5	6	9	25	36	53
Southampton	40	6	8	6	27	26	6	6	8	22	40	50
Tottenham Hotspur	40	9	5	6	26	23	3	6	11	12	25	47
Norwich City	40	7	5	8	26	26	5	4	11	14	26	45
Derby County	40	6	7	7	18	17	4	6	10	17	28	43
West Ham United	40	6	9	5	23	21	3	6	11	17	31	42
Charlton Athletic	40	7	7	6	23	21	2	8	10	15	31	42
Chelsea	40	7	11	2	24	17	2	4	14	26	51	42
Portsmouth	40	4	8	8	21	27	3	6	11	15	39	35
WATFORD	40	4	5	11	15	24	3	6	11	12	27	32
Oxford United	40	5	7	8	24	34	1	6	13	20	46	31

No	DATE			COMPETITION	OPPONENTS	HOME	AWAY	ATTENDANCE
1	August	Sat	15	Football League, Division 1	WIMBLEDON	1-0 W		15,344
2		Wed	19	Football League, Division 1	Nottingham Forest		L 0-1	14,527
3		Sat	22	Football League, Division 1	Manchester United		L 0-2	38,582
4		Sat	29	Football League, Division 1	TOTTENHAM HOTSPUR	1-1 D		19,073
5	September	Sat	5	Football League, Division 1	NORWICH CITY	0-1 L		11,724
6		Sat	12	Football League, Division 1	Sheffield Wednesday		W 3-2	16,144
7		Sat	19	Football League, Division 1	PORTSMOUTH	0-0 D		13,277
8		Tue	22	Football Lge Cup, 2nd Round, 1st Leg	Darlington		W 3-0	5,005
9		Sat	26	Football League, Division 1	CHELSEA	0-3 L		16,270
10	October	Sat	3	Football League, Division 1	Coventry City		L 0-1	16,111
11		Tue	6	Football Lge Cup, 2nd Round, 2nd Leg	DARLINGTON	8-0 W		8,186
12		Sat	17	Football League, Division 1	Southampton		L 0-1	11,933
13		Sat	24	Football League, Division 1	Everton		L 0-2	28,501
14		Wed	28	Football League Cup, 3rd Round	Swindon Town		D 1-1	13,833
15		Sat	31	Football League, Division 1	WEST HAM UNITED	1-2 L		14,225
16	November	Tue	3	Football Lge Cup, 3rd Round replay	SWINDON TOWN	4-2 W		13,378
17		Sat	7	Football League, Division 1	Queens Park Rangers		D 0-0	12,101
18		Sat	14	Football League, Division 1	CHARLTON ATHLETIC	2-1 W		12,117
19		Tue	17	Football League Cup, 4th Round	Manchester City		L 1-3	20,357
20		Sat	21	Football League, Division 1	Oxford United		D 1-1	7,811
21		Tue	24	Football League, Division 1	Liverpool		L 0-4	32,396
22		Sat	28	Football League, Division 1	ARSENAL	2-0 W		19,584
23	December	Sat	5	Football League, Division 1	Derby County		D 1-1	14,516
24		Sat	12	Football League, Division 1	LUTON TOWN	0-1 L		12,152
25		Sat	26	Football League, Division 1	SHEFFIELD WEDNESDAY	1-3 L		12,026
26		Mon	28	Football League, Division 1	Portsmouth		D 1-1	15,003
27	January	Fri	1	Football League, Division 1	Tottenham Hotspur		L 1-2	25,235
28		Sat	2	Football League, Division 1	MANCHESTER UNITED	0-1 L		18,038
29		Sat	9	FA Cup, 3rd Round	HULL CITY	1-1 D		12,761
30		Tue	12	FA Cup, 3rd Round replay	Hull City (after extra time)		D 2-2	13,681
31		Sat	16	Football League, Division 1	Wimbledon		W 2-1	6,848
32		Mon	18	FA Cup, 3rd Round, 2nd replay	HULL CITY	1-0 W		15,261
33		Sat	23	Football League, Division 1	NOTTINGHAM FOREST	0-0 D		13,158
34		Mon	25	Full Members Cup, 3rd Round	Ipswich Town (after extra time)		L 2-5	7,466
35		Sat	30	FA Cup, 4th Round	Coventry City		W 1-0	22,479
36	February	Sat	6	Football League, Division 1	Norwich City		D 0-0	13,316
37		Sat	13	Football League, Division 1	LIVERPOOL	1-4 L		23,838
38		Sat	20	FA Cup, 5th Round	Port Vale		D 0-0	22,483
39		Tue	23	FA Cup, 5th Round replay	PORT VALE	2-0 W		18,539
40		Sat	27	Football League, Division 1	Coventry City		L 0-1	12,052
41	March	Sat	5	Football League, Division 1	SOUTHAMPTON	0-1 L		11,824
42		Sat	12	FA Cup, 6th Round	Wimbledon		L 1-2	12,228
43		Sat	19	Football League, Division 1	West Ham United		L 0-1	16,015
44		Sat	26	Football League, Division 1	EVERTON	1-2 L		13,503
45		Tue	29	Football League, Division 1	Chelsea		D 1-1	11,240
46	April	Fri	1	Football League, Division 1	QUEENS PARK RANGERS	0-1 L		16,083
47		Mon	4	Football League, Division 1	Charlton Athletic		L 0-1	6,196
48		Sat	9	Football League, Division 1	OXFORD UNITED	3-0 W		10,045
49		Tue	12	Football League, Division 1	Newcastle United		L 0-3	16,318
50		Fri	15	Football League, Division 1	Arsenal		W 1-0	19,541
51		Tue	19	Football League, Division 1	NEWCASTLE UNITED	1-1 D		12,075
52		Sat	30	Football League, Division 1	DERBY COUNTY	1-1 D		14,181
53	May	Mon	2	Football League, Division 1	Luton Town		L 1-2	10,409

League ever-presents: J. McClelland, G.M. Porter (including one substitute appearance)
Most appearances in total: J. McClelland & G.M. Porter (including two substitute appearances) 52 out of 53   Most goals in total: M. Allen 9
Hat-tricks: None   Penalty goals: M. Allen 1, K.F. Jackett 1
Sent off: None
Full international appearance(s) this season: G.P. Hodges (Wales), K.F. Jackett (Wales), J. McClelland (Northern Ireland)

	Agana, P.A.O.	Allen, M.	Bardsley, D.J.	Blissett, L.L.	Chivers, G.P.S.	Coton, A.P.	Gibbs, N.J.	Hetherston, P.	Hill, R.W.	Hodges, G.P.	Holden, R.W.	Holdsworth, Dean C.	Holdsworth, David G.	Jackett, K.F.	Kuhl, M.	McClelland, J.	Morris, M.J.	Porter, G.M.	Powell, C.G.	Pullan, C.J.	Rees, M.J.	Rimmer, S.A.	Roberts, I.W.	Rostron, J.W.	Rumble, P.	Senior, T.J.	Sherwood, T.A.	Sterling, W.R.	Terry, S.G.	Thomas, R.C.	Own goals
Apps	12	16	4	17	14	37	30	2	2	22	10	0		32	4	40	39	39		2	3	9	18	33		22	9	17	6	1	
Subs	+3	+6		+8				+3	+2	+2		+2		+1				+1				+2	+7	+4		+2	+4	+4		+3	
Goals	1	3		4						3	2			2			1	3				1	2			1		2			2
Apps	4	8		5	5	11	9	3		9		0	1	9		12	12	11	0	1	2		4	12	1	7	7	7	3		
Subs	+1	+2		+4		+1	+1					+1					+1	+1					+2			+2		+1			
Goals	2	6		1			2	2		2				1			1	3					1			4			1		1
1	X		X	R1		G	X							X		X	X	X					S	X		X					
2	X	S	R	X		G	X		S					R		X	X	X						X		X					
3	X					G	X							X		X	X	X					S	R		X		R			
4	X		X	X		G	X		R					X		X	X	X1					S	S		R					
5	X		X	X		G	X		R					R		X	X	X					S	S		X					
6	S				R	G	X									X	X	X1					X	X		R1	S	X1	X		
7				S	X	G	X									X	R	X					X	X		X		X	X		
8				S	R	R	G		X1	S						X	X	X1					X	X		R1		X	X		
9				S	X	X	G		X	S						X	R	X					X	R		X		X	X		
10	X					G	X			X						X	X	X					S	X		R		X	X		
11	S1			X1		G	X1	X2		X1						X	X	X					R1	X					X1		
12	S			X		G	X		R	X				S		X	X	R					X	X					X		
13	X					G	X			X						X	X	S					R	X		X	X				
14	R1	X				G	X			X						X	X	S					S	X		X	R				
15	R	X1				G	X			X						X	X	X						X		X	S				
16		X1		S		G	X			X1				X		X	X1	X1						R		X					
17		X		X		G	X			X				X		X	X	X					X			X					
18		X1				G	X			X				X		X	X	X					X1	X		X					
19		X1				G	X			X				X		X	X	X						X		X	R	S	S		
20		R	X1	X		G				X				X		X	X	X					R			S	S	X	S		
21		X	X	X		G				X				X		X	X	X						S		R	R	R	S		
22		R	X1	X		G				X				X1		X	X	X						X		X	X		S		
23	S	X	X	X		G				R1				X		X	X	X	X							X	X				
24		X		X	R	G				X		S		X		X	X	X						X		R	X	S			
25	X	R		X		G	X	S						X		X	X	X					R	X		S					1
26	X1	S		X										X		X	X	X		R	G		X			X		X			
27		X		X					S	R				X		X	X1	X			G					X		X	R		
28	X	S		X						X				X		X	X	R			G					X	R	S			
29	X	S1		X						X				X		X	X	X			G					R	X				
30	R	S1	X	X		G				X				X1p		X	X	X						X		X			X		
31		X1p	X	X		G				X						X	X	X						X		X		X	X1		
32		X1	X	X		G				X						X	X	X						X		X		X	X		
33		X	X	X		G				X				X		X	X	X						X		X		X			
34	X							X	R			S	X						S	R	G		X			X	X1	X	X		1
35		X		R	R	G	S			X				X		X	X	X						X		X	S1		X		
36		X		S		G	X		R					X		X	X	X						X		X	X	X			
37		X	S1			G	X							X		X	X	R	S				R	R		X	X	X			
38		X		S		G	X							X		X	X	R						X		X	X	X	X		
39		R		S		G	X							X		X	X	X1						X		X	X1	X	X		
40		R		S		G	X							X	X	X	X	X						X		X		X			
41		S		S		G	X			X				X		X	X	X					R	X		X		X			
42		X1	X	X		G	X			X				X		X	X	X						X		S	X		R		
43		R		X		G	X							X		X	X	X						X		S	X	X	X		
44		R		X		G	X			X				X		X	X	X1						X				X			
45				S		G	X		S	R				X		X	X	X					R1	X		X		X			
46				S		G	X			R				X		X	X	X					X	X		X		X			
47		S		X		G	X				X			X		X	X	X					X			X		S	R		
48						G	X		X2	X1				X	X	X	X	X						X		X	X	X			
49						G	X		X	X					R	X	X	X	S				X			X	X	X			
50						G	X		R	X1				X		X	X	X					X	X		X	X	X		S	
51						G	X		R	X				X1		X	X	X					X	X		X	X	X		S	
52						G	X		R	X	S			X		X	X	X					R	X1		X	X			S	
53						G	X		S	X				X		X	X	X					X	X		X	X	R		R	1

-185-

1988/89

Football League position: 4th out of 24 in Division 2 – lost on 'away goals' rule in promotion play-off semi-final
Manager: Steve Harrison

		HOME					AWAY					
	Pl	W	D	L	For	Ag	W	D	L	For	Ag	Pts
Chelsea	46	15	6	2	50	25	14	6	3	46	25	99
Manchester City	46	12	8	3	48	28	11	5	7	29	25	82
Crystal Palace	46	15	6	2	42	17	8	6	9	29	32	81
WATFORD	46	14	5	4	41	18	8	7	8	33	30	78
Blackburn Rovers	46	16	4	3	50	22	6	7	10	24	37	77
Swindon Town	46	13	8	2	35	15	7	8	8	33	30	76
Barnsley	46	12	8	3	37	21	8	6	9	29	37	74
Ipswich Town	46	13	3	7	42	23	9	4	10	29	38	73
West Bromwich Albion	46	13	7	3	43	18	5	11	7	22	23	72
Leeds United	46	12	6	5	34	20	5	10	8	25	30	67
Sunderland	46	12	8	3	40	23	4	7	12	20	37	63
AFC Bournemouth	46	13	3	7	32	20	5	5	13	21	42	62
Stoke City	46	10	9	4	33	25	5	5	13	24	47	59
Bradford City	46	8	11	4	29	22	5	6	12	23	37	56
Leicester City	46	11	6	6	31	20	2	10	11	25	43	55
Oldham Athletic	46	9	10	4	49	32	2	11	10	26	40	54
Oxford United	46	11	4	8	40	34	3	6	14	22	36	54
Plymouth Argyle	46	11	4	8	35	22	3	8	12	20	44	54
Brighton & Hove Albion	46	11	5	7	36	24	3	4	16	21	42	51
Portsmouth	46	10	6	7	33	21	3	4	14	20	41	51
Hull City	46	7	9	7	31	25	4	5	14	21	43	47
Shrewsbury Town	46	4	11	8	25	31	4	7	12	15	36	42
Birmingham City	46	6	4	13	21	33	2	7	14	10	43	35
Walsall	46	3	10	10	27	42	2	6	15	14	38	31

New league opponents: Leeds United

Home-and-away league doubles
For – 5 (Birmingham City, AFC Bournemouth, Hull City, Walsall, West Bromwich Albion)
Against – none

Divisional changes at end of season: Chelsea, Manchester City & Crystal Palace to Division 1; Shrewsbury Town, Birmingham City & Walsall to Division 3; Middlesbrough, West Ham United & Newcastle United from Division 1; Wolverhampton Wanderers, Sheffield United & Port Vale from Division 3

All Matches: Won 27, Drew 18, Lost 15, Goals 89-64

Highest Score: 5 (Match 53)

No	DATE			COMPETITION	OPPONENTS	HOME	AWAY	ATTENDANCE
1	August	Sat	27	Football League, Division 2	BIRMINGHAM CITY	1-0 W		12,656
2		Mon	29	Football League, Division 2	West Bromwich Albion		W 1-0	10,242
3	September	Sat	3	Football League, Division 2	Crystal Palace		W 2-0	10,474
4		Sat	10	Football League, Division 2	PLYMOUTH ARGYLE	3-0 W		12,040
5		Sat	17	Football League, Division 2	Ipswich Town		L 2-3	14,644
6		Tue	20	Football League, Division 2	BRADFORD CITY	2-0 W		12,296
7		Sat	24	Football League, Division 2	Leicester City		D 2-2	10,957
8		Wed	28	Football Lge Cup, 2nd Round, 1st Leg	Leicester City		L 1-4	9,512
9	October	Sat	1	Football League, Division 2	SWINDON TOWN	2-3 L		11,657
10		Tue	4	Football League, Division 2	OLDHAM ATHLETIC	3-1 W		10,038
11		Sat	8	Football League, Division 2	Leeds United		W 1-0	15,657
12		Tue	11	Football Lge Cup, 2nd Round, 2nd Leg	LEICESTER CITY	2-2 D		9,087
13		Sat	15	Football League, Division 2	BRIGHTON & HOVE ALBION	1-1 D		12,126
14		Sat	22	Football League, Division 2	Stoke City		L 0-2	7,878
15		Tue	25	Football League, Division 2	BARNSLEY	4-0 W		10,356
16		Sat	29	Football League, Division 2	Walsall		W 1-0	6,682
17	November	Sat	5	Football League, Division 2	CHELSEA	1-2 L		17,631
18		Tue	8	Full Members Cup, 1st Round	LEICESTER CITY (after extra time)	2-0 W		3,626
19		Sat	12	Football League, Division 2	Manchester City		L 1-3	21,142
20		Sat	19	Football League, Division 2	Shrewsbury Town		D 1-1	4,621
21		Tue	22	Full Members Cup, 2nd Round	WEST HAM UTD (won 4-2 on penalties)	1-1 D		6,468
22		Sat	26	Football League, Division 2	HULL CITY	2-0 W		10,404
23	December	Sat	3	Football League, Division 2	Sunderland		D 1-1	16,330
24		Sat	10	Football League, Division 2	OXFORD UNITED	1-1 D		10,437
25		Tue	13	Full Members Cup, 3rd Round	NEWCASTLE UNITED	2-1 W		6,186
26		Sat	17	Football League, Division 2	Blackburn Rovers		L 1-2	8,808
27		Mon	26	Football League, Division 2	PORTSMOUTH	1-0 W		15,224
28		Sat	31	Football League, Division 2	AFC BOURNEMOUTH	1-0 W		14,006
29	January	Mon	2	Football League, Division 2	Plymouth Argyle		L 0-1	12,142
30		Sat	7	FA Cup, 3rd Round	Newcastle United		D 0-0	24,086
31		Tue	10	FA Cup, 3rd Round replay	NEWCASTLE UNITED (after extra time)	2-2 D		16,431
32		Sat	14	Football League, Division 2	WEST BROMWICH ALBION	2-0 W		15,168
33		Mon	16	FA Cup, 3rd Round, 2nd replay	Newcastle United (after extra time)		D 0-0	28,370
34		Wed	18	FA Cup, 3rd Round, 3rd replay	NEWCASTLE UNITED (after extra time)	1-0 W		15,115
35		Sat	21	Football League, Division 2	Birmingham City		W 3-2	6,396
36		Sat	28	FA Cup, 4th Round	DERBY COUNTY	2-1 W		20,078
37	February	Sat	4	Football League, Division 2	Oldham Athletic		L 1-3	6,364
38		Sat	11	Football League, Division 2	LEEDS UNITED	1-1 D		13,439
39		Tue	14	Full Members Cup, Quarter-Final	QUEENS PARK RANGERS (lost 1-2 on penalties)	1-1 D		8,103
40		Sun	19	FA Cup, 5th Round	NOTTINGHAM FOREST	0-3 L		18,044
41		Sat	25	Football League, Division 2	Brighton & Hove Albion		L 0-1	9,522
42		Tue	28	Football League, Division 2	Barnsley		D 2-2	6,163
43	March	Sat	4	Football League, Division 2	MANCHESTER CITY	1-0 W		15,747
44		Sat	11	Football League, Division 2	Chelsea		D 2-2	22,188
45		Sat	18	Football League, Division 2	Bradford City		L 1-2	10,003
46		Fri	24	Football League, Division 2	CRYSTAL PALACE	0-1 L		15,095
47		Mon	27	Football League, Division 2	Portsmouth		D 2-2	9,364
48	April	Sat	1	Football League, Division 2	IPSWICH TOWN	3-2 W		12,054
49		Tue	4	Football League, Division 2	BLACKBURN ROVERS	2-2 D		8,667
50		Sat	8	Football League, Division 2	AFC Bournemouth		W 1-0	9,766
51		Tue	11	Football League, Division 2	STOKE CITY	3-2 W		9,086
52		Sat	15	Football League, Division 2	Swindon Town		D 1-1	9,828
53		Sat	18	Football League, Division 2	WALSALL	5-0 W		9,777
54		Sat	22	Football League, Division 2	LEICESTER CITY	2-1 W		11,262
55		Sat	29	Football League, Division 2	Hull City		W 3-0	5,225
56	May	Mon	1	Football League, Division 2	SUNDERLAND	0-1 L		13,499
57		Sat	6	Football League, Division 2	SHREWSBURY TOWN	0-0 D		10,052
58		Sat	13	Football League, Division 2	Oxford United		W 4-0	6,573
59		Sun	21	Division 2 Play-off Semi-Final, 1st Leg	Blackburn Rovers		D 0-0	14,028
60		Wed	24	Division 2 Play-off Semi-Final, 2nd Leg	BLACKBURN ROVERS (after extra time)	1-1 D		13,852

League ever-presents: A.P. Coton, N.J. Gibbs   Most appearances in total: A.P. Coton 60 out of 60   Most goals in total: P. Wilkinson 21
Hat-tricks: None   Penalty goals: G.M. Porter 5, N.D. Redfearn 1. In the penalty shoot-outs at the end of Matches 21 & 39, successful kicks were taken by G.M. Porter, W.H. Falconer & J. McClelland (Match 21) and N.D. Redfearn (Match 39).
Sent off: K.F. Jackett (Match 26)   Full international appearance(s) this season: J. McClelland (Northern Ireland)
(The players' League totals below include the two Play-off matches.)

	Bamber, J.D. //	Blissett, L.L.	Coton, A.P.	Falconer, W.H.	Gibbs, N.J.	Henry, L.A.	Hodges, G.P.	Holden, R.W. //	Holdsworth, Dean C.	Holdsworth, David G.	Jackett, K.F.	McClelland, J.	Miller, P.R. //	Morris, M.J. //	Porter, G.M.	Pullan, C.J.	Redfearn, N.D.	Richardson, L.J. //	Rimmer, S.A. //	Roberts, I.W.	Rostron, J.W. //	Sherwood, T.A. //	Sterling, W.R. //	Thomas, R.C.	Thompson, G.L.	Wilkinson, P.	Own goals
Apps	16	3	48	32	48	1	25	32	2	27	41	45	22	2	42	1	14	9	1	13	7	14	3	17	17	46	
Subs	+2			+3			+2		+10	+8	+3				+2					+11		+5		+3	+4	+1	
Goals	3	1		5	1		5	6	2	2		1			10		3			6		2		2	7	18	1
Apps	4	1	12	8	11		2	11	0	8	9	7	8		9	1	9		0	2	1	10	2	0	6	11	
Subs				+3			+1	+1	+1	+1	+1	+1			+1		+6					+2			+1		
Goals	1						1	2							2		3			1					3	1	
1	X1		G	X	X		X	X			X	X		R	X										S	X	
2	X		G	X1	X		X			X	X	X			X							X				X	
3	X		G		X		X	X		X	X	X			X1								X			X1	
4	X1		G	X	X			R		X	X	X			X1p									S		X1	
5	X		G	X	X		X			X	X	X			X					R2				S		X	
6	X		G	X	X		X2			X	X	X			X					X						X	
7	R		G	X	X		X			X	X	X			X1							S	X			X1	
8	R		G	X			X			X	X	X			X	R						S	S			X1	
9	X		G	X	X		S	X1		X	X	X			X1					R						X	
10		X1	G		X		X	X		X	X	X			X							X				X2	
11	S	X	G		X		X1	R		X	X	X			X							R	S			X	
12	X1	R	G	X	X		R			X					X			S1		X		X	X	S			
13	S		G		X		R			X	X	X			X1p			R				X	S			X	
14		X	G		X		X			X	X	X			X					S		X		R		X	
15	R		G	X1	X		X1			X	X		X		X					S1				X		X1	
16	X		G	X	X		X			X	X		X		X							S		X		X1	
17	R		G	X	X		X			X	X		X		X							S		X		X1	
18	X		G	X	X		X1	X	R	X	S	X			X1p							S				R	
19	X		G	X	X		X	X	S	R	X	R			X1							S				X	
20	X1		G	X	X		S	R		X	X	X			X							S	R			X	
21	X		G	S	X		R	S		X	X	X			X		R					X				X1	
22	X		G		X		X			X	X	X			X		X					X1				X1	
23	X		G		X		X			X	X	X			X		X					X1				X1	
24	R		G	S	X		X			X	X	X			R		X					X				X1	
25			G	S	X		S	R1		X	X	X			R		X					X				X1	
26			G		X		X	X	S1	X	X	X			X		X					X				R	
27			G		X			X		X	X	X			X	X1						X		X			
28			G	X	X			X1		X	X	S			R		S		X			X		X		R	
29			G	X	X			R	S	X	X	S			X		X						X	R			
30			G	X	X			X		X	X	X			X		X					X		X	X		
31			G	X	X			X		X	S	X	R		R		X2p					S		X	X	X	
32			G	X	X			X1		X	X	X			X							X		X1		X	
33			G	X	X			X		X	X	X			X							S		X	R	X	
34			G	X	X			X		X	S	X	X	R	X							S		X	R		1
35			G	X	X			X		X	X	X	X		X							S		X	R2	X1	
36			G	X	X			X1		X	X	X	X		X							S		X	X	R	
37			G	X	X			R		X	X	X			X1							S		X	X	X	
38			G	X	X			R		X	X	X			X							S		X	X	X1	
39			G	S	X			X	S	X	X		X		X		R1p					X		X	X	R	
40			G		X			X		X	X	X	X		X		R					S		X	X	X	
41			G		X	X	X			X	X	X			X			X		X					R	S	
42			G	S	X		X1	X		X1	X	X			X			R		X					S	X	
43			G	X	X		X	X		X		X			X			X		X1					S	X	
44			G	X	X		X	X		X	S	X			X			R		R1					S	X1	
45			G	X	X		X	X		X	S	X			X			X		X						X1	
46			G	R	X		X	R		X	S	X			X			X		X					S	X	
47			G		X	X1		S	S1	X		R	X	X	X			X						X	R	X	
48			G		X	X1		X		X1		X			X			X						X		X1	
49			G	X	X			X		X	X	X	X		X			R						X1	S1	R	
50			G	X	X			X		S	X	X	X		X									R	X1	X	
51			G	X1	X		X1		S	S	X	X	X		X1									R	X	R	
52			G	X	X			X	S		X	X	X1		X									R	X	X	
53			G	X	X			X		X	X	X			X2p			R1						R1	X1	X1	
54			G	X	X	R	R		S1	S	X	X	X		X									X		X1	
55			G	X1	X			X		X	X	X	X		X									X	X1	X	1
56			G	X	X			R		S	X	X	R		X							S		X	X	X	
57			G	X	X				S	X	X	X			X					X			X	R	X		
58			G	X2	X					X	X	X			X		X			S1				X	R	X1	
59			G	X	X			S	S	X	X	X			X			R						X		X	
60			G	X	X			S	S	X	R	X			X	X1		R						X		X	

- 187 -

1989/90

Football League position: 15th out of 24 in Division 2
Manager: Steve Harrison (Matches 1-41), Colin Lee (Matches 42-52)

New league opponents: None

Home-and-away league doubles
For – 2 (Middlesbrough, Portsmouth)
Against – 4 (Sheffield United, Swindon Town, West Bromwich Albion, West Ham United)

Divisional changes at end of season: Leeds United, Sheffield United & Sunderland to Division 1; AFC Bournemouth, Bradford City & Stoke City to Division 3; Sheffield Wednesday, Charlton Athletic & Millwall from Division 1; Bristol Rovers, Bristol City & Notts County from Division 3

All Matches: Won 15, Drew 17, Lost 20, Goals 65-70

Highest Score: 7 (Match 25)

		HOME					AWAY					
	Pl	W	D	L	For	Ag	W	D	L	For	Ag	Pts
Leeds United	46	16	6	1	46	18	8	7	8	33	34	85
Sheffield United	46	14	5	4	43	27	10	8	5	35	31	85
Newcastle United	46	17	4	2	51	26	5	10	8	29	29	80
Swindon Town	46	12	6	5	49	29	8	8	7	30	34	74
Blackburn Rovers	46	10	9	4	43	30	9	8	6	31	29	74
Sunderland	46	10	8	5	41	32	10	6	7	29	32	74
West Ham United	46	14	5	4	50	22	6	7	10	30	35	72
Oldham Athletic	46	15	7	1	50	23	4	7	12	20	34	71
Ipswich Town	46	13	7	3	38	22	6	5	12	29	44	69
Wolverhampton Wanderers	46	12	5	6	37	20	6	8	9	30	40	67
Port Vale	46	11	9	3	37	20	4	7	12	25	37	61
Portsmouth	46	9	8	6	40	34	6	8	9	22	31	61
Leicester City	46	10	8	5	34	29	5	6	12	33	50	59
Hull City	46	7	8	8	27	31	7	8	8	31	34	58
WATFORD	46	11	6	6	41	28	3	9	11	17	32	57
Plymouth Argyle	46	9	8	6	23	25	5	5	13	28	40	55
Oxford United	46	8	7	8	35	31	7	2	14	22	35	54
Brighton & Hove Albion	46	10	6	7	28	27	5	3	15	28	45	54
Barnsley	46	7	9	7	22	23	6	6	11	27	48	54
West Bromwich Albion	46	6	8	9	35	37	6	7	10	32	34	51
Middlesbrough	46	10	3	10	33	29	3	6	14	19	34	50
AFC Bournemouth	46	8	6	9	30	31	4	6	13	27	45	48
Bradford City	46	9	6	8	26	24	0	8	15	18	44	41
Stoke City	46	4	11	8	20	24	2	8	13	15	39	37

No	DATE			COMPETITION	OPPONENTS	HOME	AWAY	ATTENDANCE	
1	August	Sat	19	Football League, Division 2	PORTSMOUTH	1-0 W		10,164	
2		Tue	22	Football League, Division 2	Oldham Athletic		D 1-1		6,230
3		Sat	26	Football League, Division 2	Oxford United		D 1-1		5,664
4	September	Sat	2	Football League, Division 2	LEICESTER CITY	3-1 W		10,252	
5		Sat	9	Football League, Division 2	Sunderland		L 0-4		15,042
6		Sat	16	Football League, Division 2	PORT VALE	1-0 W		8,445	
7		Tue	19	Football Lge Cup, 2nd Round, 1st Leg	Bolton Wanderers		L 1-2		6,856
8		Sat	23	Football League, Division 2	West Ham United		L 0-1		20,728
9		Wed	27	Football League, Division 2	Newcastle United		L 1-2		17,040
10		Sat	30	Football League, Division 2	MIDDLESBROUGH	1-0 W		10,102	
11	October	Tue	3	Football Lge Cup, 2nd Round, 2nd Leg	BOLTON WANDERERS	1-1 D		8,452	
12		Sat	7	Football League, Division 2	WEST BROMWICH ALBION	0-2 L		10,444	
13		Sat	14	Football League, Division 2	Brighton & Hove Albion		L 0-1		9,260
14		Tue	17	Football League, Division 2	AFC BOURNEMOUTH	2-2 D		9,013	
15		Sat	21	Football League, Division 2	Blackburn Rovers		D 2-2		7,950
16		Sat	28	Football League, Division 2	SHEFFIELD UNITED	1-3 L		11,623	
17		Tue	31	Football League, Division 2	Ipswich Town		L 0-1		12,587
18	November	Sat	4	Football League, Division 2	Hull City		D 0-0		4,718
19		Sat	11	Football League, Division 2	PLYMOUTH ARGYLE	1-2 L		9,401	
20		Sat	18	Football League, Division 2	Leeds United		L 1-2		26,921
21		Tue	21	Full Members Cup, 2nd Round	Ipswich Town		L 1-4		5,078
22		Sat	25	Football League, Division 2	WOLVERHAMPTON WANDERERS	3-1 W		12,736	
23	December	Sat	2	Football League, Division 2	Portsmouth		W 2-1		7,933
24		Sat	9	Football League, Division 2	OLDHAM ATHLETIC	3-0 W		9,399	
25		Sat	16	Football League, Division 2	BRADFORD CITY	7-2 W		8,554	
26		Tue	26	Football League, Division 2	Barnsley		W 1-0		7,357
27		Sat	30	Football League, Division 2	Stoke City		D 2-2		13,228
28	January	Mon	1	Football League, Division 2	SWINDON TOWN	0-2 L		13,708	
29		Sat	6	FA Cup, 3rd Round	WIGAN ATHLETIC	2-0 W		10,069	
30		Sat	13	Football League, Division 2	OXFORD UNITED	0-1 L		10,040	
31		Sat	20	Football League, Division 2	Leicester City		D 1-1		11,466
32		Sat	27	FA Cup, 4th Round	Sheffield United		D 1-1		19,435
33		Tue	30	FA Cup, 4th Round replay	SHEFFIELD UNITED	1-2 L		13,922	
34	February	Sat	10	Football League, Division 2	Port Vale		L 0-1		7,063
35		Sat	17	Football League, Division 2	SUNDERLAND	1-1 D		9,093	
36		Sat	24	Football League, Division 2	Wolverhampton Wanderers		D 1-1		16,187
37	March	Sat	3	Football League, Division 2	LEEDS UNITED	1-0 W		13,468	
38		Wed	7	Football League, Division 2	Middlesbrough		W 2-1		14,008
39		Sat	10	Football League, Division 2	NEWCASTLE UNITED	0-0 D		12,069	
40		Tue	13	Football League, Division 2	WEST HAM UNITED	0-1 L		15,682	
41		Sat	17	Football League, Division 2	West Bromwich Albion		L 0-2		9,915
42		Tue	20	Football League, Division 2	BRIGHTON & HOVE ALBION	4-2 W		8,487	
43		Sat	24	Football League, Division 2	AFC Bournemouth		D 0-0		6.737
44		Sat	31	Football League, Division 2	BLACKBURN ROVERS	3-1 W		9,096	
45	April	Sat	7	Football League, Division 2	IPSWICH TOWN	3-3 D		11,158	
46		Tue	10	Football League, Division 2	Sheffield United		L 1-4		14,653
47		Sat	14	Football League, Division 2	Swindon Town		L 0-2		8,520
48		Tue	17	Football League, Division 2	BARNSLEY	2-2 D		7,289	
49		Sat	21	Football League, Division 2	Bradford City		L 1-2		5,964
50		Tue	24	Football League, Division 2	STOKE CITY	1-1 D		8,073	
51		Sat	28	Football League, Division 2	Plymouth Argyle		D 0-0		8,564
52	May	Sat	5	Football League, Division 2	HULL CITY	3-1 W		9,827	

League ever-presents: A.P. Coton
Most appearances in total: A.P. Coton 52 out of 52   **Most goals in total:** P. Wilkinson 16
Hat-tricks: None   **Penalty goals:** G.P. Hodges 3, G.M. Porter 3
Sent off: W.H Falconer (Match 13), R.C. Thomas (Match 15), N.J. Gibbs (Match 41)
Full international appearance(s) this season: G.P. Hodges (Wales), I.W. Roberts (Wales)

Season totals

	Allison, W.A.	Ashby, B.J.	Bazeley, D.S.	Coton, A.P.	Drysdale, J.	Falconer, W.H.	Gibbs, N.J.	Harrison, G.R.	Henry, L.A.	Hodges, G.P.	Holdsworth, Dean C.	Holdsworth, David G.	Jackett, K.F.	McClelland, J.	Penrice, G.K.	Porter, G.M.	Pullan, C.J.	Redfearn, N.D.	Richardson, L.J.	Roberts, I.W.	Robson, M.A.	Roeder, G.V.	Soloman, J.R.	Thomas, R.C.	Thompson, G.L.	Wilkinson, P.	Williams, G.
Apps	6	14	0	46	18	23	41	2	7	35	0	44	16	1	29	31	1	10	31	8	1	44		30	7	43	18
Subs	+1	+4	+1		+2	+7		+1	+2		+4		+1			+1	+3	+2	+1	+1		+1		+2	+6		
Goals		1				3		1	7	1	3				12	4		1	1			1		6	1	16	
Apps		3		6	1	2	6		5	4		5	2		4	6	1	1	2	3		6	1	2	1	3	2
Subs		+1																		+1				+1	+2	+1	
Goals									1						2	1				2				1			

Match appearances

Match	Allison	Ashby	Bazeley	Coton	Drysdale	Falconer	Gibbs	Harrison	Henry	Hodges	Holds. Dean	Holds. David	Jackett	McClelland	Penrice	Porter	Pullan	Redfearn	Richardson	Roberts	Robson	Roeder	Soloman	Thomas	Thompson	Wilkinson	Williams
1				G			X			S	X	X				X		X	X			X		X	R	X1	
2				G		S	X			S1	X	X				X		X	R			X		X	R	X	
3				G		S	X			S	X	X				X		X	R			X		X1	R	X	
4				G			X				X	X				X1p		X	X			X		X	X1	X1	
5				G		S	X			S	X	X				X		R	X			X		X	X	X	
6				G			X				X	X				X		X	X	X		X		X		X1	
7				G			X				X	X				X		X	X	X1		X		X		X	
8				G		S	X		S	X	X	X				X			R	R		X		X		X	
9				G		S	X			X	X	X				X			R	X		X		X		X1	
10				G			X	X	S	X	X	X				X				X		X		X		R1	
11				G			X	X	R	R	X	X				X			S	X1		X		X	S		
12				G			X	X		X	X	X				S			X	R	R	X		X	S		
13	S			G			X	X		R	X	X				X		S	X			X		R		X	
14	X			G			X			R	X1	X				X1p		S	X			X		X		X	
15	X			G			X			X	X1	X				X			X			X		X		X1	
16	X			G			X			X	X	X				X1			X			X		X		X	
17				G	X		X			R	X	X				X		X		X		X			S	X	
18				G	X		X			X	X	X				X		X		R		X			S	X	
19				G	X	X	X				X	X				X			X1			X			X	X	
20				G	X	X	X				X				R1	X		S	R			X			S	X	
21		S		G	X	X	X			X					X1	X	R					X	X	S		R	
22		X		G		X1	X			X					X1	X			X			X				X1	
23		X		G		R	X			X					X1	X	S		X			X				X1	
24		X		G			X			X1	X		R		X1	X	S		X			X				X1	
25		X1		G			X		X1	X					X	X		X1	X1			X				X2	
26		X		G			X		X	X					X	X		X				X				X1	
27		X		G			X		X	X1					X	X		X				X				X	
28		X		G			X			R	X	X			X	X		X				X	S			X	
29		X		G			X		X	X1		X			X	X						X		X1		X	
30		X		G			X			X		X		X	X	X			X			X		X			
31		X		G			X			X	X	X			X	X			X	X		X1					X
32		X		G			X		X	X	X				X1	X				R		X		S			X
33		X		G			X		X	R	X				X	X1p						X		X	S		X
34		X		G	R	S	X				X				X	X		X				S		R	X	X	X
35		X		G		S	X		X						X	X						X		X1		X	R
36				G	X	X	X		X		X				X	X						X		X		X1	
37				G			X		X		X				X	X						X		X1		X	
38		S		G			X		R	X2p	X				X	X		R	S			X		X		X	
39				G	X	X	X			X	X				X							X		X		X	
40	R	R		G			X				X				X	X	X	X	S			X	S	X	S	X	
41				G	X	X	X		X		X				X	X						X		X		X	
42				G	X	X	X			X1	X				X			R1				X		X1	S	X1	X
43				G	X	X	X			X	X				X	X						X		X		X1	X
44				G	X	X	X				X		X1	S	X1			R				X		X		X1	X
45		S		G	X	X		X		X2#	X				X	X1						X		X		X	R
46		X		G	X	X					X				X1							X		X		X	X
47		S		G	S	X	X	R			X				X	X						X		X		X	R
48				G	X	X	X				X				X	X						X		X1		X1	X
49	X			G	X	X1	X				X				X	X						X		S		R	X
50	R			G	S	X	X	S			X				X			R				X		X1		X	G
51		X		G	X	X	X				X				X				X			X				X	X
52		S	S	G	X	X1	X			X					X2							X		R		X	

1990/91

Football League position: 20th out of 24 in Division 2
Manager: Colin Lee (Matches 1-20), Steve Perryman (Matches 21-50)

New league opponents: None
Home-and-away league doubles
For – 1 (Charlton Athletic)
Against – 5 (Brighton & Hove Albion, Bristol City, Newcastle United, Notts County, West Ham United)
Divisional changes at end of season: Oldham Athletic, West Ham United, Sheffield Wednesday & Notts County to Division 1; West Bromwich Albion & Hull City to Division 3; Sunderland & Derby County from Division 1; Cambridge United, Southend United, Grimsby Town & Tranmere Rovers from Division 3
All Matches: Won 12, Drew 15, Lost 23, Goals 47-70
Highest Score: 3 (Match 44)

	HOME					AWAY					
	Pl	W	D	L For	Ag	W	D	L For	Ag	Pts
Oldham Athletic	46	17	5	1 55	21	8	8	7 28	32	88
West Ham United	46	15	6	2 41	18	9	9	5 19	16	87
Sheffield Wednesday	46	12	10	1 43	23	10	6	7 37	28	82
Notts County	46	14	4	5 45	28	9	7	7 31	27	80
Millwall	46	11	6	6 43	28	9	7	7 27	23	73
Brighton & Hove Albion	46	12	4	7 37	31	9	3	11 26	38	70
Middlesbrough	46	12	4	7 36	17	8	5	10 30	30	69
Barnsley	46	13	7	3 39	16	6	5	12 24	32	69
Bristol City	46	14	5	4 44	28	6	2	15 24	43	67
Oxford United	46	10	9	4 41	29	4	10	9 28	37	61
Newcastle United	46	8	10	5 24	22	6	7	10 25	34	59
Wolverhampton Wanderers	46	11	6	6 45	35	2	13	8 18	28	58
Bristol Rovers	46	11	7	5 29	20	4	6	13 27	39	58
Ipswich Town	46	9	8	6 32	28	4	10	9 28	40	57
Port Vale	46	10	4	9 32	24	5	8	10 24	40	57
Charlton Athletic	46	8	7	8 27	25	5	10	8 30	36	56
Portsmouth	46	10	6	7 34	27	4	5	14 24	43	53
Plymouth Argyle	46	10	10	3 36	20	2	7	14 18	48	53
Blackburn Rovers	46	8	6	6 26	24	6	4	13 25	39	52
WATFORD	46	5	8	10 24	32	7	7	9 21	27	51
Swindon Town	46	8	6	9 31	30	4	8	11 34	43	50
Leicester City	46	12	4	7 41	33	2	4	17 19	50	50
West Bromwich Albion	46	7	11	5 26	21	3	7	13 26	40	48
Hull City	46	6	10	7 35	35	4	5	14 22	53	45

No	DATE				COMPETITION	OPPONENTS	HOME	AWAY	ATTENDANCE	
1	August	Sat	25		Football League, Division 2	MILLWALL	1-2 L		11,541	
2		Tue	28		Football League, Division 2	Plymouth Argyle		D 1-1		7,734
3	September	Sat	1		Football League, Division 2	West Ham United		L 0-1		19,872
4		Sat	8		Football League, Division 2	BRIGHTON & HOVE ALBION	0-1 L		7,487	
5		Sat	15		Football League, Division 2	Sheffield Wednesday		L 0-2		22,061
6		Sat	22		Football League, Division 2	NOTTS COUNTY	1-3 L		7,973	
7		Wed	26		Football Lge Cup, 2nd Round, 1st Leg	Norwich City		L 0-2		7,720
8		Sat	29		Football League, Division 2	Ipswich Town		D 1-1		11,351
9	October	Tue	2		Football League, Division 2	HULL CITY	0-1 L		6,448	
10		Sat	6		Football League, Division 2	MIDDLESBROUGH	0-3 L		8,057	
11		Tue	9		Football Lge Cup, 2nd Round, 2nd Leg	NORWICH CITY	0-3 L		6,148	
12		Sat	13		Football League, Division 2	Blackburn Rovers		W 2-0		7,060
13		Sat	20		Football League, Division 2	Charlton Athletic		W 2-1		5,892
14		Tue	23		Football League, Division 2	PORTSMOUTH	0-1 L		8,247	
15		Sat	27		Football League, Division 2	OXFORD UNITED	1-1 D		7,521	
16	November	Sat	3		Football League, Division 2	Bristol City		L 2-3		11,576
17		Sat	10		Football League, Division 2	Oldham Athletic		L 1-4		12,410
18		Sat	17		Football League, Division 2	BRISTOL ROVERS	1-1 D		8,285	
19		Tue	20		Full Members Cup, 1st Round	BRISTOL ROVERS	1-2 L		3,076	
20		Sat	24		Football League, Division 2	Newcastle United		L 0-1		13,774
21	December	Sat	1		Football League, Division 2	BARNSLEY	0-0 D		7,839	
22		Wed	5		Football League, Division 2	West Bromwich Albion		D 1-1		7,657
23		Sat	8		Football League, Division 2	PLYMOUTH ARGYLE	2-0 W		6,361	
24		Sat	15		Football League, Division 2	Millwall		W 2-0		8,910
25		Sun	23		Football League, Division 2	Leicester City		D 0-0		16,290
26		Wed	26		Football League, Division 2	PORT VALE	2-1 W		8,084	
27		Sat	29		Football League, Division 2	SWINDON TOWN	2-2 D		11,233	
28	January	Tue	1		Football League, Division 2	Wolverhampton Wanderers		D 0-0		18,159
29		Sat	5		FA Cup, 3rd Round	Shrewsbury Town		L 1-4		5,327
30		Sat	12		Football League, Division 2	WEST HAM UNITED	0-1 L		17,172	
31		Sat	19		Football League, Division 2	Brighton & Hove Albion		L 0-3		8,339
32	February	Sat	2		Football League, Division 2	SHEFFIELD WEDNESDAY	2-2 D		10,338	
33		Sat	16		Football League, Division 2	Bristol Rovers		L 1-3		5,736
34		Sat	23		Football League, Division 2	OLDHAM ATHLETIC	1-1 D		8,230	
35	March	Sat	2		Football League, Division 2	Barnsley		L 1-2		6,755
36		Sat	9		Football League, Division 2	NEWCASTLE UNITED	1-2 L		10,018	
37		Tue	12		Football League, Division 2	Hull City		D 1-1		5,815
38		Sat	16		Football League, Division 2	IPSWICH TOWN	1-1 D		7,732	
39		Tue	19		Football League, Division 2	BLACKBURN ROVERS	0-3 L		6,913	
40		Sat	23		Football League, Division 2	Middlesbrough		W 2-1		14,583
41		Sat	30		Football League, Division 2	Port Vale		D 0-0		6,661
42	April	Mon	1		Football League, Division 2	LEICESTER CITY	1-0 W		10,078	
43		Sat	6		Football League, Division 2	Swindon Town		W 2-1		9,699
44		Sat	13		Football League, Division 2	WOLVERHAMPTON WANDERERS	3-1 W		12,014	
45		Tue	16		Football League, Division 2	Notts County		L 0-1		6,168
46		Sat	20		Football League, Division 2	CHARLTON ATHLETIC	2-1 W		10,178	
47		Tue	23		Football League, Division 2	WEST BROMWICH ALBION	1-1 D		15,054	
48		Sat	27		Football League, Division 2	Portsmouth		W 1-0		10,074
49	May	Sat	4		Football League, Division 2	Oxford United		W 1-0		8,437
50		Sat	11		Football League, Division 2	BRISTOL CITY	2-3 L		13,029	

League ever-presents: D.B. James, P. Wilkinson
Most appearances in total: P. Wilkinson 50 out of 50   **Most goals in total:** P. Wilkinson 18
Hat-tricks: P. Wilkinson (Match 44)   **Penalty goals:** G.M. Porter 2, P. Wilkinson 1
Sent off: G. Williams (Match 3), D.G. Holdsworth (Match 7), J. McLaughlin (Match 12), D.S. Byrne & K.B.L. Dublin (Match 25), W.H. Falconer (Match 31)
Full international appearance(s) this season: A.M. Meola (USA), P. Nicholas (Wales)

League summary

	Ashby	Bazeley	Butler	Byrne	Callaghan	Denton	Devonshire	Drysdale	Dublin	Falconer	Gavin	Gibbs	Harrison	Holdsworth	Inglethorpe	James	Kennedy	McLaughlin	Meola	Nicholas	Penrice	Porter	Pullan	Roeder	Soloman	Thomas	Wilkinson	Williams	Own goals
Apps	20	1	10	16	6	0	23	25	43	32	8	34	4	15	1	46	13	24		15	12	40	1	30	5	15	46	21	
Subs	+3	+6		+1	+6	+2	+1	+5		+3	+5		+2				+5			+2	+5	+1	+3	+3	+9		+3		
Goals			1	2	1		1			4		2					3	1			5	4		1		1	17	2	
Apps	2	1		1			2	2	3	3	2	1	3	1	3	1	2	1			1	4		2		2	4	3	
Subs		+2					+1							+1		+1										+1			
Goals									1																	1			

Match appearances

#	Ashby	Bazeley	Butler	Byrne	Callaghan	Denton	Devonshire	Drysdale	Dublin	Falconer	Gavin	Gibbs	Harrison	Holdsworth	Inglethorpe	James	Kennedy	McLaughlin	Meola	Nicholas	Penrice	Porter	Pullan	Roeder	Soloman	Thomas	Wilkinson	Williams	Own goals
1		S					X		X	X			R			X	G	X1	X			S				R	X	X	
2		S							X	X						X	G	X	X1			X		X		X	X	R	
3		R						S	S							X	G	X	X			X				X	X	X	
4							R	S	R	X	X					X	G	S	X			X				X	X	X	
5									X	X	X					X	G	S	X			R		X		X	X		
6		S							X	R	X1		R			X	G		X			X				X	X	S	
7		S							X	X	X					X	R	G	X			X				X	X		
8									X	X	X					X	R		X		S	X				X	X1	X	
9								R	R	X	S					X	G		X		X	X				S	X	X	
10	X	S					X			X	R					X	G		R			X		S		X	X	X	
11	R	X					X	S·		X			X			S	G		X			R				X	X	X	
12	X						X1			X	X						G	X	X			S				X	X1	R	
13	X						X			X	X						G	X1	X			S				X	R1	X	
14	X						R			X	X						G	X	R			S		S		X	X	X	
15		S								X	X	X	X			X						R		X		X	X1	X	
16							X	S	X	R	X	S	X1			G						X1				X	X	R	
17								R	X	X			X	R	X1	G	X					X		S	S	X	X		
18		S	R				X	X					X	X	X	G	X1					X					X		
19	S		X					X	X				X	X	X		X	G				X				R	X1		
20			X							X			X	X		G	X	X				X					X	X	
21			X				X			X			X	S	R	G	X	X				S		X			X	R	
22			X				R	S		X			X			G	X	X				X1p		X			X	X	
23			X				X	R	X	S			X			G	R	X				S		X			X2		
24			X				X	X	X				X			G	S	X			R1	X					X1		
25	S		X				R	X	X				X			G	S	X			R	X					X		
26	X						X	X	X	R			R			G	X1	X				X				S1	X	S	
27			R1				X	R	S				X			G	X1	X				X				S	S	X	
28			R				R		X	S			X			G	X					X		X		S	X	X	
29	X						R		X	X1			X			G	S	X				X		X		S	X	R	
30	X						X			X	S		X			G	X					X		X		R	X	X	
31	X						X			X	S		X	S		G	X					X		X		R	X	R	
32	S						X	X	X				S		X	G	R				R1	X				X	X1	X	
33	X		X					X	X		S					G	S	X				X	X1p	R			X	R	
34	X		R		S		R	X	X				X			G						X		X		S	X1		
35			R				X						X			G						X1		X		S	S	X	
36							X	R	X				X			G				X		X		X		S	X1		
37	S		X	X				X	X				X			G				X		X		R			X		1
38			X	X				X	X				X			G				X		X		X			X		1
39			R	X			S	X	X				X			G				X		X		X			X		
40	X		S1	R	S			R	X				X			G				X		X1					X		
41	X	R		S				X	X	R			X			G				X		X				X	S		
42	X	R		X				X	X				X			G				X		X				S	X1		
43	X	R1		S1				X	X	X			X			G				X		X			S	X	R		
44	X	X		R				X	X				X			G				X		X			S		X3p		
45	X	X							X	X			X			G				X		X				X	X		
46	X	X		S				R	X	X2			X			G				R		X				X	S		
47	X	X							X	X			X			G				X		X			X1	X	X		
48	X	R		S					X	X1			X			G				X		X				X	X		
49	X	X		S					X	X			X			G				X		X				X	R1		
50	X	X		S					X	X			X			G				X		X				R	X	X2	

1991/92

Football League position: 10th out of 24 in Division 2
Manager: Steve Perryman

	HOME					AWAY					
	Pl	W	D	L	For	Ag	W	D	L	For	Ag	Pts

	Pl	W	D	L	For	Ag	W	D	L	For	Ag	Pts
Ipswich Town	46	16	3	4	42	22	8	9	6	28	28	84
Middlesbrough	46	15	6	2	37	13	8	5	10	21	28	80
Derby County	46	11	4	8	35	24	12	5	6	34	27	78
Leicester City	46	14	4	5	41	24	9	4	10	31	31	77
Cambridge United	46	10	9	4	34	19	9	8	6	31	28	74
Blackburn Rovers	46	14	5	4	41	21	7	6	10	29	32	74
Charlton Athletic	46	9	7	7	25	23	11	4	8	29	25	71
Swindon Town	46	15	3	5	38	22	3	12	8	31	33	69
Portsmouth	46	15	6	2	41	12	4	6	13	24	39	69
WATFORD	46	9	5	9	25	23	9	6	8	26	25	65
Wolverhampton Wanderers	46	11	6	6	36	24	7	4	12	25	30	64
Southend United	46	11	5	7	37	26	6	6	11	26	37	62
Bristol Rovers	46	11	9	3	43	29	5	5	13	17	34	62
Tranmere Rovers	46	9	9	5	37	32	5	10	8	19	24	61
Millwall	46	10	4	9	32	32	7	6	10	32	39	61
Barnsley	46	11	4	8	27	25	5	7	11	19	32	59
Bristol City	46	10	8	5	30	24	5	3	15	25	47	54
Sunderland	46	10	8	5	36	23	4	3	16	25	42	53
Grimsby Town	46	7	5	11	25	28	7	6	10	22	34	53
Newcastle United	46	9	8	6	38	30	4	5	14	28	54	52
Oxford United	46	10	6	7	39	30	3	5	15	27	43	50
Plymouth Argyle	46	11	5	7	26	26	2	4	17	16	38	48
Brighton & Hove Albion	46	7	7	9	36	37	5	4	14	20	40	47
Port Vale	46	7	8	8	23	25	3	7	13	19	34	45

New league opponents: None

Home-and-away league doubles
For – 2 (Grimsby Town, Plymouth Argyle)
Against – 3 (Derby County, Southend United, Wolverhampton Wanderers)

Divisional changes at end of season: Ipswich Town, Middlesbrough and Blackburn Rovers to Division 1; Plymouth Argyle, Brighton & Hove Albion and Port Vale to Division 3; Luton Town, Notts County and West Ham United from Division 1; Brentford, Birmingham City and Peterborough United from Division 3. **(Division 2 was renamed Division 1.)**

All Matches: Won 19, Drew 12, Lost 21, Goals 57-56

Highest Score: 5 (Match 52)

No	DATE			COMPETITION	OPPONENTS	HOME	AWAY	ATTENDANCE
1	August	Sat	17	Football League, Division 2	WOLVERHAMPTON WANDERERS	0-2 L		13,547
2		Tue	20	Football Lge Cup, 1st Round, 1st Leg	SOUTHEND UNITED	2-0 W		6,231
3		Sat	24	Football League, Division 2	Newcastle United		D 2-2	22,440
4		Wed	28	Football Lge Cup, 1st Round, 2nd Leg	Southend United		D 1-1	3,802
5		Sat	31	Football League, Division 2	CAMBRIDGE UNITED	1-3 L		8,902
6	September	Tue	3	Football League, Division 2	Barnsley		W 3-0	6,500
7		Sat	7	Football League, Division 2	MIDDLESBROUGH	1-2 L		8,715
8		Sat	14	Football League, Division 2	Brighton & Hove Albion		W 1-0	8,741
9		Tue	17	Football League, Division 2	Blackburn Rovers		L 0-1	9,542
10		Sat	21	Football League, Division 2	CHARLTON ATHLETIC	2-0 W		8,459
11		Tue	24	Football Lge Cup, 2nd Round, 1st Leg	Everton		L 0-1	8,284
12		Sat	28	Football League, Division 2	Swindon Town		L 1-3	8,863
13	October	Wed	2	Full Members Cup, 1st Round	SOUTHEND UNITED	0-1 L		1,700
14		Sat	5	Football League, Division 2	GRIMSBY TOWN	2-0 W		6,970
15		Tue	8	Football Lge Cup, 2nd Round, 2nd Leg	EVERTON	1-2 L		11,561
16		Sat	12	Football League, Division 2	Bristol City		L 0-1	7,882
17		Sat	19	Football League, Division 2	SOUTHEND UNITED	1-2 L		6,862
18		Sat	26	Football League, Division 2	Plymouth Argyle		W 1-0	4,090
19		Tue	29	Football League, Division 2	MILLWALL	0-2 L		7,366
20	November	Sat	2	Football League, Division 2	Sunderland		L 1-3	12,790
21		Wed	6	Football League, Division 2	OXFORD UNITED	2-0 W		4,785
22		Sat	9	Football League, Division 2	LEICESTER CITY	0-1 L		9,271
23		Sat	16	Football League, Division 2	Bristol Rovers		D 1-1	5,064
24		Sat	23	Football League, Division 2	PORTSMOUTH	2-1 W		8,135
25		Sat	30	Football League, Division 2	Port Vale		L 1-2	5,777
26	December	Sat	7	Football League, Division 2	DERBY COUNTY	1-2 L		8,302
27		Sun	22	Football League, Division 2	BARNSLEY	1-1 D		7,522
28		Thu	26	Football League, Division 2	Millwall		W 4-0	9,237
29		Sun	29	Football League, Division 2	Cambridge United		W 1-0	8,439
30	January	Wed	1	Football League, Division 2	TRANMERE ROVERS	0-0 D		9,892
31		Sat	4	FA Cup, 3rd Round	Swindon Town		L 2-3	9,817
32		Sat	11	Football League, Division 2	NEWCASTLE UNITED	2-2 D		9,811
33		Sat	18	Football League, Division 2	Wolverhampton Wanderers		L 0-3	14,175
34		Fri	24	Football League, Division 2	Tranmere Rovers		D 1-1	6,187
35	February	Sat	1	Football League, Division 2	Southend United		L 0-1	7,581
36		Sat	8	Football League, Division 2	PLYMOUTH ARGYLE	1-0 W		7,260
37		Sat	22	Football League, Division 2	PORT VALE	0-0 D		6,602
38		Sat	29	Football League, Division 2	Derby County		L 1-3	14,052
39	March	Sat	7	Football League, Division 2	IPSWICH TOWN	0-1 L		9,199
40		Wed	11	Football League, Division 2	Oxford United		D 0-0	5,808
41		Sat	14	Football League, Division 2	SUNDERLAND	1-0 W		8,091
42		Tue	17	Football League, Division 2	Ipswich Town		W 2-1	12,484
43		Sat	21	Football League, Division 2	Leicester City		W 2-1	14,519
44		Sat	28	Football League, Division 2	BRISTOL ROVERS	1-0 W		7,496
45		Tue	31	Football League, Division 2	BRIGHTON & HOVE ALBION	0-1 L		7,589
46	April	Sat	4	Football League, Division 2	Middlesbrough		W 2-1	13,669
47		Sat	11	Football League, Division 2	BLACKBURN ROVERS	2-1 W		10,522
48		Sat	18	Football League, Division 2	Charlton Athletic		D 1-1	7,477
49		Mon	20	Football League, Division 2	SWINDON TOWN	0-0 D		9,911
50		Wed	22	Football League, Division 2	Portsmouth		D 0-0	14,417
51		Sat	25	Football League, Division 2	Grimsby Town		W 1-0	6,483
52	May	Sat	2	Football League, Division 2	BRISTOL CITY	5-2 W		10,582

League ever-presents: K.B.L. Dublin
Most appearances in total: K.B.L. Dublin 52 out of 52   **Most goals in total:** L.L. Blissett 12
Hat-tricks: None   **Penalty goals:** G.M. Porter 4, J. Drysdale 1
Sent off: J. McLaughlin (Match 1), N.J. Gibbs (Match 18)
Full international appearances this season: S.J. Morrow (whilst on loan to Watford) (Northern Ireland), P. Nicholas (Wales), L.M. Nogan (Wales)

	Ashby, B.J.	Bazeley, D.S.	Blissett, L.L. //	Butler, S.	Devonshire, A.E. //	Drysdale, J.	Dublin, K.B.L.	Gibbs, N.J.	Hessenthaler, A.	Holdsworth, David G.	Inglethorpe, A.M.	James, D.B. //	Johnson, R.M.	Kennedy, A.J. //	Lavin, G.	McLaughlin, J. //	Morrow, S.J. //	Nicholas, P. //	Nogan, L.M.	Porter, G.M.	Putney, T.A.	Soloman, J.R.	Thomas, R.C.	Waugh, K.
Apps	18	25	34	28	0	36	46	43	35	33	0	43	1	4	0	22	7	25	23	34	26	19	1	3
Subs	+3	+9	+8	+15	+1	+1					+2		+1	+3	+1		+1			+10	+2	+10	+4	
Goals		6	9	8		5		1	2	2			1		1		1		5	8	2			
Apps	2	5	5			2	6	6	4	1		6		2		5	1	6		6	6	3	0	
Subs		+2	+1	+1																		+1	+1	
Goals		1	3											1						1				
1	S		S	X		X	X					G		R		X	X	X		X	X		R	
2			X1	X		X	X					G		R		X				X1	X	X	X	
3		R	R1	X		X	X					G				X	X	X1		X	X	S	S	
4			X	X		X	X					G		X1		X				X	X	X		
5	R	S	X1	X		X	X					G		R			X	X		X	X		S	
6		R1	R1	S		X	X					G		X1		X	X			X	X		S	
7		X	X	S		X	X					G		R		X1	R	X		X	X		S	
8		X	R	X1		X	X					G			S	X	X	X		R	X		S	
9			X	X		X	X	X				G			S	X	R	X		X	R		S	
10	S	R	R	X1		X	X	X1				G			S	X				X	X		X	
11	X	R	S			X	X	X				G				X				X	X		X	
12		R	X	X	R	X	X	X				G				X				X	X1	S	S	
13	X	S	X			X	R	X				G				R	X	X		X	X		S	
14		X	X			X	X	X1				G				X				X	X1			
15		S1	X	X		X	X	X	R			G				X				X	X			
16		S	R	X	S	X	X	X	R			G				X				X	X			
17		X	X	R		X	X					G				X	S	X		X1p	X			
18		X1	R	S		X	X	X				G				X				X	X			
19		X	X	S		X	X	X				G				X				X	R			
20		X	X	S	R	X	X	X				G				X				X1	X			
21		S1	X	R			X	X	X	X		G				X				X1p	X			
22		S	X	X		S	X		X	X		G				R				X	R	X		
23	X	X	X1	R		X	X		X	X		G								X		X	S	
24	X	R	X2	S		X	X		X	X		G				X				R		X	S	
25	X	R	X			X	X		X	X		G				X				X1			S	
26	R	X	X1	S		X	X		X	X		G				R				X		S		
27		S	X			X	X		X	X		G				X				X1	X	R		
28		S		X2		X1	X	X	X	X		G				R				R	X1	S	X	
29		R	S	X1		X	X	X	X	X		G	X							X		X		
30		S	X	X		X	X	X	X	X		G			S					R		X		
31		S	X2	X		X	X	X	X	X		G								R		X		
32		S	R	S		X	X	X	X	X1										X1p	X	X		G
33			X	S		X	X	X	X	X						X				X	R			G
34			X	S1		X	R	X	X							X				X	X	X		G
35	S		X	S		X	X	R	X	X		G				X				R	X	X		
36			X1	S		X	X	X	X	X		G				X				X	R	X		
37			X	S		R	X	X	X	X		G				X			R	X	X	X	S	
38			X	S		R	X	X	X	X		G				X				X1	S	R	S	
39	X		X	X		X	X	X		X		G								X	X	X		
40	X		R	S		X	X	X		X		G								X	X	X		
41	X		R	S		X	X	X		X		G			S					X	R1p	X		
42	X	S	X	X		X2	X	X		X		G								R		X		
43	X	X		X1		X	X	X		X		G								X1		X		
44	X	R	S	R		X1p	X	X		X		G								X	S	X		
45	R	X		X		X	X	X	X	X	S	G								X	S	R		
46	X	R	S	X1		R	X	X	X	X1		G								X	S	X		
47	X	R2	S	X		X	X	X	X	X		G								R	S	X		
48	X	R	S	R		X	X	X	X	X		G								X1	S	X		
49	X	R	R			X	X	X	X	X	S	G								X	S	X		
50		X		X		X	X	X	X			G								X	S	X	R	
51	X	R	S			X	X	X	X			G								X1	S	R		
52	R	X1	S1	R		X1	X	X1	X	X		G								X	S	X1		

- 193 -

1992/93

Football League position: 16th out of 24 in Division 1
Manager: Steve Perryman

New league opponents: None

Home-and-away league doubles
For – 2 (Bristol Rovers, Sunderland)
Against – 4 (Grimsby Town, Leicester City, Swindon Town, West Ham United)

Divisional changes at end of season: Newcastle United, West Ham United & Swindon Town to FA Premier League; Brentford, Cambridge United & Bristol Rovers to Division 2; Crystal Palace, Middlesbrough & Nottingham Forest from FA Premier League; Stoke City, Bolton Wanderers & West Bromwich Albion from Division 2.

All Matches: Won 16, Drew 15, Lost 22, Goals 65-85

Highest Score: 4 (Match 15)

		HOME					AWAY					
	Pl	W	D	L	For	Ag	W	D	L	For	Ag	Pts
Newcastle United	46	16	6	1	58	15	13	3	7	34	23	96
West Ham United	46	16	5	2	50	17	10	5	8	31	24	88
Portsmouth	46	19	2	2	48	9	7	8	8	32	37	88
Tranmere Rovers	46	15	4	4	48	24	8	6	9	24	32	79
Swindon Town	46	15	5	3	41	23	6	8	9	33	36	76
Leicester City	46	14	5	4	43	24	8	5	10	28	40	76
Millwall	46	14	6	3	46	21	4	10	9	19	32	70
Derby County	46	11	2	10	40	33	8	7	8	28	24	66
Grimsby Town	46	12	6	5	33	25	7	1	15	25	32	64
Peterborough United	46	7	11	5	30	26	9	3	11	25	37	62
Wolverhampton Wanderers	46	11	6	6	37	26	5	7	11	20	30	61
Charlton Athletic	46	10	8	5	28	19	6	5	12	21	27	61
Barnsley	46	12	4	7	29	19	5	5	13	27	41	60
Oxford United	46	8	7	8	29	21	6	7	10	24	35	56
Bristol City	46	10	7	6	29	25	4	7	12	20	42	56
WATFORD	46	8	7	8	27	30	6	6	11	30	41	55
Notts County	46	10	7	6	33	21	2	9	12	22	49	52
Southend United	46	9	8	6	33	22	4	5	14	21	42	52
Birmingham City	46	10	4	9	30	32	3	8	12	20	40	51
Luton Town	46	6	13	4	26	26	4	8	11	22	36	51
Sunderland	46	9	6	8	34	28	4	5	14	16	36	50
Brentford	46	7	6	10	28	30	6	4	13	24	41	49
Cambridge United	46	8	6	9	29	32	3	10	10	19	37	49
Bristol Rovers	46	6	6	11	30	42	4	5	14	25	45	41

No	DATE			COMPETITION	OPPONENTS	HOME	AWAY	ATTENDANCE
1	August	Sat	15	Football League, Division 1	MILLWALL	3-1 W		9,745
2		Sat	22	Football League, Division 1	Grimsby Town		L 2-3	4,772
3		Tue	25	Football League, Division 1	Notts County		W 2-1	6,274
4		Sat	29	Football League, Division 1	DERBY COUNTY	0-0 D		9,809
5	September	Tue	1	Anglo-Italian Cup, Preliminary Round	Bristol City		L 0-1	3,588
6		Sat	5	Football League, Division 1	West Ham United		L 1-2	11,921
7		Sat	12	Football League, Division 1	NOTTS COUNTY	1-3 L		7,077
8		Tue	15	Anglo-Italian Cup, Preliminary Round	LUTON TOWN	0-0 D		5,197
9		Sat	19	Football League, Division 1	Wolverhampton Wanderers		D 2-2	13,497
10		Tue	22	Football Lge Cup, 2nd Round, 1st Leg	READING	2-2 D		4,036
11		Sat	26	Football League, Division 1	LEICESTER CITY	0-3 L		8,715
12		Tue	29	Football League, Division 1	SUNDERLAND	2-1 W		6,263
13	October	Sat	3	Football League, Division 1	Swindon Town		L 1-3	7,723
14		Wed	7	Football Lge Cup, 2nd Round, 2nd Leg	Reading		W 2-0	7,386
15		Sat	10	Football League, Division 1	BRISTOL ROVERS	4-2 W		7,624
16		Sat	17	Football League, Division 1	Brentford		D 1-1	8,490
17		Sat	24	Football League, Division 1	TRANMERE ROVERS	3-2 W		6,937
18		Sat	31	Football League, Division 1	Oxford United		D 1-1	6,234
19	November	Tue	3	Football League, Division 1	PETERBOROUGH UNITED	1-2 L		7,016
20		Sat	7	Football League, Division 1	Barnsley		W 1-0	6,193
21		Tue	10	Football Lge Cup, 3rd Round	LEEDS UNITED	2-1 W		18,035
22		Sat	14	Football League, Division 1	PORTSMOUTH	0-0 D		8,714
23		Sat	21	Football League, Division 1	Newcastle United		L 0-2	28,871
24		Sun	29	Football League, Division 1	Luton Town		L 0-2	8,341
25	December	Sat	5	Football League, Division 1	BRISTOL CITY	0-0 D		6,746
26		Wed	9	Football Lge Cup, 4th Round	Blackburn Rovers		L 1-6	13,187
27		Sun	13	Football League, Division 1	CHARLTON ATHLETIC	1-1 D		6,541
28		Sat	19	Football League, Division 1	Birmingham City		D 2-2	7,182
29		Sat	26	Football League, Division 1	Southend United		W 2-1	5,769
30		Mon	28	Football League, Division 1	CAMBRIDGE CITY	2-2 D		8,147
31	January	Sat	2	FA Cup, 3rd Round	WOLVERHAMPTON WANDERERS	1-4 L		12,363
32		Sat	9	Football League, Division 1	WOLVERHAMPTON WANDERERS	3-1 W		6,845
33		Sat	16	Football League, Division 1	Leicester City		L 2-5	12,854
34		Wed	27	Football League, Division 1	Sunderland		W 2-1	14,703
35		Sat	30	Football League, Division 1	GRIMSBY TOWN	2-3 L		6,613
36	February	Sat	6	Football League, Division 1	Millwall		L 2-5	8,847
37		Sat	13	Football League, Division 1	WEST HAM UNITED	1-2 L		13,115
38		Sat	20	Football League, Division 1	Derby County		W 2-1	15,190
39		Sat	27	Football League, Division 1	Bristol Rovers		W 3-0	5,702
40	March	Sat	6	Football League, Division 1	SWINDON TOWN	0-4 L		8,791
41		Tue	9	Football League, Division 1	Portsmouth		L 0-1	10,716
42		Sat	13	Football League, Division 1	BARNSLEY	1-2 L		5,785
43		Sat	20	Football League, Division 1	Bristol City		L 1-2	8,265
44		Tue	23	Football League, Division 1	NEWCASTLE UNITED	1-0 W		11,634
45		Sat	27	Football League, Division 1	Peterborough United		D 0-0	7,631
46	April	Sat	3	Football League, Division 1	LUTON TOWN	0-0 D		10,656
47		Tue	6	Football League, Division 1	Charlton Athletic		L 1-3	6,462
48		Sat	10	Football League, Division 1	SOUTHEND UNITED	0-0 D		7,198
49		Tue	13	Football League, Division 1	Cambridge United		D 1-1	5,106
50		Sat	17	Football League, Division 1	BIRMINGHAM CITY	1-0 W		9,186
51		Sat	24	Football League, Division 1	BRENTFORD	1-0 W		9,045
52	May	Sat	1	Football League, Division 1	Tranmere Rovers		L 1-2	8,315
53		Sat	8	Football League, Division 1	OXFORD UNITED	0-1 L		8,127

League ever-presents: K.B.L. Dublin
Most appearances in total: K.B.L. Dublin 53 out of 53   **Most goals in total:** P.A. Furlong 22
Hat-tricks: None   **Penalty goals:** J. Drysdale 5
Sent off: G. Lavin (Match 23)
Full international appearance(s) this season: None

	Alsford, J.	Ashby, B.J.	Bazeley, D.S.	Butler, S. //	Charlery, K.	Drysdale, J.	Dublin, K.B.L.	Dyer, B.A.	Furlong, P.A.	Gibbs, N.J.	Hessenthaler, A.	Holdsworth, David G.	Johnson, R.M.	Lavin, G.	Meara, J.S. //	Nogan, L.M.	Porter, G.M.	Putney, T.A. //	Sheppard, S.	Soloman, J.R.	Suckling, P.J.	Thomas, R.C. //	Waugh, K. //	Willis, R.C.	Own goal
Apps	2	33	10	2	30	37	46	0	41	7	45	38	0	24	1	40	25	16	5	34	37	1	4	28	
Subs	+3	+2	+12	+7	+2	+2		+2				+1	+1	+4	+1	+2	+8	+8		+2				+4	
Goals			1		11	6	1		19		3					11				2				2	1
Apps		3	3	2	1	7	7		6	1	5	6		6		5	4	7		5	7	1		1	
Subs			+1	+3										+1		+2									
Goals						2			3			1		1		1									

#	Alsford, J.	Ashby, B.J.	Bazeley, D.S.	Butler, S.	Charlery, K.	Drysdale, J.	Dublin, K.B.L.	Dyer, B.A.	Furlong, P.A.	Gibbs, N.J.	Hessenthaler, A.	Holdsworth, David G.	Johnson, R.M.	Lavin, G.	Meara, J.S.	Nogan, L.M.	Porter, G.M.	Putney, T.A.	Sheppard, S.	Soloman, J.R.	Suckling, P.J.	Thomas, R.C.	Waugh, K.	Willis, R.C.	Own goal
1		X	R1	S		X1p	X		R	X	X	X				X1	S			X	G				
2		X	R	S		X	X1		X1	X	X	X				X	X				G				
3		X		X		X1	X		X1	X	X	X				X				X	G				
4		R	X	S		X	X		X	X	R	X				X	S			X	G				
5		X	R	X		X	X		X	X	X			S		S	X	R		X	G				
6		X	S	R		X	X		X1	X	X	X				X	S			R	G				
7		X	X	S		X1	X		X	R	X	X				R	S			X	G				
8			R	S	X	X	X		X		X	X		X		S		R		X	G	X			
9		X				X	X		X1		X	X		X		X1	X			X	G				
10		X		S		X	X		X2		X	X		X		X	X			R	G				
11		X	X			R	X		X		X	X		S		S	R			X	G	X			
12		X				X	X		X		X2	X		X		X	X			X	G				
13	S	R	S			X	X		X1		X			X		X	R			X	G				
14			S	X		X1	X				X	X		X1		X	R			X	G				
15						X1p	X		R1		X	X		X		X2	S	X		X				X	
16				S		X	X		X		X	X		R		X1	X			X	G		R	
17				X1		X	X		X2	R	X	X		S		X	R		S	G			X		
18				S		X	X		R1		X	X		X		X	X			X	G			
19	S	R		S		R1	X				X	X		X		X	X				G			X	
20	S	X		S		X	X		X1	R	X			X		X	X				G			R	
21		X		S		X1p	X		X		X	X1		X		R	X	X			G				
22		X		S		X	X		X		X	X		X		R	R	X			G			S	
23		X				X	X		R		X	X		X		R	S	X			G			S	
24		X	S			X	X		X		X	X		R			X	X			G			X	
25		X	S			X	X		X		X	X	S			X	R	R			G			X	
26			X			X	X		X1		X	X		X		X	X	X			G				
27			S			X1	X		X		X	X		X		R	X				G			X	
28	X		S			X	X		X2		X	X		X		R	X				G			X	
29						X1	X		X		X	X		X		X				X1	G			X	
30	X					X1	X		X	R	X			X		X	S			X	G			X1	
31			X	X		X	X		X		X			X		X1	X			X	G			X	
32			X			X	X		X2		X	X		X		X1		S	G					R	
33		S				R	X		X		X	X		R		X1		S	G	X1				X	
34						X	X		X1		X	X				X		X	G	X				X1	
35						X	X		X1		X	X		X		X1		X	G					X	
36		S				X	X		X		X	R		X		X1	R		G					X	
37		X				X1	X		X		X	X		R		R	S			X	G			X	
38		X				X1	X		X1		X					X	X			X	G			X	
39		X	S			R2	X		R		X					X1	X	S		X	G			X	
40		X	S			X	R		X		X					X	X	S		R	G			X	
41		X	S			X			X		X	X				X	X	S		R	G			R	
42		X	R			R			X1		X	X		S		X	X			X	G			S	
43		X	R			X1			X		X	X		S		R	X			X	G			S	
44		X	S			X			X1		X	X				X				X			G	R	
45		X				X			X		X	X		R		X	S			X			G	X	
46		X	S			X			X		X	X		R		X	X			X			G	X	
47		X	S			X			X		X	X		R		X	X	S		X			G	R	1
48	X	X	X	S	X				X		X	X				R	X			X	G				
49	X	R	X		X				X		X	X				X1	X			X	G				
50	X	R				X1	X	X	S		X					X	X			X	G			X	
51	X					X	X1p	X	X		X					X	X			X	G			X	
52	X					X	X1p	X	X		X	X		S			R			X	G			X	
53	X					X	X	X	S		X	X		R			S	X		R	G				

1993/94

Football League position: 19th out of 24 in Division 1
Manager: Glenn Roeder

New league opponents: None

Home-and-away league doubles
For – 2 (Oxford United, Peterborough United)
Against – 4 (Nottingham Forest, Stoke City, Tranmere Rovers, West Bromwich Albion)

Divisional changes at end of season: Crystal Palace, Nottingham Forest & Leicester City to FA Premier League; Birmingham City, Oxford United & Peterborough United to Division 2; Sheffield United, Oldham Athletic & Swindon Town from FA Premier League; Reading, Port Vale and Burnley from Division 2.

All Matches: Won 17, Drew 11, Lost 25, Goals 77-93

Highest Score: 5 (Match 33)

	HOME						AWAY					
	Pl	W	D	L	For	Ag	W	D	L	For	Ag	Pts
Crystal Palace	46	16	4	3	39	18	11	5	7	34	28	90
Nottingham Forest	46	12	9	2	38	22	11	5	7	36	27	83
Millwall	46	14	8	1	36	17	9	7	9	22	32	74
Leicester City	46	11	9	3	45	30	8	7	8	27	29	73
Tranmere Rovers	46	15	3	5	48	23	6	11	6	21	30	72
Derby County	46	15	3	5	44	25	5	8	10	29	43	71
Notts County	46	16	3	4	43	26	4	5	14	22	43	68
Wolverhampton Wanderers	46	10	10	3	34	19	7	7	9	26	28	68
Middlesbrough	46	12	6	5	40	19	6	7	10	26	35	67
Stoke City	46	14	4	5	35	19	4	9	10	22	40	67
Charlton Athletic	46	14	3	6	39	22	5	5	13	22	36	65
Sunderland	46	14	2	7	35	22	5	5	13	22	36	65
Bristol City	46	11	7	5	27	18	5	9	9	20	32	64
Bolton Wanderers	46	10	8	5	40	31	5	6	12	23	33	59
Southend United	46	10	5	8	34	28	7	3	13	29	39	59
Grimsby Town	46	7	14	2	26	16	6	6	11	26	36	59
Portsmouth	46	10	6	7	29	22	5	7	11	23	36	58
Barnsley	46	9	3	11	25	26	7	4	12	30	41	55
WATFORD	46	10	5	8	39	35	4	5	14	27	45	54
Luton Town	46	12	4	7	38	25	2	7	14	18	35	53
West Bromwich Albion	46	9	7	7	38	31	4	5	14	22	38	51
Birmingham City	46	9	7	7	28	29	4	5	14	24	40	51
Oxford United	46	10	5	8	33	33	3	5	15	21	42	49
Peterborough United	46	6	9	8	31	30	2	4	17	17	46	37

No	DATE			COMPETITION	OPPONENTS	HOME	AWAY	ATTENDANCE
1	August	Sat	14	Football League, Division 1	Luton Town		L 1-2	9,149
2		Tue	17	Football Lge Cup, 1st Round, 1st Leg	Brentford		D 2-2	4,297
3		Sat	21	Football League, Division 1	BARNSLEY	0-2 L		5,937
4		Tue	24	Football Lge Cup, 1st Round, 2nd Leg	BRENTFORD	3-1 W		4,938
5		Sat	28	Football League, Division 1	Oxford United		W 3-2	5,159
6		Tue	31	Anglo-Italian Cup, Preliminary Round	LUTON TOWN	2-1 W		2,854
7	September	Sat	4	Football League, Division 1	CHARLTON ATHLETIC	2-2 D		6,925
8		Tue	7	Football League, Division 1	WOLVERHAMPTON WANDERERS	1-0 W		7,870
9		Sat	11	Football League, Division 1	Grimsby Town		D 2-2	4,783
10		Wed	15	Anglo-Italian Cup, Preliminary Round	Southend United		L 0-3	1,881
11		Sat	18	Football League, Division 1	NOTTS COUNTY	3-1 W		6,959
12		Tue	21	Football Lge Cup, 2nd Round, 1st Leg	MILLWALL	0-0 D		5,954
13		Sat	25	Football League, Division 1	SUNDERLAND	1-1 D		7,694
14	October	Sat	2	Football League, Division 1	Millwall		L 1-4	7,707
15		Wed	6	Football Lge Cup, 2nd Round, 2nd Leg	Millwall (after extra time)		L 3-4	5,381
16		Sun	10	Football League, Division 1	MIDDLESBROUGH	2-0 W		7,582
17		Sat	16	Football League, Division 1	Birmingham City		L 0-1	12,823
18		Sat	23	Football League, Division 1	BOLTON WANDERERS	4-3 W		7,492
19		Sat	30	Football League, Division 1	West Bromwich Albion		L 1-4	15,299
20	November	Wed	3	Football League, Division 1	Southend United		L 0-2	4,584
21		Sat	6	Football League, Division 1	STOKE CITY	1-3 L		7,767
22		Sat	20	Football League, Division 1	BRISTOL CITY	1-1 D		6,045
23		Sun	28	Football League, Division 1	CRYSTAL PALACE	1-3 L		7,485
24	December	Sat	4	Football League, Division 1	Stoke City		L 0-2	13,465
25		Tue	7	Football League, Division 1	Portsmouth		L 0-2	8,242
26		Sat	11	Football League, Division 1	Wolverhampton Wanderers		L 0-2	17,460
27		Sun	19	Football League, Division 1	LUTON TOWN	2-2 D		7,567
28		Mon	27	Football League, Division 1	Leicester City		D 4-4	21,744
29		Tue	28	Football League, Division 1	PETERBOROUGH UNITED	2-1 W		7,155
30	January	Sat	1	Football League, Division 1	Tranmere Rovers		L 1-2	8,271
31		Mon	3	Football League, Division 1	NOTTINGHAM FOREST	1-2 L		14,539
32		Sat	8	FA Cup, 3rd Round	West Ham United		L 1-2	19,802
33		Sat	15	Football League, Division 1	BIRMINGHAM CITY	5-2 W		7,636
34		Sat	22	Football League, Division 1	Middlesbrough		D 1-1	8,089
35		Sat	29	Football League, Division 1	Derby County		W 2-1	15,308
36	February	Sat	5	Football League, Division 1	Bolton Wanderers		L 1-3	10,150
37		Sat	12	Football League, Division 1	WEST BROMWICH ALBION	0-1 L		10,087
38		Sat	19	Football League, Division 1	DERBY COUNTY	3-4 L		8,277
39		Sat	26	Football League, Division 1	Charlton Athletic		L 1-2	7,546
40	March	Sat	5	Football League, Division 1	OXFORD UNITED	2-1 W		7,049
41		Sat	12	Football League, Division 1	Notts County		L 0-1	6,378
42		Tue	15	Football League, Division 1	GRIMSBY TOWN	0-3 L		5,109
43		Sat	19	Football League, Division 1	Sunderland		L 0-2	16,479
44		Sat	26	Football League, Division 1	MILLWALL	2-0 W		9,036
45		Wed	30	Football League, Division 1	Nottingham Forest		L 1-2	23,044
46	April	Sat	2	Football League, Division 1	LEICESTER CITY	1-1 D		8,645
47		Tue	5	Football League, Division 1	Peterborough United		W 4-3	7,734
48		Sat	9	Football League, Division 1	TRANMERE ROVERS	1-2 L		7,347
49		Tue	12	Football League, Division 1	Barnsley		W 1-0	4,380
50		Sat	16	Football League, Division 1	SOUTHEND UNITED	3-0 W		7,694
51		Sat	23	Football League, Division 1	Bristol City		D 1-1	8,324
52		Sat	30	Football League, Division 1	PORTSMOUTH	1-0 W		10,141
53	May	Sun	8	Football League, Division 1	Crystal Palace		W 2-0	28,749

League ever-presents: G. Lavin
Most appearances in total: G. Lavin 53 out of 53   **Most goals in total:** P.A. Furlong 19
Hat-tricks: G.M. Porter (Match 18), P.A. Furlong (Match 33)   **Penalty goals:** G.M. Porter 2, P.A. Furlong 1
Sent off: B.J. Ashby & J. Drysdale (Match 1), B.A. Dyer (Match 3), P.A. Furlong & D.G. Holdsworth (Match 15), P.A. Furlong (Match 17), A. Hessenthaler (Match 19)
Full international appearance(s) this season: M.S. Watson (Canada)

	Alsford, J.	Ashby, B.J.	Bailey, D.L.	Barnes, D.	Bazeley, D.S.	Charlery, K.	Digweed, P.M.	Drysdale, J.	Dublin, K.B.L.	Dyer, B.A.	Foster, C.J.	Furlong, P.A.	Harding, P.J.	Hessenthaler, A.	Holdsworth, David G.	Inglethorpe, A.M.	Johnson, R.M.	Lavin, G.	McCarthy, A.J.	Millen, K.D.	Mooney, T.J.	Nogan, L.M.	Page, R.J.	Porter, G.M.	Ramage, C.D.	Sheppard, S.	Soloman, J.R.	Suckling, P.J.	Watson, M.S.	Willis, R.C.	Own goals
Apps	7	16	2	5	6	15	26	19	30	29	6	38	1	42	28	1	22	46	8	10	10	21	4	43	11	18	21	2	17	2	5
Subs	+1	+1	+6		+4	+1			+3				+1			+8	+5		+1			+5			+2		+4			+2	
Goals	1	2	4		1	2			1	6	1	18		5			2		2			2		3		8			3		
Apps	3	4				3		2	6	7		6		6	6	1	1	7				3		7		7	6		1	1	
Subs						+1										+2	+2					+1									
Goals									3			1		1	1	1						1		2			1				
1		X		R	X		X	S				X1		X			R	X						S			G	X			
2	X					X	X	X	X1			X1			X			X									G	X			
3		X				X	X		X			X		X	X			X						X			G	X			
4		X				X	X		X			R1		X	X	X1		X						S			G	X1			
5	X1			R1					X	X		X		X	X			X						S			S	X1			
6	X							X	X1					R	X	S1	S	X						X			G	X		R	
7	X					X			X			X		X	X	S1		X						R			G	X1			
8	X					R			X			X		X	X			X						X			G	X			1
9	X	X				X			X			X		X				X						X1			G	X1			
10	X	X				S			X	X		R		X		X		X						X			G	X			
11		X				X			X	X		X2		X	X			X1						X			G	X			
12		X				X			X	X		X		X	X			X						X			G	X			
13		X1				R			X	X		X		X	X		X	X						S			G				
14		X				R			X	X		X		X	X		S	S						S1			G	R			
15		X				X	R		X			X1		X	S	S	X	R1						X1			G	X			
16		X				X	R1		X			X		X	X			X						X			G	X			
17		X				R			X			X	X	X	S	S	X	R	X					X			G	X			
18	X	X			S1				X	X		X		X		R		X						X	X3p		G	X			
19	X	X			X				X	X		X		X				X						R	X		G	X1		S	
20	X	X			X				X		X	X		X				X						X	X		G	X			
21		S			R		R	X	X1		S	X	X				X	X						X			G	X			
22					X			X	X					X			X	X						X		X1	G	X	X		
23					R			R	X			X		X	X	S		X		S1				X		X	G	X	X		
24					R			X	X			X		X	X	X		X		X				X			G	X	X		
25	S					X			X			X		X	X	X		R						X			G	X	X		
26					X			X	X			X		X	X	X		X						X			G	X			
27					G			X2			X	X		X	X	X		X						X				X			
28					G			X2	X2		X	X		X	X	X		X						R		S		X			
29					G			X	X2		X	X		X	X	X		X						X				X			
30					G			X	X1		X	X		X	X	X		X						X				X			
31					G			X	X		X	X		X	X	X		X	X	R				X				X			1
32					X	X		X	X			X		X	X	X		X						X	X1p		G		X		
33		X			G			S	X			X3p		X1	X		R	X						X		S		X			1
34		X			G				X			X1		X	X		X	X						X				X			
35		X	X		G				X			X1		X	X		R	X						X		S1		X			
36		X	X		G			S	R			X		X	X	S1		R						X		X		X			
37	X			R	G				X			X		X	X		X	X						X		X		X			
38	X1		X	X1	G	X			R			X1		X		S		X						X		X		X			
39	X		R		G	X			X			X		X		S		X						X1	X	X		X			
40	X		S		G	X	X	X				X		X1				X						R	X	X					1
41	X				G	X	X					X		X				X						R	X	X					
42			S		G	X	X					X		X	X			X						R	X	X					
43			S		G	X	X					R		X				X	X				X	X	X			X			
44		S			G	X	X	X	X			X1		X				X		X	R			X	X						1
45		S			G	X	X		X			X	X					X		X	R			X1	X						
46		S1			G	X	X					X		X				X		X	R	X	X	X							
47		S1			G	X	X1		X1			X		X			S	X1		X	R	X	X	R							
48		S1			G	X	X					X		X				X		X	R	X	X	X							
49		X			G	X	X		X1			X		X			S	X		X			X	X	R						
50		X1	S		G	X	X		X1			X		X				X		X	R1		X								
51					G	X	X		X			X	X1	X				X		X	X		X								
52		S			G	X	X		X			X	X	R1				X	X	X	R		X	S							
53					G	X	X		X			X1		X			R	X		X	X1		X	S							

1994/95

Football League position: 7th out of 24 in Division 1
Manager: Glenn Roeder

New league opponents: None

Home-and-away league doubles
For – 3 (Port Vale, Southend United, West Bromwich Albion)
Against – none

Divisional changes at end of season: Middlesbrough & Bolton Wanderers to FA Premier League; Swindon Town, Burnley, Bristol City & Notts County to Division 2; Crystal Palace, Norwich City, Leicester City & Ipswich Town from FA Premier League; Birmingham City & Huddersfield Town from Division 2.

All Matches: Won 23, Drew 16, Lost 16, Goals 62-55

Highest Score: 4 (Match 36)

		HOME					AWAY					
	Pl	W	D	L	For	Ag	W	D	L	For	Ag	Pts
Middlesbrough	46	15	4	4	41	19	8	9	6	26	21	82
Reading	46	12	7	4	34	21	11	3	9	24	23	79
Bolton Wanderers	46	16	6	1	43	13	5	8	10	24	32	77
Wolverhampton Wanderers	46	15	5	3	39	18	6	8	9	38	43	76
Tranmere Rovers	46	17	4	2	51	23	5	6	12	26	34	76
Barnsley	46	15	6	2	42	19	5	6	12	21	33	72
WATFORD	46	14	6	3	33	17	5	7	11	19	29	70
Sheffield United	46	12	9	2	41	21	5	8	10	33	34	68
Derby County	46	12	6	5	44	23	6	6	11	22	28	66
Grimsby Town	46	12	7	4	36	19	5	7	11	26	37	65
Stoke City	46	10	7	6	31	21	6	8	9	19	32	63
Millwall	46	11	8	4	36	22	5	6	12	24	38	62
Southend United	46	13	2	8	33	25	6	12	5	21	48	62
Oldham Athletic	46	12	7	4	34	21	4	6	13	26	39	61
Charlton Athletic	46	11	6	6	33	25	5	5	13	25	41	59
Luton Town	46	8	6	9	35	30	7	7	9	26	34	58
Port Vale	46	11	5	7	30	24	4	8	11	28	40	58
Portsmouth	46	9	8	6	37	28	6	5	12	22	35	58
West Bromwich Albion	46	13	3	7	33	24	3	7	13	18	33	58
Sunderland	46	5	12	6	22	22	7	6	10	19	23	54
Swindon Town	46	9	6	8	28	27	3	6	14	26	46	48
Burnley	46	8	7	8	36	33	3	6	14	13	41	46
Bristol City	46	8	8	7	26	28	3	4	16	16	35	45
Notts County	46	7	8	8	26	28	2	5	16	19	38	40

No	DATE			COMPETITION	OPPONENTS	HOME	AWAY	ATTENDANCE
1	August	Sat	13	Football League, Division 1	Sheffield United		L 0-3	16,820
2		Tue	16	Football Lge Cup, 1st Round, 1st Leg	Southend United		D 0-0	2,859
3		Sat	20	Football League, Division 1	GRIMSBY TOWN	0-0 D		6,324
4		Tue	23	Football Lge Cup, 1st Round, 2nd Leg	SOUTHEND UNITED	1-0 W		4,582
5		Sat	27	Football League, Division 1	Swindon Town		L 0-1	9,781
6		Tue	30	Football League, Division 1	WOLVERHAMPTON WANDERERS	2-1 W		10,108
7	September	Sat	3	Football League, Division 1	MIDDLESBROUGH	1-1 D		9,478
8		Sat	10	Football League, Division 1	Barnsley		D 0-0	4,251
9		Tue	13	Football League, Division 1	Oldham Athletic		W 2-0	7,243
10		Sat	17	Football League, Division 1	LUTON TOWN	2-4 L		8,880
11		Wed	21	Football Lge Cup, 2nd Round, 1st Leg	TOTTENHAM HOTSPUR	3-6 L		13,659
12		Sat	24	Football League, Division 1	READING	2-2 D		8,015
13	October	Sat	1	Football League, Division 1	Charlton Athletic		L 0-3	8,169
14		Tue	4	Football Lge Cup, 2nd Round, 2nd Leg	Tottenham Hotspur		W 3-2	17,798
15		Sat	8	Football League, Division 1	Derby County		D 1-1	13,413
16		Sat	15	Football League, Division 1	NOTTS COUNTY	3-1 W		7,008
17		Sat	22	Football League, Division 1	TRANMERE ROVERS	2-0 W		6,987
18		Sat	29	Football League, Division 1	Bolton Wanderers		L 0-3	10,483
19	November	Tue	1	Football League, Division 1	Burnley		D 1-1	11,739
20		Sat	5	Football League, Division 1	WEST BROMWICH ALBION	1-0 W		8,419
21		Sat	12	Football League, Division 1	SOUTHEND UNITED	1-0 W		8,551
22		Sat	19	Football League, Division 1	Sunderland		W 3-1	15,063
23		Sat	26	Football League, Division 1	STOKE CITY	0-0 D		9,126
24	December	Sat	3	Football League, Division 1	Tranmere Rovers		L 1-2	7,301
25		Sat	10	Football League, Division 1	Grimsby Town		D 0-0	6,288
26		Sat	17	Football League, Division 1	SHEFFIELD UNITED	0-0 D		8,919
27		Mon	26	Football League, Division 1	PORTSMOUTH	2-0 W		9,953
28		Tue	27	Football League, Division 1	Millwall		L 1-2	12,289
29		Sat	31	Football League, Division 1	PORT VALE	3-2 W		7,794
30	January	Mon	2	Football League, Division 1	Bristol City		D 0-0	9,423
31		Sat	7	FA Cup, 3rd Round	Scarborough		D 0-0	3,544
32		Sat	14	Football League, Division 1	BOLTON WANDERERS	0-0 D		9,113
33		Tue	17	FA Cup, 3rd Round replay	SCARBOROUGH	2-0 W		7,047
34		Sat	28	FA Cup, 4th Round	SWINDON TOWN	1-0 W		11,202
35	February	Wed	1	Football League, Division 1	West Bromwich Albion		W 1-0	15,754
36		Sat	4	Football League, Division 1	Southend United		W 4-0	4,914
37		Sat	11	Football League, Division 1	BURNLEY	2-0 W		9,297
38		Sat	18	FA Cup, 5th Round	CRYSTAL PALACE	0-0 D		13,814
39		Tue	21	Football League, Division 1	SUNDERLAND	0-1 L		8,189
40	March	Wed	1	FA Cup, 5th Round replay	Crystal Palace (after extra time)		L 0-1	10,321
41		Sat	4	Football League, Division 1	Reading		L 1-4	9,705
42		Tue	7	Football League, Division 1	Middlesbrough		L 0-2	16,630
43		Sat	11	Football League, Division 1	SWINDON TOWN	2-0 W		7,123
44		Sat	18	Football League, Division 1	Wolverhampton Wanderers		D 1-1	24,380
45		Tue	21	Football League, Division 1	BARNSLEY	3-2 W		6,883
46		Sun	26	Football League, Division 1	Luton Town		D 1-1	7,984
47	April	Sat	1	Football League, Division 1	OLDHAM ATHLETIC	1-2 L		8,090
48		Tue	4	Football League, Division 1	Stoke City		L 0-1	9,576
49		Sat	8	Football League, Division 1	Port Vale		W 1-0	7,276
50		Fri	14	Football League, Division 1	MILLWALL	1-0 W		6,907
51		Mon	17	Football League, Division 1	Portsmouth		L 1-2	8,396
52		Sat	22	Football League, Division 1	BRISTOL CITY	1-0 W		7,190
53		Sat	29	Football League, Division 1	Notts County		L 0-1	5,083
54	May	Tue	2	Football League, Division 1	CHARLTON ATHLETIC	2-0 W		6,024
55		Sun	7	Football League, Division 1	DERBY COUNTY	2-1 W		8,492

League ever-presents: None **Most appearances in total:** C.D. Ramage 53 out of 55 **Most goals in total:** C.D. Ramage 11
Hat-tricks: D.S. Bazeley (Match 36) **Penalty goals:** C.D. Ramage 3, T.J. Mooney 1, G.M. Porter 1
Sent off: G.M. Porter (Match 4), K. Miller (Match 7), T.J. Mooney (Match 8), D.R. Payne (Match 37), N.J. Gibbs (Match 41)
Full international appearance(s) this season: M.S. Watson (Canada)
(In Match 7, after K. Miller had been sent off with the score 0-0, a substitution was made to enable P.M. Digweed to take over in goal.)

Season summary (top block = League, lower block = Cups):

	Barnes, D.	Bazeley, D.S.	Beadle, P.C.W.J.	Connolly, D.J.	Digweed, P.M.	Fitzgerald, G.M.	Foster, C.J.	Gibbs, N.J.	Hessenthaler, A.	Holdsworth, David G.	Jemson, N.B.	Johnson, R.M.	Lavin, G.	Ludden, D.J.R.	Millen, K.D.	Miller, K.	Mooney, T.J.	Moralee, J.D.	Nogan, L.M.	Page, R.J.	Payne, D.R.	Phillips, K.	Pitcher, G.	Porter, G.M.	Quinn, M.	Ramage, C.D.	Sansom, K.G.	Shipperley, N.J.	Soloman, J.R.	Watson, M.S.	Own goals
Apps	1	22	9	0	2	1	34	9	43	38	3	27	35	1	31	44	29	23	13	4	24	15	2	41	4	44	1	5	0	1	
Subs		+6	+11	+2	+1			+2		+1	+1	+8						+1	+1	+1			+1	+2		+1			+1	+2	
Goals		4	1				2		2	1		3			1		3	4	7		9	1		3		9		1		1	
Apps	1	9		1	2		8	5	7	8		5	5		6	7	5	7	0	0	5			9		9			0		
Subs			+1													+1		+1	+1										+2		
Goals							1		2	1							1		2					2					1		

Match-by-match appearances (X = started, S = substitute, R = substitute used, G = goalkeeper; number suffix = goals):

Match	Barnes	Bazeley	Beadle	Connolly	Digweed	Fitzgerald	Foster	Gibbs	Hessenthaler	Holdsworth	Jemson	Johnson	Lavin	Ludden	Millen	Miller	Mooney	Moralee	Nogan	Page	Payne	Phillips	Pitcher	Porter	Quinn	Ramage	Sansom	Shipperley	Soloman	Watson	Own
1		X					X	X	X							G	X	X			X			X		R		S		X	
2		X					X	X	X			X				G	X	X			X			X		X					
3		X					X	X	X			X				G	X	X			X			X		X					
4		X					X	X	X			X				G	X	X			X			X		X1					
5		X					X	X	X			X				G	X	X			X			X		X					
6		X					X1	X	X			X1				G	X	X			X			X		X					
7		X			SG		X	X	X			X1		R		G	X							X		X					
8		X					X	X	X			X			X	G	X	X						X		X	X				
9		X					X		X	X1		X				G	R	X	S		X			X1p		X					
10		X			G	R			X	X		X					X1	X1			X			X		X		S			
11		X			G				X	X		X			X		X1	X			X			X		X1					1
12		X	S		G		X		X	X		X1	X				X1	X			R			X		X					
13		X					X		X	X		X				G	X	X						X		X					
14	R						X1		X	X		X	X			G	X	X	S2					X		X					
15							X		X			X	X			G	X	X	X1					X		X					
16		S					X		X			X	X			G	X	X	X1		R1			X		X1					
17							X		X			X	X			G	X	X	X2					X		X					
18	S	R					X		X			X	X			G	X				X			X		X					
19	S	S							X			X	X			G	R	X			R1			X		X					
20									X	X		X	X			G	X1	X			X			X		X					
21							X		X	X		X	X			G	X	X			X1			X		X					
22							X		X1	X		X	X			G	X1p		X1					X		X					
23							R		X	X		X	X			G	X	S	S					X		X					
24									X	X		X	X			G	X	X1	X					X		X					
25									X	X		X	X			G	X	R	X					X		X		S			
26							X		X			X	X			G	X		X					X		X		X			
27		S					X		X			X	X			G	X	R						X		X1		X1			
28		S	S				X		X			R	X			G	X	R						X		X1		X			
29		X	SR				X1	S	X			X				G	X	R						X		X1		X			1
30		X					X	X	X			X				G	X							X		X		X			
31		X			G		X	X	X				X		X		X							X		X					
32							X		X			X	X			G	X							X		X					
33		X		R			X	X	X1	R1		X	X			G						S		X		X			S		
34		X		S			X	X	X1			X	X			G		R				X		X		X					
35		X		S			X	X	X	S		R	X				X							R		X1p					
36		X3					X	X	X	X		X					X							X		X1p					
37		X1					X	X	X				S		X	G					R			X		X		X1			
38		X					X	X	X				X			G		R			X			X		X			S		
39		X					X	R	X				S		X	G								X	X	X					
40	X	X					X	X	X			X			X	G								S	R	X					
41	X	X					R	X	X	X		S			X	G	X								S1	R		X			
42		X							S	X		X			R	G	X					S		X	R	X					
43		R	S				X	X1	X			S			X	G	R							X	X1	X					
44			S				R	X	X			S	S		X	G								X	X1	X1	R	X			
45			S		X				X			X	X		X1	G	X							X1	X1	X1	R	X			
46			S				X		X			X	X			G								X1	X	X	R	X			
47			S						X			X	X			G								X	X	R		X1			
48		X					X	X	X			S	X			G								X		R					
49		X							X			X	X			G						X	X	X	S	X1					
50		R							X			X	X			G						X	X	X	R1	X	S				
51	S	R							X			X	X			G						X	X	X1	R	X					
52	S	R							X			X	X			G						X	X	X1		X					
53	S	R							X			X	X			G						X	X	S	R	X					
54	X	X1	S						X			X	X			G						X		R1							
55	X	R							X			X	X		S	G		X				X		X1		X1p					

1995/96

Football League position: 23rd out of 24 in Division 1 – relegated to Division 2
Manager: Glenn Roeder (Matches 1-33), Graham Taylor (Matches 34-51)

New league opponents: None

Home-and-away league doubles:
For – 1 (Tranmere Rovers)
Against – 6 (Barnsley, Charlton Athletic, Huddersfield Town, Ipswich Town, Leicester City, Portsmouth)

Relegated with Watford: Millwall, Luton Town

All matches: Won 10, Drew 21, Lost 20, Goals 66-76

Highest score: 6 (Match 49)

		HOME					AWAY					
	Pl	W	D	L	For	Ag	W	D	L	For	Ag	Pts
Sunderland	46	13	8	2	32	10	9	9	5	27	23	83
Derby County	46	14	8	1	48	22	7	8	8	23	29	79
Crystal Palace	46	9	9	5	34	22	11	6	6	33	26	75
Stoke City	46	13	6	4	33	22	7	9	7	28	34	73
Leicester City	46	9	7	7	32	29	10	7	6	34	31	71
Charlton Athletic	46	8	11	4	28	23	9	6	8	34	32	71
Ipswich Town	46	13	5	5	45	30	6	7	10	34	39	69
Huddersfield Town	46	14	4	5	42	23	3	8	12	19	35	63
Sheffield United	46	9	7	7	29	25	7	7	9	28	29	62
Barnsley	46	9	10	4	34	28	5	8	10	26	38	60
West Bromwich Albion	46	11	5	7	34	29	5	7	11	26	39	60
Port Vale	46	10	5	8	30	29	5	10	8	29	37	60
Tranmere Rovers	46	9	9	5	42	29	5	8	10	22	31	59
Southend United	46	11	8	4	30	22	4	6	13	22	39	59
Birmingham City	46	11	7	5	37	23	4	6	13	24	41	58
Norwich City	46	7	9	7	26	24	7	6	10	33	31	57
Grimsby Town	46	8	10	5	27	25	4	6	13	28	44	56
Oldham Athletic	46	10	7	6	33	20	4	7	12	21	30	56
Reading	46	8	7	8	28	30	5	10	8	26	33	56
Wolverhampton Wanderers	46	8	9	6	34	28	5	7	11	22	34	55
Portsmouth	46	8	6	9	34	32	5	7	11	27	37	52
Millwall	46	7	6	10	23	28	6	7	10	20	35	52
WATFORD	46	7	8	8	40	33	3	10	10	22	37	48
Luton Town	46	7	6	10	30	34	4	6	13	10	30	45

No	DATE			COMPETITION	OPPONENTS	HOME	AWAY	ATTENDANCE	
1	August	Sat	12	Football League, Division 1	SHEFFIELD UNITED	2-1 W		8,677	
2		Sat	19	Football League, Division 1	Huddersfield Town		L 0-1		10,556
3		Sat	26	Football League, Division 1	BARNSLEY	2-3 L		8,049	
4		Tue	29	Football League, Division 1	Charlton Athletic		L 1-2		8,442
5	September	Sat	2	Football League, Division 1	Grimsby Town		D 0-0		3,993
6		Sat	9	Football League, Division 1	STOKE CITY	3-0 W		7,130	
7		Tue	12	Football League, Division 1	CRYSTAL PALACE	0-0 D		8,780	
8		Sat	16	Football League, Division 1	Ipswich Town		L 2-4		11,441
9		Tue	19	Football Lge Cup, 2nd Round , 1st Leg	AFC BOURNEMOUTH	1-1 D		5,037	
10		Sat	23	Football League, Division 1	BIRMINGHAM CITY	1-1 D		9,422	
11		Sat	30	Football League, Division 1	Tranmere Rovers		W 3-2		7,041
12	October	Tue	3	Football Lge Cup, 2nd Round, 2nd Leg	AFC Bournemouth (won 6-5 on penalties)		D 1-1		4,365
13		Sat	7	Football League, Division 1	MILLWALL	0-1 L		8,918	
14		Sat	14	Football League, Division 1	Sunderland		D 1-1		17,790
15		Sat	21	Football League, Division 1	WOLVERHAMPTON WANDERERS	1-1 D		11,319	
16		Tue	24	Football League Cup, 3rd Round	BLACKBURN ROVERS	1-2 L		17,035	
17		Sat	28	Football League, Division 1	Portsmouth		L 2-4		7,025
18	November	Sat	4	Football League, Division 1	SOUTHEND UNITED	2-2 D		7,091	
19		Sat	11	Football League, Division 1	Leicester City		L 0-1		16,230
20		Sat	18	Football League, Division 1	Port Vale		D 1-1		6,265
21		Tue	21	Football League, Division 1	LUTON TOWN	1-1 D		10,042	
22		Sun	26	Football League, Division 1	NORWICH CITY	0-2 L		7,798	
23	December	Sat	2	Football League, Division 1	Millwall		W 2-1		8,389
24		Sat	9	Football League, Division 1	Birmingham City		L 0-1		16,970
25		Sat	16	Football League, Division 1	TRANMERE ROVERS	3-0 W		7,257	
26		Sat	23	Football League, Division 1	Oldham Athletic		D 0-0		5,878
27	January	Sat	6	FA Cup, 3rd Round	WIMBLEDON	1-1 D		11,187	
28		Sat	13	Football League, Division 1	HUDDERSFIELD TOWN	0-1 L		7,568	
29		Wed	17	FA Cup, 3rd Round replay	Wimbledon		L 0-1		5,142
30		Sat	20	Football League, Division 1	Sheffield United		D 1-1		12,782
31	February	Sat	3	Football League, Division 1	Barnsley		L 1-2		6,139
32		Sat	10	Football League, Division 1	CHARLTON ATHLETIC	1-2 L		8,394	
33		Sat	17	Football League, Division 1	Crystal Palace		L 0-4		13,235
34		Sat	24	Football League, Division 1	IPSWICH TOWN	2-3 L		11,872	
35		Wed	28	Football League, Division 1	Stoke City		L 0-2		10,114
36	March	Sat	2	Football League, Division 1	Reading		D 0-0		8,933
37		Tue	5	Football League, Division 1	DERBY COUNTY	0-0 D		8,306	
38		Sat	9	Football League, Division 1	OLDHAM ATHLETIC	2-1 W		10,961	
39		Tue	12	Football League, Division 1	West Bromwich Albion		D 4-4		11,836
40		Sat	16	Football League, Division 1	Derby County		D 1-1		15,939
41		Sat	23	Football League, Division 1	WEST BROMWICH ALBION	1-1 D		10,334	
42		Sat	30	Football League, Division 1	Wolverhampton Wanderers		L 0-3		25,885
43	April	Tue	2	Football League, Division 1	SUNDERLAND	3-3 D		11,195	
44		Sat	6	Football League, Division 1	PORTSMOUTH	1-2 L		8,226	
45		Mon	8	Football League, Division 1	Southend United		D 1-1		5,348
46		Sat	13	Football League, Division 1	PORT VALE	5-2 W		9,066	
47		Tue	16	Football League, Division 1	READING	4-2 W		8,113	
48		Sat	20	Football League, Division 1	Luton Town		D 0-0		9,454
49		Tue	23	Football League, Division 1	GRIMSBY TOWN	6-3 W		8,909	
50		Sat	27	Football League, Division 1	Norwich City		W 2-1		14,188
51	May	Sun	5	Football League, Division 1	LEICESTER CITY	0-1 L		20,089	

League ever-presents: None
Most appearances in total: K. Miller 47 out of 51   **Most goals in total:** C.D. Ramage 15
Hat-tricks: D.J. Connolly (Match 46 & Match 49), C.D. Ramage (Match 49)   **Penalty goals:** D.J. Connolly 2, K. Phillips 2, T.J. Mooney 1
(In the penalty shoot-out at the end of Match 12, successful kicks were taken by D.S. Bazeley, G. Pitcher, T.J. Mooney, C.D. Ramage, R.M. Johnson & K.D. Millen)
Sent off: None   **Full international appearance(s) this season:** D.J. Connolly (Republic of Ireland)

	Andrews, W.M.H.	Barnes, D.	Bazeley, D.S.	Beadle, P.C.W.J.	Caskey, D.M.	Cherry, S.R.	Connolly, D.J.	Dixon, K.M.	Foster, C.J.	Gibbs, N.J.	Hessenthaler, A.	Hill, D.R.L.	Hodge, S.B.	Holdsworth, D.G.	Johnson, R.M.	Lavin, G.	Ludden, D.J.R.	Millen, K.D.	Miller, K.	Mooney, T.J.	Moralee, J.D.	Neill, W.A.	Page, R.J.	Palmer, S.L.	Payne, D.R.	Penrice, G.K.	Phillips, K.	Pitcher, G.	Porter, G.M.	Ramage, C.D.	Simpson, C.R.	Ward, D.P.	White, D.W.	Wilkinson, P.	Own goal
Apps	0	10	35	3	6	4	7	8	26	8	30	1	2	26	17	16	9	32	42	38	17	1	16	35	9	4	26	2	28	34	0	1	9	4	
Subs	+1		+6				+4	+3		+1				+1	+3		+3	+1			+4	+8		+3			+3	+3	+1	+7	+1	+2	+1		+7
Goals		1		1		1		8		4				1	1			1	6	3				1	1		11	1	1	15			4		1
Apps			4	1			0		4					4	4	2	1	5	5	4	4		1	2	0		4	3	2	5					
Subs			+1				+1										+1			+1				+1			+1		+1						
Goals			1											1					1					1			1								
1				R					X	X				X	X1	X		X	G	S				X1		X			X						
2		S		R					X	X				X	X	X		X	G	S				X		R			X						
3			X		G	S			R	R				X	X	X		X		S				X		X2p			X						
4			X		G	S		X	S					X	X	X		R			X1			X		X			R						
5			X		G	R			X	X				X	X							S		X		X			X	X			X		
6			R						X	X				X	X				G	R1	S			X		X	S		X	X2					
7			X						X					X	X	X			G	X				X		X			X	X					
8			X						X					X	R	X			G	X				X1		S1			X	X					
9			X	X					X						X1			X	G	X	S					R	X		X	X					
10			X	R			S		X					S	X	X		X	G	X	R1								X	X					
11			S						X1					X	X	X		X	G	X1	R1			X					X	X					
12			S1						X					X	X	X		X	G	X				X			X			S	R	X			
13		S							X					X	X	X		X	G	R	R			X					S	S	X	R			
14		X							X					X		X		X	G	X	X1			X					X	X					
15		X							X					X1		X		X	G	X	X			X					X	X					
16		X							X					X		X		X	G	X	X			X			X1			X					
17		R			X	G			X					X		X				S	R			X			X1	S		X1					
18		X1							X		X			X		X			G	X	X			X			X1			X					
19		X							X					X		S	S	X	G	X	X			X			X			R					
20		X							X					X		S	X	X	G	X	S			X			X		S	R1					
21		X							X					X		X		X	G	X	S			X			R	X1		X					
22		X		X					X					X				X	G	X	X			X			X			X					
23		X					X		X					X	X				G	X				X	S		X2		R					X	
24		X					X		X					X				X	G	X				X		S	S	R						X	
25		X					X		X				X	X	X			X	G	X				X			X2p							X	1
26		X					X		X				R	X	X			X	G	X				S	R		X	S						X	
27		X					X		X					X	X	S	X	G	R1	X				S			X	R		X					
28		X			X	X			X					X	S		X	R	G					R	X		X	S		X					
29		X					S		X					X	X		X	X	G				X		X		X	R		X					
30		R1			X	X			X					X	X		X	X	G	X		X	S				X			X					
31		X			X	X	X		X						X	G	X	R		X		S1		X			X			X					
32		X					X		X		R				X	G	X			X	X1	S		X			X			X					
33		S			X	R	X	X	X					X	G	X				S	S		X				X		R				X		
34	X	S				X	X		X				X		X1	G	R			X1			R	X			S			X			X		
35	X	S				X	X		X				X		S	G	R			X			R	X			S			X			X		
36	X	X					X		X				X	X	G		S		X	X			R			X	T	S		R					
37	S	X	X				X		X				X	X	G	X	R		X	X						X		S					S		
38		X	X			S	X		X						G	X	R		X	X			X			X	X2								
39		X	X			S	X2		X						G	X	R		X	X			X			R	X2						S		
40		X					X1		X						X	G	X	R		X	X			X			X	X					S		
41		X				S	X		X						X	G	R	R		X	X						X	X1					S		
42		X				SR	X		X		X				X	G		R		X	X			X	X2								S		
43		X				X	R		X		X				X	G	X2			X	X						S	X1					S		
44		X				R			X		X				X	G	X1p			X	X						R	X	S	S					
45	X	X				X			X		X				X	G	X			X	X1						X	X1							
46	X	X			X3p	R					X				X	G	X	S		X	X	S					R	R				S2			
47	R	X			R1				X		S				X	G	X	S		X	X						X	X1					X2		
48		X			R				X		X				X	G	X	S		X	S						R	X	X	X					
49		X			X3				X		X				X	G	X			X	X3						X	X					X		
50	R	X			X1p				X		X				X	G	X			X1	X						X	X					X		
51		X			R				R		X				X	S	X	X		X	X						X	X					X		

1996/97

Football League position: 13th out of 24 in Division 2

Manager: Kenny Jackett

New league opponents: None
Home-and-away league doubles
For – 2 (Bristol Rovers, York City)
Against - none
Divisional changes at end of season: Bury, Stockport County & Crewe Alexandra to Division 1; Peterborough United, Shrewsbury Town, Rotherham United & Notts County to Division 3; Grimsby Town, Oldham Athletic & Southend United from Division 1; Wigan Athletic, Fulham, Carlisle United & Northampton Town from Division 3
All matches: Won 22, Drew 19, Lost 16, Goals 60-48
The sequence of nine consecutive away draws in the Football League (Match 18 to Match 40) is without parallel in the history of the competition.
Highest score: 5 (Match 27)

	HOME						AWAY					
	Pl	W	D	L	For	Ag	W	D	L	For	Ag	Pts
Bury	46	18	5	0	39	7	6	7	10	23	31	84
Stockport County	46	15	5	3	31	14	8	7	28	27	82	
Luton Town	46	13	7	3	38	14	8	7	33	31	78	
Brentford	46	8	11	4	26	22	12	3	8	21	74	
Bristol City	46	14	4	5	43	18	7	6	10	26	33	73
Crewe Alexandra	46	15	4	4	38	15	7	3	13	18	32	73
Blackpool	46	13	7	3	41	21	5	8	10	19	26	69
Wrexham	46	11	9	3	37	28	6	9	8	17	22	69
Burnley	46	14	3	6	48	27	5	8	10	23	28	68
Chesterfield	46	10	9	4	25	18	7	11	17	21	68	
Gillingham	46	13	3	7	37	25	6	7	10	23	34	67
Walsall	46	12	8	3	35	21	7	2	14	19	32	67
WATFORD	46	10	8	5	24	14	6	11	6	21	24	67
Millwall	46	12	4	7	27	22	4	9	10	23	33	61
Preston North End	46	14	5	4	33	19	4	2	17	16	36	61
AFC Bournemouth	46	8	9	6	24	21	7	6	10	19	25	60
Bristol Rovers	46	13	4	6	34	22	2	7	14	13	28	56
Wycombe Wanderers	46	13	4	6	31	14	2	6	15	20	42	55
Plymouth Argyle	46	7	5	11	29	33	5	7	11	18	44	54
York City	46	8	6	9	27	31	5	7	11	20	37	52
Peterborough United	46	8	6	9	27	31	3	7	13	28	47	47
Shrewsbury Town	46	8	6	9	27	32	3	7	13	22	42	46
Rotherham United	46	4	7	12	17	29	3	7	13	22	41	35
Notts County	46	4	9	10	20	25	3	5	15	13	34	35

No	DATE			COMPETITION	OPPONENTS	HOME	AWAY	ATTENDANCE
1	August	Sat	17	Football League, Division 2	AFC Bournemouth		W 2-1	7,368
2		Tue	20	Football Lge Cup, 1st Round, 1st Leg	Walsall		L 0-1	2,659
3		Sat	24	Football League, Division 2	MILLWALL	0-2 L		9,495
4		Tue	27	Football League, Division 2	PLYMOUTH ARGYLE	0-2 L		7,349
5		Sat	31	Football League, Division 2	Crewe Alexandra		W 2-0	3,655
6	September	Tue	3	Football Lge Cup, 1st Round, 2nd Leg	WALSALL	2-0 W		5,325
7		Sat	7	Football League, Division 2	STOCKPORT COUNTY	1-0 W		7,208
8		Tue	10	Football League, Division 2	Notts County		W 3-2	3,660
9		Sat	14	Football League, Division 2	Bristol Rovers		W 1-0	6,276
10		Tue	17	Football Lge Cup, 2nd Round, 1st Leg	SUNDERLAND	0-2 L		9,136
11		Sat	21	Football League, Division 2	PETERBOROUGH UNITED	0-0 D		12,007
12		Tue	24	Football Lge Cup, 2nd Round, 2nd Leg	Sunderland		L 0-1	10,659
13		Sat	28	Football League, Division 2	Shrewsbury Town		L 0-1	3,655
14	October	Tue	1	Football League, Division 2	PRESTON NORTH END	1-0 W		6,434
15		Sat	5	Football League, Division 2	York City		W 2-1	5,232
16		Sat	12	Football League, Division 2	WREXHAM	1-1 D		8,441
17		Tue	15	Football League, Division 2	BURNLEY	2-2 D		6,450
18		Sat	19	Football League, Division 2	Bury		D 1-1	4,092
19		Sat	26	Football League, Division 2	Blackpool		D 1-1	6,072
20		Tue	29	Football League, Division 2	LUTON TOWN	1-1 D		14,109
21	November	Sat	2	Football League, Division 2	BRENTFORD	2-0 W		11,448
22		Sat	9	Football League, Division 2	Rotherham United		D 0-0	3,619
23		Sun	17	FA Cup, 1st Round	Northampton Town		W 1-0	7,342
24		Tue	19	Football League, Division 2	WYCOMBE WANDERERS	1-0 W		7,657
25		Sat	30	Football League, Division 2	BLACKPOOL	2-2 D		12,017
26	December	Tue	3	Football League, Division 2	Bristol City		D 1-1	9,097
27		Sat	7	FA Cup, 2nd Round	ASHFORD TOWN	5-0 W		7,590
28		Sat	14	Football League, Division 2	Walsall		D 1-1	3,674
29		Sat	21	Football League, Division 2	GILLINGHAM	0-0 D		7,809
30		Thu	26	Football League, Division 2	NOTTS COUNTY	0-0 D		9,065
31	January	Tue	7	Associate Members Cup, 2nd Round	TORQUAY UNITED	2-1 W		2,298
32		Sat	18	Football League, Division 2	Preston North End		D 1-1	8,735
33		Tue	21	FA Cup, 3rd Round	OXFORD UNITED	2-0 W		9,502
34		Mon	27	Football League, Division 2	Luton Town		D 0-0	7,428
35	February	Sat	1	Football League, Division 2	ROTHERHAM UNITED	2-0 W		10,657
36		Wed	5	FA Cup, 4th Round	Manchester City		L 1-3	24,031
37		Sat	8	Football League, Division 2	Brentford		D 1-1	8,679
38		Tue	11	Assoc Mem Cup, Southern Quarter-Final	BRISTOL CITY	2-1 W		3,142
39		Tue	18	Assoc Mem Cup, Southern Semi-Final	PETERBOROUGH UNITED	0-1 L		4,941
40		Sat	22	Football League, Division 2	Wycombe Wanderers		D 0-0	8,438
41		Tue	25	Football League, Division 2	SHREWSBURY TOWN	2-0 W		6,378
42	March	Sat	1	Football League, Division 2	BRISTOL CITY	3-0 W		8,539
43		Tue	4	Football League, Division 2	Peterborough United		L 1-2	4,200
44		Sat	8	Football League, Division 2	Gillingham		L 1-3	7,385
45		Sat	15	Football League, Division 2	WALSALL	1-0 W		7,818
46		Tue	18	Football League, Division 2	BRISTOL ROVERS	1-0 W		6,139
47		Sat	22	Football League, Division 2	Millwall		W 1-0	8,713
48		Sat	29	Football League, Division 2	AFC BOURNEMOUTH	0-1 L		10,019
49		Mon	31	Football League, Division 2	Plymouth Argyle		D 0-0	6,836
50	April	Sat	5	Football League, Division 2	CREWE ALEXANDRA	0-1 L		12,441
51		Tue	8	Football League, Division 2	Chesterfield		D 0-0	4,258
52		Sat	12	Football League, Division 2	YORK CITY	4-0 W		7,645
53		Mon	14	Football League, Division 2	Stockport County		L 0-1	7,164
54		Sat	19	Football League, Division 2	Wrexham		L 1-3	3,437
55		Thu	24	Football League, Division 2	CHESTERFIELD	0-2 L		6,411
56		Sat	26	Football League, Division 2	BURY	0-0 D		9,017
57	May	Sat	3	Football League, Division 2	Burnley		L 1-4	8,259

League ever-presents: None
Most appearances in total: N.J. Gibbs 56 (including two substitute appearances) out of 57   **Most goals in total:** T.J. Mooney 12
Hat-tricks: D.J. Connolly (Match 27)   **Penalty goals:** T.J. Mooney 2, D.S. Bazeley 1, D.J. Connolly 1
Sent off: R.M. Johnson (Match 18), S.L. Palmer (Match 36), K. Phillips (Match 54), C.D. Ramage (Match 55)
Full international appearance(s) this season: D.J. Connolly (Republic of Ireland)

	Andrews, W.M.H.	Armstrong, S.C. //	Bazeley, D.S.	Chamberlain, A.F.R. //	Connolly, D.J. //	Easton, C.J.	Flash, R.G. //	Gibbs, N.J.	Johnson, C. //	Johnson, R.M.	Lowndes, N.P.	Ludden, D.J.R. //	Millen, K.D.	Miller, K. //	Mooney, T.J.	Noel-Williams, G.R.E. //	Page, R.J.	Palmer, S.L.	Penrice, G.K. //	Phillips, K.	Porter, G.M. //	Ramage, C.D.	Robinson, P.P.	Scott, K. //	Slater, S.I.	Talboys, S.J.	Ward, D.P.	White, D.W. //	Own goals
Apps	16	15	38	4	12	17	0	43	1	35	0	18	42	42	33	9	35	40	22	13	6	10	8	6	13	2	7	19	
Subs	+9		+3		+1		+1	+2		+2	+3	+2			+4	+16	+1	+1	+10	+3		+1	+4		+3	+1		+3	
Goals	4		3		2	1		1		2			2		12	2		1	1	3		3			2	1		3	2
Apps	5		10		4	4		11		6	0	6	7	11	8	2	11	11	4	0	2	1	4	2	4	0	1	7	
Subs	+2				+1	+1				+2	+1				+1				+2	+2		+1	+1		+1				
Goals	2		4		5										1	1				1								1	
1	S		X		R1			S		X			X	G	X		X		X			R			X			X1	
2			X		X			X		X			X	G	X		X	X	S			R						X	
3			X		R			S		X	R		X	G	S		X	X	S			X			R			X	
4	R		X				X	X		X			X	G	X		X	X		X								X	
5	R		X	G				X	S	X			X		X1		X	X1		X								X	
6	R1		X					X	S	X			X	G	X		X	X			X1							X	
7	R		X					X	S	X			X	G	X1p		X	X			X							X	
8	X1		X					X					X	G	X2		X	X			X							X	
9	R		X					X		S			X	G	X		X	X	S			R						X1	
10	R							X					X	G	X		X	X	X			X	S					X	
11	R		X					X		S			X	G	X		X	X	X			X	SR					R	
12	R		R					X		X			X	G	S	X	X	X	X						S			X	
13			X		S			X		X			X	G	X	R	X	X							S			R	
14	S		X		R			X		X			X	G	X		X	X										X1	
15	X1		X					X		X			X	G	X		S	X	R1									X	
16	R		X					X		X			X	G	X1p	S	X	X										X	
17	X1		X					X		X1			X	G	X		X	X	S			R							
18	R1		X					X		X			X	G	X		X	X				S						X	
19			X					X		X			X	G	X1		X	X										X	
20	R		X1					X		X			R	G	X	S	X	X	X					S				R	
21	R		X		X			X1					X	G	X1	X	X	X	R					S				S	
22			X		X			X		X			X	G	X	R	X	X	X									S	
23	S		X1		R	X		X		S			X	G	X		R	X				X						X	
24	R		X		X1	R		X		X			X	G	X	S	X	X				X						X	
25			X		R			X		X			X1	G	S	S1	X	X				X		X				R	
26	S		X					X		X			X	G	X	R1	X	X				X		R				S	
27		X2		S3	X			S		X			X	G	R	X	X	X	X			X		R					
28			X	R	X	X1		S		S			X	G	X		X	X				X		X					
29	S	S	X		X	R		X		X			X	G			X	X				R							
30	S	R	R		X	X		X		X			S	G			S	X	X			X		X					
31		X	X1p		X			X		X			X	G	X		X1	X	X					X			X		
32		X		X	X			X		X			X	G	X1	S	X	X	R					X			X		
33		X		X1	S			X		X			X	G	R		X	X						X			X1		
34	S	X	X		R			X		X				G			X	X						X	X	X			
35	R	X	X1					X		X				G			X	X	X	S				X1	X				
36	S	X			X			X		X	X			G			R1	X					S	X	X				
37	S	X	X					X		X	X			G			R	X					X1		X				
38	R1	X1p			X	X		X		X	X			G			X	X		S			X	X					
39	R	X			X	X		X		X	X			G			X	X	S	S			R	X					
40	S	X			R	X		X	X	X			G			X		X	X				X						
41		X1			X	X		R	X	X			S				X	R1				S		X					
42		X			X	X		X		X			G			S	X		X	X2			X	R				1	
43		X			X	X		S	X	G	X1		S	X	X		X	R	R										
44		X			X	X		X		G	R		S			X	X	X				X1		X					
45		X	R		X	X		X		G	R1		S			X	X			S			X						
46		X	X		X	X		R		G	R1	S		X	X	S	X												
47		X	X		X	X		X		G	X	S	X	X			R											1	
48		X	X		R	X		X		G	R	S		X	X	X				S	R								
49		X	S		X	X		X		G	X		R	X	X	X		S											
50		R	R		X	X		X		G	S		X	X	X		X		S										
51	S	X			X	X		X		G	X		X	X			R	X	X										
52	R	R	S		X1	X		X		G	X1		X	X	S		X2		X										
53	R	X			X	X		X		G	X		X	S	X	S	X												
54		X			X	X		X		G	S		X	R	X	X1	X												
55		R		G	X	X		X		X			X		X	S	X	S	X	R									
56		X	X	G	X	X		X					X	R	X	X	X	S											
57		X	G		X	S	X			X			X1	R	S	X		X				R	X						

1997/98

Football League position: 1st out of 24 in Division 2 – promoted to Division 1
Manager: Graham Taylor

New league opponents: Wigan Athletic

Home-and-away league doubles
For – 6 (AFC Bournemouth, Brentford, Bristol Rovers, Carlisle United, Chesterfield, Fulham)
Against – none

Promoted with Watford: Bristol City and Grimsby Town

All Matches: Won 27, Drew 21, Lost 8, Goals 77-52

Highest Score: 4 (Matches 14 & 19)

		HOME					AWAY					
	Pl	W	D	L	For	Ag	W	D	L	For	Ag	Pts
WATFORD	46	13	7	3	36	22	11	9	3	31	19	88
Bristol City	46	16	5	2	41	17	9	5	9	28	22	85
Grimsby Town	46	11	7	5	30	14	8	8	7	25	23	72
Northampton Town	46	14	5	4	33	17	4	12	7	19	20	71
Bristol Rovers	46	13	2	8	43	33	7	8	8	27	31	70
Fulham	46	12	7	4	31	14	8	3	12	29	29	70
Wrexham	46	10	10	3	31	23	8	6	9	24	28	70
Gillingham	46	13	7	3	30	18	6	6	11	22	29	70
AFC Bournemouth	46	11	8	4	28	15	7	4	12	29	37	66
Chesterfield	46	13	3	7	31	19	3	10	10	15	25	65
Wigan Athletic	46	12	5	6	41	31	5	6	12	23	35	62
Blackpool	46	13	6	4	35	24	4	5	14	24	43	62
Oldham Athletic	46	13	7	3	43	23	2	9	12	19	31	61
Wycombe Wanderers	46	10	10	3	32	20	4	8	11	19	33	60
Preston North End	46	10	6	7	29	26	5	8	10	27	30	59
York City	46	9	7	7	26	21	5	10	8	26	37	59
Luton Town	46	7	7	9	35	38	7	8	8	25	26	57
Millwall	46	7	8	8	23	23	7	5	11	20	31	55
Walsall	46	8	5	10	26	16	4	4	15	17	36	54
Burnley	46	10	9	4	34	23	3	4	16	21	42	52
Brentford	46	9	7	7	33	29	2	10	11	17	42	50
Plymouth Argyle	46	10	5	8	36	30	2	8	13	19	40	49
Carlisle United	46	8	5	10	27	28	4	3	16	30	45	44
Southend United	46	8	7	8	29	30	3	3	17	18	49	43

No	DATE			COMPETITION	OPPONENTS	HOME	AWAY	ATTENDANCE
1	August	Sat	9	Football League, Division 2	BURNLEY	1-0 W		11,155
2		Wed	13	Football League Cup, 1st Round, 1st Leg	Swindon Town		W 2-0	6,271
3		Sat	16	Football League, Division 2	Carlisle United		W 2-0	7,395
4		Sat	23	Football League, Division 2	BRENTFORD	3-1 W		10,125
5		Tue	26	Football League Cup, 1st Round, 2nd Leg	SWINDON TOWN	1-1 D		7,712
6		Sat	30	Football League, Division 2	Preston North End		L 0-2	11,042
7	September	Tue	2	Football League, Division 2	Plymouth Argyle		W 1-0	5,141
8		Sun	7	Football League, Division 2	WYCOMBE WANDERERS	2-1 W		12,100
9		Sat	13	Football League, Division 2	CHESTERFIELD	2-1 W		11,204
10		Tue	16	Football League Cup, 2nd Round, 1st Leg	SHEFFIELD UNITED	1-1 D		7,154
11		Sat	20	Football League, Division 2	Gillingham		D 2-2	7,780
12		Tue	23	Football League Cup, 2nd Round, 2nd Leg	Sheffield United		L 0-4	7,511
13		Sat	27	Football League, Division 2	YORK CITY	1-1 D		13,812
14	October	Sat	4	Football League, Division 2	Luton Town		W 4-0	9,041
15		Tue	14	Football League, Division 2	Bristol Rovers		W 2-1	8,110
16		Sat	18	Football League, Division 2	MILLWALL	0-1 L		12,530
17		Tue	21	Football League, Division 2	FULHAM	2-0 W		11,486
18		Sat	25	Football League, Division 2	Grimsby Town		W 1-0	5,699
19	November	Sat	1	Football League, Division 2	BLACKPOOL	4-1 W		9,723
20		Tue	4	Football League, Division 2	Southend United		W 3-0	4,001
21		Sat	8	Football League, Division 2	Walsall		D 0-0	5,077
22		Sat	15	FA Cup, 1st Round	Barnet		W 2-1	4,040
23		Tue	18	Football League, Division 2	OLDHAM ATHLETIC	2-1 W		8,397
24		Sat	22	Football League, Division 2	Northampton Town		W 1-0	7,373
25		Sat	29	Football League, Division 2	WIGAN ATHLETIC	2-1 W		9,455
26	December	Tue	2	Football League, Division 2	Wrexham		D 1-1	3,702
27		Sat	6	FA Cup, 2nd Round	Torquay United		D 1-1	3,416
28		Tue	9	Associate Members Cup, 1st Round	Fulham		L 0-1	3,364
29		Sat	13	Football League, Division 2	BRISTOL CITY	1-1 D		16,072
30		Tue	16	FA Cup, 2nd Round replay	TORQUAY UNITED (after extra time)	2-1 W		5,848
31		Sat	20	Football League, Division 2	AFC Bournemouth		W 1-0	6,081
32		Fri	26	Football League, Division 2	Wycombe Wanderers		D 0-0	8,090
33		Sun	28	Football League, Division 2	PLYMOUTH ARGYLE	1-1 D		11,594
34	January	Sat	3	FA Cup, 3rd Round	SHEFFIELD WEDNESDAY	1-1 D		18,306
35		Sat	10	Football League, Division 2	Burnley		L 0-2	9,551
36		Wed	14	FA Cup, 3rd Round replay	Sheffield Wednesday (lost 3-5 on penalties)	D 0-0		18,707
37		Sat	17	Football League, Division 2	PRESTON NORTH END	3-1 W		10,182
38		Sat	24	Football League, Division 2	Brentford		W 2-1	6,969
39		Sat	31	Football League, Division 2	Chesterfield		W 1-0	5,975
40	February	Sun	8	Football League, Division 2	GILLINGHAM	0-2 L		10,498
41		Sat	14	Football League, Division 2	LUTON TOWN	1-1 D		15,182
42		Sat	21	Football League, Division 2	York City		D 1-1	4,890
43		Wed	25	Football League, Division 2	Millwall		D 1-1	7,126
44		Sat	28	Football League, Division 2	BRISTOL ROVERS	3-2 W		12,186
45	March	Tue	3	Football League, Division 2	WALSALL	1-2 L		8,096
46		Sat	7	Football League, Division 2	Blackpool		D 1-1	5,237
47		Sat	14	Football League, Division 2	SOUTHEND UNITED	1-1 D		10,750
48		Tue	17	Football League, Division 2	CARLISLE UNITED	2-1 W		7,274
49		Sat	21	Football League, Division 2	Oldham Athletic		D 2-2	5,744
50		Sat	28	Football League, Division 2	NORTHAMPTON TOWN	1-1 D		14,268
51	April	Sat	4	Football League, Division 2	Wigan Athletic		L 2-3	4,262
52		Sat	11	Football League, Division 2	WREXHAM	1-0 W		12,340
53		Mon	13	Football League, Division 2	Bristol City		D 1-1	19,141
54		Sat	25	Football League, Division 2	GRIMSBY TOWN	0-0 D		14,002
55		Tue	28	Football League, Division 2	AFC BOURNEMOUTH	2-1 W		12,834
56	May	Sat	2	Football League, Division 2	Fulham		W 2-1	17,114

League ever-presents: A.F.R. Chamberlain
Most appearances in total: A.F.R. Chamberlain & T.J. Mooney 54 out of 56   **Most goals in total**: P.H.J. Kennedy 13
Hat-tricks: P.H.J. Kennedy (Match 20)   **Penalty goals**: R. Rosenthal 2 (In the penalty shoot-out at the end of Match 36, successful kicks were taken by by J.B. Lee, P.H.J. Kennedy & R.M. Johnson)
Sent off: J.B. Lee (Match 2 & Match 11)   **Full international appearance(s) this season**: R.J. Page (Wales)

Summary (two competition sets)

Stat	Andrews W.M.H.	Bazeley D.S.	Chamberlain A.F.R.	Day C.N.	Easton C.J.	Foley D.J. //	Gibbs N.J.	Grieves D.L.	Hazan A.	Hyde M.A.	Johnson R.M.	Kennedy P.H.J.	Lee J.B.	Ljung P.-O. //	Lowndes N.P.	Melvang L.M. //	Millen K.D.	Mooney T.J.	Noel-Williams G.R.E.	Page R.J.	Palmer S.L.	Pluck C.J.	Robinson P.P.	Rooney M.J. //	Rosenthal R.	Slater S.J. //	Smith T.W.	Talboys S.J. //	Thomas D.J.	Ward D.P.
Apps	0	14	46		8	2	34			7	40	42	34	35		1	4	38	45	27	41	32	1	14	24	9	0	0	8	
Subs	+2	+2			+4	+6	+4			+3						+3			+11		+9				+8		+1	+2	+8	
Goals		3					1	1		4	7	11	10			1	1	6	7		2			2	8				3	
Apps	0		8	2	2		8	1		9	9	9	8		1	2	1	6	9	7	7	8	6	1	2	1	5	3	0	1
Subs	+2				+1											+1			+2		+1		+1			+1		+3	+1	
Goals										1		2							4						3					

Match-by-match

Match	Andrews	Bazeley	Chamberlain	Day	Easton	Foley	Gibbs	Grieves	Hazan	Hyde	Johnson	Kennedy	Lee	Ljung	Lowndes	Melvang	Millen	Mooney	Noel-Williams	Page	Palmer	Pluck	Robinson	Rooney	Rosenthal	Slater	Smith	Talboys	Thomas	Ward
1			G				X			X	X	X	X1					X	X	X	X					X				
2			G				X			X	X	X	X					X	X	X1	X				S1	R				
3			G			R				X	X1	X1	R					X	X	X	R	S			S	X		S		
4	S		G							X	X1	X				R1	X1	X		X	S				X	X			R	
5	S		G							X1	X	X				X	R	X	X	X	S				R	X				
6	S		G			X				R	X	X						X	X	X	X				R	R	S	S		
7			G							X	X	X	X			X		X	X1	X					X					
8			G			S				X1	X	X	X1			R		X	X	X					R					
9			G							X	X	X	X1					X	X	X					X1					
10	S		G							X	X	X1	X					X	R	X	X				X					
11			G			S				X	X1	X	X			R			X	X	X	R			X1p	S				
12			G	S			X					X						X			X	X			R	X				
13			G			R				X	X	X	X1					X	X	R	X	S				X	S			
14			G				X				X1	X2						X	X	S	X	X				R	X		X1	
15			G				X			X	X	X1						X	X	S	X	S				X1p	X		X	
16			G			R				X	X	X						X	R	S	X	S				X			X	
17	X		G							X	X		X					X	X	X	X			X1		X1				
18	X		G							X	X		X					X	X	X	R	S		X		X1				
19	R		G		S					X	R1	X	R2					X	X	X	X			X		X1				
20			G				X				X	X3	X					X	X	R	X	X				X			S	
21			G				X				X	X	X					X	X	R	X	X				X			S	
22			G				X			X	X	X	R					X	X	X	X				X2				S	
23			G				X			X	X	X						X1	R	X	X		S		R		S		X1	
24			G				X			X	X	X1						X	X	X	X				X				X	
25			G				X			X	X	X						X1	X	X	X				X				X1	
26			G				S			X	X	X						X	X	X	R	S			X1				R	
27			G				X			X	X	X	R			S		X	X	R1	X	S			X				R	
28			G	X					X				X	X	X						X	X	X	X				R		S
29			G				X			X	X	X	X					X	X	S1	X				R					
30			G				X			X	X	X	X					X	X	X2	R	X		S			SR			
31			G				X			X	X	X1	X					X	X	X	X				X					
32			G				X			X	X	X	X					X	X	X	X				X					
33			G				X			X	X	X	X			S		X	X1	X	X				R					
34			G	X			X			X	X	X1	X			R		X	X		X								S	
35			G	R			X			X	X	X	X			R		X	X	S		X			S					
36			G				X			X	X	X	X					X	X	R		X			X				S	
37			G				X		R	X1	X	X2	X					X	X		X	S			X					
38			G				X		R	X	X1	X						X	X1		X	R			S				S	
39			G				X			X	X		X					X	X	S1	X	X			X				R	
40			G				X			X	X	X	R					X	X	R	X	S			X				S	
41			G				X			X	X		X					X	X	S	X	X			X1		R			
42			G		S		X			R	X		X			S		X	X		X	S1		R		X	R			
43			G			S	X			X	X		R					X	X1	X	X	X			X					
44		S	G		R	R	X				X							X	X1	X1	X	X			X1	S				
45		S	G		R	R	X				X							X	X	R1	X	X			X	S				
46		X1	G		X		X				X		X					X	X	X	X	X			R					
47		R	G		R		X			X1	R		S		S			X	X	X	X	X			S					
48		R1	G		X	S	X			X			X					X	X		X	X1			X					
49		X1	G		R	S	X1		S	X			X					X	X		X	X			R					
50		X	G			S	R		S	X	X1	R	X					X	X		X	X			X					
51		X	G		S1				S	X1	X	X	R					R	X	S	X	X			R					
52		X	G		S		X		R	X	X	R	R1					X	X	S	X	X			S					
53		X	G				X		R	X		X	X1					X	X	S	X	X			X					
54		X	G		X	S	X		R	X		X	R					X	X	S	X	X			X					
55 *		X	X						R	X	X	X	X1					X	X	R1		G			S		X			
56		X	G				S			X	X	X	X1					X	X	R1		R			S					

* As part of a light-hearted ploy to enable the player to wear all 14 shirts during the season, S.L. Palmer was
nominated as goalkeeper for Match 55, but changed places with A.F.R. Chamberlain immediately after the kick-off

PART FOUR

Wartime

1915/16

LC = London Combination (Watford finished 10th in a league of 12 clubs)
LCS = London Combination Supplementary Competition (Watford finished 7th in a league of 14 clubs)
F = Friendly
56 players were used in the 38 matches (Most appearances - F.J. Gregory & R.G. Williams 38. Most goals - H. Smith 16)

Date			Status	Opponents	Result		Att	Scorers
Wed	1	Sep	F	Sherwood Foresters	H	W6-4		H. Smith (3), Pte Brown, A. Green, A.E. Mallett
Sat	14	Sep	LC	Fulham	H	L 2-4	2,000	J.J.S. McLauchlan (pen), J.H. Taylor
Sat	11	Sep	LC	Clapton Orient	A	L 0-2	5,000	
Sat	18	Sep	LC	Chelsea	A	L 0-1	10,000	
Sat	25	Sep	LC	Millwall	H	L 0-3	2,000	
Sat	2	Oct	LC	Croydon Common	A	W2-1		J.J.S. McLauchlan, A.J. Tyler
Sat	9	Oct	LC	Arsenal	H	W1-0		J.J.S. McLauchlan
Sat	16	Oct	LC	Brentford	A	W2-1	4,000	G. Coomber, H. Smith
Sat	23	Oct	LC	West Ham United	H	L 2-3	3,000	J.J.S. McLauchlan (2 pens)
Sat	30	Oct	LC	Tottenham Hotspur	A	L 0-3	3,000	
Sat	6	Nov	LC	Crystal Palace	H	W7-1		J.H. Taylor (4, inc 1 pen), E.J. Wright (2), G. Coomber
Sat	13	Nov	LC	Fulham	A	L 3-4		H. Smith, J.H. Taylor, E.J. Wright
Sat	20	Nov	LC	Clapton Orient	H	W3-1		G. Coomber, V.F. Gregory, J.H. Taylor
Sat	27	Nov	LC	Chelsea	H	L 0-3	2,000	
Sat	4	Dec	LC	Millwall	A	L 0-4		
Sat	11	Dec	LC	Croydon Common	H	W3-0	700	H. Smith (2), G. Meekin
Sat	18	Dec	LC	Arsenal	A	L 1-3		G. Meekin
Sat	25	Dec	LC	Queens Park Rangers	H	W5-1	1,500	H. Smith (3), G.W.N. Edmonds (2)
Mon	27	Dec	LC	Queens Park Rangers	A	L 1-3		H.H. Pantling
Sat	1	Jan	LC	Brentford	H	W3-1		O.H. Gregory, H. Smith, G.F. Meagher
Sat	8	Jan	LC	West Ham United	A	L 1-5		W. Miller
Sat	15	Jan	LC	Tottenham Hotspur	H	L 0-1	1,500	
Sat	22	Jan	LC	Crystal Palace	A	D 1-1	800	H. Smith
Sat	29	Jan	F	Luton Town	A	L 1-3	2,500	V.F. Gregory
				(In aid of the Footballers' Battalion Comforts Fund)				
Sat	5	Feb	LCS	Arsenal	A	D 1-1	7,000	W.G. Ashmole
Sat	12	Feb	LCS	Queens Park Rangers	H	W6-0	2,000	W.G. Ashmole (2), G. Coomber (2), J.H. Taylor (2)
Sat	19	Feb	LCS	Crystal Palace	A	L 0-1		
Sat	4	Mar	LCS	Croydon Common	A	L 0-3		
Sat	11	Mar	LCS	Fulham	H	W2-0		F.J. Gregory, T. Knighton
Sat	18	Mar	LCS	Queens Park Rangers	A	D 2-2	2,000	G. Eames, E.J. Wright
Sat	25	Mar	LCS	Crystal Palace	H	W4-0		E.J. Wright (2), T. Knighton, J.J.S. McLauchlan
Sat	1	Apr	LCS	West Ham United	A	D 2-2	8,000	T. Knighton (pen), E.J. Wright
Sat	8	Apr	LCS	Croydon Common	H	L 0-2		
Sat	15	Apr	LCS	Fulham	A	L 0-2		
Fri	21	Apr	LCS	Luton Town	H	W2-1	4,000	H. Smith (2)
Mon	24	Apr	LCS	Luton Town	A	L 1-3	5,000	H. Smith
Sat	29	Apr	LCS	Arsenal	H	W2-1	1,000	F.J. Gregory, H. Smith

Sat	6	May	LCS	West Ham United	H	L 0-2	3,500	

(Cassio Road was unavailable for this match, and it was played at West Ham United's ground)

1916/17

LC = London Combination (Watford finished 11th in a league of 14 clubs)
71 players were used in the 39 matches (Most appearances - C.W. White 36. Most goals - F. Morris 27 in 14 games)

Sat	2	Sep	LC	Southampton	A	L 0-5	3,500	
Sat	9	Sep	LC	Clapton Orient	H	D 2-2	1,200	W.F. Edwards, H. Smith
Sat	16	Sep	LC	Fulham	A	L 0-7		
Sat	23	Sep	LC	Queens Park Rangers	H	W 2-0	1,000	W.F. Edwards (2)
Sat	30	Sep	LC	West Ham United	A	D 2-2	8,000	H. Smith (2)
Sat	7	Oct	LC	Tottenham Hotspur	H	L 0-2	2,000	
Sat	14	Oct	LC	Crystal Palace	A	W 1-0		R. Cavanna
Sat	21	Oct	LC	Brentford	H	W 4-2		F. Morris (3), C.W. White
Sat	28	Oct	LC	Chelsea	A	L 2-3	9,000	F. Morris (2, inc 1 pen)
Sat	4	Nov	LC	Arsenal	H	L 2-4		F. Cotterill, W.F. Edwards
Sat	11	Nov	LC	Luton Town	A	L 2-3		W.F. Edwards, C.W. White
Sat	18	Nov	LC	Portsmouth	H	W 1-0		H. Smith
Sat	25	Nov	LC	Southampton	H	D 0-0		
Sat	2	Dec	LC	Clapton Orient	A	D 1-1		E.J. Wright
Sat	9	Dec	LC	Fulham	H	L 2-8		W.F. Edwards (2)
Sat	23	Dec	LC	West Ham United	H	L 1-3		G.W.N. Edmonds
Mon	25	Dec	LC	Millwall	A	L 0-3		
Tue	26	Dec	LC	Millwall	H	L 1-6		W. Stanton
Sat	30	Dec	LC	Tottenham Hotspur	A	L 0-3	3,000	
Sat	6	Jan	LC	Crystal Palace	H	D 2-2		G. Coomber, H. Smith
Sat	13	Jan	LC	Brentford	A	L 1-4		W. Alderson
Sat	20	Jan	LC	Chelsea	H	L 0-3	250	
Sat	27	Jan	LC	Arsenal	A	D 1-1		W. Hastings
Sat	3	Feb	LC	Luton Town	H	D 0-0		
Sat	10	Feb	LC	Portsmouth	A	L 0-3	3,000	
Sat	17	Feb	LC	Queens Park Rangers	A	L 1-2		F. Morris
Sat	24	Feb	LC	Portsmouth	H	W 9-0		F. Morris (6, inc 1 pen), W.F. Edwards (2), C.W. White
Sat	3	Mar	LC	Millwall	A	D 2-2	6,000	W.F. Edwards, F. Morris
Sat	10	Mar	LC	Brentford	H	W 5-2		F. Morris (3, inc 1 pen), H. Smith (2)
Sat	17	Mar	LC	Chelsea	A	D 2-2	5,000	W.F. Edwards (2)
Sat	24	Mar	LC	Fulham	A	L 2-7		H. Smith (2)
Sat	31	Mar	LC	Queens Park Rangers	H	L 1-2		H. Geeson
Fri	6	Apr	LC	Luton Town	H	L 4-7	3,000	F. Morris (3, inc 1 pen), G.W.N. Edmonds
Sat	7	Apr	LC	Portsmouth	A	L 3-8	4,000	C.W. White (2), R. Brown
Mon	9	Apr	LC	Luton Town	A	L 0-3	4,000	
Sat	14	Apr	LC	Millwall	H	W 5-3		F. Morris (4), W.F. Edwards
Wed	18	Apr	LC	Fulham	H	W 4-2	500	F. Morris (3), N. Robertson
Sat	21	Apr	LC	Brentford	A	L 1-2	1,000	F. Morris
Sat	28	Apr	LC	Chelsea	H	L 3-6		W.F. Edwards, H. Smith, C.W. White

1918/19

After nearly two seasons of inactivity, the club resumed operations after the First World War with four friendly matches in April 1919. A normal season of peacetime football took place in 1919/20.

Sat	5	Apr	F	Luton Town	A	L 1-3	2,000	H. Smith
Sat	12	Apr	F	Luton Town	H	W 6-2		C.W. White (3, inc 1 pen), G.H. Barnes, H. Price, A. Wright
Sat	19	Apr	F	Northampton Town	H	W 4-2	3,000	G.W.N. Edmonds (2), F.J. Gregory, C.W. White
Tue	22	Apr	F	Northampton Town	A	D 2-2		G.W.N. Edmonds, G.W. Squire

1939/40

FL = Football League, Division 3 (South) - null & void after 3 matches, owing to outbreak of war
RLSA = Regional League South, A Division (Watford finished 4th in a league of 10 clubs)
RLSD = Regional League South, D Division (Watford finished 3rd in a league of 10 clubs)
LC = League Cup (Preliminary Round, one leg - subsequent rounds, two legs)
F = Friendly
29 players were used in the 49 matches (Most appearances - W. Davies 49. Most goals - T.G. Lewis 29)

Sat 19 Aug F   Luton Town   H W2-1   5,887   W. Davies (pen), T.G. Lewis
                  (In aid of the Football League Jubilee Benevolent Fund)

Sat 26 Aug FL   Queens Park Rangers   A D 2-2   11,174   D.R. Evans, T.G. Lewis
J. McHugh (goal); R.V. O'Brien & B.E. Dabbs (full-backs); A. Woodward, J.H. Armstrong & T.W. Postlethwaite (half-backs); T.J. Jones, T.A. Barnett, T.G. Lewis, D.R. Evans & W. Davies (forwards)
Wed 30 Aug FL   Mansfield Town   H L 1-2   4,900   W. Davies
J. McHugh (goal); R.V. O'Brien & B.E. Dabbs (full-backs); A. Woodward, J.H. Armstrong & T.W. Postlethwaite (half-backs); T.J. Jones, T.A. Barnett, W.G.M. Law, D.R. Evans & W. Davies (forwards)
Sat 2 Sep FL   Clapton Orient   H D 1-1   4,850   W.G.M. Law
J. McHugh (goal); R.V. O'Brien & D.J. Lewis (full-backs); A. Woodward, J.H. Armstrong & A.G. Reed (half-backs); T.J. Jones, T.A. Barnett, W.G.M. Law, P.J. Curran & W. Davies (forwards)

Sat	30 Sep	F	Northampton Town	H	W4-0	2,187	W. Davies (pen), T.J. Jones, T.G. Lewis, T.C. Walters
Sat	14 Oct	F	Charlton Athletic	H	W2-0	2,091	T.A. Barnett, T.J. Jones
Sat	21 Oct	RLSA	Clapton Orient	H	L 1-2	2,693	R.V. O'Brien
Sat	28 Oct	RLSA	Crystal Palace	A	D 3-3	2,461	W. Davies, T.J. Jones, T.G. Lewis
Sat	4 Nov	RLSA	Norwich City	H	W4-1	2,709	W. Davies (2), T.J. Jones, T.G. Lewis
Sat	11 Nov	RLSA	Tottenham Hotspur	A	L 2-8	4,981	T.A. Barnett (2)
Sat	18 Nov	RLSA	Millwall	H	W2-0	3,140	T.A. Barnett, T.J. Jones
Sat	25 Nov	RLSA	West Ham United	A	L 0-5	5,400	
Sat	2 Dec	RLSA	Southend United	A	W2-1	3,000	T.A. Barnett, T.G. Lewis
Sat	9 Dec	RLSA	Arsenal	H	L 1-3	10,381	T.G. Lewis
Sat	16 Dec	RLSA	Charlton Athletic	A	L 1-5	1,646	T.G. Lewis
Sat	23 Dec	RLSA	Clapton Orient	A	-- 1-2	400	T.G. Lewis
			(Abandoned after 57 minutes, owing to fog)				
Mon	25 Dec	RLSA	Crystal Palace	H	W5-1	3,157	W. Davies (3), T.G. Lewis, own goal
Tue	26 Dec	RLSA	Norwich City	A	L 2-3	4,350	T.A. Barnett (2)
Sat	30 Dec	RLSA	Tottenham Hotspur	H	W6-1	2,219	W. Davies (3), T.J. Jones, T.G. Lewis, T.C. Walters
Sat	6 Jan	RLSA	Millwall	A	D 1-1	4,564	T.C. Walters
Sat	13 Jan	RLSA	West Ham United	H	W3-1	3,989	T.A. Barnett, T.J. Jones, T.G. Lewis
Sat	20 Jan	RLSA	Southend United	H	W4-0	1,642	T.C. Walters (2), T.G. Lewis, R.V. O'Brien (pen)
Thu	8 Feb	RLSA	Arsenal	A	D 2-2	996	T.G. Lewis, T.C. Walters
Sat	10 Feb	RLSD	Aldershot	H	W3-0	2,529	T.G. Lewis (2), T.J. Jones
Thu	15 Feb	RLSA	Clapton Orient	A	W2-1	509	T.G. Lewis (2)
Sat	17 Feb	RLSD	Clapton Orient	A	D 1-1	1,243	W. Davies
Sat	24 Feb	RLSD	Southend United	H	W4-2	2,779	T.C. Walters (2), W. Davies, T.G. Lewis
Sat	2 Mar	RLSD	Bournemouth & Boscombe Ath	A	D 1-1	2,692	W. Davies (pen)
Sat	9 Mar	RLSD	Crystal Palace	H	W5-2	4,611	W. Davies (2), T.A. Barnett, E.W. Lager, A. Woodward
Wed	13 Mar	RLSA	Charlton Athletic	H	W3-0	1,085	E.W. Lager (3)
Sat	16 Mar	RLSD	Reading	A	L 2-5	3,500	W. Davies (pen), own goal
Fri	22 Mar	RLSD	Queens Park Rangers	H	D 1-1	7,537	T.A. Barnett
Sat	23 Mar	RLSD	Norwich City	A	L 0-2	4,270	
Mon	25 Mar	RLSD	Queens Park Rangers	A	L 0-2	6,258	
Sat	30 Mar	RLSD	Brighton & Hove Albion	H	W4-2	3,174	T.A. Barnett (2), T.C. Walters (2)
Sat	6 Apr	RLSD	Aldershot	A	W3-2	5,000	T.G. Lewis (2), T.C. Walters
Sat	13 Apr	LC	Northampton Town	A	D 1-1	4,799	T.G. Lewis
Wed	17 Apr	LC	Northampton Town	H	W2-1	2,441	W. Davies (pen), T.G. Lewis
Sat	20 Apr	LC	Southend United	A	L 1-3	3,650	W. Davies
Sat	27 Apr	LC	Southend United	H	L 1-3	4,025	W. Davies (pen)
Wed	1 May	RLSD	Reading	H	W3-0	994	W. Davies, T.G. Lewis, T.C. Walters

Sat	11	May	RLSD	Clapton Orient	H	D 2-2	1,691	W. Davies (pen), A. Woodward
Mon	13	May	F	Bedford Town	A	W 4-1	991	T.G. Lewis (2), W. Davies (pen), T.C. Walters
Mon	18	May	RLSD	Norwich City	H	D 0-0	1,697	
Wed	22	May	F	An FA XI	H	L 1-3	1,554	J.C.R. Smith

(In aid of Red Cross funds. The Watford team was designated "A Herts FA XI")

Tue	25	May	RLSD	Bournemouth & Boscombe Ath	H	W 7-1	1,230	T.A. Barnett (2), R.V. O'Brien (2), W. Davies, T.G. Lewis, T.C. Walters
Wed	29	May	RLSD	Crystal Palace	A	L 1-2	2,335	T.C. Walters
Sat	1	Jun	RLSD	Brighton & Hove Albion	A	D 2-2	1,000	A.J. Duncombe, T.G. Lewis
Sat	8	Jun	RLSD	Southend United	A	D 2-2	741	W. Davies, T.G. Lewis

1940/41

SRL = South Regional League (Watford finished 8th in a league of 34 clubs)
FLS = Football League South (Watford and Brighton & Hove Albion both claimed the championship of this league of
*   eight clubs, and the dispute was settled by a challenge match)*
FLSC = Football League South Challenge Match
LC = League Cup (two-leg matches)
F = Friendly
49 players were used in the 44 matches (Most appearances - T.A. Barnett & R.F. Williams 43. Most goals - T.G. Lewis 29)

Sat	17	Aug	F	Royal Army Medical Corps	H	W 9-1		A.J. Duncombe (4), T.G. Lewis (2), T.A. Barnett, W. Davies, T.J. Jones
Sat	24	Aug	F	Royal Army Service Corps XI	H	-- 0-0		

(Interrupted by an air-raid warning after 7 minutes, and abandoned when the RASC team was recalled to duty)

Sat	31	Aug	SRL	Portsmouth	H	L 1-2	1,015	W. Davies
Sat	14	Sep	SRL	Aldershot	H	W 3-1	1,084	W. Davies, T.G. Lewis, R.F. Williams
Sat	21	Sep	SRL	Aldershot	A	L 1-2	3,000	T.G. Lewis
Sat	28	Sep	SRL	Southampton	A	W 5-2	500	W. Davies (3, inc 2 pens), T.G. Lewis, R.F. Williams
Sat	5	Oct	SRL	Millwall	A	L 0-3	500	
Sat	12	Oct	SRL	Crystal Palace	H	L 1-2	1,665	own goal
Sat	19	Oct	SRL	Southampton	H	W 3-2	1,551	H.H. Lewis (2), T.A. Barnett
Sat	26	Oct	SRL	Northampton Town	A	L 1-2	3,500	T.A. Barnett
Sat	2	Nov	SRL	Southampton	A	W 4-0	1,000	J. Brown (2), T.G. Lewis (2)
Sat	16	Nov	SRL	Millwall	H	D 1-1	1,178	H.S. Miller
Sat	23	Nov	SRL	Brighton & Hove Albion	A	D 1-1	750	A.R. Brown
Sat	30	Nov	F	Royal Artillery XI	H	W 3-2	491	T.A. Barnett (2), T.J. Jones (pen)
Sat	7	Dec	SRL	Brighton & Hove Albion	H	W 4-0	1,160	T.J. Jones, T.G. Lewis, K. Walshaw, T.C. Walters
Sat	14	Dec	SRL	Southend United	A	W 3-1	700	T.G. Lewis (2), A.R. Brown
Sat	21	Dec	SRL	Southampton	H	W 4-2	1,072	H.H. Lewis (3), T.J. Jones
Wed	25	Dec	SRL	(am) Luton Town	H	D 2-2	2,743	H.H. Lewis (2, inc 1 pen)
Wed	25	Dec	SRL	(pm) Luton Town	A	L 1-4	1,689	H.H. Lewis (pen)
Sat	28	Dec	SRL	Southend United	H	D 1-1	1,222	H.H. Lewis (pen)
Sat	11	Jan	SRL&FLS	Southend United	H	W 8-2	855	T.S.E. Robinson (3), A.R. Brown (2), T.J. Jones, H.H. Lewis, H.S. Miller
Sat	18	Jan	SRL&FLS	Bournemouth & Boscombe Ath	A	W 5-2	204	H.H. Lewis (3), T.J. Jones (2)
Sat	25	Jan	SRL&FLS	Southampton	H	W 7-1	608	T.A. Barnett (2), H.H. Lewis (2), A.L. Pease (2), R.F. Williams
Sat	1	Feb	SRL&FLS	Portsmouth	A	L 1-7	1,500	W. Davies
Sat	8	Feb	SRL&FLS	Brighton & Hove Albion	H	D 2-2	1,236	T. Galley (pen), H.S. Miller
Sat	15	Feb	LC	Fulham	H	W 4-1	3,637	C.J. Drinkwater, E.N. Jones, H.H. Lewis, own goal
Sat	22	Feb	LC	Fulham	A	L 1-2	2,500	H.H. Lewis
Sat	1	Mar	LC	Arsenal	H	L 0-4	10,884	
Sat	8	Mar	LC	Arsenal	A	L 0-5	4,427	
Sat	15	Mar	SRL&FLS	Southend United	A	W 3-2	750	T. Galley, E.N. Jones, T.G. Lewis
Sat	22	Mar	SRL&FLS	Southampton	H	W 2-0	1,410	T.A. Barnett (2)
Sat	29	Mar	SRL&FLS	Bournemouth & Boscombe Ath	H	W 5-0	1,200	T.G. Lewis (2), T. Galley (pen), T.J. Jones, H.H. Lewis

Sat	5 Apr	SRL&FLS	Luton Town	H	L 2-6	2,561	T.A. Barnett, T.G. Lewis
Sat	12 Apr	SRL&FLS	Norwich City	H	W7-1	1,800	T.G. Lewis (4), T. Galley, H.S. Miller, W. Saunders
Mon	14 Apr	SRL	West Ham United	A	L 0-2		
Sat	19 Apr	SRL&FLS	Norwich City	A	L 4-5	1,289	T.G. Lewis (3), A. Woodward
Sat	26 Apr	SRL&FLS	Portsmouth	H	W6-0	2,005	T.G. Lewis (4), T. Galley (pen), W. Saunders
Sat	3 May	SRL&FLS	Brighton & Hove Albion	A	L 2-4	2,500	H.H. Lewis, T.G. Lewis
Sat	10 May	SRL&FLS	Luton Town	H	L 0-1	1,728	
Sat	17 May	SRL	Queens Park Rangers	A	L 2-4	1,900	W. Davies (pen), H.H. Lewis
Sat	24 May	SRL	Queens Park Rangers	H	D 3-3	1,674	T.G. Lewis (2), T.A. Barnett
Sat	31 May	FLSC	Brighton & Hove Albion	A	L 1-4	2,500	T.G. Lewis
Mon	2 Jun	F	Shorts Sports, Strood	A	L 3-6	2,000	C.J. Walker (3)
Sat	7 Jun	SRL	Aldershot	A	L 1-3	1,884	R.F. Williams

1941/42

LL = London League (Watford finished bottom of a league of 16 clubs)
LWC = London War Cup - Group Qualifying Competition (Watford finished 3rd in a group of four clubs)
83 players were used in the 36 matches (Most appearances - T.J. Jones 35. Most goals - D. Westcott 8)

Sat	30 Aug	LL	Tottenham Hotspur	A	L 0-5	5,074	
Sat	6 Sep	LL	Portsmouth	H	L 1-5	4,000	T. Galley
Sat	13 Sep	LL	Chelsea	H	L 1-3	4,473	A.G. Biggs
Sat	20 Sep	LL	Charlton Athletic	A	L 1-5	3,660	A.G. Biggs
Sat	27 Sep	LL	West Ham United	H	L 0-8	3,991	
Sat	4 Oct	LL	Clapton Orient	H	D 2-2	1,516	T. Galley, H. Waller
Sat	11 Oct	LL	Aldershot	A	L 1-8	3,000	F. Briggs
Sat	18 Oct	LL	Millwall	A	L 2-4	2,500	D. Westcott (2)
Sat	25 Oct	LL	Arsenal	H	W3-1	5,328	T.J. Jones, M. Killourhy, T. Morris
Sat	1 Nov	LL	Queens Park Rangers	A	W5-1	3,000	D. Westcott (5)
Sat	8 Nov	LL	Reading	H	D 0-0	4,000	
Sat	15 Nov	LL	Brighton & Hove Albion	A	D 2-2	4,000	F.H. Broome, T. Robinson
Sat	22 Nov	LL	Brentford	H	L 1-6	3,969	M. Killourhy
Sat	29 Nov	LL	Crystal Palace	A	L 1-6	4,800	T.G. Lewis
Sat	6 Dec	LL	Fulham	H	L 3-5	1,715	T.A. Barnett, J.A. Cringan, H.H. Lewis
Sat	13 Dec	LL	Tottenham Hotspur	H	L 1-2	3,035	G.D. Egan
Sat	20 Dec	LL	Portsmouth	A	L 1-7	4,500	J.E. Griffiths (pen)
Thu	25 Dec	LL	Chelsea	A	D 2-2	4,132	J. Brown, T. Morris
Sat	27 Dec	LL	Charlton Athletic	H	L 1-2	2,789	T. Morris
Sat	3 Jan	LL	West Ham United	A	L 1-4	3,000	E.N. Jones
Sat	10 Jan	LL	Clapton Orient	A	L 0-2	1.450	
Sat	31 Jan	LL	Arsenal	A	L 0-11	4,701	
Sat	14 Jan	LL	Reading	A	L 1-5	3,500	M. Killourhy
Sat	21 Feb	LL	Brighton & Hove Albion	H	W 7-1	783	T.J. Jones (2), M. Killourhy (2), E.N. Jones, F.J. Kurz, T.G. Lewis
Sat	28 Feb	LL	Brentford	A	L 3-5	3,110	H. Hutton (2), E.C. Lancelotte
Sat	7 Mar	LL	Crystal Palace	H	W2-1	1,030	D. Halford, T.G. Lewis
Sat	14 Mar	LL	Fulham	A	W3-1	2,463	H. Hutton, T.J. Jones, C.J. Wipfler
Sat	21 Mar	LWC	Charlton Athletic	H	L 1-4	2,592	F.J. Kurz
Sat	28 Mar	LWC	Tottenham Hotspur	A	L 2-5	4,627	M. Killourhy, D. Westcott
Sat	4 Apr	LWC	Charlton Athletic	A	W1-0	3,152	C. Dougall
Mon	6 Apr	LWC	Tottenham Hotspur	H	D 0-0	4,541	
Sat	11 Apr	LWC	Reading	H	W6-0	2,187	F.J. Kurz (4), J. Brown, M. Killourhy
Sat	18 Apr	LWC	Reading	A	L 0-3	3,000	
Sat	25 Apr	LL	Aldershot	H	L 1-5	2,087	own goal
Sat	2 May	LL	Queens Park Rangers	H	L 0-5	1,721	
Sat	9 May	LL	Millwall	H	W1-0	1,686	E.N. Jones (pen)

1942/43

FLS = Football League South (Watford finished 17th in a league of 18 clubs)
LCS = League Cup (South) Qualifying Competition (Watford finished 3rd in a group of 4 clubs)
F = Friendly
86 players were used in the 36 matches (Most appearances - T.J. Jones 32. Most goals - E.N. Jones 12)

Sat	29	Aug	FLS	Millwall	H	L 3-4	1,884	T.G. Lewis (2), E.N. Jones (pen)
Sat	5	Sep	FLS	Reading	A	L 2-3	3,293	E.N. Jones, T.G. Lewis
Sat	12	Sep	FLS	Southampton	A	L 1-4	4,000	J. Morris
Sat	19	Sep	FLS	Brighton & Hove Albion	H	D 1-1	2,104	A. Driver
Sat	26	Sep	FLS	Aldershot	A	L 0-4	3,000	
Sat	3	Oct	FLS	Brentford	A	L 0-3	3,950	
Sat	10	Oct	FLS	Charlton Athletic	A	L 0-7	3,400	
Sat	17	Oct	FLS	Clapton Orient	H	L 2-3	1,545	J. Morris (2)
Sat	24	Oct	FLS	West Ham United	A	L 0-3	4,940	
Sat	31	Oct	FLS	Portsmouth	H	W4-2	1,971	C. Broadhurst, E.N. Jones, A.S. White, own goal
Sat	7	Nov	FLS	Crystal Palace	H	W5-3	1,975	F.R. Jones (2), E.N. Jones (pen), T.J. Jones, T.W. Robinson
Sat	14	Nov	FLS	Fulham	A	L 0-2	3,005	
Sat	21	Nov	FLS	Tottenham Hotspur	A	L 0-6	5,459	
Sat	28	Nov	FLS	Millwall	A	D 3-3	2,873	B.C. Loom (3)
Sat	5	Dec	FLS	Reading	H	L 2-5	1,790	F.J. Kurz (2)
Sat	12	Dec	FLS	Southampton	H	L 3-4	1,762	H. Ware (2), E.N. Jones
Sat	19	Dec	FLS	Brighton & Hove Albion	A	L 1-2	3,000	B.C. Loom
Fri	25	Dec	FLS	Luton Town	A	W2-0	2,500	E.N. Jones, J. Morris
Sat	26	Dec	FLS	Luton Town	H	L 1-2	3,547	W. Lane
Sat	2	Jan	FLS	Aldershot	H	W5-3	1,622	D.K. Martin (2), H. Jackson, T.J. Jones, A. Weir
Sat	9	Jan	FLS	Brentford	H	W2-0	2,177	H. Jackson, T.J. Jones
Sat	16	Jan	FLS	Charlton Athletic	H	L 3-5	2,564	E.N. Jones (2), J. Morris
Sat	23	Jan	FLS	Clapton Orient	A	L 3-4	1,812	T.G. Lewis (2), D.K. Martin
Sat	30	Jan	FLS	West Ham United	H	W3-2	2,274	D.K. Martin (2), H. Jackson
Sat	6	Feb	FLS	Portsmouth	A	L 2-6	5,000	T.J. Jones, D.K. Martin
Sat	13	Feb	FLS	Crystal Palace	A	W2-0	2,750	E.N. Jones, D.K. Martin
Sat	20	Feb	FLS	Fulham	H	L 1-4	2,280	W.H. Brown
Sat	27	Feb	FLS	Tottenham Hotspur	H	L 0-3	2,096	
Sat	6	Mar	LCS	West Ham United	A	L 1-6	2,000	H. Jackson
Sat	13	Mar	LCS	Arsenal	A	L 1-4	7,500	E.N. Jones (pen)
Sat	20	Mar	LCS	Brighton & Hove Albion	H	D 1-1	2,184	D. Westcott
Sat	27	Mar	LCS	West Ham United	H	D 0-0	3,246	
Sat	3	Apr	LCS	Arsenal	H	D 1-1	8,726	E.N. Jones
Sat	10	Apr	LCS	Brighton & Hove Albion	A	W5-0	1,500	H. Jackson (2), J. Hughes, J. Morris, own goal
Sat	17	Apr	F	Aldershot	A	L 2-4	2,000	H. Jackson, J. Morris
Mon	26	Apr	F	Queens Park Rangers	A	L 2-3	1,000	E.N. Jones, C.E. Williams

1943/44

FLS = Football League (South) (Watford finished 15th in a league of 18 clubs)
LCS = League Cup (South) Qualifying Competition (Watford finished 3rd in a group of 4 clubs)
F = Friendly
70 players were used in the 37 matches (Most appearances - T.J. Jones 31. Most goals - J. Brain & W. Davies 12)

Sat	28	Aug	FLS	Millwall	H	L 1-4	2,470	T.W. Smith
Sat	4	Sep	FLS	Reading	A	L 2-8	4,304	H. Jackson, L.H. Warner
Sat	11	Sep	FLS	Southampton	H	W6-1	2,508	W. Davies (2), H. Jackson (2), T.J. Jones, own goal
Sat	18	Sep	FLS	Queens Park Rangers	A	L 1-3	5,885	H. Jackson
Sat	25	Sep	FLS	Aldershot	A	D 3-3	4,500	A.R. Lowes, J. Milburn, J. Shaw
Sat	2	Oct	FLS	Brentford	A	L 1-4	6,720	R. Ross
Sat	9	Oct	FLS	Charlton Athletic	H	D 2-2	4,102	W. Davies, T.J. Jones
Sat	16	Oct	FLS	Clapton Orient	H	W6-1	2,886	J. Brain (3), W. Davies (2, inc 1 pen), W.H. Brown

Sat	23 Oct	FLS	Arsenal	A	L 2-4	8,033	J. Brain, H. Jackson
Sat	30 Oct	FLS	Portsmouth	A	W3-2	8,159	J. Brain (3)
Sat	6 Nov	FLS	Crystal Palace	H	L 2-4	3,783	D. Westcott (2)
Sat	13 Nov	FLS	Fulham	A	D 0-0	3,901	
Sat	20 Nov	FLS	Tottenham Hotspur	A	L 2-4	8,499	R. Walls (2)
Sat	27 Nov	FLS	Millwall	A	L 3-4	1,651	J. Brain, W. Davies, J.L. Loughran
Sat	4 Dec	FLS	Reading	H	L 3-5	3,078	W. Davies (2), J. Brain
Sat	11 Dec	FLS	Southampton	A	L 1-4	3,600	R. Walls
Sat	18 Dec	FLS	Chelsea	H	W1-0	2,229	J. Brain
Sat	25 Dec	FLS	Luton Town	A	W3-2	7,000	H. Jackson (3)
Mon	27 Dec	FLS	Luton Town	H	L 1-2	5,558	G. Guest
Sat	1 Jan	FLS	Queens Park Rangers	H	D 2-2	4,483	W. Davies (2)
Sat	8 Jan	FLS	Crystal Palace	A	L 0-1	5,000	
Sat	22 Jan	FLS	Brentford	H	D 4-4	2,759	W. Davies (2), J. Brain, L.H. Warner
Sat	29 Jan	FLS	Charlton Athletic	A	D 1-1	3,000	T.J. Jones
Sat	5 Feb	FLS	Clapton Orient	A	D 0-0	2,000	
Sat	12 Feb	FLS	Arsenal	H	L 0-2	7,887	
Sat	19 Feb	LCS	West Ham United	A	W2-1	4,500	W.H. Brown (2)
Sat	26 Feb	LCS	Chelsea	H	L 0-3	5,282	
Sat	4 Mar	LCS	Southampton	A	L 1-3	6,000	A.S. White
Sat	11 Mar	LCS	West Ham United	H	W2-1	4,257	J. Brain, H. Jackson
Sat	18 Mar	LCS	Chelsea	A	D 1-1	14,440	H. Jackson
Sat	25 Mar	LCS	Southampton	H	L 1-4	3,440	H. Jackson
Sat	1 Apr	FLS	Portsmouth	H	L 1-3	2,281	A. Younger
Sat	8 Apr	F	West Ham United	A	L 2-4		S.N. Baines (2)
Mon	10 Apr	FLS	Aldershot	H	W2-1	4,880	R.F. Williams (2, inc 1 pen)
Sat	22 Apr	FLS	Chelsea	A	L 1-2	5,586	J. Stone
Sat	29 Apr	FLS	Fulham	H	L 3-6	2,196	G. Guest (2), S.N. Baines
Sat	6 May	FLS	Tottenham Hotspur	H	D 1-1	2,655	G. Guest

1944/45

FLS = Football League (South) (Watford finished 10th in a league of 18 clubs)
LCS = League Cup (South) Qualifying Competition (Watford finished bottom of a group of 6 clubs)
F = Friendly
64 players were used in the 38 matches (Most appearances - W. Saunders & R.F. Williams 33. Most goals - T.G. Lewis 24)

Sat	26 Aug	FLS	Southampton	A	L 0-9	7,000	
Sat	2 Sep	FLS	Crystal Palace	H	L 2-4	1,410	S.N. Baines, H. Jackson
Sat	9 Sep	FLS	West Ham United	H	D 3-3	3,842	J. Brain, H. Jackson, J.L. Wrigglesworth
Sat	16 Sep	FLS	Reading	H	D 2-2	3,695	J. Brain, H. Jackson
Sat	23 Sep	FLS	Aldershot	A	L 0-1	4,395	
Sat	30 Sep	FLS	Fulham	H	L 1-2	4,840	J. Brain
Sat	7 Oct	FLS	Clapton Orient	A	D 4-4	2,000	T.G. Lewis (2), H. Jackson, F. Jones
Sat	14 Oct	FLS	Brentford	A	L 1-4	5,387	J. Brain
Sat	21 Oct	FLS	Portsmouth	H	W3-0	3,520	J.L. Wrigglesworth (2), T.G. Lewis
Sat	28 Oct	FLS	Chelsea	H	L 1-6	7,730	T.G. Lewis
Sat	4 Nov	FLS	Luton Town	A	W3-2	4,462	J.L. Wrigglesworth (2), T.G. Lewis
Sat	11 Nov	FLS	Brighton & Hove Albion	H	W5-1	2,853	T.G. Lewis (2), J.L. Wrigglesworth (2), S.N. Baines
Sat	18 Nov	FLS	Arsenal	A	L 0-4	7,910	
Sat	25 Nov	FLS	Charlton Athletic	H	W3-2	4,326	H. Jackson (pen), T.G. Lewis, J.L. Wrigglesworth
Sat	2 Dec	FLS	Southampton	H	W2-1	4,451	T.G. Lewis, J.L. Wrigglesworth
Sat	9 Dec	FLS	Crystal Palace	A	W3-2	5,897	T.G. Lewis, R.F. Williams, J.L. Wrigglesworth
Sat	16 Dec	FLS	West Ham United	A	L 2-6	7,000	S.J. Bennett, J. Milburn (pen)
Sat	23 Dec	FLS	Millwall	A	D 3-3	3,500	T.G. Lewis (2), R.F. Williams
Tue	26 Dec	FLS	Millwall	H	-- 0-3	3,345	
			(Abandoned after 60 minutes, owing to fog)				
Sat	30 Dec	FLS	Reading	A	L 2-4	3,037	J. Milburn (pen), J. Stone
Sat	6 Jan	FLS	Aldershot	H	L 1-3	3,261	R.F. Williams

Sat	13 Jan	FLS	Fulham	A	W 2-0	3,616	H. Jackson, J. Tivendale
Sat	20 Jan	FLS	Clapton Orient	H	L 0-3	1,906	
Sat	3 Feb	LCS	Charlton Athletic	A	D 1-1	5,500	H. Jackson (pen)
Sat	10 Feb	LCS	Chelsea	A	L 1-3	12,027	T.G. Lewis
Sat	17 Feb	LCS	Southampton	H	L 1-6	4,124	T.W. Smith
Sat	24 Feb	LCS	Charlton Athletic	H	L 2-6	4,130	W. Davies, J. Milburn (pen)
Sat	3 Mar	LCS	Chelsea	H	L 0-2	5,992	
Sat	10 Mar	LCS	Southampton	A	L 1-2	12,000	S. Hooper
Sat	17 Mar	FLS	Portsmouth	A	W 4-3	9,000	H. Jackson (2), P.J. Curran, S. Walker
Sat	31 Mar	FLS	Luton Town	H	D 1-1	4,636	T.G. Lewis
Mon	2 Apr	F	Northampton Town	A	D 3-3		J.H. Browne (2), T.G. Lewis
Sat	14 Apr	FLS	Brighton & Hove Albion	A	L 2-3	3,000	J. Stone, S. Walker
Sat	21 Apr	FLS	Arsenal	H	W 3-2	5,980	H. Jackson (2), S. Walker
Sat	28 Apr	FLS	Charlton Athletic	A	D 3-3	3,462	T.G. Lewis (3)
Sat	5 May	FLS	Chelsea	A	W 4-3	1,896	T.G. Lewis (3), B.A.G. Jezzard
Sat	12 May	FLS	Millwall	H	L 1-2	2,838	T.G. Lewis
Sat	19 May	FLS	Brentford	H	W 5-1	2,563	H. Dykes (3), T.G. Lewis (2)

1945/46

3SN = Football League, Division 3 South (North) (Watford finished 4th in a league of 11 clubs)
3SNC = Football League, Division 3 South (North) Cup Qualifying Competition (Watford finished 10th in a group of 11 clubs)
FAC = FA Cup
F = Friendly
47 players were used in the 46 matches (Most appearances - R. Gray 45. Most goals - T.G. Lewis 27)

Although normal Football League operations were not resumed until 1946/47, the FA Cup restarted this season (on a two-leg basis throughout), with only registered players eligible for selection.

Sat	25 Aug	3SN	Norwich City	A	L 1-8	7,000	T.G. Lewis
Wed	29 Aug	3SN	Northampton Town	H	W 4-2	2,768	B.A.G. Jezzard (2), M. Edelston, T.G. Lewis
Sat	1 Sep	3SN	Norwich City	H	W 2-1	4,842	T.G. Lewis, K. Saunders
Sat	8 Sep	3SN	Mansfield Town	H	W 2-1	4,649	B.A.G. Jezzard, T.G. Lewis
Sat	15 Sep	3SN	Mansfield Town	A	W 2-1	4,500	T.J. Jones (2)
Mon	17 Sep	3SN	Northampton Town	A	L 0-3	5,969	
Sat	22 Sep	3SN	Southend United	A	L 2-6	6,210	T.G. Lewis, own goal
Sat	29 Sep	3SN	Southend United	H	L 0-1	5,266	
Sat	6 Oct	3SN	Walsall	H	W 2-1	4,781	R. Gray (2 pens)
Sat	13 Oct	3SN	Walsall	A	W 3-0	3,924	W. Beckett, W.H. Brown, B.A.G. Jezzard
Sat	20 Oct	3SN	Port Vale	A	L 1-2	7,607	R. Gray
Sat	27 Oct	3SN	Port Vale	H	D 2-2	5,528	T.G. Lewis (2)
Sat	3 Nov	3SN	Ipswich Town	H	W 4-3	5,021	W. Beckett, P.J. Curran, C.J. Drinkwater, T.G. Lewis
Sat	10 Nov	3SN	Ipswich Town	A	L 2-4	9,500	W. Beckett, B.A.G. Jezzard

Sat 17 Nov FAC   Southend United   H D 1-1   5,808 W. Davies
1st Round, 1st Leg - G.P. Bland (goal); R.V. O'Brien & W.T. Harris (full-backs); P. Gillespie, J. Shaw & R. Gray (half-backs); T.J. Jones, W. Davies, T.G. Lewis, W. Beckett & C.J. Drinkwater (forwards)
Sat 24 Nov FAC   Southend United   A W 3-0   7,200 T.G. Lewis (2), R. Gray
1st Round, 2nd Leg - G. Mee (goal); R.V. O'Brien & T.J. Jones (full-backs); P. Gillespie, J. Shaw & R. Gray (half-backs); B.A.G. Jezzard, W. Beckett, T.G. Lewis, W. Davies & C.J. Drinkwater (forwards)

Sat	1 Dec	3SN	Queens Park Rangers	H	L 0-2	11,215	

Sat 8 Dec FAC   Bromley   A W 3-1   5,092 R. Gray (pen), B.A.G. Jezzard, own goal
2nd Round, 1st Leg - G. Mee (goal); R.V. O'Brien & T.J. Jones (full-backs); P. Gillespie, J. Shaw & R. Gray (half-backs); B.A.G. Jezzard, W. Beckett, T.G. Lewis, W. Davies & C.J. Drinkwater (forwards)
Sat 15 Dec FAC   Bromley   H D 1-1   5,481 R. Gray (pen)
2nd Round, 2nd Leg - G. Mee (goal); R.V. O'Brien & T.J. Jones (full-backs); P. Gillespie, J. Shaw & R. Gray (half-backs); B.A.G. Jezzard, W. Beckett, T.G. Lewis, W. Davies & C.J. Drinkwater (forwards)

Sat	22 Dec	3SN	Clapton Orient	H	W5-2	2,883	T.G. Lewis (4), C.J. Drinkwater
Tue	25 Dec	3SN	Notts County	H	W7-2	3,589	T.G. Lewis (4), P.J. Curran, C.J. Drinkwater, A. Weir
Wed	26 Dec	3SN	Notts County	A	W2-1	17,174	W. Davies (2)
Sat	29 Dec	F	Polish Air Force	H	W6-2	2,130	T.G. Lewis (3), W. Davies, C.J. Drinkwater, A. Weir
Tue	1 Jan	3SN	Queens Park Rangers	A	D 1-1	6,447	W. Davies

Sat 5 Jan FAC Nottingham Forest A D 1-1 15,394 own goal

3rd Round, 1st Leg - G. Mee (goal); R.V. O'Brien & L. Gallimore (full-backs); P. Gillespie, J. Shaw & R. Gray (half-backs); W. Davies, A. Weir, T.G. Lewis, W. Beckett & C.J. Drinkwater (forwards)

Wed 9 Jan FAC Nottingham Forest H D 1-1 7,008 T.G. Lewis (after extra time)

(Abandoned after 53 minutes of extra time, owing to rain and bad light)

3rd Round, 2nd Leg - G. Mee (goal); R.V. O'Brien & L. Gallimore (full-backs); P. Gillespie, J. Shaw & R. Gray (half-backs); W. Davies, W. Beckett, T.G. Lewis, P.J. Curran & C.J. Drinkwater (forwards)

Thu	10 Jan	3SN	Clapton Orient	A	L 0-4	1,500	
Sat	12 Jan	3SNC	Cardiff City	H	L 1-7	7,821	T.G. Lewis

Wed 16 Jan FAC Nottingham Forest -- W1-0 6,500 own goal (after extra time)

3rd Round replay (at Tottenham Hotspur) - G. Mee (goal); R.V. O'Brien & L. Gallimore (full-backs); P. Gillespie, J. Shaw & R. Gray (half-backs); W. Davies, A.Weir, T.G. Lewis, P.J. Curran & C.J. Drinkwater (forwards)

Sat	19 Jan	3SNC	Cardiff City	A	W2-0	10,000	W. Beckett, W. Davies

Sat 26 Jan FAC Birmingham City A L 0-5 23,973

4th Round, 1st Leg - G. Mee (goal); R.V. O'Brien & L. Gallimore (full-backs); P. Gillespie, J. Shaw & R. Gray (half-backs); W. Davies, A. Weir, T.G. Lewis, P.J. Curran, C.J. Drinkwater (forwards)

Wed 30 Jan FAC Birmingham City H D 1-1 5,277 R. Gray (pen)

4th Round, 2nd Leg - G. Mee (goal); R.V. O'Brien & L. Gallimore (full-backs); P. Gillespie, J. Shaw & T.J. Jones (half-backs); W. Davies, A. Weir, R. Gray, P.J. Curran & C.J. Drinkwater (forwards)

Sat	2 Feb	3SNC	Clapton Orient	A	L 3-4	5,922	W. Davies, T.G. Lewis, own goal
Sat	9 Feb	3SNC	Northampton Town	H	W1-0	4,647	W. Davies
Sat	16 Feb	3SNC	Northampton Town	A	L 1-4	5,527	W. Davies
Sat	23 Feb	3SNC	Notts County	A	L 1-2	10,921	T.G. Lewis
Sat	2 Mar	3SNC	Notts County	H	W6-2	1,373	R. Gray (2), W. Beckett, W. Davies, T.G. Lewis, A. Weir
Sat	9 Mar	3SNC	Queens Park Rangers	H	L 1-3	8,665	W. Beckett
Sat	16 Mar	3SNC	Queens Park Rangers	A	L 1-2	9,868	T.G. Lewis
Sat	23 Mar	3SNC	Norwich City	H	W2-1	5,269	W.L. Dunderdale, A. Weir
Sat	30 Mar	3SNC	Norwich City	A	L 0-3	10,924	
Sat	6 Apr	3SNC	Ipswich Town	H	L 0-1	4,317	
Sat	13 Apr	3SNC	Ipswich Town	A	D 2-2	9,846	W.L. Dunderdale (2)
Fri	19 Apr	3SNC	Clapton Orient	H	W2-0	3,435	W.L. Dunderdale (2)
Sat	20 Apr	3SNC	Mansfield Town	H	L 0-3	5,431	
Mon	22 Apr	3SNC	Mansfield Town	A	L 0-1	7,616	

PART FIVE

Friendlies from 1896/97

THE following list contains friendly matches played from the time the club joined the Southern League - except wartime friendlies, which can be found in Part Four. Matches played in private are not included. Attendances, where known, are listed in the right-hand column.

1896/97

Sep	12	Chesham Generals (h)	W 4-3	200
Oct	10	Anerley (h)	W 2-1	
	21	Enfield (h)	W 2-0	
	24	Civil Service (h)	W 3-2	
Nov	4	Royal Veterinary College (h)	D 1-1	
Dec	26	Watford St Mary's (h)	L 1-2	2,000
	28	Kettering Combination (h)	D 3-3	200
Feb	24	Aldenham School (h)	D 2-2	100
Mar	10	St Bartholomew's Hospital (h)	D 2-2	
Apr	19	Woolwich Arsenal Reserves (h)	L 0-6	
	22	Old Rossalians (h)	L 0-3	

1897/98

Sep	4	West Ham Garfield (h)	L 0-1	200
	11	Civil Service (h)	L 1-3	100
	25	London Welsh (h)	L 1-2	
	29	Bowes Park (h)	W 4-0	
Oct	6	Casuals (h)	L 1-3	
	9	Watford St Mary's (a)	L 1-2	2,500
	13	2nd Life Guards (h)	W 3-0	
	20	R.G.P. Wymer's XI (h)	W 5-1	
	27	St Bartholomew's Hospital (h)	W 5-1	
Nov	3	2nd Scots Guards (h)	L 1-4	
	10	Aldenham School (h)	D 4-4	
	13	St Albans (h)	W 5-0	2,000
	24	Royal Veterinary College (h)	W 6-2	
Dec	25	2nd Scots Guards (h)	W 4-1	700
	27	Sheppey United (h)	L 1-3	2,000
	28	Bishop Auckland (h)	L 1-2	400
Jan	8	Chesham Generals (h)	W 4-1	800
Feb	16	1st Scots Guards (h)	W 2-1	200
	19	Wolverton L&NWR (h)	D 6-6	1,000
	23	Aldenham School (h)	W 2-1	
	26	Small Heath (h)	D 2-2	2,000
Mar	12	Chesham (h)	W 3-2	1,000

Mar	26	Watford St Mary's (h)	W 3-1	1,800
Apr	9	Wolverton L&NWR (h)	W 4-1	1,200
	11	Scottish Amateurs (h)	W 3-2	3,000
	12	Thornaby Utopians (h)	W 5-1	250
	16	2nd Scots Guards (h)	W 4-1	700
	20	Luton Town (h)	D 2-2	2,000
	27	Watford St Mary's (h)	W 2-0	750
	30	West Bromwich Albion (h)	D 1-1	2,000

1898/99

Sep	3	Reading Amateurs (h)	W 8-0	1,500
	7	1st Coldstream Guards (h)	W 4-0	500
	10	Ilford (h)	W 5-0	1,000
	17	Richmond Association (h)	W 3-1	1,500
Nov	5	Queens Park Rangers (a)	D 2-2	3,500
	12	Chatham (h)	L 1-4	1,000
	30	Casuals (a)	L 2-4	
Dec	3	West Norwood (h)	W 4-1	600
	26	Crewe Alexandra (h)	L 1-3	3,000
	27	Metropolitan Railway (h)	W 6-0	200
	31	Fulham (a)	W 3-0	600
Apr	3	Middlesbrough (h)	D 2-2	2,000
	4	Luton Town (h)	D 3-3	1,000
	15	Queens Park Rangers (h)	W 2-0	1,200
	19	Apsley & District (a)	W 7-2	400
	26	Rest of Bucks & Contiguous Counties League (h)	L 3-4	1,000
		(benefit match for the professionals)		
	29	St Albans (h)	W 3-0	1,500

1899/1900

Sep	2	London Caledonians (h)	W 3-1	1,200
	6	Eastleigh (h)	D 1-1	250
	13	1st Scots Guards (h)	-- 8-2	
		(abandoned after 75 minutes, owing to bad light)		
	16	Barking Woodville (h)	W 6-0	1,000
	20	2nd Coldstream Guards (h)	W 2-1	

Date	Opponent	Result	Attendance
Sep 23	3rd Coldstream Guards (h)	W 4-1	
Oct 11	Luton Town (h)	W 4-3	1,000
21	Folkestone (h)	W 3-1	750
Nov 27	Queens Park Rangers (a)	L 0-4	
Dec 23	Grays United (h)	W 12-0	500
26	Crewe Alexandra (h)	D 1-1	1,000
Mar 24	Sheppey United (h)	L 0-2	1,500
Apr 7	Richmond Association (h)	L 3-7	700
11	Queens Park Rangers (h)	L 0-3	250
16	Darlington (h)	L 2-5	2,000
25	Rest of Bucks & Contiguous Counties League (h)	D 0-0	
28	Chesham Town (h)	W 5-1	

1900/01

Date	Opponent	Result	Attendance
Sep 3	Chesham Town (a)	W 3-0	250
12	Richmond Association (h)	W 8-1	500
26	West Norwood (h)	W 6-1	200
Oct 17	Herts FA XI (h)	W 4-2	
Dec 25	Bishop Auckland (h)	W 5-3	
26	Burton Swifts (h)	W 5-1	3,000
Feb 25	Luton Town (a)	L 0-3	
Mar 16	Queens Park Rangers (h)	L 2-4	750
27	Luton Town (h)	L 1-3	
Apr 5	Chesham Town (h)	W 4-0	1,500
8	Darlington (h)	W 5-1	1,500
13	Rushden (h)	W 6-0	500
20	Burslem Port Vale (h)	D 0-0	
24	West Ham United (h)	L 0-1	50

1901/02

Date	Opponent	Result	Attendance
Sep 2	Luton Town (a)	L 0-5	2,000
4	Luton Town (h)	D 1-1	2,000
25	Brentford (h)	W 3-0	200
Oct 23	Hertfordshire FA (h)	W 2-1	350
Nov 7	Brentford (a)	D 1-1	150
Dec 14	Doncaster Rovers (h)	L 1-4	
25	Kettering Combination (h)	W 8-0	
26	Oxford City (h)	D 2-2	1,500
	(benefit match for the professionals)		
Mar 5	Aldenham School (a)	W 4-0	
22	Luton Town (h)	W 6-2	1,000
29	Millwall (a)	L 1-6	2,000
Apr 17	Cheshunt (h)	D 2-2	50
26	Richmond Association (h)	W 4-1	
30	Preston North End (h)	L 1-3	

1902/03

Date	Opponent	Result	Attendance
Sep 1	Civil Service (h)	W 3-2	500
3	Luton Town (h)	D 2-2	1,000
8	Luton Town (a)	L 0-3	1,000
Nov 15	Grays United (h)	W 4-1	
Dec 26	Bishop Auckland (h)	L 1-4	1,000
Feb 7	Oxford City (h)	L 1-2	500
Apr 10	Kensington Town (h)	W 5-1	
11	Darlington (h)	W 7-0	
13	Scottish Amateurs (h)	W 6-0	1,500

1903/04

Date	Opponent	Result	Attendance
Sep 1	Civil Service (h)	D 1-1	400
2	Luton Town (a)	L 0-3	2,000
7	New Brompton (a)	D 1-1	
9	Luton Town (h)	W 3-0	1,000
Sep 16	Hampstead (h)	W 2-0	
19	South West Ham (h)	W 11-0	
Oct 6	Bedfordshire Regiment (h)	W 8-0	
28	New Brompton (h)	W 2-1	400
Nov 7	Millwall Reserves (h)	W 6-0	500
25	Ilford (h)	W 4-2	
Jan 30	Vulcans (h)	W 13-0	150
Mar 26	Lincoln City (h)	W 2-0	2,500
Apr 1	Leicester Fosse (h)	W 2-1	3,500
2	Northampton Town (h)	W 5-1	2,500
4	French Professionals (h)	W 9-1	3,000
21	Ilford (a)	W 4-3	

1904/05

Date	Opponent	Result	Attendance
Sep 1	Civil Service (h)	W 3-0	800
Feb 4	Northampton Town (h)	W 1-0	1,500
Mar 4	Clapton (h)	W 2-1	1,000

1906/07

Date	Opponent	Result	Attendance
Apr 17	Apsley & District (a)	L 2-3	1,000

1907/08

Date	Opponent	Result	Attendance
Sep 4	Luton Town (h)	W 4-0	2,000
9	Luton Town (a)	L 0-2	
Feb 1	Clapton Orient (h)	W 4-1	
Apr 29	Southend United (a)	L 0-6	
30	Croydon Common (a)	L 1-5	

1909/10

Date	Opponent	Result	Attendance
Feb 14	Chesham Town (a)	W 9-3	

1910/11

Date	Opponent	Result	Attendance
Sep 1	Luton Town (a)	L 2-7	
7	Luton Town (h)	W 3-2	1,600
Oct 3	Treharris (a)	L 1-4	

1911/12

Date	Opponent	Result	Attendance
Sep 6	Luton Town (a)	L 2-7	
Nov 8	Herts County (h)	W 4-2	

1912/13

Date	Opponent	Result	Attendance
Oct 12	Luton Town (a)	D 1-1	
Jan 11	Luton Town (h)	W 2-0	
Apr 9	Tottenham Hotspur (h)	D 0-0	2,000

1913/14

Date	Opponent	Result	Attendance
Jan 10	Brentford (h)	W 2-1	
Apr 13	Newport County (a)	L 1-2	

1914/15

Date	Opponent	Result	Attendance
Jan 16	Luton Town (a)	D 1-1	
Feb 6	Luton Town (a)	L 1-2	1,000
May 1	Military XI (h)	W 4-1	

1919/20

Date	Opponent	Result	Attendance
Oct 15	Luton Town (a)	W 3-1	2,000
Jan 10	Merthyr Town (a)	-- 0-0	2,000
	(abandoned after an hour, owing to heavy rain)		
Apr 9	Mid Rhondda (a)	W 3-2	
15	Pontypridd (a)	-- 3-2	
	(abandoned after 80 minutes, owing to waterlogged pitch)		
28	Luton Town (h)	W 4-0	
	(Alex Stewart benefit match)		

1920/21

Date	Opponent	Result	Attendance
Sep 22	Tottenham Hotspur (h)	W 4-2	4,500
	(in aid of the family of the late Tom Coulson, trainer)		
Dec 18	Norwich City (a)	L 2-4	1,500
Mar 9	Queens Park Rangers (h)	W 4-1	
	(Fred Gregory/Skilly Williams benefit match)		

Apr	28	Hertfordshire FA (at St Albans)	L 1-3	4,000

1922/23

Dec	2	Queens Park Rangers (h)	D 1-1	1,500
Mar	14	Luton Town (a)	W 4-2	800
Apr	12	Hertfordshire FA (at St Albans)	W 5-2	
	18	Luton Town (h)	L 0-2	

1923/24

Dec	1	Cambridge University (h)	L 0-3	3,000
Apr	28	Luton Town (a)	L 0-1	300
	30	Luton Town (h)	D 2-2	100

(Fred Gregory benefit match)

1924/25

Apr	28	Chelsea (h)	L 1-2	2,000

(Fred Foxall benefit match)

1925/26

Jan	9	Queens Park Rangers (a)	W 3-2	5,000

1927/28

Apr	25	St Albans City (h)	W 4-3	2,951

(Frank Smith benefit match)

1928/29

Sep	13	St Albans City (a)	W 5-4	2,500

1929/30

Apr	30	Queens Park Rangers (h)	L 3-5	1,100

(George Prior benefit match)

1932/33

Nov	26	Corinthians (h)	W 3-2	4,477
May	3	Luton Town (h)	L 2-5	1,000

(Arthur Woodward benefit match)

1933/34

Dec	9	Doncaster Rovers (a)	L 2-3	1,500
May	2	The Army (h)	W 4-1	500

1934/35

Apr	29	Luton Town (a)	D 4-4	1,000

1935/36

Sep	8	Ajax (Amsterdam) (a)	W 2-0	6,000
Oct	23	Holland (a)	L 1-2	22,000

1936/37

Sep	28	Fulham (h)	W 2-0	1,369

(Tommy Barnett benefit match)

Jan	30	Chesterfield (a)	L 0-4	

1937/38

Oct	14	Tottenham Hotspur (at Bury St Edmunds)	D 3-3	

1938/39

Aug	20	Luton Town (a)	L 1-2	9,103

(in aid of the Football League Jubilee Benefit Fund)

Feb	15	A Netherlands XI (a)	W 4-1	10,000
Apr	19	Wisbech Town (a)	W 3-0	
May	6	Wealdstone (a)	D 1-1	

1947/48

Dec	20	Bath City (a)	L 1-2	
May	8	Edgware Town (a)	W 3-1	

(for the Edgware Charity Cup)

1948/49

Dec	11	Ipswich Town (a)	D 2-2	3,153
May	11	Edgware Town (a)	L 1-2	

(for the Edgware Charity Cup)

1950/51

Apr	30	Star XI (h)	D 2-2	2,281

(Joe Harper benefit match)

May	10	National Luxembourg (h)	W 5-1	3,232
	12	Wealdstone (a)	W 4-2	

1951/52

Dec	5	Headington United (a)	L 3-4	7,000

1952/53

Mar	9	Gloucester City (a)	W 3-2	1,400
	18	Hereford United (a)	L 0-2	4,413
	23	Worcester City (a)	W 2-1	
Apr	27	London All-Star XI (h)	L 2-4	6,373

(Tommy Eggleston/Jimmy Jones benefit match)

1953/54

Oct	13	Luton Town (h)	D 1-1	12,294

(The first floodlit match at Vicarage Road. This and all subsequent matches v Luton Town in this section up to and including 30th April 1962, and also that played on 10th May 1983, were for the Rigby Taylor Cup.)

	19	Pegasus (h)	W 2-1	11,005
	27	Stoke City (h)	W 4-2	11,212
Nov	10	Brentford (h)	W 4-1	11,538
Dec	12	Southampton (h)	D 1-1	5,212
Jan	9	Northampton Town (a)	L 0-3	2,877
	25	Hajduk (Yugoslavia) (h)	W 1-0	11,524
Feb	8	FC Wien (Austria) (h)	W 1-0	7,268
	19	Middlesbrough (h)	W 3-1	6,513
	22	Portuguesa des Desportos (Brazil) (h)	L 2-5	14,105
Mar	15	England Amateur XI (h)	W 2-1	7,744
	24	Luton Town (a)	L 1-4	6,122
Apr	6	All-Star XI (h)	D 3-3	18,000

(Jimmy Kelly/Phil Nolan benefit match)

1954/55

Oct	12	Borussia (Dortmund) (h)	W 4-1	12,430
	19	Port Vale (h)	W 2-1	7,790
	25	Simmering (Vienna) (h)	-- 1-0	7,267

(abandoned after 57 minutes, owing to fog)

Nov	1	Vienna Athletic (h)	W 2-0	4,968
	30	Liverpool (h)	W 3-2	4,699
Feb	15	Leeds United (h)	W 2-0	6,328
Mar	14	Luton Town (h)	L 0-2	6,185
	22	St Mirren (h)	D 2-2	4,010
Apr	4	Third Lanark (h)	W 2-1	3,625
	20	Southall (a)	D 0-0	6,000
	28	Kings Langley (a)	W 6-2	
May	3	All-Star XI (h)	W 7-3	10,000

(Benefit Fund match - part proceeds to reserve player Harry Bennett, retired owing to injury)

	7	Berkhamsted Town (a)	W 8-1	1,800

1955/56

Oct	10	Blackpool (h)	L 1-4	9,391
Nov	7	Cardiff City (h)	W 5-2	3,388
Jan	27	Mansfield Town (a)	W 5-4	3,190
	31	Sturm Graz (Austria) (h)	D 1-1	644
Feb	7	St Albans City (h)	W 4-0	1,143
	14	Peterborough United (h)	W 1-0	1,708
Mar	12	Luton Town (h)	L 0-2	4,648
Apr	10	All-Stars XI (h)	W 6-1	4,709

(Jimmy Wilson benefit match)

	19	Rampa (Uruguay) (h)	W 4-2	5,651
	30	Peterborough United (a)	D 2-2	3,155
May	2	Hemel Hempstead Town (a)	W 3-2	1,300

1956/57

Oct	16	Falkirk (h)	W 2-1	3,583
Jan	4	Brentford (a)	W 2-0	2,650
	26	Luton Town (h)	L 3-4	6,644
Feb	7	Headington United (a)	W 2-0	3,000
	19	Ex-Watford XI (h)	D 1-1	1,908

(Ernie Bateman/Johnny Meadows/
Frank Mitchell benefit match)

Mar	18	All-Star Managers XI (h)	W 2-1	3,120

(Ernie Bateman/Johnny Meadows/
Frank Mitchell benefit match)

Apr	4	Celtic (h)	L 0-4	9,712
	16	Kings Langley (a)	W 5-2	
	24	Hemel Hempstead Town (a)	W 7-2	
May	2	All-Star XI (h)	L 3-5	3,472

(Ernie Bateman/Johnny Meadows/
Frank Mitchell benefit match)

1957/58

Nov	25	All-Star XI (h)	W 4-2	1,775

(Colin Bateman/Roy Brown/Maurice
Cook/Bill Shipwright benefit match)

Jan	4	Chelmsford City (a)	L 2-3	2,251
Mar	4	British Army (h)	W 3-2	2,771

(Colin Bateman/Roy Brown/Bill Shipwright benefit match)

May	1	Kings Langley (a)	W 6-1	

1958/59

Apr	30	All-Star XI (h)	L 4-5	3,048

(George Catleugh/Peter Walker benefit match)

1959/60

Oct	20	Fulham (h)	L 2-7	9,728
Dec	2	Folkestone (a)	D 1-1	1,100
Jan	4	Margate (a)	W 5-2	1,950
	25	Margate (a)	D 2-2	1,328
Feb	16	Ramsgate Athletic (a)	W 2-1	
May	6	Charlton Athletic (h)	L 2-3	2,688

1960/61

Aug	13	British Olympic XI (at Uxbridge)	L 1-2	
Nov	21	Margate (a)	W 4-2	1,071
Jan	2	Ramsgate Athletic (a)	W 4-1	
Mar	2	Nottingham Forest (h)	D 1-1	3,340
	20	Luton Town (h)	W 2-1	3,296
May	1	Herts FA XI (h)	W 5-1	1,761
	4	Swansea Town (h)	L 1-3	1,657

1961/62

Aug	14	Kettering Town (a)	W 5-2	2,500
Feb	5	Slovan Bratislava (h)	W 3-1	4,219
	14	Wealdstone (a)	W 3-2	3,000
	19	FA Amateur XI (h)	D 0-0	2,943
Apr	30	Luton Town (h)	W 2-0	1,431

1962/63

Aug	4	Cambridge United (a)	W 3-1	1,500
	11	Brentford (a)	D 0-0	
	14	Aldershot (h)	W 4-2	
Nov	20	Ramsgate Athletic (a)	L 1-2	

1963/64

Aug	8	Newry Town (a)	W 5-0	
	12	Distillery (a)	W 5-2	
	13	Gillingham (h)	L 0-1	3,267
	17	Brentford (a)	D 2-2	

Sep	24	Oxford United (a)	W 4-1	3,442
Nov	12	East Anglian Cup XI (at Wealdstone)	W 7-0	
Feb	17	Romford (a)	D 2-2	
Apr	14	Arsenal (h)	W 1-0	8,253

(George Catleugh testimonial match)

	28	Bedford Town (a)	W 2-1	2,249

1964/65

Aug	8	Oxford United (h)	L 1-2	3,569
	12	Oxford United (a)	D 1-1	5,000
	15	Bedford Town (a)	W 4-3	1,317
	17	Coventry City (h)	L 0-1	3,914
Dec	5	Southend United (a)	L 1-2	1,138
Feb	8	Wealdstone (a)	W 2-1	2,000
Mar	30	St Albans City (a)	D 1-1	
Apr	5	Hendon (a)	W 3-2	

1965/66

Aug	7	Southall (a)	W 4-0	
	14	Leyton Orient (a)	W 5-0	
	16	Chelmsford City (a)	W 2-1	2,500
Nov	1	England Amateur XI (h)	W 3-1	2,600
	10	Canterbury City (a)	W 3-2	960
Mar	14	Slough Town (a)	W 4-1	2,000
May	3	West Herts Select XI (at Berkhamsted)	W 3-1	

1966/67

Aug	6	Gravesend & Northfleet (a)	W 2-1	650
	8	Chelmsford City (a)	L 0-1	1,483
	12	Wealdstone (a)	W 2-1	1,000
	15	Brentford (h)	D 0-0	
Sep	12	England Amateur XI (h)	W 4-1	1,070
Oct	3	Corinthian-Casuals (h)	W 7-0	933

(for the Sheriff of London Shield)

Nov	23	Ramsgate Athletic (a)	W 4-1	512

1967/68

Aug	5	Luton Town (a)	D 1-1	5,360
	8	Norwich City (h)	L 1-2	3,483
Oct	16	Great Britain Olympic XI (h)	W 3-2	1,270
Nov	6	West Ham United (h)	W 3-2	8,792

(Dave Carr testimonial match)

Feb	12	Great Britain Olympic XI (h)	L 0-1	
May	13	Luton Town (h)	D 1-1	5,967

(testimonial match for Pat Molloy, trainer)

1968/69

Jul	30	Hartlepool (a)	L 0-1	3,382
Aug	2	Darlington (a)	L 0-1	1,112
	5	Bradford City (a)	W 2-1	2,157
Jan	22	A Jersey XI (a)	W 1-0	3,500
May	8	Arsenal (h)	L 1-2	15,229

(Ken Furphy testimonial match)

	31	Sliema Wanderers (Malta) (a)	W 3-0	
Jun	1	Valetta (Malta) (a)	W 2-1	

1969/70

Jul	26	Morton (h)	W 2-1	5,452
	28	Waterford (a)	D 1-1	
	30	Evenwood Town (a)	W 3-0	500
Aug	1	Darlington (a)	L 2-3	
	4	Bohemians (Prague) (h)	W 5-1	5,483
Sep	8	Folkestone Town (a)	W 3-1	600
Dec	9	Gornik Zabrze (Poland) (h)	D 0-0	8,544
Feb	18	First Tower United (Jersey) (a)	W 6-1	250

1970/71

Aug	1	Chesterfield (a)	W 2-1	
	3	Bradford City (a)	D 0-0	3,408
	8	Rotherham United (a)	D 0-0	6,188
Nov	23	Great Britain Olympic XI (h)	L 2-4	1,999
Jun	10	Brno (Czechoslovakia) (a)	L 1-3	10,000
	12	Liberac (Czechoslovakia) (a)	D 1-1	2,000
	14	Bohemians (Czechoslovakia) (a)	L 0-1	

1971/72

Jul	31	Rotherham United (h)	W 4-0	
Aug	4	Bohemians (Prague) (h)	W 1-0	
	7	Notts County (h)	D 3-3	4,597

1972/73

Jul	29	Nottingham Forest (h)	L 1-2	3,280
Aug	1	Exeter City (a)	W 3-1	1,442
	5	Reading (a)	L 0-4	2,370
	7	Hillingdon Borough (a)	L 0-2	
	9	Dover (a)	L 0-1	675
May	1	Wolverhampton Wanderers (h)	D 2-2	6,244
		(testimonial match for Pat Molloy, trainer)		
	7	Hillingdon Borough (a)	L 2-3	
	8	Marlow Town (a)	L 0-2	

1973/74

Aug	11	Rotherham United (a)	D 1-1	1,618
	18	Luton Town (h)	L 1-2	4,651
Sep	25	Boreham Wood (a)	W 5-0	1,700
Oct	29	Wealdstone (a)	W 5-2	
		(John Pearce benefit match)		
May	6	Oxford United (at Clanfield)	L 0-1	
		(for the Clanfield Cup)		
	7	Wolverhampton Wanderers (h)	W 3-2	5,728
		(Duncan Welbourne testimonial match)		

1974/75

Aug	3	Harlow Town (a)	W 2-0	
	5	Millwall (h)	W 1-0	
	7	Hillingdon Borough (a)	W 3-1	
	10	Lincoln City (a)	W 1-0	800
Jan	24	Tottenham Hotspur (h)	L 2-3	7,475
Feb	14	Morton (h)	D 0-0	1,521
May	6	Sheffield United (h)	D 2-2	2,740
		(Johnny Williams testimonial match)		

1975/76

HSC = Herts Senior Cup (Watford were runners-up)

Aug	2	Wimbledon (a)	W 4-2	
	6	Aldershot (h)	W 6-1	1,254
	9	Weymouth (a)	L 1-3	
Dec	10	Boreham Wood (a) *(HSC)*	W 3-2	739
Feb	18	Tring Town (h) *(HSC)*	W 5-0	852
Mar	10	Queens Park Rangers (h)	L 0-6	5,734
		(Ian Morgan testimonial match)		
	23	Letchworth Town (a) *(HSC)*	W 2-1	600
Apr	30	All-Star XI (h)	L 1-4	1,500
		(testimonial match for Ron Rollitt, club secretary)		
May	3	Hemel Hempstead Town (a)	W 2-1	400
	4	Bishops Stortford (at Hitchin)*(HSC)*	L 1-3	

1976/77

KCC = Kent Charity Cup

Jul	31	Luton Town (h) *(KCC)*	L 0-1	3,357
Aug	3	Portsmouth (a) *(KCC)*	L 2-4	2,690

Aug	7	Oxford United (h) *(KCC)*	W 3-0	1,759
May	16	Hillingdon Borough (a)	W 3-0	
	20	Wealdstone (a)	W 2-1	1,500

1977/78

HSC - Herts Senior Cup (Watford won it. The first-team was fielded in the Quarter-Final and Final only.)

Jul	30	Oxford United (h)	W 3-0	
Aug	3	Shrewsbury Town (a)	L 0-1	
	5	Colchester United (a)	W 2-1	719
	8	Barnet (a)	D 1-1	720
Sep	19	Berkhamsted Sunday Lge XI (at Tring)	W 6-2	
Feb	27	Barnet (h) *(HSC)*	W 5-1	1,798
May	5	Wembley (a)	W 2-0	500
	8	Tring Town (h) *(HSC)*	W 2-1	1,700

1978/79

Jul	29	Morton (a)	L 1-5	3,640
Aug	1	Clydebank (a)	W 1-0	806
	3	Airdrieonians (a)	W 3-1	
	8	Wolverhampton Wanderers (h)	L 0-2	5,226
Nov	1	Scarborough (a)	D 1-1	1,146
Feb	5	Denmark Under-21 (h)	W 2-0	3,536
May	11	Sochaux (France) (a)	D 0-0	
	15	Old Lincoln XI (a)	W 2-0	2,544
	22	Gibraltar XI (a)	W 1-0	2,000

1979/80

Jul	28	Morton (a)	L 1-2	3,500
	30	St Mirren (a)	L 0-2	3,600
Aug	1	Airdrieonians (a)	L 2-3	1,500
	3	Ayr United (a)	D 2-2	2,000

1980/81

Jul	29	Torquay United (a)	W 3-0	1,149
	31	Plymouth Argyle (a)	D 1-1	1,527
Aug	2	Exeter City (a)	W 2-0	1,546
Feb	9	Red Star (Belgrade) (h)	D 2-2	6,127
Mar	16	Vancouver Whitecaps (h)	W 1-0	10,071
May	11	Bognor Regis Town (a)	D 2-2	1,200

1981/82

Aug	4	Hitchin Town (a)	W 4-0	407
	6	Boreham Wood (a)	W 3-2	
	8	Barnet (a)	W 1-0	
May	10	Brentford (a)	W 2-1	2,089
	11	Lokeren (Belgium) (h)	W 2-1	4,393

The next six matches were played on tour in Australia, New Zealand and Malaysia

	20	Victoria State XI (a)	W 4-0	7,000
	23	New Zealand World Cup XI (a)	W 1-0	18,000
	26	New Zealand World Cup XI (a)	D 1-1	21,000
	29	New Zealand World Cup XI (a)	W 2-0	
Jun	2	Malaysia National XI (a)	W 6-1	
	4	Kuala Trengganu (a)	W 4-0	

1982/83

Jul	29	Valerengen (Norway) (a)	W 5-1	2,066
Aug	2	Kongsvinger (Norway) (a)	W 9-0	
	4	Kvik (Norway) (a)	W 4-0	2,000
	5	Hamerkameratene (Norway) (a)	L 1-2	
Nov	3	Burton Albion (a)	W 5-0	1,727
Nov	29	Exeter City (a)	W 6-1	2,046
Mar	28	Corinthian-Casuals (h)	W 6-1	3,686
		(for the Sheriff of London Shield)		

Apr	19	Israel Olympic XI (h)	D 2-2	3,034
May	10	Luton Town (h)	W 4-0	7,225

(Ross Jenkins testimonial match, and
for the Rigby Taylor Cup)

	19	Team America (in Jamaica)	D 1-1	33,000
Jun	1	Chinese National XI (a)	W 3-1	80,000
	5	A Shanghai XI (a)	W 2-1	40,000
	7	Chinese National XI (a)	W 5-1	70,000

1983/84

Aug	13	Reading (a)	L 1-2	1,352
	16	Swindon Town (a)	W 5-0	1,800
	18	Colchester United (a)	L 1-2	961
	20	Oxford United (a)	L 3-4	2,378
Oct	11	Israel Olympic XI (a)	L 0-1	

1984/85

Aug	4	Dumbarton (a)	L 1-2	4,000
	6	Morton (a)	W 3-2	4,000
	11	Linfield (a)	W 4-2	

The next two matches were part of a four-club knock-out
tournament in Majorca

	17	Barcelona	L 1-2	22,000
	18	Real Mallorca	L 1-2	30,000
	21	Grimsby Town (a)	D 2-2	2,189
Sep	19	Phil Neale XI (at Lincoln)	D 1-1	2,134
Nov	7	Burton Albion (a)	W 6-0	1,005
Dec	4	Chesham United (a)	W 3-1	3,000
Apr	3	Chalfont St Peter (a)	W 2-0	2,500
May	20	Blackpool (a)	W 5-2	4,000
	30	Sheffield Wednesday (in Bangkok)	D 0-0	2,000

(lost 2-3 in penalty shoot-out)

1985/86

Aug	6	Aldershot (a)	W 3-0	870
	8	Swindon Town (a)	W 3-0	2,224
	10	Hull City (a)	L 0-2	3,900
Sep	17	Luton Town (a)	D 1-1	2,120
	30	Irthlingborough Diamonds (a)	W 7-1	893
Oct	22	Harlow Town (a)	W 9-1	900
Nov	12	Hertfordshire FA (h)	W 4-0	383
Dec	2	St Albans City (a)	W 3-1	600
Feb	15	Exeter City (a)	W 4-0	804

1986/87

Jul	27	Jarbo (Sweden) (a)	W 3-1	1,420
	28	Norrstrands (Sweden) (a)	W 1-0	1,660
	31	Nora (Sweden) (a)	W 1-0	
Aug	3	Krylbo (Sweden) (a)	W 8-0	2,046
	4	Vasteras (Sweden) (a)	D 1-1	2,363
	5	Heart of Midlothian (a)	L 1-2	8,500
	9	Portsmouth (a)	L 0-3	2,269
	11	Corby Town (a)	W 3-0	2,240
	13	Millwall (a)	L 1-2	1,605
	16	Stoke City (a)	D 0-0	2,199
Sep	29	Chelsea (h)	W 3-2	2,675

(Tom Walley testimonial match)

Oct	20	Hungerford Town (a)	W 10-0	276
Dec	1	March Town (a)	W 9-0	600
Jan	6	Exmouth Town (a)	W 6-0	1,406
	17	Reykjavik Select XI (Iceland) (a)	D 1-1	850
Feb	17	Dorking (a)	W 3-0	1,264
Mar	18	Sao Paolo (Brazil) (in Trinidad)	D 1-1	22,000

(lost 5-6 in penalty shoot-out)

May	12	Heart of Midlothian (h)	W 4-3	4,402

(Steve Sherwood testimonial match)

The next five matches were part of an eight-team tournament
for the Great Wall of China Cup, which was won by Watford

	23	North Korea XI (in Nanjing)	W 1-0	
	25	Hubei (in Nanjing)	W 2-0	
	27	China National XI (in Nanjing)	W 2-0	30,000
	29	Liaon Ning (in Shanghai)	W 1-0	
	31	China National XI (in Shanghai)	W 2-0	

(after extra time)

1987/88

Jul	21	Jaro (Finland) (a)	W 5-0	2,178
	23	Tegs SK (Sweden) (a)	W 9-0	
	25	Hudiksvalls ABK/Iggesund HIF (Sweden) (a)	W 7-0	
	28	GIF Sundsvall (Sweden) (a)	W 4-2	2,561
	30	Anundsjo (Sweden) (a)	W 5-1	2,453
Aug	5	AFC Bournemouth (a)	W 4-3	3,037
	9	Crystal Palace (a)	W 2-1	2,976
Sep	7	RAF Uxbridge (a)	W 3-0	500
Nov	30	Northampton Town (a)	L 2-3	1,879
Jan	6	Tunisia (a)	W 2-1	15,000

1988/89

Jul	30	Dawlish (a)	D 0-0	640
Aug	2	Exeter City (a)	D 1-1	1,170
	6	Bristol Rovers (a)	W 3-0	984
	13	Gillingham (a)	W 2-1	1,500
	16	Luton Town (h)	W 3-1	7,213

(Luther Blissett testimonial match)

	19	Chester City	D 0-0	1,858

1989/90

Aug	4	Exmouth Town (a)	W 2-1	800
	7	Exeter City (a)	L 2-3	1,356
	10	Halifax Town (a)	D 1-1	857
	12	Dulwich Hamlet (at Fisher Athletic)	W 3-0	100
	14	Aston Villa (h)	L 1-6	4,775

(Kenny Jackett testimonial match)

Oct	9	Burgess Hill Town (a)	W 2-0	1,200
Dec	5	Merthyr Tydfil (a)	W 4-0	1,083
May	20	Hamrun Spartans (Malta) (a)	L 1-3	700

1990/91

HSC = Herts Senior Cup (first team fielded in 2nd Round)

Jul	26	Oskarshamm AIK (Sweden) (a)	W 1-0	734
	28	Virserums SGF (Sweden) (a)	W 8-0	400
	30	Raslatts SK (Sweden) (a)	W 2-1	2,461
Aug	1	IFK Orby (Sweden) (a)	W 7-0	752
	2	BK Astrio (Sweden) (a)	L 0-2	
	4	Gallstad AIS (Sweden) (a)	W 2-0	645
	11	Norwich City (h)	D 1-1	2,871
	15	Hibernian (a)	L 2-3	3,132
	18	Reading (a)	L 0-2	1,746
Jan	29	Ware (h) (HSC)	W 3-0	366

1991/92

Jul	18	Kuwait Olympic XI (at Woodside)	L 0-1	
	20	Eid (Norway) (a)	W 2-1	
	23	Televag (Norway) (a)	W 3-2	
	25	SK Brann (Norway) (a)	W 3-0	
	27	Follese (Norway) (a)	L 1-2	650
Aug	3	Norwich City (h)	W 2-0	2,111

Aug	7	Arsenal (h)	L	1-3	10,019
	9	Queens Park Rangers (h)	L	1-4	2,969

1992/93

Jul	18	Elburton Villa (a)	W	2-0	700
	19	Dawlish (a)	W	7-0	450
	21	Buckfastleigh (a)	W	5-0	450
	23	Saltash United (a)	W	4-1	
	25	Torquay United (at Kingsteinton)	D	0-0	1,600
	31	Kettering Town (a)	L	0-2	691
Aug	4	Barnet (a)	L	1-3	1,357
	8	Tottenham Hotspur (h)	L	0-1	5,567

1993/94

Jul	17	Saltash United (a)	W	1-0	
	20	Truro City (a)	W	3-1	
	22	Tiverton Town (a)	W	3-0	
	24	Taunton Town (a)	W	4-3	
	27	Corby Town (a)	W	4-1	
Aug	4	Queens Park Rangers (h)	D	1-1	5,078

(Nigel Gibbs testimonial match)

	7	Swansea City (a)	D	2-2	2,019

1994/95

Jul	22	Colchester United (a)	W	2-1	568
	25	Leyton Orient (a)	L	2-3	1,419
	27	Chelsea (h)	L	0-1	7,079

(Gary Porter testimonial match)

Aug	3	Fulham (a)	D	1-1	1,502
	6	Tottenham Hotspur (h)	D	1-1	14,021

1995/96

Jul	24	Jonsereds IF (Sweden) (a)	D	1-1	200
	26	Kungshamns IF (Sweden) (a)	D	1-1	350
	27	Herrljünja SK (Sweden) (a)	W	3-0	550
	29	Ränneslovs GIS (Sweden) (a)	W	5-0	250
	31	Swedish Select XI (a)	W	7-0	909
Aug	1	TG&IF (Sweden) (a)	D	3-3	700
	5	Tottenham Hotspur (h)	L	0-2	7,354

1996/97

Aug	2	Chesham United (a)	W	2-0	1,764
	6	Oxford United (h)	W	1-0	2,632
	9	Cambridge United (h)	W	3-0	1,802
May	16	Arsenal (h)	L	1-4	7,470

(testimonial match for Les Simmons, groundsman)

1997/98

The next two matches were played in Kaunus, Lithuania, as part of a four-club knock-out tournament

Jul	12	Vladikavkaz (Russia)	L	1-2	
	13	Jas Bardejov (Slovakia)	D	1-1	

(lost 4-5 in penalty shoot-out)

	16	Fakenham Town (a)	W	4-0	
	22	FC Hameenllinna (Finland) (a)	W	1-0	2,500
	26	FC Rips (Finland) (a)	W	2-0	
	29	Keski-Suomi All-Stars (Finland) (a)	W	4-0	
Aug	2	Wimbledon (h)	L	1-3	3,663
May	11	Petahtikva (Israel) (a)	L	0-1	

PART SIX

Players' Career Records

THE following career records are for all players used in peacetime competitive matches to the end of the 1997/98 season. 'Career Span' indicates the calendar years of the first and last peacetime appearance. 'League' refers to both Southern League and Football League matches (including Test Matches and Play-off matches). 'Others' includes the South-Eastern League, but only those games in which the first-team was fielded (see introduction to Part Three). Figures after '+' are appearances as a used substitute. Penalty-shoot-out goals are excluded. The playing position is that in which the player usually appeared for Watford, and the abbreviations used are: G (goalkeeper), D (defender), FB (full-back), WH (wing-half), CH (centre-half), HB (half-back), M (midfielder), F (forward), W (winger), IF (inside-forward), and CF (centre-forward).

	Position	Career Span	LEAGUE Apps	LEAGUE Goals	FA CUP Apps	FA CUP Goals	OTHERS Apps	OTHERS Goals
C.J. (Chris) Adams	W	1954-1956	75	5	6	1	1	
L.E. (Laurie) Adams	IF	1952	1					
P.A.O. (Tony) Agana	W	1987-1988	12 +3	1	2		2 +1	2
V.D. (Vic) Akers	FB	1975	22		1		3	
E. (Ned) Allan	FB	1902-1903	20		1		3	
W. (Watty) Allan	IF	1900-1901	18	1	1			
D.S. (Doug) Allder	W	1977	1					
Derrick S. Allen	W	1956	6	1	2		2	
Malcolm Allen	F	1985-1988	27+12	5	6 +8	6	4 +1	2
Wayne A. Allison	F	1989-1990	6 +1					
Julian Alsford	CH	1992-1993	9 +4	1			3	
H.G. (Andy) Anderson	W	1896	8	2	1		4	
J.O. Anderson	F	1894			1		2	1
T.C. (Tommy) Anderson	F	1957-1965	73	14			2	2
L.T.A. (Len) Andrews	F	1924-1925	38	6	2	1		
Wayne M.H. Andrews	F	1996-1997	16+12	4	0 +2		5 +2	2
H.A. (Harry) Anstiss	IF	1923-1924	18	5	4			
Arthur O. Ardley	WH	1894-1898	10		3		8	
S. Craig Armstrong	FB	1997	15					
G.J. (Gerry) Armstrong	F	1980-1983	50+26	12	5 +2	2	11 +3	5
J.H. (Jimmy) Armstrong	CH	1933-1939	187	2	14		15	
W.B. (Wally) Armstrong	CF	1927	1					
Thomas E. Ashbridge	IF	1913-1914	21	9	2	5		
Barry J. Ashby	CH	1989-1994	101+13	3	4		8 +1	
William G. Ashmole	F	1920	1					
C.L. (Charlie) Aston	FB	1905-1908	104	1	6		29	
Bryan H. Atkinson	D	1955-1956	20		1			
Paul G. Atkinson	W	1983-1984	8 +3		0 +2			
Duncan S. Auld	WH/F	1897	2		1			
A.W. Ayling	F	1896-1897	3				1	1
Ernest F. Bacon	WH	1920-1921	12					
G.R. Bacot	F	1889					2	1
George H. Badenoch	WH/W	1903-1906	80	9	9	1	36	7
H.O. (Bert) Badger	WH	1906-1908	54	5	2		13	2
John J. Bagshaw	CH	1921	14					

Name	Pos	Years						
Dennis L. Bailey	F	1994	2 +6	4				
A. Guthrie Baker	G	1897-1900	51		9		16	
J.S. (Jimmy) Baker	HB/IF	1925-1926	9	2				
J.D. (Dave) Bamber	F	1988	16 +2	3			4	1
H.E. (Bertie) Banks	IF	1903-1904	19	21	2	1	11	11
W.G. (Bill) Barber	WH	1957-1960	25		1		2	
David J. Bardsley	FB	1983-1987	97 +3	7	13 +1	1	7	1
Cecil Barnard	CF	1921	2	1				
C. Barnes	W	1904-1906	5	1	1	1	3	
David Barnes	FB	1994-1996	16		1			
Edward Barnes	G	1920	1					
George H. Barnes	W	1922-1924	5	1				
J.B. (Jack) Barnes	W	1931-1933	75	11	8			
John C.B. Barnes	W	1981-1987	232 +1	65	31	11	32	9
Peter Barnes	WH	1960-1962	10					
T.A. (Tommy) Barnett	IF	1928-1939	395	144	36	16	11	3
R.J. (Bob) Barnshaw	CH	1914-1921	58	4	3			
Ernest Barsby	D	1909-1910	4					
Frank Barson	CH	1928	10	1				
Harry Barton	CF	1903-1905	34	26	5		18	17
E.J. (Ted) Bassett	W	1919-1921	70	9	3			
Colin Bateman	FB	1954-1957	50		6			
E. (Ernie) Bateman	CH	1955-1956	23		1		1	
W.H. (Billy) Bates	W	1948-1949	13	1				
W.A. (Bill) Baxter	HB	1971-1972	11				1	
John T. Bayley	D	1900	4				2	
Darren S. Bazeley	F/FB	1990-1998	151+49	19	11 +1	3	18 +5	3
T.H. (Tuggy) Beach	F/D	1897-1902	40	16	9	2	12	4
Peter C.W.J. Beadle	F	1994-1995	12+11	1			1	
Roger J. Beament	G	1957	1					
S. (Syd) Beaumont	WH/F	1909-1911	27	1			3	3
W. (Bill) Beckett	IF	1945-1947	7	1	8	1		
Martin Becton	F	1909-1910	20	2	1		3	
Edmund Beevor	F	1891-1892					4	
John Bell	CF/IF	1924-1926	20	6	1			
R.M. (Bobby) Bell	FB	1957-1964	268	2	23		12	
H. (Bert) Bellamy	WH	1921-1923	36	2	1			
E.E. (Ted) Bennett	G	1953-1956	81		5			
M.D. (Micky) Benning	W	1959-1962	103	14	14	1	5	
Arthur C. Betts	FB	1907-1910	93		7		5	
D.G. (Dave) Bewley	FB	1953-1956	113	1	7			
W. (Billy) Biggar	G	1904-1910	217	1	17		49	1
C.R. (Charlie) Billington	CH	1957	14		1		2	
Charlie D.V. Birse	HB	1946-1947	7		2			
W. (Bill) Black	CF	1937-1938	16	3			4	4
Albert G. Blake	WH	1929-1933	28		1			
G.P. (Pat) Bland	G	1945			1			
Luther L. Blissett	F	1976-1992	369+46	148	32 +2	15	50 +4	23
M.J. (Mike) Block	W	1966-1967	11 +2	2				
Alfred Blyth	FB	1896-1897	3					
Reuben Blyth	WH	1895-1897	18		2		6	
J. (Johnnie) Blythe	WH	1911-1913	44		5		1	
Ian R. Bolton	D/M	1977-1983	233 +1	28	15	2	37 +1	6
Dennis J.T. Bond	M	1964-1977	271 +1	38	13	2	16	2
Dennis Booth	M	1977-1980	97 +3	2	6		11	
J.D. (Jimmy) Bowie	IF	1952-1955	125	39	5	1	1	
Stuart C. Brace	W	1965-1966	16	4	2	2		
Arthur D. Bradford	FB	1896	1					
Henry Bradford	W	1896	1					
J.H. (Jack) Bradshaw	IF	1919	1					
John Brandon	F	1895			1			
C. Bray	FB	1905					1	

Name	Pos	Years	App	Gls	App	Gls	App	Gls
B. (Ben) Brelsford	FB	1928-1930	25	1				
Guy A. Bristow	CH	1974-1976	18+5					
J. (Jimmy) Broad	CF	1926	1	1	1			
J. (Joe) Brooks	FB	1903-1907	106		8		53	2
M. (Matt) Broughton	W	1904-1907	14				1	
G.F. (George) Brown	CF/IF	1905-1906	3				2	
H. Roy Brown	F/CH	1953-1957	142	40	5	1	1	
J. (Joe) Brown	F	1937-1938	6	2			3	1
J.A. Brown	F	1889-1890					2	
R.H. (Bobby) Brown	F	1961-1963	28	10	2	1		
T.G. (Tommy) Brown	IF	1949-1953	108	11	5	1		
W. (Roland) Brown	W	1901-1904	57	4	4	1	12	2
W. (Bill) Brown	FB	1928-1935	220		21		8	
W.W. (Billy) Brunt	G	1890-1900	6				5	
C. (Chris) Bulling	HB	1911-1914	60	4	8		2	
Harold M. Bulling	FB	1911-1915	99	1	4		5	
F. (Freddie) Bunce	W	1955-1962	150	34	19	3	8	5
Eric R.C. Burgess	D	1964	3					
R. Burgess	FB	1897			1			
A. (Alf) Burr	HB	1893					2	
E. Busby	W	1897	10	2			2	
David Butler	FB	1970-1975	168	2	8	1	10	
S. (Steve) Butler	F	1991-1992	40+22	9	1		6+4	
John T. Button	WH	1897	3					
David S. Byrne	W	1990-1991	16+1	2			1	
Nigel I. Callaghan	W	1980-1991	215+19	42	25+1	3	35+3	7
J.W.H. (Joe) Calvert	G	1948	5					
Harry J. Capell	FB	1886-1888			4		7	
T.A.E. (Tommy) Carpenter	G	1950-1951	4					
D. (Dave) Carr	F	1965	10	3				
J.E.C. (Jimmy) Carr	W	1913-1914	18				1	
J.H. (Jack) Carter	CF	1933-1934	15	7	2	1		
W. (Wilf) Carter	WH	1920-1925	126	4	5			
Norman Case	CF	1950-1951	10	4				
Darren M. Caskey	M	1995	6	1				
Keith B. Cassells	F	1978-1980	6+6		1+1		2+1	
Francis J.A. Cassidy	M	1983					0+1	
George C. Catleugh	WH	1954-1964	293	15	19	1	15	1
Walter Catlin	CF/IF	1898					1	
J. (Jimmy) Chalmers	W	1901-1902	30	5	2	1		
Alec F.R. Chamberlain	G	1996-1998	50		5		3	
W. (Billy) Chapman	W	1928-1934	210	10	22		1	
K. (Ken) Charlery	F	1992-1993	45+3	13	1		3+1	
C.T. (Charlie) Chase	F	1946-1948	16	1				
Dennis Cheney	W	1948	18	5				
Steve R. Cherry	G	1995	4					
Gary P.S. Chivers	D	1987-1988	14		4		1	
C. (Sammy) Chung	F/HB	1957-1965	220	22	19	2	6	
G.C. Clark	D	1890-1891					3	
C.E. (Chris) Clarke	W	1966	1+1					
Tracey W. Clarke	F	1897-1898	12	2	1	2		
F.L. (Fred) Cleaver	F/HB	1908-1910	39	8	2	1	3	
A.E. (Archie) Clement	FB	1930-1931	14					
Peter T. Coffill	M	1975-1977	56+7	6	3	1	1+2	
Ephraim Colclough	F	1900-1901	17	1				
Arthur Coles	FB	1893					1	
Percy Coles	F	1888-1895			7	2	19	7
Walter S. Coles	F	1887-1895			12	10	25	30
W.T. (Theo) Coles	WH	1921	1					
E. (Ernie) Colledge	W	1924	1					
A.N. (Tony) Collins	W	1950-1957	107	9	5	1	1	1
R.M. (Mike) Collins	G	1958-1959	43		3		3	

Name	Pos	Years						
David J. Connolly	F	1995-1997	19 +7	10	3 +3	4	2	1
Maurice Cook	F	1953-1958	208	68	10	9	6	4
R.K. (Bobby) Cook	W	1951-1952	53	8	3	1		
W.H. (Billy) Cooke	FB	1954	10					
E. (Eddie) Cother	F/HB	1898-1899	8	1	1		6	
J.W. (Jack) Cother	FB	1898-1905	111		12		18	3
A.P. (Tony) Coton	G	1984-1990	235		32		24	
M.J. Cottam	F	1892					2	2
Frank Cotterill	F	1909-1910	13	4	2	2	1	
Ernest H. Cottrell	F	1901-1903	38	12	1		2	
Albert C. Cousins	F	1911	2				1	
Wilfred J. Coutanche	FB	1921-1923	6					
R. (Bob) Cowan	F/WH	1928-1929	6	1				
John M. Cowen	G	1965-1967	17					
A.G. Cox	WH	1899	1					
L.D. (Laurie) Craker	M/D	1973-1976	60 +6	4	2 +1		3	
J. Cramb	G	1913					1	
R.J. (Ron) Crisp	WH/F	1961-1965	89	14	5		7	3
Peter H.L. Croker	FB	1952-1953	23		3			
W. Croom	W	1905					1	1
H. (Bert) Crownshaw	CH	1909-1913	1				1	
J.F.(Jimmy) Crussell	IF	1925	1					
H. (Harry) Culverhouse	F	1891			2	2		
R. Horace Cumner	W	1948-1950	62	7	4			
J. (Johnny) Curran	G	1957-1958	30		1		2	
P.J. (Pat) Curran	IF	1946			4			
A.W. (Tony) Currie	M	1967-1968	17 +1	9	2		0 +1	
George H. Cutts	G	1921-1923	5		1			
B.E. (Ben) Dabbs	FB	1938	3					
William Dackers	D	1902-1903	26	1	2		1	
Malcolm O. Dalrymple	G	1974	5					
R.G. (Ron) Daly	IF	1950	3		1			
Arthur Daniels	W	1926-1930	136	16	10	1		
Alfred R. Darvill	CF	1925	1					
George Davenport	D	1896-1899	47	1	1		5	
Graham G. Davies	G	1947-1948	9					
Robert Davies	WH	1910-1911	15		2		1	
T. (Tom) Davies	WH	1933-1937	58	3	3		7	
W. (Taffy) Davies	W/IF	1931-1950	283	69	29	3	13	3
J. Davis	FB	1903-1904	1				1	
J. (Joe) Davison	FB	1927-1931	135	2	12			
Albert Day	CF	1949	4	1				
B.J. (Jimmy) Day	F	1952	3					
C.N. (Chris) Day	G	1997					2	
Roger A. Day	IF	1962	1					
E.J. (Eddie) Denton	M	1991	0 +2					
W.G. (Bill) Devan	IF	1933-1937	90	33	5	1	6	1
W. (Willie) Devine	W	1958-1959	30	6			1	
Alan E. Devonshire	M	1990-1991	23 +2	1	1		1	
H.J. Dewey	HB	1890-1891			2		4	
L.F. (Len) Dewick	G	1924	7					
J.W. Dickson	F	1888-1890			7	4		
Perry M. Digweed	G	1993-1995	28 +1		1		1	
Kerry M. Dixon	F	1996	8 +3					
T. (Tommy) Dixon	IF	1911-1913	72	21	8	4	2	1
W. Dodds	F	1893					2	1
David M. Donald	W	1913-1914	22	3	2			
Gary Donnellan	W	1981					0 +1	
Herbert J. Dow	W	1896-1897	5					
R.D. (Bobby) Downes	W	1974-1979	192 +7	18	9		21 +1	4
C.F. Drake	W	1902	1					
C.J. (Charlie) Drinkwater	W	1945-1947	1		9			

Name	Pos	Years						
George B. Drury	F	1948-1949	35	3	1			
W. (Billy) Dryden	IF/CF	1913-1914	20	8			1	
Jason Drysdale	FB	1989-1994	135+10	11	2		12 +1	2
Keith B.L. Dublin	D	1990-1994	165 +3	2	4		18	
R.A. (Reg) Dudley	FB	1950	1					
J.R. Dukes	HB	1888					1	
W.L. (Len) Dunderdale	CF	1938-1948	74	34	7	4		
Arthur T.B. Dunn	F	1891-1892					2	3
Bruce A. Dyer	F	1993-1994	29 +2	6	1		6	3
J. Barry Dyson	F	1968	38	19	1		1	
T.G. (Terry) Eades	CH	1976	4					
W. (Wally) Eames	F	1901-1907	61	11	5	6	17	16
M. (Mike) Early	W	1946	5	1				
Clint J. Easton	M	1996-1998	25 +4	1	3 +1		3 +1	
R.J. (Ray) Eastway	FB	1951-1952	12		2			
S.L.L. (Sam) Eaton	F	1905-1906	11	1	1	1	12	2
A.W. (Doss) Ebden	CH	1907					2	
Keith Eddy	D/M	1966-1972	239 +1	26	19	3	15	2
Derek J. Edmonds	G	1971	15					
George W.N. Edmonds	CF	1913-1927	107	57	5	3		
H.R. (Harry) Edwards	WH/IF	1899	7				2	1
T. (Tommy) Eggleston	WH/FB	1948-1952	177	6	9			
J.A.E. (Jimmy) Eggleton	CH	1923-1926	48	2	4			
A.J. (Jack) Elkes	CH	1933	9	1				
F.C. (Fred) Ellis	WH	1931-1932	30	1	7			
S. (Sam) Ellis	CH	1977-1978	30 +4	4	1		5	1
Barry Endean	F	1968-1971	72 +5	28	13	8	2 +1	1
J.C. (Jack) English	FB	1912-1913	33		3		1	
George A. Ephgrave	G	1951	4					
B.R. (Roy) Evans	IF	1951	2	1				
D. Ralph Evans	F	1937-1948	88	30	8	2	5	4
Hugh Evans	IF	1952-1953	7	2				
Jethro Evans	CF	1912-1913	11	1	3		1	
Charlie Ewington	FB	1934-1936	12					
John Fairbrother	CF	1959-1963	40	19	3	2	3	1
Mark P. Falco	F	1986-1987	33	14	7	2	1	
W.H. (Willie) Falconer	M	1988-1991	87+13	12	6	1	7 +3	
John D. Farley	W	1971-1974	97 +8	8	5 +1	1	4	
T. (Tot) Farnall	WH	1900-1902	30	1	4	1	1	
A.L. (Les) Farnen	CH	1946-1949	77	4				
Alec Farrall	M	1966-1967	47 +1	8	5	3	3	
Albert E. Farrow	WH/W	1908-1909	9					
F. (Tiny) Fayers	HB	1908-1910	64	2	5		1	
W. Fellows	WH	1899-1901	19				8	
John J. Ferguson	W	1929-1930	4					
George E. Ferne	W	1900	4	1				
Sidney Field	CF	1905					1	
W. (Bill) Findlay	WH	1932-1936	128	6	9		4	
K.D.W. (Ken) Fisher	HB	1947-1951	106	2	4			
Peter Fisher	IF	1936	3	1				
Gary M. Fitzgerald	CH	1994	1					
Richard G. Flash	M	1997	0 +1					
George K. Fleming	F	1958-1959	27	10	4		1	
Eli Fletcher	FB	1926-1927	23		2	1		
L. (Len) Fletcher	CF	1935-1938	36	22	6	3	3	1
William Flint	F	1910-1911	17	4	3	3	3	3
Dominic J. Foley	F	1998	2 +6	1				
Colin J. Foster	CH	1994-1996	66	7	6		6	1
Cyril J. Foster	IF	1925-1928	70	24	1			
J. (Jack) Foster	CF	1905-1907	57	29	2	1	20	9
Arthur T. Foxall	WH/W	1923-1924	3	1				
F.H. (Fred) Foxall	W	1923-1924	32	2	3			

Name	Pos	Years	App	Gls	App	Gls	App	Gls
Albert Francis	W	1924	1					
John J. Frankish	CH	1913	2				1	
Paul L. Franklin	D	1981-1986	32		5		5 +1	
Colin J. Franks	M/F	1969-1973	99+13	8	7	1	3 +2	
John W. Fraser	IF	1962-1964	24	3	4		1	1
Graham E. French	W	1964	4					
E.W. (Eddie) Fuller	HB	1927-1929	55		4			
John P. Furie	D	1967	0 +1					
Paul A. Furlong	F	1992-1994	79	37	2		10	4
K. (Ken) Furphy	FB	1964-1968	95 +6	1	6		4	
George M. Furr	F	1906-1909	37	3	4		5	3
V.R. (Vic) Furr	W	1925	1					
George Fyfe	WH/F	1905-1910	119	7	9		29	4
A.E. (Bert) Gale	WH	1901-1910	4		1		1	
L. (Len) Gallimore	FB	1937-1946	64		11		5	
C. (Charlie) Gallogly	D	1952-1954	47					
Terry G. Garbett	M/F	1966-1971	196 +4	46	21	4	10	
R.H. (Ray) Garbutt	CF	1950-1951	22	8	1			
W.E. Gardner	F	1887			1			
Alan H. Garner	CH	1975-1979	200	15	10	1	22	
Brian Garvey	HB	1965-1970	179 +1	2	11 +1		9	
J.T. (Johnny) Gavin	W	1958-1959	43	12	3	1	2	
Mark W. Gavin	W	1990-1991	8 +5					
J.M. (Jimmy) Gay	FB	1930	4		1			
A.J. (Tony) Geidmintis	FB	1976-1978	48 +1		5		7	
George Gemmell	CF	1912-1913	6	1				
Frank R. George	G	1964-1965	10					
R.S. (Ricky) George	F	1964-1965	4		1			
Nigel J. Gibbs	FB	1983-1998	364+12	5	39 +1		36	2
Peter L. Gibbs	G	1976	4					
Frank A. Gibson	W	1946	1					
W. Gibson	F	1888					1	
P. (Pat) Gillespie	WH	1945-1947	6		10			
J.M. (Jimmy) Gilligan	CF	1981-1985	18 +9	6	5	1	6 +3	6
C.E. (Charlie) Gladwin	FB	1919-1920	12					
J. Walter Glew	FB	1897-1898	11					
J.A.G. (Jimmy) Gooch	G	1956-1957	43		1		1	
M. (Micky) Good	CH	1899-1901	42	6	7	1	5	4
John Goodall	IF	1903-1907	62	14	7	3	23	19
K.G.A. (Ken) Goodeve	D	1974-1976	67	4	1		5	1
E. (Ted) Goodier	HB	1935	1					
Peter J. Gordon	IF	1958-1960	43	13	3		3	
Peter J. Goy	G	1964-1965	27		1		2	
L. (Les) Graham	IF	1955-1957	90	26	4	6	2	1
J.J. (Jack) Gran	WH	1900					1	
M. (Micky) Gray	F	1947	10	3				
R. (Ron) Gray	WH	1945-1946	16		13	4		
Albert Green	IF	1913-1915	48	13	2		2	
F. Green	CF	1896	1					
George E. Green	WH	1894-1896	3		3		7	
H. Rodney Green	CF	1968-1970	19+11	8	1 +1		0 +1	
Brian A. Greenhalgh	F	1975	17 +1	1	0 +1		2	1
Robert P. Greenslade	WH	1901-1903	31				1	
A.C. (Tony) Gregory	W/WH	1960-1963	107	14	8	3	4	
F.J. (Fred) Gregory	D	1911-1926	311	13	22	4	3	
V.F. (Val) Gregory	WH	1911-1920	155	13	6	3	2	
J. (Jock) Grieve	WH	1909-1911	62	1	6		5	
T. (Tom) Grieve	W	1904	1					
Daniel L. Grieves	M	1997					1	
W.J. (Billy) Grimes	F	1906-1907	15	3	1	1	6	
Arthur Grimsdell	HB	1911-1912	36	3	5	1	1	
E.F. (Ernie) Grimsdell	FB	1913-1920	15					

Name	Pos	Years						
J.P.G. (Joe) Groome	CF	1927-1928	17	14				
Henry W. Grover	D	1886-1889			2		7	
Gordon Haigh	IF	1951-1952	29	5	2	2		
R. (Dixie) Hale	M	1967-1970	95 +3	7	8 +1	3	6	
H.A. (Harry) Hall	W	1897	2		1			
E. Halsey	F	1886-1887			3	1	2	1
Andrew Hamilton	W	1900-1901	6	1				
J. (Jock) Hamilton	HB	1901-1902	30	3	2			
John Hamilton	F	1967	7 +1	2			3	
J.E. (Jack) Hamilton	F	1921	2					
Richard W. Hammett	G	1900-1901	33		3			
E.A. (Tony) Hapgood	W	1953	1					
A. Harding	D	1901-1903	12		3		1	
Paul J. Harding	M	1993	1 +1					
C.B. (Charlie) Hare	CF	1898-1900	43	23	12	12	16	24
Herbert M. Harford	FB	1893-1895			2		7	
T.C. (Tommy) Harmer	IF	1960-1962	63	6	7	1	4	
-- Harper	IF	1906					1	
Ivor R. Harper	IF	1952	3					
J.J. (Joe) Harper	D	1946-1952	159	1	11			
George A. Harris	W	1962-1966	162 +1	55	10	3	5	2
John Harris	F	1925-1926	29	5	3			
W.T. (Tommy) Harris	W/FB	1936-1948	94	6	8			
A. Harrison	F	1894					1	
C. (Bangy) Harrison	F	1893					2	2
Gerald R. Harrison	M	1990	6 +3				1	
H. (Dabber) Harrison	HB/F	1896-1897	8	1			2	1
S.J. (Steve) Harrison	FB	1978-1981	82 +1		9		10	
J. (Jack) Harrop	FB	1956-1960	111		6		7	
J. (Johnny) Hartburn	W	1949-1951	66	19	5	2		
Barry Hartle	IF	1958-1960	39	7	6	1		
T.W. (Tom) Hartley	IF	1948	6	1				
Howard Harvey	CF/IF	1901-1903	39	4	3		1	
William Hastings	W	1914-1915	34	6	1		1	
S.T. (Sam) Hatton	FB	1914					1	
Harry Hawkins	IF/WH	1937-1938	5				4	
N.S.C. (Norrie) Haywood	CF	1933	1					
Alon Hazan	M	1998	7 +3					
David M. Heard	W	1960					1	
M.R. (Mick) Henderson	FB	1979-1982	50 +1		4		11 +1	
W. (Billy) Hendry	D	1898	5					
Liburd A. Henry	F	1989-1990	8 +2	1	3		2	
J. (Jimmy) Hernon	IF	1954-1956	43	10	2	1	1	
A. (Andy) Hessenthaler	M	1991-1996	195	12	5	2	17	1
J. Arthur Hetherington	W	1938	8	1				
Peter Hetherston	F	1987-1988	2 +3		1		2 +1	2
J.T. (Joe) Hewitt	G	1927-1931	104		6			
J.C. Hibbert	F	1891-1892					2	
A.W. (Bill) Hicklin	WH	1947-1948	21	5	2			
H.W. (Bert) Higgins	G	1902-1910	45		2		21	
S.W. (Sid) High	W	1948-1949	7	3				
D.R.L. (Danny) Hill	M	1996	1					
J. (Johnny) Hill	W	1897-1900	65	25	10	1	18	11
M. Hill	CF	1897	1				1	
Richard W. Hill	M	1987	2 +2					
W. Ralph Hills	W	1927-1929	30	3	1			
J.L. (Jimmy) Hindmarsh	CF	1907-1908	10	4				
A. (Alf) Hitch	CH	1906-1908	69	2	3		8	1
Sydney G. Hobbs	F	1894-1897	18	8	3	1	7	6
F. (Frank) Hoddinott	CF	1919-1921	52	29	2	3		
S.B. (Steve) Hodge	M	1995	2					
Glyn P. Hodges	M	1987-1990	82 +4	15	8	1	7 +1	3

Name	Pos	Years	App	Gls	App	Gls	App	Gls
Cornelius Hogan	CH	1901	2					
R.W. (Rick) Holden	W	1988-1989	42	8	6	1	5 +1	1
Dean C. Holdsworth	F	1987-1989	2+16	3			0 +2	
David G. Holdsworth	CH	1988-1996	249+11	11	14 +1	1	28	2
Peter B. Holland	F	1928-1930	21	3	1			
T. (Tom) Holland	G	1930-1932	62		11			
H. Hollingshead	FB	1896	4		1		2	
C.C. (Cliff) Holton	CF/IF	1958-1966	144	96	17	7	5	2
S. (Stan) Hopkinson	G	1947	1					
Oscar A. Horne	W	1909	5				2	
F.Y. (Fred) Horner	G	1902	27		2		1	
Arthur Horsfield	CF/CH	1975-1977	78	16	4		1	
F. (Fred) Horsman	FB	1919-1924	132		6			
A. Horton	F	1890-1892			3		5	2
W.F. Horton	HB	1887			1			
Leslie G. Hosier	W	1906					2	2
A.J. Houghton	HB	1892			1			
W.G. (Billy) Houghton	WH	1964-1966	48	2	3	1		
Trevor A. How	FB	1975-1979	90 +1	2	3		7	
George A. Howard	D	1906-1907	1				3	
R.M. (Bobby) Howfield	F	1957-1963	92	22	5	2	4	1
A. (Archie) Hubbard	F	1908-1909	50	18	3	2		
A.E. (Ted) Hufton	G	1932	2					
Roger V. Hugo	F	1965-1966	24 +1	6			1	
George H. Hunt	CH	1947-1949	35					
S.C. (Stan) Hurst	W	1936-1937	29	12	1		2	2
Micah A. Hyde	M	1997-1998	40	4	5		4	1
F.H.S. Iles	F	1890-1891					2	1
John H. Iles	W	1897	1					
A.M. (Alex) Inglethorpe	F	1990-1994	2+10	2			2 +3	1
William J. Inglis	HB	1932-1933	12					
Derek V. Irvin	F	1968	0 +2	1				
R. (Bob) Irvine	CF/IF	1933-1934	22	2	1		1	1
E. (Ernie) Ison	W	1932	3	1				
Frank Jackett	WH	1949-1953	14					
K.F. (Kenny) Jackett	D/M	1980-1990	330 +7	25	38 +1	5	51 +1	4
W. (Billy) Jackson	W	1935	4	1				
David B. James	G	1990-1992	89		2		7	
George C. James	CF	1930-1933	83	67	11	9		
William H. Janes	W	1899	2	1			2	
A. (Alf) Jebb	HB	1912-1913	38		3		2	
Alec Jeffrey	HB	1900-1901	18		3			
Nigel B. Jemson	F	1995	3 +1					
Ross A. Jenkins	CF	1972-1983	312+27	118	18 +1	5	36 +4	19
P.A. (Pat) Jennings	G	1963-1964	48		3		1	
W.J. (Billy) Jennings	CF	1970-1974	80+13	33	3		4	4
George Jewett	D	1927-1928	29					
Bedford A.G. Jezzard	F	1945			3	1		
Richard I. Jobson	M/D	1982-1984	26 +2	4	0 +1		8 +1	
C. (Chris) Johnson	M	1996	1					
David N.C. Johnson	W	1981-1983	4 +3				3 +4	
George A. Johnson	WH/IF	1937-1938	23	8	2	1		
George E. Johnson	CH	1938	1					
J. (Joe) Johnson	FB	1920-1924	94	1	8			
Richard M. Johnson	M	1991-1998	144+20	13	11 +2		14 +2	1
Maurice J.G. Johnston	F	1983-1984	37 +1	23	7	4	1	
Bryn E. Jones	FB	1963	2					
B.J. (Jimmy) Jones	FB	1947-1954	158		9			
B.R. (Bryn) Jones	FB	1963-1966	90 +1	1	3		5	
D. Oswald E. Jones	IF	1938	2					
J. (Jimmy) Jones	WH	1904-1905	7				4	
Ormond H. Jones	G	1936	8					

Name	Pos	Years	App	Gls	App	Gls	App	Gls
Trevor Jones	W	1949-1950	15	2	1	1		
T.J. (Tom) Jones	F	1935-1946	118	23	13	3	6	1
W. Morris Jones	IF	1951-1952	27	7	1			
H. (Harry) Jordan	CH	1898-1899	1				2	
Roger D.W. Joslyn	M	1974-1979	178 +4	17	9 +1		21 +1	4
Basil H. Joy	F	1895			1			
Norman H. Joy	WH	1896	1					
M.T. (Mike) Keen	WH	1972-1975	124 +2	5	5		5	1
F. (Frank) Kelly	W	1905-1909	46	5	4	3	19	6
J. (Jimmy) Kelly	WH	1950-1954	119	4	4			
William B. Kelly	IF	1910-1911	29	8	2		3	1
A.J. (Andy) Kennedy	F	1990-1991	17 +8	4	0 +1		3	1
The Rev John Kennedy	FB	1889					1	
J.J. (Jim) Kennedy	CH	1913-1915	51	3	1		1	
Peter H.J. Kennedy	M	1997-1998	34	11	5	1	4	1
M.J. (Mike) Kenning	W	1972-1973	35 +6	2	3	1		
H. (Harry) Kent	CH	1909-1913	63	6	6	3	3	
E. Kilner	W	1912-1913	5					
F. King	IF	1896	1					
S. (Sid) King	G	1893-1897	24		5		16	
T.H. (Tommy) King	G	1955-1956	20		1		1	
W. Kingham	CF	1913					1	
R.J.S. (Badger) Kirby	F	1922	1					
J. (Jim) Kirkpatrick	FB	1927	9					
Martin Kuhl	M	1988	4					
Peter Kyle	CF	1909-1910	12	4	1			
R.W.J. (Dick) Lacey	F	1923	3	1				
David B.P. Laing	W	1937-1938	15	5	2		2	1
R.S. (Bobby) Laing	F	1950-1952	60	8				
W.H.C. (Billy) Lane	CF/IF	1932-1935	124	68	3		9	9
B.P. (Bunny) Larkin	WH/IF	1962-1964	49	3	5		3	
Gerard Lavin	FB	1992-1995	121 +5	2	6		14 +1	1
W. (Billy) Law	W	1906-1908	63	7	3		17	1
Norman Lawson	FB	1960					1	
J.M. (Jimmy) Lawton	CF	1967-1968	10 +3	1	1		1 +1	2
J. (Jimmy) Leaver	CH	1926-1927	35	3				
J. (Jack) Lee	W	1924-1925	8					
Jason B. Lee	F	1997-1998	35 +1	10	4		4	
W. (Don) Lees	HB/F	1904-1905	6	2	1		7	5
Walter J. Lees	CH	1968-1976	220 +6	10	17	1	10	
F.J.S. (Fred) Le May	W	1932	4					
K.G. (Ken) Lesslie	W	1948	7	1	1	1		
B. (Bernie) Lewis	W	1967-1970	41 +10	9	3		3	
D.J. (Jim) Lewis	FB	1931-1939	111		5		8	
Thomas Lewis	W	1920	1					
T. George Lewis	FB/CF	1936-1946	25	11	9	4	8	3
J.S. Lidderdale	FB	1894			1		3	
J.Y. (Jimmy) Lindsay	M	1971-1973	64 +1	12	1		7	1
T. (Jock) Lindsay	W	1930	7		2	1		
W. (Billy) Lindsay	FB	1903-1906	59		9		27	
J. (Jimmy) Linton	G	1959-1963	71		13		4	
F. Spencer Lister	W	1897-1899	11	3	1			
C.E. (Charlie) Livesey	CF	1962-1964	64	26	6	1	1	1
Per-Ola Ljung	FB	1997					1	
Frank W. Lock	FB	1955-1957	42	1	2		1	
Arthur Lockett	FB	1908-1912	141	1	13		5	
J.H.P. (Jan) Lohman	M	1981-1986	51 +12	6	9 +2	3	5 +2	1
Clive I. Lomas	D	1966	6 +1					
W. (Duke) Lovett	F	1895			1			
Alfred M. Low	D	1889-1891			1		2	1
A. Roy Low	F	1967-1968	25 +1	4				
H.P. (Harry) Lowe	IF	1929-1935	120	41	10	6	7	

Name	Pos	Years	App	Gls	App	Gls	App	Gls
Nathan P. Lowndes	F	1996-1998	1 +6		1 +1		1 +1	
Dominic J.R. Ludden	FB	1994-1997	28 +5		2 +1		5	
R. (Ray) Lugg	M	1969-1972	51 +8	3	5	2	3	1
George Lunn	CH	1947	5		2			
Thomas J. Lynch	G	1937	2					
Frank Lyon	FB	1902-1903	14					
H. (Bert) Lyon	IF/CF	1901-1902	30	12	2	2		
J. (Jimmy) McAnearney	IF	1963-1966	84 +2	19	1		1	
Patrick McArdle	W	1910-1911	11		1		2	
F. (Frank) McAvoy	CH	1902-1903	23	2	1		1	
Neil McBain	CH	1928-1931	85	5	9			
Alan J. McCarthy	FB	1993-1994	8 +1					
Kevin J. McCarthy	M	1975-1977	35 +1	1			2	
D. (Dave) McCartney	CH	1903-1906	82	13	9	1	41	8
John McClelland	CH	1984-1990	187	3	32		14 +1	
Albert McClenaghan	D	1978	2					
J.C.F. (Jimmy) McCrae	HB	1926	2					
T. (Tom) McCready	FB	1963	1		2			
Dennis McCrystal	G	1950	1					
Robert G. McCulloch	W	1925	14	2				
L. (Larry) McGettigan	W	1971-1974	40+10	3	1		4	
M.J. (Mick) McGovern	F	1972	4				1	
Robert McGuire	W	1914-1915	3					
J. (Jock) McHugh	G	1933-1939	38		2		4	
David McKinley	F	1908-1909	23	5	3	1		
C.F. (Mac) Maclachlan	IF	1895-1896	1		3	1	2	2
J. (Jimmy) MacLaine	CF/IF	1908-1911	99	27	8	8	5	
J. (Jim) McLaren	G	1933-1939	194		14		18	
Joseph J.S. McLauchlan	CF	1913-1914	20	8	1		1	
J. (Joe) McLaughlin	CH	1990-1992	46	2	1		6	
T.P. (Tommy) McMillan	F	1956-1958	33	13			3	2
F.A. McMorran	WH	1914-1915	6		1			
J. (Jack) McNee	IF	1897-1900	62	32	9		18	12
V. (Vince) McNeice	CH	1957-1964	231		22	1	10	
F.C. (Frank) McPherson	W/CF	1928-1936	94	67	8	8	4	2
R. (Bobby) McWilliams	W	1930-1931	22	1				
Laurence Mahon	HB	1913	10		1			
A. (Sandy) Main	WH	1904-1907	67	1	8		32	
S.T. (Sam) Malpass	FB	1947-1949	41					
T.J. (Terry) Mancini	CH	1961-1965	66 +1		6		3	
R.J. (Ben) Marden	W/CF	1955-1956	41	11			1	1
Edgar H. Mariette	FB	1889-1894			5		5	
Leo S. Markham	F	1972-1975	22+11	3	1 +1			
William A. Markland	FB	1919-1920	13					
I. (Ike) Marsh	CF/WH	1897-1898	23	5	5	1	1	1
William Marshall	CH	1922	2					
Dennis Maskell	W	1951-1952	5					
H.M. (Harry) Matthew	WH	1903	10				2	1
J.F. (Jimmy) Maxwell	W	1926	4	1				
F.M. May	F	1896					2	
Alan K. Mayes	F	1974-1979	110+23	31	5 +4	1	11 +4	4
J.A. (Johnny) Meadows	WH/IF	1951-1960	222	42	14	4	8	3
James S. Meara	M	1993	1 +1					
Gordon Mee	G	1945-1946			8			
Colin Meldrum	FB	1960-1962	32		3		5	
T. (Terry) Melling	F	1966-1967	23 +1	5	4	2	2	
Lars M. Melvang	FB	1997	4	1			1	
A.M. (Tony) Meola	G	1990					1	
Keith Mercer	F	1973-1979	109+25	46	6	4	10 +4	3
H. (Harry) Middleton	F/HB	1911-1912	23	5			1	
W.P. (Dossie) Miles	CH	1929-1930	14	1	3			
Keith D. Millen	CH	1994-1998	153 +1	5	14		10	

Name	Pos	Years						
H.E.J. (Ted) Miller	F	1922	2					
Kevin Miller	G	1994-1997	128		10		13	
Paul R. Miller	CH	1988-1989	22	1	5		3	
Peter S. Miller	IF	1930-1931	14	1	2	1		
R.B. (Rev) Miller	F	1922	1					
H.J. (Harry) Mingay	G	1927	2		1			
Frank R. Mitchell	WH	1952-1957	193		12		3	
T.W. (Tommy) Mitchell	W	1912-1914	60	9	3		2	
J. (Joe) Moffat	HB	1908-1909	18					
T.J. (Tommy) Mooney	D/F	1994-1998	155 +8	29	10 +1	1	16	1
J. (Jack) Moore	W	1909-1910	20	2	3	2		
S.F.P. Moore	F	1888			1			
Jamie D. Moralee	F	1994-1996	40 +9	7	5		6 +1	
J. (Jack) Moran	FB	1932-1935	100		6		5	
E. (Tom) Morgan	WH	1935-1938	108	6	5		12	2
Ian A. Morgan	W	1973-1974	15 +1	1	2			
J. S. (Taffy) Morgan	CF	1902-1904	15	9	1		2	1
L. (Lew) Morgan	FB	1946-1947	50		4			
W. (Billy) Morgan	WH	1903-1904	20	9	2	1	13	4
H. (Harry) Morris	F/HB	1925-1928	50	4				
Mark J. Morris	CH	1987-1989	41	1	7		5	1
P.J. (Pat) Morrissey	F	1971-1974	101 +6	27	5	1	5	1
G.D. Morrison	HB	1889-1890			4	1	2	
S.J. (Steve) Morrow	D	1991	7 +1				1	
G.D. (Geoff) Morton	G	1948-1951	107		6			
Philip H. Morton	F	1887-1888			2	1	5	2
A.S. (Alf) Moule	CF	1928-1929	11	4				
A.E.P. (Eddie) Mummery	F/HB	1921-1925	119	23	7			
J. (Jack) Munn	F	1891			1			
Stewart Munn	HB	1901-1904	37		2		7	
J. (Jimmy) Murray	IF	1902-1903	27	6	2		2	2
J. Edward Myers	G	1897	3					
Warren A. Neill	FB	1996	1					
James R. Ness	CF	1911	4	2			1	
Robert T. Newman	IF	1922	1					
T.B. (Tommy) Niblo	F	1906-1907	30	8	2		10	3
K.W. (Ken) Nicholas	FB	1959-1964	198	4	19	2	2	
Peter Nicholas	M	1991-1992	40	1	1		5	
G.F. (Fred) Nidd	FB/G	1900-1902	55		5			
W. (Bill) Nock	F	1898	3	3				
Gifton R.E. Noel-Williams	F	1996-1998	36+27	9	6	4	3 +1	1
Lee M. Nogan	F	1991-1994	97 +8	26	2	1	6 +4	3
P. (Phil) Nolan	F/CH	1947-1954	91	8	4			
G.W. (George) Norman	CF	1912	8	4				
E.J. (Joe) North	CF/IF	1926-1927	6					
M.T. (Mick) O'Brien	CH	1931-1933	61	5	10	1		
R.V. (Vic) O'Brien	D/F	1934-1946	179	9	23	1	19	1
R.J.G. (Ralph) Oelofse	FB/CH	1953-1954	15					
H.S. (Harry) Oliver	FB/CH	1948-1952	122	2	6	2		
K. (Ken) Oliver	F	1963-1964	58	26	4	2	1	
Joseph H. Orme	G	1911-1913	13				1	
W. (Billy) Orr	D	1906-1907	5				7	
John F. Osborn	G	1897	5					
E.J. Osborne	WH	1897	2					
J. (Johnny) Osborne	WH/IF	1948-1949	34	13	1			
David Ovenstone	W	1937	1				1	
Brian E. Owen	W	1963-1970	148 +5	17	11	3	4 +2	
M.D. (Mike) Packer	D	1968-1973	57+11	2	6 +2		1	
F.W. (Fred) Packham	W	1926-1927	5					
R. Padley	F	1903					1	
Robert J. Page	CH	1993-1998	100 +5		9 +1		11	1
Fred Pagnam	CF	1921-1927	144	67	13	7		

Name	Pos	Years						
C.A. (Charlie) Palmer	FB	1981-1984	10	1			8	
F. (Fred) Palmer	WH	1907-1910	16				3	2
S.L. (Steve) Palmer	M/D	1995-1998	107+10	4	7+1		12+1	
Thomas Pangborn	IF	1901-1902	24	5	2			
H. Harold Pantling	FB/WH	1911-1914	35		2		2	
J.M. (Jack) Papworth	CF	1925	27	12				
Henry J. Paris	D	1896-1897	6					
R. (Dick) Parker	CF	1927-1928	13	2	1	1		
F. Parkes	F	1888-1891					5	
R. (Bob) Parkinson	CF	1900-1901	15	5				
Martin Patching	M	1979-1983	24+1	3	3+1	2	6+1	1
A.M. (Sandy) Pate	FB	1965-1967	14+1					
Robert B.J. Paten	W	1897	1	1				
T. (Tommy) Paterson	IF/WH	1952-1954	45	7	3			
J. (Johnny) Paton	W	1952-1955	84	17	7			
J.A.J. (Jim) Paton	FB	1929-1930	5					
T.G. (Tommy) Paton	IF/WH	1948-1952	141	1	8			
John R. Paull	FB	1892-1899	13		6		12	
Derek R. Payne	M	1994-1996	33+3	1	2+1		3	
C.H. (Charlie) Peacock	D	1886-1894			13		28	1
John Pearce	D	1971	0+1					
J. (Joe) Penney	HB	1891-1895			4		14	
Gary K. Penrice	F	1989-1997	67+15	19	5	1	4+2	1
F. (Fred) Pheby	F	1906					1	
Kevin Phillips	F	1995-1997	54+5	23	2		2+2	1
Harold J. Phipps	CH	1952-1953	47					
W.E. (Bill) Pick	W	1930-1931	26	5	4			
H.J. (or W.J.) Pickin	HB	1886			1			
L. (Les) Pilkington	W	1950-1951	5					
W. Pillon	W	1907					1	
G. (Geoff) Pitcher	M	1995-1996	4+9	2	2		1+1	
Colin J. Pluck	D	1997	1				1	
Gary E. Plumley	G	1987			1			
Brian E. Pollard	W	1977-1979	68+3	8	4+1		8+1	
Richard J. Poole	F	1976-1977	3+4	1			2	
William A. Poole	CF	1923-1925	42	8	1	1		
A. (Andy) Porter	WH	1960-1963	72	4	5		3	
Gary M. Porter	M	1983-1996	364+38	46	25+2	3	40+3	7
Malcolm Poskett	F	1980-1982	57+6	17	5+1	6	11	8
S.J. (Poley) Poulton	HB	1887-1891			8	1	15	
C.G. (Cliff) Powell	CH	1988					0+1	
J. (Jimmy) Poxton	W	1934-1935	23	9	2		1	1
Hugh Prentice	CF	1910	1					
C. Pretty	F	1892			1	1		
John D. Price	FB	1959	22		3		1	
J.L. (Jack) Price	F	1900-1901	26	6	3	3		
Neil Price	FB	1982-1984	7+1		2		2+1	
George Prior	FB	1924-1930	174		15	3		
Keith B. Pritchett	FB	1976-1982	133+7	9	10		20+1	3
John Proudfoot	CF	1902	12	5	1			
C.J. (Chris) Pullan	FB/M	1987-1990	5+7				3	
Trevor A. Putney	M	1991-1993	42+10	2	2		11	
Frederick T. Putterill	IF	1896-1897	4				1	1
David A. Pygall	IF	1956-1960	20	2			1	
M. (Mick) Quinn	F	1995	4+1					
Andrew T. Ralston	D	1905	2	1				
Craig D. Ramage	M	1994-1997	99+5	27	7		8+1	2
John E. Rand	IF	1926-1927	6					
A.G. (Andy) Rankin	G	1971-1979	299		13		17	
B. (Bill) Ratcliffe	CH	1948-1949	24		1			
C.R. (Charlie) Rattray	W	1934-1935	19		3	1	4	
H.A. Rauthmell	HB	1895					1	

Name	Pos	Years	League Apps	League Gls	Cup Apps	Cup Gls	Other Apps	Other Gls
William Ray	IF	1897-1898	20	10				
E. (Ernie) Reading	F	1904-1905	6				4	1
Neil D. Redfearn	M	1988-1989	24 +2	4	6	3	4	
A.G. (Alf) Reed	WH	1935-1939	126	5	7		12	
M.J. (Mel) Rees	G	1987-1988	3		1		1	
J. (Jimmy) Reid	IF	1905-1906	19	7	3	2	13	7
J. (John) Reid	W	1956	1	1				
M.J. (Micky) Reid	CF	1952-1953	19	8				
George G. Reilly	CF	1983-1985	46 +2	14	8	4	5	1
J. (Jack) Reynolds	W	1907-1908	27	4	1		1	
J.W. (Joe) Reynolds	WH	1930	6					
P.J. (Pat) Rice	FB	1980-1984	112	1	10		14 +1	
D. (Dave) Richards	FB	1931-1933	35		8			
Ian P. Richardson	F	1983-1985	5 +3	2			6 +1	3
J.W. (Jack) Richardson	WH	1897-1909	166	2	16	3	35	3
Kevin Richardson	M	1986-1987	39	2	7		4	
Lee J. Richardson	M	1989-1990	40 +1	1	1		1 +1	
F.W. (Fred) Riddell	F	1908-1909	6					
T. (Tommy) Rigg	G	1946-1948	80		5			
Stuart A. Rimmer	F	1988	10	1			0 +1	1
A.W. (Alex) Ritchie	W	1933-1934	17	3				
R. (Bob) Ritchie	IF	1949	1					
Alan D. Rivers	D	1967	0 +2					
Iwan W. Roberts	F	1986-1990	42+23	9	1 +6		9 +2	3
J. (Joe) Roberts	W	1926-1927	20	5				
T. (Tommy) Roberts	FB	1954	1					
L.V. (Len) Robertson	IF	1946	6	2				
F.C. (Fred) Robins	CH	1894-1899	46	2	8	1	15	1
E. Robinson	CH	1913	1					
Paul P. Robinson	FB	1996-1998	22+12	2	3 +2		3	
R. (Reg) Robinson	HB	1937-1938	2				5	
Mark A. Robson	W	1989	1					
William N. Roe	FB	1887-1888			4		4	
Glenn V. Roeder	CH	1989-1991	74 +4	2	3	1	5	
Peter M. Ronald	IF	1914-1921	99	29	3		1	
Mark J. Rooney	D	1997					1	
Ronny Rosenthal	F	1997-1998	24 +1	8	2	2	3 +1	
R. (Bobby) Ross	WH	1946-1947	33	6	2			
J.W. (Wilf) Rostron	W/FB	1979-1989	306+11	22	43 +1	2	41 +2	6
Brian Rowan	D	1971-1972	8 +4		1			
Paul Rumble	FB	1988					1	
D.P. (Dave) Russell	G	1926	7					
George H. Russell	FB	1926-1927	12	1				
J. (Jack) Rutherford	G	1931-1933	31		1			
John J. Ryden	HB	1961-1962	24	1			2	
John Sanchez	WH	1960-1961	19					
Arthur E. Sans	W	1906					1	
K.G. (Kenny) Sansom	FB	1994	1					
R.F.E. (Reg) Saphin	G	1951-1954	57		2			
A.A. (Alf) Sargent	G	1886-1890			10		16	
F.A. (Freddie) Sargent	F	1886-1895			9	7	32	39
W.A. (Alec) Sargent	D	1886-1892			12		24	1
Herbert J. Saunders	G	1909	2					
James E. Saunders	G	1910	4				1	
R. (Ron) Saunders	F	1964-1965	39	18			2	
W. (Bumper) Saunders	IF	1896-1900	33	19	2	1	9	7
Harry Savage	W	1921-1922	7	1				
H. (Harry) Scott	IF	1933	1					
Keith Scott	F	1997	6	2			2	
Stewart M.A. Scullion	W	1966-1976	304 +8	49	22	3	14	3
Frank B. Searle	WH	1933	4		1			
Trevor J. Senior	F	1987-1988	22 +2	1	3 +1	2	4 +1	2

Name	Pos	Years						
A. (Albie) Sharp	FB	1898-1901	58	1	11	2	13	
Ivan G. Sharpe	W	1908	7	1				
J.W. Sharpe	F	1890			1	1		
Arthur Shaw	D	1955	3					
John Shaw	D	1945-1946			9			
Edward Shawcroft	CF	1921	1					
Simon Sheppard	G	1993-1994	23		1		6	
W. (Bill) Sheppard	IF	1927-1929	89	37	6	2		
S. (Steve) Sherwood	G	1977-1987	211	1	23		35	
T.A. (Tim) Sherwood	M	1987-1989	23 +9	2	9		8 +2	
J.H. (Bert) Shinner	FB	1909-1910	18				4	
Neil J. Shipperley	F	1994-1995	5 +1	1				
W.K. (Bill) Shipwright	FB/CH	1954-1959	146		7		6	
James Short	CF/IF	1920-1921	21	7				
George F. Simons	FB	1905	1					
Colin R. Simpson	F	1996	0 +1					
S.F. (Steve) Sims	CH	1978-1987	169 +2	5	21		26 +1	3
Roy Sinclair	M	1969-1972	32+11	3	1		2	
Lee Sinnott	D	1983-1987	71 +7	2	11		6	
Arthur H. Skilton	F	1908-1910	15	5			2	
R. (Reg) Slade	FB	1921-1929	119		5			
R. (Bert) Slater	G	1965-1969	134		9		9	
Stuart I. Slater	M	1996-1998	22 +8	1	3		4	
T. Arthur Slater	G	1933	29		1			
R. (Bobbie) Slaughter	IF	1894-1900	33	18	8	7	15	9
David Small	W	1951-1952	5					
Neil Smillie	W	1985-1986	10 +6	3	2	1	1	
Albert Smith	G	1929	5					
A. (Tony) Smith	F	1966-1967	3					
C. (Chris) Smith	D	1910-1912	32		1		2	
E.E. (Bert) Smith	CH	1925-1927	50	1	5			
E.W.A. (Eddie) Smith	IF	1953-1955	38	12	4	1		
Frank W. Smith	IF/WH	1921-1931	319	30	22	1		
G. Smith	WH	1902-1904	3				2	
George Smith	CH	1931	1					
Harry Smith	CF	1908-1913	35	15			1	1
J. (Jack) Smith	CF/IF	1960-1961	20	8	3			
J.K. (Joe) Smith	FB	1931	1					
J. Trevor Smith	IF	1947	10		2			
Lionel Smith	FB	1954-1955	7					
R. (Ron) Smith	FB	1955	2				1	
T.W. (Tommy) Smith	F	1997	0 +1		0 +1			
W.A. (Bill) Smith	G	1959	10					
T. Albert Soar	W	1906-1908	33	3	2	1	10	
Jason R. Soloman	M	1989-1994	79+21	5	1		14 +1	1
W. Spearing	FB	1893					1	
R.E. (Ron) Spelman	W	1963-1965	40	3	3		1	
F. (Fred) Spiksley	W	1906	11	5			1	
Arthur Squires	W	1909-1913	106	20	10	5	5	
S.M. Stanley	F	1888			1			
T. (Tom) Steel	FB	1898-1899	1		1		1	
Eric G. Steele	G	1979-1984	51		4		10	
G.G. (Geoff) Steiner	FB	1952	3					
J. (Jimmy) Stephenson	W	1922-1927	195	18	14	2		
Worrell R. Sterling	W	1983-1988	82+12	14	18	2	7 +3	1
A. (Alex) Stewart	FB	1910-1915	149	3	11	1	6	1
John Stirk	FB	1978-1979	46		3		11	
K.S. (Ken) Stockley	WH	1949-1950	1		1			
A. (Fred) Stokes	WH	1931-1933	38		4			
A.F. (Alf) Stokes	IF/CF	1961	14	2			2	1
J. Stokes	F	1890					1	
Peter R. Storer	G	1959	9					

Name	Pos	Years	App	Gls	App	Gls	App	Gls
J. (Jock) Strain	HB	1921-1927	178	6	15			
J.H. (Jimmy) Strain	CH	1957	3					
Robert C.M. Strouts	F	1894-1895			1		4	
J. Acworth Stuart	F	1889			3	1	5	1
Perry J. Suckling	G	1992-1993	39		1		6	
H. (Hugh) Surtees	W	1947-1949	14	1	2			
R.L. (Bobby) Svarc	F	1977	1					
J. (Jack) Swan	IF/CF	1925-1927	54	27	5	4		
Brian E. Talbot	M	1985-1986	46 +2	8	8		3	
S.J. (Steve) Talboys	M	1996-1997	2 +3				1 +1	
W.S. (Wally) Tattersall	W	1910-1912	64	11	8		3	
L. (Les) Taylor	M	1980-1985	167 +5	13	21	3	18	4
S.S. (Toby) Taylor	F	1894			1		2	3
J. (Jimmy) Tennant	W	1902-1905	83	15	9	6	26	12
Steve G. Terry	CH	1980-1988	160	14	20 +1	1	26 +1	5
William Tervit	IF	1900	1					
F. Theobald	IF	1910-1911	3					
David J. Thomas	F	1997-1998	8 +8	3	1 +3			
D.W.J. (Dave) Thomas	CF	1948-1950	105	39	6	4		
Roderick C. Thomas	W	1988-1992	65+21	9	0 +1		5 +3	
Cyril A. Thompson	CF	1951-1953	78	36	5	5		
Garry L. Thompson	F	1988-1990	24+10	8	7 +1		0 +1	
W. (Bill) Thompson	G	1946-1947	9		2			
Arthur Thurley	CH	1932	4					
T. (Tommy) Tierney	F	1904					2	
H.F. (Bert) Tinklin	W	1936	8				2	
A.E. Tooley	FB	1904-1906	1				4	
A. Tooms	FB	1889					1	
George Toone	HB	1919-1924	178		12			
A.H. Town	F	1887					1	
Charles Tracey	W	1930-1931	3	1				
R. (Ray) Train	M	1978-1982	91 +1	3	9		9 +2	1
Patrick Trainer	IF	1904					1	2
J. (Jimmy) Trotter	IF/CF	1931-1932	4	1				
A. Docwra Turner	W	1899	4	1			1	
John A. Turner	G	1929-1930	13		3			
Peter Turner	IF	1904-1907	99	20	9	2	43	16
R. (Bob) Turner	CH	1902	2					
E.D. (Dave) Underwood	G	1952-1963	176		12		6	
E. Dennis H. Uphill	CF	1959-1960	51	30	7	6	1	
J.A.G. (Johnny) Usher	F/WH	1946-1948	23	3	3	1		
S.J. Valentine	F	1886-1887			1		3	
H.J. (Harry) Vanner	W	1928	2					
E.A. (Algy) Varley	W	1898-1901	42	9	6	1	12	3
T.H. (Tommy) Varty	F/WH	1950-1951	34	5	1			
E.E. (Ted) Villiers	HB	1888-1892			7		16	
John Wakefield	IF	1897	1					
A. (Andy) Walker	CH	1930	2					
M.S.G. (Micky) Walker	G	1968-1973	137		14		8	
Paul G. Walker	M	1972	2 +1		1			
Peter M. Walker	F	1954-1962	172	37	7	2	11	5
R.W. (Ron) Walker	F	1955	3					
Thomas Walker	CF/IF	1908	15	5				
George Waller	G	1901	7		2			
J.T. (Tom) Walley	WH	1967-1977	214 +3	17	16		15	1
E.E. (Ernie) Wallington	W	1921-1922	51	5	2			
-- Walmesley	G	1903	1					
J.T. (Jimmy) Walsh	FB	1974-1977	60 +5		1		4	
J. (Johnny) Walter	D	1905-1906	1				7	1
T.C. (Tom) Walters	CF	1935-1938	57	24	2	1	7	6
D. (Dai) Ward	IF	1962-1963	59	31	5	1	2	
Darren P. Ward	CH	1996-1997	8		1		0 +1	

Name	Pos	Years						
John P. Ward	F	1979-1981	22 +5	6	1 +1		1	
H.G. Wardale	FB	1892					1	
Keith D. Warn	G	1960	3					
J. (Jack) Warner	IF/WH	1926-1930	110	22	5	3		
T. (Tommy) Waterall	W	1914-1921	108	19	4	1	1	
George Waterman	F	1886-1888			4		7	2
F. Watson	HB	1894					1	
Mark S. Watson	CH	1993-1995	18		1 +2			
John G. Watt	D	1972	0 +1					
Keith Waugh	G	1992-1993	7					
J. (Joe) Webster	G	1910-1914	131		13		4	
J. (Jimmy) Weedon	WH	1897	12				2	
George B. Weeks	FB	1932	1					
A. (Alex) Weir	F	1945-1946	1		4			
Duncan Welbourne	FB/WH	1963-1974	404 +7	22	28	2	17 +1	1
C.F. Welch	W	1902	1	1				
W.H. Wellings	F	1886-1887			3		3	2
Colin West	CF	1985-1986	45	20	8	3	2 +1	
C. (Charlie) Wheeler	F	1892-1895			1		10	5
H. Wheeler	F	1886-1888			2	1	3	5
W. (Billy) Wheeler	W	1909-1911	24		1		1	1
C.W. (Charlie) White	IF	1909-1925	345	81	27	5	8	2
Devon W. White	F	1996-1997	28+10	7	2	1	5	
F. White	F	1891					1	1
H.W. (Bertie) White	F	1900	10	6	2	1		
R.N. (Bob) White	CF	1930-1932	20	16	4	4		
T.H. (Tommy) White	F	1909	3		1	1		
Vincent H. White	WH	1923-1924	7	1				
R.G. (Ron) Wigg	F	1970-1973	91 +6	20	4 +2	4	6 +1	3
-- Wigzell	IF	1904					1	
H. (Harry) Wilbourn	W	1928	2					
Harry M. Wilcox	IF	1900-1901	29	2	3	2		
J.B. Wildman	F	1890			1			
Fred Wilkinson	WH	1919-1921	72	1	2			
Gilbert G. Wilkinson	CF	1927-1928	9	2				
J. (or T.B.) Wilkinson	F	1892			1			
J.T. (Jack) Wilkinson	W	1921-1923	61	7	4			
Paul Wilkinson	F	1988-1995	139 +1	51	8 +1		10	4
S.C. Wilks	F	1892			1			
Alan Williams	CH	1965-1966	43	4	2		2	
Gary Williams	FB	1990-1991	39 +3		3		2	
J.R. (Johnny) Williams	FB	1964-1975	371 +3	2	26		19	
K. (Ken) Williams	IF	1947	2					
R.G. (Skilly) Williams	G	1913-1926	323		17		1	
T.J. (Tommy) Williams	W	1961-1962	12	6			2	1
W.L. (Bill) Williams	IF	1936	1					
Roger C. Willis	M/F	1992-1993	30 +6	2	1		1	
J. (Jack) Wilson	FB	1896-1900	23		1		4	
J.T. (Jimmy) Wilson	F/WH	1951-1957	49	12	2		1	
Robert D. Wilson	WH	1923	1					
William Wilson	IF	1931	1					
C.J. (Charlie) Wipfler	W/IF	1937-1947	35	8	3	1	3	
R.K. (Dick) Wise	CH	1896-1897	5		1		1	
H. (Micky) Wood	WH/F	1896-1901	94	9	10		20	5
David Woodfield	CH	1971-1973	14 +1				1	
Albert G. Woodison	IF	1956-1958					2	
L.C. (Lew) Woodroffe	F	1947-1951	63	6	1			
C.M.P. (Charlie) Woods	W	1970-1972	40 +2	3	1		3	1
Dennis J. Woods	W	1962-1963	13	2				
H.A. (Gayler) Woods	W	1909	3					
J. (Jack) Woods	D/G	1888-1893			6		9	
Arthur Woodward	WH	1926-1939	391	16	29	2	12	1

Name	Pos	Years						
Joseph H. Woodward	G	1926	2					
W. Woodward	D/F	1890			1		1	
Arthur Woolliscroft	IF	1930-1933	63	14	4	2		
J.E. (Ted) Worrall	FB	1925	4					
Eric S. Worthington	F	1949-1950	24	4	6			
W. (Willie) Wragg	WH/FB	1901-1902	18		2			
A. (Ticker) Wright	HB	1920	1					
Arthur R.L. Wright	F	1894-1897	1				1	
J. (Jocky) Wright	IF	1907-1908	27		1		1	
Norman Wright	W	1935-1936	21	3	4	2	1	
Richard G. Wright	CF	1894-1898	13	6	5	2	11	6
J. (Jack) Yates	WH	1928	2					
W. (Bill) Yates	G	1926-1929	47		2			
G. Young	CF	1908	1					
George Young	IF	1946-1949	43	5	1			

PART SEVEN

Summary of League Results

THE following summary of results against each opposing club encompasses matches only in the Southern League and the Football League, excluding Test Matches and Play-off matches. Figures for two away fixtures which were played at Watford (v 1st Coldstream Guards 1896/97 and v Chesham 1898/99) are included in the 'Away' columns. In brackets after each club's name are figures separated by a slash (eg 3/2) which represent the number of league 'doubles' (home and away wins in the same season) by Watford and by their opponents, respectively.

Opponents	First Season	HOME					AWAY					TOTAL				
		W	D	L	For	Ag	W	D	L	For	Ag	W	D	L	For	Ag
Aberdare Athletic (0/0)	1921/22	4	2	0	15	2	0	0	6	4	23	4	2	6	19	25
Aldershot (2/0)	1932/33	11	8	6	45	27	3	11	11	23	37	14	19	17	68	64
Arsenal (3/0)	1982/83	5	0	1	14	6	3	1	2	10	9	8	1	3	24	15
Aston Villa(1/0)	1969/70	4	2	0	16	9	1	2	3	6	11	5	4	3	22	20
Barnsley (0/2)	1960/61	7	6	5	26	20	5	5	8	15	23	12	11	13	41	43
Barrow (1/0)	1958/59	3	1	0	10	3	2	1	1	9	3	5	2	1	19	6
Birmingham City (2/1)	1969/70	8	1	2	19	9	2	3	6	9	18	10	4	8	28	27
Blackburn Rovers (2/1)	1969/70	4	4	3	14	16	3	4	4	10	14	7	8	7	24	30
Blackpool (0/0)	1969/70	3	1	1	12	5	1	3	1	6	8	4	4	2	18	13
Bolton Wanderers (0/0)	1969/70	4	3	0	13	6	2	1	4	7	13	6	4	4	20	19
AFC Bournemouth (5/5)	1923/24	23	10	14	65	46	11	16	20	54	83	34	26	34	119	129
Bournemouth & Boscombe Athletic - former name of AFC Bournemouth																
Bradford City (0/0)	1960/61	3	2	0	15	5	0	2	3	4	7	3	4	3	19	12
Bradford (Park Avenue) (0/1)	1907/08	3	0	2	7	8	0	3	2	5	7	3	3	4	12	15
Brentford (5/6)	1898/99	23	13	8	71	43	9	12	23	56	86	32	25	31	127	129
Brighton & Hove Albion (6/9)	1904/05	24	17	14	86	58	13	12	30	52	99	37	29	44	138	157
Bristol City (3/8)	1900/01	14	12	11	55	46	5	11	21	36	73	19	23	32	91	119
Bristol Rovers (14/3)	1900/01	37	11	9	108	54	21	12	24	75	89	58	23	33	183	143
Burnley (0/0)	1971/72	4	1	0	11	3	0	1	4	2	11	4	2	4	13	14
Bury (0/0)	1960/61	1	4	0	7	6	2	1	2	5	5	3	5	2	12	11
Cambridge United (0/0)	1973/74	3	4	1	9	5	2	2	4	10	18	5	6	5	19	23
Cardiff City (2/2)	1913/14	11	4	3	34	16	4	3	11	18	31	15	7	14	52	47
Carlisle United (1/2)	1958/59	4	3	2	16	10	1	1	7	5	16	5	4	9	21	26
Charlton Athletic (1/4)	1921/22	10	10	6	37	31	4	8	14	28	45	14	18	20	65	76
Chatham *(both matches void)*	1900/01															
Chelsea (2/1)	1979/80	3	0	5	13	16	4	3	1	15	9	7	3	6	28	25
Chesham - former name of Chesham Town																
Chesham Town (3/0)	1896/97	5	0	0	18	4	3	1	1	10	8	8	1	1	28	12
Chester (1/0)	1958/59	3	0	0	9	4	1	0	2	3	4	4	0	2	12	8
Chester City - present name of Chester																
Chesterfield (2/0)	1960/61	4	2	1	11	7	2	3	2	8	9	6	5	3	19	16
Clapton Orient - former name of Orient																
Colchester United (1/1)	1950/51	7	7	3	24	14	3	5	9	19	30	10	12	12	43	44
1st Coldstream Guards (0/0)	1896/97	1	0	0	4	0	0	1	0	3	3	1	1	0	7	3
Coventry City (6/8)	1908/09	19	5	9	74	39	8	5	20	35	66	27	10	29	109	105

Opponents	First Season	HOME					AWAY					TOTAL				
		W	D	L	For	Ag	W	D	L	For	Ag	W	D	L	For	Ag
Crewe Alexandra (3/0)	1958/59	6	0	2	20	7	5	2	1	16	10	11	2	3	36	17
Croydon Common (1/0)	1909/10	2	0	0	4	0	1	0	1	1	2	3	0	1	5	2
Crystal Palace (4/4)	1906/07	26	10	11	91	57	11	9	27	45	89	37	19	38	136	146
Darlington (1/0)	1958/59	4	2	0	9	3	1	3	2	4	3	5	5	2	13	6
Dartford (1/0)	1896/97	3	0	0	11	4	1	0	2	5	16	4	0	2	16	20
Derby County (0/1)	1980/81	2	4	2	14	10	2	4	2	11	12	4	8	4	25	22
Doncaster Rovers (2/1)	1959/60	4	0	1	18	5	2	1	2	3	3	6	1	3	21	8
Everton (0/3)	1982/83	2	1	3	13	14	0	0	6	3	15	2	1	9	16	29
Exeter City (6/5)	1908/09	25	11	10	79	43	12	10	24	52	84	37	21	34	131	127
Freemantle (0/0)	1896/97	1	0	0	3	1	0	0	1	0	5	1	0	1	3	6
Fulham (2/1)	1898/99	6	3	3	24	17	3	3	6	10	24	9	6	9	34	41
Fulham Reserves (0/0)	1903/04	1	0	0	2	0	0	1	0	3	3	1	1	0	5	3
Gateshead (1/0)	1958/59	2	0	0	10	1	1	0	1	3	2	3	0	1	13	3
Gillingham/New Brompton (10/4)	1900/01	29	15	8	107	50	12	15	25	61	86	41	30	33	168	136
Gravesend United (0/0)	1900/01	1	0	0	2	0	0	0	1	2	4	1	0	1	4	4
Grays United (1/0)	1899/1900	2	0	0	5	0	1	0	1	4	7	3	0	1	9	7
Grimsby Town (4/2)	1920/21	10	4	5	39	25	6	7	6	24	25	16	11	11	63	50
Halifax Town (1/0)	1960/61	3	5	0	11	8	1	5	2	6	8	4	10	2	17	16
Hartlepool (1/0)	1958/59	5	1	0	18	4	1	1	4	7	10	6	2	4	25	14

Hartlepool United - present name of Hartlepool
Hartlepools United - former name of Hartlepool

Opponents	First Season	HOME					AWAY					TOTAL				
Hereford United (0/0)	1973/74	1	1	0	3	2	1	1	0	2	1	2	2	0	5	3
Huddersfield Town (0/2)	1969/70	3	2	2	7	5	1	1	5	6	12	4	3	7	13	17
Hull City (1/2)	1960/61	5	5	3	25	17	1	5	7	11	22	6	10	10	36	39
Ipswich Town (0/2)	1938/39	8	6	6	32	25	3	7	10	21	37	11	13	16	53	62
Kettering (0/0)	1900/01	1	1	1	2	3	0	1	2	3	6	1	2	3	5	9

Kettering Town - present name of Kettering

Opponents	First Season	HOME					AWAY					TOTAL				
Leeds United (0/0)	1988/89	1	1	0	2	1	1	0	1	2	2	2	1	1	4	3
Leicester City (1/3)	1969/70	8	2	5	27	20	2	8	5	20	29	10	10	10	47	49
Leyton (1/1)	1906-07	3	2	1	14	9	2	2	2	7	9	5	4	3	21	18

Leyton Orient - former and present name of Orient

Opponents	First Season	HOME					AWAY					TOTAL				
Lincoln City (1/1)	1961/62	1	1	1	6	6	1	1	1	6	5	2	2	2	12	11
Liverpool (0/3)	1982/83	2	1	3	8	11	0	0	6	5	18	2	1	9	13	29
Luton Town (5/11)	1900/01	23	12	15	75	58	9	11	30	53	85	32	23	45	128	143
Maidenhead (2/0)	1896/97	3	0	1	20	5	3	1	0	10	4	6	1	1	30	9

Maidenhead United - present name of Maidenhead

Opponents	First Season	HOME					AWAY					TOTAL				
Manchester City (1/0)	1982/83	3	1	0	7	3	2	0	2	4	5	5	1	2	11	8
Manchester United (0/2)	1982/83	2	2	2	7	4	0	2	4	4	13	2	4	6	11	17
Mansfield Town (1/2)	1931/32	7	1	3	21	10	3	3	5	12	17	10	4	8	33	27
Merthyr Town (3/0)	1912/13	9	2	2	39	12	5	2	6	22	23	14	4	8	61	35
Middlesbrough (1/2)	1966/67	4	1	4	10	10	3	2	4	11	16	7	3	8	21	26
Millwall (4/11)	1900/01	18	14	21	64	71	12	13	28	55	106	30	27	49	119	177
Millwall Reserves (1/0)	1903/04	1	0	0	3	0	1	0	0	3	2	2	0	0	6	2
Newcastle United (1/1)	1979/80	4	5	2	17	12	2	3	6	11	18	6	8	8	28	30

New Brompton - former name of Gillingham

Opponents	First Season	HOME					AWAY					TOTAL				
Newport County (10/3)	1919/20	20	7	8	86	43	15	9	11	52	44	35	16	19	138	87
Northampton Town (8/4)	1901/02	29	15	10	110	56	16	13	25	53	94	45	28	35	163	150
Norwich City (0/7)	1905/06	18	18	11	71	58	6	14	27	49	103	24	32	38	120	161
Nottingham Forest (1/2)	1949/50	3	4	2	10	10	1	2	6	8	17	4	6	8	18	27
Notts County (6/3)	1930/31	13	4	7	45	31	10	1	13	35	39	23	5	20	80	70
Oldham Athletic (3/1)	1958/59	13	3	3	40	18	5	7	7	24	25	18	10	10	64	43
Old St Stephens (0/0)	1896/97	1	1	0	8	4	1	0	1	7	7	2	1	1	15	11
Orient (4/4)	1929/30	16	5	7	47	27	7	13	8	27	32	23	18	15	74	59
Oxford United (2/0)	1965/66	9	4	3	27	12	5	8	3	20	14	14	12	6	47	26
Peterborough United (1/3)	1961/62	4	2	6	18	19	3	3	6	16	25	7	5	12	34	44
Plymouth Argyle (3/9)	1904/05	14	6	17	47	47	8	13	16	31	51	22	19	33	78	98
Portsmouth (2/7)	1900/01	13	7	11	42	43	4	7	20	22	58	17	14	31	64	101
Portsmouth Reserves (1/0)	1903/04	1	0	0	6	1	1	0	0	2	1	2	0	0	8	2
Port Vale (4/2)	1938/39	13	5	4	33	20	6	6	10	21	38	19	11	14	54	58